S. WILLIAM HALPERIN, Professor of Modern History at
the University of Chicago, has taught in the History
Department since he received his Ph.D. from the University of Chicago in 1930. Born in Lithuania, he came
to the United States in 1907 and was educated in this
country. He has been Visiting Professor of History at
Ohio State University. At present he is Editor of the
Journal of Modern History, President of the Society
for Italian Historical Studies, and associated with a
number of other important historical associations. His
books include *The Separation of Church and State in
Italian Thought from Cavour to Mussolini* (1937),
*Italy and the Vatican at War: A Study of their Rela-
tions from the Outbreak of the Franco-Prussian War
to the Death of Pius IX* (1939), *Some 20th Century
Historians: Essays on Eminent Europeans* (1961),
*Diplomat under Stress: Visconti-Venosta and the Crisis
of July 1870* (1963), *Mussolini and Italian Fascism*
(1964), and *Germany Tried Democracy.*

Germany Tried Democracy

A POLITICAL HISTORY *of* THE REICH
from 1918 *to* 1933

S. WILLIAM HALPERIN

Professor of Modern History,
The University of Chicago

The Norton Library
W · W · NORTON & COMPANY · INC ·
NEW YORK

To My Mother

Books That Live
The Norton imprint on a book means that in the publisher's
estimation it is a book not for a single season but for the years.
W. W. Norton & Company, Inc.

ISBN   0   393   00280   2

PRINTED IN THE UNITED STATES OF AMERICA

7 8 9 0

PREFACE

THE story of the German republic makes depressing reading. It records the rise and fall of a venture in democracy. Had this venture succeeded, World War II might never have taken place. Its failure plunged a nation into slavery. Democracy, like peace, is indivisible. What happened in Germany had profound repercussions throughout the world. These repercussions are with us still.

In January, 1919, the republic had the support of most Germans. Fourteen years later, it was dead. The following words might well be inscribed upon its tombstone: "Here lies a noble experiment. It was sabotaged by friend and foe alike." It was sabotaged unwittingly by its friends, but the effect, nonetheless, was devastating. Allied statesmen, who should have known better, treated the new Germany as if it were a replica of the old. The honest, well-meaning men who spoke for the Social Democratic party made one mistake after another. Confusion and faintheartedness marked their tortuous course. While they blundered, the republic's inveterate enemies—the Junkers, the militarists, and one section of the industrial plutocracy—carried on with impunity. Agrarian feudalism survived in Prussia. The military caste retained its grip on the armed forces of the state. The unhampered formation of combines, trusts and cartels placed the nation's economic destiny in the hands of a few masterful men.

Throughout these years the predominance of class over national interests was almost always in evidence. Factionalism paralyzed the Reichstag and undermined respect for the parliamentary principle. Proportional representation on a national scale lent impetus to the splintering of political groups. It also increased the distance between voters and candidates. At a time when the nation hungered for effective leadership, petty bickering and the pursuit of partisan ends aggravated the sense of disunity. The decline of militancy in the trade unions and the fateful split in the ranks of German labor worked incalculable harm to the democratic cause. The runaway inflation of the early 1920's impoverished a considerable section of the middle class. It destroyed, in the process, one of the main props of the Weimar regime. The assignment of excessive powers to the president of the Reich constituted another link in this chain of tragic developments. The *coup de grâce*

v

was delivered by the great economic depression. It was this world-wide calamity which demoralized and decimated even the staunchest champions of democracy and made possible the phenomenal growth of National Socialism. Bruening's efforts to combat the depression proved futile. His fall sealed the doom of the republic. Thereafter the issue was no longer democracy versus dictatorship. It was conservative authoritarianism versus nihilist totalitarianism. The first was favored by men like Hindenburg, Schleicher, and Papen. The second represented the goal of Hitler and his brown-shirted cohorts.

The history of the German republic is replete with grim warnings. Will these warnings be heeded during the difficult years which are bound to come in the wake of World War II? Much will depend upon the answer to this question. For Germany, despite defeat and dismemberment, remains the key to the future of Europe.

The author takes this opportunity to express his deepest thanks to his wife. Her keen literary sense proved invaluable. Her unfailing encouragement made possible the completion of this book.

The footnotes in this book were inserted by the publisher to indicate credit for quoted matter.

S. William Halperin

CONTENTS

Chapter I

CROSSCURRENTS IN THE GERMAN EMPIRE
1871-1914

1

THE history of the German republic cannot be understood without reference to the earlier history of the Reich. The forces which shaped its destiny stem from an era far removed from contemporary times. Of these forces the most powerful was nationalism. It was rampant romanticism, with its emphasis on blood and race, its glorification of the past, its call for individual heroism and sacrifice, its clamorous insistence upon *Deutschland ueber Alles*. The annals of German nationalism are studded with memorable dates, but none takes precedence over January 18, 1871. On that day, in the wake of Prussia's smashing victory over France, the German empire came into being. Its birthplace was the famed hall of mirrors of the royal palace at Versailles. Here, in the presence of many distinguished personages, King William of Prussia was proclaimed German emperor. The dream of generations of German nationalists finally came true. The new Reich owed its existence above all to the genius of three men: Otto von Bismarck, the consummate statesman who steered the Prussian ship of state through manifold diplomatic shoals; Albrecht von Roon, Prussia's minister of war and indefatigable "organizer of victory"; and Helmuth von Moltke, the master strategist who headed the Prussian general staff. Encouraging them, sustaining them, were the millions of Germans from many different regions, parties and walks of life who had clung steadfastly to their vision of a united and powerful Reich. The advent of the German empire is one of the great, portentous landmarks of world history. A mighty people, industrious, disciplined and marvelously efficient, took what it thought was its rightful place in the center of the European stage. Like a somnolent giant awaking to the unsuspected strength that lay buried in his great muscles, the German people swung into a new tempo of working and living.

From 1871 to 1918, German political life remained harnessed to a constitution that was largely of Bismarck's making. This far-sighted representative of Prussian Junkerism wanted a Reich in which all power would be wielded by the central government. But the South German states objected. Predominantly Catholic, they were traditionally hostile to Prussia and fearful of her desire for complete hegemony in Germany. They insisted on the retention of a considerable measure of autonomy as the condition of their entry into the new Reich. So a federal system of government was established. Power was divided between the central authorities and the twenty-five territorial units that made up the empire. The federal character of this regime found its clearest expression in the composition and functions of the Bundesrat, the upper house of the national parliament. This body constituted the stronghold of German particularism. Its members were appointed by and represented the governments of the various states. No bill could become law without its consent. Indeed, it was the principal source of legislation.

Bismarck regarded the absolute monarchy as the ideal form of government. But in drafting the constitution, he had to take into account the wishes of the middle-class liberals who had supported his brilliantly conceived and executed campaign to unify Germany. These men wanted political democracy at home. They were very explicit on this point. To meet their demands, Bismarck made provision for a second legislative chamber, the Reichstag, to be elected on the basis of universal manhood suffrage. But the status to which this body found itself relegated proved a modest one indeed. Theoretically, its powers equaled those of the Bundesrat. In reality, it played second fiddle in the legislative domain. Moreover, the executive was completely beyond its control. It often assailed the doings of the imperial cabinet, but its criticisms were of no avail because the ministers were responsible not to it but to the emperor. It could make things rather unpleasant by refusing to vote the annual appropriations. However, the government had ways of getting around this, too. Little wonder, then, that the Reichstag came to be regarded as a mere debating society. The German empire, in spite of its parliamentary facade, was a semiautocratic state. The democratic window-dressing of the constitution of 1871 was the small price Bismarck paid to insure the continuance of arbitrary rule.

With the passage of time, the Reichstag came to be less and less an authentic expression of the popular will. When the empire was founded, the country was divided into electoral districts of approximately equal population. But in the decades which followed 1871, and especially after 1890, the rapid industrialization of the Reich produced some remarkable shifts of population. Many places that had been flyspecks on the map became heavily populated urban centers. Other places that had been comparatively populous before the onset of large-scale industrialization either showed no gain or actually lost ground. The result by 1914 was gross underrepresentation for the urban districts. But since reapportionment would have meant much heavier representation for the rapidly growing Social Democratic party, the group which, in theory at least, was committed to a program of socialism, no action to rectify the situation was taken by the dominant conservative elements.

As a loyal servant of the House of Hohenzollern, Bismarck wished to make the new Germany merely a greater Prussia. In this he was signally successful, despite the concessions he was forced to make to South German particularism. The dominant position of Prussia in the Reich was the most striking feature of the imperial constitutional system. Indeed, 1871 meant the beginning of the Prussianization of the entire German people; for it was Prussia that imposed her will, her standards and ideals, on all the other German states. Of the fifty-eight members of the Bundesrat, only seventeen, it is true, represented Prussia. But because the smallest states generally voted as she directed, she was almost always able to command a majority. To her king was given the title of German emperor. He was the chief executive of the Reich. His powers were many and imposing. He commanded the armed forces, directed foreign policy, appointed and dismissed chancellors, summoned and adjourned parliament. He lacked the power to initiate legislation or to veto measures adopted by the two houses. But in practice these limitations meant little. For as king of Prussia he named the Prussian members of the Bundesrat; and through them he was able to initiate most of the bills that were laid before parliament and to throttle legislation to which he objected. The irresponsibility of the emperor, his independence of parliamentary control, was one of the hallmarks of the constitution of 1871. The provision that his every act had to be countersigned by the chancellor was devoid of significance. For the chancellor was appointed by the emperor and responsible to him alone. So long as Bismarck held this post, a strong will prevailed at the chancellery. But the situation underwent a drastic change after his fall. When weaker men took over, the full import of their legal relationship to the emperor became manifest. The autocratic position of the chief executive was to prove the source of unmitigated disaster for the Reich, the German people and the Hohenzollern dynasty. The course of German and world history might have been different if the constitution had made the chancellor and the cabinet responsible to the representatives of the people.

The ascendancy of Prussia in the Reich became more pronounced as the years passed. By a series of treaties with most of the German states, she obtained the right to recruit, drill and command their military forces as a part of her own army. In this fashion, the indissoluble connection between the new Reich and the old military aristocracy of Prussia was strengthened enormously. Prussia's hegemony was further fortified by the gradual expansion of the vast authority vested in the central government. The latter encroached more and more upon the complex of powers assigned to the states. By 1914 it wielded an authority far greater than that which had originally been conferred upon it. The South German states objected strenuously to the overwhelming predominance of Prussia, but their efforts to combat it proved futile.

Within the Reich, Prussia stood out as the citadel of reactionary absolutism. Down to 1918 she retained the thoroughly undemocratic constitution of 1850. Under its terms, the king was complete master of the state. The Prussian Diet was a negligible quantity. It had no control whatsoever over the executive. The upper chamber consisted of individuals who sat in it by virtue either of lineage or royal appointment: Hohenzollern princes, members of former ruling families, aristocrats of less exalted rank, men of wealth, representatives of universities, religious bodies and important centers of population. This chamber labored faithfully to protect the interests of the upper classes. It had nothing whatever in common with the masses of the kingdom; at no time did it show any appreciation of their needs. The lower house was elected indirectly. The voters in each district were divided into three classes in accordance with the amount of direct taxes they paid. The result was that the masses of the population were put into a single class of voters and allowed to choose only one-third of the electors. Thus the composition of both houses of the Prussian Diet made a mockery of democracy. This oligarchical system was repeatedly assailed by liberals and socialists, but it managed to survive until the closing moments of World War I.

The ascendancy of Prussia was accompanied by the vigorous propagation of three things: the idea of the power-state, reactionary nationalism and anti-Semitism. The apostles of this trinity were many and influential. Outstanding among them was the famous historian, Heinrich von Treitschke. This gifted and eloquent man was an ardent nationalist. Throughout the 1860's he backed Bismarck's program and urged the German people to do likewise. The attainment of unity in 1871 did not mean, so far as Treitschke was concerned, that the national program had been accomplished. He believed that much hard work still remained to be done to give the German people certain things which he thought they lacked: spiritual unity, confidence in their own prowess, enthusiasm for new and even greater enterprises. In an effort to kindle pride in past achievements, he embarked upon the writing of his *History of Germany in the Nineteenth Century,* which he managed to carry to 1848 shortly before his death in 1896. His frequent contributions to the great conservative periodical, *Die Preussische Jahrbuecher,* and his impassioned orations in the Reichstag, served the same purpose: to play up Germany's greatness and stimulate the country to heroic exertions in fresh fields of endeavor. From his crowded lecture-hall at the University of Berlin, where he taught from 1874 until his death, he trumpeted his vision of the new Germany. He poured his scorn on Jews, socialists and capitalists. He decried the soft, opulent living which, in his opinion, was undermining everything simple and heroic in the German character. He lashed out furiously against the vogue of non-German political ideas, especially British notions about natural law, natural rights and popular sovereignty. Germany, he insisted, must build her own political philosophy upon foundations laid by such thinkers as Herder. States he defined as the expression of national groups and statesmen he excused from compliance with the canons of private morality. The goodness or badness of any piece of statecraft was determined by the manner in which it affected the interests of the Fatherland. Of the state itself he spoke in superlatives. It was, he never wearied of repeating, divinely inspired and divinely directed. For it but one maxim was valid: be strong. He contended almost ad nauseam that power was the prime necessity and trait of the state and that a nation must strain every nerve to build up its military strength. War was sublime, the supreme test of a nation's quality. Treitschke lauded Prussia for imposing a truly German stamp upon the non-Prussian regions of the Reich. But two enemies still remained to be fought and destroyed: provincialism and internationalism. Against the latter he railed with particular bitterness. He attacked Catholic allegiance to Rome and proletarian allegiance to Marxism. He denounced the Jews without letup. He accused them of importing into Germany such "French" ideas as rationalism and democracy and of undermining thereby the very bases of German society. They it was who disseminated all sorts of dangerous notions: that women should be emancipated, that the press should be free, that material aims should be pursued to the exclusion of spiritual ones. Treitschke idealized the German character, its loyalty, its intellectual profundity, its transcendentalism. He was a rabid imperialist. He urged expansion both eastward and westward, the creation of a powerful fleet, the acquisition of colonies. His teachings made a deep impression on important sections of the population, especially the nationalist youth, whose idol he became.

Richard Wagner, the great composer, also contributed powerfully to the development of chauvinism and racialism in Germany. He glorified everything German. He regarded the Germans as original, creative, inventive, whereas other peoples he described as purely imitative, exploiting what the Germans had produced. He dwelt on the greatness, beauty and nobility of the German spirit. The German, he contended, was superior to the Latin because he was more thoughtful, because he was concerned not with the immediate present but with the ultimate meaning of things. The German people had a great and unique mission that was rooted in the uniqueness of the German soul. This mission was nothing less than to rescue the world from the pernicious materialism which French civilization had disseminated. Wagner deplored the tendency of certain Germans of his day to ape foreign writers and artists. He wanted a German style, a German art. To this aspiration he dedicated his own incomparable genius. He gave Germany a national German music based on the hero-legends of the Teutons. In politics Wagner was militantly conservative. In later years he denounced the 1848 movement as completely un-German in character. Democracy he reviled as something alien to the German spirit, as something brought in by the French and their accomplices. He idealized the monarchical form of government. For the Jews he conceived a monomaniacal hatred. He was deeply influenced by Arthur de Gobineau's *Essay on the Inequality of the Human Races*. The Aryans, Wagner contended, were of divine descent and ordained by nature to rule. And within the Aryan group the Germans occupied the highest place because of their superior qualities—courage, pride, honor, a dislike for luxury and an innate incapacity to lie. As for the Jews, only one course remained open to them: self-destruction.

Wagner's influence was exerted not directly but through a circle of friends and followers. One of the most active members of this circle was Houston Stewart Chamberlain. This somewhat peripatetic Englishman finally settled down in Germany, married Wagner's daughter and became more German than the Germans. In 1899 he published a virulently anti-Semitic work called *The Foundations of the Nineteenth Century*. One section of the two-volume tract bears the title, "Christ not a Jew." Chamberlain's pet abominations, in addition to the Jews, were democracy and financial capitalism. His ideas made a profound impression on Alfred Rosenberg, who subsequently became the high priest of the Nazi movement. They also affected the thinking of Adolf Hitler, whom Chamberlain ecstatically hailed in 1923 as the savior of Germany.

Somewhat paradoxical was the role played by Friedrich Nietzsche, the renowned philosopher, in the development of the German power-complex. Nietzsche strongly condemned Prussianism. He reviled the Bismarckian Reich. He decried race-hatred and exaggerated nationalism and thought of himself as a good European. He had some rather unflattering things to say about the German soul and about Germany's intellectual pretensions. He spoke harshly of German philosophers and lavished praise upon the culture of France. On one occasion he wrote: "All that Europe has known of sensibility, of taste and nobility, has been the work and creation of France." Yet Nietzsche, thanks to a distorted interpretation of his teachings, became, *malgré lui,* one of the high priests of German *Machtpolitik.* Young Germans drank in the warnings and prophecies which stud the pages of his *Thus Spake Zarathustra.* His glorification of strength, his brilliant apotheosis of the will to power, were used to justify militarism, imperialism and Junkerism.

Reactionary nationalism had an ardent and persuasive exponent in the person of Adolf Stoecker, for many years court chaplain in Berlin. Stoecker was violently anti-Semitic. He regarded the Jews as alien and dangerous to everything German. He pictured the Aryans as a superior race, the embodiment of virtues that were not to be found in the rest of mankind. He tried to prove that nationalism and hatred for internationalism were entirely compatible with belief in God. He had much to say about the "national soul," which, he explained, resided in the blood of all Germans. He detested democracy and individualism. Of militarism he was a fervent champion. Stoecker was extraordinarily active. He founded a party of his own, served as a deputy in the Reichstag and the Prussian Diet and harangued innumerable audiences. His influence during the closing decades of the nineteenth century was unquestionably far-reaching.

An important place among the nurturers of the German power-complex belongs to General Friedrich von Bernhardi. In 1911 he published a book called *Germany and the Next War*. This book was widely read. It described war as a biological necessity, as something so essential to the health of mankind that it could not be dispensed with. Strong, growing peoples, it insisted, were entitled to conquer from others what they needed. Peace was condemned as being directly antithetic to the laws which governed the earth. "Without war," the argument ran, "inferior or decaying races would easily choke the growth of healthy, budding elements, and a universal decadence would follow." Besides, war was a great tonic, stimulating nations to the fullest use of their powers and bringing out the best in them.

Anti-Semitism, which loomed so large in the thinking of men like Treitschke, Wagner, Chamberlain and Stoecker, stemmed in the main from German nationalism, with its pronouncedly racialist tinge. After 1871, two additional factors intervened: the jealousy engendered by the economic success of the Jews; the identification of certain Jews with liberal and radical movements, which brought down upon the entire Jewish population the ire of conservative and reactionary elements. Anti-Semitic agitators were quick to blame the Jews for the business crash of 1873, which ushered in a prolonged economic depression. Bismarck did not hesitate to make political capital of the fact that some of his most prominent adversaries were Jews. Throughout the 1880's, anti-Semitism continued to grow. On one occasion, a gigantic petition was sent to the government. It demanded that no more Jews be permitted to enter Germany; that no Jews be allowed to hold political office or teach in the public schools. Pre-war anti-Semitism reached its peak in the elections of 1893. The various groups that made hatred of the Jews the alpha and omega of their program won sixteen seats in the Reichstag. All this helped to underline the fact that the Jews of Germany, despite their emancipation, were second-class citizens. Prior to 1914, commissions in the imperial army were consistently denied them. Only after serious losses in the war had depleted the officers' ranks were they permitted to rise in the military hierarchy. It was impossible for Jews to obtain high public office. Very few of the many who tried were able to secure university professorships. Discrimination was rife in the medical and legal professions. The advent of democracy in 1918 brought a distinct improvement in their status. But the feeling against them, far from diminishing, received new impetus from the material and spiritual travail which marked the post-war years.

The unification of Germany under Bismarckian auspices meant not only that Prussia was to rule the Reich but that the military caste which for so long had held the upper hand in Prussia was to enjoy a corresponding position in the empire. From their feudal stronghold in Prussia, the army chieftains could now look forward to a much larger field of action. New and vast resources were at their disposal. The fighting machine which they had created crushed Austria and France in the space of a few years. With all of Germany to draw on, and aided by the development of mammoth and marvelously efficient industries, they set about to build an army strong enough to conquer Europe. To insure maximum results, it was necessary to bring the entire German people under the sway of that militarism which for centuries had been a basic feature of Prussian life. Difficulties were encountered, especially in southern Germany which distrusted the Prussian oligarchs and disliked their methods and ambitions. But by 1914 the process of militarization had made deep inroads in nearly all the non-Prussian areas of the Reich. The life of practically every German was affected. It could not be otherwise. The Prussian war lords, utilizing the powers assigned to the dynasty by the imperial constitution, had their way in all matters pertaining to national defense. This was a broad realm, and necessarily so. But it was easier to harness people's bodies than to enslave their minds. Hostility to militarism and everything it signified persisted in spite of unceasing efforts to exalt it. This hostility was to be found in certain middle-class circles but above all among the masses of industrial workers. Not even the most ardent pacifists in Great Britain and the United States had a deeper loathing for militarism than the liberals and socialists of imperial Germany. This widespread antipathy to the gospel of violence and war, to the arrogance and arbitrariness of the military caste, manifested itself repeatedly during the years which preceded the outbreak of World War I.

From 1871 to 1914, the officers' corps stood at the apex of the social hierarchy. Aided and abetted by the dynasty, it exerted a decisive influence upon the internal evolution of the Reich. Within this highly privileged group the nobility predominated. Commoners could and did become officers, especially if they came from the upper middle class and possessed skills needed by the army. But between them and their aristocratic colleagues there yawned an unbridgeable gulf. German officers of the imperial era were characterized by a knightly devotion to the dynasty. They took pride in the rigid conception of honor which governed their conduct. For civilians and their mode of life they had nothing but withering contempt. An elaborate system of military academies kept the officers isolated from the rest of the population during their most impressionable years. In these institutions they received a one-sided education. They were taught to idealize force. The doctrine that might makes right was the axiom on which their whole training rested. They learned to despise democracy and humanitarianism. Socialism they were made to regard as a deadly poison which had to be combated with all the resources of the state.

Prussian militarism owed its existence to the Hohenzollerns, who labored with unfailing zeal and resourcefulness to harness land and people to the chariot of war. It owed its laurels to the members of the Junker aristocracy, those stiff-necked, class-bound feudal barons who generation after generation faithfully served their sovereign with great profit to the state and to themselves. Because almost all the higher officers of the army were drawn from their ranks, militarism and Junkerism became virtually interchangeable. But war was only one interest of the landowning aristocracy. As a class it sought to maintain the status quo in Prussia and in the Reich. Indeed, it remained throughout the imperial era the stoutest bulwark of the existing order. These men of noble lineage had much to say about their allegiance to God, king and country. No doubt they were sincere. But their prime concern at all times was to protect their class interests, to preserve the political and social preeminence which remained theirs until 1918. In this endeavor they had the indispensable backing of the dynasty, which regarded aristocrats as the only persons worthy of filling the highest posts in the government, the army and the bureaucracy. Because the Hohenzollerns set so much store by the services of the Junkers, they tried very hard to preserve the economic foundations upon which the primacy of this class rested. The maintenance of the great estates east of the Elbe thus became the special object of royal solicitude. The Prussian monarchy consequently remained until the end an unmistakably feudal state. The progress of industrialization and the emergence of new and powerful classes posed a threat to this outdated edifice; but it managed to survive until defeat on the battlefield and chaos at home brought ruin to the Hohenzollerns and to all the other crowned heads of Germany.

The Junkers were represented in the political arena by the Conservative party. This group also contained people from other classes—the bourgeoisie and the peasantry—but the landed aristocrats were invariably the dominant element. The Conservative party vigorously opposed all efforts to democratize the Prussian constitution and introduce ministerial responsibility in the Reich. It demanded protection for the rights of agriculture. It viewed with concern the mounting pretensions of the industrialists. Because the Junkers were staunch Lutherans, they championed the rights of the Evangelical church. Unctuous references to the "Christian philosophy of life" figured in most of their pronouncements. They regarded the religious school as the proper basis for popular education and as a bulwark against the rising tide of radicalism among the masses. Socialism they abhorred above all else and called unceasingly for its extirpation. They decried the "disintegrating" influence of the Jews upon German life and clamored for the expulsion of Jewish teachers from the public schools.

2

During the period from 1871 to 1914 Germany went through a colossal process of economic change which transformed her into one of the world's greatest industrial powers. So tremendous and rapid was her progress in all spheres of industrial production that there is nothing comparable to it except possibly the pace of economic advance in the United States since 1890 and the astonishing expansion of industry in the U.S.S.R. between 1928 and 1941. The wealth of the Reich increased manyfold as the number of giant factories multiplied and as more and more of the inventive genius, the inexhaustible vitality and disciplined energies of the German people flowed into industrial enterprises of every description. A new class of industrial magnates appeared, and with them powerful bankers catering to expanding industrial and commercial needs, and shipping tycoons whose globe-girding activities speedily became the envy of foreign rivals. In industry, in banking, in shipping, there developed an enormous amount of concentration, with relatively few men controlling almost everything that went on in their respective spheres. These men, disposing as they did of such tremendous economic power, came to play an increasingly influential role in the life of the nation. They brought tremendous pressure to bear on the government in an effort to secure legislation favorable to their interests. More often than not they managed to get what they wanted. Most of them were on excellent terms with Emperor William II. He had a high regard for their abilities and believed that the future of the country lay in their hands. But effective lobbying and royal patronage could not obscure the fact that commoners, no matter how successful or wealthy, were unable to attain the topmost rung in the German social and political ladder. The captains of industry did not take kindly to this state of affairs. They resented the favoritism shown the feudal aristocracy. They wanted a fair share of the responsibilities and privileges of government. Prior to 1914 they were unable to undermine the predominant position so long enjoyed by the baronial servants of the Prussian crown. There were occasional head-on conflicts between landowners and industrialists, especially over questions of tariff policy. But the two classes were almost always ready to submerge their differences in order to stand together against the common danger of radicalism from below.

The group which stood closer than any other to the new industrial plutocracy was the National Liberal party. It was composed for the most part of manufacturers, merchants and professional people. It demanded the fulfillment of all "justified" wishes of the nation, but it insisted that both the emperor and the Reichstag should retain the powers which were constitutionally theirs. It was for a big army and navy and for a vigorous foreign policy which would safeguard Germany's honor and her colonial interests. In keeping with their class bias, the National Liberals denounced feudal privilege in the bureaucracy and in the army and clamored for the wholesale admission of commoners to public office. They opposed special favors for agriculture. They demanded government regulation of consumers' co-operatives because the latter competed with private enterprise; but in the same breath they called for a minimum of state interference in the economic life of the nation. National Liberal spokesmen fought the trade unions, the principle of collective bargaining and social legislation that might reduce profits. Socialism was their chief bogey. They were ready to co-operate with all other groups against the Social Democrats. Anti-Catholic slogans, particularly denunciations of "ultramontanism," were a recurrent feature of their electioneering propaganda. With equal doggedness, they demanded protection for the rights of the Evangelical church. They favored religious instruction in the schools, but insisted that it be imparted under strict supervision by the state. Within the party there was a left wing which opposed the conservatism of the majority. This group was genuinely progressive in outlook. It was willing to co-operate with parties further to the left, including even the Social Democrats, to secure legislation which it deemed imperative in the national interest. It demanded constitutional reform. Specifically, it opposed the three-class system of voting and urged the introduction of ministerial responsibility in both Prussia and the Reich. These left-wingers called themselves "Young Liberals." Vigorously, but with scant success, they battled for their views in the party's councils. For a time it looked as if they might secede from the parent organization and seek a more congenial affiliation. The leader of the party, Ernst Bassermann, managed to prevent an open break, but he was utterly unsuccessful in his attempts to effect any sort of real reconciliation between the rival factions.

Standing immediately to the left of the National Liberals was the Progressive People's party. It was the real carrier of the great German liberal tradition which goes back hundreds of years. Bismarck's cleverly implemented hostility, together with internal dissension which resulted in frequent splits and secessions, had greatly impaired the strength of the movement. But by the eve of World War I, it had managed to win back some of the ground lost and had every reason to look forward to more prosperous times. Support for the party came primarily from the lower middle class. Professional people furnished the bulk of its leaders. The Progressives advocated significant political and social reforms, but found themselves constantly blocked by the conservative and reactionary elements. They wished to see the semiautocratic regime set up by Bismarck in 1871 converted into a truly parliamentary one. They pressed for the establishment of ministerial responsibility and the transfer of supreme authority to the elected representatives of the people. They urged the abolition of class privileges and distinctions. They insisted upon equality for all citizens regardless of origin and creed. They demanded the introduction of a democratic franchise in Prussia and the recasting of the Reichstag constituencies in accordance with recent population shifts. Anti-clerical in outlook, they worked for the liberation of education from ecclesiastical control. They detested Prussian militarism and freely criticized the officers' corps. They championed the idea of international arbitration. Some of them even urged the formation of an association of nations dedicated to peace and freedom. The party was friendly to the trade unions, to the principle of collective bargaining and to legislation for the benefit of the working classes. It was prepared to co-operate with the Social Democrats, but it had a profound antipathy for their ideology. It feared that the spread of socialism among the masses would hurt the liberal cause by forcing the upper classes to go to greater lengths to protect their interests.

3

Protestantism and Catholicism played important parts in the momentous drama which had the German empire as its stage. The Evangelical church, thoroughly national in outlook and long the submissive ally of the Hohenzollern dynasty, steadfastly supported the semiautocratic regime. It consistently preached obedience and docility. It gave invaluable aid to the Junkers, reinforcing the long-standing ties which existed between them and the peasants. It helped to impede the spread of radical ideas among the rural masses of Protestant Germany. Less uniform and definitely more spectacular was the role of German Catholicism. From the first days of the empire, the Roman church, with the enormous power and prestige of the Holy See behind it, made its influence felt. United Germany contained a Protestant majority, but it was a rather slim one, for almost half the population was Catholic, and militantly so. The strength of this imposing minority was marshaled through two powerful bodies: the ecclesiastical hierarchy, ranging from cardinals to humble parish priests, and the Center party. The latter had the unique distinction of being organized on a confessional basis, and throughout its long and eventful career in the German political arena, it fought with skill and tenacity for the interests of the church. At times, the going was very rough. This was especially true during the 1870's, when the so-called *Kulturkampf* was in progress. The trouble arose over the attitude of the German Catholics, who stressed states' rights and the federative principle in opposition to the Bismarckian-Prussian conception, which called for as much centralization as possible on the very morrow of unification. Bismarck and his aides, thoroughly steeped in the tradition of Prussian absolutism and eager to exalt the position of the Hohenzollern dynasty, succeeded in making the emperor the real power in Germany. Their anxiety to consolidate Prussia's gains made them trigger-like in their reaction to anything that seemed to run counter to their plans. In the opinion of Bismarck, the particularism of the Catholic church and its identification with separatist currents within the Reich jeopardized the newly won unity and exposed the empire to the danger of complete disintegration. To save his own handiwork, he threw himself headlong into a war to the hilt against his Catholic adversaries—and for the first time in his phenomenally brilliant career tasted the bitterness of complete and resounding defeat. The battering to which he subjected his intended victims only stiffened their will; and in the process of resisting they acquired a solidarity and discipline which distinguished their political behavior thereafter. Realizing that he was being worsted, the Iron Chancellor resolved to beat an orderly retreat. His decision was quickened by alarm over the recent spread of socialism which threatened not only the integrity of the empire but the very foundations—economic, social and religious—of German society. To combat the Marxist menace, a union of all conservative forces was imperative; and without the active co-operation of the Catholic church, with its enormous moral authority and its fierce hatred of the godless movement that was threatening to sever the masses from their traditional moorings, such a union would be woefully incomplete. And so the *Kulturkampf* was terminated and the erstwhile adversaries joined hands to meet the peril of proletarian radicalism.

Thenceforward, the role of the Center party grew steadily in importance. Consistent its conduct was, in so far as it was designed to serve the interests of the Catholic church and of the vast army of followers who marched under its political banner. But the membership of the party was, from the social and economic point of view, hopelessly heterogeneous. Inscribed upon its rolls were great landowners and lowly peasants, industrial magnates and factory workers, bankers and shopkeepers, professional men and artisans. To satisfy the needs and demands of all these components was beyond the reach of human resource. The result was a policy that was as receptive and flexible in matters economic and social as it was rigid and unrelenting in the moral and religious sphere. In the Reichstag the Center aligned itself now with one set of parties, now with another, always as expediency dictated. In the main it tended to steer a course roughly midway between that espoused by the reactionaries on the extreme right and the one urged by the liberals to its left. While the strength of other parties fluctuated, the size of the Centrist faction in the Reichstag remained substantially the same throughout successive decades. The constancy of its strength, which was at all times considerable, enabled it to play a perennially effective role, and not infrequently a decisive one, in the deliberations of the popular assembly. On many a crucial issue, the Catholic deputies held the balance of power. It was their practice on such occasions to drive hard bargains. On the whole, they exerted a steadying influence, holding the extremists in check and exhibiting a rock-ribbed intransigence of their own when vital Catholic interests were involved.

The Center stressed its loyalty to the existing constitution and its desire to see the federal character of the Reich maintained. It advocated more and more labor legislation but remained bitterly hostile to socialism. It sought to create a counterweight to that movement by organizing Catholic trade unions which by 1914 boasted a sizable membership. It was primarily fear of proletarian radicalism that prompted most Centrists to oppose revision of the Prussian constitution. They correctly assumed that the introduction of equal and universal suffrage in Prussia would redound to the advantage of the rapidly growing Social Democratic party. The Centrists' outstanding figure during the prewar years was Matthias Erzberger. This remarkable politician became the leader of the party's left wing, which urged the adoption of a more progressive program. With the support of his labor and lower-middle-class followers, Erzberger sought to wrest control from the hitherto dominant conservative elements. The outbreak of war in 1914 gave him his great opportunity. He speedily acquired a commanding position in the councils of the party. Thanks above all to him, the Centrists began to gravitate toward the democratic camp.

4

Socialist ideas made their appearance in Germany prior to 1848, but not until that year of revolutions did a working-class movement of serious proportions come into being. The cause of German labor then marked time until the energetic and imaginative leadership of Ferdinand Lassalle infused new life into the movement in the early 1860's. His premature death dealt a heay blow to the moderate and national brand of socialism which he championed, and the way was cleared for the dissemination of the Marxist ideology with its emphasis on the class struggle, social revolution and the worldwide solidarity of the proletariat. Eventually, in 1875, the two factions joined forces to form the united Social Democratic party of Germany. It was then that Bismarck, noting the rapid spread of socialism among the workers, decided to throttle the movement. The anti-socialist law of 1878 made things rather hot for the Social Democrats, but they managed to thrive on persecution and grew stronger rather than weaker. Sensing that the mailed fist alone would not accomplish his purpose, Bismarck reconsidered his strategy. He resolved to resort to the milk-and-honey technique while continuing the policy of repression. Marx had said in his famous *Communist Manifesto* that the workers of the world had nothing to lose but their chains. Bismarck made up his mind to give the workers of Germany something to lose besides their chains. Thus there came into being the social insurance laws of the 1880's which put Germany far ahead of the rest of the world so far as this type of legislation was concerned. It is rather ironic that this vast program of benefits for the workingman should have come not from a friend of labor but from its sworn enemy. It is not surprising, however, that the government should have concerned itself with questions of this sort. For state paternalism was an integral part of the Prussian tradition. Bismarck hoped that his policy would destroy the Social Democratic movement by weaning the workers from their leaders and implanting in them a feeling of loyalty to the state. This hope proved futile. The movement, instead of disintegrating, continued to grow. In 1890 Bismarck ceased to be chancellor and William II, who had notions of his own, refused to renew the anti-socialist law. An ambitious program of factory legislation sponsored by the young emperor failed to stem the socialist tide. The accelerated pace of industrialization after 1890 brought a vast increase in the number of urban workers. A seemingly endless stream of new recruits flowed into the Social Democratic camp. By 1914 the party had millions of adherents, scores of newspapers, a well-filled exchequer and an organization that had lost none of its efficiency in the process of expansion.

The rapid growth of the movement was accompanied by the emergence of new problems. The most serious of these was the intra-party controversy between the Radicals and the Revisionists. The Radicals were the party's left-wingers. They advocated mass strikes to back up the workers' demands and hasten the inevitable showdown between capital and labor. They contended that the Russian revolution of 1905 had ushered in an era of world-shaking possibilities. Catastrophe, they predicted, would overtake the capitalist system in the foreseeable future. All Europe was about to undergo a crisis of unprecedented proportions. A great war impended and social upheavals were bound to follow. It was therefore necessary for the German workers to go beyond mere election campaigns. They must not be satisfied with such piddling, ineffectual tactics. It was their duty to gird for a revolutionary struggle. They must emulate the Russian proletariat by advancing boldly upon the enemy. Outstanding among the Radicals were Rosa Luxemburg, Karl Liebknecht, Georg Ledebour and Franz Mehring. Luxemburg, a hunchbacked Polish Jewess with a mind like a razor's edge, was easily the group's brainiest and most determined leader. She was also the best versed in Marxist ideology.

The Revisionists or Reformists constituted the right wing of the Social Democratic party. They were led by Eduard Bernstein, Georg von Vollmar, Richard Calwer and Eduard David. Bernstein was their principal theoretician. In a work which appeared in 1899, he attacked the basic principles of Marxism and advanced many of the arguments employed by the bourgeois critics of socialist theory. He insisted that the orthodox Marxist position was incompatible with existing realities. He declared that the welfare of society as a whole should be placed above that of any single class. He challenged the Marxist prediction that the ownership of property would be concentrated in fewer and fewer hands. The formation of vast industrial combines was accompanied, he said, by an increase in the number of property owners. There was no indication that capitalist economy was moving toward collapse. Consequently, the theory of violence and revolution must be discarded. The Revisionists urged the party to concentrate on objectives that could be achieved in the foreseeable future. These included ministerial responsibility to the Reichstag; popular control of foreign policy; abolition of the three-class system in Prussia; the enfranchisement of women; the democratization of the army and reduction of the period of compulsory military service; decreased appropriations for the army and navy; withdrawal from the scramble for colonies; reform of the penal law in accordance with the dictates of humanitarianism; unemployment insurance and the eight-hour day in all branches of industry; graduated income, property and inheritance taxes; free elementary schooling for all. The Revisionists claimed that the proletariat would be able to get what it wanted by peaceful, gradual means. They believed in co-operation with liberals or any other bourgeois groups whenever expedient.

Arrayed against the Radicals were not only the Revisionists but the trade unions. As the latter became large and affluent, they tended to repose more and more faith in their own strength. They believed themselves capable of securing before long such desiderata as shorter working hours and minimum wage laws. They were interested not in political but in economic objectives. Their primary concern was to improve the material lot of their members. This they believed they could do within the framework of the existing capitalist system. Rash or violent action, they feared, would jeopardize everything so far gained. By 1914 their assets included two and one-half million members, considerable property and a sizable income. This was too much to stake on the outcome of desperate gambles.

The attitude of the trade unions proved decisive. Revisionism triumphed over Radicalism within the Social Democratic party. Lip-service continued to be paid to the idea of the class struggle and to other features of orthodox Marxism. But it was Revisionism that motivated the party's everyday battles in parliament and the press. The Social Democrats came to be, for all practical purposes, a party of working-class liberals. They stressed their respect for legality. They regarded violence as something evil, no matter what its purpose. They wanted freedom for all, their adversaries included. Political democracy, they kept insisting, was the thing to work for because it would bring social justice without bloodshed and revolution. Socialism remained, in theory, the ultimate goal. But it was too remote to be the sole yardstick of decisions that could not be postponed. The Social Democrats were in no hurry to assume power. They were quite content to remain indefinitely a party of opposition, criticizing the government's policies and winning ever increasing numbers of converts. They did not demand the establishment of a republic because the times seemed anything but propitious for such a change. There was very little sentiment for a republic among the masses. Besides, leading members of the party came to believe that the aims of Social Democracy could be realized under a monarchical form of government. Indeed, these men held that under certain circumstances a monarchy could be even better than a republic.

The party's faith in the efficacy of the democratic process was strengthened by the outcome of the elections of January, 1912. The Social Democrats polled 4,238,919 votes and captured 110 Reichstag seats. They thus became far and away the single strongest party in Germany. The Revisionists claimed that the party's success at the polls vindicated their moderate and evolutionary stand, particularly their contention that the interests of the working class could best be served by collaborating with bourgeois liberals. As a matter of fact, the Social Democrats were helped on this occasion by a pre-election agreement with the Progressives.

The Revisionist mood of the party was reflected in the momentous decision reached by its leaders in August, 1914. For years the Social Democrats had denounced imperialistic war and had affirmed their loyalty to pacifist principles. On August 1, 1914, Germany declared war on Russia. Two days later, she declared war on France. On August 4, Great Britain declared war on the Reich. The overwhelming majority of the German people believed that the war had been thrust upon the Fatherland by jealous and vindictive neighbors, that Germany had never wanted this war, that she was fighting to save herself from destruction. Because most Social Democrats shared this feeling, they decided to support the war. They remained as opposed as ever to imperialistic enterprises, to ventures undertaken for territorial or economic gain. But, in their opinion, this war was different. The readiness of the average Social Democrat to assume this attitude testified to the completeness with which the Revisionist spirit permeated the party. Besides, Social Democratic spokesmen had repeatedly put themselves on record as favoring the defense of the Fatherland against outside aggression, especially Russian aggression. Tsarist Russia symbolized to them everything uncivilized, barbarian and tyrannical. German civilization, they were convinced, had to be protected against this menace from the east. Thus a war against Russia could generate real enthusiasm within the nation's largest party. The average worker, like the average member of every other class, honestly believed that his country had wanted only peace, that it had been forced by the belligerence and rapacity of others to draw the sword. He was prepared to make the greatest sacrifices to avert defeat. For defeat would mean that German women and children would fall prey to Russian bestiality. It would also mean ruin for every German, regardless of class. Genuine abhorrence of war did not entail a refusal to fight once war had broken out in spite of the Reich's efforts to prevent it. The workers had one, inexorable duty: to rally to the defense of the Fatherland in its hour of need.

On August 2, 1914, the leaders of the Social Democratic party met to fix the group's attitude in regard to war credits. It was known that the Reichstag would convene two days later to vote on this matter. Only two of the men present advocated rejection of the government's request for appropriations: Hugo Haase and Georg Ledebour. All the others emphasized their desire to see the party go along with the rest of the Reichstag in approving war credits. In spite of the entreaties of their colleagues, Haase and Ledebour refused to change their minds. The decisive turn came at the meeting of the Social Democratic members of the Reichstag on the night of August 3. The discussion was acrimonious and at times extremely bitter. Those who wanted the party to sanction war credits adduced the views of Lassalle, Friedrich Engels and August Bebel in support of their contention that it was the duty of the workers to defend their country. Finally, a vote was taken. Of the 110 deputies, only fourteen favored a policy of opposition to the war. These dissenters, who were led by Haase, took their defeat very hard. But in the interests of party unity and discipline, they agreed to submit to the majority. And so, on August 4, 1914, the Social Democratic delegation in the Reichstag voted unanimously in favor of war credits. Even Karl Liebknecht, whose extreme radicalism set him apart from all the other deputies, voted yes on this occasion. The party's declaration explaining its position was read by Haase, who had allowed himself to be persuaded to discharge this role. The declaration ran as follows:

We are facing a critical time. The results of imperialistic policy, by creating a prolonged period of competitive armaments and intensifying national differences, have spread like a tidal wave over Europe. The responsibility for this falls on the supporters of this policy: we refuse to take it. Social Democracy has opposed with all its might this ominous development, and has up to the very last moment worked for the preservation of peace. . . . Our efforts have been in vain. Now we are up against the stern fact of war. The horrors of hostile invasion stare us in the face. Today we have not to decide between peace and war, but to settle the question of voting the credits necessary for the country's defense. We have now to think of millions of our countrymen who, through no fault of theirs, are involved in this crisis. . . . We regard it as our imperative duty to stand by them, to lighten their burdens and mitigate this immeasurable disaster. In case of victory for the Russian autocrat, whose hands are stained with the blood of the best of his countrymen, much, if not all, will be at stake. It is of paramount importance to prevent this danger and to insure the position and independence of our own land. . . . We will not desert our Fatherland in the hour of peril. . . . We . . . condemn all wars of aggression. We demand that, directly our security is won and our enemies are inclined to make peace, the war should end in a peace that will make friendly relations with our neighbors possible.

Chapter 2

THE PEACE RESOLUTION OF JULY, 1917

I

THE Social Democrats were in earnest when they said they wanted a just peace. Throughout the war, they demanded the unequivocal repudiation of all annexationist designs. But as time went on, dissatisfaction and unrest within the party grew. For this the nation's military leaders were mainly responsible. On August 29, 1916, Field Marshal Paul von Hindenburg, the hero of Tannenberg, was appointed head of the Supreme Command. Simultaneously, Erich Ludendorff was named his chief of staff with the rank of First Quartermaster General. Hindenburg was passive by nature. Ludendorff, on the other hand, was masterful and dynamic. In his hands Hindenburg was like putty. For all practical purposes the Supreme Command became Ludendorff's personal vehicle. He did all the thinking and deciding. Hindenburg, nominally his superior, carried out his wishes and assumed responsibility for them vis-à-vis the emperor. Ludendorff arrogated to himself not only military control but control of political affairs as well. He became, in fact, the virtual dictator of Germany. He wielded his power one-sidedly, against the masses and for the benefit of the big landowners and the industrialists. Like all other members of the military caste, he detested democracy and everything it signified. He was an unabashed annexationist. His aim was a peace of conquest. The chancellor, Theobald von Bethmann-Hollweg, was a man of moderate outlook. However, he counted for little. He had no secure following anywhere. He could not rely on the emperor, who was completely subservient to the Supreme Command. He could not rely on the Reichstag or on public opinion. As regards war aims, he entertained views which were

22

markedly different from those of Ludendorff. But he was too weak and too friendless to put them over. In November, 1916, his efforts to achieve a separate peace with Russia were foiled by the Supreme Command. In February, 1917, the military and naval chiefs overruled him on the question of resuming unrestricted submarine warfare.

Dictatorial rule by the Supreme Command and the pursuit of annexationist designs intensified the ferment within the Social Democratic party. The dissident minority clamored more insistently than ever for a change of policy. The time had come, it declared, to take up an attitude of opposition to the government's conduct of the war. But most Social Democrats demurred. They stuck to their original position, albeit with shrinking enthusiasm. They persisted in regarding the war as a defensive one and believed that it should be supported until the existence of the German people had been rendered secure. The malcontents found this attitude unendurable. They were outraged by the blatant imperialism of the military leaders. The idea of conquering other nations, they held, was not only despicable in itself but was, in addition, prolonging the war and therefore the agony of the German people. Unendurable, too, was the dictatorial behavior of the militarists, their arrogant refusal to give the people any real voice in the determination of national policies. This minority was moved by the suffering and hardships which the masses were being forced to undergo. It wished to see peace concluded at once and to this end showered the party's leaders with demands for the immediate denial of further war credits.

Matters reached a critical pass in March, 1916. Differences of opinion regarding the new emergency budget presented by the government precipitated the showdown. The majority of the Social Democratic party, led by Friedrich Ebert, declared itself in favor of voting the appropriation. Disclaiming any desire to promote plans for conquest or territorial annexation, Ebert and his friends contended that so long as the enemy refused to accept Germany's peace terms, it was their duty to stand by the government. The Fatherland, they argued, had to be defended against invasion. Defying the injunctions of the majority, a group of eighteen deputies, headed by Haase, voted no. Disciplinary action was taken against the rebels, who promptly organized themselves as a separate faction which called itself the Social Democratic Labor Association. The final break came early in 1917 when Haase and his followers formed the Independent Social Democratic party. At their initial congress in April, 1917, the Independents adopted a program which expressed opposition not only to the war policy of the government but to the existing political regime. A frontal attack on the semiautocratic Reich set up in 1871 was now in the making.

Still further to the Left stood a small group of extremists headed by Karl Liebknecht and Rosa Luxemburg. They looked upon the outbreak of the European conflict as the beginning of the collapse of capitalist society. Consequently, they called upon the workers to do everything in their power to hasten the overthrow of the existing political and social order in Germany. They described the war as a squabble between capitalists and imperialists and insisted that the masses would lose, no matter which side won. They urged the German proletariat to unite with the workers of other countries in a crusade against capitalism everywhere. The goals to which they aspired were world revolution and international socialism. In December, 1914, Liebknecht detached himself from all his party comrades in the Reichstag by voting against the supplementary war credits asked by the government. He and other members of this little band agitated incessantly for immediate termination of the war. In a pamphlet circulated in May, 1915, the group proclaimed that the foe was not on the battlefields but at home, in Germany. It singled out, as the real enemies, German imperialism, German militarism and secret diplomacy. Liebknecht and his followers called themselves Spartacists, in honor of Spartacus, the Thracian leader of the gladiators in the war against Rome in 73-71 B.C. Contact was established between the Independents and the Spartacists. The latter, as a matter of fact, were admitted to membership in the Independent Social Democratic party, but they insisted on retaining complete freedom of action. They regarded Haase and men of his type as altogether too bourgeois in outlook to be of much use in the impending struggle against capitalism. But they welcomed the weakening of the Social Democratic forces which resulted from the feud between the Independents and the majority of the party. During the first three years of the war, the Liebknecht-Luxemburg group had very little success with its revolutionary propaganda. But it kept up its campaign with undiminished energy, sure that before long its day would come. For a part of this time it was without the services of Liebknecht. In June, 1916, he was arrested and sentenced to two and a half years in prison for leading an antiwar demonstration in Berlin.

2

The Russian revolution of March, 1917, produced considerable excitement in Germany. It emboldened the Social Democrats, who hastened to press harder than ever for constitutional reform. Pointing suggestively to the fall of Tsarism, they warned the government that it could not procrastinate much longer in carrying out urgently needed internal changes. They protested strongly against Bethmann-Hollweg's decision to postpone reform of the franchise in Prussia until after the war. The impatience manifested by the nation's biggest party forced the government to reconsider its stand. However, the upshot of its deliberations fell far short of expectations. In his Easter message to the chancellor on April 8, 1917, Emperor William II did, indeed, invite proposals for electoral change in Prussia. But he made it clear that legislative action would have to be deferred until the German armies came home. He and his advisers clung to the belief that constitutional reform at this time would precipitate disturbances and thus jeopardize the war effort. The Independents kept the political pot boiling by laying before the Reichstag a resolution calling for the termination of the war and the democratization of the imperial constitution. The Progressives contributed to the excitement by joining the Social Democrats in demanding the immediate abolition of the three-class system in Prussia. Some weeks earlier, on March 29, 1917, the Reichstag had set up a special committee to deal with constitutional matters. The groundwork was thus laid for co-operative action by the Social Democrats, the Progressives and the Centrists. The latter, under Erzberger's leadership, were now beginning to abandon their prewar opposition to political change. Assistance from the National Liberals was also in prospect. The left-wingers of this party took a positive stand on the question of constitutional reform. They battled to impose their views on the right-wingers who, as the representatives of heavy industry, strenuously objected to anything that might redound to the advantage of the Social Democrats. The Conservatives, as usual, spearheaded the forces of reaction. They obdurately opposed modification of the existing order. And behind them, ready to throttle "subversive" movements of any variety, stood the all-powerful Supreme Command.

Indicative of the growing ferment among the masses was the strike proclaimed by 200,000 Berlin workers on April 16, 1917. This was the first wartime strike in the nation's capital. It was precipitated by a reduction in the bread ration announced the day before. The food situation was bad and getting rapidly worse. The kind of desperation which only a combination of hunger and disillusionment can produce forced the workers of Berlin to shake off the habit of meek obedience and resort to direct action. The strike was led by the Independents. Not to be outdone by their rivals, the Social Democrats took a more bellicose line. On April 19, they publicly welcomed the triumph of the revolutionists in Russia. They declared themselves at one with the manifesto issued by the workers' and soldiers' councils of Russia. This manifesto called for a general peace without annexations and indemnities, a peace based on the principle that all nations should be free to shape their own destiny. The Social Democrats reiterated their opposition to the expansionist designs of the chauvinist elements. They promised to do everything in their power to force the government to renounce all thought of conquest and to initiate, at the earliest possible moment, negotiations for a peace of justice and understanding. To this the Conservatives replied with a defiant blast. They declared that adoption of the demand for a peace without annexations and indemnities would spell ruin for Germany. They assailed Bethmann-Hollweg for his alleged submissiveness vis-à-vis the Social Democrats. They insisted that the nation had no choice but to strive for a victorious peace.

In May, 1917, the political struggle in Germany entered a new phase. The Centrists, the Progressives and the National Liberals—the latter were now following the line urged by their left-wingers—submitted a joint resolution to the constitutional committee of the Reichstag. This resolution called for the introduction of ministerial responsibility. Further, it stipulated that the appointment of all army officers would have to be formally approved by the minister of war. The government's reaction was distinctly negative. The emperor likewise objected. The three parties were forced to beat a retreat. But their failure could not obscure the possibilities of co-operative action. Before long another and more formidable attempt was to be made to impose the nation's will on the small ruling clique. The war had produced a marked change in the spirit of the people. There was a greater tendency to question, to criticize. Buoyed by this change, the Reichstag made ready to play a more dynamic role in the political life of the country.

3

During the initial phases of the war, Erzberger had been a rabid annexationist, rivaling even the Pan-Germans in his clamor for territorial gain. But in the spring of 1917 he changed his mind. He came to the conclusion that only by seeking a moderate peace could Germany extricate herself from her dangerous position. The entry of the United States into the war in April, 1917, had darkened Germany's chances of ultimate victory. The radical elements in Russia and the socialist parties in Germany were scoring heavily with their slogan: no annexations and no indemnities. The will to fight on was being undermined. The defection of Austria-Hungary could not long be delayed. It was against this ominous backdrop that Erzberger announced his conversion to the idea of a just peace. He spoke on July 6, 1917; his audience was the main committee of the Reichstag. The picture he painted was unrelievedly black. He called attention to the staggering financial cost of the war. He enlarged upon the steadily worsening food situation. Unrestricted submarine warfare, he warned, would fail to accomplish its purpose. Continuation of the war would lead to ruin. It was necessary to go back to the mood of August, 1914. The best way to obtain peace was to reaffirm what had been stated at the very beginning of the conflict: that Germany was fighting a defensive war, that she desired a peace by agreement which would expose no nation to oppression. This the Reichstag would have to say to the German government. It would then be up to the chancellor to make diplomatic use of such a statement. There was no need to bother about the 25,000 pan-Germans. Let them go crazy, Erzberger jeered. It would be cheaper to build asylums for them than to prolong the war.

Erzberger's speech, and especially his pessimistic allusions to what might happen if the war were not ended soon, created a tremendous sensation. For the general public had until now entertained little doubt as to the ultimate outcome. It had been going by the fact that the German armies were still deep in enemy territory, that they were still able to mount powerful offensives, that submarine warfare was officially credited with the chance of bringing Great Britain to her knees. So serious a view did the authorities take of Erzberger's broadside that they summoned the emperor and the Supreme Command to Berlin. Hindenberg and Ludendorff arrived in the capital on July 7 but left in the course of the same day because the emperor wished to handle the matter himself. William and Bethmann-Hollweg were at one in the belief that a peace move along the lines suggested by Erzberger would do the German cause more harm than good. Hence they stoutly opposed the Centrist leader. But the chancellor's arguments failed to convince those who shared Erzberger's views.

The controversy over war and peace aims precipitated a major political crisis. The steadily mounting ill feeling against Bethmann-Hollweg flared anew. The much-harassed statesman found himself the target of attacks from every quarter. The Conservatives and the National Liberals berated him for failing to take strong action against the parties of the Left. They also accused him of standing in the way of an annexationist peace. They wished to see Germany help herself to the territory and resources of other nations. Because Bethmann-Hollweg entertained more moderate views, they resolved to drive him from office. The Social Democrats, the Centrists and the Progressives were furious with him because his peace policy was not strong enough. They railed against his supine surrender to the demands of the Supreme Command. While the Conservatives denounced him for being too favorable to the idea of constitutional reform, the Social Democrats charged him with being lukewarm to it. Matters approached a crescendo when Gustav Stresemann, Bassermann's successor as leader of the National Liberals and an ardent annexationist, demanded the chancellor's resignation. The Centrists jumped to a leading position in the assault by adopting a resolution which stated that the retention of the chancellorship by Bethmann-Hollweg would render more difficult the attainment of peace. In the meantime there had been formed an inter-party committee representing the Social Democrats, the Centrists and the Progressives. This committee, which was the later Weimar coalition in embryo, gave itself an ambitious program. It proposed not only to draft a peace resolution but to work for the immediate enactment of constitutional reforms. Preeminent among these were ministerial responsibility and equal suffrage in Prussia. Moreover, the committee hoped to establish the supremacy of parliament in matters of foreign policy. Leadership in this all-important sphere was to be transferred from the cabinet to the parties controlling a majority in the Reichstag. The idea of the committee was to use the peace issue, about which the public was so exercised, to wrest concessions in the constitutional domain. This coupling of the two questions produced immediate results. At the urging of Bethmann-Hollweg, and in spite of fierce opposition by the Conservatives, the emperor agreed to make an important concession. He instructed the Prussian cabinet to prepare and submit to the Diet a measure which would do away with the three-class system. This measure was to be in effect when the next Prussian elections took place. The country was informed of the emperor's action on July 12, 1917. The committee was jubilant. But it was less successful in its efforts to obtain ministerial responsibility. On this question the emperor was absolutely adamant.

While Bethmann-Hollweg was belatedly promoting the cause of constitutional reform, his adversaries in all the leading parties were preparing the blow which, they hoped, would force him from office. They met with the German Crown Prince and told him bluntly that they and the groups they represented wished to see the chancellor go. The Crown Prince passed this information on to his father. But what actually turned the trick was the intervention of the Supreme Command. Ludendorff hated Bethmann-Hollweg and wanted him dismissed without further ado. There was one stratagem, the general knew, which could not fail: the threat that both he and Hindenburg would resign from the Supreme Command if they were not allowed to have their way. Ludendorff persuaded the field marshal to join him in requesting the emperor to relieve them of their posts. William, as Ludendorff foresaw, was hardly in a position to defy the military heroes of Germany, the only men who, according to popular belief, could insure ultimate victory. Bethmann-Hollweg hastened to submit his resignation. It was promptly accepted by the emperor. This was on July 13, 1917.

The great question now was: who should succeed Bethmann-Hollweg? Both Erzberger and Stresemann wished to see Prince Buelow reinstalled in the chancellorship. But the emperor, who remembered with bitterness that statesman's unedifying role in the famous *Daily Telegraph* Affair of 1908, would not hear of this. Admiral Tirpitz, the founder of German sea power and a strong personality, was considered. However, he, too, was *persona non grata* to the emperor. Only recently, in March, 1916, he had been dismissed from his post as head of the admiralty precisely because he had been unable to get along with William. Bethmann-Hollweg suggested Count Hertling, the Bavarian premier and a leading member of the Catholic Center. The emperor reacted favorably. Hertling seemed admirably equipped to assume the reins of government. But when the chancellorship was offered to him, he refused it. He adduced, as the reasons for his refusal, his advanced age and the promise he had given the king of Bavaria that he would remain at his present post. The name

of Count Bernstorff, the former ambassador to Washington, came up.
This time it was the military chiefs who said no. They agreed instead
on the choice of Dr. Georg Michaelis, Prussia's food commissioner.
The emperor gave his assent. The Reichstag was not consulted. The
appointment of Michaelis came as a tremendous surprise to the nation.
The average German found it difficult to understand why some better-
qualified person had not been chosen. The gravity of the situation in
which the Fatherland currently found itself was incontestable. Incontestable, too, was the need for a chancellor who would prove equal to
his heavy responsibilities. Yet a run-of-the-mine bureaucrat with very
limited experience and no reputation to speak of had been selected. It
was all very puzzling and not a little disheartening. The prestige of
the government, which had not been helped by Bethmann-Hollweg's
vacillation and dilatoriness, hit a new low. The consensus of opinion
in informed quarters was that Michaelis would not last.

On July 19, 1917, the peace resolution was introduced in the Reichstag. It ran as follows:

As on August 4, 1914, the words of the speech from the throne, 'No desire for conquest urges us forward,' hold good for the German people now,
at the beginning of the fourth year of war. Germany has taken up arms in
defense of her freedom and independence and for the integrity of her territory. The object of the Reichstag is to obtain a peace of understanding and
of lasting reconciliation between nations. With such a peace forced cessions
of territory and political, economic and financial oppression are incompatible. The Reichstag rejects all plans that may entail an economic boycott
and foster hostile feelings among the nations after the war. The freedom of
the seas must be definitely established. Only harmony in economic matters
will prepare the ground for a friendly concord among the nations. The
Reichstag will energetically sponsor the creation of international courts of
arbitration. However, so long as the enemy governments do not entertain
such a peace, so long as they threaten Germany and her allies with territorial seizures and violence, the German people will stand together as one
man, will hold on unshaken and fight till their own right and that of their
allies to live and develop have been secured. The German people are unconquerable when united. The Reichstag knows it has the concurrence of the
men who are heroically defending the Fatherland. The ever-lasting grati-
tude of the entire nation is assured them.

The resolution was adopted by a majority composed of Social Democrats, Centrists and Progressives. The opposition consisted principally
of Conservatives and National Liberals. The latter drew a sharp dis-

tinction between constitutional reform and the issue of war aims. On behalf of the first they were ready to co-operate with other parties. But, under the influence of men like Stresemann, they looked with disfavor upon any formulation of war aims which failed to take account of the expansionist wishes of heavy industry. The Reichstag's action was a slap in the face for the Supreme Command and its annexationist supporters. Ludendorff had tried very hard to prevent adoption of the resolution. But for once his objections had been swept aside. Parliament's belated manifestation of independence was an event of far-reaching importance. It shattered the political truce established in August, 1914, to facilitate the winning of the war. It foreshadowed a more aggressive role on the part of the democratic forces. Above all, it sounded the knell of the semiautocratic system of government. Clearly, a new chapter in German history was about to open.

4

How binding on the German government was the resolution of July, 1917? The answer to this question was provided by Chancellor Michaelis himself. In announcing his acceptance of the resolution, he used the qualifying phrase, "as I interpret it." This was tantamount to saying that the government would continue to do pretty much as it pleased in the realm of foreign affairs. The Supreme Command would be able to proceed unhindered with its plans for conquest and annexation. Michaelis was very pleased with the way he had handled the matter. He wrote to the Crown Prince on July 25, 1917: "The hateful resolution has been passed by 212 votes to 126. . . . I have deprived it of its greatest danger by my interpretation. One can, in fact, make any peace one likes, and still be in accord with the resolution." Even Erzberger, a leader in the fight for a just peace, displayed unabashed cynicism in appraising the practical implications of the Reichstag's action. He said to Prince Max of Baden apropos of the resolution: "You see, Your Highness, this way I get the Longwy-Briey line [demanded by German industrialists because it would give the Reich French-owned ore deposits of great value] by means of negotiation." But the German masses did not share this cynicism. They took the Reichstag's gesture seriously and expected to see it implemented in the very near future.

The challenge represented by the peace resolution was met head-on by the champions of a peace of conquest. Under the leadership of Tirpitz and Wolfgang Kapp, an East Prussian official closely associated with Junker interests, they formed the so-called Fatherland party. It was made up principally of Conservatives, pan-Germans, spokesmen for heavy industry, high army officers and leading bureaucrats. With Ludendorff's blessings, the group sought to whip up sentiment in favor of an annexationist peace. On September 2, 1917, it issued a manifesto to the nation. Many Germans, it declared, did not agree with the Reichstag majority. Everyone, of course, wanted peace. But weak-kneed peace resolutions would only prolong the war. The enemy, intent upon the annihilation of Germany, regarded such resolutions merely as evidence of the collapse of German strength. If the enemy were assured that Germany was always ready to conclude a peace of understanding, he would have nothing to lose and everything to gain by continuing the war. In order to pursue a strong national policy, the German government needed wide popular support. Hence the formation of the Fatherland party, which aimed at uniting all patriotic Germans regardless of political affiliation. It was designed to strengthen the nation's will to victory. It would not run candidates for Reichstag seats. It would disband the day peace was concluded. What it wanted above all was national unity, the elimination of internal discord, in order that victory might not be jeopardized. In this war not only the great position but the very existence of the Reich was at stake. The struggle was going well for Germany. England was in desperate straits. Fatally wounded by German submarine warfare, she was still hoping to be saved by German disaffection and disunity. But defeat would speedily overtake her if only Germany held firm and resisted all deceptive peace offers. The Fatherland did not want a peace of hunger. To obtain the kind of peace it did want, it would have to follow Hindenburg's injunction and keep its nerves under control. If the German people continued for a little while longer to put up with hardships and deprivations, they would be able to secure a "Hindenburg peace," a peace which would bestow upon Germany the rewards of hard-earned victory. Any other kind of peace would be an annihilating blow to the future of the Reich.

The Fatherland party had little success with its annexationist propaganda. The masses showed a marked preference for the program espoused in the peace resolution. The drastic steps taken by the government to discourage open opposition to the aims of the Fatherland party created keen dissatisfaction. They widened the gulf between the bulk of the nation and the jingo coalition of Junkers, militarists, industrialists and bureaucrats. The semiautocratic regime had weathered many storms since its inception in 1871. But never before had it so completely alienated the sympathies of the average citizen.

5

Michaelis turned out to be merely the tool of the Supreme Command, doing its bidding all along the line. His brief chancellorship witnessed the first manifestations of insubordination among disgruntled sailors at the great naval base of Kiel. The admiralty dealt severely with the mutineers. They were court-martialed, and on September 5, 1917, two of the ringleaders were executed. The remaining accused received long prison sentences. This provoked much ill feeling in left-wing circles. At the Reichstag session of October 9, 1917, the Independent leader, Wilhelm Dittmann, claimed that the sailors had been punished because they had dared to express political views which were unpalatable to the authorities. Michaelis replied by accusing the Independents of conducting subversive agitation among members of the armed forces. He was followed by the navy minister, Admiral Eduard von Capelle, who vigorously supported this accusation. According to Capelle, the instigators of the mutiny had informed the Independent leaders, Haase, Dittmann and Vogtherr, of what was impending and had obtained their approval. The government was obviously trying to use the trouble in the navy to discredit the left-wing elements. But this political offensive boomeranged dismally when it became known that the cabinet did not have conclusive proof for its charges. Public indignation swerved from the Independents and turned against the chancellor and the navy minister. The Social Democrats, the Centrists and the Progressives trained their oratorical guns on Michaelis. They had no love for the Independents, but they felt it their duty to censure the government for behavior which they regarded as unethical. The strongest blast was delivered by Ebert. He ended his philippic by expressing the hope that the country would soon be rid of the Michaelis government. Sensing the temper of the country, the National Liberals hastened to climb on the anti-Michaelis bandwagon. On October 23, 1917, the four parties took a most unusual step. They informed the emperor that a change in the chancellorship would be in the best interests of the country. The aggressive, purposeful behavior of the Reichstag majority bespoke the change which had come over the German political scene. Michaelis had on his side only the Conservatives and the pan-Germans. This forced his resignation on October 26, 1917.

On taking leave of the emperor, Michaelis recommended Hertling as his successor. William once again was willing, and this time Hertling, feeling that it was his patriotic duty to accept, gave an affirmative answer. The new chancellor was an experienced politician. For many years he had been a member of the Reichstag and for a time had served as chairman of the Catholic Center. He was currently chairman of the Bundesrat's foreign affairs committee and was therefore reputed to be at home in the field of international relations. He was worldly-wise, tactful and level-headed. He had strong convictions but espoused them without rabid partisanship. The choice of Hertling was an advantageous one from the emperor's point of view. By selecting a member of the Center, one of the parties in the Reichstag coalition which had voted the peace resolution and was demanding the democratization of the imperial constitution, William was making a show of regard for the principle of ministerial responsibility. At the same time he was risking little because Hertling himself was no supporter of constitutional reform. The count belonged to the conservative right wing of the Center and had little sympathy for the views of Erzberger, the party's dominant figure. To Hertling the idea of transforming the semiautocratic regime into a truly parliamentary one was anathema. Hence the appointment of Hertling was received with a conspicuous lack of enthusiasm by the Reichstag majority. But the pill was sweetened by the selection of a leading member of the Progressive party, Friedrich von Payer, as vice-chancellor. Payer was a convinced liberal and enjoyed the confidence of the Social Democrats. This appointment, to which Hertling only reluctantly assented, was another concession to the exponents of ministerial responsibility. It was welcome to socialists and liberals for yet another reason: it meant the ouster of Karl Helfferich from the vice-chancellorship. In politics Helfferich had begun as a liberal and wound up as an arch-reactionary. This alone was enough to damn him in the eyes of his erstwhile comrades. Besides, he was tactless and vindictive and had made himself extremely unpopular with most of the Reichstag deputies. That he was a talented economist, banker and administrator no one could gainsay; but this was not enough to save him from the consequences of his personal shortcomings. His departure was a victory for the majority parties. They achieved still another triumph. They forced the admission of a left-wing National Liberal and a Progressive to the Prussian cabinet, thereby setting the stage for renewed pressure in favor of constitutional reform. Thus the advent of Hertling was accompanied by changes in personnel which constituted a long step toward the attainment of real democracy in Germany.

Chapter 3

BREST-LITOVSK

I

NOVEMBER, 1917, witnessed the Bolshevist revolution in Russia. The Social Democrats, who had formerly denounced Tsarism, now denounced Bolshevist terrorism and the dictatorship of the proletariat. They recoiled in horror from violence, revolution, bloodshed, civil war, the negation of democratic principles. The triumph of the Bolshevists in Russia stirred the German masses. It made a deep impression on the Independents and caused them to move farther to the Left. It greatly increased the importance of the numerically insignificant Spartacists, for the latter took up the Bolshevist cry of all power to the soviets and made themselves for all practical purposes the German wing of the Russian revolutionary movement. From a military point of view the seizure of power by the Bolshevists could be a great boon to Germany, for the Soviet leaders, notably Nicholas Lenin and Leon Trotsky, favored immediate withdrawal from the war. For this reason Ludendorff had permitted Lenin to travel through Germany in a sealed train that returned the famous exile to the land of his birth. Russia's withdrawal would free large German forces now engaged in the east for an all-out effort in the west before the full weight of American participation could make itself felt in that all-important theater.

On November 26, 1917, after having vainly appealed to all the belligerents for a general peace, Trotsky, Lenin's foreign commissar, applied to the German Supreme Command for an armistice which would pave the way for a democratic peace without annexations and indemnities. Two days later, Russian troops were ordered to cease firing. On November 29, the German and Austro-Hungarian governments announced their acceptance of the Russian proposals as a basis for armistice negotiations. Thus, in effect, they pledged themselves to conclude peace on the basis of the formula laid down in the resolution of July, 1917. The armistice with Russia was signed at Brest-Litovsk on December 17, 1917.

The Supreme Command was now in a position to attempt a decisive blow in the west. Ludendorff realized that such an attack would be a most difficult military operation. On the whole, however, he was optimistic as to its outcome because of the end of Russian resistance in the east. In a confidential report before a Bundesrat committee on January 2, 1918, he remarked that the transfer of troops from east to west would, at long last, consolidate the military position of Germany in the Franco-Belgian theater. He referred to certain difficulties which confronted the German war machine but quickly added that the enemy was plagued by similar difficulties. He told the committee that the over-all picture was better than at any previous time and that good prospect existed of bringing the war in the west to a successful conclusion. Actually, for the first time since the outbreak of the conflict, Germany enjoyed numerical superiority on the western front. She had, in March, 1918, 192 divisions at her disposal against 180 for the Anglo-French command.

While decisive military developments were thus in the making, the process of reaching an agreement with Russia monopolized the attention of most Germans. The Reich's good faith in claiming that the war it was waging was a purely defensive one underwent the acid test in the negotiations at Brest-Litovsk. The German people and the world generally were afforded an opportunity to ascertain whether the government of the Reich considered itself bound by the language of the resolution of July, 1917. Would the authorities at Berlin forego indemnities? Would they refrain from annexing foreign territory? Would they grant independence to Poland, the small Baltic states and the Ukraine? These questions Richard von Kuehlmann, the German foreign minister, attempted to answer shortly before his departure for Brest-Litovsk. He told the leaders of the various political parties that the government proposed to pursue a policy based on the resolution of July, 1917, and in accordance with the Bolshevist formula of no annexations and no indemnities. The Centrists, the Progressives and the two socialist parties applauded Kuehlmann's statement. They were sincerely anxious to see a just peace concluded with Russia. They reflected the attitude of the bulk of the German population.

But the views and aims of Kuehlmann and of his civilian colleagues in the cabinet did not tally with those of Ludendorff. The latter continued to insist on an annexationist policy. He wanted generous slices of Polish territory which were to be converted into "protective belts" for the defense of East Prussia and Upper Silesia. The German government objected to this plan because it meant the incorporation of additional millions of Poles into the Reich. However, the Supreme Command contended that military necessity must prevail over all other considerations. Ludendorff also wished to see Courland and Lithuania converted into grand-ducal appendages of the Hohenzollern dynasty. The annexationist program of the Supreme Command was vigorously supported by the National Liberals and the Conservatives. These groups made Ludendorff's views their own and urged them in the press and from the platform.

Braving Ludendorff's wrath, Kuehlmann stood his ground. But when he tackled the problem of translating his views into concrete political and territorial terms, he backslid lamentably. At Brest-Litovsk, he became afflicted with an anxiety to placate the Supreme Command and ended by espousing a program that could not fail to facilitate the execution of Ludendorff's plans. The Bolshevist peace delegation, headed by Adolf Joffe, was informed that the Central Powers regarded as perfectly proper the decision of Poland, Courland and Lithuania, once they had withdrawn from the Russian state, to set themselves up as independent entities or seek protection by making themselves part of the German Reich. Moreover, the Central Powers made it clear that they intended to deal directly with the spokesmen of Poland, Courland and Lithuania. From these parleys Russia was to be excluded. The Bolshevist delegates were outraged. They protested loudly and bitterly, claiming that the principle of peace without annexations was being brutally violated. Discovering that complaints were vain, they resorted to threats. They declared they would call a halt to the negotiations if satisfaction were not given them. But the Germans held firm. They knew full well that the Bolshevists, confronted with the danger of counterrevolution at home and handicapped by the lack of effective armed forces, would have to capitulate or risk seeing themselves ousted from power. They were right. Negotiations were not broken off. The Russians stayed in Brest-Litovsk and suffered another resounding setback. On December 28, 1917, the German delegation rejected the Russian demand for a completely untrammeled plebiscite in Poland, Courland and Lithuania. It justified its action by arguing that the Poles,

Courlanders and Lithuanians had already made up their minds. What the German delegation neglected to point out was that the land councils arbitrarily set up in Poland, Courland and Lithuania and presuming to speak in the name of the local population were definitely unrepresentative. And they were, to boot, forced to take orders from the commanders of the German armies of occupation. Thus the Diet of Mitau, acting under German pressure, had already asked William II to accept the title of Duke of Courland. Even greater pressure was being exerted upon the Lithuanian Diet to insure its compliance with the wishes of the Supreme Command. To regard these Diets as representing the will of the local inhabitants was, therefore, to make a mockery of the principle of self-determination to which the German delegation at Brest-Litovsk persisted in paying lip-service. All this the Russian delegates clearly perceived. They realized that their conception of self-determination was vastly different from Kuehlmann's. They knew now that the Germans had absolutely no intention of concluding a peace without annexations. What the Reich was up to was old-fashioned imperialist land-grabbing thinly camouflaged with slogans and catchwords that bore a superficial resemblance to those recently coined by the Bolshevists and by the parties of the Left in Germany.

2

The Russians were not alone in bewailing the character of German policy. Socialists and liberals throughout the Reich were irate over the government's betrayal of the principles enunciated in the peace resolution. They saw now that the rulers of their country were merely using phrases like "peace without annexations" as a smokescreen behind which to conceal their expansionist designs and their utter disregard for the rights of conquered peoples. These Germans appreciated, too, the awful responsibility which the Reich was assuming in thus repudiating the idea of a just and democratic peace. So far as propaganda warfare was concerned, Germany had put herself at a fatal disadvantage vis-à-vis the Allies. They could now adduce irrefutable proof for their contention that their cause was morally superior to that of the Central Powers. The moment was indeed propitious for a resounding utterance stressing the loftiness of Allied war aims. Such a manifesto, addressed to friend and foe alike, would accomplish several things. It would bolster civilian morale in Allied countries. It would counteract Bolshevist propaganda. It would undo some of the damage wrought by the recent disclosure that the Allies, in spite of all their high-sounding talk, were out to get whatever they could in keeping with the time-honored but now supposedly discredited rule that to the victors belong the spoils. Above all, it would increase disaffection within the Reich. It would give encouragement to all those Germans who sincerely opposed the annexationist plans of the Supreme Command and wished to see the war ended at the earliest possible moment. With these objectives in mind, President Woodrow Wilson outlined the war aims of the United States in a message to Congress on January 8, 1918. He stated the American program in a series of fourteen points. These included freedom of the seas; the removal of all trade barriers; the reduction of national armaments; an "absolutely impartial adjustment of all colonial claims"; the withdrawal of foreign troops from Russian soil; the evacuation and restoration of Belgium; the evacuation and restoration of the invaded portions of France and the recovery by her of Alsace-Lorraine; the creation of an independent Poland with access to the sea; the establishment of a league of nations to protect the independence and territorial integrity of all countries.

The fourteen points seemed to foreshadow lenient treatment for Germany. There were to be no war indemnities other than those implied in the demand for the restoration of Belgium and the enemy-held regions of France. Germany was asked to surrender only Alsace-Lorraine and the indisputably Polish districts in the east. Her colonies were not to be bartered about as mere spoils of war. Her maritime and economic interests were not to be ignored. Disarmament of the victors as well as of the vanquished was in prospect. The proposed league of nations would guarantee security for all, Germany included. Full-bodied implementation of these aims would go a long way toward attenuating the stigma and penalties of defeat.

Wilson's advocacy of a just peace on this and subsequent occasions had a tremendous effect on German public opinion. Extracts from his utterances were disseminated by airplane throughout the Reich. War-weary and disillusioned Germans came to regard the American president as someone who would bring better times for them as well as for the rest of the world. Their yearning for peace grew. Wilsonian idealism thus became the Allies' most potent psychological weapon. It contributed mightily to ultimate victory.

A challenge like Wilson's could not go unanswered. Hertling sought to meet it in the speech which he delivered before the main committee of the Reichstag on January 24, 1918. The chancellor discussed the

Wilsonian manifesto point by point. He declared that in general he agreed with the American statesman. Only as regards Poland and the occupied sections of France did he voice specific reservations. Occupied French areas, he stated emphatically, constituted a valuable pawn, to be used by Germany to protect herself against forced cessions of territory which rightfully belonged to her. This was an unmistakable allusion to Alsace-Lorraine, which Germans of every shade of opinion agreed in regarding as an integral part of the Reich. Equally emphatic were Hertling's remarks on the subject of Poland. He claimed for the Central Powers the right to decide, in agreement with the Poles, the destiny of that unhappy country. Hertling professed to discern in Wilson's observations the principles which might serve as the basis of world peace. Germany, he said, could assent to these principles. But he lessened the significance of this declaration by observing pointedly that Germany's military position was more favorable than ever before, that Germany's military leaders viewed the future with undiminished confidence, and that the German armies were permeated with unimpaired zeal for battle. Leaning heavily on Ludendorff's sanguine evaluation of Germany's prospects, Hertling proceeded to voice objection to the tone of certain remarks in Wilson's address. Said he: "That is the way the victor speaks to the vanquished; that is the language of one who regards all our previous expressions of readiness for peace merely as a sign of weakness." At the close of his speech, Hertling called upon the Allied leaders to revise their program.

If you come forward with new proposals, we will examine them seriously; for our goal is nothing less than the reestablishment of a lasting general peace. But such a peace is not possible so long as the integrity of the German empire, the protection of our vital interests and the dignity of our Fatherland are not safeguarded.

On February 11, 1918, Wilson stated in general fashion the principles which, in his opinion, would have to govern the future peace. Every part of the final settlement, he urged, must be based on justice and on "such adjustments as are most likely to bring a peace that will be permanent." Peoples and territories were not to be "bartered about from sovereignty to sovereignty as if they were mere chattels and pawns in a game. . . ." All territorial arrangements resulting from the war would have to be made in the interests of the peoples concerned, and not simply as part of a deal between rival powers. The principle of national self-determination was to be given every satisfaction that could be afforded it without creating new or perpetuating old quarrels that would ultimately prove disastrous to the peace of the world. On February 25, Hertling vouchsafed a friendly reply to Wilson's latest utterance. He declared before the Reichstag that he concurred in the principles laid down by the American statesman. A general peace, he believed, could be discussed on the basis of them. However, they would first have to be recognized by all states and nations. Hertling's remarks were universally applauded in Germany but they made little impression on the Allied governments.

3

Trotsky, who replaced Joffe as head of the Soviet peace delegation, arrived in Brest-Litovsk early in January, 1918, to resume the negotiations. He proved a far more formidable adversary than his predecessor. He announced that Russia would continue to reject the German conception of self-determination for the regions under military occupation. The Bolshevist government wanted a peace that was at once democratic and just. There followed an interminable and fruitless wrangle between the Russian and German delegates. Trotsky reiterated the Russian thesis that all troops must be withdrawn from the occupied territories in order to insure completely free plebiscites. Kuehlmann retorted that the German troops would stay where they were. He insisted once again that the Poles, the Courlanders and the Lithuanians had already exercised their right of self-determination through agencies established under the supervision of the occupation authorities. On January 12, 1918, General Max Hoffmann, chief of staff in the east, stated the Supreme Command's position with unvarnished frankness. At once there was a loud outcry on the part of all those Germans who still persisted in taking seriously the language of the peace resolution of July, 1917. Indignation was strongest among the industrial workers of the Reich. These humble wage earners had reacted with ill-disguised disgust to the proceedings at Brest-Litovsk. Long imbued with the desire for a just peace, they were infuriated by the disclosure of Ludendorff's annexationist plans in the east. They wanted the war to end as soon as possible. But their military leaders' lust for conquest might well mean an indefinite prolongation of hostilities. This, however, was not their only grievance. They objected strenuously to autocratic rule and the indiscriminate invocation of martial law. They were angry over the barbaric punishment meted out from time to time to labor leaders. Above all, they were driven to the verge of des–

peration by the indescribable hardships endured in this winter of 1917-1918, the terrible "turnip winter." Radical propaganda was bound to and did become more effective. This was especially true in the Berlin area, where the Independents were strong. Many of the capital's trade unions were dominated by the so-called Revolutionary Shop Stewards (*revolutionaere Obleute*). These men were militant radicals. They belonged to the left wing of the Independents. At the same time, they maintained close and continuous contact with the Spartacists.

The ferment which gripped large sections of the German proletariat found dramatic expression in the great metal workers' strike which broke out in Berlin on January 28, 1918. The movement, led by Independents, quickly spread to other large cities. It was political rather than economic in character. The strikers called for the immediate negotiation of a peace based on the Bolshevist formula of no annexations and no indemnities. The workers, they declared, must be represented at the peace conference. They demanded adequate provision for the needy and the starving through a more rigorous control of foodstuffs and other necessities. They clamored for termination of the state of siege and demilitarization of the great national industries. They insisted upon an amnesty for all political offenders and the enactment of sweeping democratic reforms in the constitutional sphere. These demands were obviously not as revolutionary as the Shop Stewards and the Spartacists would have desired. They did not constitute an attempt to bring about socialism in Germany. But they revealed, nonetheless, an unmistakable swing to the Left among the nation's workers. Clearly, the wage-earning masses were placing themselves far in advance of their principal spokesmen, the trade-union executives and the Social Democrats. The latter found themselves from the outset in a rather difficult position. Mass strikes smacked too much of revolution to suit their moderate, gradualist tastes. They preferred less drastic means. But their hand was forced by the fact that many of the workers who participated in the strike belonged to the Social Democratic party. When these workers demanded that their party make common cause with the strikers, the Social Democratic chieftains decided it would be inexpedient to refuse. So they joined the Independents in the leadership of the movement.

The strike was put down in short order. Denouncing work stoppages in time of war as nothing less than treason, the authorities proceeded with the utmost severity. Wilhelm Dittmann, who had helped to organize the walkout in Berlin, was sentenced to five years' imprisonment. There were mass arrests; and large numbers of strikers were drafted into the army, a move which boomeranged disastrously because these unwilling recruits sought to undermine the morale of the fighting forces by spreading defeatist propaganda. The strictest kind of martial law was clamped down on Berlin. By February 3, 1918, the government had the situation well in hand.

The January strike, foreshadowing as it did the possibility of even more serious disturbances, had the effect of stiffening the resistance of the Russians to the harsh terms laid before them at Brest-Litovsk. The stalemate in the negotiations irked the emperor no end. He ordered Kuehlmann to bring matters to a head by presenting a 24-hour ultimatum to the Soviet delegation. But Kuehlmann refused because he felt the moment was unpropitious for such a move; and he forced William to back down by threatening to resign if the idea of an ultimatum were not dropped. Kuehlmann believed that the Russians, at long last, were prepared to be more tractable. He was speedily disillusioned. On February 10, 1918, Trotsky created a sensation by asserting that Russia could not sanction with her signature the conditions laid down by the Central Powers. However, he went on to say that his government, although refusing to accept a peace of annexation, considered the war ended and was ordering the demobilization of its troops on all fronts. That night the Russian delegation departed for Petrograd. Trotsky's theatrical "no peace-no war" pronouncement left the spokesmen for the Central Powers dumbfounded. At once a meeting of the German crown council was summoned; it took place at Homburg on February 13, 1918. Ludendorff demanded the immediate denunciation of the armistice with Russia and urged the emperor to order the German troops on the eastern front to keep going until all of Livonia and Estonia had been occupied. He argued that in this way a kind of *cordon sanitaire* would be created to prevent the westward spread of Bolshevism. He also pointed out that a resumption of the German advance was dictated by the necessity of safeguarding the recently concluded peace with the Ukraine, whose grain the Central Powers, plagued by an ever growing food shortage, desperately needed. The emperor was inclined to agree with Ludendorff, but Hertling and Payer dissented. Their opposition to the views of the Supreme Command was motivated by the fear that a resumption of hostilities against Russia would aggravate Germany's internal situation by alienating the socialist parties and driving the masses into the arms of the most radical elements. However, they relented after Ludendorff assured them that he had no intention of occupying Livonia and Estonia permanently and that all he had in mind was a relatively limited operation whose objective was two-fold: shortening of the front in the east in order to facilitate the forthcoming offensive in the west; and conquest of the strategically important city of Dvinsk. Kuehlmann refused to accept the views of the Supreme Command but finally allowed himself to be overruled. Thereupon the emperor declared the armistice at an end and ordered Hoffmann to set the German war machine in motion.

Hostilities against the Bolshevists were resumed on February 18, 1918. One army marched toward Dvinsk and Reval; another forged ahead in the Ukraine. In the course of these initial advances, the Germans occupied all of Estonia and Livonia without encountering resistance. The Soviet government promptly gave in. On February 20, it announced its unconditional acceptance of the terms laid down at Brest-Litovsk. Berlin replied with an ultimatum which went beyond the demands previously submitted by the Central Powers. Russia was told that she would have to give up Courland, Lithuania and Poland, evacuate Finland and the Ukraine, facilitate the return of the East Anatolian provinces to Turkey, demobilize her armed forces forthwith and discontinue her propaganda against the Central Powers. Livonia and Estonia were to be occupied by a German police force until public order and safety had been restored. Russia was given forty-eight hours to accept. Her plenipotentiaries would have to proceed at once to Brest-Litovsk and within three days of their arrival affix their signatures to the peace treaty. The Bolshevists were furious. Some of them, giving free vent to their feelings, insisted that no country could accept such devastating and humiliating terms. They said they preferred war to the kind of peace the Germans were concocting. But these hotheads found Lenin immovable. With that cold and inflexible realism which he was to display again and again, the Soviet leader declared that Russia had no choice but to capitulate. The country's military situation was utterly hopeless. If the war were resumed, everything would be lost. "You must sign this shameful peace," he said, "in order to save the world revolution, in order to hold fast to its most important and, at present, its only foothold—the Soviet Republic. . . ." After a protracted and bitter debate, he won. Early in the morning of February 24, 1918, one hour before the expiration of the German ultimatum, he dispatched a telegram to Berlin signifying his government's readiness to sign. The stage was now set for the consummation of Ludendorff's annexationist schemes.

The task of defending the policies and high-handed tactics of the Supreme Command fell to Chancellor Hertling. On February 25, 1918, that benign and cultured statesman impressed upon the Reichstag that from the beginning the nation's war aims had been the defense of the Fatherland, the maintenance of its territorial integrity and the safe-guarding of its freedom to develop economically. The purely defensive character of the war, he went on, had not been impaired by unavoidable recourse to aggressive means. This point had to be emphasized in order to prevent misunderstandings in connection with current military operations in the east. The discontinuance of peace negotiations by Russia gave the Reich a free hand vis-à-vis that country. The subsequent resumption of the German advance was not motivated by a desire for territorial conquest. Its object was to secure the fruits of the recently concluded peace with the Ukraine. But grain was not the only consideration. Germany was acting in response to Ukrainian appeals for help against the Bolshevists. Operations in other sectors of the eastern front were being undertaken in answer to similar appeals from the local inhabitants. It was therefore clear that the campaign was being waged in the name of humanity. This character it would retain. Germany had no intention of establishing herself permanently in Estonia and Livonia. She desired only to remain on friendly terms with the regimes which were taking shape there. As for Courland and Lithuania, the important thing was either to create machinery which would enable them to express their own wishes and achieve self-government or to bolster whatever machinery was already in process of formation. On the Polish issue, Germany and Austria-Hungary were in complete agreement. It was their aim to create an independent Poland which would constitute a pillar of peace in Europe. The constitutional organization of the new state could not be determined immediately. It was, at the moment, the subject of conversations between the three countries. There were difficulties of an economic nature in connection with the resurrection of an independent Poland. To these difficulties new ones had recently been added as a result of the collapse of the Tsarist regime in Russia. Specifically, the delimitation of Poland's frontiers presented serious problems. Because they feared the worst, the Poles had reacted unfavorably to the news of a peace between Germany and the Ukraine. It was to be hoped that an amicable adjustment of rival claims would be achieved. Germany, for her part, would demand only that portion of Polish territory which she regarded as indispensable from a military point of view.

On February 26, 1918, the terms of the German ultimatum to Russia were divulged to the Reichstag by a spokesman for the ministry of foreign affairs. The Conservatives and the National Liberals promptly voiced their approval. This was hardly surprising, since those two parties had consistently supported the annexationist schemes of the Supreme Command. But surprising, certainly, was the attitude of the Centrists and the Progressives. Although they had collaborated with the Social Democrats to put through the peace resolution in July, 1917, they now gave their sanction to the terms imposed on Russia. This volte-face was justified in language which revealed the moral bankruptcy of men who only seven months before had given new hope to all those Germans who aspired to a just and democratic peace. The spokesman for the Progressives declared that his party attached great importance to the reestablishment of friendly relations with Russia. However, it did not believe that this result could be achieved only by fulfilling the demands of the Bolshevists. Germany, he blandly continued, had no desire for conquests. Even more astounding and disillusioning was the language of Erzberger. The unscrupulous and mercurial Centrist leader contended that the conditions laid down in the German ultimatum were consistent with the principles proclaimed by the peace resolution. Only the Social Democrats and the Independents had the decency to denounce the German terms. Philipp Scheidemann, the Social Democrats' most effective orator, bluntly asserted that the treatment being accorded the Russians ran counter to the wishes of his party. "We are fighting," he said, "to defend our Fatherland, not to destroy Russia." He warned that revolution would be the consequence of failure to conclude a true peace. Thanks to her annexationist policy, Germany was losing her last friends abroad. But the honors in this debate went not to the Social Democrats but to their hard-hitting rivals, the Independents. On February 27, 1918, Hugo Haase delivered a speech the like of which had never before been heard in the hall of the Reichstag. Casting aside the restraints ordinarily imposed upon themselves by participants in a public discussion, especially in time of war, Haase painted a picture of German policy that made his hearers squirm. The ultimatum to Russia, he declared, was the expression of a policy of violence and, as such, was utterly incompatible with the Reichstag peace resolution. It could no longer be claimed that the German government was seeking a peace of understanding. Spokesmen for the Catholic and Progressive parties had voiced approval of the ultimatum. This showed the worthlessness of Germany's disavowal of desire for conquest. As a matter of fact, Chancellor Hertling was nothing more than a press agent for the "all-powerful" military party. He was only nominally the head of the imperial government. The real ruler of the country was Ludendorff. Thanks to him, Russia was being compelled to sign a peace treaty so bad that a worse one could not be imagined. The right of self-determination, to which so much lip-service had been paid, was being ruthlessly disregarded in the territories taken from Russia. The real aim of German policy toward the Ukraine was to repress the revolutionary forces that had wrested control of that embattled area from the anti-Bolshevist elements. Poland, whose fate was being arbitrarily determined in Berlin and Vienna, stood on the verge of still another partition. German statesmen had often said that the Reich had no desire to despoil or subjugate any other nation. With equal frequency they had accused foreign governments of wishing to destroy Germany and the German people. But today, no one outside Germany, not even the most pro-German circles in neutral countries, could abstain from laughing at such assertions and accusations. The Reich had no right to intervene in the domestic affairs of other peoples. Against this policy of violence the Independents protested and would continue to protest so long as it was practised. They would not be deterred by the fact that Germany was in a state of war.

It is very easy, in time of peace, when there is no question of coming to a decision, to speak out in purely theoretical fashion against a policy of violence. But it is the special duty of those who are sincere about this to make themselves heard when the principle involved is being put to a practical test. . . .

German imperialism was not confined to the east. The Conservatives were demanding the annexation of Belgium. Hertling had recently stated that Germany did not want to keep Belgium. But that was not really the issue. What required explaining was whether Germany was prepared to recognize the economic, financial and military independence of Belgium. About this Hertling had said nothing. A word of enlightenment was also needed about Longwy and Briey in view of the desire of Stresemann and his National Liberals to help themselves to the rich iron deposits of those areas.

Haase next turned his attention to the internal situation and to the manner in which it was being affected by disillusioning developments abroad. He charged that within Germany, as in her foreign policy, the principle of violence held sway. This was clear from the thoroughly reprehensible way in which the January strike had been handled by the government. The brutal treatment meted out to the leaders of the strike had only served to enrage and embitter the workers. The government harbored the complacent delusion that it had mastered the labor movement. Actually, the policy of putting working-class leaders into the army was very short-sighted. For every leader spirited away, two new ones would appear. Contrary to government charges, the strike was not the work of foreign agitators. It grew out of the political situation in Germany. In August, 1914, the workers had been urged to agree to a civil truce for the duration. But those who had done the urging had themselves had no intention of abiding by the terms of this truce. For these people the suspension of internal quarrels was to be a means of keeping the workers from engaging in class warfare. Throughout the war the Junkers, industrialists and merchants had unremittingly looked after their own interests. A great deal of new wealth had passed into their hands. If the workers gave up the class struggle, they would stand defenseless against German capitalism. But the decisive factor in their resolve to stage a strike was their realization, strengthened by the Brest-Litovsk negotiations, that the war was being waged for conquest and that the ruling classes of Germany were incapable of bringing about a general peace. The workers had not launched the strike in order to win some small economic advantage; they had been inspired exclusively by political idealism. Their gesture of protest had achieved its purpose. At home it had served notice on the ruling classes that the workers were fed up with being used as the tools of a policy of oppression and exploitation. It had made clear to the world the readiness of the German proletariat to work with the industrial masses of other countries for a democratic peace.

The attitude of the Social Democrats and the Independents failed to stay the rape of Russia. On February 28, 1918, the Soviet delegation arrived in Brest-Litovsk and three days later signed the treaty of peace. The final text of the document went beyond the terms of the German ultimatum, for at the last moment the Turks had insisted on the insertion of a clause which disposed, in the manner specified by them, of the fate of Ardahan, Kars and Batum. All in all, the treaty was one of the most draconian ever imposed by one nation upon another. As

John W. Wheeler-Bennett points out in his *The Forgotten Peace*, Russia lost "34 per cent of her population, 32 per cent of her agricultural land, 85 per cent of her beet-sugar land, 54 per cent of her industrial undertakings, and 89 per cent of her coal mines." Compared to the Treaty of Brest-Litovsk, the Treaty of Versailles, against which the Germans were to protest so bitterly, was mild and even generous. The Bolshevists attempted to make political capital of their enforced capitulation to the demands of the German war lords. Just before the ceremony of signing, Gregory Sokolnikov, who had succeeded Trotsky as head of the Russian delegation, eloquently restated his government's position.[1]

This is no peace of understanding and agreement, but a peace which Russia, grinding her teeth, is compelled to accept. This is a peace which, while pretending to free Russian border provinces, really transforms them into German states and deprives them of their right of self-determination. This is a peace which, while pretending to reestablish order, gives armed support in these regions to class exploitation, putting the working class again beneath the yoke of oppression which was removed by the Russian revolution. This is a peace which returns the land to the landlords and again drives the workers into the serfdom of the factory owners. . . . Under present conditions, the Soviet government . . . is unable to withstand the armed offensive of German imperialism and is forced, for the sake of saving revolutionary Russia, to accept the terms put before it. . . .

Sokolnikov's ringing challenge became a powerful weapon of Bolshevist propaganda throughout Central Europe, above all in Germany. But it failed to affect the deliberations of the Reichstag. The Treaty of Brest-Litovsk was ratified by a majority which included Centrists and Progressives. The Social Democrats, instead of ranging themselves against so flagrant a violation of the principle of no annexations, abstained from voting. They justified their strange behavior by arguing that they could not vote against a peace treaty because to do so would be to vote in favor of prolonging the war. Only the Independents, speaking for the outraged workers of Germany, voted no.

[1] Quoted in *The Forgotten Peace,* by John W. Wheeler-Bennett (William Morrow & Company).

Chapter 4

GERMANY SUES FOR PEACE

I

Military considerations had been adduced by the Supreme Command in justification of its severe policy toward Russia. But the very harshness of the peace imposed on the Bolshevists, the fact that it could be maintained only by the exercise of overwhelming force, compelled Ludendorff to keep more than a million soldiers in the east when every ounce of available strength was needed for the impending thrust in the west. Thus the great German offensive, which was designed to annihilate the Entente armies and bring the war to a victorious close before the expanding military might of the United States could make itself felt, had to dispense with the services of the legions commanded by General Hoffmann. The resultant weakening of the effort in the west contributed heavily to the ultimate outcome of the campaign. Because he had overreached himself in his dealings with the Russians, Ludendorff found himself constrained to embark upon the supreme military venture of his career without adequate first-class reserves.

The German attack began at 4 A.M. on March 21, 1918. Allied positions in the crucial Arras-Cambrai-St. Quentin-La Fère sector were promptly overrun. The success of the operation seemed assured. Jubilation swept Germany. Both Hindenburg and Ludendorff were signally honored by the emperor. The popularity of the two war lords had never been greater. But this rejoicing proved premature. The reserves which the Allies managed to rush to the scene of action turned out to be the decisive factor. The connection between the French and British armies, which Ludendorff had sought to sever, remained unbroken. On March 30, the German advance was stopped.

On April 4, Ludendorff threw new troops into the fray in an attempt to break through to Amiens, an important French base and railway center. Its capture would have unhinged the French lines. The German effort failed. Undaunted by this setback, Ludendorff opened another large-scale assault in Flanders on April 9. The British were pushed back and made to suffer heavy losses. But timely French aid prevented the attackers from achieving anything more than a local tactical success.

The German offensives of March-April, 1918, resulted in the taking of a vast amount of booty and many thousands of prisoners. Deep salients had been driven into the Franco-British lines. But the main objective of the Supreme Command had not been attained. A decisive victory over the Allies still remained to be won. The big danger for the Germans, and this Ludendorff realized, was the ever growing strength of the American forces in France. Another attempt would have to be made to overwhelm the French and British armies before the main body of American troops was encountered. After a one-month pause, during which frenzied preparations were made for a resumption of large-scale operations, a new German offensive was launched on May 27, 1918. This time the attack was directed against the French armies north of the Aisne. Once again the Germans scored a great tactical success, forcing the French back to the Marne. A decisive victory seemed within reach; but the German armies did not possess sufficient reserves to follow through, and the engagement continued well into the month of June, 1918. Undeterred by heavy losses and the fact that his overworked troops were nearing the point of exhaustion, Ludendorff decided to make one more effort. The point selected for attack was Rheims. The Germans went over the top on July 15, 1918. After a few initial successes, they were stopped cold. The French counterattacked sharply and forced the Germans back. Confronted with the danger of an Allied flanking movement that would have rendered his most advanced positions untenable, Ludendorff was compelled to order a general retreat from the Marne. The operation was completed in orderly fashion by the beginning of August, 1918. No longer able to mount new offensives, and heavily outnumbered thanks to the arrival of large American contingents, the Germans had no choice but to pursue from now on a purely defensive strategy.

On August 8, 1918, the British launched a surprise assault between Amiens and St. Quentin. Several German divisions were overwhelmed as the attackers, spearheaded by tanks, knifed their way forward. The breach in the German lines was speedily widened. Only the most heroic exertions on the part of Ludendorff's outnumbered and exhausted warriors finally brought the British to a halt. But the respite, the Germans knew, would be short-lived. The superiority of the Allies in men and matériel was bound to make things increasingly uncomfortable. Most disturbing to the Supreme Command was the deteriorating morale of Germany's fighting men. A new division which had just arrived at the front was greeted with cries of "Strikebreakers!" and "You are prolonging the war!" from battle-weary soldiers being moved to the rear.

The significance of the British victory was not lost on Ludendorff. When word of the breakthrough was relayed to him, he realized that the beginning of the end was at hand. As he later acknowledged, August 8, 1918, was "the black day of the German army in the history of this war." The situation was too critical to be kept from the emperor. Important political decisions might have to be made before further disasters overtook the armies of the Reich. A few days after the German reverse in the Amiens-St. Quentin sector, Ludendorff said to his sovereign: "We must realize that we have suffered a serious defeat." Hindenburg contributed to the gloom by reporting that Germany's Austro-Hungarian allies were nearing the end of their rope. The pessimistic attitude of the Supreme Command led the emperor to conclude that the jig was up. "I see," he said, "that we must add up accounts. We have arrived at the limit of our energies. The war must be stopped." On August 13, 1918, the two generals conferred with Hertling and Admiral Paul von Hintze, who had succeeded Kuehlmann as foreign minister. Ludendorff now took a more sanguine line. He admitted that Germany would have to confine herself to a purely defensive strategy but contended that it was still possible to break the enemy's will to fight and force him to sue for peace. Hintze was not convinced. He told Hertling that he did not share Ludendorff's optimism and insisted that diplomatic steps would have to be taken to bring the war to a close. The issue thus posed by Hintze was fully discussed the following day at a meeting of the crown council. The foreign minister urged his views on the emperor, contending that Germany was no longer militarily capable of forcing the Allies to abandon the struggle. Hindenburg promptly demurred. He was still hopeful, he said, that the German armies would be able to stand firm in France and thus win out in the end. Ludendorff also contradicted Hintze, arguing that steps toward peace should be taken only after another victory had been won in the west. The emperor, to whom the sanguine outlook of the generals must have come as a surprise, agreed to wait. Germany, he declared, must be on the lookout for the proper moment to reach an understanding with the enemy. That moment, Hertling observed when the emperor had finished, would come after Germany's next victory on the western front. A basic question of foreign policy was thus once again decided in accordance with Ludendorff's wishes.

The hoped-for victory never materialized. And instead of standing firm, the German armies continued to fall back before the mounting fury of British, French and American onslaughts. But the west was not the sole source of bad tidings. On September 15, 1918, Austria-Hungary, which was desperately seeking to get out of the war before being overtaken by irreparable ruin, invited all the belligerents to send representatives to "a confidential and non-binding discussion on basic principles." On the same day, the Allies launched a powerful offensive in the Salonika sector. The Bulgarians were overwhelmed and forced into headlong flight. Unable to make a stand anywhere, they had no choice but to sue for an armistice, which was granted them on September 29, 1918.

September 15, 1918, was clearly another "black day" for Germany; and it was altogether obvious that even worse days were in the offing. Yet Hertling made no effort to reach an understanding with the enemy. His inaction at this late date, when the victory he had been praying for was no longer a possibility, can be explained only by the fact that he had surrendered all initiative and independence of judgment to Ludendorff and simply marked time while waiting for the general to tell him what to do. Certain members of the chancellor's immediate entourage did not conceal their concern. Hintze was their principal spokesman. He took the position that the time had come to do something about initiating peace negotiations. But Hertling showed no inclination to bestir himself. Even the ominous gesture of the Austrians failed to galvanize him into action.

On September 24, 1918, Hertling and Hintze appeared before the main committee of the Reichstag and reported on the political situation. Nothing of great moment happened at this session. But on the following day the leaders of the various parties had their say. The first to take the floor was Adolf Groeber, the Centrist spokesman. His address turned out to be a veritable bombshell. It was clear, when he had finished, that the Center no longer stood behind its own chancellor.

The press underlined this point. And many newspapers went so far as to speculate about the identity of Hertling's successor.

News of Bulgaria's collapse reached Berlin on September 26. At once the political crisis precipitated by Groeber's speech deepened. For it was now apparent that the decisive blow against Germany was coming not from the west but from the southeast. The latest developments signified that the capitulation of Austria was only a question of days or weeks. And when this occurred, Germany's military position would become absolutely untenable. It would then be impossible to avoid disaster by holding in the west, for the Reich would be exposed to invasion from several other directions.

On September 28, the Social Democrats and the Progressives launched a new political offensive. They demanded the abrogation of two sections of the imperial constitution. One of these (Article 9) made it impossible for a Reichstag deputy to become a member of the Bundesrat. The other (Article 21) obliged members of the Reichstag to surrender their seats if they accepted cabinet posts. Both of these sections had for long been regarded as the chief obstacle to the parliamentarization of the German government. They stood in the way of all attempts to increase the power of the lower house. In pressing for their abrogation, the Social Democrats and the Progressives argued that such action was indispensable for the creation of a government which would be able to win the confidence of the Reichstag, organize national defense and attain a peace of understanding. The Catholic Center refused to take quite so unequivocal a stand. It declared that it could not assume the initiative in proposing the constitutional reforms in question. But it hastened to add that a considerable number of its members would vote for them in the Reichstag.

On the evening of September 28, just as he was about to leave for general headquarters in Spa, Hertling was apprised of this newest development. So far as he was concerned, the demands of the Social Democrats and the Progressives were absolutely unacceptable. He had repeatedly voiced his opposition to any tampering with the provision forbidding concurrent membership of both houses of parliament. On his way to Spa, Hertling pondered the situation. If he remained in office, he would have a fight with the Reichstag on his hands. The only alternative was to resign. This he would rather do than agree to the proposed constitutional changes. Article 9 was the cornerstone of the federative structure of the Reich. And federalism was an integral part of Hertling's political creed. Besides, he opposed the establishment of a truly parliamentary system, which was the ultimate objective of the majority parties.

Hertling arrived in Spa early in the afternoon of September 29, 1918. William was also on hand for conferences with the Supreme Command. Bad tidings awaited them. Shortly before their arrival, the military chieftains of Germany had decided that the war was irrevocably lost. It was on September 28 that Ludendorff and Hindenburg, independently of each other, reached the same conclusion: Germany must ask for an armistice without delay. They both felt that even if the German forces should be able to hold in the west, developments in the Balkans could so aggravate the over-all military position of the country as to make it completely hopeless. As usual, the decisive factor was the attitude of Ludendorff, and at this moment the once arrogant and masterful First Quartermaster General was in the grip of panic and despair. What he wanted above all was the immediate initiation of steps to mitigate the impending military catastrophe and avert the crowning humiliation of capitulation in the field. With this in mind, he insisted on certain guarantees. The conditions of the armistice, he said, must be such as to permit an orderly evacuation of the occupied territories. They must likewise be so framed as to make possible, if this should prove necessary, the resumption of hostilities along the borders of Germany.

On the morning of September 29, Hindenburg and Ludendorff conferred at length with Hintze. The two army leaders discussed the rapidly deteriorating military situation in Southwestern Europe and contended that a request for an armistice would have to be dispatched to Wilson at once. In making this request, Germany was to declare herself prepared to conclude peace on the basis of the principles laid down in Wilson's published utterances. Hintze agreed. But Ludendorff did not confine himself to a discussion of the military situation. He pointed out that revolution or chaos might ensue when the German people, without forewarning, learned that the war had been lost. The sudden realization that defeat and not victory was in the offing might deal such a shock to the nation that both the empire and the dynasty would be endangered. Only a revolution from above could stave off the threat of revolution from below. The emperor must democratize the government by broadening its base. Such a change was dictated by still another consideration. Should the Allied terms prove unacceptable, a last-ditch struggle would have to be waged. This struggle would have to take the form of a people's war. But no such

universal and wholehearted response would be possible without sweeping constitutional reforms. Moreover, lenient terms would not be obtained from Wilson unless popular rule was instituted in Germany.
In urging this point, Ludendorff was on solid ground. Recent utterances by the American president indicated that the Allies would refuse to deal with the Reich so long as it retained its semiautocratic
regime.

Their conference concluded, Hindenburg, Ludendorff and Hintze
repaired to the emperor's quarters. William agreed to an immediate
request for an armistice. He also concurred in the view that the
people should be given a larger share in the government. It was now
the turn of Hertling to be apprised of these momentous decisions. His
first act was to submit his resignation, which the emperor had no
choice but to accept. The aged statesman argued that time should be
taken to ponder the formation of a new government and the dispatch
of an armistice request. There was no need, so far as he could tell,
for undue haste. Besides, nothing could be done about an armistice
until the new government, constituted in accordance with parliamentary principles, had been formed. And there was little reason to suppose that so drastic a change could be consummated before several
days had elapsed. But Ludendorff said he could not wait. He told
Hintze that a new government would have to be in existence and
ready to dispatch the armistice request not later than October 1. The
situation, he warned, was too critical to admit of delay.

2

On September 30, 1918, in a proclamation addressed to Hertling, the
emperor announced that the chancellor's resignation had been accepted. He went on to say:

It is my wish that the German people should participate more effectively
than heretofore in the determination of the fate of the Fatherland. It is
therefore my will that men who enjoy the confidence of the nation should
partake extensively of the rights and duties of government.

The emperor had taken the first step toward the revolution from above
demanded by Ludendorff. He took the second on the morning of
October 1, 1918, when he decided to entrust the chancellorship to
Prince Max of Baden. This, from many points of view, seemed a
happy choice. The prince was a close relative of the emperor and hence

could be relied upon to stand by the Hohenzollern dynasty during the stormy days ahead. He was the heir to the throne of Baden; he therefore had an important personal stake in the preservation of the monarchical system in Germany. He was no novice at the game of politics, having at one time been active in Badenese parliamentary life. He was widely reputed to be democratic in outlook and favorable to the idea of a peace of understanding. He had come out publicly for a league of nations. He was, for these reasons, acceptable to liberals and socialists whose good will the Hohenzollern dynasty would need to survive the coming ordeal. At the same time his aristocratic lineage and class interests gave ample assurance that under his leadership there would be no plunge into wild experiments at home. With a man like Prince Max at the helm, changes marked by gradualism and compromise would be possible. Enjoying the confidence of both the Right and the Left, he might succeed in preserving as much as possible of the old order while lending his support to necessary democratic reforms. The big unanswered question was: did he possess the ability and strength to guide the German state under admittedly difficult conditions?

On the afternoon of October 1, Prince Max journeyed to Berlin to assume his new post. In his pocket he carried the outline of a program which he had hastily sketched: no peace offer, but a clear statement of Germany's war aims which would go a long way toward meeting the views of the enemy; enunciation, at the same time, of the nation's firm resolve to fight to the death if dishonorable terms were offered it. On his arrival in Berlin, Max was as yet unaware of the Supreme Command's pessimistic view of the military situation and of Ludendorff's frantic clamor for the immediate dispatch of an armistice request. He was therefore deeply dismayed to learn how matters stood and that he was expected to initiate peace negotiations without further ado. Nevertheless, he hoped that he would be able to postpone, for a while at least, the action desired by Ludendorff. But already—unbeknown to Max—a step had been taken which made it virtually impossible for the German government to alter the course fixed for it by the Supreme Command. On the night of September 29-30, Hintze had informed Germany's allies—Austria-Hungary, Bulgaria and Turkey—of the projected armistice request. The number of those who were initiated into the secrets of Germany's future policy was now very large, and in a short while the Reich's intention to sue for peace would become generally known. Under the circumstances, a change of course dictated by purely tactical considerations would fool no one, least of all the Allies. For in effect Germany had served notice that she was through, and the inferences to be drawn from such an admission were plain. All this meant that Prince Max was confronted with a *fait accompli*. He had so little room in which to maneuver that in the end he would have to go ahead with the policy demanded by the Supreme Command.

In the meantime, Ludendorff continued to press for an immediate peace overture. He warned that failure to act might result in a military catastrophe within the next forty-eight hours. Messages to this effect poured in on the German foreign office from general headquarters at Spa. They received a vigorous rejoinder from Max, whose first reaction was to stand up for his own ideas. He contended that an overhasty request for peace would be politically and diplomatically inexpedient. Time, he insisted, was needed to plan the whole thing. It was questionable whether all the implications of Wilson's fourteen points were appreciated by the German people. In any case it would be wise to wait until a new government, fashioned in accordance with democratic principles, had come into being. Max refused to be overawed by the Supreme Command's warning that the gravity of the military situation made further delay inadmissible.

At the request of the emperor, Vice-Chancellor Payer sounded the various party leaders regarding the formation of a new cabinet. The outcome of these negotiations lent support to the view that a national coalition government composed of the representatives of all the parties would not meet the needs of the moment. The impression prevailed that the best results would be obtained by recruiting the cabinet from the three majority parties and by adding the National Liberals at some later date. The Conservatives, it was generally agreed, could hardly be trusted with a share of the new leadership.

On the morning of October 2, 1918, Major von der Bussche, speaking for Ludendorff, described the desperate military situation at a closed meeting of party leaders. He stressed the point that peace overtures to the Allies must be accompanied by the formation at home of a united front which would demonstrate Germany's resolve to continue the war if the enemy should refuse to make peace or should offer unacceptable terms. Ebert, who attended this meeting, promptly closeted himself with other leaders of the Social Democratic party. The attitude of the nation's strongest political group was bound to determine the fate of the current efforts to establish a coalition government which could speak for the majority of the population. On the question of whether or not to join such a government the Social Democratic chieftains were sharply divided. One faction, led by Scheidemann, argued that the party would be committing a grave mistake if it agreed to enter Prince Max's cabinet. For years, Scheidemann pointed out, the Social Democrats had striven to make possible a peace which would not be a defeat. They had endeavored to preserve the Reich's independence and to win freedom for Germans on German soil. While working for these objectives, the party had not fared too well. Its unity had been broken and it had been compelled to make one sacrifice after another. Disregard for its wishes had led to disaster. Yet now it was being asked to take over the bankrupt inheritance of the Hohenzollerns, of Hindenburg and Ludendorff. It was being asked to accept responsibility for a defeat which resulted from the actions of militarists and Junker aristocrats, the most implacable enemies of Social Democracy. The answer to Prince Max must be an unequivocal and emphatic no.

This view was strongly contested by Ebert. He declared that the present was no time to be concerned about the fate of the party. The only thing that mattered now was to save for the German people whatever still could be saved. The very existence of the nation was at stake. At such a moment no one could stand aloof and pretend that what was going on did not concern him. The Social Democrats must place themselves at the disposal of the state, regardless of the effect which such a step might have upon their political fortunes. The majority of the party leaders sided with Ebert. Scheidemann accepted defeat gracefully, declaring that he would support the policy of collaboration. Under Ebert's leadership, the party formally announced its willingness to enter the new coalition cabinet.

While progress was thus being registered in the work of setting up a truly parliamentary government, the Supreme Command continued to insist with ever increasing vehemence that an armistice request must be dispatched forthwith. On the afternoon of October 2, 1918, the emperor made it clear to Prince Max that the demand of Ludendorff and Hindenburg would have to be acceded to. But Max fought on. He told Hindenburg that an immediate appeal for peace would prove detrimental to Germany's interests. He had a different procedure in mind. He intended, in his first speech before the Reichstag, to make an exact and forthright interpretation of Wilson's fourteen points. By showing what Germany understood them to mean, he would clear the atmosphere before an armistice was actually requested. If the Allies reacted favorably to his interpretation of the fourteen points, Germany would be justified in asking for a cessation of hostilities. But if the Allies rejected his interpretation, Germany would have no choice but to continue the struggle. Max declared that on one condition only would he agree to an immediate request for an armistice: the Supreme Command would have to state in writing that the military situation did not admit of a postponement of peace overtures until after the delivery of his speech, which was scheduled for October 4.

Hindenburg, with Ludendorff egging him on, hastened to take advantage of this opening. On the afternoon of October 3, 1918, he sent Max the following communication:

The Supreme Command adheres to its demand made on . . . September 29 for the immediate dispatch of the peace offer to our enemies. Owing to the breakdown of the Macedonian front, whereby a weakening of our reserves in the west is necessitated, and in consequence of the impossibility of making good our very heavy losses in the battles of the last few days, there no longer exists any prospect, according to human calculation, of forcing peace upon our enemies. The enemy is regularly bringing new and fresh reserves into action. The German army still holds fast and repulses all attacks with success. But the position gets worse every day, and may force the Supreme Command to make serious decisions. In these circumstances it is imperative to stop fighting in order to spare the German people and its allies further useless sacrifices. Each day that is lost costs the lives of thousands of brave soldiers.

The picture was black, but Max remained unconvinced. He warned the Supreme Command that an immediate armistice request made under the pressure of military reverses might lead to the loss of the nation's colonies and of German territory in Europe, particularly Alsace-Lorraine and the Polish districts in the east. The Supreme Command replied that the French-speaking sections of Alsace-Lorraine might be surrendered, but that the Polish districts of the Reich must be defended to the last man. Max was overruled. On the night of October 3-4, 1918, he sent to Switzerland, for delivery to Washington, a note requesting Wilson "to take steps for the restoration of peace." The German government declared that it accepted, as a basis for negotiation, the program laid down by Wilson in his fourteen points and in his subsequent pronouncements.

3

The tempo of inter-party conversations quickened after the Social Democrats indicated their willingness to serve under Prince Max. On October 4, 1918, the composition of the new government was made known to the country. In the course of the next few days, several additional appointments were announced. Six ministers were held over from the Hertling cabinet. Payer remained vice-chancellor. Wilhelm Solf, the colonial minister, not only retained his post but assumed direction of the foreign office as well. The Center was represented by Groeber and Erzberger, who were named ministers without portfolio, and by Karl Trimborn, who took over the ministry of the interior. Conrad Haussmann, a leading Progressive, was given a status identical with that of Groeber and Erzberger. Ebert turned down an invitation to join the cabinet which he had done so much to make possible. He preferred, for the time being, at least, to remain on the sidelines. Primary responsibility for interpreting to the government the wishes of the Social Democratic party devolved upon Scheidemann, who agreed to serve as minister without portfolio. Another Social Democratic spokesman, Gustav Bauer, became head of the newly created ministry of labor. The establishment of this ministry as an independent cabinet post represented the fulfillment of a desire long voiced by the trade unions. The parties of the Right were excluded. The chief of the emperor's civil cabinet, Friedrich von Berg, had attempted to win support for the idea of giving representation to the Conservatives and the National Liberals. Both of these groups had gone out of their way to underline their willingness to join the cabinet. But the Social Democrats refused pointblank to collaborate with the Conservatives. And the Centrists and Progressives, albeit with less sharpness, took a similar line. The cabinet, they urged, should be made as representative as possible of the three parties that had sponsored the peace resolution of July, 1917. The Allies might then be more inclined to negotiate an armistice with Germany.

With what kind of program would the new chancellor and his cabinet present themselves to the country and to the world? For the moment, this question overshadowed all others. Prince Max had given considerable thought to the matter. He knew pretty well what he wanted to say. He wished, for one thing, to undo the harm wrought by the overhasty request for an armistice. The enemy must be made to understand that Germany was not yet finished, that she still possessed the will and the strength to continue the war if necessary. He was also anxious to subject Wilson's peace program to a detailed analysis and to make the German point of view emphatically clear. Late on the night of October 4, 1918, Max completed the draft of his address. It was a forthright declaration. If the enemy, it warned, should insist on prolonging the war until Germany had been thoroughly humiliated and pulverized, the cost to the victors would be extremely heavy. It made Germany's interpretation of the fourteen points crystal-clear. It voiced the hope that the request for a cessation of hostilities would pave the way to an honorable peace; but it indicated that the German people would be summoned to fight on if that was what the enemy wished. Great powers of resistance still resided in the Reich. About this the Allies must not deceive themselves.

The next item of business on Max's crowded agenda was to secure the assent of the cabinet. But all the ministers consulted reacted negatively. What they objected to was the proposed analysis of the fourteen points. They argued that a detailed discussion of war aims would jeopardize the possibility of obtaining an armistice. Colonel Hans von Haeften, who represented the Supreme Command in its dealings with the government, vigorously supported this view. In the name of his superiors, he demanded that the draft be discarded. Max was convinced that his critics were wrong, that their refusal to come to grips with the implications of the Wilsonian program would prove disastrous in the end. Nonetheless, he yielded. A new speech was hastily drafted. It contained only general references to Wilson's program. Max delivered it before the Reichstag on October 5, 1918. He pointed out that in pursuance of the emperor's proclamation of September 30, Germany had experienced a basic change in her political leadership. Only the fact that the people now participated most extensively in the determination of their own destiny made it possible for him, the chancellor, to assume with confidence the burdens and responsibilities of office. His decision to serve had been greatly facilitated by the presence of influential and trusted labor leaders in the new cabinet. The co-operation of these men made it certain that the government would enjoy the support of the broad masses of the nation. Without such support, the work of the cabinet would be foredoomed. Prince Max announced his acceptance of the program recently adopted by the Social Democrats, the Centrists and the Progressives. This program demanded unconditional assent to the peace resolution of July, 1917. It urged German participation in a league of nations based on equality for all, for the weak as well as the strong. Belgium, it insisted, must be completely restored with due regard for her independence and her territorial integrity. An understanding must be sought on the question of reparation. The treaties which the Reich had concluded with Russia and Rumania should not be permitted to stand in the way of a general peace. In the Baltic provinces, in Lithuania and Poland, democratically constituted assemblies would have to be formed as soon as possible. To facilitate this, a purely civil administration would have to be introduced in those areas. And the local populations must be left free to frame their own constitutions and to determine their relations to neighboring states. Such was the program which Prince Max solemnly accepted on October 5, 1918. It was therefore hardly necessary for him to remind the country that the new cabinet consisted of men who espoused a peace of justice, who had declared themselves publicly to this effect when Germany was at the zenith of her military success.

Having underlined his aversion to the annexationist policy of the Supreme Command, Max adverted to issues that were of more immediate concern to the German people. Never again, he said, would a government be organized which did not have the confidence of the Reichstag and which did not contain leading members of that body. One of the results of the war was that for the first time the country's great parties stood united in support of a common program and were helping to determine the nation's fortunes. This development made necessary a change in the federal constitution in conformity with the sense of the emperor's recent proclamation. Moreover, a democratic franchise would have to be introduced in Prussia without delay. Because of Prussia's paramount position in the Reich, the question of her suffrage was not a local but a national issue. Important as these problems were, they constituted but one phase of the over-all picture. More than four years of bloody struggle against numerically superior foes lay behind Germany. The nation had already made heavy sacrifices; but it was prepared to make even heavier ones, if necessary, for its honor, its freedom and the wellbeing of future generations. For several months, a murderous battle had been going on in the west. Thanks to the incomparable heroism of the German army, the front was unbroken. But it was the duty of the country to make certain that this costly conflict did not last a single day longer than was necessary to achieve an honorable peace. Consequently, a request for an armistice had been sent to Wilson. It had been sent to him because he, in his address of January 8, 1918, and in his subsequent utterances, had laid down a program which Germany could accept as a basis for negotiations. In language of unmistakable sincerity, Prince Max declared that the objective to which he aspired was a just and lasting peace for all mankind. He looked forward serenely to the result of his overture. However, if the reply of the enemy should be dictated by a desire to destroy the Reich, the German people would fight on with impregnable firmness and unity. He, for one, was not afraid. He knew the magnitude of the strength which still resided in the German people. He knew, too, that this strength would be doubled when the German people realized that they had no choice but to fight for their very existence as a nation.

Prince Max's remarks before the Reichstag were supplemented by a proclamation which the emperor issued on the same day to the armed forces of the Reich. Germany, William declared, would accept only an honorable peace. It was not yet certain that there would be an armistice. In the meantime, every ounce of energy would have to be employed to resist the attacks of the enemy. The people of Germany felt strong enough to defend their beloved Fatherland.

The chancellor and the emperor had spoken. Their pronouncements exuded a confidence that was tragically at variance with existing realities. They gauged correctly the average German's love of country. But they underestimated the travail of four years of war. Two things, and two things alone, mattered to the weary and hungry masses: peace and bread.

Chapter 5

WILSON DICTATES

I

THE bulk of the nation welcomed the news that an armistice had been requested. A discordant note was sounded only by two political groups, those standing at opposite extremes: the Independents and the Conservatives. The Independents hastened to point out, through their Reichstag spokesman, Haase, that they had no quarrel with the request for an armistice; for they had long been demanding a democratic peace. But what irked them was the manner in which the job was being done. They had no confidence, they said, in the methods of diplomacy. At this historic moment, when the old discredited political system was being forced to abdicate, it was the duty of the people's representatives to take the lead. Yet the Reichstag was eliminating itself from participation in the great decisions with which the nation was confronted. Against this the Independents protested. They reposed their hopes for peace and freedom in the masses of the population.

In a manifesto addressed to all German workers, Haase and his colleagues divulged their aims. German militarism, they declared, had suffered a blow from which it would never recover. The Independent Social Democratic party had foreseen the catastrophic consequences of this militarism. It had remained loyal to the principles of democracy and socialism. It alone among the nation's political groups had voted against the Treaties of Brest-Litovsk and Bucharest. The policy of the Social Democrats, like that of the old ruling classes, had resulted in utter failure. So long as the German imperialists were doing well on the battlefield, the party of Ebert and Scheidemann had supported the

65

war policy of the government. It had done absolutely nothing to protect the workers against exploitation. But now that bourgeois society in Germany was literally falling apart, Social Democrats like Scheidemann and Bauer were made members of the cabinet. Their party was asked to join the government in order that it might preserve the existing social order. The Social Democrats accepted this task and the corollary one of organizing "national defense." They ignored the demand of international socialist congresses that the war be utilized to replace capitalism with socialism. The program formulated by the Social Democrats as the condition on which they would join the government was very modest; it did not go nearly far enough. As international socialists, the Independents aimed at the establishment of a socialist republic. Revolutionary changes were taking place throughout the world. At such a moment, leadership in every country had to be assumed by the proletariat. The methods employed by the Social Democrats could lead only to a crippling of the independent activity of the workers and to a strengthening of capitalist society. From now on the slogan of the German proletariat would have to be: unity under the unstained banner of the Independent Social Democratic party.

The press organs of the Conservative party expressed sharp disapproval of the request for an armistice. They denounced what they called the spirit of capitulation. They argued that neither the military situation nor the state of affairs within Germany justified the appeal for a truce. They berated the "democrats" who had offered their left cheek that Wilson might caress it. These "democrats" would be requited with a resounding slap that would dissipate forever the delusion that a peace of understanding was possible. The Conservatives were definitely in a belligerent mood. But under the leadership of Count Kuno von Westarp, they agreed to refrain from further discussion of the armistice request until Wilson's reply had been received. They felt it to be their duty, once the reprehensible step of asking for peace had been taken, to do whatever they could to insure the best possible results.

With one eye on Washington and the other on the mounting ferment at home, Prince Max hastened to implement his promise of democratic reforms. On October 8, 1918, the Bundesrat abrogated the constitutional stipulation obliging deputies who accepted cabinet posts to surrender their seats in the Reichstag. It also did away with certain statutory provisions which narrowly limited eligibility for the office of vice-chancellor. A week later the Bundesrat approved further modifications of the imperial constitution. These made the assent of both houses of parliament necessary for a declaration of war and for the signing of peace. On October 22, the Reichstag began its discussion of the changes sanctioned by the Bundesrat. Two days later the Prussian upper house gave proof of the fact that it, too, had read the handwriting on the wall. It gave its consent to the introduction of universal, equal and secret suffrage in the kingdom of the Hohenzollerns.

Far-reaching as these developments were, they could not compete for popular attention with the issues growing out of the peace negotiations. Wilson's reply, dated October 8, 1918, reached Berlin the following day. Did the German government, queried the American president, accept his peace terms, and was its purpose, in entering into a discussion of them, merely to agree "upon the practical details of their application?" No armistice, he went on, could be granted unless the Central Powers consented forthwith to withdraw their troops from all invaded territory. But this was not all. Wilson wanted to know whether Prince Max was speaking "merely for the constituted authorities of the empire" who until now had been conducting the war. Of the three issues posed by the American note, the second was clearly the most important. For if Germany agreed to evacuate all occupied territory before the armistice was signed, she would be without her best bargaining weapon when the peace negotiations began. The attitude of the Supreme Command had to be ascertained. The question Prince Max put to Ludendorff was this: if the present peace overture should fail, would Germany be able to continue the war until the spring? She would, Ludendorff replied, if first she obtained a breathing space. He thereby implied that the negotiations for an armistice should not be broken off. The impression prevailed that he would consent to the evacuation of occupied territories provided the other conditions were such as to enable the German armies to resume the struggle if necessary. Taking this to be the view of the Supreme Command, Max resolved to accede to Wilson's demand. Westarp and Stresemann objected strenuously. They urged the chancellor to discontinue the negotiations rather than surrender the enormous bargaining advantage which Germany enjoyed by virtue of her occupation of enemy territory. They took the position that the war in the west could yet be stabilized on non-German soil. But Max refused to be swayed by these representations. He called attention to the attitude of the Supreme Command, which was now speaking its mind more plainly. The German armies, it was saying, needed a rest; the danger of an enemy breakthrough was ever present.

The German government proceeded to draft a reply to Wilson. It answered his first question in the affirmative. But at the suggestion of the Supreme Command, it went on to express the belief that the other Allied states likewise accepted the American program. It thereby sought to make sure that Great Britain and France as well as the United States would be bound by the fourteen points and by the principles enunciated in Wilson's subsequent pronouncements. Withdrawal of the German armies from occupied territory was promised. The third issue raised by Wilson was dealt with in unambiguous fashion. The present German government, the note explained, had been formed "by conferences and in agreement with the great majority of the Reichstag." The chancellor, it was therefore clear, was speaking in the name of the German people. On October 12, 1918, after the Supreme Command had given its formal approval, the note was sent to Washington. A loud outcry ensued in Rightist circles when its contents were made public. The Conservatives, as usual, took the lead. They reaffirmed their opposition to the idea of relinquishing the occupied areas before an honorable peace had been assured. They adjured the government to protect the interests of the Reich with unflagging vigilance. The surrender of any German territory, they proclaimed, was incompatible with German honor. The country must be told that on this point there could be no compromise. The German people would applaud such a statement, for they were resolved to defend their soil to the bitter end.

The Supreme Command likewise fell prey to the fear that a dishonorable peace might be imposed upon Germany. It was concerned lest internal disunity and the growing mood of despair should aggravate the country's military difficulties and thus reduce the possibility of securing acceptable terms. It urged the government to mobilize public opinion, to do everything that could be done to stimulate the sense of national unity. The enemy had to be told in the most unequivocal language that never would Germany assent to humiliating conditions. But even that was not enough. It was imperative to make the German people see the terrible consequences of peace at any price. They would have to be constantly reminded that only two alternatives lay before them: an honorable peace or a fight to the finish.

While Prince Max was being subjected to pressure by the Supreme Command, Wilson found himself the recipient of urgent admonitions from the British and the French. On October 9, 1918, the Supreme Allied War Council drew up a statement in which the argument was put forward that evacuation of the invaded areas was not enough. The authors of the document also maintained that Allied military experts should have something to say about the formulation of armistice terms. Were Wilson to subscribe to these views, he would have to insist on harder conditions than those foreshadowed in his reply to the German government. As a matter of fact, many people in the United States and in other Allied countries were saying that Germany should be made to surrender unconditionally. Certain members of the American Senate went so far as to argue that armistice terms should not be discussed with the Germans until after the elimination of the Hohenzollern dynasty.

The exponents of a hard peace were overjoyed when they read Wilson's note of October 14, 1918. To German hopes for lenient terms this communication brought cruel disillusionment. Very ominous from the German point of view was Wilson's assertion that the Allied military leaders would be the ones to decide the armistice terms and that no arrangement would be acceptable which did not guarantee Allied military supremacy in the field. Wilson also demanded, as one of the prerequisites for an armistice, the halting of unrestricted submarine warfare, which he denounced in very strong language. The closing paragraph of the note directed attention to Wilson's statement of July 4, 1918, in which he called for the destruction of "every arbitrary power anywhere that can separately, secretly, and of its single choice disturb the peace of the world." Germany, the note went on, had hitherto been ruled by such a power. To alter it was within her choice. The attainment of peace would depend upon "the definiteness and the satisfactory character of the guarantees which can be given in this fundamental matter." Did this mean that Wilson was demanding the abdication of the emperor and the establishment of a republic? Or was he merely asking that the empire be democratized? What Wilson actually had in mind was not clear. But one thing was indubitable: confidence in Wilson's integrity was rudely jolted by the tone and contents of this communication. It was difficult any longer to believe in his good will.

The American note was published in the German press on the morning of October 16. It precipitated widespread dismay and indignation. This time all sections and shades of public opinion joined in decrying Wilson's attitude. The Conservatives denounced the note as an affront to Germany. The Progressives complained that it differed markedly from the American statesman's first communication and acidly observed that the spirit of Clemenceau and Lloyd George was coming to the fore. Even the Social Democrats, loath as they were to throw a monkey wrench into the armistice negotiations, found themselves compelled to admit that there were limits beyond which it was impossible to go. But their willingness to resist unreasonable demands proved extremely ephemeral. A few days later they insisted that Germany, despite Wilson's change of attitude, had no choice but to adhere to her present course. She would have to appeal to the moral rectitude of the Allied leaders. Overwhelmingly superior enemies confronted her; ultimate victory was no longer a possibility. It would be wrong, in these circumstances, to wage war one minute longer than was necessary. Germany was fighting for a peace that would be devoid of the germs of future wars. To the attainment of this goal she would have to dedicate all her energies from now on.

Both the German government and the Supreme Command reacted bitterly to Wilson's note. Prince Max, making no effort to conceal his disappointment, spoke of it as a "terrible document." From various parts of the country came demands that the armistice negotiations be broken off and the nation summoned to take up arms for a last-ditch stand. The chancellor called together all the political and military leaders of the Reich to discuss three questions. These he formulated as follows: 1) "Should Germany accept the severe conditions laid down in Wilson's note of October 14?" 2) "If the government decided to reject Wilson's demands, would the army be able to defend the German frontiers?" 3) "If the German front held for some weeks or months, would there be any chance of obtaining more favorable conditions then?" Discussion of these questions took place on October 17, 1918. Ludendorff and Prince Max differed sharply. The general declared himself opposed to any terms which would destroy the army's capacity to fight. Max reminded Ludendorff that all the current difficulties stemmed from the original armistice request made at the behest of the Supreme Command. He argued that the stiffer conditions now being laid down by Wilson were the result of Anglo-French pressure and that the president himself was desirous of continuing the negotiations. Ludendorff dissented, contending that Wilson had revealed his determination to throttle the Reich. Supported by Admiral Scheer, who vigorously opposed the idea of abandoning submarine warfare, Ludendorff insisted that Wilson's demands be rejected. That this would mean an abrupt and definitive termination of the negotiations was a foregone conclusion.

Ludendorff's attitude bewildered and dismayed the nation's political leaders. Could Germany, they queried, really keep fighting? Ludendorff replied that an enemy breakthrough on the western front was improbable, that, if given sufficient reinforcements, he would be able to hold. Yet only two weeks earlier he had stated that this was an impossibility, that the army needed a rest so badly that not a minute's delay could be tolerated. Ludendorff's inconsistency, coming on the heels of his recent display of nerves, shook the government's confidence in the man. True, the Allies had failed to exploit their recent successes, and a stalemate had ensued on the western front. But this stalemate was obviously only temporary; there had been no basic or important change for the better in the German military position. The untrustworthiness of Ludendorff's judgment could no longer be doubted. His new-born optimism failed to carry conviction. The political leaders decided that it was now too late to back out of the negotiations and to call upon the nation for a last-ditch stand.

In keeping with this decision, and in spite of the disapproving attitude of the Supreme Command, the government of Prince Max went ahead with the task of drafting a reply to Wilson. While it was so engaged, Ludendorff disseminated the charge that the civil authorities were making a cowardly surrender and agreeing to terms which were outrageously dishonorable. With the emphatic concurrence of Admiral Scheer, he reiterated his opposition to Wilson's demand for the discontinuance of unrestricted submarine warfare. The government refused to be bullied. When the drafting of the note was completed, it was submitted to the Supreme Command. The latter disapproved and suggested several alterations. Once again its views went unheeded. Ludendorff was furious. The government, he declared, would make itself responsible for the Reich's capitulation if it sent off this note and consented to abandon submarine warfare. Against this allegation the cabinet sharply protested. It placed the blame for the country's predicament squarely on Ludendorff and his precipitate demand for an armistice. At the request of the irate ministers, he agreed to desist from further interference in political affairs.

Thus it was that the civil authorities for the first time overrode the objections of both the Supreme Command and the Admiralty. This they did in spite of their realization that acceptance of the terms laid down in the second American note would render impossible a resumption of hostilities. The German reply of October 20, 1918, bowed to Wilson's demand that the Allied military leaders be empowered to fix the terms of evacuation. It stated that an order not to torpedo passenger vessels had been issued to all submarine commanders. It likewise gave assurance that the retreating German armies had been enjoined to refrain from the destruction of private property. It did not, however, allow Wilson's charge concerning the employment of "illegal and inhuman means" to go unprotested and asked that the matter be looked into by neutral investigators. It countered the president's demand for the destruction of "every arbitrary power" with the contention that fundamental constitutional alterations had already been instituted.

The new government has been formed in complete accord with the wishes of the representatives of the people. . . . The leaders of the great parties of the Reichstag are members of this government. In the future, no government will be able to take or continue in office without possessing the confidence of the majority of the Reichstag. The responsibility of the chancellor of the empire to the representatives of the people is being legally developed and safeguarded.

Wilson replied on October 23, 1918. Once again he insisted upon an armistice that would leave the Allies "in a position to enforce any arrangements that may be entered into" and that would render impossible a resumption of hostilities by Germany. These safeguards were necessary because, notwithstanding the constitutional changes referred to in the German note of October 20, the principle of ministerial responsibility had not as yet been fully applied. Nor was there any guarantee of the permanence of such changes as had already been instituted. The German people were still without the power to impose their will on the military authorities. The King of Prussia was still able to control the policy of the Reich. The old ruling elements still retained the "determining initiative." It was impossible to trust the word of those who until now had been in the saddle. The American government could deal only with the true representatives of the German people. If it should have to deal with "the military masters or the monarchical autocrats" of the Reich, it would have to demand, "not peace negotiations, but surrender."

This note made Prince Max very angry. It was the kind of language, he felt, that was addressed only to an enemy whose strength was regarded as broken. But he had already gone too far to be able to turn back. The negotiations would have to be continued. If they were broken off now, his cabinet would fall asunder. He needed the support of the Social Democrats, who were all for peace. Wilson had expressed reservations regarding the scope and permanence of the constitutional changes currently being effected. The thing to do now, in Prince Max's opinion, was to prove to him that Germany was being thoroughly democratized. Once that had been done, Wilson would either have to keep his word and agree to peace negotiations on the basis of the fourteen points or demand capitulation. If he should demand capitulation, he would be unmasked. This, at least, would clear the atmosphere.

2

On October 26, 1918, additional proposals for modification of the constitution were laid before the Reichstag. They were sponsored by a coalition of Social Democrats, Progressives, Centrists and National Liberals. They were designed to accomplish two things: to make the chancellor responsible to both houses of parliament, and to subordinate the military to the civil authorities. The Conservatives protested loudly. Their spokesman charged that the measures under consideration would destroy the federal character of the Reich and engender chaos. They signified, in his opinion, the elimination of the imperial command-power and the reduction of the monarch to the status of a figurehead. Moreover, these proposals were not in accord with the convictions of the Reichstag majority. They were being introduced because Wilson had so ordered. The meaning of this was clear: Germany was moving toward a state of affairs comparable to that which now existed in Russia. The Conservatives got support from no one. Their contentions and the mood which inspired them seemed utterly at variance with the exigencies of the moment. All the constitutional amendments, including those already enacted by the Bundesrat, were adopted. On October 28, 1918, they were signed by the emperor and thus became law. Germany, at long last, had become a truly parliamentary state.

In the meantime, the cabinet was pondering the wording of its reply to Wilson's latest communication. Most of the ministers, with Scheidemann and Erzberger taking the lead, insisted that the note should not be such as to imply that Germany was determined to fight on. A sharp battle at once ensued between the government and the Supreme Command. It was precipitated by Hindenburg, who, on the night of October 24, 1918, issued a manifesto to the armed forces. According to this manifesto, Wilson wanted an armistice which would leave Germany so defenseless that she would be unable to take up arms again. He was willing to make peace with Germany only if she bowed to Allied wishes as regards her internal organization. If she refused to do so, she would have to surrender unconditionally. The sum and substance of the matter was this:

Wilson's reply demands military capitulation. It is therefore unacceptable to us soldiers. It proves that the desire of our enemies . . . to destroy us continues undiminished. It also proves that our enemies talk about a "peace of justice" for the sole purpose of deceiving us and breaking our power to resist. Wilson's reply can therefore be for us soldiers only the summons to keep resisting with all our strength. When our enemies realize that the German front is unbreakable, they will agree to conclude a peace which will safeguard the future of Germany.

Hindenburg's manifesto provoked much excitement in the cabinet and in the Reichstag. It was followed by a decisive interview between the military leaders and Payer. The latter represented the ailing chancellor who was confined to his bed. Ludendorff spoke long and earnestly about all the things that were bothering him: the determination of the Allies to exterminate Germany, the folly of reposing any hope in Wilson, the danger of Bolshevism in Germany, the multiplication of popular demonstrations against army officers. He, together with Hindenburg and Scheer, declared that in view of the nature of Wilson's last note, which held out only the prospect of capitulation and a dishonorable peace, the armistice negotiations should be broken off and the nation called upon to fight to the last man. But Payer realized that it was now too late for such a course, that the masses, who wanted peace and bread, would refuse to answer such a call. Indeed, he feared that the workers might rise up and plunge the country into Bolshevism if Ludendorff were allowed to have his way. Consequently, he told the general that the negotiations would be continued.

Apprised by Payer of Ludendorff's stand, Prince Max promptly took a step which he had long been contemplating. He wrote the emperor a letter demanding that Ludendorff be asked to sever his connection with the Supreme Command. Prince Max warned that if this were not done, he would relinquish the chancellorship. He also requested William to do everything in his power to persuade Hindenburg to remain at the head of the Supreme Command. On October 26, 1918, Ludendorff, who had been informed of Prince Max's action, went to see the emperor and submitted his resignation. It was accepted. At the same time Hindenburg asked to be relieved of his post. He explained that he did not wish to be separated from his loyal and indispensable collaborator. But the emperor prevailed upon him to remain at his post by appealing to his sense of duty.

The departure of the country's most influential war lord, coupled with the retention of the immensely popular but far less forceful Field Marshal, cheered the cabinet. The armistice negotiations could now proceed without the danger of captious interference by the military. Nonetheless, the work of drafting the reply to Wilson ran into a few snags. Scheidemann wanted to make sure that the note was not too strongly worded. He was worried about the attitude of the workers who wanted peace without delay and might go over to the Independents if a defiant line were taken with Wilson. The all-important thing, he insisted, was to say nothing which might give Wilson an excuse to discontinue the negotiations. Erzberger sided with the Social Democratic leader. He argued that Germany could get a bad armistice and still emerge with a satisfactory peace treaty. However, other members of the cabinet, notably Haussmann, objected. They demanded a show of firmness. Finally, agreement was reached on the following text:

The German government has taken cognizance of the reply of the President of the United States. The President is aware of the far-reaching changes which have been and are being effected in the constitutional structure of Germany. The peace negotiations are being conducted by a democratic government whose decisive powers are permanently anchored in the constitution of the German Reich. Accordingly, the German government awaits proposals for an armistice, not suggestions of surrender. Only in this way will it be possible for the armistice to pave the way for a peace of justice of the kind indicated by the President in his pronouncements.

Payer and Haussmann were none too happy over this text. They felt it was a lame, weak-kneed affair. Prince Max, too, was not enthusiastic. However, he consoled himself with the thought that a clear-cut distinction had been drawn between armistice and surrender. Wilson would understand that he could not go too far. But the chancellor's restrained hopefulness speedily vanished into thin air. At the last moment, a serious complication developed. During the evening of October 26, 1918, before the note was sent off, word reached Berlin that the Austro-Hungarian emperor had appealed for a separate peace. The German government was thrown into a panic. The language of the note, it suddenly decided, was too strong. The precarious situation in which Germany now found herself obliged her to talk with greater circumspection. The distinction between armistice and capitulation would have to be deleted. The reply sent to Wilson on October 27, 1918, was minus the phrase, "not suggestions of surrender."

The German government had gone as far as it could to meet the wishes of Wilson. It humbly awaited proposals for an armistice. One question remained to haunt it: would the Allies insist on the abdication of the emperor? The answer turned out to be in the negative. Wilson's fourth note, which was dispatched to Berlin on November 5, 1918, made no reference to this matter. It expressed the readiness of the Allies to conclude peace with Germany on the basis of the fourteen points and of the principles laid down in Wilson's subsequent utterances. However, it did contain two reservations which were inserted at the insistence of the British and the French. The first had to do with the freedom of the seas. The second obligated Germany to pay "for all the damage done to the civilian population of the Allies and their property." The German government received the note on November 6 and promptly accepted its stipulations. A definite and formal agreement had finally been reached with the Allies.

3

In the meantime, the political pot had begun to boil in earnest. Wilson's note of October 23, 1918, was generally taken to mean that the emperor would have to go. At once a powerful movement, aimed at forcing him to relinquish the crown, set in. This movement was motivated by two things: the fear that peace would be indefinitely delayed if William remained on the throne; the hope that his abdication would result in more lenient terms. Everywhere the issue was discussed, and everywhere one could hear the cry: "Away with the emperor!" High-ranking Bavarian officials took a prominent part in this agitation. They feared that their state might become a battleground if the war did not cease forthwith. Certain newspapers defied the censors and bluntly spoke the nation's mind. The Social Democratic leaders found themselves compelled to make their position clear. Actually, they had no overwhelming desire to see the emperor ousted. They believed that the party would do extremely well under the new democratic dispensation. They were quite convinced that William's retention of the crown, now that his powers had been drastically curtailed, would not cramp their style. But they had to take cognizance of the passionate desire for peace that prevailed among the workers. They knew, too, that the long-suffering, disgruntled proletariat regarded the emperor as the main obstacle to a speedy termination of hostilities. If they went counter to this feeling, they might lose their hold on their followers and force them into the outstretched arms of the Independents and the Spartacists. This was too great a risk to take. They had no choice but to join in the clamor for William's abdication.

In keeping with this new orientation, Scheidemann on October 29, 1918, sent Prince Max a letter requesting him to advise the emperor to abdicate voluntarily. Scheidemann wrote:

There is no doubt that the great majority of the inhabitants of the German empire are convinced that the prospects of getting tolerable terms for the armistice and the peace are being ruined by the emperor's remaining in his exalted office.

William's retirement, Scheidemann went on, could only be postponed, not avoided. Consequently, it would be better if he withdrew at the earliest possible moment. But although the Social Democrats took a clear-cut stand on the issue of abdication, some of their most influential spokesmen continued to profess their loyalty to the monarchy. William's departure, they argued, would not mean the end of the monarchy. They held to the view that a thoroughly parliamentary monarchy which was committed to a broad program of social reform would be able to fulfill all the reasonable demands of the working classes. The principal advocate of this view was the party's No. 1 man, Friedrich Ebert.

With the controversy over his fate moving toward a crescendo, the emperor decided to leave Berlin. The reason he gave was that he was needed at general headquarters, that his place was with his soldiers at this crucial moment of the struggle in the west. But the real reason, apparently, was that he no longer felt safe in his own capital. When Prince Max learned of William's intention, he begged him not to go, pointing to the gravity of the situation which confronted the government and the country. The emperor, affecting an optimism about future developments which he could hardly have felt, refused to heed Max's entreaties. On the night of October 29, 1918, he left for Spa. This was one of the most grievous mistakes of his career. For at once, in the wake of his flight, there was a perceptible increase in the clamor for his abdication. The excitement took hold of all classes. Financiers, industrialists and even high army officers put themselves on record as favoring William's immediate retirement. Men of moderate views began to fear that the ill will engendered by the emperor's refusal to abdicate might culminate in the destruction of the monarchy itself. But William was not without defenders. The Conservatives ranged themselves on his side. They warned that revolution and Bolshevism would ensue if William were forced to abdicate. The Centrist members of the Reichstag likewise decried the nation-wide agitation. The Hohenzollern empire, they contended, had to be maintained as the symbol of German unity; the compulsory retirement of the emperor would result in the establishment of a republic. And to such a regime they and their followers were opposed.

Existing tensions were greatly intensified by the unconditional surrender of Austria-Hungary on November 3, 1918. This defection left the Reich to continue the unequal battle alone and exposed the south of Germany to invasion by the Allies. Feeling against the emperor attained phobic proportions. More and more Germans came to regard him as the sole obstacle to peace. In Bavaria, where the fear of invasion weighed heavily on the population, there was talk of seceding from the Reich. By his stubborn refusal to abdicate, William was discrediting not only himself but the dynasty, the monarchy and the monarchical principle. The country yearned for peace. It would allow nothing and no one to stand in the way of peace. The emperor's unwillingness to see this created a situation which strengthened the hand of the Independents and the Spartacists, who alone among the nation's political parties were advocating a republic. The position of the Social Democrats was a rather unhappy one. They did not want matters to go too far. They were satisfied with the democratic empire which had come into being late in October. They clung to the belief that the establishment of a republic was not necessary from the workers' point of view. But current developments were playing havoc with the program to which they were committed. The situation was deteriorating so rapidly that almost anything might happen. It was the hope of the Social Democrats that once the emperor had satisfied the popular demand, the crisis would stop right there and order and stability would return. They themselves had no desire to assume power. They preferred to go on being members of a coalition government headed by someone outside their own party. The all-important thing during the coming weeks and months was to move slowly and avoid extremes.

Chapter 6

THE ADVENT OF THE REPUBLIC

I

THE months which followed the strike of January, 1918, loom large in the history of the German revolutionary movement. They witnessed a gradual consolidation of the elements, made up for the most part of Independents and Spartacists, that wished to transform the Reich into a workers' state. The Revolutionary Shop Stewards did much to further the process of consolidation. This group of militant radicals had come into being during the first year of the war. Its original nucleus consisted of officials of the Berlin turners' union who did not approve of the moderate line taken by the majority of their confreres. When the Independent Social Democratic party was organized, the Shop Stewards joined it and became the dominant element in its left wing. As their movement grew, thanks to the influx of metal workers, they built up an elaborate organization which stretched from the revolutionary committee at the top to strategically placed agents in the factories and barracks. Their activities were designed to prepare the way for one thing, and one thing only: the success of the projected revolution. The Shop Stewards did not go in, as did the Spartacists and most of the Independents, for theoretical discussions. They shunned mass meetings and demonstrations. They preferred to carry on by means of propaganda brought in unobtrusive fashion directly to the individual whose sympathies were being solicited.

For their part in the strike of January, 1918, the Shop Stewards were made to suffer heavily. Their leader, Richard Mueller, and a number of his closest associates were drafted into the army and sent to the front. Deprived of the services of its key men, the movement fell upon evil days. But this recession proved short-lived. Emil Barth, who took Mueller's place, vigorously addressed himself to the task of rebuilding the organization. By April, 1918, his efforts were so successful that some of the hotheads in his entourage began to demand that a coup be attempted forthwith. Barth demurred. He took the position that failure was probable so long as the German army remained a disciplined and well directed force. Only after defeat and demoralization had undermined the nation's war machine would the moment for a putsch be at hand. Besides, the negotiations with the leaders of the Independents and the Spartacists, undertaken for the purpose of insuring common action, had not yet gone far enough. Actually, the Shop Stewards had many sympathizers among top-ranking Independents. Ledebour, in particular, was friendly to them. The Spartacists also seemed receptive to the idea of collaborating with the Shop Stewards. Nevertheless, Barth insisted that the ties which bound his group to the two radical parties had to be strengthened. To this task he devoted a great part of his energy throughout the spring and summer of 1918. Another matter likewise claimed his attention. The projected revolution could not be successful without arms. He made it his business to procure them. By various clandestine methods he managed to accumulate sizable quantities of pistols and hand grenades. Shock troops were organized and trained in the use of these weapons.

In August, 1918, when the tide of battle began to turn against Germany, Barth decided that the crucial hour was approaching. The tempo of preparations for revolution was stepped up. It was at this time that Ernst Daeumig, a prominent Independent, joined the Shop Stewards. He quickly made himself their most respected leader. To his new responsibilities he brought a keen mind and infectious enthusiasm. Propaganda was his forte. This he proved in connection with his efforts to spread subversive ideas among the troops that were kept at home for the express purpose of dealing with civilian unrest. The right wing of the Independent Social Democratic party, with Haase at its head, looked askance upon these preparations for revolution. The tactics advocated by the Shop Stewards were not to its liking. It did, indeed, sympathize with the idea of trying to set up a socialist republic, and it conceded that a revolution was inevitable. But it held that it would be folly to attempt a coup. It based its contention on the assumption that the revolution, which it visualized as a great spontaneous movement requiring little assistance from existing political groups, would not materialize until the war was over. The actual course of events was destined to prove that Haase and his friends had underestimated the tempo of the trend toward revolution.

In September, 1918, Richard Mueller was released from the army. His return to the political battles in Berlin resulted in a further strengthening of the tie between the Shop Stewards and the Spartacists. The latter were engaged in an ambitious propaganda campaign whose main objective, at the moment, was to destroy the morale of the nation's fighting forces. Germany's military reverses, culminating in the request for an armistice, created a situation which was exploited to the full by the radicals. The Independents took a bolder line. On October 23, 1918, in a speech before the Reichstag, Haase demanded the establishment of a republic. The same day saw Liebknecht's release from jail. This event, which was wildly cheered by thousands of Berlin workers, gave tremendous impetus to left-wing agitation for the overthrow of the existing political and social order. In the capital and in many other cities throughout the land, the Independents organized great demonstration meetings. At most of these the demand for a socialist republic was voiced. Liebknecht addressed several of the rallies in Berlin, and his remarks were invariably couched in the vein of Russian Bolshevism. The period of insane mass murder, he declared, was approaching its end. A new era was about to begin. The proletariat, so long the victim of exploitation and oppression, had at last become aware of its own strength. The great issue now was world revolution or world collapse. There was no need for further discussion; the time for action was at hand. The call for national defense, the last desperate gesture of the discredited ruling classes, must be answered with dictatorship of the proletariat, the extirpation of capitalism and the establishment of a workers' republic. By supporting the Russian soviets, the German republic would force other countries to do likewise; and proletarian domination of the world would begin.

The Shop Stewards hastily completed their plans for an armed uprising. A detailed plan of action was worked out for Berlin. It even indicated the streets to be used by the workers as they marched from the industrial districts to the government buildings in the center of the city. At the invitation of Barth, the leaders of all the revolutionary elements met on the evening of November 2, 1918. Liebknecht was there for the Spartacists. Haase, Ledebour and Dittmann—the latter had recently been amnestied—spoke for the Independents. The Shop Stewards were represented by Barth, Mueller and Daeumig. Barth presided. He was in a state of great excitement. He had made up his mind to oppose further delay. He was not sure about the attitude of Haase and Dittmann, but he was determined to make them go along whether they liked it or not. He told his listeners that the time for action had come. Only after the revolution would Germany be able to obtain an armistice from the enemy. "We are the ones who will bring peace," he declared. By terminating the war, the revolutionary elements would serve the cause of socialism in Germany and win the good-will of the Allies. He proposed November 4 as the day on which to strike. At once he encountered sharp opposition. Dittmann, who reflected the views of the right-wing Independents, took the lead in blasting Barth's proposal. He, too, he said, wished to see Germany radically transformed. But he objected to the manner in which Barth proposed to achieve the common aim. Enough blood, he grimly observed, had already been shed. A "revolution of the fist" would not meet the needs of the situation. Dittmann went on to accuse Barth of criminal irresponsibility and thoughtlessness. The projected uprising, he warned, would end in catastrophic failure. Even Liebknecht, who had been expounding the thesis that action could no longer be deferred, opposed Barth's plan. He did not care, he remarked, for conspiracies and putsches. He wanted mass demonstrations, strikes, sabotage, the incitement of soldiers to insubordination and desertion. Ledebour came to Barth's defense. He spoke eloquently of the need for an immediate frontal attack against the existing regime. His efforts proved futile. A vote was taken, and by a majority of two Barth's plea for action on November 4 was rejected. It was thereupon decided to postpone the revolution until November 11. Haase and Dittmann hoped that by then the war would be over. If it were, the task of establishing a republican regime would be greatly simplified.

2

Although the Spartacists were officially still a part of the Independent Social Democratic party, they busied themselves with their own preparations for revolution. Their avowed goal was the dictatorship of the proletariat; their method was the creation of workers' and soldiers' councils on the Russian model. They were aided and abetted by the Soviet ambassador, Adolf Joffe. He had arrived in Berlin in April, 1918, and had immediately established contact with the revolutionary elements. Through his office money, arms and propaganda material were made available to the radicals. This traffic was facilitated by the embassy's extensive use of its diplomatic privileges. Because of these privileges, the German authorities had no legal means of interfering with the constant flow of bags and boxes from Russia to the Reich. Independent as well as Spartacist leaders frequently visited the embassy, which sought to co-ordinate and direct the forces of proletarian extremism throughout the country. The spread of Bolshevist ideas among the members of the armed forces constituted a signal triumph for the radicals. It was among the troops stationed in the east that this propaganda achieved the greatest results. So bad did the situation become that the Supreme Command did not dare to transfer certain divisions to the west in spite of the fact that they were desperately needed there. In August, 1918, with military defeat staring them in the face, the troops in France and Belgium began to imitate their comrades in the east by showing a greater receptivity to Bolshevist ideas.

Thus both at home and on the fields of battle the agitation conducted by the Spartacists and the left-wing Independents bore ample fruit. These successes stiffened the resolve of the radicals to eschew compromise with the Social Democratic party. They regarded that party as far more reprehensible than the old ruling classes. They were convinced that only its complete defeat could insure the triumph of the revolution in Germany. The Social Democrats, for their part, viewed the results of Spartacist-Independent propaganda with unmitigated alarm. At first they had been inclined to minimize the Bolshevist danger. Now, at the close of October, 1918, they became obsessed with the fear that communism was around the corner. Their state of mind was not improved by the continual defections from their own ranks to those of the Independents. They were desperately anxious to halt the flow of aid from the Russian embassy to the radicals. Prince Max and his cabinet shared this anxiety. Their chance came on November 4, 1918, when a Soviet packing-case fell apart in one of Berlin's railway stations. Compromising literature was discovered by the police. Thereupon Joffe was informed that he and his entire staff would be deported the following morning. They were forced to leave Berlin just as the revolutionary conflagration which they had helped to make possible began to engulf the Reich.

3

Although the propaganda campaign unleashed by the Independents and the Spartacists in the summer of 1918 was not without effect on the German fleet, the principal reason for the rebellious state of mind of the crews was their passionate desire for peace. The retreat of the German armies in the west, the evacuation of Belgian ports, the sudden discontinuance of unrestricted submarine warfare and, above all, the request for an armistice, made a deep impression on the sailors. They were now obsessed with a yearning to go home as soon as possible; they virulently opposed continuation of the war. There were a few instances of disobedience, but matters really became serious only when the commanders of the fleet decided in favor of a last-ditch, do-or-die sally against the British. The plan which they worked out called for a blow which, it was hoped, would turn the tide of war and pave the way for a German victory. The prospects, in their opinion, were favorable. The principal units of the navy stood ready for action. A large number of torpedo-boats, submarines and mine-layers were on hand to lend assistance. The squadron commanders met on board the *Baden,* the flagship of the fleet, on the evening of October 29, 1918. Admiral von Hipper informed them that they were to leave port the next day with the object of relieving the land forces in Flanders. Should the British fleet be encountered, it was to be engaged in battle.

Like wildfire word spread among the crews that action against the British was impending. The officers were pleased. They itched for battle. But the rank-and-file seamen reacted very differently. They received the report with consternation and anger. They believed that their officers, whose reactionary outlook was a secret to no one, were seeking to effect the fall of Prince Max's liberal government. They suspected them, too, of wanting to sabotage the armistice negotiations and sacrifice the fleet and the lives of their men for the sake of German honor. The sailors charged that the decision to engage the British fleet had been taken by Hipper on his own responsibility and without the knowledge or approval of the government. They refused, they said, to sacrifice themselves needlessly. Some of them even talked of using force to prevent the departure of the ships. Disturbances ensued when efforts were made to translate this threat into action. A few sailors attached to the *Koenig* were arrested on the charge of inciting their comrades to insubordination. The ferment steadily increased throughout the night of October 29-30, 1918. So serious was the tumult on board the *Thueringen* and the *Helgoland* that torpedo-boats had to be stationed alongside of them in order to intimidate the demonstrators. The *Markgraf* was the scene of similar disorders. The officers attempted to persuade the mutineers that they were on the wrong tack.

They warned them not to break their oaths as members of the armed forces. But these harangues produced little perceptible effect. The rebels declared that they had lost confidence in their superiors. They insisted that the projected action against the British fleet was utterly useless. They were willing, until the armistice was signed, to defend the country's ports and coasts; but they would not participate in any operation upon the high seas.

In the face of the mutinous attitude of the crews, Hipper countermanded the order to leave port. But on the morning of October 30, he changed his mind. Feeling that he should do something to relieve the German armies in Flanders, he resolved to confine the attack mission to his torpedo-boats and submarines, whose crews seemed thoroughly reliable. The battlefleet was to accompany these vessels until they reached the belt of mines well out to sea; and there it was to remain until their return. When Hipper divulged his new plans to the squadron commanders, he heard doubts expressed as to the possibility of carrying them out. Nevertheless, he gave the order to weigh anchor. A large part of the crew of the *Thueringen* responded by putting that ship out of commission. Serious disorders also immobilized the *Helgoland*. Thereupon Hipper capitulated and ordered the fleet to remain where it was. But he was determined to use force to put an end to the mutiny. A company of marines, several torpedo-boats and one submarine were ordered into action against the *Thueringen* and the *Helgoland*. Just as fire was about to be opened, the mutineers lost heart and surrendered. About 400 sailors were taken off the two ships. The insurrection seemed to have been broken. The crews went back to work without further ado. But the calm proved extremely short-lived.

Ominous developments were already in the making at Kiel. There, on the afternoon of November 2, 1918, several hundred sailors and marines sought admission to the local trade-union building to consider ways and means of liberating the mutineers from the *Markgraf* who had been placed under arrest in the city. On orders from Admiral Souchon, the governor of the port of Kiel, the police prevented the men from entering the building. So, followed by large numbers of dock workers, they went to the near-by drilling ground and held their meeting there. Several inflammatory harangues were delivered. By far the most effective speaker was a sailor by the name of Artelt. This hitherto obscure individual brimmed over with an infectious revolutionary fervor. The time for deeds had come, he proclaimed. Militarism and every other feature of the prevailing system would have to be destroyed. If peaceful means proved inadequate, force would have to be used. Artelt's listeners became more and more excited as he proceeded. When he finished, the crowd burst into loud cheers for international socialism. The local Independents now attempted to gain control of the movement. They made arrangements for another mass meeting and vowed that they would not permit themselves to be cowed into inaction by the authorities. Souchon considered the idea of asking the army commander at Altona for help but finally decided against it.

Reports that new arrests had taken place aboard the *Markgraf* circulated in Kiel on the morning of November 3, 1918, which was a Sunday. The excitement increased at a great rate. By the late afternoon, when thousands of sailors and workers assembled on the drilling ground, some sort of explosion appeared unavoidable. The meeting was addressed by spokesmen for the Independents and the Social Democrats. But once again it was Artelt who provided the revolutionary spark. Once again the fervor which possessed him transmitted itself to his hearers. A great parade was organized. It was joined by some of the troops. Souchon promptly wired Altona for help. In the meantime, the demonstrators had begun to move toward the military prison where the mutineers were interned. A detachment of loyal sailors from one of the torpedo-boats barred the way. When their order to disperse went unheeded, the sailors fired into the crowd. Eight persons were killed and 29 wounded. Informed that the situation was now well in hand, Souchon notified Altona that he no longer needed assistance. But his optimism proved ill-founded. Instead of subsiding, the revolutionary movement became hourly more menacing. The number of loyal troops dwindled. Workers' and soldiers' councils were formed. Once again Souchon changed his mind. He sent an urgent appeal to Altona. However, a jurisdictional conflict developed between him and the general chosen to lead the counter-attack. Military action had to be delayed. While Souchon was temporizing, the armed forces still under his personal command went over en masse to the rebels. This meant that forcible resistance to the insurrection was, for the time being, at least, out of the question. Souchon decided to negotiate with the workers' and soldiers' councils. The imprisoned sailors were freed. The belated arrival of troops from Altona brought no alteration in the situation because Souchon was determined to avoid bloodshed.

The German government decided to intervene. It sent two troubleshooters to Kiel: Haussmann, the Progressive spokesman, and Gustav Noske, a leading member of the Social Democratic party and one of Ebert's most trusted lieutenants. Haussmann returned almost at once to Berlin. Noske stayed and succeeded in ousting the Independents from the leadership of the movement. But the ferment continued. On November 4 the workers of Kiel resolved to stage a general strike. Before the close of the following day the entire city was in rebel hands. Red flags were hoisted on the ships in the harbor. Noske was impressed by all this effervescence. However, he believed that the movement could still be localized. He was mistaken. The revolution spread with lightning speed. It engulfed the north and west of Germany. The government hastened to take counter-measures. Military action against the rebels was to be launched from Hanover. But the troops stationed in that city allowed themselves to be disarmed by a handful of sailors and joined the revolutionary forces. The paramount aims of the movement were peace and the establishment of a people's republic.

News of the developments along the coast produced great excitement in Berlin. The Social Democratic leaders did not dissemble their consternation. The idea of revolution was as abhorrent to them as ever. They hoped that the movement would not spread to the rest of the country. They believed that the monarchy and the Hohenzollern dynasty could still be saved if the emperor abdicated forthwith. There was general agreement on this point. But a sharp difference of opinion arose regarding the tactics to be employed. Scheidemann urged the dispatch of an ultimatum to Prince Max stating that the party would withdraw from the government if William did not at once relinquish the throne. He pointed to the growing restiveness of the masses. Every hour of delay, he warned, meant new converts to the cause of the Independents. The latter were zestfully exploiting the fact that the Social Democrats, as one of the parties represented in the government, could be charged with at least some of the responsibility for the present impasse. It was time to speak plainly and uncompromisingly. The Social Democratic party stood exposed to the danger of alienating its own followers and driving them into the arms of the radicals. This danger it could avert by assuming leadership of the revolutionary movement. It had to act to prevent the country from being taken over by the Independents and the Spartacists, whose avowed purpose was the creation of a socialist republic.

Ebert objected to the idea of an ultimatum. He could not bring himself to join the revolutionary forces. He hoped that he and his party would be spared the necessity of taking over the government at this critical moment. But such a necessity was bound to arise if the Social Democrats precipitated a ministerial crisis by withdrawing from Prince Max's cabinet. Besides, there was still the possibility of persuading the emperor to retire without subjecting the chancellor to threats. At a meeting of Social Democratic leaders on November 6, 1918, Ebert's views prevailed. Scheidemann's demand for an ultimatum was rejected. Instead a resolution was adopted which merely stated that the party expected a speedy settlement of the abdication question. Simultaneously, by means of pamphlets and newspaper articles, the Social Democrats vigorously defended the moderate program to which they were committed. The war, they pointed out, was now on the verge of termination; Wilson had declared himself ready to conclude an armistice with the German government. The overthrow of this government would endanger the peace. It would mean confusion and chaos, and these in turn would aggravate the already acute food shortage. The Social Democratic party demanded a full military amnesty, the thorough democratization of German political life and the withdrawal of the emperor. This program must not be sabotaged. It would have to be achieved by peaceful means. The workers must do everything in their power to maintain law and order. Germany must not be made the scene of conditions like those which prevailed in Russia. The emperor, for his part, must co-operate by abdicating without delay. The interests of one man should not be permitted to plunge the country into civil war.

The fact that Wilson had agreed to make peace with the government of Prince Max did not lessen the popular clamor for the emperor's retirement. The Independents and the Spartacists exploited to the full William's refusal to yield to this clamor. And their militant espousal of a socialist republic was having an effect on the industrial masses. Ebert suddenly awakened to the magnitude of the danger which threatened his party's hold on the workers. His fear that the country might go communist for want of the right kind of leadership drove him to adopt a more forceful attitude. He urged General Wilhelm Groener, Ludendorff's successor as First Quartermaster General of the army, to plead with the emperor, to warn him that only his abdication could save the monarchy and ward off the threat of civil war. The course advocated by Scheidemann was agreed upon without further ado. On November 7, 1918, the Social Democrats delivered the following ultimatum to Prince Max: both the emperor and the crown prince would have to renounce the throne; if no satisfactory reply was given by noon of the next day, the Social Democratic members of the cabinet would resign. Prince Max realized that the emperor was doomed. But there still seemed a way out on the larger question of regime. The monarchy, he believed, could be saved by assigning the crown to a blameless member of the dynasty: Prince William, infant son of the crown prince. This suggestion was supported by Ebert. It also met with favor in Progressive and Centrist circles, where fear for the future of the monarchy overshadowed all other preoccupations. On the morning of November 8, Prince Max set the new strategy in motion. He adjured the emperor to announce that he would abdicate in favor of his grandson as soon as arrangements had been completed for the establishment of a regency and the election of a national constituent assembly. Prince Max figured that the crown, by taking the initiative in posing the question of regime, would enjoy a decisive advantage in any contest for popular favor. But the emperor, heeding the advice of Hindenburg and Groener, said no.

William's attitude was nothing short of catastrophic for the royalist cause in Germany. But the decisive blow, the blow that sealed the doom of the Hohenzollern monarchy, had already been struck in Munich. There, on the afternoon of November 7, a great demonstration took place under the leadership of Kurt Eisner, an Independent who only recently had been released from jail. This remarkable man was first and foremost an intellectual; but the pressure of unusual circumstances gave him an opportunity to indulge a latent talent for action. The Independents actually constituted only a small minority in Bavaria. However, because they had been more outspoken and vociferous than any other group in demanding an immediate cessation of hostilities, they had acquired an importance far out of proportion to their numbers. Inflamed by Eisner's eloquence, the demonstrators helped themselves to arms, occupied public buildings and seized several newspaper plants. Workers', soldiers' and peasants' councils were organized. The king fled because no troops could be found in Munich who were willing to fire on the rebels. During the night of November 7-8, 1918, the Wittelsbach dynasty was deposed and a republic proclaimed. Eisner formed a cabinet with himself as premier and foreign minister. He declared his aversion to Bolshevist methods, to violence and bloodshed. He reposed faith in reason and the power of ideas. Eisner was unquestionably sincere. He was an idealist who believed that what was happening in Bavaria would ultimately make possible a better Germany and a better world.

4

Accelerated by the fall of the Bavarian monarchy, the tide of revolution continued to sweep relentlessly forward. One after the other Germany's leading cities succumbed: Cologne, Frankfurt, Stuttgart, Magdeburg, Leipzig. Nowhere was serious resistance offered. The imperial regime simply collapsed while its supporters in the middle and upper classes looked helplessly on. Berlin, however, had not yet toppled, and until it did, the triumph of the revolution could not be regarded as complete. The Social Democratic leaders knew they were sitting on a powder keg. The ultimatum to Prince Max had not only failed to pacify their followers but had antagonized the non-socialist members of the government. At the insistence of the latter, Ebert and his party comrades announced at noon on November 8 that the time-limit had been extended because of the impending signing of the armistice. They explained that they did not wish to do anything that might jeopardize the attainment of peace. While the Social Democrats procrastinated, the Shop Stewards resolved to strike. Their decision was precipitated by the arrest of Daeumig on November 8. Barth made ready to put into effect the detailed plan of operations which he had worked out weeks before. Handbills were distributed to workers and soldiers ordering them to leave the factories and barracks on the morning of November 9.

The Social Democrats realized that the zero hour was at hand. Even the most cautious of them were now ready to admit that Scheidemann had been right. They echoed his contention that the party could not swim against the current, that it must not temporize lest it lose its hold on the masses and expose the nation to the danger of Bolshevism and civil war. The whole question of strategy was once again aired at a meeting of Social Democratic leaders on the evening of November 8. The agents who represented the party in the factories of the Berlin area attended this all-important parley. The workers, they unanimously reported, could no longer be restrained. If the Social Democrats continued to disassociate themselves from the revolutionary movement, they would be overwhelmed. This settled the issue. It was decided to give the government until 9 A.M. of the next day to secure the emperor's abdication. If he were not off the throne by then, the Social Democratic members of the cabinet would resign and a general strike would be proclaimed. This decision would enable the Social Democrats to range themselves at the last moment on the side of the revolutionary forces and wrest control of the movement from the radicals.

Early on the morning of the 9th, thousands of workers left their factories and demonstrated in the streets of the capital. Calling for the establishment of a republic, they streamed into the center of the city without encountering any real resistance. Upon ascertaining, at 9 A.M., that the emperor had not yet abdicated, the Social Democratic party announced the withdrawal of Scheidemann and Bauer from the cabinet and instructed its followers to join the strike. Numerous workers' councils sprang into being. Large numbers of troops refused to obey their officers, fraternized with the demonstrating workers and organized soldiers' councils. Even the Naumburg *Jaeger,* a military detachment that had been rushed to Berlin because it was considered especially dependable, went over to the rebels. Realizing that resistance would prove futile, the authorities ordered the troops that had remained loyal to abstain from using their arms. The victory of the revolution, an amazingly easy, bloodless victory, was now complete. But jubilant crowds of workers and soldiers, displaying red flags, kept milling about in the streets. They refused to go home. This was their day, and they were determined to make the most of it.

5

Shortly after the first demonstrations began, but before the magnitude of the movement could be discerned, Prince Max informed the emperor of what was happening and once more implored him to abdicate. The sovereign, however, had other ideas. He wanted to place himself at the head of his army and lead it home to suppress the "traitors." But his generals grimly informed him that his troops would not fight. Groener and Hindenburg, reversing their earlier position, urged him to renounce his throne. They were now convinced that there was no other way to save the monarchy. William, deeply pained by the attitude of his most intimate advisers, said he would abdicate as emperor but not as King of Prussia. While a declaration to this effect was being drafted at general headquarters, a government spokesman telephoned from Berlin. He warned that the statement announcing the abdication would have to be in the capital within a few minutes. He was told that the emperor had made his decision and that it would be communicated to the government in half an hour.

Prince Max waited for the promised declaration. It failed to arrive. In a final effort to save the monarchy, he took matters into his own hands. A little before noon on November 9, 1918, he issued the following statement to the press:

> The emperor and king has decided to renounce the throne. The chancellor will remain in office until the questions connected with the abdication of the emperor, the renunciation of the throne by the crown prince . . . and the establishment of the regency have been settled. He intends to propose to the regent the appointment of Herr Ebert as chancellor and the introduction of a bill providing for the immediate election of a constituent national assembly whose duty it will be to determine the future form of government for the German people. . . .

A few minutes later Ebert, accompanied by several other Social Democratic spokesmen, went to see Prince Max. He declared that the political situation had undergone a drastic transformation during the morning and demanded that the government be entrusted to men "who possess the full confidence of the people." He promised to preserve order and to conduct the affairs of state in accordance with the constitution; but he insisted that it was now too late to set up a regency. Thereupon Prince Max, with the understanding that a constituent assembly would be convoked, yielded his office to Ebert. The latter immediately issued a manifesto urging the country to remain tranquil in order not to disturb the new government's efforts to cope with the terribly serious food shortage. In a second manifesto, he requested the bureaucracy to stay on the job.

Immediately after these preliminaries had been taken care of, Ebert and his colleagues returned to the Reichstag building and sat down to a meager lunch. A number of workers and soldiers rushed into the dining hall and insistently demanded that Scheidemann address the great crowd which had gathered outside. They told him that Liebknecht was already making a speech from the balcony of the royal palace and that he intended to announce the establishment of a soviet republic. Scheidemann needed no urging. Like all the other leaders of the Social Democratic party, he loathed Bolshevism and could imagine nothing worse than to see it installed in Germany. He rushed to the balcony of the Reichstag building and from there, at 2 P.M., he proclaimed the German republic. Satisfied that he had done the cause of democracy a good turn, he made his way back to the dining room only to find that Ebert was furious with him. "You have no right," roared the new chancellor, "to proclaim the republic. The fate of Germany—whether she is to become a republic or something else— must be decided by a constituent assembly." But it did not take Ebert long to reconcile himself to the accomplished fact. Having registered his protest, he swung round to Scheidemann's view and accepted without reservation what his impulsive lieutenant had done. That night, with even Hindenburg urging him to take to his heels, the emperor fled to Holland. However, it was not until November 28, 1918, that he formally renounced his throne. By then, every state of the now defunct German empire had cast out its ruler and become a republic.

Unquestionably most Germans wanted political democracy in November, 1918. But it is doubtful whether, had they been free to choose, they would have preferred a republic to a parliamentary monarchy. Centuries of habit and tradition had sanctified the monarchical principle. Only among the industrial workers was there a definite preponderance of republican sentiment. The rest of the country, except for the reactionary and chauvinist elements that detested democracy in any form, would have been content with a governmental system like that of Great Britain. But once the republic had come into being, these non-proletarian Germans rallied to its support. They did so not only because they could see no constructive alternative to such a course, given the circumstances in which the country found itself, but also because they believed that a republic had the best chance of obtaining acceptable peace terms from the Allies. Thus, on the morrow of the revolution, the German republic enjoyed the backing of the majority of the nation. True, the new regime had been begotten by starvation, despair, defeat and foreign dictation. It had come at a time when German fortunes were at their nadir. To many it was and remained a symbol and reminder of humiliation and defeat. It had been proclaimed by a man who had acted not from positive conviction but from a desperate anxiety to prevent something he considered worse: the triumph of Bolshevism. At the helm of the state stood a man who had consistently refused to turn against the monarchy and had made his peace with the republic only after its advent. The Social Democrats, upon whom the task of defending the republic mainly devolved, had remained divided on the question of regime until the very last. But all this was overshadowed now by the fact that the bulk of the nation wished the new order Godspeed. Overshadowed, too, for the moment was the implacable hostility of Junkers and militarists to the democratic way of life. These foes of the republic could count, from the very beginning, on the aid of certain industrialists and high-ranking bureaucrats. They could count, too, on the support of re-actionaries and chauvinists from other layers of the population. They recovered rather quickly from the shock of the revolution. They pro-ceeded in devious ways to pursue their counter-revolutionary aims. To combat this threat successfully, the republic would have to justify by deeds its right to survive. It would have to restore stability and prosperity. Above all, it would have to secure an honorable and just peace. So the fate of the republic rested not only with the people of Germany. It rested equally with the Allies. They had the power to make or break. They could give the republic an auspicious start or tie a millstone around its neck. They could welcome it as a sister-democracy or treat it as a pariah. Time alone would tell.

Chapter 7

GERMAN MILITARISM OBTAINS A NEW
LEASE ON LIFE

I

LESS than an hour after he had assumed the chancellorship, Ebert invited the Independents to join the Social Democrats in forming a new cabinet. He even expressed a willingness to give Liebknecht a ministerial post, but the Spartacist leader made it clear that he was not interested. The Independents asked for time to talk the matter over among themselves. The discussion of what to do about Ebert's invitation revealed a sharp division of opinion between the right-wingers and the Shop Stewards, who dominated the party's radical fringe. Haase, at the moment, was out of the city. So the task of upholding the moderate point of view fell to Dittmann. With characteristic vigor and cogency, he argued in favor of collaboration with the Social Democrats. Barth dissented. He declared himself opposed to dealings of any kind with men like Ebert and Scheidemann, whom he denounced as traitors to the cause of socialism. The long and acrimonious debate came to a sudden stop when Liebknecht appeared. Exhilarated by the events of this day of revolution, he demanded nothing less than the transfer of all power to the workers' and soldiers' councils. Barth took the same line. The right-wingers were far from friendly to the idea of a proletarian dictatorship on the Russian model. They wanted socialism, not sovietism. But in the end they were forced to yield. Having had their way on this all-important point, the Shop Stewards relented sufficiently to agree to short-term co-operation with Ebert and Scheidemann. A list of demands was forwarded to the Social Democrats late in the afternoon of November 9, 1918. Germany, the Independents stipulated, would have to become a "social" republic. Supreme authority would have to be vested in representatives chosen by all the workers and soldiers. Middle-class individuals were to be rigorously excluded from the cabinet. If these conditions were fulfilled, Ebert's invitation would be accepted—but on a provisional basis only. Actually, the Independents committed themselves to collaboration for no more than three days—just long enough, they said, to make possible the conclusion of an armistice with the enemy.

The Social Democrats replied that evening. The establishment of a "social" republic, they observed, was the aim of their policy, too; but this question was one which the people of Germany would have to decide by means of a constituent assembly. They made short shrift of the demand that all power be allocated to the representatives of the workers and soldiers. If this demand, they declared, meant a class dictatorship which did not have the support of the majority of the population, it would have to be rejected because it was contrary to the democratic principles of the Social Democratic party. Ebert and his colleagues likewise refused to acquiesce in the exclusion of middle-class persons. Such discrimination would complicate the already arduous task of feeding the country. As for the time-limit laid down by the Independents, it simply did not make sense. The two socialist parties would have to co-operate at least until the convocation of the constituent assembly.

The Independents gave their answer the following morning. They reiterated two of their original demands: all power to the representatives of the councils, and a cabinet composed exclusively of socialists. In addition, they insisted that nothing be done about the constituent assembly until after the social gains made possible by the revolution had been consolidated. However, they did show a more accommodating spirit by agreeing to lift the time-limit on their participation in the government. The Social Democrats did not like the stipulations regarding the councils and the constituent assembly. But because they felt the urgency of proceeding at once to the establishment of a government capable of maintaining order at home and concluding peace with the Allies, they capitulated. A six-man cabinet, called the Council of People's Commissioners, was promptly formed. Ebert, Scheidemann and Otto Landsberg represented the Social Democrats. The Independents named Haase, Dittmann and Barth as their plenipotentiaries. The Social Democrats anticipated little difficulty in working with Haase and Dittmann, whose comparatively moderate outlook was well known. But the same could not be said for Barth, who at that very moment was attempting to turn the workers' and soldiers' councils against Ebert and the Social Democrats.

Late in the afternoon of the same day, November 10, the workers' and soldiers' councils of Berlin assembled for the purpose of electing an executive committee. Ebert announced that a government representing the two socialist parties had been organized. The assembly, which was now, in theory at any rate, the nation's sovereign body, gave its sanction to the new cabinet. Then it turned to the main item on its agenda. This was the moment the Spartacists and the Shop Stewards had been waiting for. In an effort to wrest control of the new regime from the Social Democrats, they proposed the election of an executive committee composed exclusively of radicals. The names they offered were those of Liebknecht, Luxemburg, Ledebour, Barth and Richard Mueller. But this move was frustrated by the members of the soldiers' councils, most of whom had little sympathy for left-wing extremism. At their insistence, a committee consisting of twelve soldiers and twelve workers (the latter to represent both the Social Democrats and the Independents) was chosen. Liebknecht and Luxemburg refused to serve on it; they did not wish to traffic with Social Democrats. As the representative of the workers' and soldiers' councils, the executive committee regarded itself as the real repository of power in republican Germany. But the sphere of its competence was not clearly defined. And because it claimed the right to control the cabinet, which was theoretically responsible to it, friction between the two organs of government appeared unavoidable.

2

Two other developments of far-reaching importance occurred on November 10, 1918. One of these was the issuance of a proclamation by the Ebert cabinet. The purpose of this proclamation was to clarify the aims of the new regime. The preamble was a concession to the Independents:

The government created by the revolution, whose political leadership is purely socialist, is setting itself the task of carrying out the socialist program.

Actually, this was just so much eyewash. The proclamation promulgated no socialist measures. It did not go beyond the limits of the liberal democratic gospel espoused by the Social Democrats. It lifted the state of siege and restored freedom of assembly, freedom of association, freedom of speech and freedom of the press. It granted an amnesty to political offenders. It put back into effect the social insurance laws which had been suspended at the beginning of the war and ordered the reintroduction of the eight-hour day not later than January 1, 1919. Other socio-political ordinances were promised. The government undertook to provide work for the unemployed and indicated that an appropriate decree had already been drafted. The housing shortage was to be met by new construction. Steps were being taken to insure a regular food supply. Production would be maintained in all branches of the national economy. Property rights would be protected against infringement by private individuals. All public bodies were henceforth to be elected on the basis of equal, direct, secret and universal suffrage and in accordance with the principle of proportional representation. Persons of both sexes who had reached the age of 20 were to have the right to vote. These stipulations were to be effective in the elections to the constituent assembly.

All in all, the proclamation was a notable document. It signified the attainment of aims long pursued by socialists and liberals in Germany. But left-wing Independents received it with undisguised hostility. To them it was nothing more than an expression of the bourgeois ideal of political democracy, and political democracy, in their opinion, was meaningless without social democracy. What they wanted and demanded was immediate socialization of the nation's economy. Men like Haase and Dittmann took a different view of the proclamation. They felt that it was in keeping with prevailing circumstances. They were inclined to agree with Eisner, who publicly opposed hasty socialist experiments. The Bavarian premier declared that socialism was his ultimate goal, but he stressed the folly of socializing industry at a time when the productive capacity of the country was far below normal. The first thing to do, he contended, was to revive production; socialization would have to come later.

So far as the Social Democrats were concerned, the proclamation of November 10, 1918, was exactly and wholly right. They had a very definite conception of the task that lay immediately ahead, that had to take precedence over all others; and it did not include socialization. Millions of soldiers, they pointed out, would have to be demobilized and jobs found for them. The factories of the country, suddenly plunged into idleness by the discontinuance of war production, would have to start working on peacetime requirements. The single biggest problem was the shortage of food. The blockade was still in effect and domestic agricultural production was far from sufficient to meet the minimum needs of the population, already weakened by years of undernourishment. The all-important thing now was to do nothing that might create confusion. There must be no rash experiments— no drastic innovations.

The position taken by Ebert typified the attitude of the Social Democratic party. He believed in gradual, peaceful progress. He abhorred violence and bloodshed and shied away from any course which entailed the risk of precipitating them. It was necessary, he maintained, to control and restrain the revolutionary elements that had played so conspicuous a role in the developments of the last few days. Failure to do so would result in civil war and that most detestable of evils, Bolshevism. He was, above all, a fervent believer in the democratic process, in the right of the majority to decide and rule. He was prepared at all times to bow to the will of the majority, even if this meant loss of power for himself and his party. Like Eisner, Ebert insisted that socialism was his ultimate goal. But he contended that it would have to come slowly, by means of the ballot box. To attempt to institute socialization overnight was, in his opinion, to violate the basic principles of the socialist creed. He was convinced that not he and his colleagues but the radicals, the left-wing Independents and the Spartacists, with their emphasis on sovietism and class dictatorship, were the betrayers of socialism. Indeed, Ebert regarded these extremists as the most deadly enemies of the working class. To fight them, the use of every and any means was justified.

3

The Social Democrats had no armed force of their own with which to suppress the radicals. So Ebert turned to the Supreme Command. He did so in the belief that an understanding with the army leaders was the only way to save the country from Bolshevism and civil war. He got in touch by telephone with general headquarters at Spa. His party comrades were unaware of his action. Groener proved receptive. He was strongly of the opinion that the officers' corps should conclude an alliance with the Social Democrats who, after all, were moderates. The purpose of this alliance was to be twofold: to preserve the position and power of the military caste and combat the extreme Left. The monarchy, Groener felt, could not be restored. Consequently, the officers would have to make the best of the existing situation; and this they could do by assenting to a deal with Ebert. Groener had little difficulty in persuading Hindenburg to go along. The advantages which would accrue to the military caste were obvious. Besides, the field marshal, like his First Quartermaster General, detested the newly formed workers' and soldiers' councils and yearned to see them abolished. In such an enterprise, the Social Democrats would prove indispensable allies. Groener informed Ebert that Hindenburg was prepared to remain at the head of the Supreme Command. In return, the government would have to support the officers' corps.

In this fashion did the famous Ebert-Groener deal of November 10, 1918, come into being. Its importance can scarcely be exaggerated. Backed by the regular army, the Social Democrats were now in a position to suppress the radicals. The doom of German Bolshevism was apparently sealed. The old-line generals, who deeply regretted the overthrow of the monarchy, retained their powers and functions. Control of the nation's armed forces remained in their hands. This was one of the reasons why the Social Democrats never seriously attempted to create a republican army. Their alliance with the Supreme Command robbed them of freedom of action. The work of making the new Germany safe for militarism, whose destruction had been one of the principal aims of the revolution, was thus begun on November 10, 1918.

4

Early in October, the Supreme Command appointed an armistice commission in the belief that the war would soon end. General von Guendell was named head of this body. But when it became clear that the Allies would insist on severe terms, the Supreme Command took the position that the negotiations should be discontinued. It was at this juncture that Prince Max and his cabinet colleagues decided to add a civilian to the commission. They feared that a delegation composed exclusively of army men would not hesitate to use the harshness of the terms as a pretext for breaking off the negotiations. At a meeting of the cabinet on November 6, 1918, Prince Max proposed the appointment of Erzberger as the civilian member of the commission. The chancellor's move surprised Erzberger, who declared that not he but Haussmann should serve in this capacity. But the other ministers insisted. They believed that Erzberger, as the principal instigator of the peace resolution of July, 1917, was likely to be *persona grata* to the victors. Eager to play a great role and flattered by the insistence of his colleagues, Erzberger yielded. There was a certain poetic justice in this arrangement. For Erzberger had repeatedly stated that tolerable peace terms were well within the realm of possibility.

On the morning of November 7, Erzberger arrived in Spa. There he conferred with army chieftains. It was decided to drop Guendell and to name Erzberger head of the commission. This action was dictated in part by the belief that Wilson's pronounced antipathy to the "military masters" of Germany would make the Allies unwilling to negotiate with any member of the Supreme Command. At the close of the conference Hindenburg remarked to Erzberger that this was the first time in the history of the world that politicians and not soldiers were concluding an armistice. With this the field marshal declared himself completely in agreement. The Supreme Command, he laconically explained, had no more political directives to issue. As he took leave of the Centrist leader, he said: "May God be with you. Try to do the best you can for our Fatherland." The special train carrying Erzberger and the other members of the armistice commission arrived in the forest of Compiègne early in the morning of November 8. About a hundred meters distant stood the special train of Marshal Ferdinand Foch, the Allied generalissimo. At 10 A.M. Foch received the German emissaries. He had with him his chief of staff, General Maxime Weygand, Admiral Sir Rosslyn Wemyss, First Sea Lord of the British admiralty, and a few younger officers. No Americans were present. Upon what conditions, the German emissaries asked, would an armistice be granted? Foch replied: "I have no conditions to give you." When one of the emissaries sought to call his attention to Wilson's note of November 5, 1918, Foch refused to listen. "Do you wish," he queried coldly, "to ask for an armistice? If so, say so." Crestfallen, the German delegation asked for an armistice—with no strings or conditions attached. Thereupon Foch had Weygand read the main clauses of the armistice note agreed upon by the Allies on November 4. As soon as Weygand had finished, Erzberger demanded the immediate cessation of hostilities. He referred to the disorganized state of the Reich's armed forces. He talked about the revolutionary spirit which was taking hold of his country. Germany, he warned, was in imminent peril of being engulfed by Bolshevism. If she went down, the nations of Western Europe would find it difficult to protect themselves against this scourge. Only the prompt termination of Allied military operations could save the Reich and enable the

German army to reestablish discipline within its ranks. Foch said no. He declared that it was impossible to suspend hostilities before the signing of the armistice. The German delegation was given seventy-two hours in which to reply. Stressing the difficulty of communicating with the German government and the gravity of the decision to be made, Erzberger asked for a twenty-four hour extension of the time-limit. This Foch refused to grant.

The terms laid down by the Allies were unquestionably severe. Belgium, France, Luxemburg and Alsace-Lorraine were to be evacuated within fifteen days. Thirty-one days were allowed for the evacuation of the left bank of the Rhine and of the right bank to a depth of ten kilometers. The left bank was to be administered by the local authorities under Allied military control. Three of the most vital points on the Rhine—Mainz, Coblenz and Cologne—were to be occupied. The ten-kilometer zone on the right bank was to be neutralized. In the east, the German troops were to retire behind the 1914 frontiers. The Treaties of Brest-Litovsk and Bucharest were to be renounced. Huge quantities of war material, thousands of locomotives, railway cars and motor lorries, a certain number of warships and every submarine in the German fleet were to be handed over to the victors. All Allied prisoners of war were to be released immediately, but Germany was denied reciprocity in this matter. The cruellest blow was the stipulation that the blockade was to be maintained. Hunger had played a major role in Germany's collapse. It was one of the principal motivations of her frantic quest for peace. But now the door of escape from starvation was being slammed in her face.

Erzberger and his colleagues strove to secure milder terms. While they were so engaged, the revolution in Berlin toppled the government of Prince Max and a new regime came into being. This made their position vis-à-vis Foch all the more difficult. Nevertheless, they protested strongly against the fifteen-day limit for the evacuation of France, Belgium, Luxemburg and Alsace-Lorraine. They argued that the German army was in no position to comply with this demand and that if it were to attempt to do so an orderly retreat would become impossible. Besides, the situation within Germany had to be taken into account. The country was in the throes of revolution and infected with the Bolshevist virus. The most urgent need of the moment was the preservation of order. To avert the danger of Bolshevism on their own soil and to insure the solvency of their prospective debtor, the Allies would have to soften their terms. Germany was threatened with famine. It was inhuman, at such a time, to continue the blockade and seize railway cars and other badly needed transport material. Yet the Allies were saying that the blockade must go on. They were saying that more innocent women and children must die. It was on this issue that Erzberger laid the greatest stress. It was the problem to which Ebert, as the head of the new German government, devoted most of his attention. The efforts of the two men did not prove entirely fruitless. To the original armistice note there was appended a clause stating that "the Allies and the United States contemplate the provisioning of Germany to such an extent as shall be found necessary." No other important changes were made in the Allied terms, which the German military experts continued to pronounce impossible of fulfillment. But Hindenburg, who had declared that certain modifications were imperative, resigned himself to the inevitable and advised capitulation. At 5 A.M. on the morning of November 11, 1918, Erzberger, acting on instructions from Berlin, signed the armistice. In so doing, he signed his own death-warrant. Many of his countrymen never forgave him for accepting conditions which, they claimed, should have been spurned as unspeakably shameful.

November 11 brought a cessation of military operations. But the war against non-combatants went on in spite of the addendum to the blockade article of the armistice. Indeed, the blockade was even intensified for a time as a result of the closing of the Baltic, which hitherto had been open to German merchantmen and fishermen. Besides, the new military frontiers imposed by the armistice aggravated the already catastrophic dislocation of German economic life. The winter of 1918-19 was a period of incredible hardship for millions of Germans. The suffering which it brought was the more unendurable because of all that had gone before. On March 1, 1919, the plight of the country wrung from the German government this cry of distress: "We cannot feed ourselves from our own supplies until the next harvest. The blockade is eating away the vitals of our people. Thousands are perishing daily from malnutrition." The memory of this horrible experience lived on in the minds of Germans of every class. It bred a bitterness which the years assuaged but which could all too easily be resuscitated upon the first recurrence of adversity.

The Reich's post-armistice demands for the lifting of the blockade ran afoul of serious difficulties. One of the most formidable problems was the shortage of shipping space for the transport of food to Germany. At the time of the second renewal of the armistice in January,

1919, the Allies demanded the use of a considerable part of the German merchant marine. The German government believed that this was merely a trick to secure possession of the ships. It was therefore reluctant to comply. However, the pressure of circumstances forced it to swallow its misgivings. Toward the middle of March, 1919, it agreed to relinquish the ships. Thereafter food supplies began to reach the Reich in increasing quantities. The people of Germany were thus saved from a calamity of incalculable proportions.

5

Certain things are clearer today than they were at the time of the signing of the armistice. The Allies, it is now generally conceded, made a tragic mistake in agreeing to a truce at a moment when the German armies, though in retreat, were still intact and when all the fighting was still taking place on Allied soil. They should have marched to Berlin in order to make indisputably clear to the Germans the fullness and decisiveness of their defeat on the field of battle, in order to uproot the legend, so carefully nurtured in the minds of generations of Germans, that their armies were unconquerable. Nothing less would have sufficed to dissipate the nimbus, begotten by past successes, which surrounded the military caste and the system which it had created. But there was no march to Berlin. The German armies were withdrawn from the blood-soaked battlefield without having endured the agonies of a knockout blow. The soil of the Fatherland was spared the horrors of trench warfare. The Allies threw away their chance to destroy, once and for all, Germany's belief in her own invincibility. By so doing, they unwittingly helped German militarism to survive the debacle and obtain a new lease on life.

This error was compounded by Wilson's refusal to negotiate with the "military masters" of Germany. This meant, in effect, no dealings with the Supreme Command. As a consequence, the military leadership of Germany was divorced from the symbolically all-important act of submission. The odium of accepting responsibility for surrender fell not on the Supreme Command but on a civilian, Erzberger, and on the newly formed republic. How fortunate for the military caste that Hindenburg was not forced to appear before the victors and in the full view of the German people hand over his sword to Foch! Had the Field Marshal been singled out to sign the armistice, responsibility for the defeat would have fallen where it belonged. And German militarism would have been dealt a stunning blow.

The Allies played into the hands of the German war lords in still another way. When, in the months that followed the armistice, they drafted the Treaty of Versailles, they inserted in it that most controversial of articles, the war-guilt clause. By so doing, they diverted the German people's attention from the culpability of their former leaders. Public indignation, instead of being directed against those who had wanted and conducted the war, turned against the country's foreign calumniators. All patriotic citizens, regardless of class or party, felt called upon to deny the Allied charge that Germany alone was responsible for the outbreak of the war. In the endless and bitter recrimination that followed, the militarists posed as the paladins of German honor. And while they battened on the war-guilt controversy, the republic suffered incalculably. For had not its representatives signed the document which contained this intolerable lie? Those who harped on this theme chose to forget that the war-guilt clause and certain other "dishonoring" provisions of the peace had been accepted only under the threat of an Allied military invasion.

6

Almost on the very morrow of the armistice, German militarists, reinforced by right-wing politicians and publicists, disseminated far and wide the theory that the armies of the Reich had never been defeated on the battlefield, that they had been stabbed in the back by "subversive" elements at home—pacifists, liberals, socialists, communists, Jews. Hindenburg made himself a leading exponent of this theory. In the last chapter of his memoirs, which appeared in September, 1919, he wrote: "Like Siegfried, stricken down by the treacherous spear of savage Hagen, our weary front collapsed." A few months later he made the same point before a Reichstag committee investigating the causes of Germany's collapse.

In spite of the superiority of the enemy in men and material, we could have brought the struggle to a favorable issue if determined and unanimous cooperation had existed between the army and those at home. But . . . divergent interests began to manifest themselves with us. These circumstances soon led to a disintegration of our will to conquer. . . .

This charge was taken up by Hitler and countless other propagandists.

The theory of the stab in the back proved a source of endless tribulation for the German republic. Its corollary, the myth of victory in the field, helped to preserve the prestige of the army. Between them they lent powerful impetus to the resurgence of militarism in Germany.

The leaders of the republic completed the work of making Germany safe for militarism. On November 10, 1918, they had thrown away their opportunity to create a people's army upon which they could have relied to checkmate the counterrevolutionists. Their behavior thereafter was of a piece with this initial capitulation. They shrank from performing the drastic economic and social operations which might have prevented the restoration of anything resembling the pre-1918 order. Generals who did not even bother to disguise their hostility to the democratic regime were permitted to retain important commands. The Reichswehr, that small but beautifully trained army of the German republic, was placed under the direction of men who had only contempt for their civilian superiors. The indoctrination to which the soldiers were subjected stressed the virtues and values of the old imperial army. They were made to feel that their first allegiance was to their military superiors and not to the regime which they had sworn to uphold. Through their control of the armed forces, the Reichswehr chieftains eventually became one of the most powerful groups in the country.

The goal of the military caste was to make possible the establishment of a regime which would do its will, which would dedicate the resources of the state to war and conquest. An essential preliminary to the achievement of this goal was the destruction or emasculation of democracy at home. As the star of the dethroned Hohenzollerns declined, most of the officers cold-storaged their traditional monarchism. They lent their support to any movement or party which gave promise of being strong enough to carry out their program. They even stooped to dealings with low-born demagogues whom they secretly despised. In the end it was Hitler, a man far removed from their own antecedents and social milieu, who gave them what they wanted.

The 27th of November, 1918, witnessed the forging of another important link in the chain of events that made possible the comeback of the military caste. On that day the Supreme Command took action to reinforce, by means of voluntary enlistment, the armed forces of the nation that were being depleted at a great rate in response to the widespread demand for instantaneous demobilization. The formation of fighting units composed exclusively of volunteers proceeded rapidly. Within a few weeks such units were to be found in every part of the Reich. Some of them helped the police to maintain order at home. Others were active along the eastern frontier and especially in the Baltic provinces. Still others were used to bolster detachments of the regular army. This influx of volunteers into the armed forces was encouraged by the Social Democratic members of the government. At the behest of the Supreme Command, they issued a call for new recruits. They wished to have at their disposal a large military force that could be used against the Independents and the Spartacists. It was thus that the notorious Free Corps came into being. They were made up for the most part of professional soldiers and officers. These men were fanatically anti-Bolshevist, anti-socialist and anti-democratic. They hated the republic and everything it signified. They glorified militarism and the leadership principle. They were eager to fight for the restoration of the old order. Little wonder, then, that the Free Corps served as the spearhead of the counterrevolutionary forces during the first and crucial years of the German republic.

Chapter 8

CIVIL WAR IN GERMANY

I

THE Social Democrats were psychologically unprepared for the responsibilities of power. The sudden collapse of the imperial regime took them unawares. It left a void which they alone were able to fill. They assumed the burdens of office with understandable misgivings. They had no time for deliberation, no time to chart their course with the care which the situation demanded. The horrible mess bequeathed by the old ruling classes had to be cleaned up without delay. Problems of every description clamored for solution. The danger of civil war was always present. Defeat, starvation and economic dislocation cast their shadow everywhere. It was under these disheartening circumstances that the work of national reconstruction had to be undertaken. Nothing could be accomplished without a smoothly functioning administrative machine. The routine business of state had to be carried on without interruption. For this reason, Ebert retained the existing bureaucracy. He urged the Reich's civil servants to remain at their jobs, to minister as best they could to the everyday needs of the harassed population. Many individuals of militantly monarchist outlook were thus permitted to remain in positions of power and influence. This resulted in serious harm to the young republic. From the very outset, these men employed the powers vested in them to obstruct the working of popular rule. They aided and abetted counterrevolutionary movements. But not all the bureaucrats held over from the imperial regime behaved in this fashion. A good many of them made an honest effort to serve their new masters. The Kapp putsch of March, 1920, constituted a searching test. It gave the pro-republican members of the administrative hierarchy an opportunity to demonstrate their loyalty. On that occasion they were not found wanting.

2

Vulnerable to attack on the morrow of the November revolution were the Junkers and the industrial magnates. These groups felt completely helpless vis-à-vis the new regime. The owners of the great estates east of the Elbe lived in constant dread of the time, apparently none too distant, when confiscation of their properties would become the order of the day. They were in no position to resist forcible dispossession. They could expect no help from the hitherto loyal peasants, who had come in the course of the war to distrust their social superiors and to hope for something fairly serious in the way of agrarian reform. The fears of the Junkers and the hopes of the land-hungry peasants proved equally abortive. The Social Democrats, in whose hands lay the fate of the country, shrank from promoting an agrarian revolution. A sudden and wholesale redistribution of land was not part of their immediate program because they feared to do anything that might aggravate existing social tensions and impede the process of economic recovery. So the economic position of the Junkers, and the enormous power that went with it, remained intact.

Even the most naive of political observers could have predicted what followed: en masse the Junker landowners turned against the republic which had sought to placate them. They loathed democracy with its egalitarian principle, but they feared it even more. Despite the moderation of the republican authorities in matters of economic and social reform, there were radical ideas in the air; there was Russia, where the land had been turned over to the peasantry, and Bolshevist influence upon the thinking of a good many Germans was altogether obvious. The possibility that such subversive ideas about the sanctity of property, especially landed property, might be more widely entertained was like a sword of Damocles suspended over the heads of these German barons. Hohenzollern paternalism which had so loyally tended to their needs and shielded them from ruin was no more. Under the new democracy, the lowly masses, with their enormous power at the polls, could, if they so desired, expand the political revolution into an economic one. So long as the republic existed, the danger would always be there; only the destruction of the democratic system could secure them in the possession of their wealth and influence. The anti-republican forces thus enjoyed, from the very beginning, the unwavering and whole-hearted support of one of the most powerful sections of German society.

Fear for their property-rights was uppermost in the minds of the Junkers, but it was not the sole motivation of their unrelenting opposition to the new regime. The disarmament of the Reich under the terms of the Versailles settlement meant a much smaller army and consequently fewer officers; this in turn meant reduced military employment for the members of the landowning aristocracy. Moreover, the pacifist and international outlook of liberal and socialist opinion, not to speak of its corrosive agnosticism, was anathema to these rural diehards, who distrusted all innovation, especially when it emanated from the Left. Finally, political office, which had virtually been monopolized by the nobility under the pre-revolutionary regime, remained for years (in fact, until the Papen cabinet of 1932) closed to all but a favored few of this onetime elite. The reestablishment of an authoritarian regime which would safeguard their class interests and restore them to their former privileges was therefore the supreme objective of the Junkers. Nothing less could satisfy them.

3

Most of the great industrialists, like the landed aristocracy, were filled with consternation by the advent of the republic. Gone was the regime which till now had protected them against the demands of the proletariat. They feared the worst. For was not the state in the hands of avowedly anticapitalist elements? The socialization of industry seemed in the offing. To forestall such a disaster the employers were prepared to shower the workers with concessions. They would recognize the trade unions, agree to an eight-hour day, grant wage increases, subsidize social insurance and give labor an equal voice with management in the settlement of industrial disputes. They found the trade unions willing to make a deal. On November 15, 1918, a momentous compact was concluded between capital and labor. The employers recognized the trade unions as the only agencies entitled to speak for the workers and promised to withdraw their support from the so-called "yellow-dog" or company unions. The collective-bargaining agreement was henceforth to be the sole means for determining working conditions. In every factory employing more than fifty persons a workers' council was to be elected. The eight-hour day was to be introduced in all establishments without any reduction in pay. A central committee composed equally of workers and employers was to be established for the purpose of settling industrial disputes.

The trade union leaders and the Social Democratic party hailed this compact as a great victory for labor. But extremists on the Left bitterly denounced it as a deviation from the principle of the class struggle and as a betrayal of the cause of social revolution. The employers, for their part, were resolved to retract their concessions as soon as the political situation became propitious for such a move. In the meantime, they would have to abide by the terms of the compact. They knew they would not be out of danger until the elements that were clamoring for socialization had been disposed of.

This clamor for socialization was not confined to the radicals. Many rank-and-file members of the Social Democratic party talked in the same vein. They did not want to see the new regime become what they called a "money-bag republic." But their leaders continued to hold back, arguing that gradualness was of the essence. They reiterated their opposition to hasty experiments which would destroy all possibility of effecting an immediate improvement in the country's economic situation. It was above all necessary, they kept repeating, to save the starving nation from further and worse agony. For the time being, only those branches of the national economy that were ripe for socialization should be socialized. This view was formally endorsed by the cabinet on November 18, 1918. The job of studying the question and of making appropriate recommendations was turned over to a committee which came to be known as the Socialization Commission. Among its members were prominent socialists like Karl Kautsky and Rudolf Hilferding, the miners' foremost spokesman, Otto Hué, and several professional economists. The commission met for the first time on December 5, 1918. A month later it submitted a preliminary report. This was a cautiously worded document. It warned against a schematic transformation of German economy. Socialization, it pointed out, could take any one of several forms. The owners of enterprises earmarked for socialization would have to be compensated. The best results could be obtained only after thorough and methodical study of all the problems involved. In a separate report dealing with the coal industry, the commission made a number of specific proposals. These included the nationalization of all coal deposits and the subjection of marketing, price-fixing and the opening of new mines to govermental regulation. Ebert and his colleagues, anxious as they were to proceed slowly, regarded these reports as justifying procrastination.

4

From a legal point of view, sovereignty now resided in the revolutionary masses. But it had been delegated by them to the workers' and soldiers' councils. The most important of these were the ones that had been set up in Berlin. They operated through their executive committee, whose function it was to control the cabinet. The latter was far more representative of the masses than the executive committee. Together the Social Democrats and the Independents, who furnished all six members of the Council of People's Commissioners, accounted for the bulk of the German working class. The executive committee, on the other hand, was a purely local organization and most of its members were unknown outside the capital.

Amid clamorous applause from the radical elements, who were anxious to insure the establishment of a soviet regime in Germany, the executive committee took a most important step on November 23, 1918. It issued a call for a national congress of workers' and soldiers' councils. One of the chief tasks of the congress, which was scheduled to open on the 16th of December, was to be the selection of a central council. This body, it was explained, would replace the executive committee as the supreme co-ordinating agency of the conciliar system. Ebert and Scheidemann countered with a move that testified to their readiness for a showdown battle with the left-wing extremists. At their insistence the cabinet on November 29 fixed February 16, 1919, as the date for elections to a constituent national assembly and promulgated an appropriate electoral law. At once the Shop Stewards and the Spartacists charged that the revolution was being betrayed. They enlarged upon the conflict between "proletarian" and "bourgeois" democracy and castigated the latter as a sell-out to the forces of reaction. The Social Democratic leaders ridiculed these charges. They reaffirmed their unalterable aversion to sovietism and all its implications. They stubbornly rejected the idea of giving all power in the state to workers' and soldiers' councils. Once again they contended that sovereignty resided in the nation as a whole and not in any one class. To make the national will articulate, there had to be elections based on universal suffrage and a constituent assembly mirroring the wishes of the entire people.

The controversy between the rival proletarian camps raged with mounting fury during the ensuing days. The Spartacists, following the line laid down for them by Rosa Luxemburg, pressed unremittingly for a sovietized Reich. They were supported by the Shop Stewards, who vowed a fight to the finish against the plan to convoke a constituent national assembly. The moderate Independents led by Haase and Dittmann sought to steer a middle course between the extremists in their own party and the Social Democrats. They preferred a system of government which would combine the workers' and soldiers' councils with the kind of parliamentary democracy espoused by Ebert and Scheidemann. However, they demanded that the elections to the national constituent assembly be postponed until after German economy, especially agriculture and industry, had been socialized. They hoped thereby to insure a socialist majority in the assembly. The Social Democrats turned thumbs down on this demand. They argued that the effect of socialization on the political attitude of the nation was anybody's guess. Besides, to defer the elections until after socialization had been instituted would mean to defer them indefinitely. But the country could not wait. Peace had to be concluded with the Allies, and only a government which owed its existence to a democratically chosen national assembly could qualify for that task. Any delay in the attainment of peace would aggravate the country's desperate food situation and impede the settlement of difficulties which had recently arisen between Germany and Poland. It was also imperative to take up with Moscow the question of Russian support for Spartacist propaganda in Germany. Once peace had been concluded in the west, this ticklish matter could be approached with far greater prospect of success. Transcending all these considerations was the fact that a government which depended on workers' and soldiers' councils for its maintenance would prove incapable of reestablishing order and stability.

The tension between the Social Democrats and their proletarian rivals led to bloodshed in Berlin on December 6, 1918. Incited by rumors that a conservative counterrevolution was being launched, a band of left-wing extremists under Spartacist leadership began a march toward the heart of the city. Troops attached to the office of Otto Wels, the Social Democratic commander of the capital, intercepted the demonstrators, who were unarmed. Yielding to the excitement of the moment, Wels' men opened fire. Several of the demonstrators were killed and a good many more were wounded. The Spartacist leaders pounced upon this incident to fan the passions of their followers. They reiterated the charge that Ebert was guilty of counterrevolutionary activity and once again proclaimed the necessity of social revolution. The events of December 6 imposed a further strain on the tenuous government partnership between the Social Democrats and the Independents. Haas and Dittmann, who were being assailed by the left-wingers within their own party because they favored continued collaboration with the Social Democrats, found themselves ever more on the defensive.

5

The Spartacists pinned their hopes on the forthcoming congress of workers' and soldiers' councils. They counted on it to insure the triumph of sovietism in Germany. On December 16, 1918, the delegates assembled in the Prussian House of Deputies for the opening session. A great crowd, palpably under radical leadership, besieged the building and demonstrated noisily in an effort to influence the proceedings. From the very beginning, however, it was manifest that the extremists had grievously miscalculated. Not they but the Social Democrats, the alleged betrayers of the revolution, enjoyed the support of the great majority of the delegates. Liebknecht and Luxemburg received a resounding rebuff straightway when the assembly voted overwhelmingly against giving them seats. Richard Mueller, the leader of the Shop Stewards, started the verbal fireworks by denouncing the Haase-Dittmann policy of co-operating with the Social Democrats. While he was speaking, a Spartacist delegation forced its way into the hall and demanded the removal of the Ebert government, the transfer of supreme power to the workers' and soldiers' councils, the formation of a Red army and the issuance of a call for world revolution. This incursion was but the first of a whole series of interruptions which kept the congress in a continuous state of turmoil. On the following day, the bitterness between the Social Democrats and the radicals flared anew. Ledebour denounced Ebert in excoriating terms. But it was Barth who caused the greatest stir. He declared that his patience was at an end. He would have to decide very soon whether he wished to remain a member of the government. He had vainly combated Ebert's policies. He could no longer assume any responsibility for them. He wanted an immediate understanding with the Russians. The military "camarilla," he warned, was at work against the new regime and was being clandestinely supported by the

Social Democrats. This situation must not be tolerated another moment. The time to do away with the old officers' corps was now.

Ebert reacted sharply to the charge that he had established treasonable relations with the generals. He told the congress that the questions raised by Barth were not the kind that could be settled by public debate. Haase intervened at this point. He was anxious to prevent a widening of the breach between Ebert and the Independents. Consequently he suggested that action be delayed on Barth's demand for abolition of the officers' corps. The proceedings were suddenly interrupted by the arrival of a delegation of soldiers. Dorrenbach, head of the People's Naval Division, led the intruders. He demanded that the officers be disarmed, that all rank insignia be abolished, and that control of the armed forces be entrusted to a council of soldiers. He and his comrades clamored for immediate action and showed not the slightest intention of leaving until their demands had been granted. So great was the ensuing tumult that the congress was forced to suspend it labors. When it reconvened on the morning of December 18, an unexpected development occurred. Walther Lampl, the Social Democratic delegate from Hamburg, made common cause with Dorrenbach. Declaring that the time for action had come, he proceeded to introduce a number of sweeping motions. First and foremost on the list of his demands was the transfer of the powers of the Supreme Command to the cabinet and the executive committee of the workers' and soldiers' councils. He likewise insisted upon the elimination of all rank insignia, the election of officers by the soldiers themselves, the abolition of the standing army and the speedy creation of a people's militia. The friendly reception accorded Lampl's motions was a heavy blow to Ebert and to the program which he and Groener had clandestinely agreed upon. Ebert's plan to use the army to suppress left-wing radicalism would obviously come to nought if Hindenburg and Groener were denuded of their powers as top-ranking members of the Supreme Command. Such a possibility now seemed in the offing. For the fear of a militarist counterrevolution was no longer confined to the radicals; it had taken hold of important sections of the Social Democratic party. Lampl's motions were adopted by an overwhelming majority. Ebert's attempt to emasculate them by the addition of qualifying clauses proved vain. For the first time since the proclamation of the republic, the three proletarian parties stood shoulder to shoulder. But the action of the congress changed nothing. Ebert saw to that. Thanks to him, control of the army remained in the hands of

Hindenburg and Groener. And nothing was done to implement the other resolutions. German militarism was saved from what might have been a crippling blow.

On December 19, a different atmosphere prevailed in the hall of the congress. Now it was the turn of the radicals to endure some spirited tongue-lashings. The strongest speech of the day was delivered by Scheidemann. He conceded that the workers' and soldiers' councils had been a necessity and that they had accomplished many good things. But they should not, he insisted, be made a permanent feature of the nation's political system. If they were, German industry and commerce would be hopelessly undermined and the Reich reduced to ruin. The left-wing Independents and the Spartacists met the challenge head on. They offered a motion stating that under all circumstances the soviet system would remain the foundation of the constitution and that supreme legislative and executive authority would belong to the councils. The motion was decisively defeated. The vote was 344 to 98. This was one of the great turning-points of the German revolution. The representatives of the industrial masses, of the elements that had overthrown the Hohenzollern empire, had proclaimed their unwillingness to countenance a proletarian dictatorship. They had demonstrated in unmistakable fashion their preference for the moderate political program espoused by the Social Democrats. But the radical delegates, undeterred by this momentous setback, immediately resumed the struggle. They demanded that the central council, which was to be elected by the congress and which was to exercise the latter's powers until the convocation of a national constituent assembly, be authorized not only to supervise the work of the cabinet but to determine the formulation of government policies. This demand was likewise rejected by a large majority. Thereupon the radical delegates declared that they would have nothing to do with the election of the central council. This was a dramatic gesture, but its only effect was to facilitate the designs of Ebert and Scheidemann. A central council composed exclusively of Social Democrats was chosen. The moderates won still another victory when it was decided to advance the date of the elections to the national constituent assembly from February 16 to January 19, 1919. The left-wing Independents, through Ledebour, issued the warning that they would rally the masses to their side. On this note of disunity in the ranks of the German proletariat the congress of workers' and soldiers' councils came to an end.

6

Ebert was prepared for anything the radicals might attempt. Thanks to his understanding with Groener, sizable military forces, consisting of regular army troops and Free Corps units, were now at his disposal. The occasion to use them came sooner than he had expected. In the former royal palace in Berlin were some 3,000 sailors belonging to the People's Naval Division. They had come to the capital in November to protect the new revolutionary regime. Discipline within the group was not of the best. Several thefts had been committed in the palace and the government, in an effort to put a stop to this, ordered the division to move out. The sailors refused. Thereupon the government informed them that they would not receive their back pay until they did as they were told. The enraged sailors decided to take matters into their own hands. On December 23, 1918, they made their way to the chancellery and instructed the guard stationed outside the building to permit no one to go in or out. They also instructed Central not to put through any telephone calls from the chancellery. In the belief that Ebert was now safely incommunicado—actually he was not because there was a secret telephone in the chancellery which he was in the habit of using when seeking Groener's counsel—the sailors marched to the office of the city commander, seized Wels and two of his officials and took them to the Marstall, where they were held captive. Infuriated by these high-handed tactics, and desperately anxious to liberate Wels, Ebert turned to his military friends for help. They readily acceded to his request. They were glad of an opportunity to strike a blow against left-wing radicalism, with which the People's Naval Division was conspicuously identified. Shortly after midnight, Ledebour, in an effort to prevent bloodshed, hurried to the Marstall and prevailed upon Dorrenbach to release Wels. The news was promptly relayed to the chancellery, but it proved impossible to contact Ebert. The battle which Ledebour had sought to avert was now inescapable.

Early on the morning of December 24, a regular army division commanded by General von Lequis opened artillery fire on the palace and on the Marstall. After two hours of fighting negotiations were initiated. They culminated in an agreement whereby the sailors consented to withdraw from the palace as soon as the question of their back pay had been settled. The government, for its part, promised to remove Wels, who was most unpopular with his erstwhile captors, from his post as city commander. The incident had far-reaching political repercussions. The sympathies of the workers of Berlin and of the left-wing Independents were strongly on the side of the People's Naval Division. The shooting of republican sailors by anti-republican troops under the command of an old-line, aristocratic general aroused so much ire against the Social Democrats that the right-wing Independents were forced to sever the government partnership with Ebert and Scheidemann. This development signalized the end of the united socialist front in Germany. It gave powerful impetus to the already widespread dissension within the proletarian camp and increased the possibility of open civil war in the country generally. The showdown began on December 27, 1918, when Haase, Dittmann and Barth addressed a series of questions to the newly formed central council of the workers' and soldiers' soviets. They wished to know, they said, whether the council disapproved of the behavior of the Social Democratic leaders on December 23 and 24. They also wished to know whether it was prepared to insist on the enforcement of the Lampl resolutions. How, they queried, did the central council feel about the determination of Ebert and Scheidemann to rely upon old-line generals and units of the imperial army? And did the council intend to support the demand for speedy replacement of the old army by a people's militia? The reply to these questions was a foregone conclusion, thanks to the purely Social Democratic composition of the central council. The latter ranged itself squarely on the side of Ebert and Scheidemann. Thereupon Haase, Dittmann and Barth withdrew from the government. Their places were taken by Social Democrats. One of these was Noske, who became minister of war. Inasmuch as his relations with the officers' corps were extremely cordial, his assumption of this post foreshadowed even closer co-operation between the Supreme Command and the government. The resignation of the Independents threw into sharp relief one indubitable and paramount fact: all political authority was in the hands of the Social Democrats; upon them the future course of the revolution, the direction in which it moved, depended.

7

A national conference of the Spartacist League opened in Berlin on December 30, 1918. Wilhelm Pieck presided, but the outstanding personalities were Luxemburg and Liebknecht. These two battle-scarred champions of proletarian radicalism co-operated closely, but in temperament and intellectual equipment they were markedly dissimilar. Liebknecht was hot-headed and impulsive and given to what his intra-party critics called utopianism. Luxemburg was far the brainier of the two. She had an unequaled grasp of Marxist theory, but she appreciated, too, the dangers of an over-doctrinaire approach to the problem of translating theory into practice. Cool and level-headed, she spent a good deal of her time talking Liebknecht out of projects which she regarded as premature. While the ultimate ends which she envisaged were not lacking in boldness and comprehensiveness, she insisted on making sure that the means employed conformed to existing realities. This led to frequent disputes with Liebknecht, who itched for action and assented only with the greatest reluctance to counsels of prudence.

The Spartacist conference repudiated the Independents, declaring that they had forfeited their right to be recognized as the standard-bearers of the revolutionary masses. The tie between the two left-wing groups was formally dissolved. To signalize this event, the Spartacists gave their organization a new name: the Communist party of Germany. The conference devoted considerable attention to the question of what to do about the impending elections to the national constituent assembly. The discussion brought to light sharp differences of opinion regarding basic problems of strategy. Luxemburg took the position that victory for socialism could not be won by a putsch against the Ebert government. She argued that the revolutionary movement was as yet too weak to undertake so ambitious and hazardous an enterprise. A coup at this moment was bound to result in ignominious and bloody failure. For some time to come, the forces of proletarian radicalism would have to concentrate their energies on the task of preparing the masses for a second revolution. Only after the bulk of the nation's workers had been won over to the revolutionary cause could the signal for action be given. In the meantime, the party would have to make the most of whatever opportunities lay within reach. It would have to participate in the forthcoming elections and in the labors of the national constituent assembly. By so doing it would be in a better position to further its own ends. Luxemburg's reasoning convinced Liebknecht. He sided with her. But the majority of the delegates felt otherwise. They voted in favor of boycotting the elections. They wanted no part of bourgeois parliamentarism. What they did want was a putsch, and they wanted it right away.

The onrush of events seemed to presage quick fulfillment of this desire. Shortly after the withdrawal of the Independents from the cabinet, Ebert and his colleagues attempted to force the resignation

of Emil Eichhorn, the chief of Berlin's police. Eichhorn belonged to
the left wing of the Independents; between him and the Social Democrats there existed intense ill feeling. Now that the Independents were
no longer in the cabinet, the radicals tended to regard Eichhorn as
their last pillar of strength. To defend him against "traitors" like
Ebert, Scheidemann and Noske became a sacred obligation. In spite
of the pressure that was brought to bear upon him, Eichhorn stubbornly refused to resign. The Social Democratic leaders decided to
temporize no longer. One of their principal lieutenants was Paul
Hirsch, Prussia's premier and minister of the interior. At their behest
he formally dismissed Eichhorn on January 4, 1919. The Independents
accepted the challenge with gusto. They told Eichhorn to remain at
his post. The Communists promised their support. On the morning
of January 5, the two radical parties issued a joint manifesto. It ran
in part as follows:

Workers! Comrades! The Ebert government with its accomplices in
the Prussian ministry is seeking to uphold its power with the bayonet, and
to secure for itself the favor of the capitalist bourgeoisie whose interests it
has always secretly supported. The blow that has fallen upon the chief of
the Berlin police was in reality aimed at the whole German proletariat, at
the whole German revolution. Workers! Comrades! That cannot, must
not, be tolerated! Up, therefore, to a mighty demonstration! Show the
oppressors your power today, prove to them that the revolutionary spirit of
the November days is not yet dead in you. Meet today . . . to stage a
great mass demonstration! Come in your thousands! Your freedom, your
future, the fate of the revolution, are at stake. Down with the tyranny of
Ebert and Scheidemann. . . . Long live revolutionary international socialism!

The response to this summons surpassed the fears of the authorities.
A huge throng of workers, many of them armed, surged into the
streets of Berlin. The building that housed the *Vorwaerts,* official
mouthpiece of the Social Democratic party, was seized. The offices
of other leading newspapers were likewise occupied. In the afternoon
the leaders of the two left-wing parties met in Eichhorn's office to
decide what to do next. A sharp divergence of views at once manifested itself. Liebknecht, giving free rein to his yearning for revolutionary action, declared that the moment had come to launch a putsch.
He was opposed by Luxemburg and other Communist leaders who
insisted that such a coup was bound to fail. The consequences of failure, they warned, would be nothing short of disastrous for the cause

of proletarian radicalism. Ledebour sided with Liebknecht; Daeumig
and Richard Mueller supported Luxemburg. In the end the advocates
of a putsch had their way. A revolutionary committee headed by Liebknecht and Ledebour was chosen to lead the onslaught. It promptly
published a manifesto declaring the Ebert government deposed and
urging the city's workers and soldiers to support the insurrectionaries.
Simultaneously, it issued a call for a general strike.

The Social Democrats replied by proclaiming a general strike of
their own. In the appeal which they addressed to their working-class
supporters, they declared:

We refuse any longer to allow ourselves to be terrorized by lunatics and
criminals. Order must at long last be established in Berlin and the tranquil
erection of the new revolutionary Germany must be safeguarded.

On January 6 and again on the following day thousands of workers
belonging to the two rival camps demonstrated in the streets of the capital.
The Ebert government was saved by the loyalty of its followers. There
was no bloodshed because the workers on both sides had no desire to
fight each other. The excitement began to subside as it became increasingly apparent that the effort to oust Ebert and his colleagues was getting nowhere. The Independents, through their right-wing leaders
who had refused to have anything to do with the revolutionary committee, offered to call the whole thing off. Ebert countered by demanding the
evacuation of every building occupied by the radicals. But the workers
who had forced their way into the *Vorwaerts* building declared that
they would stay where they were. Dittmann endeavored to discover a
formula that would satisfy both sides. His main concern was to make
possible a peaceful resolution of the crisis. But he found Ebert less
and less willing to negotiate. The Social Democratic leader had decided to teach the radicals a lesson they would never forget. He had
made up his mind to call in the army.

The blood-letting began on January 11, 1919, under Noske's personal
direction. A Potsdam regiment shelled the *Vorwaerts* building and
forced its defenders to hoist the white flag. They came out of the
building with arms upraised and begging for mercy. Several of them
were shot forthwith; the rest were brutally manhandled. The activities of the regular troops were supplemented by those of the Free
Corps, who responded zestfully to Noske's summons. On January 15,
when complete quiet had been restored and no excuse for violence
any longer existed, Liebknecht and Luxemburg were murdered in

cold blood by cavalry officers. Total casualties exceeded one thousand. Such was "Spartacus Week" in Berlin.

Proletarian radicalism had suffered a crushing blow. But it retained enough vitality to inspire a series of sporadic uprisings throughout the ensuing months. Left-wing extremists made futile attempts in a number of places: Bremen, Brunswick, central Germany and the industrial districts of Rhenish Westphalia. The demands invariably put forward included the establishment of a soviet system of government and immediate socialization. Blood flowed freely as these uprisings were suppressed by Noske's armed minions. The Free Corps participated most effectively in the work of repression. They enjoyed the whole business immensely. They were glad of an opportunity to vent their anti-Bolshevist feelings. They believed that in liquidating the Communist elements, they were also striking a blow at the regime which had come into being as a result of the November revolution. In March, 1919, Berlin itself was the scene of another great holocaust. Noske, whose thirst for blood seemed to grow with every new blood-letting, ordered that anyone combating the government was to be shot if captured. In pursuance of this order, about twelve hundred workers were killed. Here, too, the Free Corps played a leading role. The upshot of all this was a further widening of the breach between the Social Democrats and the revolutionary workers.

8

Of unequaled dramatic intensity was the succession of events in Munich. The Bavarian elections of January 12, 1919, resulted in overwhelming defeat for Eisner. His foes, headed by the Social Democrats, demanded that he resign as premier. Eisner for a time resisted this pressure. When it became clear that no face-saving compromise was possible, he yielded. But just as he was about to announce his resignation, he was murdered by a reactionary student of Austrian origin, Count Anton von Arco-Valley. This crime, which occurred on February 21, 1919, robbed the German revolution of one of its most constructive leaders. At once political passions flared anew. The desire to answer violence with violence took hold of the radical elements. One of Eisner's followers, a worker by the name of Alois Lindner, rushed to the hall where the Diet was deliberating and shot the leading Social Democratic member of the Bavarian cabinet, Erhart Auer. He fired at other ministers but missed. As he turned to leave, an officer who happened to be present sought to bar the way. Lindner shot him, too. Bullets whistled down from the galleries; one deputy was killed. This flurry of violence was followed by other reprisals for the murder of Eisner. The authorities arrested a number of officers and aristocrats. They closed the university, which literally swarmed with youthful counterrevolutionaries of Arco-Valley's ilk. The Independents proclaimed a general strike. Control of the government was taken over by a committee on which the Social Democrats, the Independents and the Communists were represented. But the refusal of the Bavarian congress of workers', soldiers' and peasants' councils to sanction the establishment of a soviet regime led to the resignation of the Communist members of the committee. Eventually a new cabinet composed of representatives of the two socialist parties was formed by Johannes Hoffmann, the leader of the Social Democrats.

This solution proved short-lived. The establishment of a Communist regime in Hungary on March 20, 1919, made a tremendous impression on the Bavarian radicals and spurred them to greater propagandist efforts. A small group of left-wing intellectuals in Munich spearheaded this agitation. These men were not politicians in the conventional sense. They endeavored to lift themselves above considerations of class. They were idealists, dreamers; their visions of a better world were inspired by compassion for suffering humanity, by a fanatical belief in the necessity of a spiritual revolution that would completely transpose existing values. One of the leaders of this group was Gustav Landauer. He preached a compound of socialism and anarchism. The promising young writer, Ernst Toller, helped to propagate these ideas. He loathed war and militarism, and to the task of abolishing these twin scourges he dedicated himself with evangelical fervor. Behind these utopians stood hard-boiled, tough-minded Communists like Leviné, Levien and Axelrod. Their goal was the dictatorship of the proletariat.

Early in April, 1919, the Landauer-Toller group decided that the moment had come to effectuate their plans. They got the workers' and soldiers' council of Augsburg to demand the establishment of a soviet republic. The Social Democrats felt powerless to resist this demand, which was supported by large crowds of workers in Munich. In order to retain a hand in the direction of affairs, they pretended to subscribe to the Augsburg manifesto. But this artifice proved unavailing. The hard conditions laid down by the radicals and the pell-mell rush of events precluded collaboration by the Social Democrats.

On April 6, 1919, a soviet republic was proclaimed in Munich. Hoffmann, after obtaining assurances of military support from the authorities in Berlin, set up a rival government in Bamberg. A fight to the finish between the two camps appeared imminent.

The Landauer-Toller group remained in the saddle only a few days. During this interval it attempted to carry out its humanitarian program. It promulgated a new conception of art, instituted sweeping reforms in education and housing and decreed total socialization. It also proclaimed its dedication to the Kantian ideal of permanent peace. This experiment in statecraft came to an abrupt end on April 11, 1919. On that day, a group of soldiers loyal to Hoffmann sought to overthrow the new regime. Indescribable tumult and confusion followed. The Communists exploited the situation to oust Landauer and Toller and to set up a government of their own. Supreme authority was vested in a committee of fifteen headed by Levien and Leviné.

In near-by Thuringia an armed force made up of Free Corps units and regular troops was being readied for the task of suppressing the Bavarian soviet republic. This force was under the supreme command of Noske, but the direction of operations in the field was entrusted to old-line militarists. Levien and Leviné had nothing comparable at their disposal. Besides, the chaotic state of affairs in Munich—above all, the intense ill feeling that existed between the Communist oligarchs and the rest of the population—rendered adequate defense preparations impossible. Late in April, 1919, Noske's men began to move southward. On May 1, they entered Munich. The soviet regime and its leaders were ruthlessly liquidated. So fierce was the anti-Bolshevist reaction that many persons who had had nothing whatsoever to do with the Communist dictatorship were summarily executed. The commanding officers of the Free Corps were mainly responsible for these brutalities.

The middle classes of Bavaria found it hard to forget the soviet regime. The painful impression produced by the excesses of Communist rule colored their thinking for years. It drove them by the thousands into associations and leagues that vowed undying hostility to Bolshevism. This protracted Red scare created opportunities for politicians whose program encompassed much more than the suppression of communism. Every species of reaction flourished under the benevolent eye of the local authorities. Munich became the principal center of anti-republican intrigue. There monarchists freely indulged their nostalgia for the old days. There generals dreamed of the time when militarism would resume its pre-eminent position and obscure demagogues sought popularity by cursing the Jews and reviling the Allies. There Free Corps leaders planned a campaign of assassination against outstanding republicans. It was in this atmosphere of reaction and hate that Nazism was born.

Chapter 9

THE WEIMAR COALITION TAKES OVER

I

THE suppression of the Berlin radicals in January, 1919, cleared the way for the elections to the national constituent assembly. Two new political groups participated in the competition for popular favor. One of these was the Democratic party. It had come into being in November, 1918, shortly after the proclamation of the republic. It contained many erstwhile members of the Progressive and National Liberal parties, both of which had disappeared on the morrow of the revolution. From the very beginning, the Democrats were backed by the more liberal representatives of industry and finance. They also drew wide support from professional and academic circles. The party boasted many distinguished men. These included Theodor Wolff, editor-in-chief of the *Berliner Tageblatt,* one of the nation's leading newspapers; Professor Hugo Preuss, a great authority on public law and the government's foremost expert in matters constitutional; Professor Ernst Troeltsch, author of an epoch-making work in the field of religious history; Professor Max Weber, the famous sociologist, economist and historian, who subsequently resigned from the party because he disapproved of certain of its policies; his brother and fellow-sociologist, Professor Adolf Weber; Friedrich Naumann, the well known publicist and champion of social reform, who was elected leader of the party shortly before his death in August, 1919; Carl von Siemens, head of the country's greatest electrical firm; Walther Rathenau, another outstanding industrialist and a gifted essayist and philosopher as well; Hjalmar Schacht, managing director of the National Bank and former leader of the left-wing National Liberals.

The Democratic party proclaimed itself the exponent of true liberalism. It sought to rally the nation's middle-class elements in support of a program that was unequivocally pro-republican and sympathetic to the idea of economic and social reform. Indeed, it even went so far as to advocate the socialization of monopolistic industries. It came out four-square for the democratic process in government. With equal bluntness it condemned violence and terror. The founders of the party insisted on excluding anyone who, because of identification with policies that were now in disrepute, was certain to prove a political liability. Gustav Stresemann was such a person. He, like so many other National Liberals, manifested an interest in the new group; but he quickly discovered that he was unwelcome. The reason was obvious. During the war he had been a rabid annexationist and a follower of that arch-chauvinist, Admiral Tirpitz. To accept individuals like him was to invite repudiation by the overwhelming majority of the nation.

Stresemann lost little time in fashioning a political organization of his own. Under his leadership right-wing National Liberals combined with a sprinkling of Progressives to form the second of Germany's new political groups, the People's party. Many of the country's industrial magnates were among its charter members. Stresemann and his friends were immediately confronted with the necessity of defining their attitude toward the new regime. They regretted the disappearance of the monarchy. They disliked the republic; it went counter to traditions they held sacred and it had been created by representatives of the working class. They stood in constant fear of radical economic experiments. However, they had enough sense to realize that overt attempts to swim against the current would only make matters worse. They adopted wait-and-see tactics. They said they were willing, in the interests of law and order, to carry on under the existing form of government. This meant, in effect, that they were prepared to tolerate the republic so long as it managed to hold the radicals in check.

In an obvious effort to compete with the Democrats for middle-class support, the People's party framed a moderately liberal program. It declared itself in favor of a democratic suffrage. It demanded freedom of speech, freedom of the press, freedom of association and assembly. It advocated full equality of rights for all citizens regardless of origin, religion or class. It upheld the principle of private property and the right of every employer to run his own enterprise, albeit with a certain amount of co-operation from his workers. It condemned socialism and communism in very strong language; but it avowed its readiness to support legislation for the protection of the country's industrial masses.

The Conservative party changed its name after the revolution. In an effort to conform outwardly to the new emphasis on popular rule, it called itself the National People's party. But everything else about it remained substantially the same. The Nationalists stood far to the Right in German political life. They were, like their predecessors under the empire, a Junker-dominated group, but some of their most authoritative spokesmen came from the industrial plutocracy and from the intermediate strata of the bourgeosie. Army officers, high-ranking bureaucrats and right-wing intellectuals completed the party's elite. Mass support was provided by orthodox Protestant elements and by lower-middle-class people who, for a variegated assortment of reasons, looked back nostalgically to the old imperial regime and yearned for its restoration. Because of its manifest racial bias, the party attracted most of the country's anti-Semites. It endeavored to take cognizance of current realities. At the same time, it affirmed its determination to stick to its principles, which were reactionary and chauvinist in the extreme. It frankly declared its preference for the monarchical form of government. However, it promised, in working for its objectives, to utilize whatever political machinery the national constituent assembly might decide to set up. It demanded respect for property rights and protection against Bolshevism. The German "soul," it said, must be shielded from the forces which were intent upon destroying Christianity, nationality and morality. Of these forces the most deadly and insidious was Marxism.

True to the role it had played so successfully under the empire, the Catholic Center assumed a middle position. It rejected unequivocally the idea of a socialist state. The new regime, it insisted, must be a democratic republic. It thus discarded the militantly pro-monarchist attitude to which it had clung until November 9, 1918. It was prepared to share with other moderate groups the task of consolidating the republican regime. It was, as before, the stanch defender of the rights and interests of the Catholic church. In keeping with its traditional program, it demanded that the federal character of the Reich be maintained. An explicit stand on this issue was all the more necessary because of the marked intensification of particularism in Catholic Bavaria. The Center advocated a further extension of social legislation. This it did in deference to the wishes of the Christian trade unions, which provided the bulk of its labor following. But under pressure from its powerful right wing, which was composed of clericals, aristocrats and industrialists, it exhibited undisguised hostility to far-reaching economic reforms. The struggle between the party's progressive and conservative factions was nothing new; but the sharpness with which it was waged testified to the mounting social tensions within the Reich.

The three proletarian parties presented a picture of strident conflict and recrimination. Each of them went its own way, flaying the tactics of its rivals and exuding self-righteousness. The Social Democrats pointed with pride to the accomplishments of the Ebert regime. They called attention to the proclamation of November 10, 1918, and reaffirmed their faith in the aims which it set forth. They said again and again that they were for democracy, for more social legislation, for restoration of the nation's productive capacity. They urged the electorate to approve what had been done, but they emphasized their readiness to accept whatever verdict the country might pronounce at the polls. The Independents, with their left-wingers clearly in the ascendant, surpassed even the reactionaries in the bitterness with which they assailed the government. They renewed their demand for immediate and total socialization. The capitalist "class state," they trumpeted, must be transformed into a commonwealth that would serve the needs of all the people. The Social Democrats were planning to betray the revolution. Their nefarious designs could be frustrated only by an aroused proletariat. The attitude of the Communists could be summed up in one phrase: "a plague on both your houses!" They persisted in their decision to boycott the elections. The idea of vesting power in a national constituent assembly was, to their way of thinking, merely part of a carefully planned bourgeois counterrevolution.

2

Slightly more than thirty million Germans went to the polls on January 19, 1919. The results indicated that the shift toward the Left, which had begun before 1914 and which had continued throughout the war, was still very much in progress. The Social Democrats made by far the best showing. They polled almost 11½ million votes—roughly thirty-eight per cent of the total cast—and captured 163 of the assembly's 421 seats. The Center was next with 5,981,321 votes and eighty-nine seats. Third place went to the Democrats, whose strength on this occasion surpassed the expectations of even their most sanguine spokesmen. They received more than 5½ million votes and elected seventy-four candidates. The Nationalists were far behind with 2,873,523 votes and forty-two seats. The Independents, the lone representatives of proletarian radicalism in this contest, likewise ran a poor race. They attracted a total of 2,315,332 votes and emerged with only twenty-two seats. But it was Stresemann and his friends who took the worst beating of the day. Their lukewarm attitude toward the new regime alienated the republicans without satisfying the monarchists. As a result, the People's party polled only 1,633,000 votes. Thanks, however, to the intricacies of the system of proportional representation, it secured twenty-two seats in the assembly—as many as the Independents.

The outcome of the elections was a resounding victory for political democracy. The three leading parties, which were pledged to unequivocal support of the new regime, accounted for more than seventy-five per cent of all the votes cast. This gave the lie to those who doubted the German people's willingness to rally round the republic. The two parties of the Right received between them less than fifteen per cent of the total vote. The monarchist cause seemed utterly hopeless. And equally dreary appeared the prospects of left-wing radicalism. The friends of democracy had every reason to rejoice. The magnitude of their triumph was indeed most heartening. But their dedication to the cause of popular rule did not suffice to place the republic on a truly firm footing. More was needed—above all, aid from the Allies in the form of equitable peace terms and trade policies designed to promote the economic prosperity of all, victors and vanquished alike. Future swings of the political pendulum in Germany depended, to a large degree, on decisions reached in London, Washington and Paris.

On February 3, 1919, the central council of the workers' and soldiers' soviets formally handed over its powers to the national constituent assembly. In so doing it expressed the wish to see Germany become a unitary state, with all the remnants of federalism and states' rights done away with. It also declared itself in favor of incorporating the workers' and soldiers' councils into the constitutional framework of the republic in order to protect the interests of labor and insure the democratization of the armed forces. This transfer of powers removed all doubt as to the sovereign status of the national assembly. By the same token it dealt a further blow to the cause of sovietism in Germany.

Weimar was chosen as the meeting place of the national assembly because there was too much tumult and disorder in Berlin. Besides being a safer place, Weimar was the shrine of German liberalism. As such, it was ideally suited to play host to the authors of a democratic constitution. Ebert opened the assembly on February 6, 1919. The revolution, he declared, had been directed against an anachronistic and distintegrating regime based on force. Now the German people were returning to the path of legality. Only by resorting to parliamentary methods could they promote necessary economic and social changes without, at the same time, ruining the country. The national assembly was Germany's sovereign. Divine-right kings and princes were gone forever. The German people were free at last, and free they would always be. This freedom was their only consolation. It was also the only road to recovery from suffering and defeat. Germany lost the war, but for this the revolution was not responsible. It was the government of Prince Max that asked for an armistice. It could not have done otherwise after the collapse of Germany's allies and in view of the Reich's military and economic situation. The revolution disavowed all responsibility for the misery into which the country had been plunged by the imperial regime and its arrogant militarists. The revolution was likewise not to blame for the terrible food shortage which plagued the land. Those who insisted that it was could not explain away the hundreds of thousands of women, children and old men who had died because of the hunger blockade. The plan of the Allies to impose upon Germany a peace of hate and violence deserved the sharpest kind of protest. The German people could not be made the wage slaves of other countries for twenty, forty or sixty years. Only international co-operation could heal the fearful ravages wrought by the war in all Europe. Germany's enemies, according to their own testimony, fought to destroy "Kaiserism." That objective had been achieved; "Kaiserism" had been forever done away with. This was proved by the existence of the national assembly. The Allies fought to destroy militarism, but it too was no more. (At this point the Independents shouted: "You are reestablishing it!") They said they were battling for "justice, freedom and permanent peace"; but the armistice terms were extraordinarily harsh, and they were being carried out with ruthless severity. Although Germany was no longer able to resume hostilities, 800,000 German prisoners of war were still being denied their freedom. The Allies justified the armistice terms by arguing that they had been formulated in the expectation that they would be imposed upon the Hohenzollern empire. But how could one justify

the Allies' action in making those terms more and more onerous for
the young republic, which was trying desperately to fulfill all its obligations? The Allies would do themselves a terrible disservice if they
pushed Germany too far. The government of the republic preferred
the most awful privation to dishonor. Germany sued for an armistice
because she reposed faith in the principles enunciated by President
Wilson. It was now up to the Allies to give Germany the Wilsonian
peace to which she was entitled. The German republic and its people
asked only to be admitted as equals into the League of Nations and
to be given a chance to acquire a respected position within that organization.

The provisional government, Ebert went on, took over a bankrupt
concern when it came to power in November, 1918. It had done everything possible to overcome the dangers of the transitional period and
to initiate the process of economic recovery. It was the duty of the
nation's industrialists to exert themselves without stint in order to
revive production. It was also the duty of the workers to devote all
their energies to the tasks upon which they were engaged. Only
greater output could save the country. As for socialism, it would have
to wait until high production levels had been reached. But there was
no room, in a period of acute national need, for private monopolies
and excessive profits. Consequently, the government planned to do
away with profits in any industry which was ripe for socialization.
Although the future looked bleak, there was reason to have faith in
the creative ability of the German people. They could be trusted to go
forward with eyes fixed on their great goal: to establish a strong
democracy and to endow it with a genuinely social spirit; to set up a
regime based on justice, truth and equality.

On February 11, 1919, after enacting a provisional constitutional law,
the assembly elected Ebert president of the Reich. In his acceptance
speech, he declared that he would strive with all his might to live up
to the responsibilities of his new office. He promised to refrain from
partisanship, to treat all alike. He would regard himself as the representative of the entire German people, not as the leader of a party.
But, he observed with characteristic candor, he was a son of the working class. He had grown up in the world of socialist ideas. He had not
the slightest intention of disavowing either his origin or his convictions.
Adverting to some of the problems that confronted the country, he
insisted that freedom could exist only when there was order. Any attempt to establish rule by violence, no matter who made it, would be

fought to the last. This was intended to be a warning to the Communists and the left-wing Independents.

Ebert promptly requested his old comrade, Scheidemann, to form a cabinet. The Independents made the Social Democratic leader's task a bit less complicated by announcing that they were not interested in joining a coalition ministry. Indeed, they went so far as to say that they would not participate in any ministry until the "present regime of violence" had been ended and until all the members of the government had demonstrated their readiness to safeguard the accomplishments of the revolution against counter-action by the "bourgeoisie" and the "military autocracy." The cabinet organized by Scheidemann contained the representatives of three parties: the Social Democrats, the Democrats and the Centrists. These groups constituted the so-called Weimar coalition, which held sway during the initial period of the German republic. Only one member of the new cabinet had no party affiliation. He was Count Brockdorff-Rantzau, former minister to Denmark. He had been put in charge of the foreign office in December, 1918, and remained at this post under Scheidemann. He was, in spite of his aristocratic lineage, a man of genuinely liberal outlook. He had strong convictions on the subject of the future peace. He was prepared to fight for them with all the resources at his command. Scheidemann was assisted by five of his party associates. Noske continued as minister of war. Bauer returned to the ministry of labor. Landsberg, who had acquitted himself creditably as a member of the Council of People's Commissioners, was designated minister of justice. One of Social Democracy's most respected spokesmen, Rudolf Wissell, consented to serve as minister of national economy. The key ministry of food and agriculture went to another party stalwart, Robert Schmidt. Preuss, the Democratic leader, took over the ministry of the interior. The Centrists were represented by three men. By far the most articulate and influential of these was Erzberger, who once again was named minister without portfolio. Exploiting to the full his multitudinous connections and his party's strategic position in the national assembly, he made himself feared by friend and foe alike. Johannes Bell, a Catholic leader of outstanding character, was appointed colonial minister. The third member of the party to take office under Scheidemann was Johann Giesberts, who became postmaster general.

The new government announced a comprehensive program. It included peace in accordance with Wilson's fourteen points; the admission of Germany to the League of Nations on the basis of equality with other countries; the simultaneous disarmament of all nations; the prevention of war through compulsory arbitration of international disputes; educational opportunities for all Germans, including the very poorest; the creation of an army resting on democratic foundations; recognition of the right of civil servants to form collective-bargaining associations; freedom of speech and of the press; freedom of religion, learning and art. Scheidemann explained and defended this program in a speech that was vigorously applauded by the overwhelming majority of the nation. Germany, he said, had finally achieved liberty within her borders. It was imperative that no form of enslavement be imposed upon her from without. This point could not be stressed too much. An oppressed Germany would be a misfortune and a danger for the entire world. But if she were left free to act, she would find the strength to help others as well as herself. The debate that followed afforded the spokesmen of the various parties an opportunity to indicate how they and their comrades felt about the main issues of the day. The Centrists once again emphasized that they wanted a democratic and not a socialist republic. The Democrats protested against the calumnies heaped upon the German people by their enemies abroad. Leading Nationalist deputies had words of praise for the imperial regime. "We are still convinced," they said, "that the monarchy is the best form of government for Germany." Their allusions to the revolution reflected a stubborn unwillingness to accept as final their recent discomfiture at the polls. A spokesman for the People's party likewise denounced the revolution, asserting that the Social Democrats had shown themselves incapable of governing alone. He underlined the importance attached by his party to the preservation of private enterprise. At the close of the discussion the Scheidemann government won a vote of confidence. The two parties of the Right and the Independents constituted the opposition. That politics makes strange bedfellows was to be demonstrated time and again throughout the history of the German republic.

4

In April, 1919, while the Weimar assembly was wrestling with the diverse and complex problems that claimed its attention, the second national congress of workers' and soldiers' deputies convened in Berlin. Spokesmen for the Independents once again demanded that the political and social reconstruction of Germany be effected in accordance with soviet principles. They envisaged a system which would bestow primacy upon the nation's manual and intellectual workers. This system was to function by means of political and economic councils. The hierarchy of political councils was to extend from the purely local bodies in individual communities to the topmost organ, the national congress of councils, which was to have all political power. It, in turn, was to elect a central council which would appoint and control the members of the cabinet. The economic councils were to be chosen in the factories on the basis of occupation. They, too, were to form the base of a vast pyramid at the apex of which there was to be a national economic council. These bodies were to supervise the operation of the factories and institute socialization.

The Social Democratic delegates vigorously opposed this plan. They argued that it was impracticable, that it would lead, not to socialism, but to confusion and chaos. The final upshot of the whole business, they warned, would be a dictatorship operated not by the workers or the councils but by a handful of terrorists. They proposed instead that there be set up, alongside of the political parliament, an economic one representing the entire nation—employers and employees alike—and constituted on occupational lines. This proposal was adopted by a very large majority. Before adjourning, the congress enjoined the central council to devise a new method for electing members of the workers' councils. The purpose of this injuction was to eliminate certain distressing irregularities which had recently come to light. The central council got busy and in August, 1919, submitted a scheme which was promptly denounced by the Independents and the Communists. The two radical parties went so far as to urge their followers to boycott all elections conducted in accordance with the proposed scheme. They reiterated most emphatically that only in a soviet republic could the sovereignty of the workers' councils become a reality. The controversy led the central council to take a very important step. It decided, in October, 1919, to dispense with new elections. This marked, for all practical purposes, the end of the conciliar movement in Germany. True, certain proletarian extremists refused to abandon the hope of implanting in the Reich something akin to Russia's brand of sovietism. They continued for a time to propagandize for their objective. But the disintegration of the workers' and soldiers' councils that had sprung from the revolutionary soil of Germany in November, 1918, was already an accomplished fact. This decided the issue.

While the battle for a workers' state was being fought and lost, the Weimar assembly sought to come to grips with the dynamite-laden question of socialization. This it did out of fear of the restlessness that still permeated large sections of the working class. On March 13, 1919, two arresting laws were passed. One of these authorized the Reich to take over enterprises deemed ripe for socialization. The owners were to receive proper compensation. The second law transferred the management of the country's coal industry to a national commission consisting of mine-owners, workers and consumers. Actually, however, control remained where it had been: in the hands of the owners. This fact robbed the law of real significance. Subsequent efforts to rectify the situation by giving increased authority to the consumers came to nought. On April 15, 1919, the assembly made another spectacular move. It created a commission which was empowered to run the potash industry subject to supervision by the state. But, as in the case of the coal industry, the owners retained control; the commission became a mere figurehead. In supporting this program, the majority of the deputies went along with the Social Democrats. The latter continued to insist that socialization should be confined to industries which had acquired a monopolistic character. Beyond that they refused, for the time being, to go, reiterating their now familiar plea that nothing be done which might impede or wreck current efforts to restore the country to its normal productive capacity. The Independents flatly rejected the idea of partial socialization. They wanted the government to go all the way in the direction of collectivism. But their demands were opposed by all the other parties in the assembly. The issue became a focal point of controversy within the cabinet in May, 1919. Wissell, who had taken the lead in urging the adoption of a planned economy, submitted a scheme for socialization worked out by himself and one of his departmental aids. The scheme was rejected by the cabinet. Wissell resigned a few months later. He was succeeded by Schmidt, who had been directing the ministry of food and agriculture. In keeping with his party's desire to concentrate on monopolistic enterprises, Schmidt prepared a plan for the socialization of the electrical industry. He laid it before the assembly in August, 1919. It was adopted in December of the same year, but almost nothing was done to enforce its provisions. Thus, more than twelve months after the revolution, the exponents of partial socialization had little to show for their efforts. German industry not only retained its monopolistic character but managed, during the ensuing years, to extend the process of concentration. Control of the nation's economic life became the prerogative of a few men. The manner in which they used their power was to go a long way toward determining the ultimate fate of the German republic.

Chapter 10

VERSAILLES

I

IN APRIL, 1919, the German government laid down a number of instructions to be used by its representatives at the Paris peace conference. It stressed the point that Wilson's program, which it regarded as binding on both sides, would have to be made the basis of the peace. It demanded a free plebiscite in Alsace-Lorraine. It rejected the separation of the Saar and the left bank of the Rhine from the Reich. It likewise insisted on keeping the great coal mines of the Saar under German control. As regards the frontier with Poland, the Scheidemann government felt that a plebiscite was indicated in one area only, Posen. Here alone, it held, was the population indisputably Polish. West Prussia could not be ceded because that would mean the severance of East Prussia from the Reich. The cession of Upper Silesia was also inadmissible because the large amount of coal produced there was vital to Germany's existence and because the people of the region would be adversely affected by union with Poland. The latter would receive privileges from the German government which would take care of her need for free access to the sea. A Polish corridor to Danzig was out of the question. Northern Schleswig's right to self-determination by means of a plebiscite was conceded. German territories now occupied by Allied troops would have to be evacuated when peace was concluded. The American note of November 5, 1918, was to be the basis for any settlement of the reparation question. This meant payment only for damage to civilians and their property. The blockade, which was still in effect except for carefully stipulated food supplies, would have to be lifted promptly. Germany would have to regain control of her merchant fleet. In her economic relations with other countries, she would not allow herself to be fettered or handicapped. Her colonies, which had been overrun by Allied armies, would have to be returned to her. She asked only that the principle of equality be adhered to in this matter. She was prepared to serve as a mandatory under international supervision if the other colonial powers consented to do likewise. Unilateral disarmament of the Reich was rejected. Disarmament would have to be carried out on an international scale and in accordance with the principle of reciprocity. Germany definitely favored the formation of a League of Nations; she was sympathetic to the idea of settling international disputes by means of arbitration. She wished immediate admission to the League on the basis of equality with other countries. As for the Allied charge that Germany alone was responsible for the outbreak of the war, it would have to be denied forcefully and unequivocally.

Armed with these instructions, the German delegation, headed by Brockdorff-Rantzau, arrived in Versailles on April 29, 1919. The reception accorded it was far from friendly. The Allied terms were presented on May 7. No oral discussion was permitted. All observations had to be made in writing, and for this a maximum period of fifteen days was allowed. The high-handed tactics employed by the victors gave rise to the charge, which was to be repeated time and again in later years, that this was a "dictated" peace. That the Allies committed a serious psychological blunder in excluding the Germans from the peace conference until the treaty had been drafted and in denying them the privilege of negotiating orally is now generally admitted. German chauvinists of every description, and especially the Nazis, zestfully exploited this blunder. They made it one of the principal themes of their anti-republican propaganda.

The terms themselves were severe, to say the least. Alsace and Lorraine were to revert to France. German territory west of the Rhine was to be occupied by Allied troops for at least fifteen years to insure execution of the treaty. If Germany fulfilled all her obligations, the territory would be evacuated piecemeal: the Colonge area at the end of five years, the Coblenz area at the end of ten, and the Mainz area at the end of fifteen. The left bank of the Rhine and the right bank to a depth of fifty kilometers were to be permanently demilitarized. The Saar basin, one of Europe's richest prizes because of its great coal deposits, was to be governed for fifteen years by a commission representing the League of Nations. The mines were given to France to compensate her for the destruction wrought in her own coal fields. At the close of the fifteen-year period, the inhabitants of the Saar would decide, by means of a plebiscite, whether they wished to remain under the League, unite with France or return to Germany. If they should vote in favor of the last of these alternatives, Germany was to repurchase the mines. Belgium received the districts of Moresnet, Eupen and Malmédy. In the last two, the local population was to be permitted to indicate how it felt about this change of sovereignty. Plebiscites were also to determine the fate of Schleswig, the northern section of which was claimed and ultimately obtained by Denmark.

Far greater were the territorial losses which Germany was asked to accept in the east. Poland, France's protégé and satellite, was to get industrially rich Upper Silesia, most of Posen and West Prussia (the latter constituting the so-called Polish Corridor), and extensive rights in Danzig, which was to be set up as a Free City under the protection of the League of Nations. East Prussia was thus to be completely cut off from the rest of the Reich. In addition, the port of Memel was detached from this outpost of Germanism, but it was not formally awarded to Lithuania until 1923. The union of Austria with the Reich would have made up for these losses. Both countries were overwhelmingly favorable to such a merger, and they took steps to effect it when they drafted their republican constitutions. But the peace treaty with Germany, and the Treaty of Saint Germain subsequently concluded with Austria, explicitly forbade *Anschluss* except with the consent of the Council of the League. Germany's territorial losses in Europe were paralleled by the sacrifices she was forced to make outside the Continent. Articles 118 and 119 of the document submitted to her representatives on May 7, 1919, demanded the surrender of all her colonies.

The Allies, professing a high-minded and widely applauded desire "to render possible the initiation of a general limitation of the armaments of all nations," sought to reduce Germany to military impotence. Her army was not to exceed 100,000 men. This force was to be devoted "exclusively to the maintenance of order within the territory and to the control of the frontiers." The Great German General Staff was to be dissolved. The manufacture of munitions was to be rigidly curtailed. All war material in excess of the amounts allowed by the Allies was to be surrendered. A strict ban was imposed upon the importation and exportation of arms and upon the manufacture and importation of poisonous gas. Military airplanes, armored cars and tanks were also placed in the category of things forbidden. Universal compulsory military service was to be abolished. Members of the armed forces were to be recruited on a voluntary basis. The period of enlistment was to be twelve years. This was designed to prevent the creation of a large trained reserve by means of a rapid turnover of personnel. Officers were to serve for twenty-five years, and there was to be only one military school for each arm of the service. Article 177 was an integral part of the Allied scheme to prevent the military resurgence of Germany. It ran as follows:

Educational establishments, the universities, societies of discharged soldiers, shooting or touring clubs and, generally speaking, associations of every description, whatever be the age of their members, must not occupy themselves with any military matters. In particular, they will be forbidden to instruct or exercise their members, or to allow them to be instructed or exercised, in the profession or use of arms. These societies, associations, educational establishments and universities must have no connection with the Ministry of War or any other military authority.

German naval power was to be reduced to innocuous proportions. At its disposal there were to be not more than six small battleships, six light cruisers, twelve destroyers and twelve torpedo boats. The possession of submarines was explicitly forbidden. Inter-Allied Commissions of Control were to supervise German compliance with the disarmament clauses of the treaty. They were to be established on German soil. They were to be free to go to any part of the country and were to receive from the German government whatever assistance they might need to accomplish their missions. The Reich was likewise to facilitate any investigation that the Council of the League might deem necessary.

The treaty terminated the commercial agreements which had enabled Germany to trade with other countries on advantageous terms. She was thus effectually barred from Allied markets. But that was not all. The Allies bestowed upon themselves the right to most-favored-nation treatment in the German market for a period of five years. This meant a one-way traffic at the expense of a country that was being forced to surrender a large part of its human and economic resources. It meant the denial of indispensable sources of revenue to a nation that was being saddled with heavy financial obligations. To make matters worse, Germany was to be deprived of almost all her foreign financial holdings, and her merchant fleet was to be reduced to less than one-tenth of its pre-war size.

Article 227 served notice that the Allies would ask the Dutch government to surrender the former emperor for trial. This was in keeping with their charge that inexcusable atrocities had been perpetrated by Germany in the course of the war. Of greater immediate significance were Articles 228-230. They imposed upon Germany a most extraordinary obligation: that of acknowledging the right of the Allies to try individuals "accused of having committed acts in violation of the laws and customs of war." All such persons were to be handed over to the Allies by the government of the Reich. They were to have the right to name their own counsel. If pronounced guilty, they would receive appropriate punishment. The Allies added insult to injury by stipulating that the German government would have to furnish the evidence needed "to ensure the full knowledge of the incriminating acts, the discovery of offenders and the just appreciation of responsibility."

To justify their claim to reparation for the damage wrought by Germany, the Allies drew up Article 231, the famous war-guilt clause of the Treaty of Versailles. It stated:

The Allied and Associated Governments affirm and Germany accepts the responsibility of Germany and her allies for causing all the loss and damage to which the Allied and Associated Governments and their nationals have been subjected as a consequence of the war imposed upon them by the aggression of Germany and her allies.

Because they disagreed among themselves regarding the amount Germany should pay, the Allies abstained from fixing a definite sum in the treaty. The authority to do this was given to a Reparation Commission, which was to announce its decision on or before May 1, 1921. However, in the categories of claims enumerated in an Annex to this section of the treaty, such items as pensions and separation allowances were included. This was done at the insistence of the British.

2

The Allied terms horrified and infuriated the German peace delegation. They provoked explosions of wrath throughout the Reich. Germans of every class and political persuasion joined in the outcry. The general refrain was that Germany had been too trusting, that she had been deceived and tricked by men who had never intended to honor their pledges. Countless mass meetings and newspaper editorials gave expression to this feeling. The Scheidemann government, for its part,

minced no words. It instructed the peace delegation to inform the
Allies that the terms were "unfulfillable, unbearable and ruinous for
Germany." Simultaneously, it issued a proclamation denouncing the
treaty and stressing the fact that its provisions were not in accordance
with the promises made in the pre-armistice agreement. The nation
was adjured to stand firm and united in the face of this attempt to
annihilate Germany. All public entertainment was suspended for a
week in order to signalize the country's disappointment and sorrow.
Scheidemann stoked the fires of public indignation by branding the
treaty a "document of hatred and delusion." Ebert spoke in a similar
vein. He called the proposed settlement a "peace of violence." He
assured his compatriots that it would not be signed in its present form.
Through the Berlin representative of the Associated Press, he addressed
a personal appeal to the United States. He argued that the Allied
terms were not only a perversion but a complete negation of Wilson's
fourteen points. In spite of this, the German people continued to cling
to the ideas so fervently espoused by the high-minded American statesman. Ebert begged the United States to come to the aid of the young
German republic. He warned that if American democracy gave its
sanction to the Allied terms, it would be making itself a party to political oppression. It would be abandoning the principle of fair play and
befouling the democratic cause.

The national assembly, which had not met since April 15, 1919, was
convened on May 12 in Berlin. The keynote speech was delivered by
Scheidemann. Once again he stressed the total dissimilarity between
the Allied pre-armistice pledges and the conditions now proposed. Wilson, he declared in anguished tones, had disillusioned everyone. It was
impossible any longer to trust him. The future appeared bleak indeed.
Germany was being commanded to slave for others. She was being
robbed of some of her fairest provinces, despite the wish of these mar-
tyred areas to remain part of the Reich. She was being deprived of
her foreign trade, so vital to her economic well-being. Her enemies
were helping themselves to her natural resources. They were forcing
her to assume a reparation burden that no nation could bear. They
were fettering her with restrictions that no sovereign state could tolerate. Said Scheidemann:

I ask you: who can, as an honest man, I will not say as a German, but
only as honest, straightforward man, accept such terms? What hand would
not wither that binds itself and us in these fetters? . . . We have made

counterproposals; we shall make others. We see, with your approval, that our sacred duty lies in negotiation. This treaty, in the opinion of the government, cannot be accepted.

Tumultuous and prolonged applause greeted this statement. Through their respective spokesmen, the Social Democratic, Centrist, Democratic, Nationalist and People's parties denounced the Allied conditions and joined the government in pronouncing them unacceptable. The Independents likewise decried the treaty. But they refused to take the view that it had to be rejected. Their attitude, they explained, was motivated by the desire to avert a renewal of the war. As for the treaty, it would be changed beyond recognition by the impact of "world revolution." The Independents were not alone in insisting that indignation was one thing and that the power to offer military resistance was another. On May 15, 1919, the government let it be known that no one in authority entertained the insane idea of summoning the nation to take up arms again. Even General Groener, it was explicitly stated, had not the slighest intention of calling for a war of liberation.

3

During the weeks which followed the presentation of the Allied terms, the German peace delegation strove with might and main to secure modifications. Following the line laid down by their superiors, Brockdorff-Rantzau and his comrades charged that this was an unjust and vindictive peace, a peace of violence and revenge. "Our enemies," they complained, "have repeatedly professed that they are not making war on the German people but on an imperialistic and irresponsible government. . . . Today, after the radical political changes that have taken place in Germany . . . , our enemies no longer face an irresponsible German government but the German people, who control their own fate." Germany was now a democracy. She had sloughed off the militaristic spirit. But all this had been disregarded by the authors of the treaty. The terms were in flagrant contradiction with the fourteen points and with Wilson's other pronouncements of the pre-armistice period. This was all the more reprehensible in view of the fact that the American statesman's program had been solemnly accepted by both sides as the basis of the future peace.

The Germans hotly denied that they were solely responsible for the war. This issue provided them with one of their most telling arguments, and they used it for all it was worth. They sought to undermine the moral foundations of the entire territorial and economic settlement by charging that the treaty was based on a falsehood. On the specific subject of reparation they minced no words. They declared that they were being asked to sign a blank check. They were being asked to assume financial obligations, the full extent of which had not been disclosed to them. Moreover, the inclusion of such things as pensions and separation allowances in the reparation bill constituted an inexcusable violation of the Allies' pre-armistice promise to seek indemnification only for damage done to civilians and their property. As for the Reparation Commission, its members were to be named solely by Germany's enemies. The whole financial scheme was designed to enslave the German people for a generation or more.

Vociferous, too, were the protests against the transfer of large segments of German territory to the Poles. The question of the eastern frontier exercised the Germans mightily. It was complicated by longstanding antipathy between Teuton and Slav. In the areas of West Prussia and Posen that were to go to Poland, the Germans were economically dominant. They controlled local industry and held a commanding position in the domain of agriculture. They were better educated and trained than their Slavic neighbors. They had nothing but contempt for the Poles, whose reputation for inefficiency had long been the butt of innumerable German jokes. According to German statistics, this territory contained about three million persons, of whom a distinct majority—something like two-thirds—were Poles. This, however, did not deter the Germans from pronouncing the projected cession wholly and cruelly unjust. They wailed that the creation of a Polish corridor stretching southward from the Baltic would separate East Prussia from the rest of the Reich. They dwelt on the moral iniquity and economic impracticability of such a separation. They talked in much the same vein about what was in store for Danzig. The city, they pointed out, was overwhelmingly German in character. Its retention by the Reich would be strictly in accordance with the Wilsonian principle of self-determination. The legitimate economic needs of Poland could be satisfied without subjecting Danzig to non-German rule. The proposed allocation of Upper Silesia to Poland also infuriated the Germans. This district was one of their key industrial areas. It furnished twenty-three per cent of their coal, eighty per cent of their zinc and a considerable portion of their iron. The population was mixed. The cities and towns were predominantly German; the rural areas were overwhelmingly Polish. German brains and money had developed the industries of the region. The peace delegation bitterly assailed the Allied proposal. It adduced ethnographic, economic and historical considerations in support of its position. It warned that the loss of the province would impair Germany's ability to pay reparation and would lead to irredentist agitation.

The Germans invoked the principle of self-determination in denouncing the separation of Memel from the Reich. Upon it they based their protest against the refusal of the Allies to permit an Austro-German union. They cited it as justfication for their contention that Eupen, Malmédy and Moresnet should remain German. They used it in assailing the re-cession of Alsace-Lorraine to France. They argued that to settle the fate of Alsace-Lorraine without ascertaining the wishes of the local inhabitants was to create "a new wrong."

Another enormity in the eyes of the Germans was the stipulation that they surrender all their colonies. They called attention to the fact that the fifth of Wilson's fourteen points promised a "free, open-minded, and absolutely impartial adjustment of all colonial claims." They contended that no adjustment could be considered impartial so long as Germany was not given a chance to plead her case. Colonies, the peace delegation insisted, were an economic necessity for Germany. They were a source of raw materials; they constituted a market for manufactured goods; they provided a haven for the mother country's surplus population. Besides, Germany had the right "to co-operate in the joint task which devolves upon civilised mankind of exploring the world scientifically and of educating the backward races. In this direction she has achieved great things in her colonies. . . . Germany has looked after the interests of her natives." She was prepared to administer her colonies according to League principles—as a mandatory, perhaps. Actually, the peace delegation showed little respect for the truth when it discussed the economic aspects of this question. For the German colonies had been of negligible importance as a source of raw materials; and their capacity to absorb German exports had likewise been minuscule. As an outlet for surplus population, they had been a complete fizzle. Fewer than 20,000 Germans had migrated to these outposts of the Fatherland in something like thirty years. The thing that mattered most to the Germans was the element of prestige. They felt that Germany, as a great power, was entitled to have colonies. Without them she would lose standing and find herself depressed to the rank of a second-class state.

No feature of the treaty irked the Germans more than the provisions regarding the so-called "war criminals." They contended that the contemplated prosecution of the former emperor was devoid of any legal basis. The German government, they warned, "cannot allow a German to be placed before a foreign special tribunal, to be convicted on the basis of an exceptional law promulgated by foreign powers solely against him, on the principles not of right, but of politics, and to be punished for an action which was not punishable at the time it was committed." They likewise objected to the idea of handing over the other "war criminals" to the Allies. Most Germans looked upon the men in question as individuals who had served their country according to their lights and to the best of their ability. The worst that could be said about them was that they had made mistakes, and for these their own compatriots would hold them accountable. To turn such men over to foreign judges whose motive was not justice but revenge was both unfair and intolerable. Accordingly, the peace delegation informed the Allies that the Reich could not comply with their request. "German honor," it remarked, "obviously demands the refusal of this proposition." Moreover, a section of the German criminal code forbade the extradition of German subjects.

The Germans took strong exception to the commercial restrictions laid down in the treaty. England, they were well aware, was utilizing the Allied victory to banish the threat to her own commercial predominance which pre-war Germany had represented. As for France, she was intent upon weakening her enemy in every possible way. Her policy embraced the economic as well as the military, territorial and financial spheres. It was therefore with passionate urgency that the peace delegation addressed itself to this question. Germany's foreign trade, it charged, was to be "excluded from every field of activity." She was being deprived of the opportunity to procure from others the raw materials she needed. Her products were being denied entry into foreign countries. The delegation summed the matter up as follows:

None of these measures ... can be justified from the standpoint of reparation. They offer, it is true, great advantages to the rival merchant who will compete with the German merchant abroad, but they do nothing towards repairing the damages which Germany has bound herself to make good. They can only be understood on the assumption that the Allied and Associated Powers intend to stamp out German commercial competition.

The Germans demurred to unilateral disarmament. They were willing, they said, to comply with the military and naval clauses of the treaty provided the other powers likewise reduced their armaments and did away with universal conscription. They objected to foreign supervision of the process of disarmament. They felt that the powers vested in the Inter-Allied Commissions of Control constituted an infringement of German sovereignty. The whole business of playing host to snoopers from other countries was galling to German pride. Bitterly resented, too, was the Allied plan to occupy the Rhineland for fifteen years. The peace delegation pointed out that Germany was now militarily too weak to menace her neighbors. It insisted that occupation would either diminish or destroy Germany's ability to fulfill her reparation obligations. The unity of the Reich would likewise be jeopardized. Therefore, Germany had no choice but to demand the evacuation of the occupied territory not later than six months after the signing of the treaty.

4

While Brockdorff-Rantzau and his colleagues were waging their battle for concessions, back at home significant changes of mood began to manifest themselves. The continuance of deplorable conditions throughout the Reich and the fear that the war might be renewed, with horrible consequences for Germany, caused a break in the ranks of those who till now had been united in their demand for rejection of the Allied terms. Within the cabinet, the Social Democrats and the Democrats remained adamant in their insistence upon rejection. But the Center, under the influence of Erzberger, began to veer away from this uncompromising line. It was Erzberger who first broached the idea of retreat. Ambitious, resourceful and energetic, he labored to win over his own party and the cabinet to his point of view. He even threatened to resign from the government if it persisted in its refusal to sign the treaty. Rejection of the Allied terms, he held, would mean nothing less than political chaos and economic ruin. Only peace and total elimination of the blockade could save the unity of the Reich. Once the treaty had been signed, the government would be able to nip in the bud the separatist movements in the Rhineland (which the French, with an eye to the dismemberment of Germany, were encouraging) and check the spread of Bolshevism. Refusal to sign would bring an Allied invasion of Germany; and this, in turn, would bring civil war, Bolshevism and partition of the Reich. A few members of

the cabinet were convinced by Erzberger's arguments, but the rest
stuck to their guns and held out for rejection. Least receptive to the
idea of capitulation was the Democratic party. It threatened to withdraw from the government if a decision in favor of signing should be
reached. Most of the ministers were, like Erzberger, alive to the danger
of separatism and Bolshevism, but they could not bring themselves to
accept terms which outraged all their patriotic sensibilities. The cabinet, unable itself to settle the question, passed the buck to the parties
of the Weimar coalition. They were asked to decide. Erzberger managed to persuade a good many, but not all, of the members of his
party. This he did by advocating acceptance of the treaty minus the
so-called "points of honor"—Articles 227 to 231, which had to do with
"war criminals" and war-guilt. But the Social Democrats and the
Democrats remained solidly in favor of rejection.

5

The Allies did not take kindly to the Reich's outcry against
the treaty. They resented Brockdorff-Rantzau's voluminous and
barbed criticism of their handiwork. The German foreign minister
made matters more difficult by assuming a defiant attitude. The victorious powers were unanimous in regarding Germany as the aggres-
sor. All around them were evidences of the destruction she had
wrought. The bitterness engendered by years of bloody warfare could
hardly subside overnight. Public opinion in France and England demanded vengeance. Little wonder, then, that the Allies were not in
a forgiving mood. On June 16, 1919, they replied to the German
counterproposals. They made only a few concessions, the most important of which was provision for a plebiscite in Upper Silesia. On
all other major issues, they refused to budge. Germany, they solemnly
reiterated, was responsible for the outbreak of the war and for "the
savage and inhuman manner in which it was conducted." She would
have to make reparation for the wrongs committed. "War criminals"
would have to be extradited for trial. The peoples who had suffered
at Germany's hands required, for a time, protection against German
competition in the markets of the world. The fact that Germany had
undergone a revolution made no difference. The German people supported the policies of their government during the war and could not
now expect to escape the consequences of defeat. The Allies declined
to give Germany immediate admittance to the League. She would

first have to prove two things: that she intended to fulfill the conditions of the treaty; and that she had become a peace-loving nation. Adverting to specific features of the treaty, the Allies contended that the terms which they had formulated were both just and in harmony with the pre-armistice agreement. They defended the territorial settlement in Europe. They refused to modify their reparation terms. They reaffirmed their determination to strip Germany of all her colonies. In so doing, they added insult to injury by charging that she was unfit to govern backward peoples. The disarmament of Germany, they argued, would "facilitate and hasten the accomplishment of a general reduction of armaments." It was their intention to initiate negotiations with a view to adopting a plan for general disarmament. But the effectuation of such a plan would depend in large measure on the fulfillment by Germany of her own obligations.

The Allies described the note of June 16, 1919, as their "last word." An answer would have to be given within five days. Failure to accept the treaty would lead to Allied action to enforce its terms. The German delegation at Versailles at once made ready to leave. But before its departure it requested and obtained a forty-eight-hour extension of the time limit. Brockdorff-Rantzau and his colleagues reached Weimar on June 18 and promptly submitted a report to the cabinet. They pointed out that the Allied note of June 16 contained only concessions of secondary importance. Consequently, they felt it to be their duty to advise rejection of the treaty. The nation's military leaders assumed a similar attitude. Hindenburg spoke their mind when he said that as a soldier he preferred "honorable defeat to a shameful peace." But when quizzed regarding the possibility of armed resistance, the Field Marshal was forced to admit that Germany had little chance of winning out. His reply to the government's query was explicit enough.

In the event of a resumption of hostilities, we would be able to reconquer the province of Posen and hold our frontiers in the east. In the west, because of the numerical superiority of the Allies and their ability to envelop both our flanks, we can hardly count on being successful if our enemies should attack in earnest. A favorable outcome for all our operations is therefore very doubtful.

In spite of this pessimistic appraisal of the situation, the military chieftains persisted in their demand that the treaty be rejected. They even threatened to leave the government in the lurch if it should decide to sign. However, in order to save the country from Bolshevism, they finally consented to remain in harness if the "points of honor" were deleted.

The decision was squarely up to the three coalition parties. Rallying behind the leadership of Erzberger, the majority of the Centrists declared they would accept the treaty if the Allies agreed to do three things: drop the war-guilt charge, forget about the "war criminals" and modify the economic clauses. This declaration was issued after Erzberger had assured his party and the cabinet that the Allies would not insist on retaining Articles 227 to 231. Most of the Social Democrats now executed an about-face. Taking their courage in both hands, they went much farther than the Centrists. They said that, although they would demand the elimination of the section on "war criminals," they were prepared to advocate acceptance of the treaty even if the Allies refused to make this concession. The Democrats, however, remained unanimously opposed to signing. Scheidemann conferred with the leaders of the three parties on the evening of June 19, 1919. He asked them to unite in support of the Centrist program. He explained that Germany would refuse to sign if the Allies rejected the conditions laid down by the Catholic group. The pros and cons were heatedly discussed until the early hours of the morning. No agreement could be reached primarily because the Democrats continued to hold out for unconditional rejection. In the face of this impasse, and because he personally was opposed to signing, Scheidemann resigned. Ebert wanted to do likewise because he, too, believed that the treaty should be rejected. But his party comrades managed to convince him that his resignation would plunge the country into chaos and strengthen the hand of the Bolshevists. He decided to remain at his post.

The formation of a new government proved far from easy. The Democrats were the chief stumbling block. They categorically refused to join any ministry that would agree to sign the treaty. After carefully canvassing the situation, the Social Democrats and the Centrists decided to organize a cabinet without the Democrats. On June 22, 1919, with the deadline for signing only 24 hours away, Gustav Bauer announced that he had succeeded in forming a new government. Hermann Mueller, a leading Social Democrat and a man of unimpeachable integrity, assumed direction of the nation's foreign policy. The ministry of finance was assigned to Erzberger. Noske remained minister of war. Bauer promptly informed the national assembly that the formation of the new cabinet had been made possible by the desire of the Social Democrats and the Centrists to spare the country the horrors of internal chaos. The government, he sadly declared, had no choice but to accept this "peace of injustice." He emphasized that all the members of the assembly, regardless of how they might vote on the issue before them, were at one in denouncing the treaty. After making a final protest against the document, he asked the assembly to vote on a resolution declaring Germany's readiness to sign but explicitly rejecting Articles 227 to 231. The resolution was adopted by a vote of 237 to 138. The opposition consisted of the Nationalists, the People's party and the Democrats. On the evening of June 22, the Allies were informed of the Reich's qualified acceptance of the treaty. They replied immediately. Their language was blunt and uncompromising. The time for discussion, they said, was over. No qualifications or reservations would be countenanced. Germany had to accept or reject the treaty as a whole. With less than 24 hours remaining before the expiration of the Allied ultimatum, Bauer requested an extension of 48 hours. The answer was a categorical no. The moment was indeed a desperate one. Over the country hung the peril that the army might refuse to abide by the decision to which the government was being inexorably driven. This peril was enhanced by the attitude of Noske. He aligned himself with the generals. He told the cabinet that he would rather see Germany overrun by foreign armies than accept Articles 227 to 231. To make matters worse, the Centrists, Erzberger included, formally decided not to accept the treaty if those articles were retained. This was the situation on the morning of June 23. An answer had to be given to the Allies not later than 6 P.M.

In desperation, Ebert turned to Groener. He asked him for his opinion regarding the possibility of armed resistance. Groener confirmed what Hindenburg had already said. But, unlike the Field Marshal, he advised capitulation. The country, he averred, had no choice but to accept the enemy's terms. At Groener's suggestion, Noske swallowed his misgivings and appealed to the army to stand by the government. The national assembly was hurriedly convened. The majority of the deputies, putting the welfare of the country before all other considerations, authorized the government to sign unconditionally. The Nationalists, the People's party, most of the Democrats and a section of the Center made up the opposition. Two hours before the expiration of the ultimatum, the following note was sent to the Allies:

The government of the German republic is overwhelmed to learn from the last communication of the Allied and Associated Powers that the Allies are resolved to enforce, with all the power at their command, the acceptance even of those provisions in the treaty which, without having any material significance, are designed to deprive the German people of their honor. The honor of the German people cannot be injured by an act of violence. The German people, after their terrible sufferings during these last years, are wholly without the means of defending their honor against the outside world. Yielding to overpowering might, the government of the German republic declares itself ready to accept and to sign the peace treaty imposed by the Allied and Associated governments. But in so doing, the government of the German republic in no wise abandons its conviction that these conditions of peace represent injustice without example.

Hindenburg handed in his resignation. Noske did likewise in order to show that he, too, could not stomach the dishonoring provisions of the treaty. However, he was persuaded by Ebert and other leading Social Democrats to remain in the cabinet. On June 24, the government issued a proclamation to the country. It declared that its decision to sign had been made under duress and with but one thought: to spare the defenseless nation further suffering. The conditions of the treaty would have to be fulfilled. However, those Germans who were now to be separated from the Reich would never be forgotten. During the trying days ahead, the country would have to work and heed the call of duty. Otherwise, there would be, not peace, but war once again. A delegation headed by Mueller journeyed to Versailles. There, on June 28, 1919, it signed the treaty. The ceremony took place in the very same hall where, forty-eight years before, the German empire had been proclaimed.

The Treaty of Versailles dealt a staggering blow to the German republic. Instead of using their power as victors to help democracy in Germany, the Allies made its position infinitely more difficult. They refused to recognize the fact that the November revolution had transformed the Reich into a state in which the people were sovereign. They treated as of no account the impressive victory which moderate republicanism had won in the elections of January, 1919. They persisted in regarding the Germany of Ebert and Scheidemann as in no essential regard different from the Junker-dominated Germany of 1914. What they failed to see was that the consolidation of democracy in Germany was the first prerequisite of European and world peace. In their anxiety to weaken and fetter Germany, they overlooked the all-important fact that nowhere were there stancher believers in Wilsonian idealism than the men and women who composed the parties of the Weimar coalition. These men and women were the natural allies of democrats and internationalists the world over. That they were, from the very beginning, placed on the defensive in their own country may, in large measure, be ascribed to the blindness and vindictiveness of the Allies at Versailles.

The Treaty of Versailles strengthened enormously the hand of the reactionaries and provided them with a propaganda weapon of supreme and lasting effectiveness. In their disappointment and bitterness, millions of Germans who had acquiesced in the new regime as the sole means of escape from an intolerable predicament turned away from it in disgust. They gave themselves up to an unbridled hatred of the men who had democratized the Reich and accepted the peace. They listened with morbid satisfaction to the antirepublican canards circulated by the Nationalists, who exploited their golden opportunity with complete unscrupulousness and consummate skill. The theory of the stab in the back made rapid headway, above all in middle-class circles; and the damage it did then and in subsequent years to the republican cause proved irreparable. The country was told by right-wing politicians and journalists that only the old ideals and methods that had made Germany great in the past could restore her to dignity, strength and prosperity. The leaders of the new regime were pictured as traitors and cowards who cared nothing for Germany and callously permitted her to be humiliated and bled white by her foes. These things were believed by many Germans, and so it was that during the months which followed the signing of the treaty, a change came over the Reich. The opposition to the republic, which only a short while before had lacked mass support, became strong enough to challenge the moderate parties. And there was noticeable a stiffening of attitude toward the Allies, a growing determination to stand up to them and to answer pressure with defiance.

Chapter 11

THE WEIMAR CONSTITUTION AND THE STRUGGLE
OVER THE FACTORY COUNCILS

I

THE making of peace was the national assembly's most dramatic accomplishment. However, far more of its thought and energy went into the drafting and discussion of the constitution which was to regularize the existence of the German republic. As the assembly proceeded with its labors, it encountered manifold difficulties. Some of these sprang from the unhappy state of the country. Others stemmed from the exaggerated expectations to which the convocation of the assembly gave rise. The obstructionist attitude of the oppositional parties and a general penchant for prolixity engendered further complications. For weeks the controversy over the signing of the treaty diverted attention from the task of endowing the country with a new governmental structure. In spite of these obstacles and distractions, the men at Weimar not only persevered but accomplished their work with commendable speed. On July 31, 1919, the new constitution was adopted. The vote was 262 to 75. The opposition consisted almost entirely of Nationalists, Independents and members of the People's party. The constitution was promulgated on August 11. Ebert continued as president. The Bauer government remained in charge of the nation's affairs. The assembly did not disband. In September, 1919, it moved to Berlin. There it legislated not only on matters connected with the effectuation of the constitution but on a host of other issues that required immediate attention. Its achievements testify to the German people's capacity for self-government even under circumstances which were always trying and not infrequently desperate.

The principal author of the Weimar constitution was Professor Hugo Preuss. He and his collaborators borrowed a good many ideas from foreign countries, notably France, Switzerland and the United States. But they were guided primarily by German precedents. They made a conscious effort to preserve those features of the Bismarckian constitution which were likely to function satisfactorily under a truly popular regime. They retained the term *Reich*, with all its imperial associations, to denote the republic as distinguished from the individual *Laender* or states. They also drew upon the abortive Frankfurt constitution, one of the interesting by-products of the revolutionary movement that rocked Germany in 1848.

Many conflicting interests were represented in the national assembly. Besides, no single party controlled a majority of the seats. The Weimar constitution therefore had to be and was a compromise. One of the issues which had to be settled on a give-and-take basis was that of the unitary state versus the federal state. Preuss himself was an ardent exponent of the *Einheitsstaat* and proposed the dismemberment of Prussia as the initial step toward such unification. But the opposition proved too strong. The federative principle was retained. This was a victory for the South German states, whose fear of Prussia's hegemonic designs showed no sign of diminishing. However, the exponents of a unitary solution did not emerge empty-handed. Under the new constitution, the national government enjoyed far more power than its imperial predecessor. The legislative authority vested exclusively in the Reich was enormous. It embraced such things as foreign relations, national defense, tariff and monetary policies, citizenship, immigration and emigration, communications. Moreover, the Reich was given unlimited but not exclusive power to deal with a great many other matters. These included civil and criminal law, judicial procedure, poor relief, the press, the right of association and assembly, the protection of mothers and children, public health, labor, expropriation and socialization, commerce, banking, industry, railways and internal navigation, the theater and the cinema. The Reich could levy taxes "in so far as they are claimed in whole or in part for its purposes." It could take measures to protect public order and safety. It could lay down "fundamental principles" in regard to education, the rights of religious bodies, land distribution and colonization, housing, the taxing power of the *Laender*. The latter were thus shorn of many of the prerogatives which they had been permitted to retain in 1871. The principle governing this lopsided division of powers between the federal government and the states was stated succinctly in Article 13: "As long as, and in so far as, the Reich does not make use of its powers of legislation, the *Laender* shall retain the power of legislation. This does not apply to the power of legislation which belongs exclusively to the Reich." The restricted powers reserved to the *Laender* underwent further diminution during the ensuing years, thanks to the national government's tendency to legislate on subjects that were within the areas of concurrent action. Especially gratifying to the exponents of a unitary system was the stipulation that national laws were to be superior to the laws of the states. A supreme judicial tribunal was to settle all disputes as to whether a local law was in harmony with a similar law enacted by the Reich. The *Laender* were to enforce national laws unless the Reich specified otherwise. But the national government was to have the right to supervise the work of enforcement. It could, in exercising this right, lay down general directives and send commissioners to the local authorities. The result was an appreciable extension of Berlin's control over officials of the states. Besides, the national government made it a practice to entrust to its own agencies the enforcement of all legislation dealing with matters which were exclusively within its domain. As a consequence of all this, the trend toward administrative centralization, which had been so much in evidence prior to 1918, became even more marked under the republic. Germany became less and less a federal state and more and more a unitary one; but it was not until after the advent of Hitler that the last remnants of states' rights were done away with.

The modest position accorded the *Laender* by the makers of the Weimar constitution was underlined by still other provisions of the document. Section one of Article 48 stipulated that if a state should fail to live up to the obligations imposed upon it by the constitution or by national laws, the president of the republic might use armed forces to bring that state into line. The *Laender* were to be represented in the Reichsrat, the upper house of the national legislature, but this body had far less authority than the imperial Bundesrat. The lower house, its name unchanged, was given the dominant position in the legislative field. The two chambers were on an equal plane so far as originating or revising bills was concerned, but in the matter of their enactment the Reichsrat was made distinctly subordinate to the Reichstag. Moreover, there was the all-important fact that the cabinet was to be responsible to the Reichstag alone. This meant popular control of the executive and therefore of the general direction of national policy.

Like its predecessor under the empire, the Reichstag represented the country as a whole. But whereas the old Reichstag had been elected on the basis of manhood suffrage, the new one was to be chosen by all citizens, male and female alike, who were 20 years of age. Another innovation was the stipulation that the elections were to be conducted in accordance with the principle of proportional representation.

The makers of the Weimar constitution proceeded on the assumption that a powerful president was essential to the well-being of the republic. True, some of the deputies argued that it would be wise to dispense altogether with a chief executive. A weak president, they said, would be a superfluity; a strong one, on the other hand, would endanger the very existence of the republic. But they were overruled. The assembly accepted the proposals put forward by Preuss, who took the position that the country would need a chief executive powerful enough to serve as a counterweight to parliament. Preuss pointed out that the president, in addition to keeping tab on the legislature in the name of the nation, would serve as a unifying symbol and endow the government which he headed with a greater measure of dignity. He would be, as Preuss put it, "a definite center, an immovable pole," in the new democratic regime. In keeping with this conception of the presidency, Preuss and his collaborators rejected the idea of having the chief executive elected by the two houses of parliament sitting together as a national assembly. They held that this procedure was all right for France, where the president was scarcely more than a figurehead. But it would not do for Germany, where the chief executive would have to receive his mandate directly from the people if he were to fulfill the role of counterpoise to the powerful Reichstag. Preuss had to contend with the doubts and fears of those who argued that some kind of dictatorship might grow out of this method of choosing the president. He himself recognized the danger implicit in the system he was advocating, but he clung to the belief that a weak executive would be more harmful to German parliamentarism than a strong one. Once again his views prevailed. "The president of the Reich," Article 41 stipulated, "shall be elected by the whole German people."

The Social Democratic deputies in the national assembly wished to see the presidential term limited to five years. They were also anxious to make it impossible for any individual to hold the office more than twice. Their attitude was motivated by the fear that unless such safeguards were incorporated into the constitution, the country might find itself saddled with something approximating a life presidency. But

Preuss demurred. The republic, he insisted, would need stability and continuity of policy in order to make headway in the face of party discord and inevitably recurrent cabinet crises. Consequently, a longer presidential term and no limitations as to eligibility for reelection were indicated. On this issue, too, he had his way. The chief executive was to serve for seven years and was made indefinitely reeligible. He was given a formidable array of functions. He represented Germany in international relations. He had the power to make treaties and alliances. He appointed and removed the chancellor and other members of the national government. He was the supreme commander of the armed forces and appointed and removed all military officers. He could dissolve the Reichstag and, if he so wished, subject any law enacted by parliament to a popular referendum. Above all, he was given broad emergency powers under paragraph two of Article 48. This famous provision stated: "If public safety and order are seriously disturbed or threatened . . . , the president of the Reich may take such measures as are necessary to restore public safety and order. If necessary, he may intervene with the help of the armed forces." But this was not all. He was clothed with authority to suspend temporarily the extensive civil liberties guaranteed elsewhere in the constitution. However, paragraph three stipulated that all emergency measures taken by the president were to be repealed if the Reichstag so ordered. The fourth paragraph rounded out this remarkable article by authorizing the governments of the *Laender* to exercise, "in case of imminent danger," emergency powers similar to those bestowed upon the president of the Reich.

The authors of the Weimar constitution gave further evidence of their penchant for a strong executive. Following the example set by Bismarck, they assigned to the chancellor a dominant position within the cabinet. Not the ministry as a whole but the chancellor was to lay down "the general course of policy." Each of his colleagues was to conduct the affairs of his department in accordance with these directives. In actual practice, however, the ministers were far more than mere errand-boys for the chancellor. They tended, from the very beginning, to play an important part in the formulation of cabinet decisions. Only when the chancellor happened to be a man of unusual strength did he monopolize the responsibilities of government and completely overshadow his subordinates.

Another significant feature of the Weimar constitution was the provision for popular initiative and referendum. When the idea of the

popular initiative was first broached in the national assembly, it precipitated an acrimonious debate. The plan formulated by Preuss contained no mention of any arrangement which would have permitted
a certain quota of voters to sponsor a legislative proposal and secure
action upon it by the electorate as a whole. The only group that came
out wholeheartedly for such a scheme was the Social Democratic party.
It managed, on this occasion, to have its way in spite of the strenuous
opposition offered by the parties of the Right and by some of the more
conservative elements in both the Centrist and Democratic camps.
The plan finally adopted bestowed upon one-tenth of the nation's
qualified voters the right to bring forward, by means of a petition,
either an ordinary bill or an amendment to the constitution. The
measure was first to be submitted to parliament by the cabinet. If it
was then enacted in the usual manner, it became part of the law of the
land. If, however, it failed to secure the necessary majority, the nation
would have to be called upon to accept or reject it. The referendum
had smoother sailing in the national assembly. It received general
approbation from the very outset, and provision for it was made with
the support of an overwhelming majority of the deputies.

The economic sections of the Weimar constitution represented a
compromise between socialist principles, to which the Social Democrats
continued to pay lip-service, and the bourgeois ideology of the Centrists and the Democrats. A number of provisions reflected the doctrinaire radicalism of the country's strongest party. The exercise of
property rights, it was stipulated, must at the same time serve the
public good. The distribution and use of the soil were to be controlled
by the state in such a way as "to prevent abuse and to promote the object of assuring to every German a healthful habitation. . . ." Landed
property might be expropriated if its acquisition were deemed essential
to the achievement of certain socially desirable ends. Unearned in-
crements in the value of land "shall inure to the benefit of all." The
country's natural resources and "all economically useful forces of nature" were to be placed under the supervision of the state. The Reich
was authorized to transfer to public ownership "private economic enterprises suitable for socialization." It was also empowered to combine
them "in the interests of collectivism." Every German was to be accorded an opportunity to earn a livelihood "by productive work." The
national government was to exert itself in behalf of the international
regulation of labor's legal status "to the end that the entire working
class of the world may enjoy a universal minimum of social rights."

The more moderate outlook of the Centrists and the Democrats likewise received ample expression in the constitution. Thanks to the influence of these groups, the economic liberty of the individual was explicitly assured. Private property and the right of inheritance were guaranteed. Expropriation was to be permissible only if it redounded to the public good, if it was based on existing law and was accompanied by just compensation to the owner. Legislation favorable to the interests of the middle class was promised.

The Weimar document was thus a hodge-podge of precepts drawn from the socialist and liberal credos. This confusion as to economic objectives and the unresolved conflict of class interests proved the Achilles' heel of German democracy. They transcended in significance the structural shortcomings of the constitution itself. Of these shortcomings the most fateful were the introduction of proportional representation and the excessively broad grant of emergency powers to the chief executive. The Social Democrats were the chief exponents of proportional representation. They had been grossly underrepresented in the imperial Reichstag and were determined to do everything they could to prevent the same thing from happening again. They were also genuinely convinced that no other system of representation could insure a more faithful expression of the popular will. In practice, however, the proportional plan turned out to be a hindrance rather than a help. It resulted in so great an increase in the size of the Reichstag that the efficiency of that body was seriously impaired. Proportional representation operated to the disadvantage of individuals without political affiliations. Many outstanding persons of independent outlook were thus denied an opportunity to participate in the work of the national government. Striving for the maximum number of seats, the various parties drew up extremely lengthy lists of candidates. Many of these aspirants to political office were totally unknown to the electors, yet the latter had no choice but to vote for the party list as a whole. A personal relationship between the candidate and the voter was rendered impossible. This could not fail to affect adversely the functioning of the democratic process. Above all, proportional representation encouraged the formation of far too many political parties. The existence of numerous "splinter" groups created confusion and paralyzed the national will. It often impeded the organization of cabinets and subjected the parliamentary system to unnecessary strain. It helped to produce impasses which in turn facilitated the advent of authoritarian rule. During the closing years of the republic, when co-ordinated effort and national unity were crying needs, the Reichstag found itself hamstrung by party dissension. True, the constant bickering and struggle that characterized German politics stemmed primarily from the conflict of classes. The nature of the system of representation was obviously a secondary factor. But it cannot be denied that the consequences of social disunity were aggravated by the operation of the proportional plan.

When the constitution was being drafted, Germany was knee-deep in civil war. Disorders which threatened the very existence of the moderate republic were occurring with ominous frequency. The defenders of the new regime decided that the executive branch of the government would have to be given authority to deal summarily with unruly individuals or groups. Such was the purpose of paragraph two of Article 48. The authors of this provision had no intention of empowering the president to act arbitrarily or irresponsibly. They were manifestly anxious to prevent such abuse of the executive authority. But they were driven, by the circumstances of the moment, to the conclusion that risks of this sort would have to be taken. It is, of course, customary in democratic countries to make provision for the use of emergency powers in times of crisis. However, the discretionary authority vested in the German president was so broad that it could readily be converted into an instrument for dealing with almost any type of contingency. The president alone was to decide when "public safety and order" were being threatened; and the elasticity of such terms as "safety" and "order" opened up all sorts of possibilities for dictatorial action within the letter of the law. It was one thing to invoke emergency powers in combating actual or impending physical disorders. It was quite another to invoke them in dealing with the kinds of economic or political difficulties to which even the most stable of democratic societies from time to time fall prey. Article 48 was a double-edged sword. It could be used to defend the existing order, but it could just as readily be used to destroy it. In the hands of anyone intent upon substituting authoritarianism for the more cumbersome processes of democracy, it could be the beginning of the end of individual freedom and popular rule.

2

Although the Social Democratic leaders obdurately opposed any system of government under which all political authority would be vested in workers' councils, they had, long before the revolution, advocated the establishment within the factories of councils representing the workers and sharing with the employers the power to determine working conditions. The idea of setting up factory councils acquired new life immediately after the establishment of the republic. But it encountered the opposition of the trade-union executives, who feared that the strong position which was theirs as a result of the capital-labor accord of November 15, 1918, might be jeopardized. However, they finally withdrew their objections and consented to go along provided the factory councils did nothing of which the unions disapproved. In March, 1919, the German government and the Social Democratic party concluded a formal agreement which was designed to pave the way for the requisite legislative action. The key provision of this agreement ran as follows:

There shall be legally regulated workers' representation to supervise production, distribution, and the economic life of the nation, to inspect socialized enterprises, and to contribute towards bringing about nationalization. A law providing for such representation shall be passed as soon as possible. It must make provision for the election of industrial workers' and employees' councils, which will be expected to collaborate on an equal footing in the regulation of labor conditions as a whole. Further provision must be made for district labor councils and a Reich labor council which, in conjunction with the representatives of all other producers, are to give their opinions as experts before any law is promulgated concerning economic and social questions. They may themselves suggest laws of this kind. The provisions outlined above shall be included in the constitution of the German republic.

In April, 1919, the Reich minister of labor acted to implement this agreement. He asked a specially constituted committee of economic experts to prepare a system of labor law based on the principles of social democracy. The committee was to concern itself with a number of matters. These included the creation of workers' councils in the factories, the establishment of labor courts and the formulation of the collective bargaining contract. While the committee was deliberating, the makers of the Weimar constitution took matters into their own hands. They outlined, in Article 165, the essential features of what was designed to be an ambitious experiment in economic democracy. The language of this article was most explicit.

Workers and employees shall be called upon to co-operate with employers, and on an equal footing, in the regulation of wages and working conditions, as well as in the entire field of the economic development of the forces of production. The organizations on both sides and their agreements shall be recognized. Workers and employees shall, for the purpose of looking after their economic and social interests, be given legal representation in factory workers' councils, as well as in district workers' councils . . . and in a workers' council of the Reich. District workers' councils and the workers' council of the Reich shall meet with the representatives of employers and other interested population groups as district economic councils and as an economic council of the Reich for the purpose of performing economic functions and for co-operation in the execution of the laws of socialization. District economic councils and the economic council of the Reich shall be constituted so that all important economic and social groups will be represented in them in proportion to their economic and social importance. The national ministry shall, before proposing drafts of politico-social and politico-economic bills of fundamental importance, submit them to the economic council of the Reich. The economic council of the Reich shall itself have the right to initiate drafts of such bills. If the national ministry fails to assent, it shall nevertheless present the draft to the Reichstag accompanied by an expression of its views.

The comprehensive organizational program set forth in this article was never fully carried out. Workers' councils were set up in the factories and a provisional economic council was established for the Reich as a whole. But even the adoption of these measures was preceded by bitter and prolonged controversy.

The bill for the creation of factory councils was laid before the national assembly in the summer of 1919. The two parties of the Right opposed it. So did the Independents, but for vastly different reasons. They regarded the measure as a poor substitute for the far-reaching program which they espoused. They were convinced that it was part of a carefully devised plan to sabotage the revolution. The battle waged by conservative opponents of the bill centered on the following points: Should the members of the council be given the right to inspect the books of the firm? Should they be accorded representation on its board of directors? And should they be permitted to share with management authority in such matters as the hiring and firing of workers? The People's party and the Nationalists said no to all three questions and spoke up vigorously for their point of view. The parties of the Weimar coalition were in favor of granting the workers representation on the board of directors. They collaborated to secure the adoption of a provision making such representation mandatory. But they did not agree on the question of giving the members of the council the right to inspect the company's books. The Social Democrats took a strongly affirmative stand on this issue. However, their allies failed to support them and so they were overwhelmingly defeated. They had to be content with a substitute clause authorizing the councils to request permission to see the firm's balance-sheet. Information so obtained was not to be divulged. The Social Democrats were equally unsuccessful in their efforts to obtain for the workers some measure of control over the hiring and firing of factory personnel. The councils were given only a very limited right to entertain appeals in such cases. They might negotiate with the employer, and if no agreement was reached, they could either drop the matter or submit it to a board of arbitration.

While the bill was being discussed in the national assembly, conservative circles throughout the country launched a virulent campaign against it. The powerful federation of German industrialists (*Reichsverband der Deutschen Industrie*) took a prominent part in this campaign. Much more spectacular were the tactics employed by the radical opposition. As the measure neared its last hurdles, the left-wing Independents and the Communists issued a call for a protest demonstration. In answer to this summons, a great throng of workers assembled in front of the Reichstag building on January 13, 1920. The authorities made it clear that they would stand for no nonsense. Trouble speedily developed. The police opened fire on the crowd. Forty-two persons were killed and 105 wounded. The feud between the Independents and the Social Democrats flared to a new pitch of intensity. Indescribable bitterness took hold of those sections of the working class that had already been estranged by the failure of the Social Democrats to institute total socialization. The enemies of the republic exulted. They knew, if the workers did not, that the principal casualty on this occasion was German democracy.

On January 18, 1920, the hotly contested bill received final sanction. The vote was 213 to 62. Once again the Independents aligned themselves with the Nationalists and the People's party. The measure went into effect on February 4. It was an elaborate statute, consisting of 106 articles. It authorized the formation of councils in all enterprises, both public and private, employing at least twenty persons. Salaried employees as well as factory workers were to have representation. In establishments employing fewer than twenty persons, a "shop chairman" was to be elected. The councils were given a wide assortment of functions. They were to suggest ways and means of maximizing efficiency. They were to collaborate with management in introducing new labor methods. Upon them rested the obligation of preventing "violent disturbances" and of encouraging the use of arbitrative machinery for the settlement of industrial disputes. Another of their duties had to do with the fixing of shop regulations in agreement with the employer and within the limits laid down by the collective bargaining contract. The councils were, in short, to foster harmonious relations between management and labor. At the same time, however, they were charged with the task of protecting the workers' right of combination. The prevention of accidents and the elimination of unhealthful conditions generally likewise loomed large in the list of their responsibilities. Noteworthy, too, were the functions assigned to them in connection with housing and the administration of pension funds.

The law for the establishment of factory councils was supposedly a compromise arrangement. Actually, it was nothing of the sort. The workers surrendered almost completely the right of comanagement. The councils were denied the power to make and enforce decisions. They could act only with the assent of the employers on matters related to the most vital and controversial aspects of capital-labor relations. The privilege of being represented on boards of directors meant very little because the workers' spokesmen always constituted a small minority. Moreover, the councils were not to trespass on the preserves of the trade unions or in any way serve as substitutes for them. Indeed, the law explicitly safeguarded the right of the unions "to represent the interests of their members." It was therefore no accident that the trade unions came to exercise complete control over the councils. This in turn engendered friction between organized and unorganized workers in the same factory. The fact that there were many divergent, ambiguous and inaccurate interpretations of the law made matters no easier. Workers often tried to get more than they were entitled to, while employers, with equal frequency, sought to withhold concessions which the law made obligatory. Numerous disputes arose, but most of them were settled amicably.

Instead of turning next to the formation of the intermediate councils envisaged in Article 165 of the constitution, the German government centered its attention on the apex of the hierarchy. A provisional economic council of the Reich came into being as a result of legislative action taken in May, 1920. It met for the first time on June 30. The problem of according representation to the nation's manifold interests and groups "in proportion to their economic and social importance" proved extremely difficult. The following distribution was finally agreed upon:

	NUMBER OF REPRESENTATIVES
Agriculture and forestry	68
Industry	68
Commerce, banking and insurance	44
Small business and handicrafts	36
Transport and postal services	34
Consumers	30
Government	24
Civil service and professions	16
Market industries and fisheries	6

There were employers and workers in the enterprises covered by most of these categories, and the principle laid down was that of equal representation for the two groups.

In spite of its avowedly transitory character, the provisional economic council of the Reich showed no disinclination to come to grips with a host of urgent questions. It pondered such things as the length of the working day, social insurance and the status of house-servants. It probed the intricacies of tariff policy and reparation. Those of its members who spoke for the working classes invariably endeavored to broaden the scope of measures designed to benefit their constituents. But in almost every instance, they encountered sharp opposition from the employers' representatives. Some of the council's stormiest sessions were provoked by differences of opinion regarding the establishment of a system of arbitration for dealing with industrial disputes. This controversy, and several others like it, brought out the fact that the balance of power rested with the twenty-four members appointed by the government. The council, which was intended to be a purely economic parliament, thus became merely one more instrument of the state. Recognition of this fact led the Free trade unions affiliated with the Social Democratic party to question the usefulness of the entire experiment.

From the very beginning, the provisional economic council of the Reich sought to facilitate the creation of the intermediate agencies foreshadowed in Article 165. However, the difficulties which ensued proved insurmountable. The principal stumbling block was the status of local employers' associations, particularly the chambers of commerce. The trade unions insisted upon their abolition. They argued that the continued existence of such bodies would reduce the district economic councils to complete impotence. The employers refused to dissolve their associations. The government sided with them. The trade unions clung to their position. As a consequence, the establishment of district economic councils was indefinitely postponed.

Chapter 12

THE KAPP PUTSCH

I

THE Treaty of Versailles saddled the Reich with many new problems. One of the most explosive of these was created by the Allied demand for the extradition of "war criminals." This somewhat elastic category comprised many individuals who were distinctly unpopular in their own country. But the desire of the Allies to get hold of them speedily obscured their sins and invested them with an aura of martyrdom. It became a patriotic duty to shield the nation's wartime leaders from the vengeance of their foreign persecutors. So strong was the feeling against extraditing them that any government which should endeavor to comply with the demand of the Allies was certain to be forced out of office. The Bauer cabinet was well aware of this. On December 18, 1919, it secured the enactment of a law designed to spare the susceptibilities of the German people. Under its provisions, the government obligated itself to open legal proceedings against all individuals designated by the Allies. However, the trials were to take place, not abroad, but in Germany. They were to be conducted by the supreme court at Leipzig. The Allies were warned that if they insisted on extradition, insuperable difficulties would be created.

In the meantime, the Allies had been busily engaged in compiling lists of "war criminals." They wound up with no fewer than 895 names. But they knew they would have to yield on the issue of extradition. This they acknowledged in February, 1920, when they informed the German government that they would not interfere, that they would allow the Reich authorities to assume responsibility for the proceedings against the individuals in question. However, they reserved the right to scrutinize the results with a view to determining the honesty and sincerity of the German government. An inter-Allied commission would be set up to collect evidence regarding the perpetration of war crimes, and this material would be forwarded to the German authorities. Moreover, the fact that Germany was to be allowed to take care of this business did not imply abrogation of the extradition clauses of the treaty. Should there be convincing grounds for believing that the accused had been permitted to escape the punishment they deserved, they would be compelled to stand trial in foreign courts. The German government, through its foreign minister, Hermann Mueller, promptly gave assurance that everything would be done to insure impartial trials. Early in March, 1920, the necessary arrangements were completed. The Bauer cabinet and the Social Democrats who dominated it had won a notable victory. German "honor" had been successfully defended. The Nationalists, who had been exploiting the Allied demand for extradition to heap abuse upon the government and the republic, were robbed of an excellent talking point. However, they had plenty of others and their campaign of vilification in no way diminished. The proceedings against the "war criminals" turned out to be something of a farce. A list of 45 test cases was presented to the government of the Reich. But no more than twelve were actually tried, and of these only six resulted in convictions.

The prestige which the Bauer cabinet derived from the successful handling of this issue was in part offset by the disaster which overtook one of its ablest and most dynamic members. Erzberger was the *bête noire* of the Nationalists. It was they (to be more exact, their pre-revolutionary selves, the Conservatives) who had been exposed by him in 1906, in connection with the colonial scandals of that year. It was they who thereafter had repeatedly been made to feel the whiplash of his caustic tongue. It was they who had most strongly opposed the peace resolution of July, 1917, for which Erzberger was primarily responsible. They reviled and cursed him because he had signed the humiliating armistice of November, 1918. His role during the hectic weeks which preceded the signing of the Treaty of Versailles was remembered by them with a bitterness that nothing could assuage. He had managed also to infuriate the great coal and steel magnates, headed by Hugo Stinnes. Stung by the strictures of a spokesman for the People's party, which championed the interests of Stinnes and his fellow-capitalists, Erzberger had warned the captains of industry that their halcyon days were over. He was blunt and often exasperatingly tactless. Where others might have stepped with caution and chosen the least dangerous course to achieve the object in view, Erzberger waded in with an abandon that did little credit to his political sagacity. Bitter adversaries he had aplenty, but none was more implacable than Karl Helfferich. This able but self-important and quarrelsome man had had a distinguished career before the revolution. He had made a great reputation as an authority on monetary theory. He had held important posts in the government and during a very large part of the war had served as vice-chancellor. Because he had been mainly responsible for the Reich's financial difficulties in the years which preceded the collapse of the old regime, Helfferich brought down upon himself reproaches and accusations from many directions. But no one denounced him as furiously and unmercifully as Erzberger, and between the two men there had sprung up an enmity which time and the impact of revolutionary events had served only to intensify.

Restless, itching for action and power, and unawed by the animosities which he was perennially stirring up, Erzberger utilized his position as minister of finance in the Bauer cabinet to make himself the center of another fierce controversy. In the summer of 1919, he introduced a number of "soak-the-rich" tax measures. He justified them in a blistering speech which sent a tremor of panic through all those who stood to lose the most. The ensuing debates in the assembly and in the country at large were marked by unbridled acrimony and spite. Reactionary and conservative circles pressed into service every means at their disposal in an effort to discredit Erzberger. Helfferich, who had been waiting for just such a moment, gleefully joined in the hue and cry. In a series of newspaper articles he charged that Erzberger had been involved in unsavory financial transactions. The nature of the accusations and the ruthlessness with which they were pressed forced Erzberger to sue his tormentor. The trial opened in January, 1920, and a few days later an unsuccessful attempt was made on Erzberger's life. On March 12, the court rendered its verdict. Helfferich was forced to pay a small fine because he was found technically guilty of slander; but the court held that most of the charges against Erzberger were true. This meant that Erzberger was finished politically. He promptly withdrew from the cabinet. His fall caused wild rejoicing among the enemies of democracy. It gave them new strength and hope. It robbed the Center party of one of its most progressive leaders and correspondingly strengthened the position of its conservative wing. Erzberger's fate was therefore more than a personal tragedy. It was a tragedy for all who shared his political convictions, for the system and philosophy of government enshrined in the Weimar constitution. Erzberger's shortcomings were beyond question. But, in spite of them, he had performed yeoman's service on behalf of the new regime. In later years, his absence was to be sorely felt.

2

Erzberger's political demise came at a moment when powerful military elements were girding for an onslaught against the Weimar system. The signing of the peace treaty on June 28, 1919, had caused widespread indignation in army circles. So strained did the relations between Groener and a section of the officers' corps become that the general felt impelled to resign from the Supreme Command. His departure was deeply regretted by Ebert. During the summer and autumn of 1919 the feeling among disgruntled officers hardened into a resolve to set up a military dictatorship. The leader of this clique was General Baron Walther von Luettwitz, who commanded the troops stationed in the Berlin area. Luettwitz regarded himself, now that Hindenburg had retired from active service, as the most authoritative spokesman of the military caste. He believed that the existing political regime, in which the traditionally anti-militarist Social Democrats held the upper hand, constituted a perennial threat to the interests of the officers' corps. Consequently, it would have to be removed. The government, in his opinion, had forfeited its right to lead the nation when it accepted the Treaty of Versailles unconditionally. If it remained in office, it would end by destroying the country. Upon the officers' corps rested the obligation of rescuing Germany from the perils which beset her. Bolshevism was by far the greatest danger. Of this Luettwitz and the men around him were unshakably convinced. They regarded a Russo-German war as imminent and therefore sought to do everything in their power to prevent a reduction in the armed strength of the Reich. In assaying the chances of a *coup*, Luettwitz exhibited a shockingly inadequate grasp of political realities. He wished to have Noske on his side, but was prepared to dispense with his support if necessary. He was ready to defy the bulk of the nation. He even persuaded himself that he did not need the help of the two right-wing parties. Control of the army, he felt, would be enough.

Another leading member of the conspiratorial clique was Major Waldemar Pabst. This veteran cavalry officer was ambitious, energetic and keenly interested in politics. He worked out a plan according to which Noske was to seize power and establish a military dictatorship with the aid of the army. But Noske refused to co-operate, declaring that any attempt to rule against the will of the masses would end in disaster. Thanks to Pabst, other individuals were drawn into the plot. One of these was Colonel Max Bauer, Ludendorff's former adjutant and an old hand at the game of intrigue. Wolfgang Kapp, the East Prussian official who had collaborated with Admiral Tirpitz in establishing the Fatherland party, was slated to be the head of the new government. He maintained close and continuous contact with Ludendorff. The erstwhile war lord expressed complete sympathy with the aims of the conspiracy but requested that he be allowed to remain in the background.

Luettwitz and Kapp counted heavily on the unfavorable reaction of the army to the Allies' demand for speedy execution of the disarmament provisions of the treaty. They figured that irate officers and men, faced with the prospect of dismissal, would be willing to go to almost any lengths to prevent the disbanding of their units. If they were encouraged to resist the Allies' demand, a conflict between them and the government was bound to ensue. Such a conflict would precipitate the fall of the existing regime. The machinations of the conspirators gave rise to rumors that a putsch was impending. Ebert and Noske were inclined to view the situation without alarm. They professed to believe that the army could be trusted and that the republic was therefore in no serious danger. Scheidemann did not share this optimism. With increasing sharpness he called attention to the likelihood of a reactionary counterrevolution and demanded that something drastic be done to curb the military. Ebert and Noske rejected this demand. They persisted in regarding left-wing radicalism as much more dangerous than the forces of reaction. What the nation needed most, they maintained, was maximum industrial production. This could only be insured by repressive measures against the fomenters of strikes and other labor disturbances.

3

The time was approaching when the Reich would have to institute drastic cuts in the strength of its armed forces. According to the terms laid down by the Allies, the German navy on March 10, 1920, was not to exceed 15,000 men while the army was to be reduced to 200,000 by April 10. To meet these figures, the German government found itself obliged to dismiss without further ado between fifty and sixty thousand men. Orders to this effect were issued and distributed to commanders in every branch of the service. Among the units earmarked for dissolution was the naval brigade commanded by one of the nation's most notorious Free Corps leaders, Captain Hermann Ehrhardt. This brigade, which had the reputation of being a most effective fighting organization, had played a prominent part in the suppression of the Bavarian soviet republic. It was now stationed at Doeberitz, just outside Berlin. Ehrhardt went to Luettwitz and told him that his men were disturbed over the prospect of imminent dismissal. What, he queried, should he do? Luettwitz's answer was most reassuring. He declared that he would not allow the brigade to be disbanded. Ehrhardt reminded him that the order to disband had already been issued. That, retorted Luettwitz, was something he would take care of.

Word quickly got around that Luettwitz had decided to defy the government. One of the first to react was General Hans von Seeckt, head of the *Truppen Amt,* the new agency installed in the place of the Great General Staff which had been abolished by the Treaty of Versailles. Seeckt hurried to Luettwitz to ascertain the truth of the report. He defended the government, pointing out that it was acting under irresistible foreign pressure. Luettwitz, when asked whether he intended to execute a *coup d'état,* disingenuously replied in the negative. General Walther Reinhardt, who, as chief of the army command, topped the republic's military hierarchy, also intervened. Without circumlocution, he asked Luettwitz whether he would respect the constitution. Luettwitz's reply was evasive. But there was nothing ambiguous about what he said at a military review in Doeberitz on March 1, 1920. He would not, he reiterated on this occasion, permit the dissolution of the Ehrhardt brigade.

The Nationalists and the People's party were intrigued by the possibility of a counterrevolution. They sympathized wholeheartedly with the aims of Luettwitz and his associates. But several considerations motivated their decision to stand aloof. They did not regard Kapp as the person best suited to lead the movement. They were inclined to agree with Noske that any attempt to rule against the will of the vast majority of the nation was bound to fail. They did not care to share with the conspirators the risks attendant upon so hazardous an enterprise. If, contrary to expectations, the putsch should succeed, they were prepared to cast aside all reserve and identify themselves completely with the counterrevolutionary forces. In the meantime they hoped to achieve, by less dangerous means, the goal which Kapp and Luettwitz had in view. They believed—and there was ample evidence to support this conviction—that the time was propitious for action to lessen the influence of the hitherto dominant Social Democrats. Conservatism was palpably on the increase in Germany. And at the other end of the political axis the Independents were daily gaining adherents at the expense of their working-class rivals. Confident that new elections would bring an appreciable increase in their parliamentary representation, the Nationalists and the People's party planned to introduce a motion calling for the dissolution of the national assembly not later than May 1, 1920. They also made ready to demand the formation of a cabinet of "experts" in the belief that such a move would redound to their advantage. Finally, they were determined to urge the immediate enactment of a law to govern procedure in presidential elections. In preparing to press for the adoption of such a law, the two right-wing parties had a special object in view. Hindenburg was now being mentioned for the first time in the pan-German press as a presidential possibility. His admirers among the Nationalists openly referred to him as the white hope of the royalists, as the man whose job it would be to facilitate the restoration of the monarchy. One thing was beyond doubt: the Field Marshal was immensely popular. The defeat of 1918 had tarnished many a military reputation, but Hindenburg's had remained unsullied. He was still idolized as the hero of Tannenberg, the greatest victory won by German arms in the course of the war. He was gratefully remembered as the man who had brought the armies safely home after the signing of the armistice. Now, as a retired general, he lived with exemplary modesty. He kept himself aloof from the swirl of politics, making no effort to trade on his popularity. With such a man as their candidate for the presidency, the monarchists had an excellent chance to win. All this was not lost on the supporters of the republic. The parties that constituted the Weimar coalition contained many individuals who opposed the direct popular election of the president. They feared that it would lead to some form of dictatorship. They wished to see the Reichstag given the power to choose the chief executive. This could be done by amending the constitution. The parties of the Right were alarmed by such talk. They regarded the retention of direct popular election as essential to the success of their plans.

On March 4, 1920, Luettwitz conferred with Oskar Hergt, a leading Nationalist, and Rudolf Heinze, a spokesman for the powerful right wing of the People's party. Neither the general nor the conservative bloc had sought this contact; it came about at the suggestion of Colonel Arens, a high-ranking police official who wished Luettwitz to see how devoid of political support his contemplated putsch would be. As Arens foresaw, the conference gave little comfort to Luettwitz. The latter explained to his visitors that the troops were in a rather dangerous state of mind because of mass dismissals from the service. "The government," he went on, "must be made aware that it is acting irresponsibly in permitting the last pillars of the state to be undermined. If the Free Corps are dissolved and, in addition, half of the regular army is disbanded, the country will be left defenseless vis-à-vis the threat of Bolshevism." Hergt and Heinze asked what would happen if the Allies insisted on compliance with the military clauses of the treaty. Obedience to the Allies, Luettwitz retorted, must not be carried to the point of disregarding Germany's vital necessities. The dissolution of the Free Corps and further reductions in the size of the regular army would have to be postponed. The two party leaders pointed out that the government would refuse to do anything of the sort. They warned the general that if he laid down an ultimatum, he would jeopardize the efforts of the Nationalists and the People's party to bring about the speedy dissolution of the national assembly and to hasten the election of a new president. Luettwitz declared himself in sympathy with this program but said he doubted the possibility of putting it through by parliamentary means. He would rather rely on his troops. His guests demurred. The masses, they contended, would not support a military coup. They urged Luettwitz to postpone his ultimatum. This he agreed to do provided all went well with the demands which the Nationalists and the People's party were about to lay before the national assembly. But on March 9, 1920, those demands were overwhelmingly rejected. Luettwitz hurried to Hergt. The latter was obviously disappointed. Nevertheless, he continued to counsel patience. The campaign against the government, he said, was just beginning. It would be madness to rush matters. If, in spite of this warning, Luettwitz got himself involved in an open conflict with the government, the two conservative parties would not support him.

Hergt's words fell on deaf ears. Luettwitz, his mind made up, informed Kapp that a showdown was imminent. In an effort to obtain a clear picture of the chances of success, Kapp proceeded to institute inquiries regarding the attitude of the army. He was assured that on the whole it was favorable to the conspirators. His informants were less sanguine on the subject of the police, but they did intimate that some assistance might be forthcoming from this quarter, too. The government, for its part, attempted to keep close tab on the situation. It was not unduly alarmed. It believed it could count on the loyalty of military leaders like Reinhardt and Seeckt. With such men on its side, it would be able to cope with the rebellious members of the officers' corps. Nonetheless, certain precautions were taken. Noske sent his chief of staff, Major von Gilsa, to ascertain the attitude of Ehrhardt. The latter made it clear that he would obey Luettwitz's orders. Without further ado, Noske took a step which was designed to stop the counterrevolutionaries in their tracks. He withdrew the Ehrhardt brigade from the military jurisdiction of Luettwitz and placed it under the command of Admiral Adolf von Trotha, who was in charge of the nation's naval forces. This action brought matters to a head. Luettwitz saw Ebert and Noske on March 10. He demanded a number of things: the cessation of dismissals from the German army; the removal of Reinhardt from his post as chief of the army command; the resubjection of the Ehrhardt brigade to the control of the area commander. Noske sternly rejected these demands and warned that he would not hesitate to cashier any general who rendered himself suspect. Instead of taking this warning to heart, Luettwitz proceeded to make additional demands. These, it turned out, were identical with the ones formulated by the parties of the Right and rejected by the national assembly only the day before. Ebert replied that the matters in question were the concern of the political authorities. Luettwitz's parting remark left little doubt as to his intentions. He had come, he said, to deliver a warning. If anything unpleasant happened, the responsibility would not be his. Noske needed no more convincing that the situation was serious. On the following day, he removed Luettwitz from his command. Simultaneously, he ordered the arrest of Kapp, Bauer and Pabst. But the three men, forewarned of what was in store for them, managed to elude the police. They prepared to strike. Last-minute arrangements were hurriedly attended to. The Ehrhardt brigade was to spearhead the assault. The government, for its part, was far from idle. It labored to place the capital in a state of readiness for whatever might happen.

4

March 12, 1920, was a day of mounting excitement. Berlin seethed with rumors that the Ehrhardt brigade was about to go into action against the government. Noske sent Trotha to Doeberitz with instructions to ascertain Ehrhardt's intentions and to bring him to his senses if possible. The captain refused to deny or confirm the report that his brigade was about to march. His men, he told the admiral, were asleep; complete quiet prevailed in the encampment. This message Trotha relayed to Noske. But at 10 P.M., in accordance with pre-arranged plans, the brigade set out for Berlin. Noske hurriedly dispatched emissaries to negotiate with Ehrhardt. They returned with an ultimatum from the rebel leader. Among the demands put forward were those originally made by the two parties of the Right. The remaining stipulations called for the reinstatement of Luettwitz, the removal of Noske and the assignment of his post to a general. The government was given until 7 A.M. to reply. This short reprieve proved a godsend for Ebert and the members of the cabinet. It gave them time to consider appropriate countermeasures. Noske summoned the top-ranking military leaders and told them that Ehrhardt's ultimatum was unacceptable. He wished to proceed against the rebels. But first he wanted to know where the officers stood. Only two of those present—Reinhardt and Gilsa—declared themselves ready to defend the government. The spokesman for the unco-operative majority was Seeckt. German soldiers, he said, must not be allowed to fire upon each other. If a pitched battle did take place, the rebels would win. They had the support of large sections of the police. Noske thus learned, to his consternation, that the generals, who always managed to find enough troops to quell left-wing radicals, could not bring themselves to take action against reactionary foes of the republic.

The attitude of Seeckt and his colleagues foredoomed any attempt to defend Berlin militarily. The next move was up to the cabinet. Reinhardt, to the surprise of the ministers, asked that all available troops be ordered to proceed against the rebels. His request was voted down. He replied to this rebuff by resigning as chief of the army command. At the suggestion of Eugen Schiffer, the Democratic vice-chancellor, the cabinet decided to leave Berlin. If it remained in the capital it would be taken captive and the fight against the rebels would be stymied. Schiffer declared his willingness to stay behind and serve as the government's representative. He was authorized to inform Ehrhardt that the ultimatum had been rejected. Berlin was still wrapped in early morning darkness when the members of the government, headed by Ebert, departed by automobile for Dresden. But shortly before their departure, a decisive step was taken: the workers of the land were called upon to stage a general strike. The hurriedly composed manifesto ran as follows:

Workers, comrades! The military putsch is under way! The Ehrhardt naval brigade is marching on Berlin in order to force a transformation of the government. These mercenaries, who fear disbandment, want to put reactionaries in the various ministerial posts. We refuse to bow to this military pressure. We did not make the revolution in order to acknowledge once again the bloody rule of mercenaries. We will make no deal with the Baltic criminals. Workers, comrades! . . . Use every means to prevent this return of bloody reaction. Strike, stop working, strangle this military dictatorship, fight . . . for the preservation of the republic, forget all dissension! There is only one way to block the return of William II: to cripple the country's economic life! Not a hand must move, not a single worker must help the military dictatorship. General strike all along the line! Workers, unite!

This call was issued in the name of the Social Democratic party. It was communicated without a moment's delay to every section of the Reich. Ulrich Rauscher, chief of the chancellery's press bureau, sought to give added weight to the document by appending to it the names of the Social Democratic members of the government. This he did without consulting the individuals in question; there was no time for such formalities. The manifesto presented German Social Democracy in a new role. In the past the party had almost invariably frowned on the use of the general strike. But in the desperate situation which now obtained, there seemed no other way to save the republic.

Early on the morning of March 13, 1920, the Ehrhardt brigade arrived at the Tiergarten in Berlin and there awaited the government's reply. The police, far from interfering with the rebels, shouted words of approval. As soon as he learned that the ultimatum had been rejected, Ehrhardt ordered his men to occupy the government buildings and hoist the old imperial colors. No resistance was encountered. Kapp proclaimed himself chancellor. Luettwitz assumed the ministry of war and named General Ernst von Wrisberg, one of his closest friends, chief of the army command. Traugott von Jagow, former police chief of Berlin, was made minister of the interior. The insurgents sustained a serious blow when Seeckt refused to place himself at their disposal. His example was followed by a number of staff officers attached to the ministry of war.

5

The mantle of leadership now rested on the shoulders of Wolfgang Kapp. His career until this moment had been far from distinguished. He had spent the best years of his life as a provincial bureaucrat. He had served, faithfully but not brilliantly, the interests of his Junker masters. He was the son of a German liberal, Friedrich Kapp, who had migrated to the United States in 1848. There Wolfgang was born. Domiciled at an early age in the land of his forebears, he grew up to be a fanatical chauvinist and pan-German. During the war he had repeatedly attacked Chancellor Bethmann-Hollweg, even going so far as to accuse that statesman of being secretly in the employ of the British government. Kapp was regarded in his own circles as a man of iron will. Actually, however, he was given to vacillation. This trait cropped up directly he assumed power and contributed significantly to the failure of the putsch.

In their first manifesto to the nation, the rebels announced that they were establishing a government of "order, freedom and action." Order was clearly their primary concern. They instructed army commanders throughout the land to proceed against all foes of the new regime and to keep the press tightly muzzled. Simultaneously, however, they attempted to curry favor with the industrial masses by promising far-reaching concessions to labor. It was one thing to issue pronunciamentos and make promises; it was quite another to get on with the urgent tasks of administration. Key bureaucrats in some of the ministries flatly refused to co-operate with Kapp. The Reichsbank said no to his frantic requests for money. Some of his subordinates, especially those in charge of the press bureau, proved hopelessly incompetent. To make matters worse, an inspired purposefulness reigned in the camp of his enemies. The Independents, the Democrats and the Centrists aligned themselves with the Ebert-Bauer government and backed the call for a general strike. Only the Communists stood aloof. Insisting that there was no real difference between people like Ebert and Kapp, Noske and Luettwitz, they disassociated themselves from the strike call and announced a policy of neutrality. But this one note of discord was drowned out by the great roar of approval which came from the German proletariat. The trade unions responded magnificently to the appeals of their leaders. By the late afternoon of March 14, 1920, the greatest strike the world had ever seen was a reality. The economic life of the country came to a standstill. In the face of this stupendous demonstration of proletarian unity and discipline, the Communists relented and climbed on the bandwagon. Kapp attempted to break the strike. He issued a stringent decree "for the protection of labor peace." He made picketing a capital offense. But his efforts proved totally ineffectual.

In the meantime, the Ebert-Bauer government, from its temporary refuge in Dresden, issued a proclamation designed to give further impetus to the nation-wide movement of resistance. The cabinet, the proclamation asserted, had left Berlin in order to avoid bloodshed. As for the putsch, it would collapse very shortly. Until that happened, every German citizens would remain under obligation to be loyal and obedient to the legal government which alone was entitled to give orders. The Kapp-Luettwitz regime stemmed from an act of violence perpetrated by a few men; as such it was bereft of authority both at home and abroad. True, certain officers had broken their oath and had rallied to the support of the rebels. But the army as a whole would be well advised not to follow their example. This warning was only partially successful. In its attitude toward the Kapp-Luettwitz regime, the army split on regional lines. The units stationed in the eastern provinces aligned themselves with the rebels; those stationed in the west and south remained loyal to the Ebert-Bauer government. The local authorities, too, were divided. Bavaria, Wuerttemberg and Baden declared their solidarity with the legitimate government, but some of the other *Laender* went over to the insurgents.

Of considerable importance was the attitude of the two right-wing parties. They had plenty of unkind things to say about the Bauer cabinet. They accused it of seeking to retain power in contravention of the constitution and ascribed the current upheaval to this alleged disregard for legality. They adopted a different tone when speaking of the rebels. But their allusions to Kapp were too guarded to commit them to any particular course of action. They had evidently decided that wait-and-see tactics would serve their interests best so long as the fate of the putsch remained in doubt.

At the suggestion of Ludendorff, who was one of the insurgents' behind-the-scenes advisers, Kapp promised to stage new elections as soon as order had been restored. He hoped thereby to win the active support of the Nationalists and the People's party. His calculation seemed sound enough. The conservative bloc was shouting to high heaven that the composition of the national assembly no longer reflected the popular will. But Kapp's adversaries gave him no chance to profit by this gesture. The legitimate government, which had moved to Stuttgart, issued a call for the immediate convocation of the national assembly. On March 16, Schiffer conferred with spokesmen for the parties of the Weimar coalition. He got them to agree on the following points: a date for new elections would have to be set without delay; the constitutional provision for popular election of the president was not to be tampered with; the Bauer cabinet was to be reorganized at the earliest possible moment. This agreement produced the intended effect. Having gotten what they wanted, the two parties of the Right decided that Kapp, whose prospects grew hourly darker, had become a liability. They advised him to discuss terms with his foes. At the behest of his superiors, Pabst went to see Schiffer. The latter laid down hard conditions. He demanded the withdrawal of Kapp and Luettwitz and the removal from Berlin of every soldier who had participated in the putsch. The Bauer government added a few stipulations of its own. It insisted on the dissolution of the Ehrhardt brigade and the subjection of all troops in the Berlin area to the command of a trustworthy general.

The morning of March 17, 1920, found Kapp in a very unhappy frame of mind. The Berlin police and some of the troops supporting his regime were demanding his resignation from the chancellorship because they wanted Luettwitz, their favorite, to assume supreme authority. Realizing that his position had become thoroughly untenable, Kapp decided to capitulate. That very morning, at 10 A.M., he announced his resignation. He explained his decision in the following proclamation to the country: "After the Bauer government resolved to fulfill the basic political demands whose rejection led on March 13 to the establishment of the Kapp government, Chancellor Kapp regards his mission as accomplished and is resigning. . . ." He added that he was transferring full executive power to Luettwitz. He closed with an allusion to the need for a united national front against the "destructive danger of Bolshevism."

The legitimate government at Stuttgart exulted over Kapp's departure, but it refused to have anything to do with Luettwitz. Spokesmen for all the political parties except the Independents and the Communists met in Berlin to consider the situation. Stresemann, who was working to bring about some sort of modus vivendi between the rival camps, contrived to have Luettwitz present. But the Social Democrats refused to sit at the same table with the general and walked out. Luettwitz did not help matters by insisting that he be permitted to retain the chancellorship for at least two weeks. However, late in the afternoon of March 17, he yielded to the urgent counsels of certain of his fellow-generals and submitted his resignation. Together with Kapp and other high-ranking insurgents, he promptly left Berlin. Schiffer took charge of affairs in the name of the Bauer government. That evening Ebert, at the suggestion of Reinhardt, appointed Seeckt acting chief of the army command.

6

The principal reason for the failure of the Kapp putsch was the general strike. The virtually total paralysis of the country's economic life created insuperable difficulties for the insurgents and doomed their enterprise from the very beginning. Organized labor's display of solidarity on this occasion proved that its will to act was equal to its comprehension of the issues involved. Notice was served upon the enemies of German democracy that the spirit of revolution still lived among the industrial masses. The events of March, 1920, demonstrated conclusively that a united and dynamic proletariat was essential to the preservation of the republic. In making common cause with the Social Democrats, the Independents had placed their concern for the national welfare above party considerations. And even the Communists, whose divisive tactics were soon to bear fruit, had been forced to go along. Other factors contributed to the failure of the putsch. These included the loyalty of certain bureaucrats in the ministries of war, finance and the interior to the legal government of the Reich; the refusal of several outstanding military leaders, headed by Seeckt, to place their services at the disposal of the insurgents; the ambiguous, do-nothing attitude of the parties of the Right; the personal shortcomings of Kapp himself.

The leaders of the putsch fared variously. Kapp and Max Bauer fled the country. Ailing and dispirited, Kapp eventually gave himself up. He died in prison on June 12, 1922, while awaiting trial. Bauer stayed away until he was amnestied. Luettwitz severed his connections with the army and settled down to a quiet existence in Schweidnitz. Ehrhardt found a haven in Munich, where he identified himself with secret terrorist organizations. Jagow was tried in 1921 and sentenced to five years' imprisonment. He was amnestied in 1924, thanks to the clemency so often displayed toward men of his stripe.

7

Although the Kapp putsch proved a complete fiasco, it made possible
a victory of lasting importance for the reactionary elements in Bavaria.
When General Arnold von Moehl, who commanded the armed forces
in the Munich area, heard of the happenings in Berlin, he decided to
launch a coup of his own. During the night of March 13-14, 1920, he
informed Hoffmann, the Bavarian premier, that it would be impossible
to guarantee the safety of the government unless all political authority
was vested in the army command. Hoffmann promptly assembled his
cabinet and urged rejection of the general's ultimatum. But most of
the ministers shrank from such a course. They supported the proposal
put forward by the Democratic leader, Ernst Mueller-Meiningen, who
suggested that Moehl be allowed to have his way and that Gustav von
Kahr, the governor of the province of Upper Bavaria, be entrusted with
the administration of civil affairs. Thereupon Hoffmann resigned; his
colleagues had no choice but to do likewise. At once a committee
representing the socialist parties, the trade unions and the factory
workers' councils issued a call for a general strike. In explaining its
action the committee declared: "The Junker reaction is here. We must
fight it together. We must preserve the socialist republic." On March
16, Kahr was elected premier by the Bavarian Diet. The Social Democratic deputies decided, by a vote of 32 to 8, to spurn representation in
the new government. They charged that Kahr, by working with
Moehl on the night of March 13-14, had made himself politically unacceptable. This action marked the definitive end of Social Democratic
participation in Bavarian cabinets. The mainstay of Kahr's ministry
was the Bavarian People's party. It had recommended his election as
premier. It supported with enthusiasm the conservative program to
which he was committed. On a good many national questions, this
group did not see eye to eye with its parent organization, the Catholic
Center. In the elections to the national assembly, it had campaigned
under the Centrist banner. But it had subsequently severed this tie and
struck out on its own. It did not relish the progressive outlook of the
Center's left wing. Besides, an independent status in the national
legislature would afford it a better opportunity to indulge its particularist bias.

On the morrow of Kahr's election to the premiership, the leaders of
the strike, sensing the futility of further overt resistance, ordered their
followers to go back to work. While calm was thus being restored in

Munich, momentous developments seemed to be in the making in Stuttgart, the capital of near-by Wuerttemberg. There, on March 18, 1920, the national assembly convened. About 200 deputies were present. Of these only three were Nationalists and only one belonged to the People's party. Chancellor Bauer delivered the main address. Adverting to the putsch, he declared that German democracy had won a complete victory. But the country, he went on, had not yet regained stability. An ominous increase in communist activity was evident. Bloody clashes were occurring in certain sections of the Reich, and responsibility for this unfortunate state of affairs rested squarely upon the shoulders of Kapp and Luettwitz. Bauer's closing words were addressed to the Allies. He implored them not to aid the chauvinist elements in Germany by making impossible demands upon the Reich. The ensuing debate turned out to be a most lively affair. The honors for plain and vigorous speaking went to Scheidemann. He demanded a thorough purge of the Reichswehr. Every officer who had shown himself unreliable must be dismissed, he said. And all those who had aided and abetted the conspirators must be drastically punished, even to the extent of being deprived of their property. To this the spokesmen for the parties of the Right demurred, but they were careful at the same time to emphasize their loyalty to the Weimar constitution.

Directly the national assembly adjourned, Noske, drawing attention to Scheidemann's speech, submitted his resignation. This he did in response to pressure that was being exerted by certain elements within his own party. For some time Scheidemann supported by several of his Social Democratic colleagues, had been denouncing the war minister's pronounced predilection for members of the officers' corps. Hitherto Noske had always managed to come out on top, thanks to the support given him by the majority of his party's representatives in the national assembly. But now the mood of the Social Democratic deputies was grim; they were inclined to be less tolerant of Noske and his coddling of militarist counterrevolutionaries. Giving free vent to their feelings, they called for the establishment of a supreme people's court in Leipzig which would be charged with the task of trying the members of the Kapp government. They demanded, in addition, the creation of six lower people's courts whose function it would be to chastise local Kappists by confiscating their property.

8

In the meantime, a basic divergence had developed between the leaders of organized labor and the parties of the Weimar coalition. The general strike, these parties contended, had completely achieved its purpose—reestablishment of the Weimar system—and should therefore be terminated forthwith. But the trade unions felt otherwise. They wanted more than a mere return to the regime which they had rescued. They insisted on a number of sweeping reforms and indicated they would refuse to call off the strike or permit the Bauer government to resume office until their demands had been granted. They had their way. On March 20, 1920, the day the German government returned to Berlin, the three parties and the trade unions concluded the following nine-point pact: 1) The composition of new governments in Prussia and the Reich was to be determined only after agreement with the trade unions, which were to be accorded "a decisive voice in the formulation of economic and socio-political legislation." 2) All those who had participated in the putsch were to be immediately disarmed and punished. 3) Guilty persons were to be removed from all public administrative offices and from managerial posts in industrial establishments. Their places were to be taken by "trustworthy leaders." 4) Administrative reform "on a democratic basis" was to be instituted at once with the approval of the trade unions. 5) Existing social legislation was to be expanded, and new statutes, which would guarantee "complete economic and social equality" to the working classes, were to be enacted. A "liberal civil service law" was to be passed forthwith. 6) The socialization of those branches of the national economy "that are ripe for it on the basis of the recommendations of the Commission on Socialization" was to be initiated without delay. The Coal and Potash Syndicates were to be owned by the government. 7) All available foodstuffs were to be effectively controlled and, if necessary, seized. Profiteering was to be severely repressed. 8) "Associations of counterrevolutionary troops" were to be disbanded. Their duties were to be assigned to military organizations composed of "trustworthy republican elements of the population, particularly organized manual workers, clerical employees and civil servants. . . ." 9) Noske and the Prussian minister of the interior, Wolfgang Heine, who had likewise submitted his resignation, were to withdraw from public office.

The program laid down in this agreement was ambitious, to say the least. The first point was particularly arresting. Its effectuation would have made the trade unions the final authority on questions of economic and social policy. The administrative and managerial purge demanded in Point Three was likewise an objective of revolutionary proportions. Point Five, with its reference to "complete" equality in the economic and social spheres, suggested nothing less than a redistribution of the nation's wealth. This contrasted sharply with the relatively modest request put forward in Point Six, which in essence was merely a reaffirmation of the program advocated by the Social Democrats. Familiar, too, was the demand in Point Eight for the creation of a truly republican army. Had the agreement of March 20, 1920, been carried out, German democracy would have been placed on a much surer footing, and the subsequent history of the Reich might have followed a vastly different course. There was no lack of understanding of what the situation called for, of what had to be done to preserve the republic. But the requisite will, courage and leadership were conspicuously absent. Once again a golden opportunity was thrown away.

Announcement of the nine-point pact was accompanied by a proclamation from the trade unions declaring the general strike at an end. But the situation was suddenly complicated by the refusal of the Independents to sign the proclamation. They wanted, they said, to think the matter over before making up their minds. They were not sure that the time had come to call off the strike. The Communists assumed a more militant stand. They took issue with the authors of the proclamation, insisting that the strike should not be terminated until certain conditions had been fulfilled. These included the arming of the workers and the complete subjugation of the reactionary officers' clique. Swayed by the attitude of the Independents, most of the workers in the Berlin area refused to heed the back-to-work order. The trade-union leaders and their Social Democratic allies urged the Independents to put aside partisan considerations and come out four-square for the proclamation. The strike, they wailed, was being unnecessarily prolonged. The Independents countered with the contention that the nine-point agreement represented labor's minimum program. Further concessions, especially in the military realm, would have to be granted to insure the preservation of the republic. When Bauer stated his readiness to consider such concessions, the Independents declared themselves satisfied and agreed to support the proclamation. The Communists, however, persisted in their demand that the strike be continued. It was in the face of violent opposition from them that the workers of Berlin decided on March 23, 1920, to return to their jobs.

In the meantime, Noske's letter of resignation had been lying unanswered on the president's desk. For obvious reasons, Ebert was reluctant to dispense with the services of his hard-boiled minister of war. He was just as vulnerable as Noske to the charge of partiality to reactionary militarists and of excessive severity to radicals of the Left. Were he to get rid of Noske, he would, in a sense, be repudiating the policy of collaboration which he and Groener had inaugurated on November 10, 1918. Yet he, like Noske, was still convinced of the rightness of that policy. Ebert's position was therefore a painful one. But the pressure to which he was subjected was now too great to be resisted. On March 22, 1920, he finally gave in and accepted Noske's resignation. The Social Democratic party's choice for the vacated post was its chairman, Otto Wels. But he declined the honor, preferring the less arduous duties of a party functionary. With no other candidate of their own ready to hand, the Social Democrats acquiesced in the appointment of Otto Gessler, a member of the Democratic party. There was something grimly ironic about the substitution of Gessler for Noske. For the new minister of war promptly fell under the spell of the military. The generals found him a willing tool. Through him they acquired more and more influence in all matters pertaining to national defense. They used him to make themselves increasingly independent of parliamentary control. Gessler held this post during the greater part of the republic's abbreviated career: from March, 1920, until January, 1928. Under the cover which he provided, the military caste was able, with comparative impunity, to tighten its hold on the Reichswehr and thus make itself the strongest power in the state.

The resignation of Noske necessitated a further reshuffling of the cabinet. But this process ran afoul of insuperable difficulties, with the result that the entire ministry was forced to resign on March 26, 1920. Mindful of their decisive role in frustrating the Kapp putsch, the trade unions now came forward with the contention that one of their leaders should be made chancellor. But Carl Legien, head of the Free trade unions and organized labor's most powerful figure, declared that he was not interested. A similar attitude was expressed by Wissell, whose name had also been suggested by the trade unions. Thereupon Hermann Mueller was asked to form a new government. This he did on March 27. His cabinet, which was destined to be short-lived, consisted of Social Democrats, Democrats and Centrists. Resolution of the ministerial crisis in the Reich had its parallel in Prussia. There, too, the parties of the Weimar coalition collaborated to fashion a new government. This reshuffle brought to the fore two of the strongest personalities in the Social Democratic party: Otto Braun, who assumed the premiership, and Carl Severing, his choice for the post of minister of the interior. For years—in fact, until 1932, when they were both ousted by Chancellor Papen—Braun and Severing played a vital role in German political life. They were admired by their party comrades and respected by most of their adversaries.

On March 29, Mueller announced his program before the national assembly. Germany, he declared amid applause from the Left, was in need of a thorough house-cleaning. Her administrative system and her economic life would have to be democratized. This was in keeping with the government's firm resolve to fulfill the demands of the trade unions. Specific reforms were already being envisaged. These included a new law for the settlement of industrial disputes, more adequate provision for the victims of the war and the adoption of broadly conceived labor and civil service codes. Mueller talked at considerable length about the all-important subject of socialization. He pointed out that socialization of the electrical industry had been agreed to in principle and that government operation of the mining industry was being contemplated. Indeed, he went so far as to indicate that complete nationalization of the Coal and Potash Syndicates was only a matter of time. Gessler supplemented the chancellor's remarks by promising that the Kappists would be punished and that the Reichswehr would be reconstructed along democratic lines as soon as it had been purged of unreliable elements.

9

In most parts of Germany the collapse of the Kapp putsch had been followed by the restoration of public order. But the situation was very different in the Ruhr. Here the anti-Kapp strike staged by the workers had played into the hands of left-wing Utopians. These radicals were not content with checkmating the putschists. Their aim was social revolution, and to its accomplishment they dedicated themselves with fanatical zeal. They managed to obtain control of several important localities, including Essen, Duesseldorf, Muelheim, Elberfeld and Oberhausen. They organized a Red army which proved strong enough to force the withdrawal of the regular troops stationed in the area. They were quelled early in April, 1920, after a series of bloody encounters with the Reichswehr.

Chapter 13

GERMANY MOVES TOWARD THE RIGHT

I

THE disturbances in the Ruhr had a dramatic sequel. In the course of its operations against desperately resisting remnants of the Red army, the Reichswehr moved into the demilitarized zone. By way of reprisal, French troops proceeded on April 6, 1920, to occupy Frankfurt a. M., Darmstadt, Hanau and Dieburg. Still other localities were occupied during the next twenty-four hours. The commander-in-chief of the Allied armies of occupation in the Rhineland, General Degoutte, issued an explanatory proclamation. The German government, he charged, had yielded to the pressure of the "military party." It had ordered "a sudden offensive . . . against the working class of the Ruhr." In so doing, it had violated one of the most important provisions of the Versailles Treaty. The government of France was therefore compelled to intervene. Its action was not inspired by hostility to the working-class population of the Ruhr. Its sole purpose was to insure compliance with the terms of the treaty. Occupation of the newly overrun localities would be terminated as soon as the Reichswehr had evacuated the demilitarized zone.

The Mueller government reposed no trust in these assurances. It regarded the French action as a move designed not only to sever the occupied area from the rest of the country but to encourage particularist and separatist movements in the Catholic west and south of Germany. Such movements were of long standing, and of long standing, too, was France's desire to dismember the Reich. German suspicions were further aroused by the hypocritical attitude of French army leaders. They were, by and large, reactionary in their social outlook. But now, because it suited their purpose to do so, they decried the Reichswehr's punitive operations against the workers of the Ruhr. It all added up, in the eyes of Berlin, to a nefarious scheme that accorded with everything else French Germanophobes were attempting. The Mueller government minced no words. It denounced the French invasion as an irresponsible tampering with the peace of the world, as an unprovoked act of aggression, as a violation of the Treaty of Versailles, as an act of brutal militarism. Senegal Negroes, it lamented, were stationed in the University of Frankfurt and standing guard before the Goethe-House, one of Germany's most sacred cultural shrines. The British government strongly supported the German protest. Rather than risk alienating their all-important ally, the French decided to yield as gracefully as possible. But it was not until May 17, 1920, that the last French troops were withdrawn from the recently occupied zone.

Although on this question England and France had shown themselves to be on opposite sides of the fence, no such disagreement subsisted between them on current issues raised in connection with the disarming of Germany. They chafed at the Reich's slow-motion procedure in reducing its army to treaty strength. They were irked by the existence of the Free Corps and demanded the immediate dissolution of these formidable fighting units. One of their principal complaints had to do with the establishment of the so-called *Einwohnerwehr* or Citizens' Corps. These semi-military organizations had come into being in 1919. Their purpose was to preserve public order in areas which had been the scene of communist disturbances. They were predominantly conservative in character. Most of their members were middle-class people who lived in constant dread of the Bolshevist menace and needed little urging to take the law into their own hands. Their fear of communism was often coupled with antipathy to the republic and a pronounced sympathy for counterrevolutionary aims. This was above all true in Bavaria, where the Citizens' Corps were exceptionally numerous and militant. The existence of such organizations constituted a flagrant violation of the treaty. The Inter-Allied Commission of Control pointed this out in a note which demanded the immediate dissolution of the *Einwohnerwehr*. The note was published on April 7, 1920. The next day, Erich Koch, Germany's minister of the interior, brought the matter to the attention of the *Laender*. He asserted that the note was full of inaccuracies. Nevertheless, Germany had no choice but to desist from further representations. She was obliged to urge the states to facilitate prompt fulfillment of the commission's demand. At once there were loud protests from many sections of the country. The excitement was greatest in Bavaria. Here the reactionary elements had a field day. Striking a patriotic pose, they flayed the "Marxist" republic and its leaders. They adjured Kahr to defy Berlin. They argued that the Citizens' Corps were a bulwark against Bolshevism and must under no circumstances be sacrificed. Some of them went so far as to accuse the German government of planning to turn Bavaria over to the Communists. Kahr was delighted to make himself the champion of the *Einwohnerwehr*. A stanch monarchist and conservative, he enjoyed the prospect of a brisk encounter with the authorities in Berlin. He told them that the Allied ultimatum would have to be rejected. He buttressed this statement with the warning that Bavaria might withdraw from the Reich if the Citizens' Corps were abolished. A prolonged impasse followed. Not until June, 1921, did Kahr yield. Under pressure from his more moderate supporters, who feared the consequences of a head-on conflict with the Reich, he finally ordered the disarming of the *Einwohnerwehr*.

The Allied demand for dissolution of the Free Corps produced another grave crisis. The deadline set was May 31, 1920, and the German government did its best to comply. It did not underestimate the difficulty of its task. It was aware of the efforts being made by the leaders of the Free Corps to preserve their formations. It knew that they would actively resist the order to disband. In an attempt to intimidate them, it announced stern measures against all persons guilty of urging members of the Free Corps to defy the authorities. It prescribed similar penalties for anyone who organized or joined unauthorized military associations. Nevertheless, the order to disband proved impossible to carry out. The Free Corps went underground. For years they maintained a clandestine existence, deriding the law which decreed their demobilization. They specialized in conspiracy and murder. They were never in want of arms and ammunition. They had powerful friends who looked after their needs and stoked the flames of their hatred for the republic. Bavaria was their principal haven. It gave shelter to many of their most desperate characters. These included Captain Ehrhardt and the members of his brigade.

2

On June 1, 1920, Seeckt was appointed permanent chief of the army command. He was one of Germany's foremost soldiers. In his new capacity as head of the Reichswehr, he showed himself to be a first-class statesman and administrator. He was, in respect of family, background and training, a typical member of the Prussian military caste. But, thanks to extensive travel in Europe, his outlook and interests were far broader than those of most German officers. He possessed, to an extraordinary degree, the ability to size up people and make them do what he wanted. He was realistic almost to the point of cynicism. He took things as they came and hewed to the line of compromise whenever controversy impended. He kept his own counsel. Even his closest associates habitually referred to him as the "Sphinx." During the war he served, for a time, as Field Marshal Mackensen's chief of staff. In the autumn of 1917, he was made head of the Turkish general staff. This interlude enabled him to establish connections which were to prove extremely useful in later years. On his return to the Reich in 1918, he found no dearth of demand for his services. After acting as military adviser to the German peace delegation, he was entrusted with important work in connection with the reorganization of the armed forces. It was while he was so engaged that the Kapp putsch came along and removed the last barrier that stood between him and the highest military post in the land.

On June 3, 1920, in Seeckt's presence, the ranking officers of the Reichswehr took an oath of loyalty to the Weimar constitution. But it was not the republic they were thinking of when they took this oath. They were pledging allegiance to the German state, which they revered as the indestructible symbol and embodiment of power, as the uniquely perfect expression of the principle of authority. The democratic, humanitarian ideology which underlay the Weimar constitution was, in their eyes, alien to this conception of the state.

3

The national assembly had much unfinished business to dispose of when it resumed work after the Kapp putsch. One of its most urgent tasks was to determine the procedure to be followed in presidential elections. On May 4, 1920, it adopted the following plan: The candidate receiving a majority of the votes was to be declared elected. If, however, no one obtained a majority on the first ballot, there was to be a run-off contest between the two highest candidates. Actually, this law was never put into practice. In March, 1925, shortly before the presidential election necessitated by the death of Ebert, a substitute measure was enacted. It, too, specified that there was to be a second balloting if no candidate emerged with a majority. But under the new arrangement, the contest at this stage was not to be confined to the two highest competitors. All the candidates further down on the list, and new ones as well, were to be eligible to participate in the race. And the individual receiving the largest number of votes, regardless of whether it was a majority, was to be declared president of the Reich.

The national assembly held its last session on May 21, 1920. Its disappearance evoked few regrets. The many solid achievements to which it could point with pride were lost sight of. Most Germans preferred to dwell on its mistakes and shortcomings. They refused to take into account the difficulties under which it had labored. The sourness of their mood was enhanced by a combination of economic ills. Depreciation of the currency was already under way, and it was accompanied by a sharp rise in the cost of living. Particularly alarming was the recent boost in the price of bread. Unemployment was increasing. The bad news was not confined to the home front. Almost daily the nation received reminders of its low estate in the realm of foreign affairs. Virtually unnoticed, therefore, went the national assembly's eleventh-hour attempts to deal with such matters as education for the masses, the mediation of industrial disputes and the reorganization of the country's railway administration. Quietly, without fanfare and ceremony, it voted itself out of existence.

The election campaign which followed differed markedly from the last. In January, 1919, the champions of the republic had been on the march. Their cause had stood at the zenith of its popularity. Now they were on the defensive. The nation blamed them for all its troubles: the harsh peace terms, the subsequent reverses of German diplomacy, the steadily deteriorating economic situation. Discontent and disillusionment were particularly rife among the middle classes. The Treaty of Versailles had dealt the first blow to their faith in the existing political order. It was followed by the fall of the mark and the spread of lawlessness at home. The government seemed incapable of coping with these evils. The impression grew that financial chaos and political instability were the inescapable consequences of popular rule. It is therefore hardly surprising that large sections of the German bourgeoisie turned against the republic.

The middle classes were not the only ones to desert the Weimar regime. A very considerable segment of the proletariat decided to transfer its allegiance to the Independents. These workers railed against the government's failure to alleviate the hardships of the poorer classes. They decried its harsh treatment of left-wing radicals and its unwillingness to crack down on avowed enemies of the revolution. But their principal complaint was the lack of progress toward social-ization. For this they blamed the Social Democratic party, which until now they had faithfully supported. As Friedrich Stampfer so aptly puts it in his *Die vierzehn Jahre der ersten deutschen Republik,* "The Weimar coalition was a candle that burned at both ends."

The excellent prospects of the Independents were scarcely marred by the decision of their rivals on the extreme Left to participate in the elections. The Communists were as yet organizationally too weak to capitalize on the growing disaffection among the workers. But they were not unduly disturbed; they looked ahead to better times. The rough treatment they had received at the hands of the authorities and the failure of successive left-wing uprisings in 1919 led them to revise their strategy. They were now convinced that putschism would get them nowhere. They saw, too, that their boycott of the elections to the national assembly had been a mistake. They were prepared, for the next few years, at any rate, to concentrate on boring-from-within tactics. They would make use of all agencies and groups that might prove useful to their cause. They would participate actively in the work of the Reichstag and of other public bodies. They would in-sinuate themselves into the trade unions and the factory councils with the object of controlling them eventually. The masses would gradually be readied for the day of revolution. The ideas vainly espoused by Rosa Luxemburg shortly before her death were henceforth to be the party's guiding principles.

The elections of June 6, 1920, proved that the German republic, after only a year and a half of existence, was losing ground at an alarming rate thanks to foreign intransigence and domestic tensions. The most devastating setback was sustained by the Democratic party. It emerged with only 2,202,334 votes (its total in January, 1919, was 5,653,618), and its parliamentary representation dropped from seventy-four to forty-five. This marked the beginning of a tailspin for middle-class liberal-ism which continued almost uninterruptedly until the extinction of the republic. Since Allied maltreatment of Germany played so large a part in initiating this tailspin, it was only natural that the beneficiaries should be the two chauvinistic groups on the Right. Between them they captured practically all the malcontents in the Democratic camp. The Nationalists increased their popular following from 2,873,523 to 3,736,778 and elected sixty-six deputies as compared with forty-two in the national assembly. Far more spectacular were the gains scored by the People's party. Whereas in January, 1919, it had polled only 1,633,-000 votes, it emerged on this occasion with 3,606,316; and the number of its successful candidatures jumped from twenty-two to sixty-two. Next to the Democrats, the elections' most serious casualty was the Social Democratic party. Its popular vote fell from 11,466,416 to 5,614,-456. It lost fifty-one seats but remained, with 112, by far the largest parliamentary group. Thanks to these wholesale defections from the Social Democratic banner, the Independents became the nation's second-strongest party. They attracted 4,895,317 supporters, more than double the number recorded in January, 1919, while their parliamentary representation rose from twenty-two to eighty-one. The Communists' first bid for popular favor proved a complete fiasco. They polled 441,995 votes and wound up with exactly two seats. They remained, nonetheless, a power to be reckoned with because of their close relations with left-wingers in the camp of the Independents. The Catholic Center came out of the contest appreciably weakened. But its losses were light compared to those suffered by the other members of the Weimar coalition. The combined vote of the Center and the Bavarian People's party, which was now operating independently, was 1,268,769 less than the total amassed in 1919. Of greater immediate importance was the fact that the eighteen deputies elected by the Bavarian People's party were not at the disposal of the Center. The latter had to remain content with sixty-eight seats, but they sufficed to give it a strategic position in the parliamentary arena.

The elections of 1920 were a milestone in the history of the republic. They reflected a trend that was to dominate German politics during the next few years. The swing to the Right placed new opportunities within the reach of the Nationalists and the People's party. It enabled them to play a major role in the struggles that were to determine the inner evolution of the Reich. Of far-reaching significance in this connection were the evanescent character of middle-class liberalism, the weakened position of the Social Democrats and the persistence of disunity in the ranks of the nation's proletariat. The composition of the new Reichstag boded ill for the future of German parliamentarism. The coexistence of a formidable conservative bloc, a depleted middle-of-the-road coalition and a greatly strengthened radical contingent gave rise to apprehensions that were not confined to chronic pessimists.

4

As a result of the elections, the parties of the Weimar coalition lost their majority in parliament. They now controlled only 225 seats out of a total of 466. Under the circumstances, Chancellor Hermann Mueller had no choice but to resign. This he did on June 8, 1920. But as the spokesman of the party that was still the nation's largest, he was asked by Ebert to attempt the formation of a new cabinet. Mueller gladly complied because he knew how much was at stake. The impressive comeback registered by the parties of the Right was an unmistakable omen. Would those who had the most to gain from the preservation of democratic institutions heed the handwriting on the wall? Would they bury past differences and stand shoulder to shoulder in the face of this new threat? The answer lay with the Independents. Till now they had categorically refused to co-operate with the non-socialist parties. If they persisted in this attitude, they would force upon the country a cabinet far more conservative than any of its predecessors. If, however, they consented to make common cause with the parties of the Weimar coalition, a socialist-liberal-Catholic majority would be assured; and those who were either openly hostile or lukewarm to the republic would continue to remain outside the government. Mueller stated the issue clearly when he invited the Independents to join the Social Democrats, the Democrats and the Centrists in forming a new cabinet. He pointed out that only a coalition government that had been strengthened by the addition of Leftist elements could defend the republican system against attacks from the Right, preserve the eight-hour day and all the other social gains of the revolution, and carry out a foreign policy that was in harmony with the democratic and pacifist sentiments of the great majority of the German people.

The Independents spurned this appeal. With doctrinaire stubbornness they clung to their dogma of class war. They could not, they said, enter a coalition government which sought to reestablish the "capitalist economy of exploitation," which was reviving and strengthening militarism in order to suppress the proletariat. Were they to join such a government, they would be lending support to the counterrevolutionary program; they would be betraying the faith of the masses who had voted for them in order that they might continue to fight for the destruction of "capitalist-militarist class rule." Should the further progress of the revolution necessitate the formation of a purely socialist government, the Independents would join it, but on the following conditions: they must be given more than half of the ministerial posts, and their program must be made the foundation of cabinet policy.

On receipt of the Independents' reply, Mueller informed Ebert that his efforts had proved futile. Heinze, who represented the People's party in these negotiations, was asked to canvass the situation. He immediately invited the Social Democrats to discuss with him the possibility of a *mariage de convenance* between his followers and the Weimar coalition. It was now the turn of the Social Democrats to say no. They notified Heinze that they could not participate in any government which contained Rightist elements. They seized this opportunity to censure the attitude of the Independents. The latter, they charged, had made themselves responsible for a state of affairs that could only lead to the formation of a purely bourgeois ministry.

The crisis was finally terminated when Konstantin Fehrenbach, one of the most respected members of the Center, assumed the chancellorship. This occurred on June 25, 1920. Inasmuch as Fehrenbach had agreed to include members of the People's party in his cabinet, the Social Democrats refused to join it. But they assured the new chancellor that they would tolerate his government so long as it did nothing to merit their displeasure. The Democrats, for their part, agreed to collaborate with the People's party on one condition: the Fehrenbach cabinet must accept the Weimar constitution as the cornerstone of its program. Would the People's party agree to this? The answer was largely up to Stresemann. Although, with characteristic realism, he had bowed to the inevitable when the Weimar system came into being, he had never concealed his monarchist predilections. But he was now convinced that the interests of big business, which his party was pledged to protect and promote, could prosper in a republic that disavowed its revolutionary antecedents and moved steadily to the Right. A conservative democracy in which radical economic experiments were eschewed and property rights respected was entirely acceptable to Stresemann and to most of his friends. Such a democracy was already in process of formation. To make sure that the process continued in spite of pressure from the Left, the People's party would have to join other bourgeois groups in buttressing the existing regime. Accordingly, Stresemann assented to the condition laid down by the Democrats. The parties represented in the Fehrenbach cabinet issued a joint statement announcing their resolve to work for the reconstruction of Germany on the basis of the Weimar constitution. They promised to combat all attempts to overthrow the republic. They declared themselves opposed to class rule and class privileges. They said they wanted harmony and understanding between the various layers of German society. The manifesto closed with an appeal to the Reichswehr and the bureaucracy. Upon them, it insisted, rested the obligation of supporting the government and the constitution.

The advent of the Fehrenbach cabinet opened a new chapter in the annals of the German republic. Ever since November 9, 1918, the Social Democratic party had been the dominant element in successive governments. Throughout this period it had, without interruption, provided leadership and assumed responsibility. But now, less than two years after the proclamation of the republic, it found itself stripped of its commanding position and compelled to see the leadership of the nation pass into other hands. It was neither in the government nor against it. It disapproved the inclusion of the People's party but refused to assume an attitude of opposition lest, by so doing, it should jeopardize the very existence of the republic. The ambiguity of its position stemmed logically from the confusion which all along had marked its thinking about ultimate objectives. The predicament into which it had maneuvered itself could not fail to affect adversely the fortunes of the democratic cause in Germany. However, the damage was in part offset by the behavior of Stresemann and his political associates. The People's party had some of the country's best brains and the resources of heavy industry at its disposal. Its new attitude toward the republic was therefore of the utmost importance. The sincerity of this attitude was still open to question, but its mere enunciation gave fresh hope and encouragement to all those who believed that the well-being of Germany was bound up with the preservation of popular rule. As a matter of fact, the People's party did keep its word. In spite of pressure from its right-wing elements, it drew ever closer to the Weimar regime. True, it remained obdurately conservative on economic and social questions. In the political sphere, however, its conduct was marked by respect for the constitution. For this Stresemann was mainly responsible. Thanks to a remarkable capacity for growth and adaptation, he developed a progressively more liberal outlook and became a faithful servant of the republic. It was only after his death that the right-wingers regained their ascendancy over the party and gradually led it back into the authoritarian fold.

Fehrenbach belonged to the left wing of the Catholic Center. He was forward-looking, a genuine republican and sincerely friendly to labor. He declared that he would continue the foreign policy inaugurated by his Social Democratic predecessors. He promised to reorganize the Reichswehr in such a way as to make it a more faithful instrument of the popular will. The existing laws on socialization would be loyally enforced and new ones submitted for consideration. Attention would be given to the formulation of a comprehensive scheme of unemployment insurance; indeed, steps were already being taken to secure appropriate legislative action. It was the purpose of his cabinet, Fehrenbach asserted, to govern with and not against the working classes. The co-operation of all citizens, regardless of occupation, was imperative. The chancellor's plea for support had one unexpected and sensational result: it elicited from Nationalist spokesmen a declaration to the effect that their party accepted the Weimar constitution. The honesty of this declaration was questionable, to say the least; and the subsequent actions of the party more than justified the skepticism with which this belated conversion to democratic principles was generally received. But one thing was clear: the Nationalists had come to the conclusion that the republic, barring unforeseen developments, was likely to survive for the time being. This being so, they decided that they would have to work for their antirepublican objectives within the framework of the existing regime.

Fehrenbach's performance fell far short of his promises. The Reichswehr was purged of some of its antirepublican elements, but the much discussed democratization of the army was never effectuated. The nation's military forces were permitted to remain under the control of men whose outlook was distinctly authoritarian. Action on the unemployment insurance bill was postponed. The Commission on Socialization, which had met right after the collapse of the Kapp putsch, produced two proposals. One was the work of those members of the commission who favored full socialization. The other came from the exponents of a planned economy. The People's party, faithful to the interests of big business, blocked action on both proposals. Fehrenbach had declared, shortly after taking office, that a permanent Economic Council of the Reich would be set up. This pledge was never fulfilled. What had been heralded as a significant experiment in economic democracy was thus denied an opportunity to demonstrate its possibilities. At the same time, the formation of giant industrial combines went on apace. The principal beneficiary of this process was Stinnes. He became, during the early 1920s, the most powerful figure in German economic life.

5

The Independents were heartened by their recent success at the polls. They looked forward to the time, which they thought not far distant, when they would be able to obtain complete ascendancy over the labor movement in Germany. Within the party itself, the revolutionary left wing was now firmly in the saddle. Sovietism and the dictatorship of the proletariat, to be achieved by force if necessary, were proclaimed as the paramount objectives. Only when the work of socialization had been completed and rendered safe for all time would the dictatorship be discontinued. Enthusiasm for Soviet Russia ran high. A powerful section of the party, led by Daeumig, went so far as to demand immediate affiliation with the Third International. But the majority of the party, though friendly in principle to the idea, agreed only to authorize negotiations with the Moscow agency. It refused to commit itself until it knew the conditions of admission to the Comintern. Moscow's terms proved hard. Nevertheless, Daeumig and his friends persisted in their demand. The right wing of the party took issue with them, and a veritable cat-and-dog fight ensued. The showdown occurred at the party congress in Halle in October, 1920. The left-wingers, who controlled a majority of the delegates, sided with Daeumig and early in December combined with the Communists to form the United Communist party of Germany. The right wing endeavored to carry on as before and maintained the Independent Social Democratic party as a separate political group. Between it and the Social Democrats a gradual rapprochement took place. This foreshadowed a final regrouping of the proletarian forces in Germany in accordance with the only distinction that now made any sense, the distinction between Social Democrats and Communists.

The leaders of the United Communist party were determined to avoid foolhardy adventures. In keeping with the strategy formulated by Bolshevist spokesmen before the elections of 1920, they insisted that the signal for an armed uprising ought not to be given until conditions in the country were propitious for such a move. But events beyond their control suddenly provoked them into taking the very opposite line. In March, 1921, a group of miners working in the Mansfeld district took up arms against police detachments sent in to establish order. Because the Communist party had not instigated the rising, it could easily have washed its hands of the entire affair. Instead, it decided that the miners must not be left in the lurch. It issued a call for a general strike in the hope that the working masses of the country would make common cause with the rebels. But the proletariat failed to bestir itself. The uprising in Mansfeld and in the surrounding industrial districts proved a miserable fiasco. Moscow, convinced that world revolution was for the time being an impossibility, advised the German Communists to revert to peaceful methods and to continue to make the greatest possible use of the parliamentary machinery of the state. This advice the party, somewhat deflated by its recent discomfiture, was glad to heed.

Chapter 14

FOREIGN AFFAIRS: REPARATION, UPPER SILESIA AND RAPALLO

I

ON APRIL 27, 1921, the Reparation Commission discharged the duty which had been assigned to it by the Treaty of Versailles. It informed the Germans that their reparation bill amounted to 132 billion gold marks. This was far in excess of what the Germans felt they were capable of paying, but their efforts to secure concessions proved utterly futile. Convinced that there was nothing more it could do, the Fehrenbach cabinet resigned on May 4. On the following day, while the Reich was still without a government, the Allies made known their position in a stiffly worded ultimatum. They gave Germany six days to announce her unconditional acceptance of the figure fixed by the Reparation Commission. Failure to do so, they warned, would be followed by Allied occupation of the Ruhr. Germany's political leaders had to think hard and act quickly. They were, of course, agreed that the Reich would never be able to pay the sum demanded. But opinions differed as to how to meet the immediate situation. The Nationalists, putting party advantage before the country's welfare, took the easy patriotic line. They declared themselves unwilling to saddle Germany with so unbearable a burden. The People's party was divided. The Social Democrats and the Center were at one in their conviction that the threat of invasion left Germany no choice but to capitulate. They feared that refusal to accept the reparation settlement would give the foreign enemies of the Reich a pretext for seizing still more German territory and inflicting even greater suffering upon the German people. The Democrats, after some hesitation, swung round to this point of view. The parties of the Weimar coalition now hurried to renew their partnership. They formed a cabinet which took office on May 10, 1921. It was headed by Josef Wirth, one of the most admirable political figures of the Weimar period. Like Fehrenbach, Wirth belonged to the left wing of the Center. He was a stanch republican and an enthusiastic exponent of social reform. He was popular in working-class circles; his warmest admirers included Social Democrats and even Independents. Within his own party, however, he had plenty of trouble. He found himself almost constantly at loggerheads with the right-wingers. These conservatives, many of whom were men of wealth and social position, disliked Wirth's wholehearted devotion to the interests of the lower classes. They were bitterly anti-Marxist and wished to see the Center take up an attitude of uncompromising opposition to the Social Democrats. Many and serious were the difficulties which dogged Wirth while he held the chancellorship. But the principal weakness of his position as head of the government was his inability to keep his reactionary confrères in line.

With the Allied ultimatum due to expire very shortly, Wirth had no time to lose. On the day his cabinet took office, he appeared before the Reichstag to urge acceptance of the settlement laid down by the Reparation Commission. Rejection of the ultimatum, he warned, would mean the destruction of Germany. With the aid of the Independents, who agreed that the Reich had no choice but to yield, Wirth obtained a majority. He promptly informed the Allies that Germany was prepared to do their bidding. This episode is instructive. Throughout the history of the republic, the parties identified with the Weimar regime repeatedly assumed responsibility for unpopular decisions forced upon the country by the Allies. The opponents of the republic, on the other hand, were careful to have nothing to do with the making of such decisions. They posed as incorruptible patriots who refused to acquiesce in any tampering with German interests. As a consequence, they enjoyed enormous advantages in the give-and-take of propagandist warfare.

2

Next to Wirth himself, the outstanding personality of the new cabinet was Walther Rathenau, who had been put in charge of the ministry for reconstruction. Wirth and Rathenau saw eye to eye on most of the basic issues of the day. This was especially true in regard to questions of foreign policy. The two men were at one in their belief that Germany could not improve her position by pursuing a policy of resistance. They held that the only way to attenuate her difficulties was to offer proof of her good faith. She would have to convince her former enemies that she no longer merited their hostility. Moreover, by making an honest effort to live up to her obligations, she would demonstrate beyond the shadow of a doubt the utter impossibility of carrying out the terms of the reparation settlement. The important thing, according to Wirth and Rathenau, was to bring about a better all-around understanding of the true state of affairs. The Allies believed that Germany could pay the sum demanded of her. What they questioned was her willingness to do so. The German people, on the other hand, were inclined to object to paying anything at all because they took too black a view of their own situation. The purpose of the policy of fulfillment advocated by Wirth and Rathenau was to win the good will of the Allies by making them see the limits of Germany's capacity to pay, to instill a healthier attitude in the German people by restoring their confidence in themselves and to prepare the way ultimately for a comprehensive understanding between the Reich and the victors of 1918.

The opposition to the policy of fulfillment was led by the Nationalists. They sought to exploit for their own political purposes the universal resentment against the onerous terms imposed by the Allies. For the policy of fulfillment and appeasement the Nationalists wished to substitute resistance and intransigence. In their attacks on the government they stopped at nothing. Because Rathenau was a Jew and hence more vulnerable than the other members of the cabinet, they concentrated much of their fire upon him. They strove to drive him from office by impugning his personal integrity and his patriotism. Anti-Semitism was their most potent weapon, and they used it unsparingly. Wirth stood loyally by his friend. He extolled Rathenau as a man of impeccable patriotism who was honestly attempting to do what was best for his country. He tried to shame the Nationalists into changing their tactics. His pleas and admonitions were of no avail.

The Nationalists were ever ready to resort to slander and vituperation in an effort to discredit their enemies. But they shrank from violence. Assassins they themselves could not be. But there were others, for the most part youthful fanatics, who were prepared to translate verbal attacks on leading republicans into a program of direct action. What followed was a veritable reign of terror against all individuals who had had anything to do with the signing of the peace,

who stood out in the liberal and socialist camps, or who were suspected of giving information to the Inter-Allied Commissions of
Control. On June 10, 1921, Karl Gareis, the leader of the Bavarian
Independents and an outspoken opponent of the illegal semi-military
associations maintained by right-wing extremists, was murdered in
Munich. A month later, Captain Ehrhardt and several members of
his brigade founded a secret society known as "Organization C." The
purposes of the group were three in number: 1) to combat the "anti-
national" Weimar constitution; 2) to set up secret Vehm tribunals
which would order the execution of "traitors"; and 3) to liquidate
parliamentarism, Social Democrats and Jews. Its first important victim
was Erzberger. The two men who murdered him on August 26, 1921,
had taken part in the Kapp putsch. Like so many other participants
in that ill-starred affair, they had found a friendly haven in Bavaria.
As members of "Organization C," they operated under the direction
of Captain Manfred von Killinger, likewise a former Kappist. The
murderers managed to escape, but Killinger and six other members of
"Organization C" were apprehended and charged with complicity in
the crime.

The assassination of Erzberger evoked a tremendous outcry in Germany. Much of this wrath converged on the Bavarian government,
which was assailed for its readiness to give protection to reactionary
gunmen. Feeling against Kahr and his ministerial colleagues mounted
sharply when it was learned that the murderers had set out from
Munich and had subsequently passed through the city in their precipitate flight to Hungary. The Nationalists, who were morally
responsible for the crime, unabashedly joined the other parties in de-
ploring it. Backed by an aroused public opinion, the German government bestirred itself. On August 29, it promulgated a decree designed
to discourage incitement to acts of violence against republican leaders.
But this measure proved utterly inadequate. The Nationalists resumed
their campaign of hate. Bavaria defied the wishes of the national government and refused to take action against the right-wing extremists
who continued to enjoy her hospitality. It was a foregone conclusion
that further outrages would be committed. However, the incident was
not entirely without beneficent issue: it created a situation which forced
Kahr to resign. On September 21, 1921, he was succeeded as Bavarian
premier by Count Hugo Lerchenfeld, a man of moderate outlook who
made no secret of his intention to support the Wirth cabinet.

3

The plebiscite which was to decide the fate of Upper Silesia took place on March 20, 1921. 707,122 persons voted for remaining with Germany, while only 433,514 indicated a preference for Polish rule. Berlin at once took the position that there could no longer be any question of Germany's right to retain the province. It insisted, too, that Germany must be permitted to keep all of Upper Silesia, since the area was an economic unit and would suffer heavily from dismemberment. Furthermore, German capital and German engineering had developed Upper Silesia's rich natural resources, and the industrial brains in the region were definitely German. In this connection the Reich was wont to remind the world of the Poles' reputation for inefficiency, a reputation which Lloyd George had in mind when he remarked that giving Upper Silesia to the Poles was equivalent to giving a clock to a monkey. Backed, as usual, by the French, the Poles sharply contested Germany's demand. They insisted on getting all the localities which had voted for Poland. Of the total number of communes in Upper Silesia, 699, for the most part rural, contained pro-Polish majorities, while 754 were preponderantly pro-German. It was finally decided to divide the region on the basis of the distribution of the vote. The inter-Allied commission in charge of the matter now undertook the arduous and thankless task of drawing a boundary in accordance with that decision. Its labors proved futile. The French members favored a line which would have delighted the Poles but which would have had little recognizable relationship with the outcome of the plebiscite. The British members, whose sympathies were patently pro-German, favored an award which would have gone far toward meeting the expectations of the Reich. The Italians discreetly took a middle position.

The thorny issue was passed on to the League of Nations. After procrastinating a bit, the Council of the League decided to accept the report of a special committee appointed to study the question. The recommendations of this committee advised a division of Upper Silesia that was palpably in disaccord with the outcome of the plebiscite. On October 20, 1921, the Reich was notified that Poland was to receive a little less than half of the province. This section contained 350,000 Germans. But even more important was the fact that it contained most of Upper Silesia's mines, mills and furnaces. This was a crippling blow to German economy, and the Wirth cabinet promptly resigned.

In so doing, it gave expression to the indignation which swept the
country when the award was made known. In his letter of resignation,
Wirth pointed out that his government had honestly sought to effect
an improvement in Germany's relations with the Allies. It had demonstrated its willingness to do what it could to fulfill the terms of the
treaty. It had consented to assume very heavy obligations in the hope
of a just solution of the Upper Silesian question. This hope had been
cruelly disappointed. The Allies had dictated a settlement which
robbed Germany of something that was rightfully hers. It would now
be more difficult to continue the policy of fulfillment. Consequently,
the cabinet had decided to withdraw. Ebert asked Wirth to form a
new government. The Centrist leader complied, and so another cabinet representing the parties of the Weimar coalition came into being.
A few months later, on January 31, 1922, Wirth appointed Rathenau
foreign minister. That assumption of this post would lead to an intensification of the campaign against him Rathenau knew very well.
As a matter of fact, his friends took it upon themselves to warn him
that his life would be in danger. But he refused to be dissuaded. He
accepted Wirth's invitation because he believed that the country needed
his services.

4

From the moment he assumed his new responsibilities, Rathenau
found himself called upon to make a decision of far-reaching importance. The question at issue had to do with the advantages of an
eastern as opposed to a western orientation of German foreign policy.
This matter had been the subject of continuous debate ever since the
signing of the Treaty of Versailles. The Social Democrats and the
moderate bourgeois groups favored a western orientation. Left-wing
radicals, as was to be expected, demanded a rapprochement with
Soviet Russia. And—to prove once again the dictum that politics
makes strange bedfellows—they were supported on this issue by a considerable section of the Nationalist party and by outstanding representatives of the military caste. In urging closer relations with Russia,
these Junker aristocrats and old-line generals went on the assumption,
which was by no means confined to them, that Germany's main effort
must be directed toward an eventual squaring of accounts with France.

Seeckt headed the advocates of an eastern orientation. France, he
maintained, was pursuing toward the Reich a policy of extermination.
All attempts to reach an understanding with her were therefore bound

to fail. Under the circumstances, another Franco-German war was inevitable. So much for the situation in the west. Things were vastly different in the east. There, Seeckt pointed out, Germany and Russia had a common aim: the extinction of Poland. They were both interested in restoring the frontier of 1914. The Russians loomed as potential allies. In her dealings with them, Germany must act accordingly. She must do what she could to strengthen them, for by so doing she would strengthen herself. She must help them develop their armament industries in order to obtain, for future use, adequate sources of war material—especially of the kind denied her by the Treaty of Versailles. Moreover, a friendly Russia would enable Germany to withstand blockade and avoid having to fight on two fronts.

Seeckt was convinced that the rapprochement with Russia would have to begin in the economic sphere. A political rapprochement would follow. And ultimately, he hoped, relations between the two countries would take the form of an out-and-out military alliance. For the time being, of course, Germany would be in no position to resist the French actively. She would have to content herself with preparations for an eventual resumption of the struggle. When the right moment came, and with Russia as a friend and ally, she would be able to crush her traditional foe and regain her position as a world power. According to Seeckt, Germany and Russia would constitute an unbeatable combination. He warned that they must never again make the mistake of fighting each other. Those who sought to build a wall between them were only serving the interests of Germany's enemies. Seeckt detested Bolshevism, but he did not permit his personal feelings to blur his perception of Russia's usefulness as an ally. Unlike a great many of his countrymen, he did not believe that the Reich would become Bolshevized if it went in for a policy of close collaboration with Moscow. Germany, he was sure, would be able to preserve her own institutions and way of life while working with Russia for purely external ends.

In keeping with his conviction that an economic rapprochement would have to come first, Seeckt gave his blessing to the Russo-German commercial treaty concluded in the spring of 1921. At the close of the following September, secret negotiations were inaugurated with Leonid Krassin, head of the Russian trade delegation. The purpose of these negotiations was to push, with German aid, the expansion of Russia's war industries. Seeckt, at the express wish of the Russians, who evidently decided he was one man they could trust, personally conducted the negotiations. He never lost sight of his paramount objective: a military understanding with Moscow. The kind of quid pro quo the Reich would be expected to offer was not difficult to divine. The Russians manifested a great and sustained interest in the development of the Reichswehr. They hoped, quite evidently, for German assistance in organizing and training their officers' corps.

Seeckt had to know in advance that the German government would co-operate fully in effecting closer relations with Russia. He got the assurances he wanted. Of particular significance was the attitude of Baron Adolf von Maltzan, head of the East European division of the German foreign office. Maltzan, like Seeckt, was all for an understanding with Russia. The general found him an unfailing and ardent collaborator. Somewhat more tempered but nevertheless firm support for Seeckt's position came from Wirth. The latter was disturbed by the apparent futility of trying to extract concessions from the western powers. He therefore agreed that the Reich would be well advised to explore other possibilities. With Wirth and Maltzan on his side, Seeckt was well fortified. Rathenau remained to be dealt with. He had no excess of enthusiasm for the general's proposals, but he agreed nonetheless to support them. He, too, could not blink the fact that the policy of fulfillment and appeasement had so far proved barren. He conceded that Germany would have to try other ways of improving her international position while continuing to show a conciliatory and accommodating spirit in her dealings with London and Paris. Moreover, as a representative of big business, he appreciated the enormous economic advantages which might flow from a rapprochement with Russia. Finally, he figured that a Russo-German accord might lead to the diplomatic isolation of France, which at the moment was at loggerheads with Great Britain.

In April, 1922, Wirth and Rathenau went to Genoa to attend an international economic conference organized by the British government. In near-by Rapallo, on the sixteenth of that month, they concluded a treaty of friendship with Georghy Chicherin, the Soviet foreign minister. The signatories agreed to reestablish normal diplomatic and consular relations. They likewise agreed to a mutual renunciation of reparation claims. The Reich consented to waive indemnification for losses sustained by German subjects as a result of the abolition of private property in Russia. Eveything possible was to be done to facilitate Russo-German trade. The signing of this pact was, of course, welcomed by Seeckt, but, ironically enough, it took place without his knowledge. The Treaty of Rapallo came as very unpleasant surprise to France and Great Britain. Their first reaction was a compound of anger and fear. They professed to see in this accord between Europe's principal outcasts a menace to the Continental status quo. The French were particularly bitter, and they voiced their objections in no uncertain terms. For most Germans, this was a great and exciting moment. They were literally thrilled by the news of what had happened at Rapallo. They applauded the signing of the treaty as the beginning of a new era of opportunity for German foreign policy. They were delighted to see their country terminate its diplomatic isolation and thereby strengthen its bargaining position vis-à-vis France and Great Britain. In their opinion, the pact with Russia meant that Germany was about to pursue an independent and dynamic course abroad. She was climbing back to a position of prestige and authority among the nations of Europe.

Leading spokesmen for the Social Democratic party did not join in the general chorus of approval. The provocative and theatrical manner in which the treaty had been sprung on the Genoa conference irked them. Besides, they feared that the Russians would now be able to flood the country with Bolshevist propaganda and play havoc with the German trade unions. But that was not all. They contended that Germany's efforts to win the good will of the rest of the world, to prove the genuineness of her desire to fulfill her international obligations and achieve an understanding with her former enemies, had suffered a staggering blow. They even had visions of Allied reprisals. Both Wirth and Rathenau shared this uneasiness regarding the reaction of other countries; they, too, did not rule out the possibility of retaliation by the French. Their fears proved groundless. So much, however, was certain: the Treaty of Rapallo greatly strengthened the position of Premier Poincaré and his Germanophobe followers in France. These intransigent foes of the Reich could now say: "We told you so. The Germans are not to be trusted. They have but one thought: revenge. They are already planning to start another war. In self-defense, the Allies must insist on rigid enforcement of the Treaty of Versailles." This state of mind was soon to have tragic consequences for Germany in connection with reparation.

5

Shortly after the signing of the Treaty of Rapallo, Seeckt and the Russian general staff concluded a secret agreement that was of great significance for the subsequent development of the Reichswehr and the Red Army. Under the terms of the Treaty of Versailles, Germany was forbidden to have tanks and military airplanes. No amount of study in officers' training schools could take the place of actual experience in the use of these indispensable weapons of modern warfare. In the opinion of Seeckt and his associates, Russia, Germany's friend and future ally, was ideally suited to provide German specialists with an opportunity to acquire such experience. The agreement between the Reichswehr command and the Soviet military leaders was strictly a mutual affair. In return for giving Seeckt what he wanted, the Russians were to receive a stipulated sum annually. In addition, their army was to be trained by German experts. These arrangements, which remained in effect for years, worked out very well for the U.S.S.R. The value of German instruction has been demonstrated by the showing of Stalin's armies in World War II. The Reichswehr likewise profited enormously. It was granted extensive training privileges within the framework of the Soviet war machine. It set up tank and artillery units which were attached to the Red Army but which carried on under German direction. It maintained its own military aviation schools. In Soviet factories, far from the probing gaze of the Inter-Allied Commission of Control, German armament firms experimented with the manufacture of airplanes, tanks, heavy guns and poisonous gas. Obviously, all this could not begin to make up for the limitations, as regards matériel, which the Treaty of Versailles imposed. But it did facilitate, after Hitler's advent, the transition to all-out rearmament.

Seeckt was a brilliant and indefatigable organizer. His job as head of the Reich's army was to make bricks without straw. What he managed to accomplish under admittedly difficult conditions evoked fervid praise abroad as well as at home. The Reichswehr was hopelessly inferior in numbers and equipment to the armies of even such countries as Poland and Czechoslovakia. But it possessed extraordinary mobility and was attuned to a fluid conception of strategy. The training it received was probably the best in Europe. In terms of per capita cost, it was the most expensive thing of its kind in the world. Seeckt stressed the development of initiative in the individual soldier. Each member of the army was to be regarded as a potential leader, as a future officer who would come into his own after the treaty limitations had been removed and conscription introduced. The Reichswehr, Seeckt insisted, must be kept out of politics and politics out of the Reichswehr. Strict enforcement of this precept was necessary in the interest of maximum efficiency. He had little regard for the Free Corps because they lacked discipline, dabbled in politics and tended to follow individual leaders. In spite of this desire to keep the army free of political entanglements, Seeckt made certain political values the basis of his program. Specifically, he sought to imbue the Reichswehr with the spirit and traditions of the old imperial army. He packed the officers' corps with young men from the so-called better families. They accepted with enthusiasm the twin principles of authority and hierarchy. There was little room in their minds, and even less in their hearts, for the ideology of Weimar.

Chapter 15

ADOLF HITLER AND THE BEGINNINGS
OF NATIONAL SOCIALISM

I

THE months which followed the assassination of Erzberger were a period of mounting violence against republican leaders. Youthful fanatics, incited by the propaganda of the Nationalist party and of a myriad of smaller, less prominent right-wing groups, took the law into their own hands. They had many outstanding personalities on their list of prospective victims. These included men like Ebert, Scheidemann and Rathenau. That such lawlessness was on the increase was due in no small measure to the attitude of the German judiciary. Most of the higher magistrates were holdovers from the imperial regime. The establishment of the republic failed to affect their deep-rooted monarchist sympathies. They disliked liberals and radicals and looked with thinly veiled approval on the machinations of the anti-republican elements. They had a double standard for political crimes. When the offenders were to the left of the center, they could expect and received little mercy. When they belonged to right-wing organizations, they were generally treated with marked leniency. This encouraged the reactionary enemies of the republic to continue their vendetta.

The Nationalist press was full of slanderous charges against leading Social Democrats. It repeatedly declared that Scheidemann had enriched himself while in office. It pictured him as the owner of baronial estates and country mansions. It spoke in like vein of Ebert. Actually, both men were in very modest circumstances, but the truth was of no importance to their calumniators. The latter were seldom prosecuted;

and when penalties were inflicted, they were almost always ridiculously light. A direct outgrowth of this campaign of vilification was the attempt on Scheidemann's life early in June, 1922. Certain Nationalist newspapers, dispensing with the hypocritical reserve usually displayed by the party's organs on such occasions, actually blamed the former chancellor for what had happened. But the great bulk of the country's press denounced the outrage which, as subsequent investigations showed, was the work of youthful desperadoes belonging to "Organization C." While the incident was still being discussed, the German judiciary gave further proof of its tenderness for right-wing gangsters. On this occasion, the beneficiary of its one-sided conception of justice was Captain Killinger. He was accused of aiding the murderers of Erzberger. The court acquitted him, holding that no punishable charge had been proved.

At a time such as this, with would-be assassins on the loose and notorious characters like Killinger getting off scot-free, it was rather dangerous for a prominent republican to venture into the streets. And it was almost suicidal to visit Munich, the principal hotbed of reaction. Yet this was exactly what Ebert decided to do. He was anxious to iron out some of the perennial difficulties between the Reich and the Bavarian government and felt that his chances of succeeding would be greatly improved if he made the trip. His arrival in Munich on June 12, 1922, proved the signal for numerous skirmishes between Leftists and Rightists. Demonstrations protesting his presence were staged and one Reich flag was burned. Very different was the reception accorded Field Marshal Hindenburg when he visited Koenigsberg on June 11. Great throngs paid him homage, and the local Reichswehr, against the explicit wishes of the government, organized a parade in his honor. There were a few clashes, too, but they could not mar the impressiveness of the welcome given the venerable war lord.

2

Among the groups that helped to foment the disturbances in Munich was the National Socialist party led by Adolf Hitler. The future dictator of Germany was born in Branau-am-Inn, a border town in Upper Austria, on April 20, 1889. His father, Alois Schicklgruber, was the illegitimate son of a lowly peasant woman. Not until January, 1877, when he was nearing his fortieth birthday, did he assume the name of Hitler. Adversity and frustration were the hallmark of his youth. For a long time he eked out a meager livelihood by plying the shoemaker's trade. Eventually, he achieved his heart's desire: he became a customs official. He now had dignity and security.

Young Adolf's education was spotty for the simple reason that he followed his own bent and contemptuously ignored those parts of the curriculum that failed to arouse his interest. He worked hard on subjects that attracted him—notably geography and history—and did well in them, according to his own testimony. He was taught history by a man with pan-German views who idealized Bismarck and the Hohenzollerns and depicted world events as a saga of Teutonic heroism. The boy proved a most receptive pupil. He not only swallowed this romanticized version of the past but clung to it fanatically forever after. He did not get along with his father. The latter wanted him to go into the Austrian civil service. The boy refused. He detested the very thought of regular work. He made up his mind that he would be an artist. To this his father vehemently objected. The quarrel which ensued became more and more acrimonious. It was ended only by the death of Alois Hitler in January, 1903, a few months before his willful son attained his fourteenth year.

When he was eighteen, Adolf Hitler went to Vienna, his heart set on gaining admission to the Academy of Fine Arts. He was unable to pass the entrance examination. Frustrated and embittered, he went home to attend his bedridden mother, the only person in all the world to whom he was deeply attached. She died in December, 1908, leaving him foot-loose and penniless. Now began the most wretched period of his life. For three years he languished in the squalor and misery of a men's hostel in Vienna. All the nationalities and classes of Austria were represented in the heterogeneous aggregation of paupers who shared these quarters with him. He took an instant dislike to his Jewish companions in misfortune. He found them different from the Germans, a group apart. Thus did anti-Semitism strike root in the being of Adolf Hitler.

He had a hard time keeping body and soul together. He did little water colors and got a friend of his to peddle them around. He begged. He shoveled snow. He worked as a building-trades laborer. Still averse to regular employment and despising the sort of thing he was doing, he proved unable to hold any job for long. Instead of probing into his own character for the explanation, he blamed the socialists and trade-unionists for his troubles. His feeling toward these imaginary enemies, with whom he seems to have argued at great length about political and economic questions, developed into a full-blown persecution-complex. Because Karl Marx, the father of socialism, was a Jew, and because Jews were prominent in the Austrian socialist movement, socialism and Judaism became one and the same thing to Hitler. He vented upon both of them a hatred that grew more consuming as his own prospects darkened. Socialism, he convinced himself, was simply a plot on the part of international Jewry to dominate the workers and enslave the world. He devoured the writings of French and German racialists. From them he learned that the Jews were an inferior species. This discovery dovetailed neatly with the needs of his sagging ego. He abhorred the hodgepodge of nationalities which was Austria. He detested Vienna, where Jews prospered while he fought a losing battle against poverty and degradation. In his eyes the city became the symbol and embodiment of racial impurity. It was no place for him.

In 1913, Hitler moved to Munich. Here he felt at home. But life in the Bavarian capital, though an improvement over his sojourn in Vienna, turned out to be no bed of roses. He did cheap water colors, painted picture post cards—and nurtured his persecution-complex. When war broke out in the summer of 1914, he welcomed the holocaust as an escape. Years later he wrote:

To me those hours came like a redemption from the vexatious experience of my youth. Even to this day I am not ashamed to say that, in a transport of enthusiasm, I sank down on my knees and thanked heaven from an overflowing heart. . . .

He enlisted in the Bavarian army, thus forfeiting his Austrian citizenship. He fought in the trenches for four years. What he went through as a soldier did his twisted, morbid personality no good. His fighting record was sufficiently distinguished to win him the Iron Cross. But he did not rise above the rank of corporal. His captain regarded him as "hysterical" and hence unfit to be a commissioned officer.

The armistice found Hitler psychologically unprepared for civilian life. Like so many of his wartime comrades, he dreaded going back to the monotonous and pedestrian existence he had led before the outbreak of the conflict. He craved excitement and action. He was impelled by a vague yearning for power. War had provided an outlet for his drives. His paramount need now was to find another channel for them. He turned to politics.

3

The revolution of 1918 filled Hitler with horror. He reviled its authors with frenetic fury. Even before the stab-in-the-back legend began its poisonous journey throughout the length and breadth of the Reich, he had embraced its message. By pinning the label of traitor on Jews and socialists, he added new fuel to his pre-war hatreds. His bitterness knew no bounds when he saw the Communists take over Bavaria and establish a soviet republic. He blamed the Jews for this crime against the German race. His gloom gave way to wild exultation when the Reichswehr and the Free Corps butchered the Bolshevists and smashed their movement. Munich, where he was stationed while awaiting demobilization orders, acquired in his eyes a new luster and significance. It was now without question the spiritual capital of the only Germany that counted: the Germany that had been treacherously felled by the November revolution.

At this juncture, Hitler was assigned to the commission of inquiry which busied itself with the task of compiling a list of persons to be shot for supporting the Communist regime. The military chieftains who commanded the counterrevolutionary forces in Bavaria remained in actual control of that bastion of reaction. They were enormously encouraged by their decisive victory over the Reds. They lived for only one thing: to destroy the republic and restore an authoritarian-militarist regime. They had plenty of helpers and sympathizers in Munich. The city fairly swarmed with Free Corps men and secret organizations of a militantly reactionary character. One of these organizations was the Thule Society, which sported the swastika as its symbol and published a scurrilous anti-republican and anti-Semitic sheet, the *Muenchener Beobachter*. Army officers closely identified with the Free Corps stood ready to give moral and financial aid to any group that pursued counterrevolutionary aims. Before long Ludendorff settled down in Munich and participated zestfully in the intrigues against the republic. The leaders of the Bavarian Reichswehr were astute enough to see that their one chance of success lay in acquiring a mass following. They themselves had no contact with the masses and were psychologically incapable of establishing one. They knew this would have to be done by someone else, someone who understood the people and whom the people would understand and trust.

Hitler's military superiors quickly discovered that he had a talent for public speaking. They decided to employ him as an "education officer."

His task it was to popularize the army's conception of nationalism. The real purpose of his harangues was to foment hostility to the republican regime. While serving in this capacity, his attention was called to an obscure political group headed by one Anton Drexler, a locksmith by trade. The Munich Reichswehr wanted Hitler to find out what he could about Drexler's followers. The group, which had in all some forty members, called itself the German Workers' party. It preached a compound of chauvinism and pseudosocialist radicalism. It refused to acknowledge that the war had ended or that the Reich had been defeated. This, together with the economic doctrines expounded by the party, appealed to Hitler. Besides, Drexler's group seemed to be exactly what the militarists wanted. It had been affiliated with the Fatherland party during the war. It was pan-German in outlook. It pandered to the masses with its talk about the rights of the under-privileged and thus gave promise of becoming the spearhead of a truly popular movement. The Reichswehr chieftains encouraged their Austrian hireling in his resolve to engage in politics. The link between the military caste and this little band of demagogues was established when Hitler, at Drexler's invitation, joined the party in July, 1919. He became the seventh member of its inner political "cell."

Gottfried Feder and Dietrich Eckart attached themselves to this coterie of schemers and dreamers shortly after Hitler appeared on the scene. Feder was a civil engineer with a flair for slogan-thinking. He provided the "scientific" ideas. He denounced the "slavery of interest" and demanded its abolition. He was for public ownership of land, the substitution of German for Roman law and the nationalization of banks. He distinguished between "Christian" capital, which was na-tional and productive, and "Jewish" capital, which was international and non-productive. The first was to be retained; the second done away with. Hitler embraced this gospel enthusiastically. He obtained further particulars about Jewish "internationalism" from that notorious forgery, *The Protocols of the Elders of Zion*. Eckart was a poet and dramatist with strongly monarchist leanings. He had translated Ibsen's *Peer Gynt* into German and was now dabbling in Nordic folklore. He hated Jews, communists and democrats. From him the party got its slogan: "Germany, Wake Up!" He kept saying that the nation must divest itself of pride of purse and return to its former simplicity. The general welfare, he insisted, must be put before self-interest. He had a way with young men. For them he painted a roseate picture of things to come. He conjured up visions of a reinvigorated and masterful

Reich treading anew the paths of greatness with a modern Caesar at its head. Eckart had long and frequent conversations with Hitler. In matters of rhetoric and composition he was the Austrian's mentor; but the stylistic imperfections of such writings as *Mein Kampf* indicate that the pupil made little progress. Eckart, long addicted to excessive eating and drinking, succumbed to his bodily ills in 1923. His principal contribution to the movement's fund of ideas was a violently anti-Semitic tract called *Bolshevism from Moses to Lenin*.

Hitler developed no great fondness for the majority of his party comrades. He found them unaware of the value of propaganda and unduly anxious to avoid unfavorable publicity. They were opposed to big meetings. They wished to do nothing which might result in friction with socialist and communist workers. This timorousness, this absence of a dynamic will to power, aroused Hitler's contempt. He dismissed as fatuous nonsense Drexler's belief that the ideas toward which the party was groping with the aid of study and discussion would spread even if no efforts were made to disseminate them. He held that the truth or falsity of an idea was not what determined its popularity. As he saw it, the only thing that mattered was propaganda: elaborate, sustained and inflammatory propaganda. Hitler finally had his way.

4

The German Workers' party was without a comprehensive program when Hitler joined it. This its board of strategy felt to be a handicap in the competition for popular favor. So a committee consisting of Hitler, Feder, Eckart and Drexler drafted a twenty-five-point pronouncement and laid it before a meeting of the party on February 24, 1920. This program was designed to win the support of many and diverse elements of the population: pan-Germans, anti-Semites, the lower middle class, war veterans, peasants, workers with strongly nationalist sympathies. It was to serve as the cornerstone of a movement which would rally to its standard every German with a grudge against the republic. The first point was written by Hitler himself. "We demand," it stated, "the union of all Germans in a Greater Germany on the basis of the right of all peoples to self-determination." A leading tenet of Wilsonian idealism was thus invoked to justify old-style pan-Germanism. The program went on to demand equality of rights for the German nation, the abrogation of the Treaties of Versailles and St. Germain, and the return of Germany's colonies. It declared that only persons of German blood were to be citizens of the Reich. Jews, accordingly, were to be excluded from participation in the political life of the country. Their connections with the press were to be destroyed. The migration of Jews into Germany was to be halted, and those who had arrived after August 2, 1914, were to be deported forthwith. The party, it was explained, "combats the Jewish materialistic spirit within us and without us. . . ." War was likewise declared on the "corrupting parliamentary system which allocates jobs on the basis of party considerations and in disregard of moral character and capacities."

The authors of the program pilfered liberally from socialist ideology. The state, they asserted, must provide employment for its citizens. The distribution of rights and duties must be based on the principle of equality. Intellectual or manual work was the first obligation of every German. The interests of the individual must be subordinated to the common welfare. All income which was not the result of labor or effort of some kind would have to be done away with. This meant, first and foremost, abolition of the "slavery of interest." The confiscation of all wartime profits and the nationalization of trusts were likewise called for. The single biggest sop to the wage-earning class was the demand that workers be permitted to share the profits of industry. The aspirations of petty shopkeepers and small businessmen, who were especially numerous in Munich, did not go unheeded. Point 16, unquestionably one of the most significant sections of the program, asked for "the creation and preservation of a healthy middle class." It urged "the immediate communalization of the big stores and their transfer, at moderate prices, to small entrepreneurs." Finally, it demanded "a most benevolent attitude toward small enterprises," which were to receive help in the form of orders placed by the Reich, the *Laender* and the municipalities. Point 17 expressed a similar solicitude for the well-being of the debt-laden peasantry. Without circumlocution it called for "a thorough land reform adapted to our national needs; a law permitting the expropriation, without indemnities, of land serving the commonwealth; the abolition of the system of mortgages; and a ban on speculation in real estate." The program had a good deal to say about certain other features of German life. It envisaged an overhauling of the educational system with an eye to the "exigencies of practical life" and to the need for inculcating the idea of the state. It demanded more adequate provision for public health, the subsidization of all organizations interested in physical training for the young and the replacement of the professional army by one truly national in character.

The party espoused what it called "positive Christianity," but explicitly disavowed any ties with a particular religious sect. Point 25 contained another of Hitler's pet ideas. It insisted on the establishment of a unitary regime, with all authority concentrated in the hands of the central government. And not the *Laender,* but "professional chambers" were to execute the laws enacted by the Reich. Hitler thus served notice on the Bavarian particularists that he would not countenance any impairment of national unity.

Because it was anxious to do everything possible to make a favorable impression on the masses, the party decided to change its name. In April, 1920, it officially labeled itself the National Socialist German Workers' Party (NSDAP). Armed with a program and name that seemed to meet the specifications of demagoguery, the Nazis, as the members of the party came to be called, set out to win new converts. At once they encountered difficulties. Their single biggest headache was the lack of funds. The situation, it was obvious from the outset, could be remedied by contributions from wealthy persons obsessed with the fear of communism. But prospective donors were scared off by the supposedly socialist character of the movement. To reassure them Hitler declared in August, 1920: "For National Socialists it goes without saying that industrial capital, since it creates values, will remain untouched. We combat only Jewish international loan capital." This pronouncement meant that Point 13, which demanded the nationalization of all trusts, was being discarded. On May 22, 1926, a general assembly of the party declared the twenty-five-point program "immutable." But less than two years later, Hitler, in an effort to curry favor with the big landowners, retracted the original demand for agrarian reform. On April 13, 1928, he issued the following statement "to clear up false interpretations" of Point 17:

In view of the fact that the NSDAP believes in the principle of private property, it is self-evident that the phrase "expropriation without indemnities" refers only to the creation of legal means whereby land which was acquired in illegal ways or which is not being administered to the best interests of the nation might be expropriated if necessary. This is directed primarily against Jewish land-speculation companies.

Hitler's readiness to tamper with the twenty-five points did not prevent him from invoking them whenever anything could be gained thereby. As an expression of pan-Germanism, racialism and pseudo-radicalism, they continued to embody the grand strategy of the National Socialist movement.

Shortly after joining the party, Hitler emerged as its foremost orator. His ability to excite an audience was nothing short of phenomenal. He seemed to cast a hypnotic spell over his listeners. They were trans-fixed by the fanaticism that shone from his smoldering eyes and drove his voice to shrieking crescendoes. They responded to the utter sin-cerity of the man, to the complete absence of those artifices that are the stock-in-trade of most political orators. But though he spoke with the fury of one possessed, he never forgot the purpose for which he was speaking. He played upon the Germans' sense of injury, their pride and desire for revenge. He pandered to their craving for a scapegoat. He flayed the Jews, the "slavery of interest" and the Treaty of Ver-sailles. No less vitriolic were his attacks on the "November criminals," the republic and the Weimar system. The Jews were his favorite whip-ping boy. He called them back-stabbers, profiteers, contaminators of German virtue. They were to blame for everything: the "attack" on Germany in 1914, the defeat, the harsh peace terms. They were, at one and the same time, Bolshevists and plutocrats, Marxists and predatory capitalists. They were mongrels, parasites and pimps, unfit to breathe Teutonic air. By trickery and deceit, they had managed to wrest from the Germans their birthright in every field of endeavor. For the bene-fit of the underdogs of German society, Hitler expatiated on the crimes of "international" capitalism and big business, being always careful to single out the alleged wrongdoings of Jewish bankers and merchants. The party, he repeatedly declaimed, was for the exploited worker and the downtrodden peasant. It was also anxious to improve the status of the small shopkeeper, who was being forced to the wall by competition from the big department stores. Hitler reserved his most passionate outbursts for the Versailles-*Diktat*. He magnified Allied vindictiveness. He denounced the "war-guilt lie" and railed at other unpopular features of the peace: reparation, disarmament, the frontiers with Poland and the loss of the colonies. There was nothing original in what Hitler said. His diatribes conformed in content to the oratory of protest which hundreds of Germans were disgorging in those days. Yet there was no one quite like him among the obscure rabble-rousers who held forth in Munich's innumerable beer halls. His personal idio-syncrasies and the strangely hypnotizing quality of his harangues stamped him as a demagogue apart.

The National Socialist party enjoyed advantages which were not shared by the many similar groups that mushroomed in these early postwar years. Hitler's prowess as a speaker and the patronage of the Bavarian Reichswehr constituted invaluable assets. Immeasurably helpful, too, was the co-operation received from Ernst Poehner, Munich's chief of police, and from Wilhelm Frick, one of his subordinates and an ardent National Socialist. The triumph of the Fuehrer principle within the movement proved another source of strength. It was in the summer of 1921 that Hitler made himself the absolute master of the party. The Nazis were also aided by their Storm Troops: the *Sturmabteilungen* or SA. This hard-bitten fighting force was founded in November, 1921. Its precursors were the detachments of husky young men who served as bodyguards for party leaders, maintained order at mass meetings and ejected persistent hecklers. The SA consisted largely of former Free Corps men. Most of these had belonged to Ehrhardt's brigade and were currently members of "Organization C." The Storm Troops became the battering-ram of the movement. Upon them devolved the duty of launching the offensive which, Hitler hoped, would some day carry the party to power.

5

Of far-reaching importance was the friendship which developed between Hitler and another leading member of the party, Captain Ernst Roehm. This redoubtable, battle-scarred warrior was well known locally as the head of an association of Bavarian officers called the "Iron Fist." This group attempted to terrorize republicans and unquestionably had a hand in some of the political murders of the early 1920's. Roehm was an able and ambitious fellow. He was political adviser to Colonel—later General—Franz von Epp, who commanded all infantry troops stationed in Bavaria. With the connivance of certain Allied officers attached to the control commissions, Roehm built up secret stores of arms which were to serve the counterrevolutionary cause. He wished to make the army supreme in Germany and hoped some day to become head of the nation's military establishment. He had already gained virtual ascendancy over the remnants of the Free Corps in Bavaria and planned to use this initial success as a stepping-stone toward bigger things. He was courageous to the point of recklessness, and this quality was to stand him in good stead during the trying years ahead. He was likewise an excellent organizer and disciplinarian. He helped to create the embryo of an efficient party machine. He brought into the movement a considerable number of officers and soldiers, most of whom had already seen action with the Free Corps. At the same time he maintained his contacts with the Reichswehr, coordinating his party activities with the counterrevolutionary aims of the military caste.

Of even greater significance was the tie which coupled Hitler's fortunes with those of Captain Hermann Wilhelm Goering. This blustering, apparently jovial and horseplay-loving showpiece of the Nazi museum of political personalities comes from a good family; in this respect his background is decidedly different from that of most Nazi leaders. His father was a retired governor of German Southwest Africa. In keeping with his decision to enter the military profession, Goering attended the Prussian Cadet Academy at Karlsruhe and subsequently underwent further training at Berlin-Lichterfelde. He became an aviator during the war and performed brilliantly in combat. In 1918 he shot down his twentieth plane and received the *Pour le Mérite*, the highest military decoration in the gift of the Hohenzollern monarchy. When the war ended, his renown as an ace was second only to that of Germany's supreme hero of aerial warfare, Baron von Richthofen. The armistice was a great tragedy for Goering; it terminated the thrill-packed existence he had been leading and reduced him to the status of a nobody. Immediately after the cessation of hostilities, he declared to a group of fellow-aviators: "We must be proud of what we have done. We must desire another such struggle. We must never forget this desire." Psychologically incapable of accepting the antimilitarist and anti-war spirit that now pervaded the country, Goering got into trouble with working-class people in Berlin who subjected him, his uniform and his medals to serious indignities. From this moment forward, he was obsessed with hatred for the proletariat and an unquenchable desire for revenge. To give free vent to this hatred and to fulfill this desire, he would need power, and thereupon he resolved that power someday he would have. He found the new republican, democratic Germany intolerable. So he left the country, vowing never again to set foot on its soil. He found employment in Sweden as a pilot for the Svenska Lufttraffick. While thus engaged, he met Karin von Kantzow, a niece of the immensely wealthy Count Eric von Rosen. This beautiful but epileptic lady was married to a Swedish lieutenant and had an eight-year-old son by him. With characteristic directness and energy, Goering went after Karin, took her away from her husband and married her. She had money, and this enabled the hitherto impecunious aviator to change his plans. Encouraged by Karin, who had boundless faith in his future, Goering returned to Germany in 1921. While in Munich, he chanced to hear one of Hitler's daily harangues and forthwith decided to join the National Socialist movement. His first assignment was to give the SA an efficient military organization. This task he discharged with energy and skill. By 1923, the 6,000 men who made up the Storm Troops were ready for action. Goering's capacity for leadership and the utter ruthlessness with which he pursued his ends won him a high place in the inner councils of the party. He became one of Hitler's most trusted subordinates and ultimately No. 2 man of Nazidom.

Swarthy, beetle-browed Rudolf Hess occupied a unique place in Hitler's entourage. He was born in Egypt, the son of a German merchant. At the age of fourteen he was sent to the Reich to prepare himself for a business career. During the war he saw continuous service at the front and rose to the rank of lieutenant. He took a keen interest in political and social questions from the moment he returned to civilian life. His hatred of the republic led him to join the Thule Society, which never wearied of parading its anti-Marxist and anti-Semitic attitude and frequently became involved in brawls with local Communists. Hess heard Hitler speak in 1920, and the effect upon him, as upon so many others, was electrifying. The two men struck up a close friendship. Before long, Hess became Hitler's private secretary. He was fanatically devoted to his chief, whose ambitions and whims he served with self-effacing fidelity. As Hitler's confidant and *alter ego*, he wielded an influence that reached into every section of the party.

Alfred Rosenberg likewise stood high in the Nazi hierarchy. He was born in Estonia, which formed part of the Tsarist empire until 1917. His people were middle-class traders of German descent. In this outpost of Teutonic civilization he eagerly imbibed the tenets of German nationalism and imperialism. He received his education in Russian schools. The outbreak of war in 1914 found him in Moscow where he was completing the course of study prescribed for architects and draughtsmen. The Bolshevist revolution elicited from him no words of disapproval so long as he remained on Russian or Baltic soil. During some of the tensest moments of the upheaval he taught drawing at a school in Riga. He was finally forced to flee. He arrived in Munich in 1919 and promptly offered his services to Eckart. On the strength of a few tracts he had recently scribbled, he was commissioned to write a series of propaganda pamphlets. What impressed Eckart was the man's fierce hatred of Jews and Bolshevists. It was through Eckart that Rosenberg met Hitler. The latter immediately fell under the spell of the young Balt. For hours the two conversed. Rosenberg talked about the Germanic master race, the mystical attributes of blood, the sacred right of Teutons to rule the world, the beauties of violence and war, the biological and spiritual inferiority of the Jew, the debilitating effects of Christian love and humility, the need for a pagan-Nordic religion based on the dynamics of heroism. Hitler listened enthralled. Rosenberg became one of his most intimate and cherished advisers. In 1921 the Munich Reichswehr, at Roehm's suggestion, presented the party with a weekly newspaper, the *Voelkischer Beobachter*. Rosenberg was made the editor of this hitherto unsuccessful sheet. In its columns he aired his views on race, religion and foreign policy. In later years he achieved international notoriety as the ideological high priest of Nazism. His *Mythus des XX Jahrhunderts* (Mythos of the Twentieth Century), which appeared in 1930, achieved a position second only to that of Hitler's *Mein Kampf* among the authoritative tracts of the movement. But during the early period of his career as a Nazi, his principal claim to distinction among the party's scribes was his unfailingly venomous attitude toward Soviet Russia.

6

The growth of the movement was far from phenomenal. In November, 1923, when Hitler and Ludendorff staged their famous beer-hall putsch, the total membership of the National Socialist party did not exceed 15,000. Most of the new recruits came from the lower middle class. One of the smaller political groups swallowed up by the Nazis during this early period was the German Socialist party headed by Julius Streicher, a Nuremberg schoolmaster with a violently anti-Semitic turn of mind. The bitter feud which developed between Hitler and Streicher was precipitated by the latter's desire to assume control of the NSDAP. The outcome of the battle was a decisive victory for Hitler. Nonetheless, the whip had to be cracked from time to time to still criticism and terminate dissension within the movement. This, and the perennial financial problems of the party, absorbed much of Hitler's attention. But all the while he kept his gaze fixed on the national scene. During the second half of 1922, the country drifted toward a crisis of overwhelming proportions. For those who hoped to fish in troubled waters unprecedented opportunities appeared to be in the making. The triumph of Mussolini's Black Shirts in Italy was hailed by Hitler and his associates as a harbinger of things to come. In Nazi and right-wing circles generally the March on Rome strengthened the belief that a similar expedition against Berlin could be staged without too much difficulty and with a minimum of disorder. All that was needed was the right moment, and that, if current storm signals were any portent, could not be far away.

Chapter 16

THE ASSASSINATION OF RATHENAU AND
ITS AFTERMATH

I

GERMAN public opinion was profoundly disturbed by developments in Upper Silesia. Early in June, 1922, German refugees streamed out of the province charging that they had been mistreated by Polish bands. On June 13, the president of the Prussian Diet issued a statement which reflected the nationwide anxiety. The Diet, he reminded the country, had denounced the Upper Silesian settlement as a brutal violation of popular will and had refused to recognize it as binding. To this position it continued to adhere, conscious of the fact that it was in complete accord with the Reichstag. The latter had assented to the settlement only under duress and had repeatedly assailed it as contrary to reason and justice. The impending separation from Germany of the Upper Silesian districts allotted to Poland was a painful reminder of other German areas exposed to a similar fate. To the inhabitants of territories already turned over to alien masters the promise had been given that they would not be abandoned; the German inhabitants of Upper Silesia could rest assured that they, too, would not be forgotten. Four days later, President Ebert, the government of the Reich and the Prussian cabinet issued a joint proclamation. The sad moment was at hand, they wailed, which for three years Germans had feverishly struggled to hold off. On this day a part of Upper Silesia was being incorporated into a foreign state in spite of the fact that the statesmen and experts of all countries had pronounced the province indivisible. A precious bit of German soil, which after centuries of toil had been brought to a peak of economic productivity, was being torn away from the Fatherland. In the plebiscite which the Allies had conceded—one of the few modifications of the original peace terms—a large majority had voted in favor of remaining with Germany. Nonetheless, the Allies had decided to partition the province, ignoring the German government's efforts to show that such a step was both politically and economically wrong. The Reich wished to thank the people of Upper Silesia for their loyalty; it shared completely the feelings which they were experiencing at this moment.

The proclamation had the effect of heightening public tension; specifically, it gave fresh impetus to the hatred of republican leaders who, according to right-wing propagandists, were responsible for the Upper Silesian tragedy. Almost simultaneously, the Reich ministry of the treasury published an inflammatory statement regarding the cost to Germany of the Allied occupation of the Rhineland. The burden of the statement was that Germany was being systematically exploited and embezzled, that all sorts of unnecessary expenditures were being run up by the occupation authorities in callous disregard of Germany's desperate financial straits. For months German newspapers had been publishing stories written in a similar vein. The result of all this, as anyone could have foreseen, was a new crescendo of popular indignation. To make matters worse, the newspapers were also spreading reports to the effect that the Allies planned new moves in the Rhineland. They were pictured as determined to extend the demilitarized zone to points east of the fifty-kilometer line laid down by the Treaty of Versailles.

Irate Germans wanted a scapegoat, and the man ideally suited to play this role was the foreign minister, Rathenau. As a Jew, a liberal and an exponent of the policy of fulfillment, he was uniquely vulnerable. The systematic campaign of vilification against him had convinced many of his compatriots that he was the archvillain. Helfferich, unrepentant over his contribution to the chain of events which culminated in the assassination of Erzberger, led the outcry against Rathenau. In arrogating to himself the role of public prosecutor, Helfferich enjoyed the backing of his own Nationalist party and of the youthful fanatics who were bent on destroying every German champion of democracy at home and collaboration abroad. It mattered not at all to these individuals that Rathenau was striving with might and main to obtain concessions for Germany. They were unimpressed by his impassioned speech on June 21, 1922—which was destined to be his last—in favor of self-determination for the people of the Saar. They found additional justification for their blind hatred in the address which Helfferich delivered before the Reichstag two days later. His remarks on this occasion were one long diatribe against Rathenau. Said Helfferich: The German population of the Rhineland and the Saar felt betrayed. The government had given parliament false information regarding its recent negotiations in Paris. It had, without authorization from the Reichstag, handed over to others some of Germany's sovereign rights. For this it should be placed on trial. Helfferich adduced textual differences between the German and French versions of the note of May 28, 1922, in support of his charge that the government had attempted to conceal from the Reichstag the concessions allegedly granted the western powers. Actually, this charge was entirely false. For, as the government pointed out, the German version was the only one that counted.

On the morning of June 24, 1922, Rathenau left his villa in Gruenewald, one of Berlin's beautiful suburbs, for his office in the city. As usual, he rode in an open limousine driven by his chauffeur. Unnoticed by the latter, an auto, in which three young men were seated, followed. Suddenly, this auto overtook the limousine; one of the three young men got up and fired several shots at Rathenau. Critically wounded, Rathenau was rushed back to his villa; he died shortly after. News of the assassination was promptly relayed to the main committee of the Reichstag, which was then in session. Tremendous excitement ensued. The feeling which gripped people of all parties except those on the extreme Right was expressed by the spontaneous reaction of the aged Independent, Eduard Bernstein. He rushed up to Helfferich and in a fury spat out one word: "Murderer!" Actually, the belief was widespread for a time that Helfferich had knowledge of the plot and that his violent attack on Rathenau the day before the assassination constituted a kind of summing up of the reasons why the death sentence should be carried. This accusation was unfounded. The murder was hatched in "Organization C." Leading members of the Nationalist party apparently did not know of the plot and had done nothing to further it. But that they were morally responsible for the current terror against republican leaders was obvious. If Rathenau was really a traitor, as Helfferich had charged, then the men who cold-bloodedly planned and executed the murder had justification for their action which to them was more than ample. Rathenau's youthful assassins, like so many other Germans of their ilk, had been pumped full of the poison of the stab-in-the-back theory. They believed that the Reds and the Jews were responsible for Germany's defeat and collapse in 1918. They had convinced themselves that by destroying the Reds and the Jews, they would avenge the "crime" of November, 1918, and restore Germany to greatness and glory. They had been led to picture Rathenau as the leader of a group of Jewish conspirators whose aim was to introduce Bolshevism into Germany. They were familiar with the contents of the *Protocols of the Elders of Zion,* which purported to prove the existence of a Jewish plot to obtain control of the world.

The government investigators assigned to the case unearthed some interesting information about the assassins: They belonged to "good" families. They were active in secret counterrevolutionary societies— the evidence indicated that they were members not only of "Organization C" but of fighting groups associated with the racialist right wing of the Nationalist party—and at least one of them was a National Socialist. They believed that the illegal possession of arms and the formation of secret military organizations at a time when Allied control commissions were operating in Germany were the very essence of patriotism. Erwin Kern, a naval lieutenant, was one of the central figures of the plot. His companions in the auto from which the shots were fired were Ernst Werner Techow, whose uncle, an industrialist, was a friend of the Rathenau family, and Hermann Fischer, an engineer. On June 29, Techow was arrested on the estate of his uncle, who knew nothing of the young man's part in the crime. Kern and Fischer, after managing for some time to elude the police, were finally cornered on July 17. Kern was slain by his pursuers; Fischer killed himself. In October, 1922, Techow was sentenced to fifteen years in prison, but was amnestied seven years later. The thirteen other persons tried in connection with the murder fared variously. Three were acquitted; the rest were found guilty and received prison sentences ranging from eight years to less than two. All the longer sentences were eventually reduced.

The bitterness against Helfferich, who had to be protected from some of his irate colleagues in the Reichstag, was only a small part of the emotional explosion produced by the assassination of Rathenau. For days feeling ran high against all persons of conservative or reactionary affiliations. Many of those most deeply shocked and moved by the crime were quick to charge that the secret organizations of murderers that were killing one republican leader after another were able to carry on only because they had powerful protectors in the ranks of the Nationalist and People's parties. This charge seemed substantiated by the attitude of prominent Nationalists and of unregenerate right-wing elements within the People's party. The individuals in question made it clear that they did not approve of political assassinations, but they hastened to adduce all sorts of extenuating circumstances in support of the contention that the murderers should not be judged too harshly. To the youthful gunmen and their accomplices they ascribed noble, patriotic motives and argued that this side of the story should not be overlooked. The racialist wing of the Nationalist party, which had already established close contact with Hitler's National Socialists, did not even bother to disguise its solidarity with the authors of the terror. The furore which its stand provoked did not deter moderate and radical Germans from pointing an accusing finger at other culpable groups. Prominent among these was the Stahlhelm, a nation-wide association of war veterans with strongly monarchist leanings. It had been founded on December 25, 1918, by Franz Seldte, a Magdeburg manufacturer. In the words of Seldte, the purpose of the Stahlhelm was to mobilize "the spirit of the front-soldier" against the "swinish revolution." The organization grew quickly; by the close of 1920, it was reputed to have more than a million members. It was not alone the avowedly anti-republican, anti-internationalist character of this movement that made it the object of attack immediately after the assassination of Rathenau; equally damning was the fact that the Stahlhelm was currently engaged in a campaign to win over the younger generation. The object of this campaign was to perpetuate the militarist, authoritarian traditions of pre-republican days among those Germans who, through no fault of their own, had failed to undergo the "elevating" experience of front-line service.

2

On the afternoon of June 24, 1922, Wirth addressed the Reichstag. Speaking with great emotion, he lauded Rathenau and paid tribute to the service he had rendered his beloved Fatherland. Wirth insisted that the work which Rathenau had set out to accomplish—to save the German people while preserving the republican form of government—must not be interrupted. The working classes and their bourgeois allies would have to help. These elements of the population could rest assured of two things: energetic measures would be taken to combat the spread of violence and terror; social reform would be pushed as soon as the country had been freed from foreign pressure.

Wirth's remarks did not elicit from the Nationalists the kind of response he had hoped for. So, after the various party leaders had spoken, he delivered another impassioned oration. He called attention to a statement published by a member of the racialist wing of the Nationalist party. This statement charged that the German government was in the employ of the Allies and under obligation to carry out their orders. Amid thunderous applause from the moderate and left-wing parties, Wirth declared: "The enemy is on the Right."

The chancellor's eloquent speeches made him the hero of the day in the eyes of all sincere republicans; but the most significant feature of the nationwide reaction to the assassination of Rathenau was the militant attitude of the working classes. It was the Free trade unions affiliated with the Social Democratic party that took the lead in formulating a program to meet the current political crisis. This program comprised a truly formidable array of demands: immediate passage of a law for the protection of the republic; severe punishment for subversive agitators; the dissolution of anti-republican groups and the elimination of untrustworthy persons from all branches of the public service, including the judiciary and the army; a ban on the display of monarchist flags, colors and emblems and on the wearing of uniforms by former officers; the appointment of a Reich commissioner and a special panel of judges for the purpose of bringing the authors of the terror to book; the creation of a federal criminal police; legal measures to facilitate the apprehension of persons sought by the authorities; legislation which would authorize the government to confiscate property and withhold pensions; an amnesty for all political offenders except those guilty of action against the republic.

The Wirth cabinet lost little time in demonstrating its resolve to combat lawlessness with all the means at its disposal. On June 24, 1922, it published a far-reaching emergency decree for the defense of the republic. A few days later, it laid before the Reichstag a measure which prescribed extremely heavy penalties for terrorists and their accomplices. The Nationalists led the opposition, which included the Bavarian People's party and the Communists. The latter were evidently fearful that the proposed law might be used against them as well as against reactionary foes of the republic. The bill underwent a number of modifications in the course of the debate, but its essential provisions remained intact. It was adopted on July 18, 1922, by a vote of 303 to 102. The bulk of the People's party followed the line laid down by

Stresemann and joined the Social Democrats, the Centrists and the Democrats in supporting the measure.

Powerful right-wing elements in Bavaria bitterly assailed the Reichstag's action. They forced the Lerchenfeld cabinet to issue an emergency decree which virtually suspended the operation of the federal law for the protection of the republic. The Bavarian government had clearly overstepped the limits of legality, but it sought, nevertheless, to justify its action on juridical grounds. The federal law, it argued, was a violation of the fundamental rights of Germans, of democratic principles and of the Weimar constitution. Besides, it had aroused such antipathy in Bavaria that the local authorities felt obliged to promulgate a decree of their own in order to preserve law and order. The German government made no secret of its displeasure. President Ebert informed the Lerchenfeld cabinet that its decree was in conflict with the Weimar constitution and a serious blow to the unity of the Reich. He warned that he would have to take steps, in accordance with the terms of Article 48, to bring Bavaria into line. At the same time, however, he emphasized his readiness to do everything possible to reach a friendly understanding with the Bavarian authorities. Lerchenfeld hastened to assure Ebert that he, too, preferred to see matters settled amicably. Negotiations followed, and they resulted in an agreement that was eminently satisfactory to Berlin. The Bavarian government promised to abrogate its decree not later than August 18, 1922; this was the most important feature of the accord. In return, the Wirth cabinet undertook to give due consideration to the rights of the Bavarian police and judiciary. It also declared that there would be no further increase in the jurisdictional authority of the Reich. Additional concessions were made to the Bavarian government, and these the latter publicized in an effort to make its capitulation more palatable to its conservative and reactionary followers. But this gesture was of no avail. Right-wing opinion throughout Bavaria denounced the agreement with Berlin and heaped abuse on Lerchenfeld for his part in the transaction. One outgrowth of this ferment was the hatching of an ambitious plot by Roehm, Poehner and Dr. Pittinger, a physician who had become the head of a violently anti-republican organization. The three men planned, with the aid of the Bavarian Reichswehr, to force Ebert and the Wirth cabinet out of office and to install a government of their own choosing. But lack of co-ordination and mounting friction between the chief conspirators made it necessary to drop the scheme before it could be put into execution. Of far greater political signifi-

cance was the decision of the Bavarian People's party and the Bavarian
branch of the Nationalist party to draw closer to each other. This
connubium resulted, first of all, in the appointment of the notorious
Nationalist spokesman, Franz Guertner, as Bavarian minister of justice. Then, on November 8, 1922, Lerchenfeld was compelled to resign.
He was succeeded by Eugen von Knilling, a somewhat pedestrian
politician who had served as minister of education during the closing
years of the monarchy. The new premier was a mere figurehead. The
power of the state was actually wielded by men who took orders from
Kahr, now the acknowledged leader of the monarchists in Bavaria. As
a matter of fact, one of Knilling's first acts was to announce that he
subscribed to the program presented by Kahr in 1920 at the time of
the Kapp putsch. The Bavarian People's party, which was responsible
for Knilling's elevation to the premiership, quite unabashedly marshaled
its forces for an effort to restore the prerevolutionary order. It espoused
a program which called for the transfer of the government's executive
powers to an official who was to have the title of President of the State.
The obvious purpose of this maneuver was to enable Prince Rupprecht,
the Wittelsbach pretender, to establish himself on the Bavarian throne.
The strength of the reactionary elements was enhanced by the founding, on November 16, 1922, of the United Patriotic Societies (*Vereinigte
vaterlaendische Verbaende*). This fusion of Bavaria's numerous
right-wing organizations heralded the inauguration of an intensified
drive against the republic.

3

The Nationalist party underwent no change of heart during the
tension-laden weeks that followed the murder of Rathenau. Nevertheless, certain elements within it decided that it was too moderate to
suit them. These right-wingers, led by Reinhold Wulle, Albrecht von
Graefe and Wilhelm Henning, withdrew from the parent organization and founded the German Racial Freedom party. The new group
constituted, for all practical purposes, the northern outpost of the National Socialist movement. Ludendorff, who was affiliated with both
camps, provided the liaison between them. The socialists, in the
meanwhile, pondered the idea of composing the feud which for so
long had rent their ranks. Within the Independent Social Democratic
party, the trend of opinion was more and more toward reunion with
the Social Democrats. Recently, the Independents, in reply to an
inquiry from the Social Democrats, had stated that they were pre-

pared, under certain conditions, to join the Wirth cabinet. This meant that the principal bone of contention between the two groups—the question of forming ministerial alliances with bourgeois parties—had ceased to exist. The fact of the matter was that the Wirth government enjoyed the confidence of the industrial masses, and the leaders of both socialist parties were vying with each other in offering it their support. The assassination of Rathenau gave a powerful fillip to the movement for reunion; it aroused the workers to the necessity of consolidating their forces. It was out of deference to this feeling that the two parties, on July 14, 1922, formally agreed to co-operate.

Simultaneously, the People's party, under Stresemann's leadership, began to draw away from the Nationalists. With a sure sense of impending political exigencies, it decided in favor of increased collaboration with the Center and the Democrats. On July 19, 1922, the representatives of these three parties announced that they were about to conclude a working agreement. They emphasized that their co-operation would take place in a spirit of complete fidelity to the Weimar constitution. Thanks to this agreement, Stresemann's followers became part of the moderate bourgeois bloc in the Reichstag; they thus extended to the national arena the program which they had initiated in Prussia when they consented to join a coalition cabinet headed by Otto Braun. But although the People's party made ready to attenuate the rigid conservatism of its first years, it by no means went all the way in severing its connections with the past. It continued to be implacably anti-socialist; indeed, one of the factors which led it to adopt a more co-operative attitude was the hope that by so doing it might more effectively combat socialist influence upon the government of the Reich. Its left wing admittedly had a good deal in common with the Democrats, but the tycoons of heavy industry who dominated its conservative fringe remained sympathetic to the ideas enshrined in the program of the Nationalist party.

The crisis produced by the assassination of Rathenau also spurred the Center to renewed organizational efforts. Specifically, Wirth and his colleagues sought to achieve greater political unity within the Catholic fold. But their efforts failed, largely because the Bavarian People's party insisted on going its own way. This avowedly reactionary group drew most of its support from three main sections of the Bavarian population: peasants, middle-class people and bureaucrats. The Center, on the other hand, contained a large number of industrial workers enrolled in the Christian trade unions, and its policy had to take account of their wishes. This greatly limited the possibility of real co-operation between the two parties.

While the middle groups in the Reichstag were working to adapt themselves to the changing political scene, the Social Democrats and the Independents continued to move steadily toward reunion. On September 6, 1922, they published a program which was to lay the groundwork for the forthcoming fusion. Socialism, they said, was still their ultimate objective. During the immediate future, however, the energies of German labor would have to be dedicated to the task of protecting the republic. The two parties recognized that the Weimar regime offered the proletariat an excellent opportunity to advance toward its goal. Consequently, they demanded a ruthless and uncompromising struggle against all attempts to restore the monarchy. The Reichswehr, they insisted, must be transformed into a bulwark of the republic; the unity of the Reich must be consolidated. If these aims were to be accomplished, the *Laender* would have to purge their police and bureaucracy of monarchists. They would also have to democratize their administrative structure, grant self-government to their municipalities and combat the particularist-reactionary elements within their borders. Another evil to be fought was "class justice." The prevailing legal system would have to be completely recast in accordance with socialist principles. This meant that henceforth judges would have to be recruited from all layers of the population and that lay magistrates would have to be permitted to participate in the work of every branch of the judicial system. The abolition of capital punishment and the elimination of all legislation which placed women in a position of legal inferiority were also urgent necessities. Turning to the financial and economic sphere, the Social Democrats and the Independents demanded a capital levy and a redistribution of the tax burden in accordance with the capacity to pay. The Reich, they declared, must be allowed to share the profits of capitalistic enterprises. Earnings derived from speculation must be heavily taxed. Upon the government rested the obligation of seeing to it that there was enough food for everyone. It was likewise the duty of the state to encourage the construction of buildings serving a socially useful purpose. Public control of private monopolies and the socialization of key industries, especially those in the mining field, were imperative. The interests of German labor would have to be protected. This could be done in various ways: by expanding existing social legislation, maintaining the eight-hour day and safeguarding the right to strike and to form trade unions; by making adequate provision for the unemployed, establishing a unified labor code and developing the system of factory councils. Another overdue reform was the socialization of medicine. The country likewise needed a single type of school, secular in character, which would be open to Germans of every class. As for religion, it had to be declared the purely private concern of the individual citizen. The two socialist parties had a good deal to say on the subject of Germany's relations with other states. Only the spirit of international socialism, they held, could create real peace. It was necessary to continue the conciliatory foreign policy inaugurated by Wirth and Rathenau, but due consideration would have to be given to the question of whether Germany was able to transfer large sums of money to other countries. Restoration of the devastated areas of northern France and of Belgium was a moral obligation which the Reich could not shirk; it was also the indispensable means of effecting an improvement in the international sphere. However, the fact remained that Germany's desperate plight made imperative a lightening of her reparation burden. Workers of all lands had a special role to play: they would have to unite to fight imperialism and power politics; they would also have to exert unremitting pressure in behalf of a revision of the peace treaties. An international organization based on law was essential to the success of this struggle. Unity in the ranks of German labor was likewise a prime necessity. Only after such unity had been achieved would the working classes be able to fulfill their historic mission: the establishment of a socialist society.

On September 18, 1922, the annual congress of the Social Democratic party convened in Augsburg. Two days later, the Independents assembled at Gera. Everything went smoothly at Augsburg. With Ebert giving his blessing and with Wels, the party chairman, stressing the need for unity, the resolution calling for a merger with the Independents was adopted without discussion. The united party was to have three chairmen, and of these, two were to be from the majority group. The congress of the Independents ran into a number of snags. Strong differences of opinion impeded action on the main issue before the delegates. Artur Crispien, a leader of the moderate faction, spoke in favor of the merger. He likewise insisted that all anti-Fascist elements, regardless of class or political affiliation, would have to join hands to combat the peril of authoritarianism. Even the Communists, he said, found themselves compelled to support the Wirth cabinet. True, the unified Social Democratic party was making the class struggle the principal feature of its program, but there could be no denying the need for co-operation with the pro-republican bourgeois parties. One had to think thrice before embarking upon any line of action that might result in the fall of Wirth. The existence in Hungary of a government like that of Admiral Nicholas Horthy was a salutary reminder of what might happen in Germany if the workers were not careful. The same moral was pointed by recent events in Italy. There, the socialists held out against the idea of coalition and now their party was in ruins. Ledebour objected vehemently to the proposed union. He argued that such a step would prove disastrous for the simple reason that the Social Democrats had long ceased to be a revolutionary group. He contended that the Communists were far closer to the Independents than the right-wing Social Democrats. Ledebour lost out. The party, by a vote of 192 to 9, decided in favor of union. A small group, led by Ledebour and Theodor Liebknecht, a brother of Karl, refused to accept this decision and organized a faction of their own.

Immediately after the conclusion of the two congresses, a convention of the united Social Democrats took place in Nuremberg. All-out defense of the republic was once again promised. But even as the delegates pondered the party's next moves, their constituents throughout the land began to worry about something else. For the disappearance of the old split in the ranks of German Social Democracy coincided with a resumption of the drive by powerful right-wing elements to wipe out some of labor's recent gains. This drive was led by Hugo Stinnes. He argued that the time had come to increase the hours of work in industry. His efforts were seconded by Fritz Thyssen, the great steel magnate, who formally demanded the introduction of the ten-hour day. A similar line was taken by Premier Knilling and his supporters in Bavaria. The trade unions did not dissemble their alarm. They regarded the eight-hour day as one of the major accomplishments of the November revolution. They were prepared to fight hard to insure its preservation. Thus, another phase of the unending social struggle in Germany seemed in the offing.

4

In February, 1922, Ebert invited the Reichstag to fix a date for the first popular election of the nation's chief executive. For several months no action was taken. Then, in July, the various party leaders announced that some decision would be reached not later than October. The government, mindful of the difficulties that continued to stand in the way of an inter-party agreement, resolved to intervene. On October

5, it suggested that the election take place at the beginning of December. This gesture evoked mixed feelings. The Democrats and the People's party considered it ill-advised. The election, they argued, should be postponed until political passions, which were still running high, had had a chance to subside. A presidential contest at this time was bound to throw the country into even greater turmoil and prejudice its position abroad. The Nationalists, who wished to obtain control of the presidency in order to further their monarchist schemes, insisted upon an immediate election and talked about offering Hindenburg as their candidate. The Social Democrats had every reason to align themselves with the Democrats and the People's party. But they succumbed to their constitutional scruples and supported the demand for an election. Should this demand be denied, they averred, the constitution would have to be amended in order to do away with the provisional character of Ebert's incumbency. The impasse was resolved by the Center. On October 11, it recommended that Ebert's term of office be extended to the close of June, 1925. The People's party and the Democrats promptly acquiesced. The Social Democrats dropped their legalistic attitude and likewise assented. A motion incorporating the Centrist recommendation was laid before the Reichstag by the four parties. The proponents of the measure emphasized the skill and tact displayed by Ebert in the discharge of his duties. They called attention to his truly national outlook, his unwillingness to think of himself as the servant of one particular party or faction. The Nationalists took sharp issue with the pro-Ebert bloc. Speaking for his comrades, Hergt freely vented his aversion to the idea of allowing the highest office in the land to remain in the hands of a socialist. He charged that Ebert had conducted himself, not as the representative of all the people, but as the spokesman for one political group. He also assailed the three middle parties, accusing them of spineless subservience to the wishes of the Social Democrats. Hergt's uncomplimentary references to Ebert brought a spirited protest from Wirth. But they were applauded by the Communists, who made common cause with the Nationalists on this issue. The men of the hammer and sickle regarded Ebert as the tool of the counterrevolutionary elements and therefore welcomed the possibility of forcing his departure. However, the outcome of the balloting was a foregone conclusion. The sponsors of the motion secured its adoption on October 24, 1922. The vote was 314 to 76. Trying times were manifestly ahead, but at least the hurly-burly of a free-for-all struggle for the presidency had been averted.

Chapter 17

WILHELM CUNO, THE RUHR IMBROGLIO AND THE GREAT INFLATION

I

DURING the first postwar years, Germany underwent the discomforts and ultimately the horrors of monetary inflation. Recourse to the printing press in an effort to cope with ever-increasing budgetary deficits boomeranged dismally. The deficits remained and the mark tobogganed. In January, 1921, when the downward trend was already well under way, the mark was forty-five to the dollar; in December of the same year, it was 160. Germany was hamstrung by a shortage of gold. For this many things were responsible: the transfer of certain stipulated sums to other lands in fulfillment of the reparation obligation; the flight of capital, which developed when Germany's plutocrats, who refused to co-operate with their government in meeting the demands of the nation's creditors, sent large amounts of money out of the country in order to prevent them from being attached for the payment of reparation; reduced credit facilities abroad; the adverse balance of trade, which sprang from the still-depressed condition of German industry, the innumerable obstacles placed in the way of German exports by other countries, and the shortage of raw-material reserves. With every passing month, Germany's already depleted supply of gold dwindled, revenue lagged farther and farther behind expenditures, and her printing presses turned out more and more paper money that was worth less and less.

Late in 1921, the German government declared that its manifold financial difficulties made it impossible for the Reich to meet the reparation installments that were about to fall due. Stressing its inability to pay reparation without foreign loans or recourse to even more drastic inflation, it asked the Allies for a moratorium on reparation payments for the following year. In March, 1922, a partial moratorium was granted. But thereafter economic conditions in Germany, instead of improving, went from bad to worse. The mark continued to fall at a dizzy pace, the flight of capital persisted in spite of governmental efforts to halt it, and the budgetary deficits kept mounting, increased taxation notwithstanding. The plight of the nation's currency was indicative of the over-all trend of affairs. In January, 1922, the mark had been quoted at 162 to the dollar. In September, the ratio was 1,303 to 1; two months later, one dollar fetched no fewer than 7,000 marks. This inflation attained unbelievably catastrophic proportions during the ensuing year. Already, however, the rapid depreciation of the mark had brought ruin and misery to a large section of the German population. Workers found it increasingly difficult to buy necessities, and in their discontent became more receptive to communist propaganda. The middle classes likewise suffered intensely. They were to fare even worse in 1923.

The German government, contending that the decline of the mark was due exclusively to reparation, warned that complete economic collapse would ensue if reparation obligations were enforced. In July, 1922, it underscored this warning by informing the Reparation Commission that financial disaster could be averted only if Germany were granted a total moratorium on cash reparation payments until the end of 1924. The issue thus posed was of paramount significance to the German people, but their minds were momentarily diverted from it by the recrudescence of political terrorism. The murder of Rathenau was followed by an amazingly brazen attempt on the life of the liberal journalist, Maximilian Harden. This, and rumors of other attempted assassinations, intensified the prevailing nervousness. The feeling became general that anything could happen, that no one was safe any longer.

Late in August, 1922, Wirth received leading representatives of the trade unions and discussed with them the desperate economic plight of the country. He assured his anxious visitors that the policy of fulfilling treaty obligations would not be permitted to jeopardize the government's efforts to provide food for the people. A few weeks later, Wirth reiterated this point, declaring: "First bread, then reparation." The nation applauded, but the days that followed brought no attenuation of its difficulties. Toward the end of October, 1922, the

German government conferred at length with representatives of the Reparation Commission. In an effort to speed consideration of Germany's plea for financial assistance, Wirth called in an international committee of experts. The countries represented on it included Great Britain, Holland and Sweden. The committee drafted a report which stated that, in last analysis, there could be no monetary stabilization in Germany until a final solution of the reparation question had been worked out. Thereupon Wirth urged the Reparation Commission to take immediate action with a view to bolstering the mark. He suggested that an international syndicate be created with the co-operation of the German Reichsbank. This syndicate would see to it that Germany obtained a loan of at least 50 million gold marks. The money would be used to support the Reich's efforts to regain financial stability. The Reparation Commission demurred. Wirth's proposals, it said, were not sufficiently definite. On November 13, 1922, the chancellor countered with these concrete suggestions: the reparation bill should be reduced; Germany should be granted a total moratorium for three or four years; an international financial conference should be convoked at once for the purpose of working out the terms of a loan to Germany.

In the meantime, a new political crisis was brewing within the Reich. The Social Democrats had collaborated closely with Wirth and had been continuously represented in his cabinet. But in the autumn of 1922, they fell out with him over the question of including members of the People's party in a reconstructed ministry which he was likewise to head. They were worried about current efforts to do away with the eight-hour day. They were pressing for monetary stabilization. On both these issues, they found themselves opposed by leading representatives of the People's party, notably Stinnes and other spokesmen for heavy industry. The Social Democrats gave a faithful picture of their state of mind in a manifesto which they issued on October 30, 1922. They declared that under no circumstances would they permit any tampering with the eight-hour day. They contended that the most effective way to increase production in Germany at this critical hour was to stabilize the mark. Any government, they warned, which refused to act in behalf of monetary stabilization and which sought to eliminate the eight-hour day would be strongly opposed by the Social Democratic party. This was clearly distressing to Wirth; he attached the greatest importance to Social Democratic collaboration and was unwilling to retain the chancellorship without it. At the same time, however, he felt that a reconstruction of his cabinet was necessary in order to make room for members of the People's party. His aim was to establish a government which would be better able to cope with the complex financial and economic issues confronting the country. In reply to his overtures, the People's party declared itself ready to join the Social Democrats, the Centrists and the Democrats in fashioning a coalition cabinet. Wirth immediately put pressure on his old friends in the Social Democratic party, urging them to waive their objections to collaboration with the followers of Stresemann. He ran into a stone wall—and resigned. This was on November 14, 1922. Wirth was never able to recapture the influence which he wielded during his chancellorship. But the real losers were the republicans, whose confidence he enjoyed and whose interests he honestly sought to serve. Grave economic and political difficulties were threatening the very existence of the Weimar regime. His departure at such a moment could not help but be a heavy blow to German democracy.

2

In 1918, Albert Ballin, the general director of the Hamburg-American Line, committed suicide because of grief over the defeat of Germany. Forty-two-year-old Wilhelm Cuno became head of the mammoth shipping concern. He had an attractive personality and a shrewd brain. He knew how to size people up and make them like him. Above all, he was a competent executive and did extremely well in his new undertaking. He represented Germany as an economic expert at numerous international conferences. He belonged to the People's party up to the time of the Kapp putsch; he withdrew from it because he did not like its ambiguous attitude during that hectic episode. He joined no other party and thus came to rate as an independent in politics. In the autumn of 1922, his reputation, which was already considerable, reached a new high, thanks to the growing belief that only the business leaders could save the country from financial chaos and ruin. The apparent inability of the state to surmount the current monetary crisis threw into sharper relief the fact that private business concerns were forging steadily ahead. The exploits of men like Stinnes, Thyssen and Cuno made a deep impression on the nation; they underlined the futility of reposing faith in politicians who were not conversant with the intricacies of modern finance. There grew up a kind of myth about the men who headed vast economic enterprises; they were credited with a species of wizardry which would enable them, once they were at the helm of the state, to do the impossible.

On November 16, 1922, Ebert requested Cuno to form a new cabinet. The latter opened negotiations with the various party leaders, but a temporary impasse ensued because he refused to be dictated to in regard to the choice of his ministers. Finally, after the Social Democrats had reiterated their unwillingness to join a government which should include members of the People's party, Cuno succeeded in putting together a cabinet consisting almost entirely of representatives of the middle parties. Holdovers from the Wirth government were Heinrich Brauns (Center), minister of labor; Gessler, minister of war; General Groener (without party affiliation), minister of transport; Andreas Hermes (Center), minister of finance. The ministry of the treasury went to a former chief of the Reich chancellery, Dr. Heinrich Albert. The new vice-chancellor, Karl Heinze (People's party), likewise assumed the ministry of justice, a post he had held under Fehrenbach. The ministry of the interior was placed under the direction of Rudolf Oeser, a highly respected Democrat. Cuno assigned the ministry of food and agriculture to Dr. Hermann Mueller-Bonn, director of the Rhenish Agricultural Chamber, but this unquestionably capable individual was disclosed to have supported the separatist movement in 1919. So he was replaced by a non-party man, Hans Luther, mayor of Essen. The appointment which caused the greatest consternation in Social Democratic circles was that of Johannes Becker as minister of economics. Becker belonged to the right wing of the People's party, a group which included reactionary industrialists like Stinnes, Kurt Sorge and Albert Voegler. He was a member of the board of directors of the giant Rhenish Steel Corporation (*Rheinische Stahlwerke*). One of his most intimate friends was Helfferich, who from the beginning wielded a great influence upon the deliberations of the Cuno cabinet. The new chancellor had an adequate grasp of the problems that clamored for solution. He was motivated by a genuine desire to promote the country's well-being. That he managed, nonetheless, to accomplish so little may be ascribed in part to his alliance with the tycoons of German industry and finance. These men were unwilling to see him pursue a policy which might have redounded to the advantage of the nation as a whole. And he, in turn, proved receptive to their counsels.

On November 24, 1922, Cuno laid his program before the Reichstag. He echoed Wirth's dictum: "First bread, then reparation." His government, he said, was resolved to work for the proposals contained in the German reparation note of November 13, 1922. He promised to do what he could to bolster the mark and improve the country's economic position. The Social Democrats were unimpressed. They did not take kindly to Cuno. They charged that the advent of his government was a victory for capitalism and a defeat for the principles of parliamentary democracy. They reaffirmed their determination to resist all attempts to tamper with the eight-hour day. This brought a quick retort from Wilhelm Marx, the Centrist leader. The tone of his remarks attested the intensity of the ill feeling that had developed between the Centrists and the Social Democratic party as a result of the latter's refusal to go along with Wirth. The Nationalists, who were not represented in the Cuno cabinet, announced that they would support the chancellor's program. The Democrats and the People's party issued similar statements. In the course of these amenities, the Social Democrats received a tongue-lashing from Stresemann, who assailed their "lust for power" and their unwillingness to co-operate with other parties. He need not have worried. In spite of their outspoken hostility to Cuno, the Social Democrats voted in favor of his program when the discussion ended. Only the Communists and the Racialists ranged themselves against the new government.

3

Having taken over the reparation policy of Wirth, Cuno hoped for a favorable response from the Allies. The very last thing he wanted was a quarrel with the French. He had not the slightest intention of halting reparation payments. He was prepared to discuss the whole question in a positive and accommodating spirit. His principal concern was to obtain a final and fair estimate of Germany's capacity to pay. But the French, taking their cue from their Germanophobe premier, Raymond Poincaré, refused to make concessions. They had already spent billions for the restoration of war-devastated areas on the assumption that they would get every penny back in the form of reparation. If Germany defaulted, the French public would be left holding the bag; for it had bought the bonds floated by the French government to raise the sums needed for reconstruction. Poincaré and those who shared his views believed that Germany was well able to pay. All that she lacked, they held, was the will to do so. The depreciation of her currency and the bankrupt state of her finances were part of a deliberate fake, the purpose of which was to enable her to escape her obligations. Poincaré's reply to the German demand for a moratorium was therefore far from accommodating. There could be no moratorium, he said, without productive guarantees; and the productive guarantee which he and the French iron industry demanded was the Ruhr. The Franco-German frontier was not a satisfactory one from the standpoint of the Comité des Forges, France's all-powerful association of steelmakers. Most of the iron ore deposits were on the French side of the frontier, while the great coal deposits were on the German side. Hence the French desire for the Ruhr. Another consideration, so far as Paris was concerned, was the incalculable injury which the loss of this industrially crucial area would do to German economy. A weaker Reich meant a safer France. The British disagreed with Poincaré on this issue; they strongly opposed military sanctions. The American government also frowned on the use of coercive measures. It inclined to the view that Germany's capacity to pay should be reexamined and that large loans should be extended to her. It regarded military invasions of German territory as dangerous to any sensible economic solution. Britain's new premier, Andrew Bonar Law, agreed.

A meeting of the French, British, Italian and Belgian premiers took place in London from the ninth to the eleventh of December, 1922. The recommendations incorporated in the Wirth note of November 13, 1922, were unanimously rejected. But Poincaré could not get Bonar Law to accept the French thesis that the Ruhr should be occupied in order to guarantee German compliance with the terms of the reparation settlement. This difference of opinion became overnight a major diplomatic controversy. Bonar Law discussed the matter in the House of Commons on December 14, 1922. Germany, he said, had indeed failed to make the payments due, and the mark was rapidly declining. But he emphasized that he did not share the French view that this was part of a deliberate German scheme to cheat the creditor nations. He was most explicit on the subject of the Ruhr. Great Britain, he declared, could not remain indifferent to any action which would have the effect of making future reparation payments difficult, if not impossible. Bonar Law's position was supported not only by his Conservative colleagues but by Liberals and Laborites as well. On the very next day, Poincaré replied in language that left no room for doubt as to his intentions. France, he stated, preferred to act in concert with her allies. But, if necessary, she would act alone.

The only thing that stood in the way of a French invasion of the

Ruhr was the absence of a legal pretext for such action; and such a pretext could materialize only if the Reparation Commission should certify that Germany had failed to meet her obligations. This formality was speedily taken care of. On December 2, 1922, the German government had informed the Reparation Commission that it would be unable to make full timber deliveries on time and requested an extension until April 1, 1923. Poincaré made the most of his opportunity. On December 27, against the opposition of the British member, the Reparation Commission declared Germany in default. Her failure to supply 140,000 telegraph poles when they were due was adduced as justification for this action. Berlin's contention that this lag in deliveries was both involuntary and temporary had been completely ignored. Most Germans believed that a French occupation of the Ruhr was certain. That this belief was well founded was demonstrated on January 9, 1923, when the Reparation Commission voted three to one (England again furnished the opposition) in favor of a resolution declaring Germany in default on her coal deliveries. Poincaré was now ready to act.

Franco-Belgian troops, under the command of General Degoutte, moved into the Ruhr on January 11, 1923. Their function was to give protection to the committee of engineers which was to direct the operation of the mines and factories on behalf of the French and Belgian governments. A number of key cities, including Essen and Dortmund, were occupied. The British strongly disapproved of the invasion; the American reaction was likewise unfavorable. But this, at the moment, was small solace to the German government. It had to face, unaided, a mortal threat to the economic and territorial fabric of the Reich. Without hesitation, it branded the French action as illegal and adopted a policy of passive resistance. The people of the Ruhr were instructed to do nothing which might work harm to the interests of the Fatherland or facilitate the task of the invaders. Active resistance was, of course, out of the question for disarmed Germany. Besides, Cuno believed that the French would find it impossible to operate the sequestered mines and plants without assistance from the Germans. He foresaw bankruptcy for the French exchequer as a result of the high cost of the venture. Thus, in the end—so reasoned the chancellor—the French would have to withdraw from the Ruhr much the poorer and with their prestige considerably diminished. And so the German authorities enforced the policy of passive resistance with conviction and energy. The Reich coal commissioner ordered the cessation of all coal and coke deliveries to France and Belgium. Their continuance was promptly demanded by the chairman of the Franco-Belgian committee of engineers. In the name of the local mine-owners, Fritz Thyssen declined to heed this demand. Degoutte called upon the miners for help, but they refused to bestir themselves. Indignation ran high. In and outside the Ruhr the view prevailed that France was attempting to do in 1923 what she had failed to do in 1919, thanks to Anglo-American opposition—namely, to establish a Rhenish buffer state under French domination as a step toward ultimate dismemberment of the Reich. The evident determination of the invaders to foster separatism in the Rhineland and to bring about the secession of this industrially rich area engendered throughout the Reich a feeling of oneness such as had not existed since the first days of the war. Germans of every class and party called upon the government to do its utmost; they declared themselves ready, if necessary, to make the greatest sacrifices in order to frustrate the traditional foe. Even the Communists took a strongly nationalist line. They demanded a general strike, which they described as the only effective answer to the French, but their urgings fell on deaf ears. Equally fruitless was the agitation of extremists on the Right in favor of active resistance. In the occupied zone, the bulk of the population followed Berlin's instructions and refused to obey the orders of the Franco-Belgian authorities. The ban against reparation deliveries was extended to embrace all commodities; the Rhenish-Westphalian Syndicate headed by Stinnes moved its headquarters to Hamburg. Factories and mines taken over by the French lapsed into idleness because those who worked in them refused to carry on. Railway employees declined to operate lines that were no longer under German control. The struggle quickly spread to all of occupied Germany. When coal-tax and customs receipts were earmarked for seizure, local officials throughout the Rhineland received instructions to disregard the commands of their new masters. A great many of these bureaucrats were immediately ousted from their positions and forced to go to unoccupied Germany. Mass arrests became a frequent occurrence. There were clashes between the foreign troops and the local population, whereupon Degoutte ordered a more rigid enforcement of the state of siege. He likewise took over more of the local railway lines and forbade the export of coal and coke to unoccupied Germany. Berlin retaliated by suspending all railway traffic between central Germany and the regions to the west.

In February, 1923, Cuno stated that there could be no settlement of the controversy until the Ruhr had been evacuated. But the French showed no disposition to pull out. On the contrary, they heaped new injuries on old. They took possession of a number of cities in Baden and prohibited the export of metallurgical products to unoccupied Germany. The Reich authorities, nothing daunted, cited figures to show that the amount of coal the French were getting out of the Ruhr had been reduced to a mere trickle. Ebert appealed for a continuation of passive resistance, declaring that it was the duty of every patriotic German to make things more and more difficult for the invaders. The latter were unimpressed. Completely ignoring the protests of the local citizenry, they forbade the police to wear uniforms and carry arms. When Berlin enjoined defiance, the French, without further ado, disbanded the police force of Essen and banished its members. But this was not all. Every German customs official was dismissed and the whole of occupied Germany was separated from the rest of the Reich by a tariff wall. Stringent punishment was prescribed for anyone guilty of interfering with the operation of the railways. A clash between French troops and irate workers occurred on March 31, 1923, in the Krupp factories in Essen; thirteen persons were killed and thirty were wounded. The local trade unions bitterly denounced the French for this, accusing them of wishing to enslave the German proletariat. The activities of Rhineland separatists, who were being encouraged by the invaders, served to increase the tension. The Communists likewise did their bit to make matters more chaotic. They clashed with moderate working-class elements, still resistant to the idea of a general strike, and with middle-class volunteer units organized for purposes of self-defense. A terrorist note was introduced by dynamite squads who blew up bridges, railway trestles and French military trains. These squads operated at night; they were led by guides who sometimes betrayed them. It was as a result of one such betrayal that a former Free Corps leader by the name of Albert Leo Schlageter fell into the hands of the French. They found him guilty of sabotage and executed him at Duesseldorf on May ˜6, 1923. During the trial, Schlageter admitted that he had done this work for money. He also revealed the identity of some of his comrades. But the Nationalists and the Nazis eulogized him as a great hero. The German people, Hitler declared, scarcely deserved such a man.

4

For a time, Seeckt believed that the occupation of the Ruhr might be the prelude to a major war. There was talk of Polish and Czech preparations for mobilization, and German military circles felt impelled to envisage the possibility of hostilities all along the nation's eastern frontier. When Marshal Foch went to Warsaw in April, 1923, the danger of a general conflict seemed imminent. The leaders of the Reichswehr pondered all sorts of ambitious plans; they even toyed with the idea of concluding a military alliance with Austria and Hungary. Ebert, who was kept informed of what the generals were cogitating, assented to Seeckt's intention to fight back if Germany should be attacked. But Cuno, mindful of the country's military helplessness vis-à-vis France, refused to think in such terms. In order to bolster the armed strength of the Reich at this critical juncture, Seeckt resorted to the creation of illegal military formations. The Reichswehr recruited short-term volunteers and added them to the 100,000 men allowed by the Treaty of Versailles. It was in this fashion that the so-called Black Reichswehr came into being. These units, comprising about 50,000 men, were composed in large part of Free Corps veterans who had been unable or unwilling to find non-military employment.

5

Social Democratic leaders in Berlin, encouraged by the friendly attitude of the British government, began to advocate an understanding with the western powers which would pave the way for the evacuation of the Ruhr. A prominent part in the discussion of what Germany should do next was taken by Stresemann. He reprimanded the pan-Germans for their insistence that the Reich should simply stop paying reparation and tell the Allies to go to the devil. The reparation question, he maintained, could be settled by negotiation. But first the French would have to give up the preposterous idea of detaching the Ruhr and the Rhineland from Germany. It was in a spirit of sober realism that Berlin renewed its efforts to terminate the imbroglio. But the overtures which it made in May, 1923, proved fruitless because the French and Belgians refused to negotiate as long as passive resistance continued in the Ruhr. Besides, the reparation total proposed by Cuno was only one-fourth of the sum to which Germany had assented in 1921. Even the British, for all their desire to see the Ruhr business ended as speedily as possible, pronounced the German proposals unsatisfactory. A similar reply was vouchsafed by Italy. On June 7, 1923, the government of the Reich submitted new recommendations; they betokened its readiness to acquiesce in further concessions to the Allied point of view. Stanley Baldwin, who had succeeded the ailing Bonar Law as British prime minister, suggested to the other creditor states that a common reply be drafted. The authorities in London formally agreed to a reexamination of Germany's capacity to pay. They regarded the restoration of economic normalcy in the Ruhr as a step toward the pacification of western Europe. They stipulated, however, that the Reich must first abandon the policy of passive resistance. As for the investigation of Germany's capacity to pay, it would have to be undertaken by a committee of impartial experts. Occupation of the Ruhr could be terminated as soon as the economic guarantees to be demanded of Germany had been put into effect. Poincaré's rejoinder was scarcely encouraging. He pointed out that no definite proposal regarding the cessation of passive resistance had as yet been received from Germany. He wanted to know whether the English plan also applied to inter-Allied war debts. And who, he queried, was to appoint the experts? By emphasizing the competence of the Reparation Commission, he sought to restore the controversy to its original status. The ensuing negotiations between the creditor states dragged on into August. The British told France and Belgium that a linking of reparation and inter-Allied debts was inadmissible. They called attention to the fact that the reparation total fixed in 1921 had been arrived at without taking into account Germany's capacity to pay. France, Poincaré replied, was prepared to pay her debts; consequently, she would have to insist that Germany do likewise. The impasse continued.

6

The occupation of the Ruhr had a most disastrous effect upon the already sagging economy of the Reich. The isolation of this supremely vital industrial area from the rest of the country brought commercial activity to a virtual standstill and robbed the German treasury of desperately needed revenue. Suffering became general as the poison of economic dislocation spread. The decision to subsidize the passive resisters in the Ruhr was, under the circumstances, unavoidable; but its principal effect was to quicken the process of financial disorganization. The output of paper money climbed to a new high. The inflation, entering upon its climactic phase, attained the proportions of an overwhelming catastrophe. The mark sank to such fantastic depths that the barter of goods began to replace the exchange of commodities for money. Matters reached a desperate pass when farmers refused to sell their produce for worthless currency. Trucks and trains bearing food to famished city-dwellers were frequently attacked and pillaged. Such was the spectacle presented by a land that only nine years before had been one of the world's richest.

Where all this would end no one could say, but there were Germans, millions of them, who knew that their lives would never be the same again. They were the rentiers, the people with fixed incomes. They were wiped out by the inflation. Wiped out, too, were other segments of the once prosperous German bourgeoisie. Professor Arthur Rosenberg, in his *History of the German Republic*, comments as follows on this tragic development:

The systematic expropriation of the German middle classes, not by a Socialist Government but in a bourgeois State whose motto was the preservation of private property, is an unprecedented occurrence. It was one of the biggest robberies known to history.

These victims of the currency debacle were depressed into the ranks of the proletariat. They retained their bourgeois, white-collar psychology, and hence proved unreceptive to communist propaganda. But they had lost their faith in liberalism, in the philosophy of moderation, of which the Weimar regime was the symbol and the embodiment. In their anguish, they turned to the gospel of extremism preached by the reactionary foes of democracy.

The middle classes were not alone in their suffering. True, the proletariat was spared the agony of seeing its savings wiped out for the simple reason that it possessed very few assets of this kind. But the drop in real wages was nothing short of calamitous. The purchasing power of paper wages sank so low that the average worker found himself unable to procure anything like adequate supplies of food and clothing for himself and his family. The inflation dealt a staggering blow to the trade unions. It undermined their financial position and thus rendered them incapable of performing their routine functions. Benefit payments to their members had to be suspended. Collective-bargaining contracts ceased to give any protection to the workers because of the rapid changes in the purchasing power of the mark. Millions of wage-earners decided that they had nothing more to gain by retaining their membership in trade associations. They sought aid and relief elsewhere.

While the laboring and middle classes were thus made to feel the full impact of runaway inflation, debtors, real-estate operators and industrial magnates were having a field day. People who had bonds to retire, mortgages to lift or notes to pay hastened to do so with worthless currency. Real-estate values soared, and immense profits were garnered by those who knew how to play this game. Speculation attained fantastic proportions. The great industrialists likewise profited enormously. They paid off loans, hired artificially cheap labor, expanded their plants and invested in up-to-date equipment. They increased their holdings at the expense of less fortunate competitors in the intermediate reaches of the economic hierarchy. Little wonder, then, that they evinced no desire to see the inflation halted until the mark had ceased to have any value whatever.

7

The tumult and suffering caused by the occupation of the Ruhr provided right-wing extremists with a golden opportunity to harass the republic and abuse its leaders. They opened their campaign on the very morrow of the invasion. The National Socialists sought to place themselves at the head of this movement. Hitler contemptuously spurned Cuno's plea for a united national front against the French. He ridiculed the policy of passive resistance, saying it was useless unless it was backed up by active resistance or at least guerrilla warfare. What he was really worried about was the possibility that the German people, confronted by this grave threat to their existence, might achieve unity and regain their strength without him and his party. Specifically, he feared that the Social Democrats, who supported the policy of passive resistance with wholehearted enthusiasm, might emerge from the crisis with a commanding position in German affairs. To his followers and to all others who would listen, he said: "No—not down with France, but down with the traitors to the Fatherland, down with the November criminals." He accused the Jews of fomenting all the current excitement. It was their intention, he charged, to force Germany into a war which she could not possibly win.

At the close of January, 1923, Hitler ordered 5,000 members of his S.A. to assemble in Munich for a mammoth demonstration. Fearful that a putsch might be attempted, Franz Schweyer, the Bavarian minister of the interior, declared that he would not allow the demonstration to take place. At this point Roehm intervened. He prevailed upon General Otto von Lossow, who had succeeded Epp as boss of the Bavarian Reichswehr, to ask the Knilling cabinet to modify its stand.

Schweyer was compelled to yield; the demonstration took place. Hitler now sought to establish closer relations with Lossow. He urged him to mobilize the Reichswehr for a march on Berlin. He contended that the moment was propitious for such action. The general listened attentively. There was much about the mustached demagogue that intrigued and impressed him. But he, for one, had no stomach for harebrained schemes; without full-bodied support from the Reichswehr of the northern provinces, a march on Berlin was likely to prove an ignominious fiasco. In the meantime, the Bavarian Social Democrats, like their comrades in other parts of the Reich, had begun to display a more aggressive spirit. They had at their disposal a small but well disciplined semi-military force and a highly efficient political organization. Hitler resolved to neutralize this threat before it should become too dangerous; he also hoped, in so doing, to launch a drive that would not cease until the Weimar system had been overthrown. The fireworks began in March, 1923, with a National Socialist attack on the printing establishment of the *Muenchener Post*, an organ of the Social Democratic party. This was promptly followed by other acts of violence. The Social Democrats demanded the dissolution of all Storm Troop formations, but the Bavarian government refused. It did, however, promise to enforce existing laws against S.A. terrorists. Encouraged by the leniency of the authorities, the Nazis made plans to break up the great demonstration scheduled by the Social Democrats for May 1, Europe's Labor Day. To do this, weapons were needed, and Lossow was the man who possessed the authority to issue them. But the general did not care to see an upheaval started by Storm Troop irresponsibles. He refused to grant Hitler's request. The Nazis thereupon repaired to the military depots and helped themselves. On the first of May, 1923, thousands of S.A. men, equipped with rifles, machine guns and light artillery, gathered on the *Oberwiesenfeld*, Munich's mammoth drilling ground, for a march to the site of the Social Democratic rally. The city had been deluged with leaflets proclaiming that a Bolshevist putsch was imminent. When all was in readiness, the Storm Troopers, with Goering at their head, began to move. But the police and the Reichswehr were ready for them. They surrounded Goering's men, who were finally persuaded to surrender their weapons. A clash was thus averted that might easily have precipitated a state of civil war. Schweyer wanted the government to institute legal proceedings against Hitler and his comrades. But Guertner saw to it that they were not molested. The reactionary elements that controlled the

Bavarian cabinet regarded the National Socialists as indispensable allies in the struggle against Berlin and the "Reds."

Left-wing extremists likewise sought to exploit the excitement and dislocation produced by the occupation of the Ruhr. But, as usual, they had a harder time than their rivals on the Right. Early in May, 1923, the Prussian government dealt the Communists a heavy blow by denying them the right to organize their own fighting associations. However, in Saxony, where Erich Zeigner, a Social Democrat of militant outlook, was premier, this right was granted them. At once there ensued a sharp increase in the number of disorders. The tumult spread to other *Laender*. The Reich seemed on the brink of civil war. Matters were made no easier by the fact that Captain Ehrhardt, who had finally been apprehended and was awaiting trial for his part in the Kapp putsch, broke out of jail in July, 1923. It was a foregone conclusion that he would resume his terrorist activities. The Cuno government decided to intervene. It warned that all perpetrators of violence would be ruthlessly punished. But there could be little doubt that it was far more concerned about proletarian radicals than about agitators who stood to the right of center. This lop-sided approach to the problem of restoring public tranquillity caused intense dissatisfaction among the working classes, already plagued by the consequences of inflation and nationwide economic paralysis. Buoyed by the resentment of their constituents, the Social Democratic deputies in the Reichstag took a bolder line. They bluntly accused the Reichswehr of disloyalty to the Weimar constitution. They demanded official action against the German Racial party. Simultaneously, the trade-union leaders made it clear that they no longer had any faith in the Cuno government.

The final showdown began on August 9, 1923, when Cuno asked the Reichstag for a vote of confidence. Hermann Mueller, speaking for the Social Democrats, minced no words. He pointed out that the critical economic situation had engendered universal bitterness. He denounced the credit policy of the Reichsbank, claiming that it had been guilty of inexcusable imprudence ever since the inflation began and that it had robbed the nation of all incentive to save. With things as they were, the masses could not understand the chancellor's admonitions to consume less and save more. Mueller lashed out against the reactionary policies of the Bavarian government and against the agitation being conducted by right-wing extremists throughout the country. He urged the German government to institute drastic economic and financial measures. The wealthy classes, he insisted, would have to be taxed more heavily; there was no other way to insure a return to normalcy and stability. Marx, the Centrist spokesman, stressed the need for co-operation in the work of rescuing Germany from the perils which surrounded her. In the name of his party, he proposed the following program: immediate establishment of a gold fund large enough to finance the acquisition of necessary foodstuffs and to stabilize the currency; creation of new opportunities for sound investment; attainment of budgetary equilibrium by means of economy measures and heavier taxation. The Center, Marx concluded, favored giving the government full authorization to put such a program into effect. Stresemann made a significant and trenchant speech on this occasion. More was at stake, he said, than the fate of a cabinet. The maintenance of constitutionalism and the very existence of the Reich hung in the balance. Everyone was agreed that the struggle in the Ruhr should not be abandoned or relaxed. This was no longer a party issue. But any German statesman who was in a position to bring about a Franco-German economic understanding and thus free the Rhineland and the Ruhr would be committing a crime if he neglected to make the most of his opportunities. France would be ill advised to persist in her efforts to dismember the Reich. Such a policy would only sow the seeds of another war. Within Germany, many people were demanding the establishment of a dictatorship. There was a core of justice in this demand, for, as matters now stood, the government had to overcome all kinds of opposition to accomplish anything at all. But the fact remained that the Weimar constitution had proved its worth. It had given Germany stability. More could have been done if putsches and swarms of secret organizations had not kept the country in a state of turmoil. Whoever fought the present regime was running the risk of plunging the Reich into chaos and exposing it to the danger of a Bolshevist dictatorship. In order to triumph over the destructive forces which believed that their moment had come, the German nation would have to concentrate its energies on the task of strengthening the hand of the government. The Democrats agreed with Stresemann. They demanded a leader who would not shrink from unpopular measures if the need for them should arise. The Nationalist spokesman insisted that Germany should have begun to rearm after France took it upon herself to discard the Treaty of Versailles. In his opinion, the charges made against Bavaria by the parties of the Left had not been proved. But the situation in Saxony, which had a government friendly to proletarian radicals, could scarcely be worse. The German cabinet had to show a greater willingness to lead; that would be the best protection against the threat of dictatorship. The views of the Communist party were stated by Paul Froelich. The workers, he maintained, were the ones who had conducted the struggle in the Ruhr. But they had been betrayed by their employers and by the government of the Reich. Cuno and his ministerial colleagues should be tried for committing high treason in the Ruhr, for plundering the German people and for sowing the seeds of civil war. When Froelich had finished, the Communist party introduced a motion expressing a want of confidence in the Cuno government. Graefe, speaking for the Racialists, pronounced the chancellor's program utterly inadequate. Only a dictatorship, he said, could lead the country out of its present misery. This dictatorship need not come about as a result of violence. However, in view of the failure of the middle parties to measure up to their responsibilities, only two possibilities remained. Bolshevism was one of them. The other was the racial awakening of the German people.

The government's prospects brightened perceptibly when the Reichstag proceeded to pass the tax bills which had been laid before it. Only the Communists voted no. But this optimism proved short-lived. On August 11, 1923, the Social Democrats sealed Cuno's doom by declaring in the most unequivocal manner that their patience was at an end. The country, they proclaimed, needed a stronger government, one that could command the confidence and support of the masses of the nation. Of course, without the Social Democrats, the formation of a broad coalition cabinet, such as the times seemed to dictate, was impossible. So, on August 12, Cuno handed in his resignation. Ebert promptly called upon Stresemann to form a new government. A unique opportunity lay before the one-time annexationist whose career from now on was to constitute so large and brilliant a chapter in the history of the Weimar republic. One question-mark beclouded the political horizon as he went about the task of complying with Ebert's request. That question-mark was the attitude of the Social Democrats. What would they do? Would they persist in their determination to remain outside the government and thus foredoom all efforts to establish a ministry which could claim to represent the overwhelming majority of the nation? Specifically, would they continue to reject the idea of collaborating with members of the People's party? The gravity of the current crisis induced the Social Democrats to vouchsafe an answer that evoked general applause: they agreed to a multi-party alliance which was to embrace the Stresemann group as well as the Centrists and Democrats. What they had refused to give to Wirth, a proved and trusted friend of labor, they were now willing to give to a man like Stresemann. The formation of the new cabinet went forward rapidly. Brauns, Gessler and Luther were allowed to retain their posts. Oeser was shifted to the ministry of transport. Four men represented the Social Democrats: Robert Schmidt, vice-chancellor and minister for reconstruction; Wilhelm Sollmann, minister of the interior; Rudolf Hilferding, a former Independent and one of the party's leading authorities on Marxist doctrine, minister of finance; and Gustav Radbruch, minister of justice. Johannes Fuchs, a Centrist, became minister for occupied areas while his confrère, Anton Hoefle, was named postmaster general. Hans von Raumer, a member of the People's party and a well-known spokesman for the electrical industry, assumed the ministry of economics.

The advent of Stresemann to power was accompanied by signs that even more troublous times lay ahead. The Communists of the Berlin area forced a stoppage of work in the metallurgical industry and halted the operation of transport facilities. There were disturbances and strikes in many other places, notably Hamburg, Krefeld and Breslau. A more immediate threat to Stresemann's position was the action taken on August 14, 1923, by forty-three Social Democratic members of the Reichstag. They declared themselves opposed to the new coalition cabinet. They demanded a rupture of the alliance with representatives of big business and an intensified struggle against the bourgeoisie. The leaders of the Social Democratic party sought to justify their decision to serve under Stresemann. They pointed out that the situation of the country was far more critical than it had been in November, 1922, when they forced the resignation of Wirth, and that active participation in a broad coalition government was necessary in order to end the struggle in the Ruhr. As a matter of fact, the Social Democratic chieftains, though still committed in theory to the class struggle, were acutely mindful of the country's peril and insisted on subordinating purely partisan considerations to the national interest. They felt that if things were allowed to drift, unmitigated and irreparable disaster would overtake Germany and the working classes. The territorial integrity of the Reich was under attack. The French were still fomenting separatism in the Rhineland with the object of detaching that area from Germany and setting it up as a buffer state which they would be able to control. And in Bavaria there were powerful separatist tendencies, reactionary-monarchist in character, which likewise received encouragement from the French. Should the south of Germany sunder itself from the north, there would be chaos and civil war. The great mass of Germany's workers, after four years of war and five years of postwar instability, wanted a return to normalcy. The Social Democratic leaders believed that their followers had no stomach for the panaceas espoused by the Communist party. They were absolutely opposed to any alliance or deal with the Communists; they professed to be shocked by Communist efforts to establish contact with right-wing extremists. Additional factors in their resolve to co-operate with Stresemann were the increasing number of paralyzing strikes and the ominous food shortages in the cities. Hunger insurrections had broken out in several of the larger urban centers, and there were continued attempts to plunder trains and trucks bearing sorely needed supplies. The forty-three dissenting deputies were also reminded that Stresemann had been moving steadily away from the Right within his own party. The new chancellor, born the son of a Berlin innkeeper, was associated with industries specializing in the manufacture of finished goods. It was well known that this branch of the nation's economy, which employed large numbers of skilled workers, tended to be less reactionary in its political and social outlook than heavy industry, with its great combines, its handful of magnates and its vast army of unskilled workers. Moreover, there was the indisputable fact that Stresemann, in spite of his deep-seated monarchist predilections, was honestly striving to defend the republican regime and was espousing a foreign policy which was definitely in accord with the views of the Social Democratic party.

Chapter 18

FROM THE ADVENT OF STRESEMANN TO THE
HITLER-LUDENDORFF PUTSCH

I

LONG before he assumed the chancellorship, Stresemann had concentrated his attention on foreign affairs. After the signing of the Treaty of Versailles, which he had opposed, he adopted what he termed a realistic attitude. Germany's policy, he argued, must be governed by the unhappy fact that she was the underdog, that for years she would be too weak to use force to get what she wanted. In his opinion, Germany could regain her old position in Europe only by playing ball with France for as long as might be necessary. By collaborating with the victors, she would be able, step by step, to wring new concessions, reduce the burdens imposed by the Treaty of Versailles, and ultimately secure the annulment of that treaty. In the autumn of 1922, he urged the government to make overtures to Paris. He called attention to the fact that German and French industrialists had tried to reach an understanding. Anyone with sense could see, he contended, that collaboration between the capitalists of the two countries was indispensable to Germany's economic and financial recovery. Stresemann professed not to believe that all Frenchmen sympathized with Poincaré's Germanophobe attitude. He insisted that there were elements in France that appreciated the interdependence of German and French industry and desired to co-operate with the Reich. But first Germany must have a definite reparation settlement. She had to know the full extent of her obligation. Otherwise, she would remain financially sick.

Shortly after the occupation of the Ruhr, Stresemann declared that Germany must have a threefold policy. She must seek a satisfactory solution of the reparation question. She must strive for co-operation between French and German industry. She must secure a guarantee of her western frontier. Stresemann attached great importance to the third of these objectives. So long as France retained the upper hand militarily, Germany had everything to gain from a French promise to forego hostilities. A disarmed and partly dismembered Germany would never dream of attacking her powerful neighbor. Such a venture could end only in disaster. By showing her willingness to bury the hatchet, Germany would win the good will and trust of other nations. She would thus facilitate the gradual liquidation of the Treaty of Versailles. Cuno wanted to see passive resistance maintained to the bitter end. Stresemann said it should be called off as soon as it became clear that Germany's interests would be better served by other tactics. Resistance made sense to him only if it brought an acceptable reparation settlement, contributed to the inviolability of German soil and paved the way for economic recovery. It had accomplished none of these things. It had served merely to underline Germany's helplessness and the folly of recalcitrance. The moral was clear: Germany must try conciliation. The other nations had to realize the seriousness of her plight. Just a few days before he became chancellor, Stresemann warned the Allies not to take the Reich's difficulties too lightly. Bolshevism in Germany, he declared, would mean Bolshevism in Great Britain. And all Europe would go down in the process.

2

Once in power, Stresemann sought to lead the country out of the abyss into which passive resistance had plunged it. The specter of proletarian revolution added to the horror of economic chaos. Capitulation could not long be delayed. But care had to be taken to soften the blow to German pride. The nation's sense of dignity must not be offended. Under no circumstances must the sins of the French be glossed over or minimized. Stresemann kept all this in mind as he prepared public opinion for his next moves. Troubled patriots were told what they wanted to hear: abandonment of passive resistance did not mean unconditional surrender to France; Cuno's policy had outlived its usefulness; only tactics, not principles, were at stake; all that mattered now was to save the Ruhr and the Rhineland.

Resentment against France was still at fever pitch. Yet most Germans were readier than at any time since the signing of the peace to accept the reparation burden. Force was one thing they understood and respected. The Ruhr episode had deeply impressed them. They knew now that France could not be trifled with. And seared into their minds was the realization that superior military might would be on her side for years to come. Nevertheless, Stresemann speedily alienated the Nationalists and other reactionary groups when he tackled the question of reparation. He also antagonized the right wing of his own party. The reason for this was his willingness to make certain economic concessions to the French in order to insure their prompt withdrawal from the Ruhr and from the Rhineland generally. Stresemann's critics feared that he was preparing to give up the struggle without further ado and insisted that the influence exerted by the Social Democrats was responsible for this shameful state of affairs. The leaders of the Nationalist party adopted a program which amounted to a declaration of war on the policy which Stresemann was known to favor. They demanded the establishment of a virtual dictatorship within Germany; the expulsion of the French and Belgian members of the inter-Allied Control Commissions; retaliation for acts of violence committed by the army of occupation in the Rhineland; the repudiation of Germany's obligations under the Treaty of Versailles; the reintroduction of universal military conscription. Undeterred by this challenge, Stresemann continued to stress his desire for an understanding with France. Germany, he said, was willing to give France productive guarantees. However, she would have to insist on the complete restoration of her territorial sovereignty. He acknowledged his readiness to accept the Curzon note of July 20, 1923, which made the negotiation of a new reparation agreement contingent upon the prior abandonment of passive resistance. But he wanted from the western powers assurances which would make it easier for him to defend this policy within Germany. Poincaré, however, insisted that Germany would have to abandon passive resistance unconditionally.

In the meantime, the mark was continuing its downward course. The following figures on the price of the dollar tell the story:

	MILLION MARKS
August 15	2.95
August 31	13.00
September 14	97.50
October 1	345.00

As the mark tobogganed (the tempo of its descent quickened after October 1, with the result that by November 15, 1923, one dollar fetched 2,520,000,000,000 marks), the country fell prey to mounting ferment. Serious disturbances became more frequent and rumors of impending insurrections flew thick and fast. In the face of this situation, Stresemann called the cabinet together on September 22, 1923, and asked Seeckt to attend. The conferees discussed the measures which would have to be taken in the event of a putsch by extremists of the Right or the Left. The outlook was unrelievedly black. The country, it seemed, was on the verge of economic collapse, territorial disintegration and bloody civil war. Something had to be done to avert these dangers. Obviously nothing could be accomplished without first ending the Ruhr impasse. On September 24, Stresemann reviewed the whole matter at a lengthy meeting of his cabinet. He reported that his efforts to obtain certain concessions before the abandonment of passive resistance had so far proved abortive. Unconditional termination of the struggle was therefore indicated. Stresemann then conferred with the various party leaders and found all of them, with the exception of the Nationalists, in substantial accord with him. Spokesmen for important economic groups in the Ruhr likewise assumed an affirmative attitude. On September 26, 1923, the government issued a proclamation to the German people. It called attention to some of the most lugubrious aspects of the Ruhr episode: 180,000 Germans driven from their homes; more than a hundred Germans killed and several hundred imprisoned; incalculable financial loss. During the week just ended, it pointed out, subsidies to the tune of 350 million gold marks went to the victims of the invasion; twice as much would have to be spent in the forthcoming week. Production had ceased and the economic life of the country had been completely dislocated. In order to preserve the nation and the state, the German government would have to end the struggle in the Ruhr. In keeping with this decision, Berlin ordered the immediate resumption of work in the occupied areas. Two days later, it lifted the ban on reparation deliveries to France and Belgium.

The Nationalists were furious. They denounced the government's decision to call off passive resistance and demanded instead a break with France. To these attacks Stresemann replied with an elaborate defense of his program. The majority of the Social Democratic members of the Reichstag vigorously supported him. His position seemed secure, but some of his own followers suddenly upset the apple-cart.

The representatives of heavy industry who dominated the right wing of the People's party resented the direction taken by Stresemann's internal policy. They demanded the resignation of Hilferding because they wanted fiscal measures which would make things easier for them during the post-inflationary period. They were particularly angry with Raumer, their party confrère, whom they regarded as altogether too friendly to the Social Democrats. They insisted on the abolition of the eight-hour day in the hope of saddling the workers with the costs of currency stabilization. Raumer showed himself reluctant to play their game; as a consequence, he found himself subjected to terrific pressure. He finally decided to resign. This brought matters to a head. On October 3, 1923, the entire cabinet withdrew.

The long-range aims of the right wing of the People's party were to destroy the alliance between Stresemann and the Social Democrats and to effect a rapprochement with the Nationalists. For the time being, however, these industrialists concentrated on more immediate objectives. They wanted the ministries of finance and economics to go to individuals they could trust. Hilferding and Raumer, they insisted, would have to be excluded from the new cabinet. To this the Social Democrats agreed. They feared that if they didn't and were forced into the position of having to oppose Stresemann, a dictatorship of the Right might be set up in Germany. Current developments in Italy taught a lesson which could scarcely be ignored. So Raumer's post went to Colonel Joseph Koeth, who had been serving as Reich commissioner for demobilization, and Luther succeeded Hilferding as minister of finance. Count Gerhard von Kanitz severed his ties with the Nationalist party to enter the cabinet. He was put in charge of the ministry of food and agriculture. To sweeten the pill for the Social Democrats, the People's party agreed to leave the eight-hour intact. A formal compact to this effect was concluded between the leaders of all the coalition parties. The opposition consisted, as before, of Nationalists and Communists.

3

On October 6, 1923, Stresemann presented his new cabinet to the Reichstag. He spoke at considerable length about the reasons for his decision to discontinue the policy of passive resistance. He alluded to the economic impossibility of persisting in the course inaugurated by the Cuno government. He frankly acknowledged his failure to secure certain assurances from the western powers in advance of Germany's capitulation on the central issue. This failure was due to the intransigent attitude of Poincaré. Since Germany had had no choice in the matter, her decision to yield was nothing any patriotic German need be ashamed of. The courage to assume responsibility for the abandonment of passive resistance was greater proof of patriotism than the glib charges made by the opposition. Stresemann was bitter over France's refusal to negotiate a settlement of the Ruhr and reparation questions. Germany, he emphasized, had shown her willingness to make far-reaching concessions. She had even declared herself ready to mortgage all privately owned property in the Reich in order to end the economic bondage imposed upon her by the Treaty of Versailles. But negotiations, nonetheless, had not materialized. In an effort to pacify his Nationalist critics, Stresemann reiterated his determination to safeguard German sovereignty and liberate the Ruhr. His words made little impression on the die-hards of the Right. Count Westarp, the Nationalist spokesman, bitterly assailed the government's foreign policy. Germany, he charged, was being led toward another shameful capitulation. She could still save herself and her honor by refusing to negotiate with France. Westarp also decried Stresemann's readiness to collaborate with the Social Democrats. Such a policy, to his way of thinking, could not be pursued for long. In Germany, one could only govern against the Social Democrats, not with them. This brought a slashing rejoinder from Stresemann. He defended the multi-party coalition. It was, he contended, the sole means of governing Germany constitutionally. The Social Democrats had behaved patriotically ever since the beginning of the Ruhr occupation. The Nationalist demand for repudiation of the Treaty of Versailles would have to be categorically rejected. Too many people were prone to forget that the settlement of 1919 was, to a certain degree, a protection for German interests against the policy of violence now being pursued by the French and the Belgians. One thing was indisputable: Germany could not expect to improve her position by scrapping her treaty obligations. Most of the deputies entertained similar views. This became clear when the Reichstag, against the opposition of the Nationalists, the Communists and the Bavarian People's party, gave Stresemann a rousing vote of confidence.

The way was now clear for the passage of a law conferring upon the government the plenary powers it needed to cope with the current crisis. The bill in question was enacted on October 13, 1923. Just before the vote, the Nationalists and the Communists, who had been offering strenuous objections, left the Reichstag hall. The law which irked them so authorized the government to take any and all measures it deemed necessary in the financial, economic and social sphere. It might even, if it saw fit, disregard the fundamental rights of citizens laid down in the Weimar constitution. The powers granted were not, however, to embrace the regulation of hours of work. This meant that there would be no tampering with the eight-hour day. Another area of German life placed beyond the reach of the government was that of social insurance. Moreover, all measures instituted under the terms of the law were to be promptly abrogated whenever the Reichstag so requested. Monetary stabilization was the first objective; but initial efforts to attain it were impeded by political developments which threatened the very existence of the Reich.

4

The failure of the policy of passive resistance played into the hands of those who were working to bring about the permanent separation of the occupied areas from the rest of Germany. Certain French circles, made up of reactionary nationalists and militarists, continued to espouse the program vainly advocated by Foch in 1919: the creation of a Rhenish buffer state between Germany and France. But other influential French groups rejected this program and favored a policy of moderation toward Germany. This divergence of outlook was manifest in the occupied areas. While the president of the Rhineland commission, Paul Tirard, repeatedly stated his preference for cautious methods, French generals lent their support to separatist movements. They found compliant tools in a small group of Rhineland Germans led by Joseph Smeets, Adam Dorten and Joseph Matthes. Divided among themselves and opposed by the majority of the local inhabitants, the separatists would have been of negligible importance had they not received foreign aid and had not certain middle-class elements reached the conclusion that separation from the Reich was unavoidable. Economic conditions in the Rhineland became even worse right after the cessation of passive resistance, and this proved a boon to the enemies of national unity. Separatist demonstrations took place in cities like Duesseldorf, Aachen, Bonn, Coblenz, Trier, Wiesbaden and Pirmasens. But counter-action by the Prussian authorities outside the occupied zones and by the British military in Cologne put a damper on the agitation. The movement swiftly receded. Some of its most prominent leaders were assassinated. By the first part of 1924, Rhineland separatism had virtually ceased to exist.

French-supported separatism in the west was only one of several threats to the unity of the Reich. Developments in Bavaria, Saxony and Thuringia held a similar danger. Powerful reactionary elements in Munich, spearheaded by the Bavarian People's party, the bureaucracy and the Reichswehr, were nearing the point of open rebellion against Berlin. These elements had repeatedly declared that they could not co-operate with any German government which tolerated Marxism, accepted Social Democratic support and catered to labor's wishes. Denunciations of Bolshevism and Moscow were part of their propaganda stock-in-trade. They were strongly monarchist in sentiment and hoped to bring about the overthrow of the Weimar system. They were also motivated by particularism. They denied that they favored outright separation from the Reich. What they really wanted, they said, was protection for Bavaria's autonomy within the German state. This could be accomplished by a return to the constitutional system established in 1871. Should the national government refuse to mend its ways, should it refuse to make the concessions demanded, then South Germany would have to go ahead on its own and create the basis for a truly federal Reich. Shortly after the advent of Stresemann, some Bavarian extremists went so far as to call for a march on Berlin. The German government tried to persuade the Munich authorities to assume a more co-operative attitude. Toward the middle of September, 1923, the various *Laender* sent their ministers of the interior to Berlin to attend a special session of the Reichsrat. Under consideration were the manifold problems of internal administration whose urgency had been greatly intensified by the impact of the current crisis. The Reich minister of the interior presided. He declared that the German government was firmly resolved to safeguard the constitutional rights of the states. He underlined the need for national unity and implored his hearers to do everything in their power to aid the federal authorities. But Bavaria's reaction was far from reassuring. On September 16, Knilling warned that his government could not trust the new masters of the Reich. Social Democrats, he observed, had received important posts in the Stresemann cabinet. Bavaria was deeply worried. She feared that these champions of Marxism would force Germany to give in to the French. Adverting to the atmosphere of crisis that pervaded the country, Knilling disclaimed any intention of pushing matters too far. Every serious-minded politician in Bavaria, he stated categorically,

rejected the idea of separation from the Reich. The fondest hope of
Bavaria was to see the German state strengthened on a federative
basis. The fight against Bolshevism would have to be the foremost
concern of any national government that did not wish to dig its own
grave. He defended the reactionary leagues with which Bavaria
abounded. They had come into being, he explained, in order to combat
Marxist terrorism. Germany needed them; there could be no salvation
for her without a people's army as distinguished from the Reichswehr
and the police, which were not enough. Two irreconcilable philosophies
of life today confronted each other. One of these was national-German-
Christian; the other was international-Marxist. Sooner or later, a
struggle between them would ensue.

The separatist agitation in the Rhineland and the chaos produced by
the total collapse of the mark encouraged leading circles in Munich to
believe that the Weimar republic was doomed. The contest for leadership of the Bavarian counterrevolutionaries seemed to be between three
men: Kahr, Hitler and Ludendorff. Kahr had powerful backing and a
strong will. He wished to see the Wittelsbach dynasty restored. Beyond that, apparently, his program did not go. Hitler had more ambitious plans, but he was hamstrung by the hostility of Lossow, who
never forgave the Nazis for helping themselves to arms on May 1.
Ludendorff still wielded considerable influence in military circles, and
he was unquestionably anxious to regain his former preeminence.
However, two things were against him: his inability to face unpalatable realities, and the distaste with which he was regarded by the rank
and file of the population. The Reich authorities watched developments in Bavaria with growing concern. Stories appearing almost
daily in the Social Democratic and Communist press added to their
uneasiness. These stories linked Crown Prince Rupprecht, Ludendorff
and Kahr with anti-republican putschist organizations in Munich. They
also reported a conflict between Ludendorff and the Crown Prince.
The former was represented as favoring a highly centralized system of
government for Germany, while Rupprecht, true to the traditions of
Bavarian particularism, was pictured as going all out for federalism.
The atmosphere throughout Germany became increasingly that of a
country teetering on the brink of civil war. Armed clashes and belligerent demonstrations occurred in widely separated areas. Upper Bavaria was the scene of a bloody encounter between the local Stahlhelm
and Communist militiamen. The same sort of thing happened in
Dresden and Leipzig. A brief but effective general strike, intended as

a warning to the reactionary elements, was staged by the trade unions of Hamburg. In Berlin, the police raided the headquarters of the Communist party and discovered caches in which arms were stored. The Communist organ, *Rote Fahne,* was repeatedly banned.

In spite of personal rivalries, the leaders of the many patriotic associations that flourished on Bavarian soil seemed ready to join forces for a common onslaught against the republic. Unity was the keynote of the demonstration which these associations staged in Nuremberg on September 2, 1923. A great crowd, estimated by the police authorities to be in the neighborhood of 100,000, witnessed the proceedings. A number of speakers, including Hitler, flayed the German government. A new all-embracing Fighting League *(Kampfbund)* was created, and the Nazis, who planned to use it for their own purposes, promptly announced a series of mass meetings to signalize the event. Whether Hitler entertained the idea of making these meetings the opening phase of a revolution is not clear. The Knilling government decided to take no chances. It had plans of its own and did not wish to see the initiative pass into Hitler's hands. On September 26, it proclaimed a state of siege and vested dictatorial powers in Kahr, who was given the title of State Commissioner General. The official statement explaining this action declared that authority had to be concentrated in the hands of a single person in order to prevent disturbances which were likely to arise as a result of widespread disappointment over the discontinuance of passive resistance. Kahr informed Hitler that the meetings would have to be canceled. The Fuehrer was furious. He threatened to stage a bloody insurrection. In an effort to placate him, Kahr disarmed the semi-military formations of the Social Democratic party and ordered the expulsion of all Jews of foreign nationality. In the meantime, a new flareup of the perennial controversy between Bavaria and the Reich loomed on the political horizon. When the Stresemann government was apprised of the latest events in Munich, it hastened to proclaim a state of siege for all of Germany. Full executive powers were transferred to Gessler, the minister of war, who promptly delegated them to the divisional commanders of the Reichswehr. Lossow was now in a position to challenge the authority of Kahr, but whether he would do so was quite another matter.

The opposition parties made a great to-do over the government's action. Displaying unwonted solicitude for the rights of German citizens, they urged Stresemann to terminate the state of siege forthwith. Their pleas and threats were fruitless. The Nationalists, all the while, continued to denounce Marxism, blaming it for the failure of passive resistance in the Ruhr and demanding the formation of a strong government from which the Social Democrats would be excluded. The Center sharply condemned this line. It called upon its followers to repose confidence in the Stresemann cabinet, which, it contended, was strong enough to deal with would-be revolutionaries from either the Left or the Right. The Social Democratic leaders, for their part, admonished the working classes to prepare for a determined defense of the republic. The gravity of the situation became dramatically evident on October 1, 1923, when units of the Black Reichswehr stationed in Kuestrin and Spandau attempted to seize control of those two places. The rebels were led by Major Buchdrucker, who, it was well known, had been conspiring against the republic. The local garrisons frustrated the putsch, and Buchdrucker was subsequently sentenced to ten years' imprisonment. But it was a foregone conclusion that similar putsches would be attempted in the very near future. Bavaria, as usual, loomed as the principal danger zone.

A conflict speedily developed between Gessler and Kahr. Hitler's paper, the *Voelkischer Beobachter,* printed a scurrilous attack on General Seeckt, who was blamed for the suppression of the mutiny at Kuestrin and Spandau. The federal government decided that matters had gone far enough. Gessler asked Kahr to ban the newspaper. Kahr flatly refused. He wished to show that he could not be ordered about by Berlin. He was also anxious to make the Nazis more dependent on him by threatening them with reprisals while shielding them from the consequences of this particular misdemeanor. The nature of his strategy became clear when he issued the following statement to the press:

The Commissioner General does not yet see fit to suppress the *Voelkischer Beobachter* on account of its malicious and unfounded attacks. However, he had the responsible editor summoned to the Commissioner General's office, to tell him that the slightest attempt to continue the insidious policy of deprecating the purpose and intentions of the Commissioner General will meet with severe punishment.

Gessler refused to admit defeat. He turned to Lossow and ordered him to suppress the paper. Although the general had no love for the Nazis, he felt that they represented a cause which, in the existing state of affairs, ought not to be weakened. Besides, he had no desire to place himself in opposition to Kahr. Consequently, he informed Berlin that he would not carry out the order. Gessler asked Lossow to give up his post. The latter declined to do so, whereupon Gessler dismissed him and named one of his subordinates, General Friedrich Kress von Kressenstein, as his successor. At this point Kahr intervened. He publicly demanded Gessler's resignation and announced that Lossow would remain in command of the Bavarian Reichswehr. In spite of a sharp warning from Seeckt, the Commissioner General insisted on exacting from the Bavarian troops a special oath of allegiance to the Munich authorities. The German government accused Bavaria of violating the constitution, but this made little impression on Kahr. He knew that Stresemann was in no position to take strong retaliatory measures. The chancellor, at the moment, had other worries: separatist agitation in the Rhineland, the resurgence of left-wing extremism in many sections of the country, and the intra-cabinet feud between the Social Democratic and People's parties, not to speak of the inflation and all the problems connected with it. The various right-wing groups in Munich welcomed the prospect of a final showdown with the republic and its alleged masters, the Marxists. They urged Kahr to emulate Mussolini and stage a march on Berlin. Signs were not wanting that they might yet have their way. Armed bands under the leadership of Captain Ehrhardt began to assemble along the northern frontier of Bavaria for the avowed purpose of rescuing Germany from Bolshevism. Civil war and the end of the Weimar system seemed in the offing.

5

Proletarian radicalism battened on the current crisis. From the very beginning of the struggle in the Ruhr, the Communists had developed intense activity. The hardships suffered by the working classes opened up all sorts of new possibilities. Simultaneously, the growth of right-wing extremism in the wake of the Franco-Belgian invasion posed urgent problems. One of the first and most important actions of the Communist party was to undertake the organization of proletarian fighting units, known as Hundreds, for the purpose of repelling attacks by the Fascist elements. At the same time, the party sought, by means of highly nationalistic propaganda, to attract to itself the lower-class adherents of right-wing organizations. It went out of its way to demonstrate its readiness to join other parties in the fight to free Germany of foreign domination. It loudly decried the idea of giving in to Poincaré. It glorified Schlogeter and opened the columns of the *Rote Fahne* to Count Ernst Reventlow, a writer of violently reactionary outlook. It also issued a brochure which contained, side by side, essays by Karl Radek, the well-known Bolshevist leader, and Moeller van den Bruck, mentor of the "Young Conservative" movement in Germany and author of a work entitled *The Third Reich (Das dritte Reich)*. At the meeting of the executive committee of the Third International in June, 1923, the phrase, "government of workers and peasants," was substituted for "government of workers." And the word "nation" came more and more to replace "proletariat" in the pronouncements of the German Communist party.

Throughout the first half of 1923, Moscow took the view that the Reich, in spite of all the ferment and dislocation produced by the occupation of the Ruhr, was not yet ripe for revolution. The leaders of the German Communist party concurred in this view. They regarded the decisive struggle for power in Germany as something that still belonged to the distant future. They were anxious to exploit to the full the opportunities created by the current upheaval. But they set definite limits to their objectives in accordance with their sober evaluation of the situation. A small group of left-wingers within the party took a different line. They attached supreme significance to the struggle in the Ruhr. They pictured it as the beginning of a climactic battle, as the crisis which would pave the way for social revolution in Germany. However, almost everyone they talked to dismissed their ideas as sheer Utopianism.

The increasing gravity of the country's situation during the summer of 1923 and the belief that the counterrevolutionaries were about to strike led the Communist party to assume a more bellicose attitude. On July 27, it issued a call for a general anti-Fascist congress and declared that civil war was now unavoidable. Simultaneously, action was taken to strengthen the Hundreds. The leaders of the party favored a working alliance with the left-wing Social Democrats. They hoped to bolster the anti-Fascist front by recruiting a million new members. They were encouraged by Communist victories in a number of highly important trade-union elections, especially in the Berlin area. Actually, the party attained its greatest influence during the tremendous strike wave in August, 1923. Yet even now its most authoritative spokesmen did not feel that Germany was ripe for social revolution. These men believed that the coalition cabinet formed under Stresemann would succeed in tranquilizing the country.

While the Communist party pondered its next moves, the cause of proletarian radicalism appeared to be making impressive headway in various parts of the Reich, notably Saxony, Thuringia and Hamburg. Concurrently, a curious realignment began to take shape. The Social Democrats constituted the strongest group in both Saxony and Thuringia. Unlike their confrères in Prussia, these particular champions of collectivism spurned the idea of a coalition with bourgeois parties and sought to establish closer relations with the Communists. They held that such tactics would enable them to consolidate the existing democracy and undertake the building of a socialist economy. Zeigner, the Social Democratic premier of Saxony, took the lead in urging an alliance with the Communists. The proletariat, he declared, must pursue a power-policy. This necessitated a unification of all its forces. Back in May, 1923, when Severing, the Prussian minister of the interior, forbade the creation of proletarian Hundreds, the Saxon Social Democrats decided to co-operate with the Communists in organizing semimilitary formations for the defense of the republic. They hoped to pit these formations against the local Reichswehr, which was extremely hostile to Zeigner and his friends.

The far-reaching developments that came in the wake of Stresemann's advent to power finally convinced Moscow that the zero hour was at hand. The Weimar republic seemed on the verge of complete disintegration. The working classes of the Reich—so reasoned the Russians—would have to take advantage of this golden opportunity. They would have to rise up and seize control of the state. The decisive conversations took place in Moscow toward the middle of September, 1923. The strategy to be followed was discussed with leaders of the Third International. It was agreed that the factory workers' councils, which had led the big political strike in August, should spearhead the new movement.

On October 5, 1923, the Communist party announced that it was prepared to enter the Saxon and Thuringian cabinets in order to co-operate with the Social Democrats in combating the Fascist menace. Its purpose was to use the apparatus of the state to obtain control of the police and to arm the workers for the forthcoming trial of strength. The offer was accepted. In both states coalition governments were formed by the two proletarian parties. The Communists found the going unexpectedly rough. Zeigner refused to allow one of their representatives to take charge of the Saxon police. The state of siege proclaimed by Berlin on September 26 and the dictatorial powers delegated by Gessler to General Alfred Mueller, commander of the Saxon Reichswehr, placed insurmountable obstacles in the path of the would-be revolutionaries. Mueller was thorough, if nothing else. He suppressed the Hundreds and other left-wing defense organizations. He suspended the publication of every Communist newspaper in Saxony. Finally, he denuded the Zeigner cabinet of all authority over the local police. The Communists were for mobilizing the workers and resisting the Reichswehr. But the Social Democrats refused to go along. Without their co-operation, the venture was foredoomed. The idea of an armed uprising had to be dropped. Owing to the confusion of these days, the Hamburg Communists failed to learn of the change of strategy. They went ahead with their original plans. Trained proletarian shock troops, numbering only a few hundred, swung into action early on the morning of October 23, 1923. They were promptly suppressed by the Hamburg police. The great majority of the city's workers took no part in the insurrection.

Acting on orders from Berlin, General Mueller ousted the Zeigner government late in October. Heinze, still a leading figure in the People's party, was named Reich commissioner for Saxony. A purely Social Democratic ministry was formed. The course of events in Thuringia was less dramatic, but the results were the same: the Reichswehr moved in and forced the Communists out of the cabinet. Berlin's action against both these states was unquestionably illegal; each of the ousted governments had possessed a parliamentary majority. Bavaria, which had given far more provocation, was not molested. This conformed to the well established habit of according lenient treatment to right-wing rebels. The Communist party now executed another about-face. At the behest of Moscow, it returned to the path of constitutionalism. The miscarriage of its plans for a proletarian revolution seemed to preclude any other course.

6

The ouster of the Zeigner cabinet precipitated a crisis in Berlin. Unwilling to share responsibility for this flagrant breach of the democratic principle, the Social Democratic members of Stresemann's government resigned on November 2, 1923. Stresemann decided to carry on for the time being with a rump ministry. He was almost relieved, in a way, to see the Social Democrats go. Now that the government of the Reich had been purged of its Marxists, Kahr might prove more tractable. Stresemann made every effort to reach an amicable accord with the Bavarian authorities. The latter showed a willingness to explore the possibility of a compromise. They sent an emissary to Berlin. He was Colonel Hans Seisser, commander of the Bavarian police and a member of the small coterie around Kahr. He returned to Munich firmly convinced that northern Germany would not support a political uprising. Among the Bavarian conservatives there was a noticeable slackening of interest in the idea of a march on Berlin. Measures for the financial stabilization of the Reich were being formulated by the German government, and the prospect of better times gave pause to many a counterrevolutionary. Kahr and Lossow had no desire to become embroiled in a hopeless venture. But they clung to the view that the existing relationship between Bavaria and the Reich could not continue indefinitely. They believed that sooner or later a separation was bound to take place. Hitler became panicky. He feared that Kahr and Lossow, instead of helping him conquer the Reich by means of a "national revolution," were scheming merely to detach Bavaria from the rest of Germany. He made up his mind to browbeat them into supporting his plans.

On the evening of November 8, 1923, Kahr made a political address in one of Munich's innumerable beer cellars. Most of the local bigwigs, including Lossow and Seisser, attended the meeting. Shortly after Kahr began to speak, the hall was surrounded by S.A. men. The police did not interfere; Wilhelm Frick, who had remained at his post despite Poehner's departure, saw to that. Hitler, accompanied by several of his lieutenants, rushed into the hall. He mounted the platform and informed the bewildered audience that the "national revolution" had begun. Then he ordered Kahr, Lossow and Seisser to follow him into an adjoining room. He threatened to kill them, and himself, too, if they should refuse to join him in a march on Berlin. But Kahr resisted, and so did the others. Ludendorff, who had been hastily sent for, arrived at this point. He urged the three men to co-operate. This they finally promised to do. But they had no intention of keeping their word. As soon as they were permitted to leave, they went to the *Oberwiesenfeld* and concerted military measures to curb Hitler and his followers. They learned, in the course of the night, that the German government, which was aware of the developments in Munich, had delegated full executive powers to General Seeckt. The next morning they announced that the promise extracted from them at the point of a gun was null and void. Kahr ordered the dissolution of the National Socialist party and of two fighting associations affiliated with it: the *Oberland* and the *Reichsflagge*. In taking this step, Kahr declared that

Germany and Bavaria would have been plunged into chaos if Hitler's "senseless and aimless" attempt at revolution had succeeded. Simultaneously, Ebert issued the following proclamation to the people of Germany:

Whoever supports this movement is guilty of high treason. Instead of helping our brothers in the Rhineland and in the Ruhr who are fighting for Germany, certain persons are plunging Germany into misfortune, endangering her food supply, exposing her to the risk of foreign invasion and destroying all possibility of restoring economic well-being. The latest measures taken by the German government in regard to the currency have resulted, during the last twenty-four hours, in a vast appreciation of the mark in foreign money markets. Everything will be lost if this mad attempt in Munich meets with any success. In this critical hour for the German people and the German Reich, we appeal to all friends of the Fatherland to stand forth in defense of unity, German order and German freedom. All necessary measures for the crushing of this attempt and the restoration of order have been taken, and will be enforced with ruthless energy.

Seeckt, who was ready to assist in suppressing the putsch, likewise issued a manifesto. The army, he warned, would deal sternly with attacks on public order, regardless of whence they came.

Still hopeful of winning out, the rebels staged a demonstration in Munich on the morning of November 9. At the head of the advancing column marched Ludendorff, Hitler, Goering and Max Erwin von Scheubner-Richter, a German-Russian adventurer who was very close to the Fuehrer. When the demonstrators reached the center of the city, they found the way barred by strong Reichswehr and police detachments. In the course of the brief scuffle which followed, sixteen Nazis, including Scheubner-Richter, were killed. Ludendorff, who comported himself with his usual hauteur and disregard for personal danger, narrowly escaped death. He was taken prisoner, but his captors showed little relish for the task of keeping an eye on the man who symbolized to them the military greatness of imperial Germany. Hitler, unlike the general, lost his nerve. Without bothering to see how the battle was going, he jumped into a waiting car which whisked him to the safety of a friend's home in Uffing, a suburb of the Bavarian capital. The man who played host to the distressed Fuehrer on this occasion was Ernst ("Putzi") Hanfstaengel, subsequently foreign press chief of the Third Reich. For two days, Hitler enjoyed the solicitous ministrations of Hanfstaengel's mother and sister. Then the police arrested him and brought him back to Munich for trial. His subordinates had varying fortunes. Hess fled to Austria. Upon his return to Bavaria, he was tried and sentenced to a sojourn of eighteen months in the fortress of Landsberg on the Lech. Roehm and Frick were released, even though they had been pronounced guilty of the charges brought against them. Goering was seriously wounded during the skirmish in Munich. With the aid of friends, he managed to get to Austria. When the Viennese authorities prepared to extradite him, he fled to Italy. From there, he and his wife, whose health was rapidly failing, went to Sweden. Unable to work, and slipping toward utter destitution as Karin's money dwindled, Goering suffered a nervous breakdown. He became a morphine addict and was treated in several psycopathic hospitals. Not until 1927 did he regain control of himself. Toward the close of that year, he returned to Germany and resumed his association with the National Socialist movement.

On February 18, 1924, Kahr and Lossow resigned from their posts. Eight days later, the trial of Ludendorff and Hitler began. The proceedings were something of a farce. The judges were overawed by Ludendorff and treated him with a deference that bordered on servility. To Hitler they were somewhat less respectful, but him, too, they handled with a consideration that contrasted violently with the feelings they displayed when left-wingers sat in the prisoner's box. Hitler used the trial to publicize himself and to flay the "November criminals." He was permitted to make endless, impassioned and irrelevant speeches in the court-room. For the most part, his remarks were virulent diatribes against the republic and its creators. There was nothing in the atmosphere to discourage such outbursts. Toward the close of the proceedings, he made this defiant pronouncement: [1]

The army we have formed is growing from day to day, from hour to hour. . . . I nourish the proud hope that one day . . . these wild companies will grow to battalions, the battalions to regiments, the regiments to divisions; that the old cockade will be taken from the filth, that the old flags will wave again, that there will be a reconciliation at the last great divine judgment, which we are prepared to face. Then from our bones and our graves the voice of that court will speak, which alone is entitled to sit in judgment over us. For it is not you, gentlemen, who pronounce judgment upon us. The judgment is spoken by the eternal court of history, which will say what it has to say concerning the accusation that has been raised against us. What judgment you will hand down, I know. But that court

[1] Quoted in *Der Fuehrer,* by Konrad Heiden (Houghton Mifflin Company).

will not ask us: 'Did you commit high treason or did you not?' That court will judge us, the Quartermaster General of the old army, his officers and soldiers, who, as Germans, wanted and desired only the good of their people and Fatherland; who wanted to fight and die. You may pronounce us guilty a thousand times over; the goddess of the eternal court of history will smile and tear to tatters the brief of the state's attorney and the sentence of the court; for she acquits us.

The verdict of the judges occasioned no surprise. Disregarding the explicit stipulations of the law, they gave Ludendorff a blanket acquittal. Hitler was found guilty of high treason. He received the minimum sentence prescribed for such offenses: five years' imprisonment. Actually, he regained his freedom after spending only eight and a half months in jail. He was not deported, although legally he should have been. All this bore no resemblance to the treatment meted out to the Munich "Reds" in 1919. Never was the dual standard of justice, so long prevalent in Bavaria and in other sections of the Reich, more flagrantly on display.

Chapter 19

FINANCIAL STABILIZATION AND THE DAWES PLAN

I

ON OCTOBER 16, 1923, the German government acted to end the monetary crisis. It established a new bank of issue, the Rentenbank, and decreed the introduction of a new currency. Simultaneously, it took steps to balance the budget and increase the nation's productive capacity. Responsibility for the execution of this ambitious financial and economic program was placed on the shoulders of two men: Hans Luther, minister of finance, and Hjalmar Schacht, director of the Darmstadt and National Bank and a leading figure in the Democratic party. On November 12, 1923, Schacht was made special currency commissioner. His task was to stabilize the mark. He was told to do it no matter how many foreign or German toes he stepped on in the process. He took his instructions literally. Without further ado, he halted the printing of more worthless paper money. Economy measures were ruthlessly enforced. The Rentenmark, which was to serve temporarily as the nation's currency, made its appearance on November 16. It was given a value equal to that of the gold mark of prewar days. Coverage for the Rentenmark was provided by a mortgage on the country's total industrial and agricultural resources. This piece of bluff—the mortgage in reality was nothing more than that—worked beautifully. Schacht did not have long to wait for his reward. On December 22, 1923, he was appointed president of the Reichsbank, the country's leading financial institution.

The Rentenmark was sustained by the confidence of the German people. This confidence was given without stint—until pocketbooks began to be pinched. All those who suffered as a result of the curtailment of expenditures growled their dissatisfaction. The government provoked a storm of protest when it disallowed war claims, dismissed thousands of public servants, slashed salaries and proclaimed a provisional moratorium on public loans. The same kind of outcry greeted the efforts to increase the public revenue. When taxes were raised, virtually everybody grumbled. Eventually, several of these fiscal measures had to be modified or repealed. But this did not occur until their deflationary purpose had been accomplished. The healing process was accompanied by still other hardships. A stable currency encouraged saving. The demand for commodities declined. A sharp fall in prices followed. Firms that had mushroomed into existence or over-expanded during the hectic days of the inflation found the going extremely rough. A good many of them folded up, while others were forced to reduce the scale of their operations. The workers suffered, too. The number of unemployed increased at a spectacular rate, jumping from 180,000 in July, 1923, to a million and a half in December. Previous pledges notwithstanding, the eight-hour day was scrapped. Wages remained at an extremely low level throughout the winter of 1923-24. All this meant fewer members and depleted funds for the trade unions.

2

On the morrow of the Hitler-Ludendorff putsch, the Social Democrats took a more belligerent line. They demanded action against the reactionary elements that were attempting to undermine the unity of the Reich. They were especially bitter toward Kahr, who, they insisted, should not be pardoned, since he had abetted the Nazis and defied the federal authorities. Stresemann, for his part, contended that a policy of moderation was the only one that could be pursued under existing circumstances. In the course of a political address at Halle on November 11, 1923, he said:

I have been accused of want of resolution because I have not taken a stronger line against Bavaria in past disputes. In reply, I would merely say this: in the fight for the unity of the Reich, it is, in my opinion, the duty of the German government to adopt the way of peaceful understanding until the very last resort, so long as it is a conflict in which there are Germans on both sides. . . . I shall welcome the moment when the axe is buried between Bavaria and the Reich. For what we need is a united front against the world, not dismemberment within.

Stresemann's position was rendered more difficult by the hostile attitude of the Nationalists. The die-hards on the Right continued to berate him for his decision to abandon passive resistance unconditionally. They decried his efforts to induce France to negotiate a new reparation settlement. It was time, they declared, to put a stop to the policy of capitulation. Another count in their indictment was his alleged willingness to take orders from the Social Democrats. Stresemann tried to convince the Nationalists that they were wrong, but he failed completely.

The opposition parties granted the cabinet no rest. At the Reichstag session of November 20, 1923, Otto Wels gave pungent expression to the dissatisfaction that gripped Social Democratic circles. The Hitler-Ludendorff putsch, he said, had failed, but one had to reckon with the possibility of further attempts. The policy of the Stresemann government toward Bavaria, Saxony and Thuringia was entirely wrong. Were not the workers of Bavaria entitled to protection from the Reich? Kahr had destroyed their rights and suppressed the newspapers of the Left. Nothing had happened in Saxony and Thuringia to justify the treatment meted out to them. In Bavaria, local law prevailed over the decrees of the Reich. Stresemann was silent about this. He preferred to coddle Bavaria while enforcing martial law against the workers of Berlin, Saxony and Thuringia. Kahr could well give up his plan of marching on Berlin, since everything was going according to his wishes. The Social Democrats could not repose confidence in a government that had allowed matters to reach such a pass. Hergt, the Nationalist leader, spoke next. He praised the Bavarian government in the strongest terms. The foreign policy of the Reich, he charged, had shown itself to be a total failure. The domestic situation, too, was far from encouraging. For this state of affairs the German cabinet must be held strictly accountable. Stresemann took up the challenge with gusto. Once again he defended his decision to terminate the struggle in the Ruhr and to seek a friendly accord with France. In an effort to calm the ire of the Social Democrats, he pointed out that a lengthening of the working day was necessary because without it Germany would be unable to obtain a badly needed foreign loan. It was the duty of the federal government, he argued, to support the "constitutional" Kahr-Knilling regime in Bavaria regardless of its attitude toward the Reich. Moreover, the authority of the army command in Bavaria as elsewhere had to be preserved. As for the current wave of antipathy to the Reichswehr, it was due to Communist agitation and nothing else.

Stresemann's plea for support left his adversaries cold. Equally ineffective were the remarks of Gessler, who continued to resist Social Democratic demands for the speedy lifting of the state of siege. Two motions lay before the Reichstag. One of these, offered by the Social Democrats, ran as follows: The government of the Reich had rigidly enforced the state of siege in Saxony and Thuringia, even though there was no adequate reason for such a policy. But it had failed to take decisive action against the unconstitutional regime in Bavaria. Therefore, it no longer possessed the trust of the Reichstag. The second motion, which had been concocted by the Nationalists, simply stated that parliament denied its confidence to Stresemann and his associates. At Stresemann's request, the Centrists, the Democrats and the People's party introduced a pro-government resolution. It was defeated on November 23 by a vote of 230 to 155. Stresemann promptly resigned. The crisis proved extraordinarily difficult to resolve. Stresemann's followers demanded that he be reinstated in the chancellorship. The new cabinet, they added, would have to contain more right-wing people than its predecessor. The Nationalists, for their part, wanted to see one of their own leaders elevated to the chancellorship, but of this Ebert would not hear. The Centrists and the Democrats complicated matters by insisting that the Nationalist party make a statement to the effect that it accepted the Weimar constitution and Stresemann's foreign policy. Four men attempted to organize a cabinet and failed. Finally, on November 30, 1923, success crowned the efforts of Wilhelm Marx, the Centrist leader. His government was almost identical with the one that had carried on after the withdrawal of the three Social Democratic ministers. There were only two important changes: the substitution of Marx for Stresemann, who remained in charge of the foreign office; and the appointment of Erich Emminger, a spokesman for the Bavarian People's party, to the post of minister of justice. This appointment was generally interpreted to mean that some sort of compromise with Bavaria impended.

Prior to the November revolution, Marx had been a judge in Rhenish Prussia. He was of moderate bourgeois outlook and thoroughly loyal to his own party. His experience as a parliamentarian stood him in good stead as he prepared to cope with the many urgent problems that confronted his government. Widespread dissatisfaction and ferment in working-class circles loomed as his first major hurdle. Leading trade-union organizations were demanding government action in connection with the wage policies of the employers' associations. The Saxon section of the Social Democratic party, still smarting under the impact of recent events, vented its rage in a strongly worded resolution. It denounced the continued enforcement of martial law, insisting that such a policy enhanced the danger of a military dictatorship. It decried the "barbaric, arbitrary actions" of the Reichswehr and extended its sympathy to the victims of militaristic terror. Finally, it urged the Social Democratic deputies in the Reichstag to do everything in their power to secure the immediate restoration of civil liberties.

The fall of the Stresemann cabinet had voided the enabling law passed in October. Marx demanded the enactment of a new one when he addressed parliament on December 4, 1923. The government, he declared, needed plenary powers because it would have to work fast to restore the country to financial and economic stability. He warned that heavy sacrifices were unavoidable. His allusions to political issues foreshadowed a continuation of his predecessor's policies. In an effort to curry favor with Bavaria, he promised concessions which would have the effect of enlarging the powers of the *Laender*. On the subject of the state of siege, he showed himself to be utterly out of sympathy with the attitude of the working classes. Recent events, he observed, proved that the sufferings of the German people were being exploited by "criminal elements" intent on promoting their own interests. The activities of these groups had serious economic implications. Even relatively mild disturbances affected adversely the country's food and financial situation. The maintenance of order was the *sine qua non* of recovery. Consequently, the state of siege could not, for the time being, be dispensed with. It would be lifted as soon as conditions permitted.

What would the Social Democrats do? The party was divided. A good many of its deputies in the Reichstag displayed a marked unwillingness to support the Marx government, which contained not a single representative of organized labor and seemed determined to steer a conservative course. The majority felt otherwise and coerced the minority into submission. The party's point of view was explained by Scheidemann on December 5. The Social Democrats, he said, did not agree with the new chancellor in all respects. However, they did recognize the vital importance of resolving the financial difficulties which plagued the country. But one thing they would have to insist upon: speedy termination of the state of siege. With this reservation, the party would vote in favor of the enabling act. The Nationalists, the Racialists and the Communists opposed the measure, but it was adopted by an overwhelming majority on December 8, 1923.

3

The cause of political tranquillity in Germany was apparently served by the speech which Knilling made in the Bavarian Diet on December 5. He likened the Hitler-Ludendorff putsch to an attack by brigands. Hitler's aim had been a march on Berlin. Had he achieved even a temporary success, the misery of Germany would have been indescribable. But in spite of the conciliatory tone of this pronouncement, the opposition groups in the Diet combined to prevent the enactment of the plenary-powers bill introduced by the government. Knilling's defeat boosted the morale of the more militant elements in the Social Democratic party. They believed that the time had come to go forward with the long contemplated project of forming a people's army dedicated to the defense of the republic. The Reichswehr was not to be trusted. The Stahlhelm and the S.A. were a menace to the existing regime. The trade unions and the Social Democrats needed a well organized and properly directed militia of their own. Small fighting units of left-wing complexion were to be found here and there; remnants of the proletarian Hundreds still survived in Saxony and Thuringia. The initiative in fusing them into a single corps for the defense of the republic was taken by Otto Wels. Late in 1923, he summoned the leaders of all these semi-military bodies and placed the issue squarely before them. They responded enthusiastically. The organizational work involved in effecting this merger was entrusted to Otto Hoersing, the Social Democratic president of the administrative district of Saxony. Hoersing suggested the formation of a national militia, to be called Reichsbanner Black-Red-Gold, that would stand above existing parties and give protection to all groups that honestly supported the republic. Democrats and Centrists were welcomed into the new organization, which was founded at Magdeburg on February 22, 1924. But from the very beginning, Social Democrats constituted its rank and file. The growth of the Reichsbanner was rapid; a year after it came into being, it comprised no fewer than three million members. Socialists and liberals were overjoyed. They hailed the appearance of the Reichsbanner as a great boon to German democracy. It would serve, they believed, as an effective counterpoise to the Stahlhelm and the S.A. They were sure, too, that henceforth putsches from the Right would be nipped in the bud. But in their elation, they tended to overlook the fact that the counterrevolutionary forces were already powerfully entrenched in the army, the bureaucracy and the courts. They also failed to realize that the multiplication of private armies was bound to aggravate the weakness of the state. An intensification of this trend could only increase the danger of civil war. Moreover, the striking of a balance between the rival camps placed greater opportunities for decisive action within the reach of the Reichswehr. Without the support or at least the sufferance of the country's military leaders, the defenders as well as the adversaries of the status quo would find themselves completely stymied.

The early months of 1924 witnessed other significant developments on the home front. In February, the Bavarian government concluded a new accord with the Reich. It was agreed that the unity of the army command was, from now on, not to be tampered with. The oath of allegiance taken by the Bavarian Reichswehr on October 22, 1923, was declared null and void. Most Germans welcomed this compact, but other matters had already begun to monopolize their attention. The most engrossing of these was the necessity of electing a new Reichstag in the very near future. An unusually exciting campaign was anticipated. Of considerable interest in this connection was the treatment to be accorded the Communists, the Nazis and the Racialists. The three parties had been suppressed by Seeckt on November 20, 1923, and unless the ban was lifted, they would be unable to participate in the forthcoming contest. Marx was inclined to be lenient. On February 28, 1924, he took a step which paved the way for the return of these parties to the nation's political arena: he finally put an end to the rule of martial law. Shortly thereafter, the ban was removed.

4

Poincaré's unyielding attitude impeded action on the Ruhr and reparation issues during the closing months of 1923. Thereafter, however, progress was relatively rapid. This was due in considerable measure to the efforts of the British and American governments, both of which strongly favored the conclusion of a new accord with the Reich. Cheering, indeed, to the Germans was the prospect of substantial financial help from their former enemies. An international committee of experts, headed by Charles G. Dawes, the well-known American financier, was appointed by the Reparation Commission. To it was entrusted the task of investigating Germany's capacity to pay and of making appropriate recommendations. The committee met in Paris on January 21, 1924. Schacht was present. Five days later, the experts went to Berlin, where they were received by Marx, Stresemann and other government spokesmen. In order to correct certain misconceptions regarding Germany's position, Stresemann, on February 6, 1924, published a forthright article in his paper, the *Zeit*. The government of the Reich, he observed, believed that the reestablishment of German sovereignty in the Ruhr and in the Rhineland and the restoration of German trade and economic unity were the first prerequisites of any reparation settlement.

After a brief sojourn in the German capital, the experts returned to Paris. They busied themselves with the preparation of a report which was submitted to the Reparation Commission on April 9, 1924. This document constituted the basis of what came to be known as the Dawes plan. It recommended, among other things, the restoration of full economic and fiscal sovereignty to Germany. This could be accomplished only by evacuating the Ruhr. A central bank of issue, with seven Germans and seven foreigners serving as its board of governors, was to receive the reparation payments. During the first five years, these payments were to rise from one to two and a half billion gold marks annually; thereafter, they were to remain at the latter figure, subject, however, to fluctuations in the general economic condition of Germany. Deliveries in kind in the first twelve months were to be financed by an international loan of 800 million gold marks. The sums earmarked for transfer to the creditor nations were to be raised by issuing railway and industrial bonds, levying a special transport tax and appropriating a part of the ordinary revenue of the state. The operation of the plan was to be supervised by a foreign Agent General.

On April 11, the Reparation Commission asked the German government to formulate a reply to the experts' proposals. The very next day Stresemann discussed the whole matter in a speech at Schneidemuehl He said: [1]

The experts' report undoubtedly shows an effort to grasp the situation in Germany from the economic point of view and is inspired by reasonable and business-like considerations. It calls upon our people to assume heavy burdens and to permit foreign co-operation in the administration of the most important property of the Reich, the state railways. Fulfillment of these conditions will be possible only if the economic, fiscal and administrative sovereignty of the Reich is completely re-established within our ter-

[1] Quoted in *Gustav Stresemann: His Diaries, Letters and Papers,* edited by Eric Sutton (The Macmillan Company).

ritory. Only on the understanding that the sacrifices to be endured by the German people are mainly for the benefit of the population of the occupied area, and that a period of quiet and peaceful development is guaranteed to the German Reich within undisputed frontiers of German sovereignty, can the experts' report be regarded as the basis for a discussion of the proposed co-operation in the settlement of the reparation question.

With these reservations in mind, the German government, on April 15, 1924, decided to give the Reparation Commission an affirmative answer. Nine days later, England, Belgium and Italy announced their acceptance of the experts' report. Poincaré's reply was ambiguous. The negotiations were held up by his insistence that Britain, in return for the evacuation of the Ruhr, formally agree to back France in the application of sanctions against the Reich if the Germans should fail to meet their payments under the Dawes plan. The British would not hear of undertaking such an obligation. However, a victory for the coalition of the Left in the French elections forced Poincaré to resign in May, 1924. A nation-wide revulsion against the methods he had employed in dealing with the whole complex of Franco-German relations was in part responsible for this political upset. Many of Poincaré's compatriots began to realize that the occupation of the Ruhr and the policy of coercion had been a mistake. It was clear that France had failed to attain her objective. Indeed, the invasion cost her more than she was able to get out of it. Moreover, there could be no denying that an economically weakened Germany would prove a dubious source of income in years to come. The scale of payments laid down by the Allies in 1921 was now wholly out of the question. But this was only part of the story. The occupation of the Ruhr had had a deleterious effect on French finances, with the franc going into a marked decline. It had alienated opinion in Great Britain, whose support France needed to achieve the kind of security she wanted. It had evoked widespread sympathy for the Reich, brought new discredit on the Treaty of Versailles and weakened the position of the republican elements in Germany. All these considerations buttressed the conclusion that negotiation, not force, would have to provide the solution of the reparation question. But the Germanophobe elements continued, in spite of everything, to defend Poincaré's policy. They insisted that important advantages had accrued to France as a result of the invasion. German economy, they pointed out, had suffered a crushing blow and this, even if it meant reduced reparation payments in the future, was to be welcomed from the larger standpoint of French security. Besides, the Germans had been taught a salutary lesson; they were not likely, from now on, to attempt to evade their reparation obligations. Nor could the fact be overlooked that France had managed to extract 1,392,689,175 francs from the Reich. Above all, the British had been made to realize that unless they agreed to support the French demand for security vis-à-vis Germany, Europe would remain in a state of dangerous tension, and the possibility of another war would always have to be reckoned with.

Poincaré was succeeded in the premiership by the Radical Socialist leader, Edouard Herriot, who also assumed the portfolio of foreign affairs. In his address before the chamber of deputies on June 17, 1924, Herriot took a conciliatory line. He declared himself opposed to the harsh policy of his predecessor. He emphasized, however, that the Ruhr could not be evacuated until after the adoption of the Dawes report. He discussed the possibility of recalling the inter-Allied Control Commissions and of entrusting the supervision of German disarmament to an appropriate agency of the League of Nations. But first, he said, Germany would have to join the Geneva organization. When that occurred, France would be prepared to conclude a security pact. Stresemann replied two days later. He accepted Herriot's stand on the question of the Ruhr. Germany, he remarked, expected the evacuation to take place as soon as she began to make payments under the terms of the Dawes report. Her government desired only peace and friendship with other countries.

5

Heartening progress toward a solution of the reparation problem seemed in prospect. But within the Reich, political passions erupted once again as the moment for new parliamentary elections drew near. On March 13, 1924, Ebert dissolved the Reichstag. Simultaneously, Marx issued an appeal to the nation. His government, he declared, stood by its accomplishments. These included the restoration of law and order, the stabilization of the currency and the return to a sound economic life. Tranquillity at home was essential to the protection of the country's rights in the international sphere. The chancellor's remarks were pithy and to the point, but they made little impression on the opposition. The imminence of decisions which would determine the future of Germany failed to sober those extremists on the Right and on the Left who never passed up a chance to harass the existing regime. The Dawes report speedily became the paramount issue of the campaign. The Nationalists saw to that. With callous disregard for the impression which their words were bound to produce in the creditor countries, they flayed the experts' recommendations mercilessly. Germany, they charged, was being enslaved. She was sacrificing a large part of her sovereignty in financial matters. Her leading banking institutions and her railways were being placed under foreign control. It was the duty of all patriotic Germans to protect the nation's independence by rejecting this sinister scheme. The all-important thing was to elect to the Reichstag men who could be trusted to put Germany's welfare before that of her insatiable enemies. The Communists, the Nazis and the Racialists joined in the outcry against the Dawes report. They, too, painted a most depressing picture of what would happen to Germany if she permitted herself to be tricked into accepting the new reparation settlement. Stresemann endeavored to answer these charges. Germany, he contended, had to choose between further depredations in the Ruhr and the liberation of the occupied areas. The latter entailed temporary sacrifices, but they were well worth making. The government was seeking to remove, once and for all, the economic shackles which fettered the country. It also sought to win the good will of the rest of the world in order to insure the peaceful development of the Reich. Stresemann dwelt upon this theme in the great speech which he delivered at Magdeburg on April 29, 1924.[2]

We have coined the phrase: 'Through work and sacrifice to freedom.' It is of course open to anyone to say: Nonsense! Through power to freedom! Give me the power! But if I have not the power I must take what I need to achieve freedom. . . . We in the cabinet were clear that it would have been foolish, when we were asked whether we proposed to take the necessary steps to put the plan into operation, if we had replied that it was unacceptable. We should then have had the whole world against us and Poincaré would have had a free hand in dealing with us. Our affirmative answer was not at all welcome in Paris. It will be said that we have often been deceived. That is true, but the participation of the United States on this occasion suggests a better prospect that these proposals will be carried through.

The policy of the German government, Stresemann continued, was not inspired by fear of what might happen if it rejected the experts' report. It stemmed from the realization that Germany needed a few years of tranquillity, that she had to protect the inviolability of her frontiers and reestablish close relations with the inhabitants of the occu-

[2] Ibid.

pied areas. The paramount issue was political, not economic or financial.[3]

> The decision that confronts us is whether the policy of Louis XIV is to be carried out in the twentieth century . . . or whether this French imperialism is to be broken and the unity of the Reich restored. Because I today place policy before any questions of finance, I say it would be a pitiable government that did not do its utmost to get back the Rhine and the Ruhr.

Although questions of foreign policy were thus thrust into the foreground, it was the inflation and the bitterness it had engendered that decided the outcome of the elections in May, 1924. Impoverished middle-class people flocked to the banner of extremists on the Right, while great numbers of workers who had lost their jobs or who were struggling along on pitifully inadequate wages cast their lot with the champions of proletarian radicalism. The most spectacular gains were scored by the Nationalists. Their popular vote totaled 5,718,543, two million more than the number polled in June, 1920, and their parliamentary representation rose from sixty-six to ninety-six. Thanks to their alliance with certain small right-wing parties, they disposed of ten additional seats. This made them the biggest group in the new Reichstag. The showing of the Nazis and the Racialists, who supported a single list of candidates, surpassed the expectations of even their most sanguine spokesmen. They emerged with 1,924,018 votes and thirty-two seats and thus became, for the first time, a fairly important factor in national politics. The Communists, in what was, for them, an unprecedented display of strength, leaped to fourth place among the parties of the Reich. They polled 3,746,643 votes and elected sixty-two deputies. Their rivals, the united Social Democrats, fared very badly. Their popular following just topped the six-million mark, while their representation in parliament fell from 171 to 100. Equally catastrophic was the decline in the fortunes of the People's party. It attracted only 2,700,447 supporters, as compared with 3,606,316 in 1920, and it emerged with forty-four seats, eighteen less than its former total. The Democrats, who had been losing ground ever since the signing of the Treaty of Versailles, sank to a new low. The final tabulation gave them 1,658,076 votes and twenty-eight places in the new Reichstag. Only the Center, among the moderate parties, managed to hold its own. Its popular vote actually showed a slight increase, but its parliamentary deputation fell from sixty-eight to sixty-five.

[3] Ibid.

The outcome of the elections constituted a resounding victory for the adversaries of the Dawes report. All eyes were on the Nationalists. Would they continue to oppose the experts' proposals? Their first pronouncements after the elections failed to provide the answer. Instead of discussing the Dawes report, they demanded the resignation of the Marx cabinet and urged the appointment of Admiral Tirpitz to the chancellorship. Stresemann and his associates in the People's party took the view that the Nationalists would be more tractable if they were forced into a position of responsibility. The Center evinced a reluctance to serve under a Nationalist chancellor. It was not, however, averse to the idea of giving the Nationalists some representation in the government. On May 15, 1924, the cabinet met to consider the situation. It decided to remain in office until the new Reichstag assembled. The Nationalists had not yet issued a clear statement regarding their attitude to the experts' recommendations. The reason for this delay was the outcropping of serious dissension within their own ranks. The less intransigent members of the party declared themselves willing to accept the Dawes report, but whether they would be able to prevail against the opposition of the die-hards was an open question. The uncertainty was hard on everyone's nerves. The People's party declined to wait any longer. It called for the resignation of the Marx cabinet in order to enable the president of the Reich to proceed with the task of bringing into being a government which would be in accord with the new parliamentary situation. The chancellor decided to comply with this invitation. On May 26, 1924, he and all the members of his government withdrew from office. The Nationalists promptly announced their willingness to participate in the formation of a new cabinet, but insisted that they would not be bound by any previous commitments in the realm of foreign policy. Simultaneously, the People's party, the Center and the Democrats reiterated their resolve to work for acceptance of the Dawes report. They assumed, they said, that the report would be recognized as "a single and indivisible whole," that it would be interpreted "with good will," and that the stability of the German currency as well as the restoration of the Reich's economic and administrative sovereignty would be guaranteed. Ebert commissioned Marx to organize a coalition cabinet representing all the bourgeois parties, including the Nationalists. The latter proved entirely unaccommodating. They were offered several key posts in the government, but they were not satisfied. They demanded a cabinet reshuffle in Prussia. This the moderate parties would not countenance. Thereupon the Nationalists pronounced further negotiation futile. The impasse was finally ended on June 3, 1924, when Ebert asked Marx to resume the chancellorship. The Centrist leader and all his subordinates returned to their posts. The government lost no time in laying its program before the new Reichstag. In the course of the protracted debate which followed, Stresemann once again came to the defense of the Dawes report. A resolution approving the previous cabinet's acceptance of the document was adopted by a vote of 247 to 183. The Nationalists, the Communists and the Nazi-Racialist contingent ranged themselves against the resolution. The Social Democrats supported it, not because they had any fondness for Marx and his colleagues but because they wished to see the foreign policy of Stresemann upheld. Thus, although they remained outside the cabinet and strongly censured its approach to domestic issues, they stood by it for purely patriotic reasons.

The driving force behind the Nationalist opposition to the Dawes report was Alfred Hugenberg. This ambitious and unscrupulous man had had an extraordinarily successful business career. He had been, for a time, a member of the board of directors of the great Krupp firm, and was still closely associated with heavy industry. He had made huge profits during the period of the inflation, and these he used to buy up scores of provincial newspapers. He was the owner of one of the country's principal news agencies. In later years he acquired a controlling interest in UFA, the great motion picture company. He thus became the nation's most powerful figure in the domain of propaganda. Almost from the very morrow of the November revolution, Hugenberg aligned himself with the right wing of the Nationalist party. He hated socialism and the republic and worked with fanatical zeal to destroy them. He wished to see the Hohenzollerns restored because he believed that a monarchical regime would reduce labor to complete impotence. Within his own party he waged a fierce and incessant battle against those elements that were willing, in the interests of expediency, to countenance some kind of compromise with the Weimar system. He conceived a violent dislike for Stresemann and for the idea of dealing in a conciliatory spirit with the former enemies of the Reich. When the experts' recommendations were announced, he criticized them in vitriolic fashion. During the ensuing weeks and months he kept up his attacks in an effort to arouse public opinion. He utilized for this purpose the great network of newspapers that carried his influence into every corner of the land. It was his

purpose to remain at the political barricades until his fight for a policy
of intransigence and revenge had been won.

6

Stresemann's problem in seeking support for his reparation program
was made more difficult by current differences with the western powers
over the supervision of German disarmament. On December 30, 1923,
the inter-Allied Control Commission, which had been withdrawn from
Germany shortly after the beginning of the Ruhr imbroglio, informed
the Reich authorities that it planned investigatory visits to Rostock,
Berlin, Dresden, Stuttgart, Munich, Paderborn and Frankfurt on the
Main. The German government did not dissemble its displeasure.
In a strongly worded communication dated January 9, 1924, it argued
that the commission had already completed its work. The things
which still remained to be done were too insignificant to warrant more
investigatory visits. Germany had disarmed; and, under the terms of
Article 213 of the Treaty of Versailles, all supervisory functions were
from now on to be discharged by the Council of the League of Nations. Poincaré sharply dissented. He held that inter-Allied control of
German armaments would have to be restored unconditionally and on
the broadest possible basis. Britain's first labor government, headed by
Ramsay MacDonald, agreed that the resumption of military control
was necessary. But it suggested that the inter-Allied commission be
replaced by a committee of guarantee, an arrangement already in effect
as regards the German navy and German aviation. On March 5, 1924,
in the wake of a Franco-British parley, the Allies sent the German
government a detailed statement of their views. Military control, they
declared, could not yet be dispensed with. It was imperative to obtain
conclusive evidence regarding the manner in which Germany was
fulfilling the disarmament clauses of the Treaty of Versailles. Of particular interest in this connection were such matters as the organization
of the police, the production of war material and the system of recruit-
ment. The Germans replied on March 31, 1924. Article 213, they reiterated, must be invoked without delay. Moreover, the question of
whether further control was necessary ought to be settled by agreement and not unilaterally by an agency representing only the Allies.
In dealing with a nation like Germany, one could not forever put
everything on the basis of command and obedience. If the Allies permitted the Control Commission to disregard this fact, they would dis-

cover that they were making themselves the unwitting sponsors of dangerous trends within the Reich. Above all, proof must be given that continued supervision was designed not to perpetuate the present disparity between the armaments of Germany and those of her neighbors but to promote the ultimate pacification of Europe.

The Allies refused to yield. The Control Commission, they stated late in May, 1924, was entitled to remain in operation until the military clauses of the treaty had been completely carried out. And as long as that body continued to function, it alone would attend to the job of supervising German disarmament. Besides, it was up to the Allies to decide whether Germany had fulfilled her obligations in their entirety. When they had satisfied themselves that everything was in order they would step aside in favor of the Council of the League. They reaffirmed the necessity of acquainting themselves with the current state of German armaments, which for almost two years had escaped scrutiny. It was their sincere desire, they said, to terminate the business of control as speedily as possible. The contemplated inspection tour would be over in three or four months if the German authorities co-operated and if no serious derelictions were discovered. But should Germany refuse to allow the investigation, the Allies would have no choice but to demand strict enforcement of the treaty.

On June 22, 1924, Herriot and MacDonald sent a personal note to Chancellor Marx. They referred to rumors of increased activity by "nationalist and military organizations" in Germany and warned that such rumors, if true, could not fail to influence the attitude of the British and French governments. They were anxious, they averred, to transfer the work of supervision from the Control Commission to the Council of the League as soon as the various questions raised by the Allies had been solved. What was needed now was a statement by the Reich which would allay alarm and conform to the letter and spirit of existing treaty obligations. In a lengthy note dated June 30, 1924, the Germans conveyed their readiness to comply with this request. It was a mistake, they observed, to assume that new wars were to be feared in Europe because of the activity of German organizations that engaged more or less extensively in military exercises. The German government did not deny the existence of groups whose purpose it was to give physical training to the youth of the country. But these groups were acting in the belief that the universal conscription of imperial days had had educational as well as military value. Proper development of the body was the best protection against the dangers which today threatened the German youth. Athletics were being cultivated on an ever increasing scale. It was wrong to link this with alleged military preparations by Germany. The German nation rejected the idea of war. All political groups in the country were at one in holding that secret rearmament was both impossible and senseless. In keeping with this conviction, the German government had striven to disarm certain political associations that were not to be confused with organizations interested in the furtherance of outdoor sports. It was true, nonetheless, that there existed in Germany a profound bitterness over the country's present situation. This was not surprising in view of what Germany had been made to endure since the end of the war. Resentment would be far less intense and widespread if, from the outset, the Allies had pursued toward Germany a policy of understanding and had permitted her to co-operate with them as an equal. The organizations referred to by Herriot and MacDonald had come into being as a result of this resentment. But, of course, no one familiar with military matters believed that Germany was in a position to provoke an armed conflict in Europe. Her army was weaker than that of even the smallest state. She was without the newest kinds of weapons. Since the conclusion of peace, she had not produced a single cannon, and her stocks of war material were below the modest limits fixed by the treaty. Consequently, she was at a loss to understand why others should continue to regard her as a threat to the peace of Europe. The German people did not relish inter-Allied military control because it represented an infringement of their sovereignty. But they were prepared to take cognizance of the change which had recently come over the whole European picture. They believed that the western powers were ready to substitute conciliation for the policy of coercion. The sacrifices demanded of them by the Dawes report would be endurable only because they assumed that their rights would be respected and that an era of international concord was about to begin. This assumption, together with the belief that the supervision of German disarmament would soon be entrusted to the Council of the League, motivated the Reich's decision to acquiesce in the investigation planned by the inter-Allied Control Commission.

The stage was now set for speedy action on the question of reparation.

Chapter 20

THE DAWES LEGISLATION, THE LEAGUE AND
THE ADVENT OF LUTHER

I

AN INTER-ALLIED conference, which was highlighted by the presence of American representatives, opened in London on July 16, 1924. It had been summoned for the purpose of discussing the measures needed to put the Dawes report into effect. Certain related matters, such as security and inter-Allied debts, were excluded from its agenda. In his speech of inauguration, Prime Minister MacDonald sounded a conciliatory note. Germany, he said, had to be given a chance to get back on her feet. The prompt restoration of her economic and financial unity was imperative. As for her creditors, who were being asked to provide a loan of 800 million gold marks, they would have to receive adequate guarantees for the repayment of this sum. Throughout the ensuing proceedings, the American delegates played an important role. They insisted that no agreement would be acceptable which failed to obtain Germany's wholehearted approval. They demanded that she be invited to the conference as soon as the Allies had reached some sort of accord among themselves. The British and Italian representatives supported the Americans in their efforts to secure tolerable terms for Germany. Herriot defended the French point of view, which diverged in a number of respects from that of the other conferees. The question of sanctions proved a fecund source of friction. The French wished to insure swift and vigorous action against the Germans in the event of another default. They insisted on the right to go ahead themselves if collective sanctions, for one reason or another, should fail to materialize. The British, for their part, frowned on any arrangement that might engender fresh difficulties. A resolution of the conflict was facilitated by American mediation. It was decided to allow the Reparation Commission to retain the power of determining whether sanctions should be invoked in any given situation; but it was to be made a more impartial body by adding an American to its roster. This seemed an adequate compromise, but the British and American bankers were not satisfied. They feared, in spite of it, that France might someday attack Germany again; and if that happened, repayment of the 800-million-mark loan would be jeopardized. The French delegates managed to reassure the Anglo-American financiers by stating in the most categorical fashion that another invasion of the Ruhr was contemplated by no one.

The conference worked out a plan for the restoration of Germany's economic unity. It called for the speedy elimination of the administrative and commercial measures introduced in the occupied zone by the Franco-Belgian forces. The military evacuation of the Ruhr was not up for discussion, yet it was precisely the question that mattered most to the Germans. Even before the conference met, Stresemann warned the British and the French that he would be unable to cope with the opposition at home unless concessions were granted on this point. He called attention to the fact that his own party, which hitherto had supported the Dawes report, might turn solidly against it if no definite assurances were obtained regarding the date of evacuation. The Democrats were likely to do the same. Defeat of the Dawes report, he emphasized, would mean the fall of the Marx government and new elections. He explained the situation with complete frankness in a letter to Leopold von Hoesch, the German ambassador in Paris.[1]

I think a statement on the question of the evacuation of the Ruhr is really the cardinal point of the whole matter. Please, therefore, in your talks with the representatives of foreign Powers, do not leave this matter in any doubt. I fancy that it would be possible to extract a statement from the French on the evacuation of the Ruhr if, while insisting on the fact, we left the details open to discussion. I must have a final limit by which the last French soldier will have left this territory, occupied in violation of the treaty. This final limit need not be a definite day of a definite month; it can be attached to some event which is clearly involved in the fulfillment of the [Dawes] report, but I must be able to say to the German people that these territories will be free within a reasonable period, or the whole experts' plan will be flung back in my face.

[1] Quoted in *Gustav Stresemann: His Diaries, Letters and Papers,* edited by Eric Sutton (The Macmillan Company).

Herriot was inclined to be accommodating; but the intransigent attitude of certain members of his cabinet gave him pause. It was only after a good deal of prodding by the British that he finally brought himself to say that he would discuss the issue outside the regular sessions of the conference. On August 1, 1924, the Reich was invited to send representatives to London. Four days later, Marx, Stresemann and Luther arrived in the British capital. MacDonald promptly encouraged them to take up the question of evacuation with Herriot. He also supported their contention that sanctions should be invoked against Germany only in the event of deliberate default. Stresemann and Herriot had a long conversation on the evening of August 8. The French statesman remarked that he was leaving for Paris the next day. Difficulties had arisen in his cabinet as a consequence of Germany's determination to raise the question of evacuation. Stresemann stressed the importance which German public opinion attached to this issue. He said that immediately after his return to Germany, the Reichstag's committee on foreign affairs was bound to demand a statement as to when the withdrawal of the Franco-Belgian troops might be expected. Herriot agreed that the evacuation should take place "within a reasonable time." He talked in this vein when he arrived in Paris, and forthwith ran into trouble. The French minister of war, General Charles Nollet, insisted on linking the question of evacuation with that of military control. Marshal Foch likewise opposed unconditional compliance with the German demand. Herriot had to promise that the process of evacuation would not be completed before the lapse of a year; on this basis alone was he able to secure the assent of his cabinet. He returned to London only to have Stresemann tell him that German public opinion wished to see the evacuation begin at once. Herriot pointed out that he personally condemned the occupation of the Ruhr. However, he had to consider the state of popular feeling in France. All he could say at this time was that he would make every effort to accelerate the withdrawal. Stresemann refused to be put off. A year, he complained, was too long; he could not ask the Reichstag to agree to such an arrangement. A stalemate ensued when Herriot, egged on by one of his Germanophobe associates, declared that a shortening of the interval was absolutely out of the question. He did, however, consent to set a date for the beginning of the evacuation. It was agreed that the Dortmund zone would be cleared as soon as the London protocols had been signed. MacDonald and the American ambassador, Frank B. Kellogg, advised Stresemann to accept the one-year arrangement. They argued that nothing better could be extracted from Herriot. Their counsel prevailed. The German cabinet met on August 15 and gave its conditional approval to the French plan.

The international spotlight shifted to the Reichstag. Upon its members devolved the obligation of giving effect to the recommendations of the Dawes report. This they were expected to do by enacting the far-reaching measures which the German government prepared to lay before them. The most important of these measures was a bill concerning the German railways. It required a two-thirds majority because it involved a modification of certain provisions of the constitution. The Dawes legislation reached parliament on August 23, 1924. The government could count on the Social Democrats, the Centrists, the Democrats and the People's party. But in view of the numerical strength and intransigence of the Nationalist party, a hard fight seemed inevitable. One thing was certain: a two-thirds majority would be unobtainable unless a goodly proportion of the Nationalist deputies joined the government bloc. Tremendous pressure was brought to bear on the leaders of the opposition. The American ambassador in Berlin, Alanson Bigelow Houghton, took part in this behind-the-scenes campaign; so did Nationalist spokesmen from the Ruhr and a number of industrial and commercial magnates—stalwart conservatives all. They dwelt on the enormous advantages which would accrue to Germany once the Dawes plan had gone into effect. Every consideration of self-interest, they argued, dictated affirmative action by the Reichstag. But the Nationalist chieftains, backed by the Nazis and the Racialists, stood their ground. The experts' report, they said, was a second Treaty of Versailles. Tirpitz, Westarp and Hugenberg headed these die-hards. Behind them stood Ludendorff, who, as the self-appointed custodian of German honor, took delight in impugning the patriotism of the government's supporters. The outlook was far from cheering when the Reichstag debate began. Speeches in favor of the plan were delivered by Stresemann, Hilferding and other champions of a reasoned, moderate approach to the Ruhr and reparation questions. But it speedily became evident that appeals to reason were wasted on the Nationalists. Disdaining the facts and figures cited by government spokesmen, they denounced the London agreements mercilessly. Germany, they charged, was being relegated to the status of an African tribe. Never would they permit this infamous deal to go through. Thanks to them, the railway legislation failed to receive the requisite number of votes at the second reading. President Ebert threatened to dissolve the Reichstag. He was egged on by the left-wing press, which predicted that the nation would give the Dawes report overwhelming approval. In an effort to end the stalemate, the People's party resorted to a bit of political bribery. It declared that once the bills had been enacted, it would insist on having the Nationalists represented in the cabinet in proportion to their numerical strength in the Reichstag. The government employed similar tactics. It assured the Nationalists that it had every intention of making the following point clear: adoption of the new reparation scheme would imply not the slightest change of attitude toward the universally detested war-guilt clause of the Treaty of Versailles. The Nationalists relented. Their followers in the Reichstag received word that they were free to vote as they pleased. Amid shouts of protest from the Communists, the Nazis and the Racialists, forty-eight Nationalist deputies availed themselves of this freedom. On August 29, 1924, they voted in favor of the railway bill, which thus obtained the necessary two-thirds majority. The struggle over the Dawes plan ended, as it had begun, on a note of strident disunity.

The London protocols were signed forthwith. The French and Belgian governments withdrew their troops from the Dortmund zone. The customs barrier erected between the Rhineland and the rest of Germany was removed. Normal communication and transport connections were reestablished. The railroads of the Ruhr reverted to their former status. The repatriation of refugees was begun. All this evoked universal satisfaction. The industrial magnates of western Germany had special reason to rejoice. The Reich announced that it would indemnify them for the damage and losses sustained as a result of the French invasion. To Germans of left-wing persuasion, this seemed unnecessary generosity. They recalled that the inflation had been very profitable to the industrialists. But their objections were brushed aside.

In fulfillment of the promise made to the Nationalists, Chancellor Marx issued the following statement immediately after the enactment of the Dawes legislation:

The Reichstag, by the decisions taken today, has set its seal to the agreement reached in London. These are measures that will be of supreme importance for the destiny of the German people for years ahead. The government of the Reich desires to express its thanks to all members of the Reichstag who have contributed to this result. All who participated had to overcome serious misgivings and even to set aside their personal convictions.

. . . Difficult as the decision may have been in each individual case, it had to be taken if our Fatherland was to find the way to a better future. But the government of the Reich cannot and will not allow this moment, in which it is undertaking heavy obligations in fulfillment of the Treaty of Versailles, to pass by without giving clear and unmistakable expression to its standpoint regarding the question of war guilt which, since 1919, has weighed so heavily on the soul of the German people. The statement imposed upon us by the pressure of overwhelming force in the Treaty of Versailles, that Germany started the world war by her own act of aggression, is contrary to the facts of history. The government of the Reich hereby states that it does not recognize this assertion. It is a just claim on the part of the German people to be freed from the burden of this false accusation. So long as this is not done, and so long as a member of the community of nations is stamped as a criminal against humanity, a true understanding and reconciliation between the nations cannot be achieved.

These words produced a painful impression in foreign capitals. In an effort to undo some of the harm, Marx sent Herriot and MacDonald a confidential note asking them not to misunderstand his motives in raising the issue at this time. Germany, he wrote, had no desire to escape her reparation obligations. But the German people regarded themselves as innocent of the charge leveled against them, and he, their chancellor, felt morally obliged to give expression to this feeling. He likewise informed Herriot and MacDonald that a formal statement of the German attitude would be dispatched shortly to the Allied governments. However, realization of the unpleasant complications which such action would entail led the German government to reconsider the matter. Because it feared to do anything which might hinder the success of the Dawes loan, it decided, after further reflection, to postpone this step indefinitely. The loan was floated in October, 1924. It found a ready market, especially in the United States. Germany's economic position was further strengthened by the substitution of the Reichsmark for the Rentenmark and by the evacuation of the Ruhr, which was completed in July, 1925.

2

Both MacDonald and Herriot were friendly to the idea of admitting Germany to the League of Nations. The question was discussed during the London conference, and the Germans came away convinced that the necessary arrangements could be completed with a minimum of delay. However, Stresemann maintained that the Reich would have to explore the diplomatic terrain carefully before dispatching a formal application to Geneva. On September 17, 1924, he had a long talk with Viscount D'Abernon, the British ambassador in Berlin. The two men were on excellent terms; Stresemann felt that he could speak his mind freely. He told D'Abernon that Germany would balk at doing anything which might be construed as recognition of the Treaty of Versailles. German public opinion, he pointed out, regarded the Covenant of the League as an integral part of the treaty. To accept one was to accept the other. Besides, Article I of the Covenant called for the fulfillment of existing international obligations. The Treaty of Versailles came under the heading of such obligations. Consequently, acquiescence in this article would mean that Germany had assented voluntarily to the settlement of 1919. It was imperative for her government to state in advance that the obligations assumed by virtue of membership in the League did not include acceptance of the treaty and its war-guilt clause. D'Abernon declared himself opposed to the making of such a statement. For it was altogether obvious that insistence on reservations regarding Article 231 was bound to create a most unfavorable impression abroad and impede the process of admission. Matters were further complicated by the attitude of Adolf Mueller, Germany's minister in Berne. The Reich, he wrote in reply to a query from Stresemann, must demand a permanent seat on the Council of the League and a settlement of the problem of military control as the *sine qua non* of its entry into the Geneva organization.

On September 23, 1924, with Ebert in the chair, the German cabinet unanimously adopted a resolution stating that efforts should be made to secure immediate admission to the League. This action, the cabinet pointed out, was taken in the belief that such questions as the protection of minorities, the status of the Saar, general disarmament and military control could be dealt with satisfactorily only if Germany cooperated with her neighbors. However, she would have to be given rights equal to those of the other great powers. Two days later, the government of the Reich approved the text of the note that was to be sent to the countries represented on the Council of the League. Germany, the document averred, felt that the moment had come to apply for membership in the League of Nations. In order to facilitate matters, she desired to clarify certain points that to her were of decisive significance. First of all, she would have to be assured a permanent seat on the Council. Then there was the problem of what to do about Article 16, the sanctions clause of the Covenant. Ger-

many could not accept, without reservations, the obligations arising
out of this article. The reason was obvious: she was defenseless,
whereas her neighbors were armed to the teeth. Furthermore, Germany's entry into the League of Nations must not be understood to
mean acceptance of the charge that she alone was responsible for the
outbreak of the war. Finally, she would have to insist on being accorded, in due course, permission to participate in the administration
of the League's mandatory system.

On September 29, 1924, this note was communicated to the powers
concerned. Germany's demand for a permanent seat on the Council
encountered no opposition. But her objections to Article 16 of the
Covenant evoked a very different response. The members of the
Council argued that Germany's application for admission must be
made without conditions of any kind. Berlin, however, was adamant.
In a lengthy memorandum dated December 12, 1924, it insisted that a
militarily impotent Germany could not comply with the stipulations
of the sanctions clause. If she attempted to do so, she would become
"the scene of European wars conducted under the auspices of the
League." The only way out was to permit Germany "to determine for
herself the extent of her active participation" in coercive measures
against aggressors. Otherwise, she would have to surrender the sole
means of defense possessed by a helpless nation: neutrality. The
League powers undertook to study the question further, but the attitude of certain countries, above all France, was scarcely encouraging.

Germany's decision to seek admission to the League of Nations
evoked grave anxiety in Moscow. The feeling of Soviet leaders was
expressed in a letter which Chicherin, the Russian foreign minister,
addressed to Ludwig Stein, the editor of the well-known periodical,
Nord und Sued. Chicherin wrote:

Germany's policy comes into collision with the Rapallo policy. Against
her own wish, by the mere power of facts, Germany will in this way be
drawn into combinations and actions that will bring her into conflict with
us. Germany would thus sacrifice such instruments as are an element of
international strength; and Germany herself would sink into the position
of one of the instruments of the Entente policy of force.

Stresemann categorically denied that Germany was altering her policy.
He called attention to the reservations which she had formulated in
connection with the application of Article 16. He also pointed out
that Prime Minister MacDonald, who was known to be friendly to the

Soviet Union, had urged Germany to join the League. Stresemann's prime concern was to convince Moscow that Germany had no intention of aligning herself with the enemies of the Soviet Union. But the Russians remained uneasy.

3

According to the terms of the Treaty of Versailles, the Cologne zone was to be evacuated not later than January 10, 1925. Throughout December, 1924, Germany awaited word from the Allies regarding the fulfillment of this obligation. But France and Great Britain exhibited little inclination to act. The newspapers of the two countries discussed the matter at considerable length. They called attention to the recent inspection tour of the inter-Allied Control Commission. That tour, they asserted, had shown how incomplete was Germany's compliance with the military clauses of the treaty. The German press angrily insisted that the Reich had lived up to its obligations and adduced facts and figures in support of this contention. Late in December, the Allied governments put an end to the uncertainty. In response to official queries from Berlin, they declared that the Cologne zone would not be evacuated on January 10, 1925. Their decision, they explained, was based on information provided by the Control Commission. Actually, the latter had discovered large stores of forbidden arms in various parts of Germany and was consequently justified in advising that the evacuation be postponed. German disappointment and resentment were intense. But some comfort could be derived from a concurrent development. The day on which the Cologne zone was to have been cleared witnessed the lapse of Germany's obligation to give, without reciprocity, most-favored-nation treatment to the authors of the Treaty of Versailles. This meant that the Reich was now free to do as it pleased in matters of foreign trade. It meant, too, that goods from Alsace-Lorraine could no longer enter Germany duty-free. The German government promptly issued a decree specifying that henceforth most-favored-nation treatment would be extended only to those countries that accorded similar favors to the Reich. The Germans attempted to make up for lost time. During the next two years, they concluded a series of commercial treaties that conferred important benefits on the Fatherland.

4

On September 24, 1924, the leaders of the People's party urged upon Chancellor Marx the necessity of enlisting the co-operation of the Nationalists. They contended that there was no other way to insure overwhelming support for the government's foreign policy. Marx proved entirely acquiescent. He declared that he had intended, in any case, to reconstruct his cabinet in order to make room for representatives of the Nationalist party. The latter indicated a willingness to negotiate. But the Democrats and the chancellor's own party, the Center, showed little enthusiasm for the idea of collaborating with the followers of Westarp and Hugenberg. The People's party refused to be put off. It insisted on making good the pledge it had given the Nationalists just before the enactment of the Dawes legislation. Marx sought to wriggle out of his dilemma by calling for the formation of a national union cabinet. He invited the Social Democrats as well as the Nationalists to join it. Such a cabinet, he suggested, would have to undertake to do four things: enforce respect for the constitution, continue the present foreign policy, curtail expenditures on social services and expand the nation's productive capacity. The chancellor's project encountered insuperable difficulties. The Social Democrats did not relish a partnership with Nationalists. The latter felt exactly the same way about "Marxists." Nevertheless, Marx persisted. He conferred with the Social Democratic leaders. They told him that the Nationalists would first have to clarify their stand on the following issues: 1) protection of the constitution; 2) enforcement of the Washington treaty regarding the eight-hour day; and 3) maintenance of Stresemann's foreign policy. But when Marx sounded the Nationalists, he found them as hostile as ever to the idea of collaborating with Social Democrats. They wanted a government based on "Christiannational" principles. The chancellor belatedly concluded that his plan would have to be discarded. An all-bourgeois cabinet seemed the only alternative. Negotiations were resumed with the Nationalists, but this time it was the Democrats who upset the apple-cart. They vigorously opposed any extension of the cabinet toward the Right. Marx gave up. At his suggestion, the Reichstag was dissolved. The issues, as the government saw them, were stated in a manifesto published on October 21, 1924. This incisively worded proclamation called attention to the fact that the cabinet had not had a dependable majority in the old Reichstag. Its persistent efforts to achieve one had been of no avail.

This failure stemmed in last analysis from the repercussions of the economic crisis of 1923. The radical elements had become too strong as a result of the elections of May, 1924. The other parties had found it extraordinarily difficult to do any constructive work. The forthcoming contest, it was to be hoped, would remedy the situation. Now that the Dawes plan had been adopted, the foreign policy of the government would have to be placed beyond the reach of captious obstructionists. The tasks of economic reconstruction at home likewise required continuity of policy. The success of this program would be assured if all the parties committed to it supported the constitution and defended it against attack from any direction. In the new Reichstag the unifying forces would have to be stronger than those that made for disunity. The extremists on the Right and on the Left, who had co-operated to sabotage the efforts of the moderate groups, would have to be repudiated once and for all at the polls.

The Social Democratic and liberal newspapers greeted the dissolution with keen satisfaction. Conservative sheets, on the other hand, were full of righteous indignation. They attacked Marx, picturing him as wholly deficient in good will and clarity of vision. They charged that he had been, from first to last, opposed to the inclusion of Nationalists in the government. The People's party trained its guns on the Democrats. To them it ascribed the failure of the recent negotiations. It contended once again that the assumption of governmental responsibilities by the Nationalists would guarantee the continuity of German foreign policy. Stresemann himself pointed out that his efforts in the diplomatic field would be in constant jeopardy so long as the nation's strongest right-wing party remained outside the cabinet. He and his associates decried the refusal of the Democrats to collaborate with the reactionary elements. This attitude, they claimed, was an outgrowth of the class struggle; it stemmed from a mistaken conception of republicanism. According to the People's party, the current crisis had been accentuated by parliamentary short-sightedness, political doctrinairism and Leftist extremism. These were the evils that would have to be fought and conquered in the forthcoming elections. Nationalist spokesmen assailed not only their political adversaries but the forty-eight deputies of their party who voted yes on August 29, 1924. They solicited support for a "Christian, racial, national and social" program. This program comprised the following demands: a hereditary constitutional monarchy; the restoration of a "healthy" federalism; the termination of the "exclusive supremacy" of the parliamentary

principle; the election of a new Reich president; the abolition of political corruption and the expunction of the war-guilt lie; protection for
Germany's interests in connection with the implementation of the
Dawes plan; a war to the hilt against the Jews; measures to promote
the well-being of industry, agriculture and the middle class; the preservation of Christian family life and Christian education.

The Social Democrats entered the contest in a jubilant mood. For
some time they had been demanding the dissolution of the "inflation
Reichstag," confident that they would register substantial gains in
elections that were less under the influence of the recent financial and
economic crisis. A manifesto issued on October 25, 1924, revealed the
main lines of their strategy. The preservation of the republic, they
declared, constituted their paramount objective. They attacked the
Nationalist party for advocating a policy of revenge abroad and heaped
censure on the Centrists, the Democrats and the People's party for
their insistence on conservative social policies at home. The Center
reacted vigorously to these criticisms. It dwelt on the virtues of the
Marx government. It inveighed against the racialism of the extreme
Right; but it also reserved much of its campaign fire for those who
preached social radicalism and who endeavored by sundry means to
foment class animosities. The Democrats took sharp issue with the
Nationalists. They demanded an enlightened foreign policy, freedom
for Germany and the Rhineland, adequate protection for the republic
and punitive measures against its foes. They called for the application
of truly liberal principles which would put an end to conflicts of class,
caste and race.

The elections took place on December 7, 1924. The outcome was,
in the main, a rousing vote of confidence for the supporters of the
Dawes legislation. The Nazis and the Communists, who, throughout
the protracted struggle over the new reparation settlement, had never
deviated from the line of uncompromising opposition, suffered heavy
losses. The Nazis forfeited eighteen seats and thus ceased to be a
factor of any importance in national politics. The Communist representation dropped from sixty-two to forty-five. The decline in the fortunes of the two extremist groups was eloquent proof of the change
that had come over the German economic scene since the last elections.
The working classes and the petty bourgeoisie were appreciably better
off than they had been six months earlier. A stable currency enabled
the trade unions to undertake the task of winning back some of the
ground lost during the inflation. They were still in serious straits, but

the future seemed replete with heartening possibilities. As for small tradespeople, they could once again function with some semblance of normalcy. The improvement all along the line was slow but definite. The optimism engendered by the first signs of material betterment was reinforced by the growing realization that the Dawes plan was a boon to Germany. More and more Germans were ready to concede that the policy of fulfillment advocated by Stresemann had begun to pay handsome dividends. The group that derived the largest benefit from this complex of changes was the Social Democratic party. It polled 7,880,058 votes and captured 131 Reichstag seats. Thus, in slightly more than half a year, it managed to increase both its popular following and its parliamentary representation by about thirty per cent. The bourgeois supporters of the Dawes plan—the Centrists, the Democrats and the People's party—registered far smaller gains. The big surprise of the elections was the showing of the Nationalists. They not only held their own but even added seven seats to bring their total to 103. They thus remained a force to be reckoned with. However, the effectiveness of the group was undermined by the interminable feud between the Hugenberg faction, which remained intransigently opposed to any compromise with the republic, and the more realistic elements. The latter wished to co-operate with Stresemann because they knew that by so doing they would be able to secure greater protection for their class interests.

5

As soon as the election results were in, Marx resigned. Ebert, who was reluctant to see him go, suggested that he try to organize a new ministry. Marx made the attempt, but eventually had to give up. The People's party was again insisting that the Nationalists be represented. The Democrats continued to say no. The Centrists declared that Nationalist participation in the new government would be possible only if the Social Democrats promised their co-operation. An effort to set up a minority cabinet of Centrists and Democrats foundered on the opposition of the finance minister, Luther. Thereupon, at the suggestion of Stresemann, Ebert offered the chancellorship to Luther. This was on January 9, 1925. Luther promptly busied himself with the task of fashioning a government that would be able to effectuate the program inaugurated by his predecessor. He, too, encountered difficulties, but managed to overcome them. His cabinet was predominantly conservative in character. The decision of the Nationalists to take office under Luther was due in considerable measure to the attitude of Martin Schiele, their new chairman. Schiele was a well-known agrarian leader. He held that the existing democracy, how-ever distasteful, could be made to serve the needs of the landowning class. He persevered in this view in spite of the fulminations of Hugen-berg. The presence of Schiele and his comrades in the new cabinet was expected to result in more stable parliamentary support for the policies of Stresemann, who remained at the foreign office. The Centrists, after much searching of soul, finally decided to co-operate with the Nationalists. They received two cabinet posts, while the Bavarian People's party was again represented by a single minister. The Democrats refused to emulate the Centrists. Gessler continued to serve as minister of war, but solely in the capacity of expert and not as a representative of his party. However, after prolonged discussion, the Democrats decided to tolerate the new cabinet. The Social Demo-crats, on the other hand, assumed an attitude of unequivocal opposition. Between them and the parties of the Right there were three bones of contention. One of these was the length of the working day. The Social Democrats wanted a return to the eight-hour principle, which had been scrapped in 1923. Their adversaries contended that the eco-nomic needs of the country would best be served by maintaining the ten-hour day. A second issue was commercial policy. The Nationalists and the People's party clamored for high tariffs because they were anxious to boost domestic prices and increase the profits of the trusts and cartels. The Social Democrats insisted on low duties and a gen-eral reduction in the cost of living. Taxes were the third subject of controversy. The Social Democrats were eager to make things easier for the masses. Consequently, they favored the elimination of sales and wage taxes and the introduction of heavier levies on property, income and inheritances. The conservative elements, on the contrary, wished to lighten the tax burden resting on big business and on the owners of the great agricultural estates. Although heavy industry and the Junker aristocracy were frequently at loggerheads because of con-flicting class interests, they co-operated at this juncture in order to achieve their aims in the labor, commercial and financial spheres.

Chapter 21

HINDENBURG BECOMES PRESIDENT OF THE REICH

I

THE new Reichstag heard Luther on January 19, 1925. He declared that his government would seek the support of all Germans who were willing to co-operate in a positive and constructive spirit. Basic decisions would have to be arrived at with the assent of the greatest possible number of citizens. He and his colleagues in the cabinet regarded the Weimar constitution as the foundation upon which their own position rested. Consequently, they would deal sternly with any attempt to alter it by unlawful means. At the same time, they were willing to scrutinize certain provisions of the constitution with an eye to effecting needed improvements in the political life of the nation. The whole subject of the relations between the Reich and the states was ripe for re-examination. One thing the government could promise without further ado: the separate existence of the *Laender* would be respected. Another matter that required special attention was the purification of public life. In carrying out this phase of its program, the government was prepared to bolster what was best in the country's elaborate bureaucracy. In the sphere of foreign affairs, it had a great and lofty objective: the achievement of lasting peace between the nations of the world. The Dawes legislation would be loyally enforced and every obligation to other states punctiliously met. All the more deplorable, therefore, was the failure of the Allies to evacuate the Cologne zone. Their behavior represented a deviation from the terms of the Treaty of Versailles and was in flagrant conflict with the spirit of the recent reparation settlement. The German government would do everything in its power to secure the speedy liberation of the Rhineland. So long as the western districts of the Reich remained under alien occupation, the economic and political stabilization of Europe would be impossible. As for the question of membership in the League, the conditions specified by the Marx cabinet still stood. The campaign against the war-guilt lie would be continued. Germany, Luther promised, would make good use of her newly recovered commercial freedom. Her economy had to be linked with that of the rest of the world. Her exports had to be increased. Only in this way could the fulfillment of her international obligations be guaranteed. Within the Reich, maximum productivity would have to be achieved. Only in conditions of prosperity could the country's enlightened social program be maintained and extended. As regards social insurance, the year 1924 was one of regaining lost ground. It was the duty of the nation to make more adequate provision for the wage-earning classes. With this in mind, the government was planning to create more opportunities for work and to introduce a comprehensive scheme of social insurance. It was also resolved to establish labor courts, raise wage levels and improve housing conditions. Middle-class victims of the recent inflation would find that they, too, were being looked after. And for the benefit of all, rich and poor alike, a just tax policy would be instituted.

Luther's obvious effort to curry favor with the proletariat made little impression on the Social Democrats. They ranged themselves solidly against him, but his program, nonetheless, was endorsed by a vote of 246 to 160. Undeterred by this setback, the Social Democrats launched an offensive of their own. They lashed out against extremists of every hue. They urged their followers to combat all attempts to restore Junker rule. With equal gusto, they assailed the strategy of the Communists, claiming that it was responsible for the current successes of the parties of the Right. But their attacks on the government were hampered by the inescapable obligation of supporting its foreign policy. Stresemann and his far-sighted diplomacy were clearly Luther's greatest assets.

2

The closing days of January, 1925, witnessed a sharp verbal exchange between Paris and Berlin. Herriot started the fireworks by telling the French chamber of deputies that Germany had continually impeded the work of the inter-Allied Control Commissions. More than that, she had failed to disarm. She had begun to recruit short-term volunteers for military service and possessed, as a consequence, a reserve force that was entirely illegal in character. She also had at her disposal a new "defense" police, the Schupo. The latter was, for all practical purposes, a part of the Reichswehr. It contained no less than 5,000 officers of the old Germany army. It had a general staff that was housed in the ministry of the interior. France was therefore justified in insisting that she could not reduce her armies of occupation in the Rhineland until Germany had been completely demilitarized. According to Herriot, the Reich not only retained stores of forbidden arms but was actually working to increase them. Munition plants in Berlin-Spandau and elsewhere had turned out large quantities of war material. The mammoth armament firm of Krupp had so far refused to dismantle machines that were capable of producing long-range artillery. The German army, which started the last war, was staging a comeback. The Great General Staff had been reestablished. Little wonder, then, that General Seeckt talked as if the forces under his command were something more than 100,000 men without airplanes and heavy guns.

Luther retorted in a slashing address before the representatives of the foreign press. Herriot, he said, was making a mountain out of a mole-hill. This was particularly true of his charge that Germany had recruited short-term volunteers. In 1923, when the country fell prey to dangerous tension, the Reichswehr subjected several thousand students to military drill for a few weeks. But what significance could this have for other states in view of the fact that Germany no longer possessed the modern weapons of war which were essential to the conduct of military operations? Of what importance was it, after Germany's huge process of disarmament, that here and there small amounts of old war material had been discovered? From a military point of view, these violations of the treaty were of no consequence. Besides, the German government was firmly resolved to shun all irregularities. But in order to carry out its intention, it would have to see the report of the inter-Allied Control Commission. Luther's allusions to the Schupo were entirely unapologetic in tone. Germany, he declared, could not dispense with a militarized police for the simple reason that her internal situation was too unsettled. Not to be overlooked was the existence of a Bolshevist movement within the Reich. So long as the process of consolidation went forward, this movement was not likely to constitute an immediate danger. But if economic conditions should deteriorate again, the Communists would throw

themselves into a decisive struggle for power. The Reichswehr was not
strong enough to cope with a threat of this kind. It would need the
assistance of a police force capable of going into action at a moment's
notice. Luther ridiculed the charge of saber-rattling which had been
hurled at the Reich. Germany, he told his listeners, had no state-owned
armament factories; her diminutive army was without heavy artillery,
airplanes and tanks; her fortifications had been dismantled or were
wholly out of date; and her border region had been demilitarized.
Once again he bewailed the Allies' refusal to evacuate the Cologne
zone. Was Herriot, he queried, resolved to get his troops out of this
area as soon as all alleged irregularities in the matter of disarmament
had been eliminated? There was no clear answer to this question in
the French premier's speech. The reason given for deferring the evacuation had failed to impress many Germans; they suspected other
motives. The German government, for its part, wished to emphasize
that it would not reject a compromise settlement. Liberation of the
Cologne zone a few months hence would be acceptable. Because she
had disarmed, Germany felt strongly the need for security; she was
therefore interested in Herriot's allusions to this subject. Once the
problem of security had been disposed of, the solution of other international questions would follow. But real understanding and reconciliation between the powers would remain unattainable so long as
one country was branded a criminal, so long as the world failed to
realize the falsity of the charge that Germany had started the war.

3

On February 28, 1925, after a short illness, President Ebert died. He was
only fifty-four. His disappearance from the political scene was a heavy
blow to the Weimar regime. For, with all his shortcomings, he would
never have permitted the prerogatives of his office to be employed in
the service of anti-democratic ends. The instability of public opinion
in Germany, as exemplified by the results of recent parliamentary
elections, opened up disturbing possibilities in connection with the
choice of a new chief executive. The German and Prussian governments, the Social Democratic party and the trade unions hastened
to pay tribute to the man who had headed the republic ever since its
birth. But this eulogistic attitude was far from universal. The Communists were particularly disparaging. Ebert, they charged, had worked
exclusively for the bourgeoisie. He had pampered big business while

permitting the masses to be exploited. During the six years of his presidency, workers had been repeatedly jailed and their leaders persecuted. In order to suppress the German revolution, he had been ready to resort to any means, no matter how despicable. Little wonder, then, that the proletariat cursed him even after he was dead. The Social Democrats protested violently against these attacks. Feeling between the two parties became indescribably bitter. This flare-up came at a most inopportune moment. The German people, for the first time in their history, were about to discharge the duty of electing a chief executive. The reactionary and conservative forces could be expected to make a powerful bid for success in this contest. Should they manage to elect a man of their own choosing, the cause of democracy in Germany might suffer irreparable damage. To prevent such a calamity, all the moderate and left-wing parties would have to stand shoulder to shoulder. But aggravation of the long-standing feud between the Social Democrats and the Communists seemed to preclude a closing of labor's ranks. And without a united proletariat, the prospects for victory against the counterrevolutionary elements were poor indeed.

The various political parties busied themselves with the task of selecting presidential candidates. Although he preferred to remain premier of Prussia, Otto Braun allowed himself to be persuaded to serve as the Social Democratic standard-bearer. He had made an excellent record as an administrator. He commanded the respect of the industrial masses and of the rank-and-file members of his own party. There was therefore every reason to suppose that he would do well in the race for the nation's highest office. Ernst Thaelmann, a former transport worker from Hamburg, was the choice of the Communists. The other groups had a harder time making up their minds. All the nonsocialist parties, from the Democrats to the Nationalists, gave thought to the possibility of uniting behind a single candidate. An effort was made to find a suitable person. Primary responsibility for pushing this quest was assumed by a committee representing the Nationalists, the People's party and the Bavarian Populists. Friedrich Wilhelm von Loebell, a former Prussian minister of rigidly conservative outlook, headed this committee. He conferred with spokesmen for the Centrists and the Democrats. Several names were considered. The qualifications of Karl Jarres, mayor of Duisburg, received a great deal of attention. During the struggle in the Ruhr, Jarres had conducted himself with exemplary courage. He had won the applause and admiration of the entire German people. From August, 1923, to February, 1924, he had served as Reich minister of the interior. Thus, in respect of popularity and experience, he seemed to pass muster. But the Centrists would not accept him, so he had to be dropped. For a time it looked as if Gessler might be chosen. At the last moment, however, the foreign office threw a monkey wrench into the proceedings. Acting on advice from its agents abroad, it warned that other governments would react unfavorably to Gessler's election. They would jump to the conclusion that the Reichswehr was in the saddle and that Germany was treading the road that led to military dictatorship. The People's party and the Center sided with the foreign office; Gessler's name was withdrawn. It finally dawned on all concerned that they were wasting their time, that their interests and aims were too divergent to permit them to unite on a matter of such outstanding importance. Several separate candidacies at once materialized. The Nationalists and the People's party were still convinced that Jarres was their best bet. They placed his name before the electorate and worked as one in his behalf. The Bavarian Populists decided to go their own way. They rallied behind Heinrich Held, Bavaria's premier at the moment and a stanch champion of federalism. Wilhelm Marx was the choice of the Center. After Gessler had signified his reluctance to run, Willy Hellpach, head of the Badenese government, agreed to enter the race as the nominee of the Democratic party. The National Socialists offered Ludendorff as their candidate, but this they did against the wishes of the Racialists, who thought it wiser to support Jarres.

The election took place on March 29, 1925. Jarres, the only contestant to be backed by more than one party, amassed the largest number of votes: 10,787,870. Braun came next with 7,836,676. Marx was a poor third with 3,988,659. The remaining four candidates were quite definitely out of the running. Their totals ranged from Thaelmann's 1,885,778 to Ludendorff's paltry 210,968. Since no candidate had obtained a majority of the votes cast, a second election was in order, and this time a plurality would suffice. The Social Democrats were confronted with the necessity of making a decision of far-reaching importance. They were alarmed by the size of Jarres' following. Braun, they told themselves, had done very well. But they realized that neither he nor any other Social Democrat would be able to garner enough votes to emerge triumphant from a second trial of strength. Besides, they knew from past experience that it was extremely difficult to get middle-class people to vote for socialist candidates. On the other hand, working-class voters could be relied upon to follow the instructions of their political leaders, even if this involved going to the polls in support of bourgeois aspirants to public office. If the nominee of the National- ist and People's parties was to be defeated in the run-off election, the Social Democrats would have to accept a middle-class candidate and exert all their voting strength in his behalf. The most ardent exponent of this point of view was Hermann Mueller. Thanks above all to him, there came into being the so-called People's Bloc. It consisted of Social Democrats, Centrists and Democrats, and the man to whom it pledged support was Wilhelm Marx. In some respects, this was a most fortunate choice. Marx possessed sterling qualities. He was honest, conscientious and straightforward. His record as a public servant was beyond reproach. But he lacked the one thing which was essential to success in contests for popular favor: personal magnetism. Moreover, because of his religion, he was certain to lose hundreds of thousands of votes in predominantly Protestant districts.

When the People's Bloc announced its choice, the supporters of Jarres were forced to reconsider their strategy. And now a rift devel- oped between them. The People's party, under Stresemann's leader- ship, argued that Jarres would do even better in the run-off election than in the first and insisted that he be kept in the race. He was, to boot, a close friend of the foreign minister, and the People's party looked upon him as one of its own. But the Nationalists objected. They feared that Jarres was not enough of a vote-getter to be able to prevail against the candidate of the People's Bloc. They proposed in- stead the name of Field Marshal Paul von Hindenburg. However one might feel about the venerable war lord, it was obvious that he packed a tremendous political punch. The mere mention of his name evoked strong and very divergent reactions. Republican-minded Germans loyal to the Weimar constitution regarded this scion of an old Prussian family as the very embodiment of reactionary monarchism. To the outside world he symbolized the brutal militarism and limitless lust for conquest that had finally been overcome after years of bloody warfare. Foreign governments could hardly fail to regard his candidacy as a frontal thrust against the Treaty of Versailles. It was this concern over the reaction of other countries that impelled Stresemann to object most strenuously to the choice of Hindenburg. The embattled and harassed foreign minister feared that the election of a man so closely identified with the imperial regime would doom the policy of conciliation and destroy the possibility of obtaining desperately needed loans from the United States. Stresemann was able to convince his own party that the candidacy of Hindenburg would be a tragedy for Germany. The old field marshal also proved amenable. He stated without equivocation that he had no desire to run for the presidency. But Stresemann's rejoicing proved short-lived. Admiral Tirpitz persuaded Hindenburg to change his mind. This he did by appealing to his sense of duty. Stresemann refused to acknowledge defeat. He urged both Marx and Hindenburg to withdraw from the race in favor of some other candidate who might be able to command the support of all the non-socialist parties. His plea was spurned. Under the circumstances, albeit with unallayed misgivings regarding the reaction of the outside world, Stresemann and the People's party announced that they would support the field marshal. The National Socialists and the Bavarian People's party promptly issued similar statements. Although the latter, as a Catholic group, preferred Marx to a stanch Lutheran like Hindenburg, it put aside religious considerations and turned against the Centrist leader because he was backed by the Social Democrats. The Communists persisted in their lone-wolf tactics. Thaelmann, they announced, would once again be their candidate.

On April 11, 1925, Hindenburg addressed an appeal to the nation. He had decided, he said, to heed the call of patriotic Germans. He had arrived at this decision after serious reflection. He was motivated solely by a feeling of loyalty to the Fatherland. His life was an open book. He had always done his duty, even in difficult times. When this duty commanded him to serve as president of the Reich, he could not say no. As a soldier he had constantly kept in view the entire nation, not individual parties. The latter, true, were necessary in a parliamentary regime, but the head of the state had to stand above them and work independently for the weal of every German. Although he had never lost his faith in the German people and in divine providence, he no longer believed that a sudden change in the fortunes of the Reich was possible. German freedom could not be regained by war or internal insurrection. What the nation needed was sustained and peaceful work. The supreme desideratum was a purification of the country's political life. No state could prosper without public virtue and order. Ebert had never denied his Social Democratic background during the years that he served as custodian of the constitution. He, Hindenburg, was likewise not abandoning his political convictions in becoming a candidate for the presidency. At the present time, however, not the form of government but the spirit which animated it was of decisive importance. The field marshal promised to co-operate with every German who was patriotic, who sought to safeguard German dignity and who desired religious and social peace.

On the following day, Marx had his say in a manifesto which received wide circulation. The freely elected head of the state, he declared, was the symbol and protector of German unity. All groups and individuals within the country were entitled to freedom, but it was important for them to realize that they had obligations as well as rights. The nation, too, had duties to perform. First of all, it would have to regain its liberty. But it would also have to live up to the commitments it had assumed toward the rest of the world. The Weimar constitution and the black-red-gold banner of the republic pointed the way to the proper fulfillment of these obligations.

Throughout the ensuing campaign, Marx's supporters underlined their fidelity to democratic principles. Their slogan was "For the Fatherland, for the people's state, for the republic!" The Hindenburg bloc extolled its candidate as the man who symbolized "German honor, loyalty, strength and firmness." It hammered home the message that during good times and bad, he had been Germany's leader and had never been found wanting. With him once again at the helm, the people of the Reich would regain unity, glory and freedom. He, and he alone, was the country's savior. On April 26, 1925, 14,655,766 Germans—forty-eight per cent of all those who went to the polls— voted for Hindenburg. Marx's total was 13,751,615. Thaelmann trailed far behind with 1,931,151. Hindenburg thus won by the scant margin of 904,151 votes. His triumph was due to the magic of his name, to the legend which made Germans of all classes and parties regard him with pride and reverence. For, in spite of the misgivings which his name aroused in republican circles, the hulking, granite-faced field marshal was, in a very true sense, the nation's idol. His enormous popularity originated during the first weeks of the war, when a deeply grateful country acclaimed him as the man who had won the stupendous victory of Tannenberg. Actually, not he but one of his subordinates was the hero of the piece, but of this the nation knew nothing. The Hindenburg myth struck deep roots. More than six years after the signing of the armistice, it was still a mighty force. It led two and a half million Germans, who had stayed away from the polls on March 29, to shake off their lethargy and vote for the former head of the Supreme Command. Thus the advent of an old-line militarist to the presidency—an event of incalculable importance—was made possible by the least politically-minded fringe of the German electorate. These people were not greatly concerned about constitutional or ideological questions; they were swayed, first and foremost, by their adoration of the man. Of course, the outcome of the election would have been different if the Communists had given their support to Marx. It would have been different if the Bavarian People's party—which controlled about a million votes—had made common cause with the Catholic Center. Thanks to these two groups, the counterrevolution was able to attain power by constitutional means. For this, in last analysis, was the meaning of Hindenburg's election.

The monarchists were jubilant. They had visions of Hindenburg placing himself at the head of a movement to restore the Hohenzollerns and remilitarize the Reich. Their newspapers predicted that he would eliminate corruption from public life and unite all Germans for a concerted effort to cope with the tasks of internal reconstruction. The general belief in Germany and abroad on the morrow of the election was that the Weimar republic had suffered an irreparable blow. Left-wing radicals charged that the reactionaries, with the field marshal as their obedient tool, would seize the very first opportunity that came along to overthrow the democratic regime. Liberals and socialists made no effort to dissemble their alarm. Democratic organs like the *Frankfurter Zeitung* and the *Berliner Tageblatt* attributed Hindenburg's victory to the political immaturity of very large numbers of Germans. Sentimentality, they averred, had triumphed over common sense. The *Vorwaerts* was full of bitterness. It reserved almost all its ire for the Communists, insisting that their divisive tactics and their betrayal of the republic had made possible the success of the counterrevolutionaries.

The outcome of the election produced consternation in many foreign capitals, above all Paris. The French press cited the field marshal's triumph as proof that Germany could not be trusted and that another war was bound to ensue. Less unfriendly was the British reaction. Many Englishmen held that Hindenburg's accession to the presidency need not be viewed as the prelude to wholesale violations of the peace treaty. It revealed, they conceded, a state of mind which they did not like. But it was their duty, they reasoned, to judge Germany not by her emotions but by her deeds. So long as she continued to discharge her obligations faithfully, she ought not to be exposed to premature, over-hasty criticism. Stresemann endeavored to encourage this train of thought. An article which appeared in the *Zeit* pointed out that Hindenburg had repeatedly endorsed the country's current foreign policy. There was therefore not the slightest reason to fear a change of course on the part of the Reich.

The Social Democrats sought to have the election of Hindenburg declared invalid. They cited numerous reports to the effect that illegal attempts had been made to influence the voting. In many rural districts, they charged, landowners or their hirelings had forced agricultural workers and others economically dependent on them to support Hindenburg's candidacy. Nothing came of this effort. On May 11, 1925, Hindenburg arrived in Berlin. He was cheered by tremendous throngs. The Stahlhelm and other right-wing organizations provided guards of honor. The Reichsbanner took no part in these festivities. Thousands of flags were displayed to signalize the occasion, but it was the black-white-red of the empire, not the black-red-gold of the republic, that predominated.

On the following day, the induction ceremony took place in the hall of the nation's parliament. Hindenburg entered the crowded auditorium in the company of Paul Loebe, the Social Democratic president of the Reichstag. All the deputies arose with the exception of the Communists, who shouted "Down with the monarchists! Long live the soviet republic!" and departed. Hindenburg proceeded to take the oath of office. He swore to preserve the constitution and laws of the Reich. Then he replied to a short address by Loebe. The Reichstag and the president, he said, were the embodiment of that popular sovereignty which was now the foundation of Germany's national life. This, in his opinion, was the deeper meaning of the constitution which he had just sworn to uphold. He emphasized, too, the duty of the president to unite all the constructive forces in the land in a spirit of non-partisanship. His proclamation to the people was couched in a similar vein. He promised to safeguard the country's well-being and to practise justice toward all. His efforts would be designed to advance the interests of the nation as a whole and not those of a particular class or religion or party. Simultaneously, he urged the army to serve the Reich in conformity with its oath and with the duties imposed upon it by the constitution. Hindenburg thus seemed content to uphold a regime which he, a stanch believer in authoritarian rule, despised with all his being. His behavior surprised everyone. For five years, until the spring of 1930, he comported himself with the most scrupulous respect for the principles of parliamentarism. His actions throughout this period were governed by the spirit as well as the letter of the Weimar constitution. The fears which his election had aroused in republican circles gradually subsided. The monarchists were wild with rage, but there was little they could do except bide their time.

Chapter 22

LOCARNO

I

In December, 1922, the Cuno government proposed the conclusion of a Rhine security pact to allay French fear of the Reich. The signatories were to guarantee Germany's western frontiers. They were also to refrain, for a generation, from making war on one another. Poincaré turned thumbs down on the German proposal. He stigmatized it as a "clumsy maneuver." Twice during 1923, in May and September, the German government renewed the offer. Poincaré, with the struggle over reparation at its height, once again proved entirely unaccommodating. He suspected the Germans of being actuated solely by a desire to influence world opinion in their favor. On February 22, 1924, Stresemann alluded to the question in the course of an address before the Reichstag. France, he observed, had not yet accepted the idea of a Rhineland treaty which would give her the security she craved. Interested powers like Great Britain and the United States should, if at all possible, be made the guarantors of such a pact. A few weeks later, Stresemann returned to this theme. He sharply assailed a British suggestion that the Rhineland be neutralized by converting it into a buffer state under the League's protection. Such an arrangement, he declared, was absolutely out of the question. The offer made by the Cuno government still stood. Acceptance of it would, in his opinion, remove all cause for French apprehension.

The adoption of the Dawes plan lessened existing international tensions, while the discussion of the Geneva protocol cleared the atmosphere by proving that something less ambitious was in order. This protocol, which was designed to insure the peaceful settlement of all international disputes, had to be dropped because of the unfavorable attitude of the British. The latter did, however, intimate that the object in view could be attained through regional understandings. Eduard Beneš, the Czech foreign minister and one of the chief artificers of the Geneva protocol, now suggested the conclusion of treaties similar to those which had created the Little Entente. He envisaged separate pacts for each of the following areas: western Europe, central Europe, the Balkans and the Baltic-Scandinavian countries. Negotiations were initiated by the German government; they culminated in the only regional pact that actually materialized. That the idea ultimately embodied in the Locarno agreements survived its many difficulties and emerged triumphant was due in large measure to the persistence and courage of Stresemann, who was attacked every inch of the way by the German Nationalists, and to the assistance given him by Lord D'Abernon. The latter appraised English opinion for Stresemann. Moreover, the moderation of his counsel helped to counteract the German statesman's temperamental instability. Thus the friendship which had sprung up between these two men proved most fortunate for the cause of European peace.

The German government was anxious to see France get what she wanted in the matter of security. There was no better way, it felt, to insure the speedy evacuation of the Rhineland, which was its paramount aim at the moment. Besides, it feared that failure to participate in the solution of the security problem might expose the Reich to serious diplomatic dangers. Realizing that the Geneva protocol was doomed, Stresemann in December, 1924, resolved to resume his efforts in behalf of a Rhineland pact. What was in his mind at this time is apparent from the following entry in his private papers: [1]

Our problem is to prevent both the extension of time of the Rhine occupation and of an international control of the Rhine zone. This problem is so much more disquieting because it is certain that the present English secretary of state for foreign affairs appears to be partisan of an entente with France and is inclined to conclude a treaty of guarantee with that power which would be unfavorable to us. On the other hand England now has difficulties in the Orient and could, at the price of concessions to France on the Rhine, obtain the co-operation of the French in eastern questions. In that way the two powers would settle their differences at our expense. Those are the reasons that have decided us to renew the attempt made unsuccessfully by the Cuno government and by myself. . . .

[1] Quoted in *Gustav Stresemann: His Diaries, Letters and Papers*, edited by Eric Sutton, (The Macmillan Company).

On January 20, 1925, Stresemann addressed a carefully worded memorandum to the British government. His purpose was more to elicit advice regarding the procedure to be followed in advancing the German proposition than to secure London's acquiescence. He called attention to the question of disarmament and to the related Rhineland issue. These problems would prove easier to solve, he argued, if they were dealt with in an agreement designed to maintain peace between France and Germany. The latter desired to settle her difficulties with France in a spirit of friendly understanding. She favored the conclusion of a treaty which would facilitate the attainment of this objective. The offer made by the Cuno government constituted a suitable basis for such a treaty. The Reich was still prepared to accept an accord "by virtue of which the powers interested in the Rhine, above all England, France, Italy and Germany, entered into a solemn obligation for a lengthy period of time ... not to wage war against a contracting state." The United States, Stresemann suggested, should act as trustee. Germany was likewise willing to conclude treaties of arbitration with "all other states." The aim of the proposed security pact would be to guarantee the territorial status quo in the Rhineland. This was tantamount to saying that Germany was ready to regard the loss of Alsace-Lorraine as definitive. Stresemann also pointed out that the demilitarization of the Rhineland, which was prescribed by Articles 42 and 43 of the Treaty of Versailles, might be underwritten by the parties to the western pact.

London received these proposals with a noticeable lack of enthusiasm and even some suspicion. The attitude of the British government was set forth by its foreign minister, Sir Austen Chamberlain, early in February, 1925. England, he explained, could do nothing behind the back of her ally, France. Moreover, no pact was possible if its conclusion was made contingent on the evacuation of all the Rhineland zones. In any case the Geneva protocol, which was still on the international agenda, would first have to be disposed of and the British position in regard to French security defined. As a matter of fact, Chamberlain, once the decision to reject the Geneva protocol had been made, suggested to his ministerial colleagues the idea of a defensive alliance with France. But the British cabinet, swayed by the views of Lord Balfour, the venerable Conservative statesman, said no.

On February 9, 1925, Stresemann opened negotiations with the French government. The note which he dispatched to Paris was identical in every respect with the memorandum of January 20 except for the suggestion that the security pact might be so drafted as to "prepare the way for a world convention to include all states. . . ." While the French were studying the German communication, the British government made an important gesture. On March 12, 1925, Chamberlain informed the Council of the League that his government could not accept the Geneva protocol. However, he promptly added that Britain was prepared "to supplement the Covenant by making special arrangements in order to meet special ends." This meant that London looked with favor on the German proposal for a Rhineland pact. And indeed, twelve days later, Chamberlain announced that Stresemann's suggestion enjoyed the provisional support of His Majesty's government.

The French saw two advantages in connection with the treaty which Berlin seemed so eager to conclude. For one thing, it would signify German resignation to the loss of Alsace-Lorraine. For another, it would facilitate greater economic co-operation between France and Germany. Such co-operation held an important place in the calculations of French industrialists, who were currently engaged in forming cartels with their German colleagues. However, the fact remained that Germany was making no promises regarding her frontier with Poland, and a guarantee of that frontier was one of the objectives of French diplomacy. Paris made this question the pivotal issue of the ensuing negotiations with Great Britain. The French and their Polish and Czech allies feared that a guarantee of Germany's western frontiers alone would only encourage her to seek a revision of her boundaries in the east. France was therefore leery of Stresemann's proposals. She intimated that she would have to reject them unless the British proved willing to guarantee the existing frontiers between Poland and Germany. Herriot's government resigned in the midst of the negotiations. Aristide Briand, who now returned to the Quai d'Orsay, continued the attempt to elicit from London a promise to extend its guarantee to the east. Failing in this, he tried to get the British to underwrite the treaties of arbitration which the German government was willing to conclude with Poland and Czechoslovakia. Once again the answer was no. On May 28, 1925, the British government declared in all finality that it would guarantee the frontiers in the west and nothing more. The exclusion of the eastern boundaries from the proposed security pact robbed the arrangement of much of its value in French eyes. Briand, however, had no choice but to accept the British reservations, which he did in substance on June 4, 1925.

On the subject of the eastern frontiers, the attitude of Stresemann and of all his colleagues in the cabinet was marked by complete inflexibility. It was one thing to renounce Alsace-Lorraine, although even this was loudly opposed by the Nationalists. After all, so long as Germany was weak and France was strong, it would be sheer madness to try to regain those provinces. A war against France was, under existing circumstances, an absolute impossibility. So in giving up something that was for the present beyond her reach, Germany was not making a real sacrifice. But the question of the eastern frontiers was something entirely different. Never would Germany reconcile herself to her current boundaries with Poland. Never would she renounce the Corridor and the portion of Upper Silesia that had been allotted to her Slavic neighbor. Never would she give up the idea of reuniting Danzig with the Reich. No German government could abandon the claims to these areas and survive because the entire nation, regardless of party or class, felt very strongly about them. As a matter of fact, Stresemann, in confidential conversations with newspapermen and with members of the Reichstag's foreign affairs committee, stressed the point that the western pact was primarily a means of securing a revision of the eastern frontiers. But, important as it was, such a revision was only one of the advantages which the western pact was expected to confer on Germany. In a letter which he addressed to the former German Crown Prince on September 7, 1925, Stresemann wrote:[2]

In my opinion, there are three great tasks that confront German foreign policy in the more immediate future—In the first place, the solution of the reparation question in a sense tolerable for Germany, and the assurance of peace, which is an essential premise for the recovery of our strength. Secondly, the protection of Germans abroad, those ten to twelve millions of our kinsmen who now live under a foreign yoke in foreign lands. The third great task is the readjustment of our eastern frontiers: the recovery of Danzig and the Polish Corridor and a correction of the frontier in Upper Silesia. In the background stands the union with German Austria, although I am quite clear that this not merely brings no advantages to Germany, but seriously complicates the problem of the German Reich. If we want to secure these aims, we must concentrate on these tasks. Hence the security pact. . . . The most important thing for the first task of German policy mentioned above is the liberation of German soil from any occupying force. We must get the stranglehold off our neck. On that account, German policy . . . will be one of finesse and the avoidance of great decisions.

A week later, the *Hamburger Fremdenblatt* published an article in

---

[2] Quoted in *The Roots of National Socialism,* by Rohan D. Butler (E. P. Dutton & Company, Inc.)

which Stresemann gave another revealing exposition of his objectives:[3]

> Germany must be the champion of the German minorities in Europe; she must be the great motherland of the German cultural community. . . . The aim of German foreign policy must, further, be an effort towards a revision of the eastern frontier, which is today recognized in all quarters as impossible. It must also consist in backing Germany's claim to . . . colonial possessions. She must, finally, stand up for the national right of self-determination which, in the question of the union of German Austria with Germany, has been treated with unexampled cynicism by the Allies and stultified. Progress within the sphere of these foreign-political aims is not dependent on warlike resources, which Germany lacks.

These were ambitious aims; their attainment by peaceful, gradual means was dictated by Germany's military weakness. It was this weakness that determined Stresemann's approach to problems of foreign policy. It explains his anxiety to avoid an armed conflict with France, to seek a settlement of the differences between Germany and Poland without recourse to war. Stresemann clung to the belief that the peaceful reacquisition of Danzig and of the territories ceded to Poland would become possible once Germany had strengthened her diplomatic position.

From the very outset the German Nationalists were a thorn in Stresemann's side. They demanded his resignation and threatened to oust the cabinet. They continued to object to the idea of a rapprochement with France and bitterly lamented the proposed reunciation of Alsace-Lorraine. The hard-pressed foreign minister countered with a vigorous defense of his policy. He told the Reichstag on May 18, 1925, that the problem of security would be solved with the co-operation of Germany or without it. Should the latter eventuality materialize, European peace and the interests of the Reich would suffer. It was of paramount importance to make a clear arrangement in regard to the western frontier. The issue between the Reich and the Allies was not compliance or non-compliance with specific provisions of the Treaty of Versailles. It was whether equality could be denied the Reich indefinitely.

2

On June 16, 1925, the French government replied to Stresemann's overture. There could be no security pact, it asserted, unless Germany joined the League of Nations and accepted the obligations set forth in the Covenant. It emphasized that no commitments in regard to revision of the Treaty of Versailles and especially of the Rhineland clauses

[3] Ibid.

would result from the signing of the pact. The Germans were likewise given to understand that Belgium would have to be a party to the agreement and that the treaty of arbitration which they declared themselves willing to conclude with France would have to cover all categories of disputes. The Allies, the French note continued, regarded with satisfaction Germany's readiness to sign arbitration treaties with other states as well. The conclusion of such accords between Germany and those of her neighbors who would not be parties to the security pact was essential to the preservation of peace in Europe. This was an obvious reference to Poland and Czechoslovakia whose interests France was still seeking to protect as best she could.

The German cabinet at once busied itself with the task of drafting a reply. While it was so engaged, Stresemann made another effort to placate the Nationalists. The accord with the western powers, he told them, would be based on full reciprocity and equality of rights for all. Germany's views on the subject of armaments and the future status of the Rhineland would have to be taken into account by the other parties to the agreement. She would definitely refuse to join the League of Nations until the first Rhineland zone had been evacuated. Her reservations in regard to Article 16 of the Covenant had not been withdrawn. Complete freedom of action had been retained so far as the eastern frontiers were concerned; foreign intervention in this matter would not be tolerated. New commitments in the west would in no way affect the Treaty of Rapallo or any other agreement previously entered into by Germany. Such was the burden of Stresemann's assurances. But he was wasting his breath. His critics remained entirely unconvinced. The agitation against him assumed more ominous proportions. Indeed, so unpopular did he become in Nationalist circles that for a time his very life was in danger. But the Nationalists were not alone in denouncing his policy. The Communists, reflecting the attitude of the Kremlin, decried the westward orientation of German diplomacy. They accused Stresemann of being nothing more than a tool of the British who, they said, were planning to make war on Russia. The new president of the Reich was also far from enthusiastic about the impending rapprochement with the adversaries of 1914-1918. He was not opposed to the League, but he doubted whether anything except war could settle matters in Europe. However, unlike the Nationalists and the Communists, the old field marshal decided that Stresemann knew best and carefully refrained from creating difficulties.

The German government answered the French note on July 20, 1925. It acknowledged that the signing of the security pact would not obligate the Allies to modify the settlement of 1919. It insisted, however, that "the possibility of adapting existing treaties at the proper moment to changed circumstances by way of peaceful agreement should not be excluded for all time." The Covenant of the League, it averred, envisaged exactly such a possibility. Germany did not make the signing of the western pact contingent on revision of the Rhineland clauses of the treaty. But the coming into force of such a pact would represent so important an innovation that it was bound to affect "the conditions in the occupied territories and above all the question of occupation itself." The German government reaffirmed its misgivings regarding the application of Article 16 of the Covenant. There was the ever-present danger that Germany might become involved in armed conflicts between other states. Yet, as a member of the League, she would not enjoy equal rights until general disarmament had been effected. Pending the attainment of that still remote goal, an arrangement would have to be worked out which took account of the Reich's special military, economic and geographical situation. This was Germany's way of saying that she was unwilling to facilitate or participate in League action for the defense of Poland should that state be attacked by Russia. The German Nationalists had made a great hue and cry precisely over this point. The Reich, they had argued, must not allow itself to be maneuvered into the perfectly fantastic position of having to enforce military sanctions against the U.S.S.R. Stresemann was thus endeavoring to forestall further criticism on this score.

The French government proved rather unaccommodating. In its note of August 24, 1925, it reminded Berlin that the Covenant presupposed scrupulous observance of the peace treaties by their signatories and specified, as the first prerequisite for admission to the League, a sincere intention to fulfill all international obligations. It insisted anew that the provisions of the Treaty of Versailles, and above all those having to do with the occupation of the Rhineland, must not be tampered with. Germany's unconditional entry into the League constituted the *sine qua non* of a security pact. Once she had become a member of the Geneva organization, she would be entitled to present her objections to Article 16 of the Covenant. As for general disarmament, its failure to materialize could be attributed to the lack of security in Europe.

3

On September 15, 1925, the Allies invited the Reich to a conference to wind up the discussions. The German government accepted the invitation. At the same time, however, it loosed another broadside on the subject of war guilt and warned that faith in the possibility of a peaceful evolution of affairs in Europe could not be restored so long as the Cologne zone remained under military occupation. This provocative gesture, which was part of a last-minute effort to mollify the Nationalists, created a most unpleasant impression in Paris and London. The French government acidly retorted that the question of war guilt had been settled in the Treaty of Versailles. The evacuation of the Cologne zone, it contended, would be possible only after the Germans had fulfilled their obligation to disarm. The British were likewise annoyed. They declared themselves unable to understand why the German government had seen fit to bring up the question of war guilt at this particular moment. They joined the French in pointing out that neither the Treaty of Versailles nor the judgment of past events which underlay it would be affected by the conclusion of a security pact. They, too, contended that the time to evacuate the Cologne zone would come when Germany had complied with the military provisions of the treaty.

This diplomatic contretemps failed to halt the slow but steady progress toward a relaxation of Europe's tensions. On October 5, 1925, leading spokesmen for Great Britain, France, Germany, Italy, Belgium, Poland and Czechoslovakia assembled in Locarno, a picturesque Swiss town on the shores of Lake Maggiore. The outstanding personalities at this conference were Briand, Stresemann, Austen Chamberlain and Beneš. Questions which Stresemann had already raised but which he wanted clarified before assenting to the security pact were discussed in a friendly spirit. The extent to which the Reich had disarmed figured in these conversations, as did also Germany's demand that she be given equality in armaments once it had become clear that general disarmament would remain nothing more than a pipe-dream. Several matters connected with the occupation of the Rhineland received a good deal of attention. Stresemann won a major victory when he got Briand to promise that the evacuation of the Cologne zone would begin at the earliest possible moment. When the question of Germany's admission to the League came up, Stresemann resolutely defended his government's stand on Article 16 of the Covenant. The Reich, he reiterated, could not pledge itself to back Poland in a struggle against the Soviet Union; nor could it be expected to assent to the movement of foreign troops across its territory. The other conferees finally gave in. They consented to a formula whereby each member of the League was obligated to co-operate against aggressors "to an extent which is compatible with its military situation and which takes its geographical situation into account." It was thereupon agreed that Germany should join the League forthwith and that the security pact should go into effect as soon as that happened.

October 16, 1925, was the big day at Locarno. It witnessed the signing of a momentous treaty between Germany, France, Belgium, Great Britain and Italy. The contracting parties undertook to guarantee "the maintenance of the territorial status quo resulting from the frontiers between Germany and Belgium and Germany and France and the inviolability of the said frontiers as fixed by . . . the Treaty of Peace signed at Versailles on June 28, 1919." They also underwrote "the observance of the stipulations of Articles 42 and 43 of the said treaty concerning the demilitarized zone." Germany and France and Germany and Belgium bound themselves to refrain from attacking, invading or making war upon each other except in certain specific eventualities enumerated in the Locarno accord. They further agreed to settle all their disputes by peaceful means. The pact was to remain in effect until the Council of the League should decide that the Geneva organization "insures sufficient protection to the high contracting parties." The Reich signed treaties of arbitration with Poland and Czechoslovakia. The spirit of good will which marked the proceedings at Locarno was eloquently expressed by Briand when he declared: "Differences between us still exist, but henceforth it will be for the judge to declare the law. . . . Away with rifles, machine guns, cannon! Clear the way for conciliation, arbitration, peace!"

It seemed to most contemporary observers that France was the victor at Locarno. Germany had acknowledged as final the loss of Alsace-Lorraine. She had agreed to dispense with the use of force. The British at long last had consented to guarantee the security of their old ally. Italy had assumed the same obligation. France's satellites were in a stronger position thanks to their treaties of arbitration with the Reich. But it was really Germany that stood to profit most by the Locarno accords. Her sacrifices were such in name only. The territories she had renounced were lost to her anyway. The pledges she had made were a matter not of choice but of necessity for a nation that was militarily impotent. On the strength of these purely nominal concessions, she could look forward to new favors from her erstwhile adversaries: treaty revision, reduction of the reparation bill, a continuation of the foreign loans so essential to her economic recovery. There was to be no repetition of the Ruhr episode; the French, at whose mercy Germany would be for some time to come, had assured her the tranquillity she would need to put her own house in order. Persuasion and negotiation were the only means at her disposal. To get what she wanted, she would have to convince the Allies of her good will, of her sincere desire for peace and amity. Locarno had therefore served a most useful purpose.

These were things which Stresemann appreciated. But large numbers of his countrymen persisted in regarding his program as a gross betrayal of Germany's interests and honor. Ever since the summer of 1925, the Hugenberg newspaper chain had been denouncing Stresemann and the steps which led to Locarno. Right-wing propagandists repeatedly charged that the government's foreign policy would result in only one thing: the perpetuation of the Treaty of Versailles. They continued to bewail the renunciation of Alsace-Lorraine and of the border territory ceded to Belgium in 1919. Nevertheless, the Nationalist members of the cabinet joined their ministerial colleagues in approving the security pact. They were promptly reprimanded by the district leaders of their party and forced to resign from the government. All the other ministers decided to remain in office long enough to put through the Locarno accords. Stresemann hastened to assure Paris, London, Brussels and Rome that the German government had no intention of altering its foreign policy. Supported by the Social Democrats, the Centrists, the Democrats and the People's party, Luther's depleted cabinet prepared for the next phase of the battle.

On November 3, 1925, Stresemann stated the government's case in an address to the nation. He declared that the French demand for security, however strange in view of Germany's military helplessness, was a reality which had to be faced and dealt with. Had Germany failed to take the initiative in this matter, she might have found herself confronted with a Franco-British pact that would not have been to her liking. The Locarno treaties, he went on, attested a widespread resolve to substitute conciliation for the methods of Versailles. They likewise betokened a change of attitude on the part of France. The latter was abandoning the demand, put forward by Foch and others in 1919, that the Rhine be made the western frontier of Germany. She was proclaiming her determination to abstain from further incursions into German territory. She was acquiescing in an arrangement which obligated the British to protect the Reich against French aggression. All this was of paramount importance. Moreover, Germany's representatives at Locarno had stood their ground on the question of war guilt. They had reaffirmed their country's right to serve as a mandatory under the League of Nations. Happily, the powers now realized that they could not continue to make war without bringing ruin on all alike. "The attempt," Stresemann said, "to create a new and better Europe by methods of compulsion, dictation and violence has been a failure. Let us try to achieve this objective on the basis of peace and of equal rights and liberty for Germany."

Still the Nationalists and all the other adversaries of the western pact remained unconvinced. Stresemann was deeply worried. He told D'Abernon that an immediate concession on the Rhineland issue was the only thing that might induce the Reichstag to accept the treaty. The Allies took this warning to heart: they consented to evacuate the Cologne zone right away. An announcement to this effect was made on November 16, 1925. The process of evacuation was to begin on December 1; it was to be completed, if possible, by January 31, 1926. Stresemann could now face his foes with equanimity. The showdown in the Reichstag occurred on November 27. The government won handily. By a vote of 271 to 174, the nation's representatives ratified the Locarno accords and approved the idea of joining the League of Nations. The opposition consisted, in the main, of Nationalists, Communists and Nazis. A no-confidence motion sponsored by the Hugenberg group was defeated. The support given the cabinet by the Social Democrats proved the decisive factor. On November 28, the Reichsrat sanctioned the accords. There was still Hindenburg to be heard from; upon him the Nationalists pinned their dwindling hopes. But the aged president disappointed them once again by proceeding, without further ado, to sign the bills of ratification. Luther and Stresemann went to London for the formal signing of the treaties. The ceremony took place on December 1. Directly it was over, the two statesmen returned to Berlin. On December 5, the cabinet resigned.

Hindenburg expressed the hope that a ministry enjoying the broadest possible support would be formed without undue delay. The Social Democrats were asked to co-operate. They agreed to do so on certain conditions. These included ratification of the Washington agreement regarding the eight-hour day, the enactment of an unemployment insurance law and a reduction of those taxes that weighed most heavily on the working masses. The People's party refused to accept such terms. The negotiations were discontinued. Hindenburg finally requested Luther to form another cabinet. This he did, but only the three middle parties were represented. On January 26, 1926, amid signs of widespread political restlessness, Luther stated his program. He sought to conciliate the Social Democrats by promising legislation favorable to the interests of labor. The gesture proved effective. The Social Democrats decided in favor of a wait-and-see policy. They abstained from voting when the new government asked the Reichstag for an expression of confidence. This enabled Luther to squeeze through with a ten-vote margin against the opposition of Nationalists, Nazis and Communists.

Chapter 23

GENEVA, THOIRY AND THE KELLOGG-BRIAND PACT

I

On January 30, 1926, the evacuation of the Cologne zone was completed. Eleven days later, Germany formally requested admission to the League of Nations. Her government sought to quiet domestic opposition to this move by emphasizing that the Reich, as a member of the League, would be in a better position to work for revision of the Treaty of Versailles. A special meeting of the Council and Assembly of the League took place on March 8, 1926. It was called specifically for the purpose of acting on the German application. Unexpected and painful complications developed. Germany had been promised a permanent seat on the Council and assumed that the execution of this promise would be nothing more than a formality. But Poland, Czechoslovakia, Spain, Brazil, China and Persia disrupted the proceedings by demanding that they, too, be made permanent members of the Council. Two of the obstructionists, Spain and Brazil, were non-permanent members of that body; and since the latter's decision had to be unanimous, they could, and said they would, block Germany's election to a permanent seat. Despite Stresemann's patent desire to see the matter settled without haggling, prolonged lobbying and backstairs negotiation ensued. The Spaniards were backed by the British; Briand favored the Poles. Stresemann declared himself willing to go along with the French, and a termination of the unseemly squabble appeared imminent. But now Brazil balked and the Swedish member of the Council made known his inflexible opposition to Poland's candidacy. Stresemann was thoroughly disgusted. He was also worried because he knew that the Geneva contretemps would provide fresh grist for the propaganda mill of his Nationalist adversaries at home. In a fit of temper he went so far as to say that he would not have been a party to the Locarno treaties had he realized that Germany's election to a permanent seat on the Council was contingent on the grant of a similar favor to other powers. The attitude of the Swedish representative helped to bring Warsaw to its senses. However, neither Spain nor Brazil would yield, so there was nothing for it but to postpone action on the German application until September. The following compromise was eventually worked out: only Germany was to receive a permanent seat; three additional non-permanent seats were to be created and they were to be offered to Poland, Spain and Brazil. Poland accepted this arrangement; Spain and Brazil defiantly announced their withdrawal from the League. Brazil stuck to her guns; Spain ultimately relented.

In March, 1926, with Germany's entry into the League temporarily stalled by the jealousy of other powers, Stresemann returned to Berlin. As he had correctly foreseen, German public opinion reacted adversely to the unedifying proceedings at Geneva. The Nationalists, renewing their denunciations of the westward orientation, exploited the affair to heap discredit on the Locarno pacts. Stresemann defended his policy before the Reichstag. But, as usual, his words made little impression on his adversaries. Right-wing extremists accused him of all sorts of crimes, including treason. They charged that he had sold out to the enemies of Germany and that he had made a handsome pecuniary profit for himself in the process. They vowed that they would drive him from office and wreck his political career once and for all. Nationalist deputies formally demanded that Germany withdraw her request for admission to the League. They contended that the government's foreign policy had brought the nation to the brink of catastrophe. Tirpitz, Stresemann's mentor during the war and now revered by all German chauvinists, sought to effect the ouster of the cabinet. But the no-confidence motion introduced at his instigation was defeated by 260 to 141. Once again it was the Social Democrats who saved the government. On this occasion, as on previous ones, their behavior was motivated by the desire to insure continuation of the policy of fulfillment.

2

While he was being harassed by enemies at home, Stresemann found himself regarded with mounting suspicion and anxiety by the Russians.

He did not belong to those who believed that an alliance with the U.S.S.R. must be made the cornerstone of German foreign policy. He personally attached far greater importance to the establishment of satisfactory relations with the western powers. However, he did agree with Seeckt and other Reichswehr chieftains that Germany needed the friendship of Russia in order to safeguard her eastern flank. Nonetheless, Germany's current rapprochement with Great Britain and France, and especially her impending entry into the League of Nations, filled Moscow with profound uneasiness. According to the Kremlin, the British were the archenemies of the Soviet Union. The League was merely their tool, to be used by them to launch, at some future date, an international crusade against the stronghold of Bolshevism. Should such a crusade ever materialize, the attitude of the Reich would be of crucial importance. The improvement in Germany's relations with England and France and her decision to join the League were therefore an ominous portent in Moscow's eyes.

The signing of the Locarno treaties made a most unfavorable impression on the Russian government. It professed to regard the western security pact as part of a systematic plan to isolate the Soviet Union. Germany, it charged anew, was reversing the Rapallo policy and shifting from an eastward to a westward orientation in international affairs. A similar apprehension was expressed by spokesmen for the Reichswehr. These men continued to demand the closest possible accord with Moscow. They frowned on any move that might interfere with their plans for the eventual annihilation of France and Poland. Stresemann once again endeavored to convince the Soviet authorities that there was nothing anti-Russian about the Locarno agreements. The rapprochement with the western powers, he said, did not exclude the possibility of continued Russo-German amity. As for Germany's entry into the League, it did not mean that she was combining with other powers against the U.S.S.R. Article 16 was nothing to worry about. Germany would never permit herself to be dragged into an anti-Bolshevist crusade. She wished to be on good terms with both the east and the west; to choose one in preference to the other was no part of her foreign policy.

But the Russians seemed incapable of banishing their fears, so deep was their distrust of London and of the capitalist world generally. On December 21, 1925, the Soviet foreign minister, Chicherin, voiced this feeling. He said: "The Locarno agreement gives the British government an opportunity to exert powerful pressure on Germany, as a result of which Germany may be forced against her own will to change her attitude toward the Soviet government." He went on to warn Berlin that it would create a dangerous situation if it continued to postpone the opening of negotiations for a new Russo-German agreement. The delay, Stresemann hastened to explain, was due to his unwillingness to antagonize the League. This concern over Geneva's state of mind proved an easily surmountable obstacle. For, shortly thereafter, Berlin and Moscow settled down to the business of drafting a treaty of friendship. On April 18, 1926, as these labors neared completion, Stresemann told a gathering of his followers at Stuttgart that the impending agreement with Russia was an entirely proper elaboration of the Locarno pact. He repudiated, as he had so often done before, the suggestion that this pact committed German foreign policy to an exclusively westward orientation. As he saw it, Locarno stood for security and peace in Europe. It foreshadowed no hostile designs against anyone. Moreover, in the course of the conversations at Locarno, the point had been stressed that the League was not an agency for throttling the Soviet Union.

The Russo-German treaty was signed at Berlin on April 24, 1926. It confirmed and strengthened the relationship which had come into being at Rapallo. The two countries declared that they would remain in friendly contact with each other in order to insure a state of rapport on all major political and economic issues. It was agreed that if one of them should be attacked by a third power, the other would maintain a neutral attitude. An economic or financial boycott directed against one of the contracting parties was not to be supported by the other. Appended to the treaty were letters from the German and Russian foreign ministers underlining the pacific intentions of both governments. Of particular importance in this connection was the explicitly worded assurance offered by Stresemann. Should the League, he wrote, contemplate an exclusively anti-Soviet move, Germany would do everything in her power to oppose it. The treaty was to run for five years. In 1931 it was renewed for three more years, with the stipulation that it was to continue in effect thereafter unless one of the signatories should denounce it. The conclusion of this compact, which, in the opinion of some writers, converted the Russo-German friendship into a virtual alliance, won almost universal approval in the Reich. This became clear on June 30, 1926, when the Reichstag ratified the agreement with only three dissenting votes.

The Treaty of Berlin created a great sensation throughout Europe.

The initial reaction in France, Czechoslovakia and Poland was definitely unfavorable. Suspicion of Germany, and especially of her sincerity in signing the Locarno accords, flared anew. The view was expressed by many newspapers that the Locarno pact had been placed in jeopardy and that Germany's admission to the League had been rendered problematical. Poland was particularly excited. She, together with Czechoslovakia, made a meticulous appraisal of the treaty. Benesh, acting in close accord with Count Alexander Skrzynski, the Polish foreign minister, urged upon France, Great Britain and Italy the necessity of examining the bearing of the Russo-German agreement on the obligations which the Reich would have to assume when it joined the League. Of primary moment was the question whether Germany's undertaking to remain aloof from any economic boycott of Russia conflicted with the duties imposed upon members of the League by Articles 16 and 17 of the Covenant. The British reacted far less violently than Germany's immediate neighbors on the Continent. Although some adverse criticism was aired in England, most commentators seemed inclined to believe that the treaty might result in the establishment of some kind of contact between Russia and the League.

After the first wave of excitement had subsided, the French government decided to make the best of a bad situation. It joined London in accepting the Reich's claim that the treaty with Russia was complementary to, and not at all in conflict with, the agreements concluded at Locarno. It publicly subscribed to the view that there was nothing in the document to occasion alarm. But actually it continued to share the apprehensions of the Polish, Czechoslovak and Rumanian governments. All four persisted in regarding the Russo-German rapprochement as a threat to the territorial status quo. They endeavored to minimize this threat. Poland and Rumania renewed their alliance of 1921. They were careful, in so doing, to add an amendment which covered the contingency of either a Russian or German attack. Skrzynski hurried to Prague with a proposal for a Polish-Czech alliance. But his overture proved fruitless. The reason, according to the Poles, was Prague's unco-operative attitude. In June, 1926, France concluded an alliance with Rumania. She undertook to guarantee Rumania's possession of Bessarabia, an area claimed by Russia.

All this did the international atmosphere no good, but it failed to prevent fresh triumphs for the "spirit of Locarno." On September 8, 1926, Germany was admitted to the League of Nations by unanimous vote of the Assembly. Two days later she took her place as a member of the Council. Stresemann received a tremendous ovation. And indeed his words on this occasion could hardly fail to evoke enthusiastic applause. He said:

Today Germany enters a circle of states to some of which she has for decades been attached by unbroken ties of friendship, whereas others were allied against her during the great war. It is surely an event of historical importance that Germany and these latter states are now brought together within the League of Nations in permanent and peaceful co-operation. It is a fact which indicates more clearly than mere words or programs that the League of Nations may in very truth be destined to give a new direction to the political development of mankind. . . . Even before her entry into the League, Germany endeavored to promote this friendly co-operation. The action which she took and which led to the pact of Locarno is proof of this, and, as further evidence, there are the arbitration treaties which she has concluded with almost all her neighbors. The German government is resolved to persevere unswervingly in this line of policy, and is glad to see that these ideals, which at first met with a lively opposition in Germany, are now becoming more and more rooted in the conscience of the German people. . . . Only on the basis of a community of all nations, without distinction and on a footing of perfect equality, can mutual assistance and justice become the true guiding stars of the destiny of mankind. Upon this foundation alone can that principle of freedom be set for which nations and individuals are constantly striving. Germany is firmly resolved to found her policy upon these lofty ideals.

3

Thanks to Stresemann, Germany enjoyed at this moment unprecedented popularity. The hopes of peace-loving people everywhere soared. Briand and Stresemann sought to give concrete formulation to these hopes. On September 17, 1926, they quietly retired to Thoiry, a village near Geneva. Here they had a heart-to-heart conversation. Briand showed himself willing to bring about, as speedily as possible, the evacuation of all of the Rhineland and the return of the Saar to the Reich. In return Germany was to come to the assistance of the franc, which had been in dire straits for some time, by mobilizing a part of her railway bonds and turning over to France a considerable sum in gold. But this ambitious plan encountered insuperable obstacles. The French press proved hostile. A similar attitude was displayed by Briand's colleagues in the cabinet. The rapidity with which Poincaré, France's premier since July, 1926, managed to stabilize the franc, and the unfavorable American reaction to the financial scheme discussed at Thoiry, reduced to zero the value of the *quid pro quo* offered by Germany. Total evacuation of the Rhineland and the liberation of the Saar had to be postponed. A great opportunity to serve the cause of democracy and of international amity was thus lost. Stresemann was cheated of a triumph which would have bolstered his position in the Reich and cut the ground from under the Nationalist opposition. Had the Rhineland been freed in 1927, in accordance with the suggestion made by Stresemann at Thoiry, the Weimar republic would have benefited enormously. For Germans of every party would have been forced to admit that the democratic regime was serving the nation well. But this concession, like so many others vouchsafed Germany by the victors of 1918, came too late—too late to help the republic or to generate more than perfunctory good will toward the Allies.

The abolition of military control was among the topics discussed at Thoiry. Briand showed himself amenable on this issue, too, but he pointed out that the French war ministry had placed before him a large number of documents purporting to prove that the Reich was not living up to its disarmament obligations. What bothered him, he went on, was the existence of "national organizations" in Germany. He referred specifically to the activities of the Stahlhelm and asked why these activities had not been suppressed by the authorities. Stresemann did his best to reassure Briand. "A great army," he declared, "cannot be spiritually disbanded." This accounted for the fact that "memories of old war days survive in all associations of front-line fighters." However, these organizations were of no significance from the military point of view. They did not enjoy the support of the Reichswehr. They had been denounced in the Reichstag by Gessler, the minister of war. General Seeckt had made it clear that he would have nothing to do with them. The republic, Stresemann continued, had failed to take account of "the psychological needs of the masses." It was "getting hidebound in the dull black jacket of everyday life." People craved "color, joy and movement." This was why organizations like the Stahlhelm and the Reichsbanner managed to thrive.

Briand accepted Stresemann's explanation. But the matter was brought up anew by the French ambassador to Germany. Stresemann declined to recommend action against the Stahlhelm and kindred bodies. He reiterated his demand for termination of inter-Allied control. Within France right-wing opinion was strongly averse to such a step. It held that nothing should be done until Germany had furnished conclusive proof of her compliance with the military clauses of the treaty. Stresemann became impatient. He told the French ambassador on November 9, 1926, that there was no truth to the charge that a member of the German government had acknowledged the existence of collusion between the Reichswehr and the national organizations. The speedy removal of the Military Control Commission, he declared two weeks later before the Reichstag, was something which all parties in Germany insisted upon. German disarmament was a reality. The Reich expected the Allies to base their behavior on that fact. It, in return, was prepared to take action against any associations within its borders that were guilty of illegal activity. It was also ready to recognize the supervisory powers of the League Council once the commission had been dissolved. At the same time, it was the duty of Germany to reaffirm her demand for general disarmament. "We must again and again remind the world," he said, "that to allow a general freedom of armament to continue, while imposing complete disarmament and unilateral control on one state, is to create, in the long run, a situation that is at once impossible and incompatible with the principle of equality of rights within the League."

Stresemann finally had his way. On January 31, 1927, the Military Control Commission was withdrawn from the Reich and all further supervision of German armaments was entrusted to the Council of the League. The disappearance of an agency which Germans of every class and political faith had resented as a gratuitous and intolerable affront to their honor was a major victory for Stresemann. He scored again on a closely related issue. At his insistence, the League's Preparatory Disarmament Commission went to work in earnest. Its labors were designed to pave the way for an international conference whose purpose it would be to implement the Allied promise to institute a general reduction of armaments.

The outcome of the Thoiry conversation did not discourage Stresemann. In subsequent discussions with Briand he kept coming back to his demand for the complete evacuation of the Rhineland before the date specified by the Treaty of Versailles. In public statements at home, he stressed the urgency of this question. On January 27, 1927, he declared in the Reichstag: "We demand evacuation above all because it [the occupation of the Rhineland] is an insurmountable obstacle to a Franco-German understanding, and because the great ideas of the Locarno policy cannot make headway so long as this anomaly exists." He alluded to the matter again on February 1, 1928. "Our attitude," he remarked, "is dictated by positive considerations. We talk about evacuation because we should regret it if the great moment for a real understanding were not taken advantage of by the present generation in France." He was equally explicit about other questions. He stated repeatedly that Germany could not continue for long to fulfill her current reparation obligations and that the Dawes plan would have to be revised. He complained of the slow progress of the Preparatory Disarmament Commission and of the delay in recognizing Germany's claim to equality in armaments. On these issues Briand, despite strong opposition in France, assumed an accommodating attitude. But he, like all other Allied statesman, was utterly uncompromising in regard to certain other demands that were constantly being advanced by disgruntled elements in Germany. One of these concerned *Anschluss*. The union of Austria and Germany had been explicitly forbidden by the Treaties of Versailles and St. Germain. The Allies had repeatedly affirmed their determination to enforce this ban. Nevertheless, the agitation in favor of Anschluss continued. Germany's neighbors were naturally disturbed. They did not relish, too, the periodic manifestations of dissatisfaction with the eastern frontiers of the Reich. And when, on one occasion, Stresemann permitted a Nationalist member of the cabinet to intimate that a revision of those frontiers was in order, foreign capitals made no effort to dissemble their alarm. The German government likewise insisted on renewing the war-guilt controversy. In the autumn of 1927 Hindenburg went to Tannenberg to dedicate a monument commemorating the victory over the Russians. In the course of his address he said: "The accusation that Germany was responsible for this greatest of all wars we hereby repudiate. . . ." The field marshal's remark produced a most unfavorable impression outside the Reich. It served to revive doubts as to the sincerity of Stresemann's conciliatory policy. And well it might, for the foreign minister had helped to write the speech.

4

While the German government was thus indulging in provocative gestures, Briand went ahead with his efforts to safeguard the peace of Europe and of the world. On April 6, 1927, he announced his country's readiness to enter into a pact with the United States outlawing war between the signatories. Two months later the French government set its diplomacy in motion. It submitted to Washington the draft of a treaty pledging the two states to renounce war as "an instrument of national policy." The American reply came late in December, 1927. It suggested that the proposed Franco-American agreement be expanded into a multilateral one. To this the French assented. On April 13, 1928, Germany was asked to co-operate. Stresemann's response was very cordial. His government, he wrote, welcomed the attempt to achieve an understanding of this type. It believed that "the binding obligation not to use war as an instrument of national policy can only serve to strengthen the fundamental idea of the Covenant of the League of Nations and the Rhine pact." Stresemann himself was of the opinion that the agreement would give impetus to the process of general disarmament and increase the possibility of a peaceful revision of the Treaty of Versailles. On August 17, 1928, he accepted the French government's invitation to come to Paris for the signing of the pact. He was seriously ill at the time, but he decided, nonetheless, to make the trip because Frank B. Kellogg, the American secretary of state and co-author of the pact, had signified his intention of attending the ceremony. The arrival of a German foreign minister in the French capital was regarded as a historic occasion; and the friendliness of the reception accorded Stresemann made it an auspicious one as well. A large crowd assembled in the station and greeted him with cries of "Vive Stresemann!" and "Vive la paix!" These were the same people who, nine years earlier, had made Brockdorff-Rantzau and his colleagues feel like pariahs. The change which had come over a very considerable section of French opinion was a significant sign, and this Stresemann fully appreciated. The communication which he issued to the press abounded in professions of good will. It stressed the importance of the Kellogg-Briand pact and affirmed the readiness of the German people to co-operate in promoting the cause of world peace. But it also gave expression to the hope that the signing of the pact would be followed by further progress toward the solution of the problems still outstanding between France and Germany.

On August 27, 1928, the representatives of fifteen powers met at the Quai d'Orsay and affixed their signatures to a document which ran as follows:

Article I. The high contracting parties solemnly declare in the name of their respective countries that they condemn recourse to war for the solution of international controversies, and renounce it as an instrument of national policy in their relations with one another. Article II. The high contracting parties agree that the settlement or solution of all disputes or conflicts of whatever nature or of whatever origin they may be, which may arise among them, shall never be sought except by pacific means.

Briand delivered a moving address. At one point he remarked: "What greater lesson can be offered the world than the spectacle of a reunion where, for the signature of a pact against war, Germany of her own free will and on an even footing takes her place among the other signatories, her former adversaries?" The occasion was all the more striking by virtue of the fact that a German foreign minister was being welcomed on French soil by a representative of the French government. Briand spoke in glowing terms of Stresemann. "One can believe me particularly happy," he said, "to render homage to the highness of mind and to the courage of this eminent statesman who, during more than three years, has not hesitated to assume full responsibility in the work of European co-operation for the maintenance of peace."

The German press underlined the friendly reception given Stresemann in Paris but had very little to say about the pact itself. However, certain right-wing newspapers showed their anti-French bias by pointedly reserving all their praise for the Americans who, unlike the French, were credited with being sincere in their desire for international co-operation. Skeptics throughout Europe and the United States had a veritable field day. They pointed out that the pact set up no machinery for the enforcement of the ban against war and that, as a consequence, it amounted to nothing more than a pious resolution. They called attention to the fact that, at the very moment the document was being signed, western Europe, with the exception of Germany, was more heavily armed than in the months preceding the outbreak of the world war. The action of the American Senate provided an ironic footnote to the proceedings in Paris. On the very day it ratified the Kellogg-Briand pact, it commenced consideration of a bill calling for the construction of fifteen heavy cruisers.

No less disturbing was the failure of the League's Preparatory Disarmament Commission to make any real progress. The technical experts of the various countries grappled unsuccessfully with the many ticklish questions that confronted them. The attempt to distinguish between offensive and defensive weapons and to find a universally acceptable basis for the reduction of existing armaments proved as futile as it was time-consuming. Throughout these discussions, each government espoused the kind of disarmament which would work to its own advantage. Because they had a small standing army and regarded the navy as the bulwark of their national defense, the British wanted to see all foreign armies drastically reduced. The French, who relied mainly on their large standing army and a great host of trained reserves for the protection of their frontiers, insisted on retaining their overwhelming superiority vis-à-vis the Reich. The Germans vigorously supported Great Britain in her demand that the number of trained reserves be limited. To this France and the other exponents of conscription steadfastly objected. The Germanophobe followers of Poincaré decried the Anglo-German proposals. They charged that the Reich, despite all assurances to the contrary, was secretly rearming.

By April, 1927, it was clear that the technical experts were getting nowhere. They clung uncompromisingly to their rival viewpoints. With matters thus deadlocked, the Preparatory Disarmament Commission returned to the apparently hopeless task on November 30, 1927. The Soviet representative, Maxim Litvinov, caused a sensation by proposing the total and immediate abolition of all armaments. Nothing, of course, came of this gesture. The discussion reverted to the specific problems argued earlier by the experts, but once again the conflict of interests proved irresolvable. A separate Anglo-French agreement on armaments, in which the two powers made important concessions to each other in the hope that by so doing they might facilitate the conclusion of a general accord, had to be abandoned in the face of American and Italian opposition. And all the while the Germans kept railing against the unwillingness of other nations to disarm. Not until the close of 1930 did the Preparatory Commission, by a majority vote and with Russia, Germany and Italy dissenting, adopt a draft convention for the reduction of armaments. It was agreed that this convention would be laid before the general disarmament conference which opened in February, 1932.

Chapter 24

PROSPERITY, DOMESTIC CONFLICT AND NEW GAINS FOR LABOR

I

EXCEPT for the initial months of 1926, which saw a recurrence of the nation's economic ills, the period from 1925 to the close of 1928 was one of great prosperity in Germany. For this American and British loans were mainly responsible. The recipients of these loans were the Reich, the various local governments and private industry. A good part of this money had to be re-exported at once to meet reparation obligations. But many millions of borrowed marks were left for domestic consumption. The golden stream from abroad touched the life of each and every German. Private industry used its portion to expand and modernize factories and mills. The *Laender* and the municipalities poured their share into public works. Huge sums thus came to be lavished upon all sorts of enterprises that were meritorious in themselves but definitely non-essential from the economic point of view. The bureaucracy was needlessly enlarged. The Reich, the *Laender* and the municipalities increased their budgets by leaps and bounds. Mounting deficits were covered entirely by foreign credits, most of which were of the short-term variety. Since the United States was the principal source of these loans, it was obvious that every fluctuation in the economy of that country would have immediate and far-reaching repercussions in Germany. The precariousness of this artificial prosperity was enhanced by the inordinate amount of speculation that went on. Employment reached and remained at a high level after the hard winter of 1925-26. Throughout most of 1927, the number of jobless was less than a million. In the summer of 1928, it dropped to

650,000. Wages were high. For the first time since 1914, the masses of Germany enjoyed material well-being.

German production forged ahead at a phenomenal rate. Outdistancing all European competitors, the Reich achieved a position second only to that of the United States among the industrial powers of the world. And in certain vital branches of production, it even surpassed the great American republic. Significant, too, was the expansion of the merchant marine. Borrowed money was not the only reason for Germany's remarkable advance. Much of the credit belongs to those resourceful and energetic men who introduced into her industry the principles of rationalization. In 1925, the Federation of German Industry declared:

We understand by rationalization the rational employment of all technical and organizational means in order to increase the productivity of the workers to the highest possible degree. All who participate in the manufacture of commodities must seek . . . to improve, expand and cheapen production.

In carrying out this program, the leaders of German industry looked to the United States for guidance. They adopted American mass-production methods and instituted scientific management. The accelerated drift toward trustification enabled them to exercise more unified control. A strenuous effort was made to eliminate duplication and to achieve maximum standardization. With industrial chemists leading the way, new processes were developed. The state gave every possible encouragement and aid. The results surpassed the expectations of even the most sanguine.

The scale of public spending, especially on non-productive enterprises, caused serious anxiety. In May, 1927, Stresemann warned the nation against over-optimism. He pointed out that German industry was buttressed by foreign credits on which interest and amortization would have to be paid. One of the necessities of the moment, he said, was a far-reaching reduction of expenditure. In a report issued on June 10, 1927, S. Parker Gilbert, the Agent General for reparation payments, likewise criticized the financial policy of the Reich. He called attention to the increase in the federal government's disbursements, a large part of which consisted of subsidies to the *Laender* and municipalities. He elaborated upon the reasons for his dissatisfaction in a conversation with Stresemann early in October, 1927. The German government, Gilbert observed, claimed that it would be unable in the long run to meet its reparation obligations; yet at the same time it was raising the salaries of its officials. French civil servants were getting less than their counterparts in Germany. Increased remuneration for members of the bureaucracy would spur the workers to demand higher wages. Prices would then rise, and another inflation would become a real possibility. And all the while, domestic demands were mounting without an equivalent increase in exports. This was bound to produce difficulties in the not too distant future. Gilbert declared himself in favor of foreign credits for industry, but he questioned the wisdom of the loans being raised by the *Laender* and municipalities. Many of these, he held, were entirely unproductive. As for the Reich, if it continued to insist on increasing the salaries of its officials, it would have to couple such action with cuts in administrative personnel.

The German cabinet did not relish Gilbert's strictures. It argued that it was impossible to eliminate all expenditures that might be classified as unproductive or non-essential. Gilbert returned to the charge in a memorandum which he sent to the government on October 20, 1927. He flatly accused the Reich of spending and borrowing too much. He warned that a serious economic and financial crisis would ensue unless the authorities inaugurated a policy of retrenchment all along the line. According to Gilbert, the least justifiable items in the Reich's budget were the grants to the *Laender* and municipalities. He charged that the local governments were saddling themselves with inordinately large debts and demanded that their financial operations be strictly controlled. He also denounced the scale of unemployment payments and reiterated his opposition to salary increases. The German government admitted that Gilbert was right in a good many respects, but contested the validity of some of his assertions. Stresemann was inclined to go further than most of his colleagues in agreeing with Gilbert. He told a Dresden audience on October 31, 1927, that non-productive loans constituted "a heavy charge" on the nation's resources. He urged a lowering of administrative costs. This, he said, could be effected by eliminating unnecessary duplication and reducing the number of superfluous officials. The besetting evil was the maintenance of separate bureaucracies by the *Laender*. What was needed, in the interests of efficiency as well as economy, was a single administrative apparatus for the whole of the Reich.

The Germans did not like to be reminded that their economic recovery was in the main the result of foreign loans and that, when these were no longer available, the day of reckoning was bound to come. It was too easy, after so many years of uninterrupted hardship, to cling to pleasurable delusions. But the march of events was to verify, before long, the dire prophecies of men like Gilbert and Stresemann. And when that moment arrived, impetus was given to a process whose repercussions have reached into every corner of the earth.

2

The Luther cabinet which took office in January, 1926, found itself confronted with serious domestic problems. The country was in the midst of a short-lived economic crisis which was especially hard on many large business concerns and brought an alarming increase in the number of unemployed. The great economic empire built by Hugo Stinnes, who died in April, 1924, was one of the victims of this recession. The heirs of the once all-powerful magnate retained only the Ruhr coal mines which the family had owned for generations. In an effort to make things easier for harassed businessmen, the government reduced the tax burden. At once an improvement in the economic situation became apparent. Luther's position seemed greatly strengthened by this success. But, with dramatic suddenness, he became involved in a controversy which proved his undoing. The issue was the national flag. On May 5, 1926, the government promulgated a decree issued by Hindenburg and countersigned by Luther. It prescribed that all German embassies, legations and consulates outside Europe and certain ones in Europe were to display, in addition to the banner of the republic, the colors of the old empire. A storm of protest ensued. The outcry was led by the Social Democrats, but they were supported by the Democrats and the Centrists. The anger of the old partners of Weimar was directed primarily against Luther. However, Hindenburg, too, was not spared. Rumor had it that he might resign. A crisis involving the very question of regime seemed in the offing. But the events which followed proved that this was only another of the contretemps with which the story of the republic abounds. The Social Democrats introduced a no-confidence motion in the Reichstag. It was defeated. The Democrats had better luck. They sponsored a resolution expressing disapproval of the chancellor's attitude. It was passed by a vote of 176 to 146. The Nationalists abstained from voting, thus insuring the fall of a government which had attempted to please them. The Luther cabinet resigned on May 12, 1926. Hindenburg requested Gessler to try his hand at forming a new government. The perennial minister of war, who was at daggers drawn with Stresemann, quickly acknowledged failure in his quest for parliamentary support. Equally fruitless were the pourparlers which Konrad Adenauer, the Centrist mayor of Cologne, conducted with the various party leaders. In the end Hindenburg turned to the former chancellor, Wilhelm Marx, who took office on May 17. His cabinet was identical in every respect with the one which had served under Luther.

With the advent of Marx, the flag controversy subsided. But another and far more serious quarrel was already in the making. This time the question was how to dispose of the properties belonging to the former ruling families. Should the principle of expropriation without compensation be followed? Or should the princes be indemnified, and, if so, how much should they get? The matter had been debated back and forth for years and, because of these apparently irreconcilable differences of opinion, no legislative action had been taken. In the meantime the princes had taken their claims to the courts and in most cases the judges, whose sympathies were strongly monarchist, had rendered decisions favorable to the plaintiffs. The issue entered upon a new phase in the autumn of 1925 when the Social Democrats pondered the advisability of staging a popular referendum for the purpose of achieving a definite settlement. The Communists thought the idea an excellent one and promptly espoused it as their own. The two parties endeavored to establish a united front on this question. Difficulties developed because they did not see eye to eye on the nature of the proposition to be laid before the people. The Communists were for expropriation without compensation. In taking this position, they placed themselves in direct opposition to the explicitly worded stipulation contained in Article 153 of the Weimar constitution. The Social Democrats were inclined to be more generous to the former dynasts. They believed that a solution providing for limited compensation would have a better chance of winning enough popular support to make the referendum a success. But the Communists were adamant, and the Social Democrats, after some hesitation, decided to yield.

Under the terms of the constitution, a petition for a referendum had to be signed by at least ten per cent of the electorate. Between them the Social Democrats and the Communists quickly obtained three times as many signatures as they needed. The referendum was fixed for June 20, 1926. The campaign which preceded it mounted in intensity as the day of decision drew near. All the non-socialist parties, from the Democrats to the Nationalists, strongly opposed expropriation without compensation. They based their stand on the sanctity of property rights. They contended that the principle laid down in the constitution should not be disregarded just because the owners in question happened to be princes. A vote against the latter, they repeatedly declared, was a vote for Bolshevism. Hindenburg came to their support. Departing from the reserve which hitherto had characterized his attitude on most controversial issues, he warned that success for the petitioners would open the way to wholesale expropriation. Such a calamity would rob the German people of the foundation upon which their cultural, economic and political life rested. The president's intervention was bitterly resented by the supporters of the petition. Was it right, they queried, to enrich the princes at the expense of the nation?

In response to the appeals of the two proletarian parties, 14,455,184 Germans voted in favor of expropriation without compensation. This was an impressive number, but it was not enough. The constitution specified that in a referendum a majority of all qualified voters, not just of those who actually went to the polls, was required. This meant that about twenty million votes were needed to win. The Social Democrats regarded the outcome as a vindication of their original stand in favor of token compensation. Had their suggestion been followed, they argued, Bolshevism could not have been made an issue. Actually, millions of even modestly circumstanced Germans had abstained from voting for fear of being stigmatized as Reds.

3

The referendum was followed in short order by another conflict between the government and the Social Democrats. The Reichswehr was the bone of contention on this occasion. In their efforts to circumvent the military restrictions imposed by the Treaty of Versailles, army leaders had managed to obtain appropriations in various roundabout ways. The sums in question had to be allocated in the regular budget, but they were made to appear under rubrics which furnished little clue to their real purpose. In this fashion money had been secured to finance such clandestine enterprises as the training of specialists in Russia and the erection there of experimental armament plants. The Social Democrats were beginning to talk about the need for an investigation. If one were launched, the position of Seeckt could hardly remain unimpaired. But at this juncture that doughty soldier's

career as commander-in-chief of the Reichswehr came to an abrupt
end. He had committed the mistake of allowing the eldest son of the
former Crown Prince to participate as a temporary officer in the recent
army maneuvers. Disclosure of this fact and the resultant outcry of
all republican elements, who regarded Seeckt's action as an improper
gesture of friendliness to the defunct monarchy, caused the political
pot to boil over. Gessler had not been aware of the general's indiscre-
tion. When he read about it in the newspapers, he made no secret of
his annoyance. He took the matter up with Hindenburg. Ever since
the latter's elevation to the presidency, there had been ill feeling be-
ween him and Seeckt. The old field marshal insisted on being the real
head of the Reichswehr. Seeckt, for his part, resented being relegated
to second place. No compromise was possible, and Hindenburg knew
it. He therefore gladly availed himself of a pretext to get rid of his
disgruntled subordinate. In October, 1926, Seeckt was summarily dismissed. The Nationalists utilized the incident to renew their attacks
on Stresemann. They argued that the general was a "victim of the
Franco-German policy of understanding." This Stresemann hastened
to deny. In a statement published by the *Taegliche Rundschau* on
October 15, 1926, he declared that Seeckt's departure "was solely a
matter of military discipline, and was decided exclusively between the
minister of war and President von Hindenburg, without any action
on the part of the cabinet." A few days later, he informed one of his
aristocratic friends, who had questioned him on this point, that political considerations had played no part in the affair. The ouster of
Seeckt was welcomed by all genuine republicans, but if they thought
it would be followed by the establishment of parliamentary control
over the Reichswehr, they were sadly mistaken. General Wilhelm
Heye, who succeeded Seeckt, took orders from no one but Hindenburg, and the latter's opposition to civilian interference in the affairs
of the army remained as inflexible as ever. Most people regarded
Heye's appointment as a mere stop-gap arrangement. And indeed, in
1930, the command of the Reichswehr went to one of Germany's foremost soldiers, General Baron Kurt von Hammerstein-Equord.

Gessler, whose spineless conformity to the wishes of the Reichswehr
chieftains had made him extremely unpopular in labor circles, found
himself under heavy fire on the morrow of Seeckt's fall. The Social
Democrats were still intent on getting to the bottom of the Reichswehr's clandestine activities. They were also determined to press for a
general overhauling of army administration. They forced a showdown

by asking Marx to drop Gessler and reform the Reichswehr. Failure to act, they threatened, would compel them to withdraw their support from the government. Marx sought escape from his difficult position by passing the buck to the Reichstag. On December 16, 1926, that body was thrown into an uproar by Scheidemann's slashing criticism of the Reichswehr. The representatives of the Nationalist and People's parties rushed to the defense of the military. They denounced Scheidemann's speech as sheer treason and indignantly left the hall. On the following day a no-confidence motion offered by the Social Democrats was carried by a vote of 249 to 171. Another protracted cabinet crisis ensued. The Social Democrats proclaimed their readiness to join the other pro-republican parties in forming a ministry whose prime objectives would be the liberation of the Rhineland, the enactment of urgently needed social legislation and the straightening out of the Reichswehr mess. The Center assented to a coalition with the Social Democrats. But the People's party demurred, while the Nationalists warned that they would refuse to support any cabinet from which they had been excluded. A way out was finally found. The Social Democrats indicated that they would tolerate an all-bourgeois government provided its program met with their approval. At the behest of Hindenburg and the right wing of the Center, Marx proceeded to organize a cabinet. It included four Nationalists, one of whom had been guilty of very questionable behavior during the Kapp putsch.

4

The composition of the new ministry could not fail to evoke deep apprehension in liberal and socialist circles. Marx sought to dispel these fears when he presented his government to the Reichstag early in February, 1927. He went out of his way to promise due regard for the republic and its constitution. He assured his listeners that he would combat all attempts upon the existing regime. But that was not all. He undertook to maintain the policy of fulfillment, to sponsor progressive legislation in the social sphere and to banish political intrigue from the ranks of the Reichswehr. The Reichstag responded by giving his cabinet a vote of confidence.

The Social Democrats continued, nevertheless, to harbor serious misgivings. But, strangely enough, it was under the auspices of this government, so heavily weighted with conservatives, that the republic registered one of the greatest social advances of the entire Weimar era.

For years, organized labor had vainly demanded the enactment of a comprehensive scheme of unemployment insurance. On July 7, 1927, the Reichstag gave overwhelming approval to a measure which fulfilled this wish. Over sixteen million persons were made eligible to receive unemployment benefits. Assistance was to be provided for a period of twenty-six weeks. Thereafter, if the individual was still unemployed, he would have to turn to the ordinary relief agencies of the state. The amount earned by the insured during the thirteen weeks prior to the loss of his job was to determine the size of the payments. The funds to finance the scheme were to be contributed by both employers and employees. The premium in each case was to be a certain percentage of the insured's wage; one half of this sum was to be paid by the employer, the other half of the employee. Employers and employees were to be equally represented on the various boards entrusted with the administration of the program. At the top was an autonomous body called the Reich Institute for Labor Mediation and Unemployment Insurance.

The enactment of this measure caused much rejoicing in working-class circles. It was indeed a notable stride toward social democracy. Significant, too, was the concurrent extension of the system of state arbitration in industry. The government received the right to intervene in disputes between organized labor and the employers' associations. Ordinarily, such disputes were first mulled over in negotiations between the representatives of capital and labor. If these negotiations proved fruitless, the matter was submitted to a state arbitration board whose decision the disputants could accept or reject. The party which did the rejecting was free to back up its demands with strikes or lockouts. The minister of labor could, at the very outset, step in and declare the mediation board's decision binding on both sides. But such action had to be assented to beforehand by the disputants. If the latter acquiesced, they would automatically deprive themselves of the right to resort to strikes or lockouts. Failure to live up to this obligation entailed legal responsibility for all resultant damage. A hierarchy of labor courts rounded out the arbitrative machinery, which functioned fairly smoothly and prevented many strikes. It helped the workers to obtain a gradual improvement of their status without recourse to extreme measures. This, unquestionably, was one of the outstanding social accomplishments of the Weimar republic.

5

During his campaign for the presidency, Hindenburg had promised to settle needy ex-soldiers on small farms to be carved out of derelict estates in East Prussia. In 1927, a bill to implement this promise was introduced in the Reichstag. The great Junker landowners opposed it vociferously. They feared that the dismemberment of derelict estates might pave the way for wholesale land reform. They decried the bill as a step toward Bolshevism and swore that they would leave no stone unturned to insure its defeat. Casting about for the most effective means to accomplish their purpose, they hit upon a brilliant idea: the president should be made a member of the landowning class. The Junker point of view would then become his, and he would need no urging to resist unorthodox experiments. Neudeck in East Prussia had once been the ancestral property of the Hindenburgs. What could be more appropriate than to give it to the old field marshal with the compliments of the nation? The whole thing could be made the occasion for a great patriotic demonstration. The estate would be purchased by public subscription. It would be presented to the president on his eightieth birthday, which was only a few months away. Everything went according to plan. The money was raised thanks to the largess of leading industrialists. The formal presentation took place on October 1, 1927. Events proved the Junkers right. Hindenburg became the watchdog of their interests, the insurmountable obstacle to land reform in East Prussia. He was encouraged by his son, Oskar, in whom title to the estate had been vested in order to eliminate the necessity of paying an inheritance tax when the old man should die. The Junker *Landbund*, one of the most powerful pressure groups in the country, made good use of Oskar. Through him it was able to wield a decisive influence upon presidential policy.

6

In an effort to increase the secret funds at the disposal of the Reichswehr, army officers had associated themselves with a number of seemingly profitable business enterprises. One of the recipients of Reichswehr money was the Phoebus Film Company. Matters went badly with this firm. Eventually it collapsed. An investigation was launched, and it revealed some shocking things about the Reichswehr's finances. These disclosures rendered Gessler's position untenable. On January 14, 1928, after almost eight years of uninterrupted service as minister of war, he resigned. His critics exulted, but not for long. Hindenburg appointed, as his successor, none other than General Groener, the man who had replaced Ludendorff as First Quartermaster General of the imperial army. Groener was of bourgeois origin and rated as something of a liberal in army circles. However, so far as the Reichswehr and its pretensions were concerned, he was in complete agreement with Hindenburg and all the other old-line militarists. Like them, he dreamed of restoring the army to its former place in Germany society. The field marshal and his erstwhile chief of staff had been at the head of the Supreme Command during the closing moments of the empire. Now, a little more than nine years later, they were once again the two most powerful men in Germany by virtue of their control of the Reichswehr.

Chapter 25

1928: THE SOCIAL DEMOCRATS RETURN
TO POWER

I

THE initial months of 1928 witnessed the dissolution of the government coalition. Stresemann had a hand in this development. He was anxious to have at his disposal a dependable majority in the Reichstag. Without one, his efforts to win further concessions from the Allies would be seriously handicapped. He was now convinced that the Nationalists could not be relied upon to co-operate with the other parties in furthering the aims of his foreign policy. It was therefore imperative, Stresemann held, to bring the Social Democrats into the cabinet. He was opposed, on this issue, by the big industrialists in his own party. The Centrists proved more amenable. They, to be sure, had no desire for close collaboration with the Social Democrats. But, like Stresemann, they regarded the Nationalists as thoroughly untrustworthy and wished to see a more stable coalition take charge of the country's affairs. They were consequently prepared, on certain conditions, to do business with the Social Democrats. A protracted controversy over educational policy, which culminated in the defeat of a measure supported by the Centrists, gave the latter the pretext they were looking for. On February 15, 1928, they announced their withdrawal from the alliance with the Nationalists and the People's party. Six weeks later, Hindenburg dissolved the Reichstag and ordered new elections. Many urgent issues, including the much-debated question of administrative reform, had to be shelved as a result of this crisis. But at least the way was clear for the political realignment envisaged by Stresemann.

2

On May 20, 1928, the German people went to the polls. The outstanding feature of the vote was the excellent showing made by the Social Democrats. They increased their popular following from 7,880,-058 to 9,146,165 and their representation in the Reichstag from 131 to 152. It was their greatest triumph since the elections of January, 1919. The current wave of prosperity was the decisive factor in this success. It caused many voters whose political outlook was determined by the state of their pocketbooks to look for the nonce more kindly on the existing regime. And of that regime the Social Democrats were clearly the chief defenders. The working classes were getting their share of the benefits of prosperity. They had every reason to reaffirm their loyalty to the party with which they were traditionally associated. Somewhat surprising, therefore, was the success scored by the Communists. Dissension within the party and the improvement in economic conditions had made their prospects look none too bright. Yet they emerged with 3,262,584 supporters—an increase of more than 500,000 over their showing in December, 1924—and their parliamentary representation rose from forty-five to fifty-four.

The swing to the Left had its counterpart in the fate which overtook practically all the non-socialist parties. The Nationalists were far and away the heaviest losers. Their popular vote dropped from 6,205,-331 to 4,703,265. The 103 deputies who had represented them in the last Reichstag were replaced by a delegation that numbered only seventy-eight. Their gospel of hate and intransigence had won converts galore when misfortune dogged the country both at home and abroad. Things were different now. A new hopefulness was beginning to pervade the land. Germans were regaining faith in themselves. As their economic prospects brightened, as Germany's position in the world improved, they became less responsive to chauvinist and reactionary propaganda. The defeat of the Nationalists was paralleled in miniature by the further slump in Nazi strength. Hitler's political fortunes reached their nadir in the elections of 1928. The Nationalist Socialist party emerged with 809,541 votes and twelve Reichstag seats. There was no indication whatever that better days were in store for it.

The Nationalists and the Nazis were not the only ones who fared badly. The People's party lost six seats and almost 400,000 supporters. This seemed surprising in view of the fact that its leader, Stresemann, had steadily risen in the nation's esteem. But the advantages accruing

from Stresemann's diplomatic successes were offset by serious strife
within the party. Although Stresemann at all times upheld the principle of private property, he was unable to get along with the big
industrialists in his political camp. These men were perfectly willing
to back his foreign policy. But they felt that he had gone too far in
supporting the Weimar system. They were worried lest the working-
classes should regain a predominant position in German politics.
Stresemann actually toyed with the idea of organizing a new party
which should embrace all genuinely republican middle-class elements.
He believed that such a group would be able to co-operate with the
Social Democrats in maintaining a middle-of-the-road regime in Germany. This conflict between Stresemann and his industrialist colleagues remained unresolved; it contributed to the disappointing showing of the People's party in May, 1928.

The Center, too, lost ground. Its popular vote suffered a drop of
over 400,000, while its Reichstag delegation declined proportionately.
Internal disunity was likewise a factor here. The feud between the
two wings of the party had nowise abated. It raged without interruption during the pre-election months. As for the Democrats, they sustained losses which were relatively heavier than those of the People's
party and the Center. The 413,706 voters who abandoned them in
May, 1928, constituted more than one-fifth of their former popular
strength. Their parliamentary representation underwent a like reduction, dropping from thirty-two to twenty-five. The besetting difficulty
of the Democrats was not so much internal dissension as the absence
of outstanding personalities. Moreover, the party lacked militancy and
a well defined program. It contained many individuals who were
discouraged by the prospect of further failures and who were beginning
to question the wisdom of maintaining themselves as an independent
political group. Ever since its impressive showing at the polls in January, 1919, the party had suffered one defeat after another. There was
little reason to suppose that the future would bring a reversal of the
trend. Only one course seemed open: fusion with the left wing of the
People's party. This train of thought paralleled Stresemann's, but neither
he nor the leaders of the Democratic party showed any eagerness to
act. The only non-socialist group to emerge strengthened from the
1928 elections was the Economic party. Under the leadership of
Professor Johannes Bredt, it espoused a program that was blatantly
bourgeois in character. It promised the intermediate and lower strata
of the middle class protection against the encroachments of both organ-

ized labor and monopolistic big business. In December, 1924, the party had polled 1,005,746 votes and captured seventeen Reichstag seats. In 1928 the figures were 1,395,599 and twenty-three. The group was comparatively small, but in a Reichstag where coalition majorities were anything but stable, it might conceivably play a role far out of proportion to its numbers.

3

The gain registered by the Social Democrats and the drop in Nationalist strength necessitated a change of cabinet. After the Marx government had submitted its resignation, Hindenburg turned to Hermann Mueller, the veteran Social Democratic leader. The formation of a ministry did not prove easy. The People's party declared it would enter a coalition cabinet only if it were given representation in the Prussian government. But Otto Braun, the Prussian premier, firmly opposed any such arrangement. The Center was angered by Hindenburg's refusal to accept Wirth as vice-chancellor and threatened to go its own way. Eventually, both parties consented to serve under Mueller. However, the Centrists were so unenthusiastic about the whole business that their withdrawal was regarded as an imminent possibility. The Democrats and the Bavarian Populists were also invited to collaborate, and they readily agreed. The only non-party member of the cabinet was General Groener, who remained at the ministry of war. Mueller called upon some of the ablest men in his own party to assist him. Severing was named minister of the interior. Hilferding took charge of the finance ministry. The department of labor was entrusted to Wissell. The new government took office on June 28, 1928. Five days later Mueller announced his program before the Reichstag. The tone of his remarks was most optimistic. He said that the country had entered upon a period of tranquil and steady progress. "The foundations of the republic," he declared, "stand firm and unshakable." He promised a continuation of the current foreign policy (Stresemann had been retained at his old post), and demanded three things of Germany's former enemies: complete evacuation of the Rhineland, general disarmament and a definitive solution of the reparation problem. He likewise undertook to safeguard the interests of the workers, the peasants and the bourgeoisie.

Mueller's optimism regarding the status of the republic was shared by the majority of his countrymen and by many foreign observers as well. The attitude of thoughtful, well-meaning people in Great Britain and the United States was expressed by Raymond Leslie Buell, one of America's foremost students of international affairs. In his book, *Europe: A History of Ten Years,* which appeared in the summer of 1928, he wrote: [1]

> The outstanding fact in the domestic affairs of the Reich during the past four years has been the real strengthening and entrenchment of the Republic. Agitation may still go on for the return of the old imperial black-white-and-red flag instead of the black-red-and-gold standard of the Republic, but this is largely a sentimental matter, although one which the German people take much to heart. Monarchist sentiment has definitely ebbed, the moderate parties are in control. Probably only a few fanatical monarchists desire the return of the discredited Hohenzollerns. In Social Democratic philosophy, evolution has taken the place of revolution, and the party forms one of the great bulwarks of the democratic Republic today. Germany, after years of tribulation and suffering, has staged one of the most remarkable come-backs as well as conversions in history and taken her place among the truly democratic and liberal states of the world.

There seemed ample reason to take a hopeful view of the future. Nowhere did the sun of prosperity shine more beneficently than in Germany. From the economic point of view, the years 1927 and 1928 were the best of the Weimar era. The recent electoral success of the Social Democrats and the setback suffered by the right-wing elements provided further cause for optimism. Heartening, too, to the friends of the republic was the almost invariably correct attitude so far displayed by President Hindenburg. Moreover, new and far-reaching concessions from the Allies were in prospect; their materialization was bound to give an additional boost to the stock of the Weimar regime. At the same time, however, certain very real dangers continued to lurk on the political horizon. One of these was the commanding position of the Reichswehr. So far it had, in the main, refrained from meddling in politics; but this policy was shortly to be reversed, with disastrous consequences for German democracy. Another potential threat to the republic was the great economic power wielded by the rabidly reactionary Junker aristocracy; and of more immediate concern was the close tie between this group and the president of the Reich.

Serious trouble for the republic was likewise foreshadowed by the attitude of certain industrialists. The discovery that the bark of the Social Democrats was more deadly than their bite and that social revolution was far from their thoughts had occasioned profound relief to

[1] *Europe: A History of Ten Years,* by Raymond Leslie Buell (The Macmillan Company).

the small coterie of men who directed the country's giant combines. But this was hardly enough to reconcile all of them to the democratic regime. For under the republic the workers could pull their weight at the polls and thus make the state harken to their demands for economic and social reforms. Under the republic trade-unionism thrived as never before and gave an unmistakable demonstration of its purposefulness in connection with the establishment of unemployment insurance and compulsory wage arbitration. Proletarian radicalism had its ups and downs, but even in its moments of decline it afforded enough tangible evidence of its existence to frighten the guardians of the great vested interests. Actually, the leaders of industry in Germany were not greatly concerned about forms of government per se; they were ready to tolerate any regime so long as it permitted them to accumulate wealth and retain it. A thoroughly conservative republic subservient to the great business interests would have been altogether satisfactory to them. But the trouble with the German republic was that it was not conservative. How could it be with millions of socialists and trade unionists on the alert to protect the working masses? So long as such potent weapons as collective bargaining and the right to strike remained in the hands of German labor, there could be no tranquillity for employers, no secure enjoyment of profits, no settlement of industrial disputes uniquely on management's terms. But the root of the evil, from the point of view of some of these industrialists, was not trade unionism but the political system which made it possible, i.e., democracy. So long as the workers were left free to do as they pleased, as was the case in a democracy, they would be able to marshal their enormous strength in defense of their class interests and threaten the bases of the existing economic order. Once democracy had been emasculated or discarded, trade unionism would be without its indispensable political safeguards and could be destroyed at will. The conclusion reached by one section of the nation's industrial plutocracy was that the republic would have to be eliminated. This conclusion was reinforced by the knowledge that the fiscal policies of a democratic state were necessarily unpredictable, varying as they did with the shifts of power in the national legislature. The possibility always existed that radical ideas might prevail in the matter of taxation. Social legislation was another consideration; it tended to be expensive, and the greater part of the costs was usually borne by the rich. Then there was the ever-present danger of Bolshevism. The republic, by its very nature, was incapable of extirpating the Communist party; such high-handed tactics were alien to the democratic process.

Many of Germany's great industrialists did not share this antipathy to the republic. They remained, until the last, loyal to the democratic regime. But the authoritarian-minded magnates, whose most typical representative was Fritz Thyssen, clung steadfastly to their counter-revolutionary aims. From the morrow of the November revolution, these men had pinned their hopes on two groups: the People's party and the Nationalists. But both had proved sorely disappointing. Under Stresemann's leadership, a considerable section of the People's party was veering more and more toward honest support of the republic. As for the Nationalists, they were clearly incapable of fostering a mass movement sufficiently powerful to sweep the republic before it.

This was the situation which confronted Thyssen and his friends in the summer and autumn of 1928. Before long, however, a violent lurch of the economic pendulum—the greatest depression of all time—was to lend powerful impetus to National Socialism; and when this happened, new opportunities for political action presented themselves to the anti-republican members of the industrial plutocracy. The power of these men, and of German industry generally, had of late increased enormously thanks to further strides in the direction of monopoly capitalism. The intermediate years of the Weimar period witnessed the formation of the largest combines in German history. In 1925, the *I.G. Farbenindustrie* (the German Dye Trust) came into being as a result of the merger of six leading firms in this field. A year later, four of the biggest steel companies of western Germany pooled their resources to organize the *Vereinigte Stahlwerke* (the United Steel Works). Similar developments took place in other branches of the country's economy.

The process of trustification dealt a heavy blow to the power of the trade unions, the principal bulwark of the republic. As regards the number of their members and the size of their funds, the trade unions were very well off at this time. But their real strength declined. This was indicated by the decreasing efficacy of the strike. The monopolistic position of the great industrial combines affected the social stratification of the land. The percentage of unskilled and semi-skilled workers rose. At the opposite end of the proletarian ladder, there was a significant increase in the number of foremen and supervisors. The wage-earning class came to have an ever larger proportion of office workers, many of whom preferred affiliation with non-socialist organizations and were addicted to a bourgeois outlook on political and social questions. The trade-union cause was harmed appreciably by all this. It suffered, too, from the mounting tendency of the state to regulate business enterprises. Such regulation had the effect of making labor more subservient and less interested in self-help. Still another factor was the spread of bureaucratization within the unions. This increased the conservatism of the movement and alienated the younger, more radical workers. The most palpable weakness of German labor stemmed from the existence of two proletarian parties. Not only did this split the working classes; it divided them into two hostile camps which fought each other practically without let-up until the closing moments of the republic. The principal victim of this feud was German democracy.

4

Acting on the strength of authorization granted by the previous Reichstag, the Mueller government announced on August 10, 1928, that work on the first of four pocket battleships (10,000-tonners permitted by the Treaty of Versailles) would begin forthwith. A loud and widespread outcry ensued. Some of the protesters argued that the type of warship in question was a waste of money because it would be helpless against the larger and more powerfully armed vessels at the disposal of leading maritime states. Others, especially labor spokesmen, were motivated by pacifist and anti-militarist sentiments. They insisted that the money should be spent not on weapons of war but on socially useful projects. They pointed specifically to the thousands of working-class children who were still suffering from the effects of years of malnutrition and urged that the funds earmarked for the construction of the battleship be used to feed these unfortunates. So strong was the feeling in proletarian circles that the Social Democrats had no choice but to intervene. In November, 1928, they introduced a motion demanding that the construction of the battleship be postponed. Groener threatened to resign if the Reichstag acquiesced in this demand. Mueller and his Social Democratic colleagues in the cabinet found themselves in a difficult situation. In the end they yielded to considerations of party discipline and solidarity. They reversed their earlier position and made common cause with the proponents of delay. But the motion was defeated by a vote of 257 to 202. The issue brought to a head long-standing discussions within the Social Democratic party regarding the attitude it should assume on the question of armaments. The matter was threshed out at the group's annual congress in the following year. On this occasion the party reaffirmed its detestation of war. It vowed that it would resist with all its force any government of the Reich which might seek to pursue an aggressive course. The resolution that was adopted demanded further disarmament on the part of Germany. But—and here the ambivalence engendered by national loyalties was evident—the party insisted that the republic needed a Wehrmacht strong enough to protect the Reich's neutrality and the manifold accomplishments of the German proletariat..

While the Social Democrats were thus grappling with one of the paramount issues of postwar politics, the Nationalists girded themselves for a renewal of their attacks on the republic. The keynote of the campaign was sounded by the Brandenburg section of the Stahlhelm in September, 1928. This group issued the following proclamation:

We hate the present regime . . . because it has made it impossible for us to liberate our enslaved Fatherland, destroy the war-guilt lie and win needed Lebensraum in the east. We declare war against the system which today rules the state and against all those who support this system by a policy of compromise.

A month later the Nationalists chose Hugenberg as their leader. In comparison with the press and film magnate, previous chairmen of the party were the very quintessence of moderation. Hugenberg continued to harbor a fanatical hatred of everything and everyone connected with the Weimar regime. He persisted in regarding democracy and Marxism as cancerous growths that had to be ruthlessly excised. Under his direction, the Nationalists embraced a program that left no room for collaboration with the middle parties.

In December, 1928, the Center also elected a new chairman. The contest between the conservative-clerical elements and the left wing led by Wirth and Adam Stegerwald, the principal spokesman of the Catholic trade unions, resulted in a victory for the former. The party's choice fell on Monsignor Ludwig Kaas, who had never been enthusiastic about co-operating with the Social Democrats. The position of the Mueller government, which needed Centrist support to survive, was weakened by this development. The split within the People's party foreshadowed additional complications. Thus, despite their victory in the recent elections, the Social Democrats were in imminent danger of losing their grip on the leadership of the nation.

Chapter 26

NATIONAL SOCIALISM IN TRANSITION

I

HITLER was moved to the Landsberg fortress at the beginning of April, 1924. His brief sojourn there was by no means an unpleasant interlude. The Bavarian government treated him as an honored guest. His quarters were comfortable and his jailers friendly. He received a constant stream of visitors who listened deferentially to his impassioned orations. But Hitler did not take kindly to this enforced idleness. He wished to be back in the political arena, reassembling and reinvigorating the forces which had fared so badly on November 9, 1923. Yet he had to watch developments from afar, and what he saw displeased and depressed him. He relinquished the leadership of the party, quarreled and broke with Ludendorff and settled down to the writing of a work which for years had been germinating in his brain. It was while he was in jail that he composed the first part of his famous autobiography, *Mein Kampf*. The remainder was completed in 1926, more than a year after his release. At Landsberg Hitler received indispensable help from his fellow-inmate and amanuensis, Rudolf Hess. The latter was familiar with the ideas of Professor Karl Haushofer, a leading exponent of geopolitics. The influence of these ideas, which dovetailed nicely with Alfred Rosenberg's phobic hatred of Russia and Hess's passion for dismemberment of the U.S.S.R., is perceptible in the second part of *Mein Kampf*. According to Hitler, the policy to be pursued toward Russia constituted "perhaps the most decisive matter of German foreign relations as a whole." A "folkish" community, he wrote, would have to guarantee "the existence on this planet of the race embraced by the state." This it could do by "establishing between the number and growth of the population, on the one hand, and the

367

size and value of the soil and territory, on the other, a viable, natural relationship." A nation could achieve "freedom of existence" only if it possessed an area of sufficient magnitude. It was the duty of the National Socialist movement to eliminate the present disproportion between the population of the Reich and the extent of its territor . "We direct our gaze," the future dictator proclaimed, "toward the lands in the East . . . if we talk about new soil and territory in Europe today, we can think primarily only of Russia and her vassal border states."

There were but two countries, in Hitler's opinion, that might become the allies of Germany. They were Great Britain and Italy. England no longer had any desire to crush Germany. Her main concern was to limit "the unbounded French drive for hegemony." Italy was likewise opposed to further increases in the might of France. The interests of both the British and the Italians were therefore in some measure identical with "the conditions of existence of the German nation." Toward the traditional enemy across the Rhine Hitler exhibited fierce animosity.[1]

France is, and remains by far, the most terrible enemy. This people, which is constantly becoming more Negrofied, constitutes . . . a grim danger for the existence of the European white race . . . For Germany . . . the French danger means an obligation to subordinate all considerations of sentiment, and to reach out the hand to those who, threatened as much as we are, will not tolerate . . . France's drive toward dominion.

If the German nation wished to escape extermination, it would have to recognize this implacable enemy and be prepared to strike him with all its strength. It would also have to realize that the territories lost in 1919 could be regained only by force of arms.

The attacks on Jews, Marxism, Bolshevism and democracy followed the usual pattern. The author of *Mein Kampf* charged that the Jews were seeking to conquer the world. They were, he asserted repeatedly, the eternal and insatiable enemies of everything German. Marxism he described as a Jewish scheme "to exclude the overwhelming importance of the personality in all domains of human life and to replace it by the numerical weight of the masses." This corresponded, in the political sphere, to the parliamentary form of government. Its counterpart, in the economic sphere, was trade-unionism "that does not actually serve the interests of the employees but exclusively the destructive intentions of the international world Jew." Racialism, on the other hand, recognized the importance of the individual and made him the pillar of

[1] *Mein Kampf*, by Adolf Hitler (Houghton Mifflin).

society. That government was best which gave predominant influence to "the best heads of the national community." The state must rest upon "the principle of personality." It was not for the majority to make decisions; that was the prerogative of one man.

Hitler's autobiography was obviously the product of a mind crazed with hate and twisted by a deep-seated Messianic complex. Parts of the work revealed a certain cunning, an intuitive understanding of human irrationality and an uncanny insight into certain aspects of domestic and international politics. Perhaps the best known portion of *Mein Kampf* is that which deals with propaganda. Here Hitler was in his element.[2]

To whom has propaganda to appeal? To the scientific intelligentsia or to the less educated masses? It has to appeal forever and only to the masses! ... The task of propaganda lies not in a scientific training of the individual, but rather in directing the masses toward certain facts, events, necessities, etc., the purpose being to move their importance into the masses' field of vision. The art now is exclusively to attack this so skillfully that a general conviction of the reality of a fact, of the necessity of an event ... is created. But ... its effect has always to be directed more and more toward the feeling, and only to a certain extent to so-called reason. All propaganda has to be popular and has to adapt its spiritual level to the perception of the least intelligent of those toward whom it intends to direct itself. ... The great masses' receptive ability is only very limited, their understanding is small, but their forgetfulness is great. As a consequence of these facts, all effective propaganda has to limit itself only to a very few points and to use them like slogans until even the very last man is able to imagine what is intended by such a word. As soon as one sacrifices this basic principle and tries to become versatile, the effect will fritter away, as the masses are neither able to digest the material offered nor to retain it.

Mein Kampf became the Nazi bible, the chief spiritual arsenal of the movement. For years party propagandists drew upon it to refurbish their old familiar themes. After Hitler's advent to power, it was made required reading for all good citizens of the Third Reich. Its impact on millions of Germans, especially the youth, was incalculable.

2

Hitler was amnestied in December, 1924. In that same month, the Nazis' representation in the Reichstag dropped from thirty-two to fourteen. So poor did the prospects of the party appear that several of its best known members hastened to contract other political affiliations. What was left of the movement was split wide open and endowed

[2] Ibid.

with means so modest that little more than a shadow existence could be maintained. Hitler dedicated himself to the task of rebuilding and strengthening the party. He did so in the face of a widespread belief that National Socialism was finished. The year 1925 saw the beginning of that great wave of prosperity which made most Germans feel that at long last their sufferings were over. In such an atmosphere, Hitler could not find a ready market for his gospel of hate. His difficulties were aggravated by his craving for worshipful subservience from those about him. He quarreled with some of his intimate associates. Even Roehm, who had worked so closely with him from the earliest days of the movement, found his megalomaniac demands intolerable. In the spring of 1925, the two men had a violent argument which was precipitated by Roehm's blunt charge that only flatterers and sycophants were acceptable to the Fuehrer. When Roehm, in a contrite mood, asked for a renewal of their friendship, Hitler wrapped himself in stony silence and refused to answer. Eventually, a reconciliation was effected on Hitler's terms. A few years later, Roehm went to Bolivia where he served as military adviser to the chief of that country's armed forces. Upon his return to Germany in 1930, he became head of the SA. This was a post for which he was well suited. However, his qualities as a leader were vitiated by strong homosexual desires which he indulged with brazen openness. He surrounded himself with dissolute young men whose frequent orgies did the party's reputation no good.

One of the relatively few men who remained loyal to Hitler throughout this difficult period was his former rival, Streicher. Hess, Frick, Rosenberg and Feder also stood by their care-ridden leader. This nucleus was strengthened when Goering returned to Germany. Newcomers were drawn into the party's inner circle. Of these the most dynamic and able was Gregor Strasser, one-time apothecary who had risen to prominence during Hitler's imprisonment. Strasser was a superb organizer. This talent stood him in excellent stead when he undertook the task of establishing Nazi outposts in various sections of northern Germany. He labored indefatigably to provide the movement with an adequate administrative apparatus. At the same time he built up a personal following by securing the appointment of several of his cronies to key positions in the party hierarchy. Prior to his fall from grace in December, 1932, he wielded an influence second only to that of the Fuehrer himself. In contradistinction to Hitler, who detested the masses, Strasser possessed genuine revolutionary enthusiasm. He took seriously the pseudo-socialist parts of the Nazi program. He had given up his modest pharmacy and joined the movement because he idealized National Socialism as the champion of Germany's little men, the perennial victims of economic exploitation. It symbolized for him the striving of all underprivileged human beings for better social conditions. The Nazi gospel, in his opinion, struck exactly the right note. He found orthodox socialism distasteful and Bolshevism abhorrent; but this did not prevent him from drawing heavily upon Marxist ideology. Giving free vent to his zeal for reform, he advocated an economic program which could not fail to appeal to the underdogs of German society.

Other rising figures in the party were Robert Ley and Paul Josef Goebbels. Ley, the future leader of the German Labor Front, was an industrial chemist who headed the Nazi cell in Cologne. Goebbels—dark, short, wizened and club-footed—was born and brought up in the small community of Rheydt, near Duesseldorf. He was seventeen when the war broke out, but his physical deformity kept him out of the army. He attended several universities and aspired to a literary career. His efforts as a writer brought him nothing but rejection slips. Frustrated and embittered, he joined the National Socialist party in 1924 and was assigned to the editorial staff of one of its weeklies. He attached himself to Strasser, who took a fancy to the young journalist and made him his protégé. The two men sought, with the aid of Otto Strasser, Gregor's brother, to push the movement farther and farther to the Left. They demanded the destruction of capitalism and the establishment of a "corporate" socialist society. They declared themselves ready to co-operate with the revolutionary elements in other lands—Russia, India and China—in order to bring about the fulfillment of this demand. On one occasion, Goebbels insisted that there were no essential differences between National Socialism and Communism. "You and I are fighting one another," he wrote in a letter to one of his Bolshevist adversaries, "but we are not really enemies. Our forces are split up and we never reach our goal." To this radical palaver Hitler took violent exception. He contended that the party must make itself the protector of private property and free enterprise. The issue was debated at a parley of district leaders in February, 1926. Goebbels suddenly deserted Strasser and aligned himself with Hitler. The latter became extremely fond of his new devotee. He made him Gauleiter for Berlin and editor of *Der Angriff,* a Nazi sheet published in the capital.

Goebbels' elevation to top rank among the party's spokesmen was to have far-reaching consequences. The little man from Rheydt possessed abilities which were invaluable to a struggling political group. He wielded a trenchant and vitriolic pen. He was a peerless slogan-maker. He could stump with the party's best. He was the most artful propagandist in the movement. Like Hitler, he had an intuitive understanding of mass psychology. He shared the Fuehrer's conviction that man thinks not with his mind but with his passions and prejudices. Goebbels' formula was simple: find out what people hate and make them hate it more. He dismissed truth, accuracy and consistency as irrelevant to the art of mass persuasion. He made a science of lying. He endeavored, by the simple but devastatingly effective process of repetition, to convert falsehoods into incontrovertible truths. Following closely the Fuehrer's directives, he made propaganda the battering-ram of political warfare. The Russian Bolshevists and the Italian Fascists had been doing this for a long time, but Goebbels, when he became the Third Reich's minister of propaganda, made them look like rank amateurs.

3

In an effort to strengthen his hold on the party and to purge it of unreliable elements, Hitler established the Committee for Examination and Adjustment *(Untersuchungs—und Schlichtungs-Ausschuss)*. This body, which came to be known as the Uschla, went into operation in 1926. Its principal task was to investigate infractions of party regulations and acts of insubordination vis-à-vis Hitler and other leaders of the movement. The punishment meted out ranged from curtly worded reprimands to expulsion from the party. Major Walter Buch, head of the Uschla, and his two assistants, Ulrich Graf and Hans Frank, performed their duties ruthlessly and in a spirit of fanatical devotion to the person of the Fuehrer.

Hitler's quarrel with Roehm in 1925 and the temporary loss of the latter's services resulted in serious difficulties for the SA, which was then in process of reorganization. It was at this moment that Hitler decided to create a special guard which would be unswervingly loyal to him. To this body he gave the name of *Schutz Staffel* (defense corps) or SS. Its members were carefully chosen. They wore resplendent black uniforms, and upon their belts was inscribed the motto: "Loyalty is my honor." The SS was encouraged to regard itself as the élite of the party. It looked down on the SA, which it contemptuously dismissed as an army of gutter-snipes. Hitler conferred upon the SS the unique honor of protecting the party's sacred "blood banner" of 1923. It was given the task of spying on the movement and of ferreting out unworthy persons. Membership in the SS became a mark of distinction and was universally coveted within the party. Up to 1929, the growth of this élite guard was slow. But in that year it was placed under the direction of Heinrich Himmler, and thereafter its numbers increased by leaps and bounds. Himmler, who, as head of the dread Gestapo, was to become Nazi Germany's most powerful figure, was born in Munich in 1900. His father was a school teacher, and he himself, with his rimless pince-nez, had the air of a mild-mannered pedagogue. He entered the army at the age of seventeen, but was never assigned to front-line duty. After the war, he studied agriculture at the University of Munich with the idea of becoming an experimental farmer. He joined the Nazi party and participated in the putsch of 1923. However, he was so obscure that the authorities made no effort to molest him. He served for a time as Gregor Strasser's secretary, then established himself on a poultry farm not far from Munich. It was from this rustic existence that he was called to undertake the task of reorganizing and expanding the SS. The talents which Himmler brought to this task were mediocre. But he had a boundless capacity for hard work and a virtual mania for precision and thoroughness. Above all, he was inspired by a fanaticism that provided him with ready answers to all questions of policy and procedure. From the very outset, he laid down the maxim that the paramount aim of the SS must be to protect the Fuehrer. He drew heavily upon the ideology of the medieval Order of Teutonic Knights. SS men were to make loyalty, honor, obedience and courage the canons of their behavior. Himmler was a passionate believer in the doctrine of Nordic superiority. This doctrine governed the requirements for admission to the SS. Each candidate had to furnish proof of a racially acceptable ancestry going back five or six generations. He had to pass physical and biological tests designed to establish his right to belong to the racial élite. This pretorian guard of the Nazi movement became Hitler's strongest weapon. He used it unsparingly to enforce subservience to his will.

4

In August, 1927, the Nazis staged their first Party Day at Nuremberg. It was attended by 20,000 persons. Hitler and Rosenberg were among the featured speakers. The Fuehrer bewailed the prosperity-begotten "optimism" which was making the German masses deaf to Nazi appeals for sympathy and support. He enlarged, in this connection, on the stultifying influence of Marxism. Rosenberg's remarks were a double-barreled attack on the "Elders of Zion" and American finance. "The gold currency of the Jewish world state," he declaimed, "must be overthrown. This would be the strongest blow against Wall Street, which would then have waged the world war for nothing." In language that was reminiscent of Houston Stewart Chamberlain's diatribes on the same subject, he called for a war to the death against the international bankers who, he charged, had battened on the misery of Europe.

On May 19, 1928, a few hours before the German people went to the polls to elect a new Reichstag, Hitler told a Nazi rally:

If Fate should give us the power, we shall use it to cleanse the nation of its enemies, and we hope that God will give us the strength to achieve our ultimate destiny on this earth. It will not be denied us. . . . We shall grow into a mighty army of termites, before the final hour comes. . . .

But the elections proved a sore disappointment to the Fuehrer and his aids. They resulted in a further reduction in the party's strength and made possible the advent of a Social Democratic chancellor. There seemed little reason to believe that the immediate future would bring any improvement in the fortunes of the movement. Hitler worked hard to revive the flagging spirits of his followers. He contended that the current reverses were but the prelude to victory. It took far more courage, he proclaimed, to oppose a regime than to serve it. The Nazi program, because it was "radical" in character, was bound to attract fearless, danger-loving men. The fact that these men found the state, the parties and public opinion arrayed against them did not mean that they would fail. On the contrary, it rendered their future success all the more inevitable. They were the élite, and one day they would prevail. If the masses were to join the party, National Socialism would suffer. For the movement, as distinguished from its supporters, would always have to constitute a small portion of the total population.

The twelve Nazi deputies in the Reichstag were captained by Goering, who spent most of his time making propaganda for the party among the upper strata of German society. It was at this juncture that Joachim von Ribbentrop placed his services at Hitler's disposal. The man who eventually became foreign minister of the Third Reich was born in the Rhineland, the son of a retired army officer. After the war, he engaged in the lucrative business of selling superior French wines in Germany. Ribbentrop made excellent use of his social contacts. He married the daughter of the Reich's biggest producer of sparkling wines and became a partner in his father-in-law's concern. As he grew more and more affluent, he showed less and less liking for the republic. He joined the Nazi movement and promptly set out to crush his Jewish competitors in the wine business. Prior to January, 1933, Ribbentrop proved useful to Hitler in many ways, but above all as a link between the party and some of the wealthiest men of western Germany.

Chapter 27

TOWARD A NEW REPARATION SETTLEMENT

I

THE Dawes plan represented a signal advance in three respects: it subjected disputes regarding the fulfillment of reparation obligations to an impartial tribunal; it made the Allies responsible for the handling of the transfer problem; and, above all, it was a negotiated agreement between Germany and the Allies—the first agreement of this kind to be concluded since the war. But from the German point of view, the plan was not altogether satisfactory. Its principal shortcoming was its failure to fix the total reparation bill. Theoretically, Germany was still bound to pay 132 billion gold marks. Yet it was conceded by most competent observers outside of Germany that payment of this huge sum was out of the question. A corollary objection to the Dawes plan was its silence on how many years annuities would have to be paid. Finally, the Germans disliked the foreign control to which they were being subjected. They had agreed to it only because their plight in 1924 made immediate financial aid imperative. Besides, they had been given to understand that the arrangement in question was not to be permanent.

After the adoption of the Dawes plan, Germany paid reparation according to schedule. But she repeatedly demanded to know how long she would have to pay and what the total bill would be. She also made it clear that she wished to see foreign supervision ended in the very near future. Gilbert supported the German stand in his report of December, 1927. He took the position that there could be no satisfactory solution of the reparation problem until the Reich's demands had been met. In a report issued six months later, he reaffirmed the necessity of arriving at a final computation of Germany's reparation obligation. He contended that such a settlement would benefit not only Germany but the creditor states as well. In July, 1928, the German ambassador to France discussed with Premier Poincaré the question of revising the Dawes plan and at the same time alluded to Germany's desire for the speedy evacuation of the two remaining Rhineland zones. Poincaré's reaction was not encouraging. The revision of the Dawes plan, he said, would depend on the attainment of a final settlement of the question of inter-Allied war debts. Of decisive importance was the attitude of the United States, which, in the past, had not been very co-operative. Besides, nothing could be done until after the American presidential elections in November.

During his visit to Paris for the signing of the Kellogg pact, Stresemann conferred with Briand. The veteran French statesman was in an optimistic mood. He declared that he had finally succeeded in convincing French public opinion that there was no longer any sense in continuing the occupation of German territory. It was his feeling that the German government should bring the question before the meeting of the League of Nations in September. Stresemann also saw Poincaré. The latter insisted that the occupation of the Rhineland was primarily designed to guarantee the payment of reparation. Hence, he went on, a solution of the question of evacuation would be possible only when a settlement regarding reparation and inter-Allied war debts had been reached. The last word rested with the American government. It would have to decide whether it was willing to be as generous to the Allies as the latter were expected to be to Germany.

Because Stresemann was too ill to go to Geneva in September, 1928, Chancellor Mueller assumed leadership of the German delegation. He found Briand non-committal when he pressed for immediate evacuation of the Rhineland. The French statesman now talked the language of Poincaré. He echoed his chief by declaring that the people of France regarded the occupation of German soil as surety for the payment of reparation. He suggested further that the matter be handled through the usual diplomatic channels. Mueller, however, argued that the question should be dealt with at once by the statesmen assembled in Geneva. In his opinion, the evacuation of the Rhineland and the payment of reparation were separate and distinct matters; one could be considered without dragging in the other. Julius Curtius, the Reich's minister of economics, stressed the same point in the course of an address before the German Bankers' Association. The cabinet, he remarked, was demanding the prompt evacuation of all of the Rhineland. Justice and common sense were on its side. The fulfillment of its request should not be made dependent on the conclusion of a new reparation accord. The people of the Rhineland did not relish the idea of "purchasing" evacuation. Nevertheless, the Reich was prepared at all times to discuss the financial issue with the creditor countries.

Mueller found the British sympathetic to the German point of view. They declared their willingness to see the occupied areas liberated without delay. The French, however, continued to insist that the question of evacuation could not be disposed of without a concurrent reparation settlement. Mueller was honest and well-meaning, but he was not richly endowed with tact. He proceeded to make things more difficult for himself by publicly bemoaning the failure of Germany's neighbors to disarm. That was not all. Disregarding the ordinary diplomatic amenities, he scored what he called the "double face" of international politics. Stung by this reproach, Briand, who had had to endure similar charges of duplicity in the French chamber of deputies, retorted with unusual sharpness. He declared on September 10, 1928, that he was ready to make all possible concessions. But no responsible statesman, he went on, could at this time advocate total and immediate disarmament. The assertion that Germany had disarmed was not entirely correct. Certain of her obligations had not been fulfilled. Her army of 100,000 men consisted of commissioned and non-commissioned officers. And behind this force stood a large mass of well disciplined civilians and an industry that had enormous productive capacity. The factories that turned out peacetime goods were also equipped to manufacture the weapons of war.

This verbal exchange created quite a sensation. But the efforts to reach an understanding continued. Finally, on September 16, 1928, the representatives of France, Germany, Great Britain, Belgium, Italy and Japan agreed to the following compromise: negotiations were to be initiated on the question of evacuation; a committee of financial experts, representing the six powers, was to tackle the reparation problem and make recommendations for "a final and comprehensive settlement"; an international control commission was to be appointed for the Rhineland. The German government regarded this agreement as a step in the right direction. It insisted, however, that the United States would have to be represented if the discussions were to prove fruitful. Even while it was underlining the importance of American participation, it received a sharp reminder of the difficulties that lay ahead. On

September 30, 1928, Poincaré made an important address at Chambéry. He said that France should get enough from the Germans to pay her foreign debts and meet the cost of repairing all the damage wrought during the war. The dictates of prudence made it imperative for her not to throw away the "pawns" which she now held.

The ensuing weeks brought further proof of the gap which separated the French and German positions. The authorities in Berlin wanted the experts to make a careful examination of the Reich's capacity to pay. They believed that a considerable lightening of the reparation burden would result from the experts' deliberations. The French persisted in their demand that inter-Allied war debts as well as reparation be taken into account in determining Germany's financial obligations. They repeated that they would consent to take a cut in reparation if their American creditors agreed to make a similar sacrifice. Stresemann fell prey to one of his periodic fits of despair. The Allies, he told Gilbert on November 13, 1928, had apparently decided to put forward certain minimum demands. This meant that the experts would be unable to act independently and impartially. The American government could not cancel or reduce its claims. To make matters worse, foreign opinion was sadly mistaken about economic conditions in the Reich. Stresemann emphasized this point.

Germany's capacity to pay is overestimated abroad. Germany gives a false impression of prosperity. The economic position is only flourishing on the surface. Germany is in fact dancing on a volcano. If the short-term credits are called in, a large section of our economy would collapse. The existing taxes cannot be permanently borne. Agriculture is in serious condition, and heavy industry is only making progress under difficulties.

2

The German Nationalists jumped into the fray with their usual gusto. Pointing to the fact that Germany's foreign trade balance was adverse, they argued that the exodus of funds from the Reich should not be allowed to continue. Once again they vilified Stresemann. Under his leadership, they charged, Germany could be counted on to neglect her real interests. It was the duty of the opposition to do everything in its power to save the country "from a new act of enslavement, from a new inflation, from new sanctions and occupations in the west and in the east, from the danger of being made the battlefield of the world." A full-dress debate on foreign policy took place in the Reichstag on November 19 and 20, 1928. Stresemann opened the proceedings with an elaborate defense of the government's diplomatic program. Germany, he said, was not alone in regarding the continued occupation of the Rhineland as incompatible with the recent trend of European affairs. Her failure to secure satisfaction on this question had caused widespread disappointment. She would, of course, maintain her claim and insist that it was in no way dependent upon the solution of other problems. Germany was resolved not to purchase evacuation with political or financial concessions to foreign powers. It was her hope that the absence of any connection between reparation and evacuation would be generally recognized. For then, and then only, would the liberation of the Rhineland become possible. All parties in Germany were at one in viewing the course of current negotiations on evacuation as a blow to the cause of international understanding and good-will. Of late, some Germans had gone so far as to say that the foreign policy of the Reich was a total fiasco. True, this policy had recently suffered a reverse, but it was unfair to condemn it for that reason alone. The opposition argued that Germany must seek support for her rights and interests wherever such support could be found. Actually, the government was more realistic than those who believed that Germany could regain her position as a great power merely by issuing protests and talking boastfully. It was clearing the way for the demands which Germany would make in the future. There were no diplomatic ties which would have to be broken in order that Germany might be free to reach new understandings. The government of the Reich had never been hindered, in its efforts to protect the nation's interests, by excessive concern for the rights of others. Conversely, foreign countries were of no mind to give Germany the kind of assistance she needed. One should not be led astray by possibilities that had no basis in fact. Even if the future should show that the Allies were no more willing than heretofore to grant Germany's demands, the latter would be compelled, because she had been stripped of arms, to continue the policy of understanding and friendliness. Any other course would jeopardize the existence of the Reich. So far as disarmament was concerned, Germany reaffirmed the views recently stated by Chancellor Mueller at Geneva. Reparation was now the most important issue confronting German diplomacy. In order to do their work well, the experts would have to be free from political partisanship; they would have to be guided solely by sound economic and financial considerations.

The Nationalists, as usual, were entirely unconvinced. One of their spokesmen, Count Westarp, made charges galore. The Locarno treaties, he said, were now worthless. England, by virtue of her close relationship with France, was no longer capable of serving as an impartial guarantor of the Reich's western frontier. France was threatening the security of her disarmed neighbor. She was increasing her armaments on an unlimited scale. She was using German reparation money to erect powerful fortifications along her eastern frontier. She was keeping her troops in the Rhineland, staging maneuvers on German soil and seeking to perpetuate Allied control of the demilitarized zone. In all this she enjoyed the connivance of the British. Under the circumstances, Germany could hardly be expected to retain any faith in the western security pact. The Nationalists, for their part, were unwilling to support the three-point agreement concluded at Geneva on September 16, 1928. Negotiations in the matter of reparation would attain satisfactory results only if the experts were given a free hand in drawing up their recommendations. American participation was essential, but Germany would have to oppose any attempt to link reparation and inter-Allied war debts. The Nationalists were not optimistic about the current parleys. One thing had to be made indubitably clear: if impossible demands should be presented, the answer would have to be no.

Mgr. Kaas, speaking for the Center, likewise asserted that Germany's foreign policy was a failure. But the purpose of the Reichstag debate, he went on, was to increase the authority of the government in such measure as to insure success in the difficult negotiations that lay ahead. Although the recent discussions at Geneva had produced little in the way of tangible results, they represented an improvement over the old diplomatic methods. Welcome indeed was Chancellor Mueller's clear statement on the question of disarmament. The German government would have to adhere to its resolve to sign nothing which was financially and economically unfeasible. All attempts by France to subject the Rhineland to international control after 1935, the terminal year of the period of occupation, would have to be strongly resisted. The conclusion of a military alliance between England and France would mean the end of the Locarno policy. For the present, however, Germany had no reason to alter her course. If certain things materialized, she would have to reconsider the situation. But it would be a great mistake to abandon all at once the line pursued hitherto.

The Democrats had nothing but praise for Stresemann. The Locarno policy, they stated, had justified itself by disposing of the question of security and by facilitating a solution of the reparation and evacuation problems. The Economic party was less enthusiastic but definitely favorable. Speaking in its behalf, Bredt stressed the need for a united national front vis-à-vis the rest of the world. The recent achievements of German diplomacy, he conceded, were not exactly brilliant. But as between a policy of understanding and a policy of force, one had no choice but to opt for the former. The People's party was represented in the debate by Werner von Rheinbaben, who explained why his group sided with the foreign minister. Everyone in Germany, he remarked, could, with a clear conscience, endorse the demands put forward by Westarp. But what really counted was the fact that might prevailed over right. Of course, Germany would have to ask for the restoration of her territorial and financial sovereignty. At the same time, however, it was well to remember that the Locarno policy had proved extremely advantageous. To discard it would be the height of stupidity. One could accomplish nothing without negotiation. Germany would be obliged to exert all possible pressure upon France and England. As to the question of reparation, greater progress would be possible if internal political differences were tabled. For this reason, the no-confidence motion introduced by the National Socialists was to be deplored. As usual, the Social Democrats rallied to the defense of Stresemann's foreign policy. Their spokesman, Rudolf Breitscheid, admitted that Germany had not gotten very far with her demands during the last few years. But gains had been registered in the effort to safeguard the peace of Europe.

The debate closed on November 20, 1928. The government was upheld by a vote of 219 to 98. That Stresemann's personal position was stronger as a result of this victory became apparent a few days later when the People's party unanimously re-elected him as its leader. On this occasion, he vigorously defended the policy of collaborating with the Social Democrats. He described this policy as a *mariage de raison,* pure and simple. He also urged a cabinet reshuffle in Prussia to make room for representatives of his party.

In December, 1928, the League Council met at Lugano, Switzerland. There the foreign ministers of France, Great Britain and Germany continued to discuss the appointment of a committee of experts. Stresemann was still pessimistic. Once again he voiced the fear that the experts would not be free to do as they pleased. There was a danger, he said, that they might have to comply with directives from their respective governments. Briand sought to reassure Stresemann on this point. The experts, he asserted categorically, would be given an opportunity to make up their own minds, and none of the governments represented would be in a position to ignore their findings. The procedure followed when the Dawes plan was drafted would be repeated. First the experts would examine the economic aspects of the question. Then the governments would make the necessary political decisions. On December 15, Briand, Stresemann and Chamberlain issued a joint communiqué. They affirmed their intention to continue the present negotiations and to achieve a complete and definite solution of the problems bequeathed by the war. A week later, Germany and her creditors formally agreed that American participation would be desirable. They also announced that the experts would not be bound by official instructions of any kind. Schacht was named head of the German delegation. He attended the first meeting of the committee of experts, which took place in Paris on February 9, 1929. The United States was represented by two men; one of these, Owen D. Young, was unanimously chosen chairman of the committee. The experts promptly settled down to the business at hand; but so complex and vast were the problems which they were called upon to solve that fully two months elapsed before anything definite in the way of proposals emerged from their deliberations.

3

In the meantime, a serious political crisis began to take shape in Germany. When Mueller became chancellor in June, 1928, he sought to revive the so-called Great Coalition extending from the Social Democrats on the Left to the People's party and the Bavarian Populists on the Right. But for months he had to be content with a "cabinet of personalities" that was theoretically independent of the political parties. In January, 1929, Mueller renewed his effort to found the ministry upon the principles of parliamentary government. At once he encountered serious difficulties. The People's party reiterated its demand for a simultaneous reconstruction of the Prussian cabinet. It was determined to secure representation in the government of the largest state of the Reich and made this the condition of any deal with Mueller. The Center, which had only one seat in the federal cabinet, now insisted on three and presented an ultimatum to that effect. When the People's party objected, the Center withdrew from the government.

This was on February 6, 1929. The Mueller cabinet found itself in an
awkward position. It remained in office while further attempts were
made to effect an adjustment of the differences between the People's
party and the Center. The latter continued to hold out for three cabinet posts; with equal doggedness, the People's party demanded two
portfolios in the Prussian ministry. Each of the disputants felt that
the other was asking too much.

The persistence of the crisis alarmed Stresemann. The committee
of experts was already at work in Paris. In order to be in a position
to deal effectively with the difficult problems that were bound to arise,
the German government would have to end the current deadlock
forthwith. Late in February, 1929, Stresemann discussed the situation
at a meeting of the central committee of the People's party. Under the
prevailing parliamentary system, he contended, members of the Reich
cabinet did not have to be party men and government posts did not
have to be distributed in accordance with the numerical strength of the
various political groups in the country. The assumption and resignation of a ministerial office should be determined by the personal responsibility of the incumbent to the Reichstag. The individual minister,
not his party, must decide. If the parties should reject this principle
and insist on treating the ministers as if they were mere puppets, to be
put forward or withdrawn at will, liberalism would go by the board.
The Mueller cabinet, it was true, had at the moment no majority in
the Reichstag; but this did not mean that it was incapable of administering the affairs of state. When the Dawes plan was being worked
out, the government of the Reich did not have a majority behind it.
Nevertheless, in the end, the plan received parliamentary sanction.
It was, of course, desirable to give greater strength to German foreign
policy. But it was dubious whether the Center, which had deserted the
cabinet, was motivated by such considerations. The present government must not resign. If it did, the German experts now in Paris
would be robbed of the "moral support" they needed.

I hold it to be the duty of those who stand at the helm to remain in their
place, even when heavy seas are breaking over the ship, and the crew are
mutinous. The sense of personal responsibility towards the state stands
higher than any party considerations.

Stresemann warned that the struggle for power being waged by the
various political factions was alienating the masses and especially the
youth. Rumors were current of illegal attempts to establish a dictator-

ship in Germany. But the country was "still very far from Fascism."
Hindenburg was not the kind of man who would lend himself to such
an enterprise. What was needed was a modification of the parliamentary system whereby party considerations would be made subordinate to the needs of the nation.

Stresemann's plea was followed by a continuation of the effort to
achieve a simultaneous reconstruction of the Reich and Prussian cabinets. No progress whatsoever was made toward a settlement of the
Prussian issue. Important elements in the People's party were so embittered that they came out flatly in favor of abandoning the government to the Social Democrats and of forming a great "national"
opposition. Stresemann strongly disapproved of any such move; there
were the reparation negotiations in Paris to consider. But because he
had reason to believe that this time his views would not prevail, he
seriously pondered the advisability of withdrawing from the party.
There seemed no other way to demonstrate his complete lack of sympathy with the idea of making common cause with Hugenberg's
Nationalists and the Stahlhelm. Stresemann made no attempt to dissemble the fact that he and many of his party comrades no longer saw
eye to eye on certain basic questions. These men were getting restive;
they did not relish the thought of remaining in the government. They
wished to be free to consort with right-wing extremists and disseminate
"patriotic" propaganda. They had their hearts set on making saber-
rattling speeches which obviously could not be backed up with force
but which were sure to evoke popular applause. They disliked working with the Social Democrats. This attitude, Stresemann argued, was
most unfair. In a letter which he addressed on March 13, 1929, to one
of his closest political associates, he wrote:

On the Right, the word traitor is used in connection with the Social
Democrats, as though it could be applied to a party which had perhaps the
highest percentage of dead in the war, and on which we had to rely for
support when votes were taken against the Poles in the east, and against
the separatists in the west.

The fact that the People's party was becoming more and more the
subservient organ of the big industrialists, who constituted its right
wing, disturbed Stresemann profoundly. He also resented the grudging tolerance with which many of his followers now regarded his
foreign policy. He wished to see the country support the moderate
parties, which were courageous enough to assume responsibility. If

the country were to do this, the Nationalist party, with which real collaboration was impossible, would eventually disintegrate. It had been his aim "to provide a bridge between the old Germany and the new" and to foster, in so doing, a greater sense of national unity. But too many members of the People's party seemed to prefer the chauvinist-reactionary program espoused by the Stahlhelm and the Nationalists.

In April, 1929, the prolonged effort to form a Great-Coalition cabinet was finally crowned with success. Three members of the Center joined the government, which from now on had at its disposal an apparently secure majority in the Reichstag. The Prussian question remained unsolved. Stresemann did not resign from the People's party. His followers, in spite of their doubts as to the direction in which he might lead them, gave him a vote of confidence. He could now concentrate his attention on the great tasks of foreign policy. Of these the most urgent was the achievement of a satisfactory reparation settlement.

After weeks of hard work, the experts representing the creditor states reached an agreement among themselves. They incorporated their conclusions in a memorandum which was submitted to the German delegates on April 13, 1929. According to these proposals, the Reich was to pay annuities ranging from 1.7 to 2.4 billion gold marks for a period of seventy-four years. Schacht countered with an offer which showed how far apart even supposedly impartial experts could be. The Germans declared themselves willing to pay annuities of 1.65 billion marks for not more than thirty-seven years. And the making of this—from the Allied point of view—unattractive offer was to materialize only if the following conditions were fulfilled: foreign financial control would have to be abolished; Germany's capacity to pay would have to be increased appreciably; and she would have to obtain additional foreign loans or be given access to raw materials overseas. Some stormy sessions followed, and for a time it looked as if the negotiations would be broken off. On May 4, 1929, Young suggested a compromise plan which the Germans accepted with reservations. But now it was the turn of the creditor states to balk. They insisted on certain modifications. To these the Germans objected strenuously. The result was another deadlock. Matters, however, were finally straightened out, and on June 7, 1929, the report of the experts was signed. Under the terms of this document, Germany was to make payments over a period of fifty-nine years. 1700 million marks were to be due the first year. Thereafter the annuities were to mount until a maximum of 2428.8 million marks was reached in 1966. During the remaining twenty-two years, the average payment was to be between 1600 and 1700 million marks. Even with interest and other charges taken into account, the total bill was considerably less than the original Allied claim of 132 billion gold marks. The process of removing reparation from the political to the financial sphere had been begun with the adoption of the Dawes plan. The Young plan facilitated further progress in this direction by providing for the establishment of the Bank of International Settlements. This institution was to be controlled by the central banks of the countries involved, including Germany. The sums due were to be obtained from tax and railway receipts. All foreign controls set up under the Dawes plan were to be abolished. The prosperity index was also discarded. A clause was inserted authorizing revision of the plan in the event of a serious emergency in Germany. The creditor states promised to reduce Germany's liabilities if the United States should consent to cancel a part of the inter-Allied debt.

Chapter 28

THE STRUGGLE OVER THE YOUNG PLAN

I

SEVERAL days before the Young plan was signed in Paris, the German Nationalists prepared to resume their obstructionist tactics. They sought first of all to initiate a full-dress debate on what had been accomplished so far by the experts. By way of reply, Chancellor Mueller revealed that the German delegates in Paris were strongly opposed to any premature discussion of the reparation issue. The Nationalists completely ignored this admonition. On June 15, 1929, they announced the strategy which they intended to follow in combating the Young plan. They were going to lay before the people the draft of a law explicitly repudiating the war guilt "lie" upon which the Allied claim to reparation was based. Five days later, the powerful Federation of German Industry gave its blessings to Hugenberg and his followers. The Young plan, it charged in a strongly worded resolution, placed unbearable burdens upon the German people. The committee of experts had allowed itself to be swayed by political considerations.

The German cabinet was not intimidated. On June 21, 1929, it unanimously accepted the Young report as the basis for discussion at the forthcoming international conference on reparation. It also called for a simultaneous solution of all other questions inherited from the war. Three days later, the debate which the Nationalists had been demanding so vociferously took place in the Reichstag. Count Westarp opened the proceedings with a caustic address. He reminded his listeners of the circumstances under which the Treaty of Versailles had been signed. Slavery and humiliation, he wailed, had for ten years been the destiny of the German people. And now the Reich was confronted with the fateful question of accepting or rejecting the

Young plan. The German people were being asked to saddle themselves with crushing financial burdens for a period which would not end until seventy years after the close of the war. Nothing could be more dangerous than to assume that the era of power politics was over and that an epoch of eternal peace and good-will was about to begin. As long as Stresemann and the middle parties maintained their alliance with the Social Democrats, their attitude on foreign affairs would be governed by "socialist illusionism and internationalism." This was perhaps the principal reason for the failure of the Locarno policy. The negotiations undertaken in September, 1928, were designed to further the interests of the creditor states rather than those of Germany. The latter had asked for an impartial investigation of her capacity to pay. Her adversaries insisted on political transactions. The Young plan was therefore unacceptable. Before it came up for ratification, the government would do well to submit to the Reichstag all the material used by the German experts and also the entire correspondence between them and their superiors in Berlin. However, even without such data, one could see that the experts' proposals were impossible of execution. If the government felt otherwise, if it believed that the plan could be carried out, then it must at least demand, as the condition of acceptance, the immediate evacuation of the Rhineland and the Saar.

Stresemann replied to this attack with moderation and restraint. The central issue, he said, was whether revision of the Dawes plan would benefit Germany. The Nationalists were insisting that it would be better to do nothing about the Dawes plan, that the wisest course was to wait and let the world see how impossible were the demands that were being made upon Germany. Compliance with their counsel would plunge the country into an economic crisis of such proportions that the entire middle class might be wiped out. This, it was hardly necessary to point out, would be an unmitigated calamity. It was easy for Hugenberg to say that parliament should be abolished. But it was far more praiseworthy to accomplish useful work with the aid of parliament. In a recent address before the students of the University of Marburg, Hugenberg had discussed the economic difficulties which were likely to arise if the Young plan were rejected. He had remarked on this occasion: "Better for a time, until the hour of freedom comes, to be proletarians along with the rest of the nation than to be arrayed against our people as the stewards and hirelings of foreign capital." He had also stated that the nation would be able to attenuate the crisis simply by being heroic. If the matter were really so simple, the

German people would not object to being heroic. But the truth was that Germany's obligations would have to be fulfilled in order not to jeopardize the unity of the Reich. It was easy enough for Hugenberg to say: "Onward through the crisis! Let us all be proletarians for a while!" But those who possessed economic power would not suffer; others would foot the bill, as the Ruhr episode had demonstrated. That episode showed, too, that the German people had overestimated their capacity to cope with the economic consequences of a policy of intransigence. The assertion that the experts had been subjected to political pressure was refuted by the testimony of the experts themselves. The main question, Stresemann repeated, was whether the Young plan would bring an improvement in Germany's situation. The German government did not regard the experts' recommendations as an ideal solution. But one had to judge them in the light of current realities. A permanent commission of control for the Rhineland was absolutely out of the question. No German, of course, would ever subscribe to the charge that his country was solely responsible for the outbreak of the war. But the Germans were not alone in feeling this way. Their attitude was shared by people throughout the world, including many Englishmen and Frenchmen. German governments had often denied the Allied charge. Then why, he queried, was this question, on which all Germans were agreed, being exploited to create dissension in the country? Besides, it was incorrect to say that reparation was the consequence of a single clause of the treaty. In reality, it was the consequence of defeat.

During the ensuing debate, Stresemann received invaluable support from the Social Democrats. Speaking in their behalf, Breitscheid defended the Young plan. He did, however, point out that the financial obligations which it imposed would be much more difficult to discharge if Germany failed to regain complete sovereignty over all her territories. Total evacuation of the Rhineland was therefore imperative. The return of the Saar to Germany also had to be discussed without delay. The Centrists took a more uncompromising line. They stressed the heavy burdens which the Young plan entailed and warned that they would accept them only if the Allies agreed unconditionally to evacuate the Rhineland. They also insisted upon a satisfactory solution of the Saar and minority questions. The Communists said, in effect: "A plague on both your houses!" They bitterly assailed the Nationalists. Westarp's speech, they contended, had been designed merely to conceal the responsibility of his own party for Germany's "enslavement," which began with the adoption of the Dawes plan. They charged that Westarp and Stresemann were working together and that all the bourgeois parties were uniting with the Social Democrats in order to establish a common front against Soviet Russia. The People's party declared that it would reserve judgment on the Young plan until the experts' proposals had been exhaustively examined. It demanded, in the meanwhile, greater protection for the rights of German minorities and recognition of Germany's right to colonies. The Economic party, like the Centrists, made the evacuation of the Rhineland the condition of affirmative action on the Young plan. The Democrats echoed Stresemann's criticism of Hugenberg's tactics. The new reparation settlement, they said, would have to be followed by the speedy liberation of all the western districts still under alien control and by an improvement in the status of minorities throughout Europe. The great mission of Germany was to espouse the idea of international co-operation. The exponents of violence would find that their gospel precluded a successful fight against the war guilt "lie." No one had as yet shown that there was any road to freedom for Germany other than the policy of understanding originally advocated by Rathenau.

Stung by Stresemann's reproaches, the Nationalists pressed their attack with greater fury. One of Hugenberg's principal lieutenants, Baron Axel von Freytagh-Loringhoven, asserted that the government's foreign policy consisted in perpetuating the catastrophe which had overtaken the Reich in 1918. Germany, as Mussolini once pointed out, had shown herself to be France's most loyal ally in the League of Nations. Even the people who till now had believed in Stresemann were beginning to waver. For it was apparent that he would continue to lead Germany from one failure to another. Posterity would regard him as the man who stubbornly pursued a will-o'-the-wisp, who nailed Germany to the cross of Versailles and rendered her resurgence impossible.

On June 28, 1929, in the midst of the controversy with the Nationalists, the German government issued the following proclamation:

This is a day of sorrow. Ten years have passed since Germany's peace delegates were forced to sign at Versailles a document which was a bitter disappointment to all friends of justice and true peace. For ten years the treaty has been a burden upon all sections of the German people, upon the life of the spirit and the national economy, upon the labor of workers and peasants. Hard work and unity of outlook on the part of all Germans were needed to ward off the most serious repercussions of the Treaty of Versailles, which threatened the existence of our Fatherland and the economic well-being of all Europe. Germany signed the treaty without thereby acknowledging that the German nation started the war. This charge makes it impossible for our people the regain their tranquillity and undermines the feeling of trust between the nations. We know we are at one with all Germans in denying the accusation that Germany alone was responsible for the war and in entertaining the belief that the future belongs to the idea of a true peace which must be based not on dictation but on the unanimous and honest conviction of free and equal peoples.

This eloquent statement was universally applauded. But it brought no change in the tactics of the Nationalists and their allies.

2

During the ensuing weeks, the German cabinet gave its attention to the task of compiling material for the forthcoming conference on reparation. Simultaneously, the Poincaré government sought to prepare French public opinion. On July 17, 1929, Briand declared in the chamber of deputies that France desired a final settlement of both the reparation and Rhineland questions. He warned, however, that if Germany should fail to live up to her financial obligations after the Rhineland had been evacuated, and if France, nonetheless, should be forced to pay her debts, Franco-German relations would be seriously impaired. Prospects for a mutually satisfactory accord between the two countries brightened considerably when Poincaré, who was seriously ill, resigned the premiership on July 26. He was succeeded by Briand, who asked for and obtained a vote of confidence on the eve of his departure for The Hague, where the conference on reparation was to be held.

This conference, which turned out to be a rather stormy affair, opened on August 6, 1929. From the first Stresemann insisted that political as well as financial and economic questions would have to be dealt with. But the *enfants terribles* of the meeting were not the Germans but the English. Philip Snowden, Britain's fiery chancellor of the exchequer and leader of his country's delegation, flatly demanded for England a greater percentage of the receipts under the Young plan. Resistance to this demand precipitated a crisis which almost wrecked the proceedings. Finally, on August 28, the conferees reached an agreement. Snowden, who got nearly everything he asked for, subsided, and the Young plan was saved. While the financial squabble was in progress, Stresemann strove for action on the Rhineland issue. He found the British willing to discuss specific dates for the commencement and completion of the process of evacuation. But the French strategy, in the beginning, at least, was one of evasion. Stresemann was told that the French general staff had not yet worked out a plan for removing the 50,000 soldiers stationed in the second and third Rhineland zones. Another complicating factor was the effort of the French delegates to make the solution of the financial problem the prerequisite for evacuation. Against this attempt to link the two questions Stresemann strongly protested. He also urged Briand to drop the idea of setting up a Rhineland commission. He underlined the bad impression which the creation of such a body would produce in Germany. In the end he had his way. He also scored a resounding success on the question of evacuation. It was agreed that the withdrawal of the forces of occupation would begin on September 15, 1929, and would be completed not later than June 30, 1930.

3

The weeks which preceded the opening of the Hague conference witnessed mounting activity by the German adversaries of the Young plan. On July 9, 1929, a national committee was formed for the purpose of organizing a plebiscite which would afford the German people an opportunity to repudiate the new reparation settlement and the war-guilt "lie." The committee was headed by Hugenberg, Hitler, Seldte, the Stahlhelm leader, and Heinrich Class, chairman of the pan-German League. Powerful elements at once rallied to its support. These included spokesmen for the nation's agricultural interests as well as members of the industrial plutocracy. For the first time since the founding of his party, Hitler found himself in possession of really abundant funds. The money came from Hugenberg and the Nationalists, who were anxious to give the Nazis a chance to display their skill as rabble-rousers. The Fuehrer and his subordinates gave ample proof of their talent for vituperation throughout the battle over the Young plan. But they had their own ideas about what to do with the money. They used it to equip and expand the SA and the SS. For there was no telling when another such windfall would come along.

In September, 1929, the Hugenberg-Hitler committee published the draft of a measure entitled "A Law against the Enslavement of the German People." The document denounced the war guilt clause of the treaty and demanded its abrogation. With this demand all Germans, to be sure, were in agreement. Section III of the bill was quite another matter. It stated categorically that no further reparation obligations were to be assumed. But far more controversial was Section IV. It declared that the chancellor, the members of the cabinet and their plenipotentiaries would be punishable for treason if they assented to new financial commitments.

Feverish efforts were made to get people to sign petitions in favor of the "freedom law," as this measure came to be known. Nationalist and Nazi spokesmen concentrated their fire on the long-term character of the Young plan. Germany, they complained, was being asked to assume the utterly fantastic obligation of paying through the nose for fifty-nine years. They pictured the new reparation scheme as a millstone around the neck of the nation. Its adoption, they warned again and again, would mean economic servitude for future generations. In the end the country would lose its autonomy and sink to the level of a "colony," languishing under the whip of alien capitalists and slaving to enrich others. These arguments were advanced by men who hoped to make their campaign against the Young plan the prelude to an all-out assault upon the democratic regime. As on similar occasions in the past, the real target was not the issue of the moment but something much bigger: the republic itself.

The opponents of the Young plan were assisted by Dr. Schacht. As Germany's ranking delegate on the Young committee, he had strenuously fought the proposals of the creditor states and had achieved a certain amount of popularity in the process. However, because he had finally been induced to sign the original text of the Young plan in Paris, he had fallen from grace and alienated his conservative friends. So when Stresemann subsequently made a few concessions at the Hague conference, he pounced upon this as a pretext for repudiating his signature. He aligned himself openly with Hugenberg, Hitler and the Stahlhelm. A few months later, he resigned as head of the German Reichsbank.

The campaign against the new reparation settlement fizzled. No amount of calumny or misrepresentation could obscure one portentous fact: the Allies had promised Stresemann that they would evacuate the Rhineland completely by June, 1930. While this concession would have made more of an impression on German public opinion if it had come a few years earlier, it was nonetheless an effective talking point in combating the propaganda of the opposition. Again and again the country was told that the liberation of the Rhineland five years ahead of time had been made possible by the government's acceptance of the Young plan. Stresemann himself did not live long enough to taste the fruit of victory. He died on October 3, 1929, and so the brunt of the struggle had to be borne by others. The very violence of the language employed by the Nationalists and the Nazis helped to discredit them. The charges they made were so preposterous and so full of venom that many persons otherwise disposed to agree with them turned away in disgust.

It was therefore hardly surprising that the sponsors of the "freedom law" were able to obtain only 4,135,350 signatures, just a little more than the minimum number required to send it to the Reichstag. A bitter fight now developed between Hugenberg and certain members of his own party. These men objected to the penal section of the measure. They were just as uncompromising as Hugenberg in their hostility to the Young plan. But they held that he had allowed his vindictiveness to get the better of him when he threatened to punish as traitors officials of the Reich whose only offense was their willingness to accept the experts' report. The anti-Hugenberg elements in the party were led by Captain Gottfried Treviranus, one of the more promising younger men and a great favorite with Hindenburg, who had entered the fray with an unequivocal denunciation of Section IV. Treviranus and his friends were convinced that the policy of unremitting and intransigent opposition pursued by Hugenberg had ceased to be politically expedient. They felt that a more constructive and positive line would have to be taken if the party and its program were to be saved from complete and irreparable ruin. Even the big landowners began to entertain misgivings regarding the possible consequences of Hugenberg's strategy. These stalwart Junkers shared the press magnate's abhorrence of the republic. They feared, however, that his refusal to work out some sort of modus vivendi with such safely conservative groups as the People's party and the Catholic Center might have disastrous consequences. So fanatical was Hugenberg's hatred of the republic and everyone associated with it that a deviation from the tactics so far employed by the Nationalists was improbable as long as he remained at the helm. But in an effort to meet the criticism of his adversaries, Hugenberg let it be known that the party was not committed to a policy of blind opposition. It was always prepared, he said, to enter a "non-Marxist" government. For the time being, however, it would have to adhere to its present course.

Hugenberg defended Section IV of the "freedom law" and categorically refused to discard it. At the congress of the Nationalist party, which took place in Cassel on November 22-23, 1929, Hugenberg stated his views more fully. The "Paris tribute plan," he averred, would usher in an era of terrible suffering and bondage. In the past, Germany had been forced to assume certain obligations. But now the situation was very different. The Young plan was being accepted voluntarily by men who were moved by partisanship and cowardice. Spokesmen for the middle parties were making soothing promises. They were saying that once the Young plan had been put into effect, a "government of order" would be established. But if the Nationalists were to participate in a "government of order" whose task it was to enforce the terms of the Young plan, they would be betraying their country and making a mockery of their pledges. Their one rule of conduct must be to do nothing which might contribute to the enslavement of the German people.

4

The "freedom law" was laid before the Reichstag on November 25, 1929. Although its rejection was a foregone conclusion, the government was far from idle. Indeed, it marshaled all the arguments it could think of in an effort to put the Hugenberg-Hitler maneuver in the worst possible light. It charged that the sponsors of the bill were attempting to chart for their country a course of action which was bound to result in utter failure. Successive governments had solemnly repudiated the war-guilt accusation and had endeavored with mounting success to make clear to the world the real causes of the conflict. The present government was resolved to do everything in its power to effect a final settlement of this question; but it must be allowed complete liberty in the matter of when and how to proceed. The "freedom law" represented an unwarranted interference with the work of the state and, if enacted, would do incalculable harm. Most reprehensible was Section IV. It impugned the patriotism of those who were responsible for German foreign policy in recent years. The prime aim of that policy had been the speedy liberation of the Rhineland. In the course of the consequent diplomatic exchanges, it had become clear that the evacuation of the occupied areas was dependent on a concurrent solution of the reparation problem. Hence rejection of the Young plan would relegate the Rhineland issue to its former unsatisfactory status. In addition it would destroy all possibility of achieving a quick settlement of the question of the Saar. True, one could validly object to certain features of the Young plan; but the fact remained that all in all it was a distinct improvement over the Dawes plan. Germany would have to pay less than before and she would be freed from all foreign financial control.

The debate in the Reichstag was opened on November 29 by Curtius, Stresemann's successor as foreign minister and a close friend and party colleague of the deceased statesman. Curtius explained that he, and not Severing, the Social Democratic minister of the interior, was stating the government's case in order to avoid giving the impression that the present issue was simply one between Marxists and non-Marxists. He denounced the "freedom law" as an attack on the authority of the state and affirmed the unanimous resolve of the cabinet and the parties supporting it to repel this attack. It was his task, he said, to defend and continue the foreign policy inaugurated by his distinguished predecessor. All the shouting about the war-guilt "lie" was a bit of patent dishonesty. Successive foreign ministers had vigorously protested against this clause of the treaty. The present government would carry on in the same way, conscious that time was on its side. Rejection of the "freedom law" would not mean that the Reichstag majority accepted the war-guilt charge. It, like the government, the president and the great majority of Germans, unequivocally repudiated that accusation. But it was impossible to conduct foreign policy by means of plebiscites. The principle of leadership, which Hugenberg and his associates constantly extolled, would be destroyed if basic questions of foreign policy were referred to the masses and made the football of politics. Many members of Hugenberg's own party were rebelling against him because they felt that the use of such methods was bound to plunge the country into chaos. It was rank nonsense to organize a plebiscite in order to establish the fact that the German people did not want to pay reparation. Of course they preferred not to pay. The only real question was whether they would or would not have to pay. If Hugenberg could so manage things as to free Germany from all necessity of paying, he would make himself the savior of his country. The Young plan was admittedly far from an ideal arrangement; but it must be remembered that once it became operative, the Rhineland would be completely evacuated and foreign control over the area would cease. The agreement to this effect reached at The Hague would be faithfully lived up to by France. The task of the moment was to demonstrate, by defeating the "freedom law," that parliament and the nation wished to see the present foreign policy continued. Germany's future course in world affairs must be based on awareness of the fact that a free, equal and prosperous Reich was indispensable to the peace of Europe. A policy whose objectives were international understanding and peace was called for under existing circumstances. Germany was obviously in no position to impose her will on others. She could obtain what she wanted only by co-operating with her neighbors. But such co-operation would be impossible if the sponsors of the "freedom law" had their way.

Hugenberg did not rise to answer Curtius. He delegated this task to one of his subordinates, who adduced all the now familiar arguments against the Young plan and buttressed them with citations from a recent speech by Schacht. If a choice had to be made between a "Dawes crisis" and a "Young crisis," he and his comrades preferred the former. The Reichstag was now ready for the question. Its response to the government's appeal left nothing to be desired. The "freedom law" was overwhelmingly rejected. Each of its sections was voted on individually. When Section IV came before the house, twenty-three of the seventy-eight Nationalist deputies abstained from voting. The rebellious minority consisted of the young conservatives led by Treviranus; the agrarians who clustered around Schiele, the president of the *Landbund*; and the small but vocal trade-union wing of the party. Hugenberg retaliated with characteristic severity. At a meeting of the party's executive committee on December 3, 1929, he engineered the expulsion of three prominent members of the Treviranus group. Treviranus and two of his closest associates promptly resigned from the party, and their example was followed by six more dissenters, including the well known Berlin university professor, Dr. Otto Hoetzsch. On December 10, Treviranus issued a statement in which he declared that he and his friends had withdrawn from the Nationalist party because they disapproved of Hugenberg's policy and because they had been denied freedom to act in accordance with their convictions. They regarded themselves as the true carriers of the ideas embodied in the Nationalist program. It was their purpose to serve the Fatherland by translating truly conservative principles into political action. They hoped to create a non-partisan national front which would deliver the country from its present misery. A few days later the Treviranus group gave further proof that its quarrel with the Nationalists was not over immediate issues but over broad, basic questions of policy. It announced that it would vote against the Young plan. It likewise professed itself morally obliged to oppose the Mueller government. On both these matters it stood shoulder to shoulder with the parent organization.

The rejection of the "freedom law" by the Reichstag meant that the measure was now to be submitted to the people. A heated campaign preceded the plebiscite, which took place on December 22, 1929. Hugenberg and Hitler suffered a humiliating defeat. To win they needed more than twenty-one million votes. They actually secured less than six million.

The Nationalist party was losing ground throughout the country, thanks above all to Hugenberg's ultra-reactionary outlook and sterile negativism. The quarrel with the young conservatives constituted a serious threat to the very existence of the party. A more tractable man than Hugenberg might have endeavored to repair the breach, which steadily grew wider. On January 28, 1930, the People's Conservative Association came into being. It consisted of the Treviranus group and of nine additional deputies who belonged to the reactionary Christian National Peasant party. The founders of the association defined their aims in rather grandiloquent terms. Treviranus underlined the necessity of battling for freedom, equality and security. The new party, he observed, would have to keep increasing its membership until it ceased to be a minority group. The Young plan he pronounced unacceptable because it failed to assure Germany the possibility of working in tranquillity and peace to discharge her reparation obligation. As for internal politics, it was clear that the parties of the Right had failed in their efforts to build up a power comparable to that of the parties of the Left. Mindful of this fact, the People's Conservative Association planned to strike out in new directions. It was convinced that the future belonged to a revivified conservatism, a conservatism dedicated to the task of providing for Germans the kind of life which would enable them to move forward without hindrance. Since this task could not be accomplished through the old parties, new political alignments were necessary.

Another spokesman for the Treviranus group, Moritz Kloenne, addressed himself to the social question in an obvious bid for labor support. He said:

The era of wage slaves is over in Germany. It is desirable that the workers should be fully aware of their strength and their destiny in the new state. ... The workers are neither commodities nor paid servants but co-owners of the Fatherland. ... Co-operation between labor and capital must be based on freedom of action for both sides. The workers must themselves decide whether they will establish a partnership with their employers or follow trade-union principles. The first great synthesis of our time, the social synthesis, inheres in honest collaboration between workers and employers. Another necessary synthesis which I foresee embraces the Christian faiths, North and South, laborers and intellectuals, cities and peasants, agriculture and industry. . . . I am convinced that the Germany of the future will be neither Communist nor National Socialist. Radicalism has been rejected by the overwhelming majority of those engaged in industry. . . . We seek to unite, under the conservative banner, all who feel themselves at one in this striving for the inner renewal of our people, for the liberation of our Fatherland.

A certain Walther Lambach, who likewise held forth on this occasion, pursued the same line of thought. "We recognize," he declared, "the various occupational associations and trade unions. But we seek their merger in an honest working partnership. Our purpose is to make sure that the struggle of individuals and groups for economic success will not lead to a weakening of the state and the nation." Another speaker pointed out that the new movement relegated the question of form of government to a secondary place. Professor Hoetzsch hailed the People's Conservative Association as the champion of "Tory democracy." He promised that it would espouse social reform and absolute equality for the "non-Marxist" working class.

5

In February, 1930, the Reichstag turned its attention to the laws which were required to effectuate the terms of the Young plan. The opposition was made up of the Nationalists, the Treviranus group, the Nazis and the Communists. This time, Hugenberg, rather than one of his lieutenants, stated the Nationalists' case. He began by reminding the house that in 1922 he had warned the country of what was impending in the Ruhr. At once there was great commotion in the Reichstag. Wels, the Social Democratic leader, cried out: "You made a pretty penny out of the invasion of the Ruhr!" For this he was promptly reprimanded by the presiding officer. From the Nationalist and Nazi benches came catcalls and insulting epithets directed at the Social Democrats, and one of the Nazi deputies, Franz Stoehr, was ejected from the hall. When some semblance of quiet had been restored, Hugenberg continued. The issues raised by the Young plan, he declared, affected the very freedom and unity of the German people. The Reich was asked to assume obligations which were impossible of fulfillment. And these demands were being made at a time when the country was in the throes of a grave political and economic crisis. The Communists were preparing for an armed uprising. Marxism and Bolshevism were alien to Germany, and the strength to overcome them was still available. But the prerequisite of success in such an undertaking was rejection of the new reparation settlement. If, nevertheless, the experts' plan should be accepted, "the will to freedom and to Christian German culture" would ultimately save the nation. While the battle against Marxism was being fought, the state and the national economy would have to be rebuilt. In the meanwhile, however, the non-Marxist parties could avert catastrophe by voting against an arrangement that was even worse than the Treaty of Versailles. Professor Hoetzsch underlined the difficulty of securing a revision of the Young plan, which, he insisted, imposed intolerable burdens upon the German people. He also decried the failure of the Allies to return the Saar to Germany. The Communist spokesman enlarged upon the international implications of the deal between Germany and her creditors. He reiterated his party's charge that the western powers were preparing to launch a crusade against Soviet Russia. Stoehr called upon Hindenburg to dissolve the Reichstag in order to give the nation an opportunity to register its disapproval of the Young plan. Breitscheid upheld the government in one of the best speeches of his career. He urged parliament to put aside partisan considerations. Germany, he pointed out, had improved her international position appreciably since the signing of the Treaty of Versailles. She had not yet attained her final objective, but the path she was following would lead her to it. The advocates of the policy of fulfillment had been cursed and crucified. Persecution had laid low men like Erzberger and Rathenau, Ebert and Stresemann. When factual arguments proved of no avail, the opponents of the Young plan resorted to lies. This was clear from the way they presented the war-guilt issue. The Social Democratic party had never accepted the contention that Germany was solely responsible for the outbreak of the war. However, it had never maintained that those who governed Germany in 1914 were the only innocent parties. The Young plan had its drawbacks, but its rejection would mean continued enforcement of the Dawes plan; and this in turn would plunge Germany into an economic crisis of appalling proportions.

The efforts of Hugenberg and his allies proved futile. The bills were passed on March 12, 1930. Simultaneously a no-confidence motion introduced by the Communists was rejected by a vote of 277 to 169. The Nationalists still refused to acknowledge defeat. They put pressure on Hindenburg in an attempt to dissuade him from signing the bills. But once again the old man proved a sore disappointment to them. Following the dictates of his conscience, he affixed his signature to the measures on March 13. At the same time he issued a statement giving the reasons for his actions. After mature reflection, he said, he had come to the conclusion that, in spite of its many shortcomings, the Young plan was a distinct improvement over the Dawes plan. It also represented an important step forward on the road that led to the liberation and recovery of Germany. He had received many letters from opponents of the plan begging him not to do something which would besmirch his name. His answer to these pleas was that he had been taught, as a member of the old army, to do his patriotic duty regardless of personal considerations. Now that the parliamentary battle was over, all Germans would have to unite in the service of the Fatherland.

Chapter 29

THE GREAT DEPRESSION AND THE ADVENT OF
HEINRICH BRUENING

I

GERMANY's prosperity proved short-lived. As early as the beginning of 1929, she began to feel the impact of serious economic difficulties. At this juncture, there were already more than two million unemployed —a tremendous increase over the figure for the first eight months of 1928. The national exchequer was virtually empty, revenues were commencing to decline sharply and foreign loans were hard to get. The dire prophecies of men like Gilbert and Stresemann, who had urged the country to spend less, seemed about to come true. The Nationalists, the big-business wing of the People's party and the Economic party began to agitate against high wages and the unemployment insurance act, claiming that they were responsible for the nation's financial troubles. Leading employers' associations demanded the reduction of unemployment payments, the reintroduction of the means test and the denial of unemployment insurance benefits to seasonal and domestic workers. To this clamor the Social Democrats, with Chancellor Mueller in the van, offered firm resistance. They conceded that certain abuses had developed in connection with the administration of the unemployment insurance program; but they contended that the fault lay not with the program itself but with the steadily deteriorating economic situation of the country. They declared themselves unalterably opposed to any reduction in unemployment benefits. They suggested that one constructive step would be to increase the premiums from three to three and one half per cent.

A committee of experts was appointed to go into the whole question.

It finally decided, against the wishes of its Social Democratic members, to recommend lower unemployment payments as well as higher premiums. The non-socialist parties supported these recommendations, but the Social Democrats refused to yield. A bill incorporating their views was introduced in the Reichstag. Among its most ardent opponents were the industrial magnates who dominated the right wing of the People's party. Stresemann was too ill to take an active part in this struggle. Nevertheless, and against the explicit orders of his doctor, he dragged himself to a meeting of his party's Reichstag delegation in order to urge support for the bill. This was on October 2, 1929. The long-standing friction between Stresemann and the right-wingers manifested itself with exceptional sharpness during the meeting. Stresemann's main concern was to prevent the disruption of the coalition cabinet and to save his party from the clutches of the reactionary elements. He stated his position with all the eloquence at his command. His adversaries refused to be persuaded. A poll of those present showed that the group was evenly divided. But Stresemann won a tactical victory when it was decided that the party would abstain from voting on the measure. This insured passage of the bill and continuance of the Mueller cabinet in office. However, for the German republic and for men of good will generally, it was a costly victory. Early on the following day, Stresemann succumbed to a stroke brought on by his exertions. His death greatly reduced the possibility of effecting a fusion of all the moderate middle-class elements. Yet never was such an alignment more urgently needed.

2

Germany's financial difficulties at this moment were already grave enough to cause widespread and mounting concern. But they became immeasurably worse as a result of developments far from her own borders. Heralded by the crash of October, 1929, on the New York Stock Exchange, an economic depression of record-shattering proportions began to engulf the world. It spread with irresistible momentum. Its lightning struck everywhere, but nowhere more swiftly than in highly industrialized countries like the United States, Great Britain and Germany. Upon the latter the depression descended early and with terrific impact. By the spring of 1930, all the symptoms of economic malaise were in evidence. The tempo of industry, which had been so phenomenal during the past few years, slackened markedly. Prices and wages began to decline. Unemployment continued to increase. Bankruptcies and foreclosures became everyday occurrences. The biggest blow of all was the drying up of Germany's sources of foreign credit. Her prosperity from 1925 to 1929 was in large measure the artificial result of huge loans from abroad. When no more loans were forthcoming, the props were literally taken from under the business boom, which came down like a house of cards. But this was only one, although the biggest factor. High tariff barriers all over the world were keeping German exports out. The United States, Great Britain, and France were cutting into Germany's markets. Russia, which had been so lucrative a preserve for German industry before 1914, was still largely inaccessible. Rationalization had reduced the demand for labor, and the worldwide fall of agricultural prices was wiping out the recent gains of the peasantry. The net result was a sharply decreased purchasing power at home.

Everybody suffered. Wage earners, as usual, were hard hit. The lucky ones were able to keep their jobs at greatly reduced rates of pay. The rest found themselves dependent on a slender dole or completely destitute. The streets were cluttered with hungry men seeking employment, while at home their families clamored for food as the grip of starvation closed relentlessly around them. Equally desperate was the plight of the lower middle class: petty shopkeepers, modest rentiers, clerks, intellectuals, professional people. The workers at least had their trade unions to fight for them; they had unemployment insurance to cushion the first impact of adversity. But the people just above them in the social hierarchy were completely defenseless because they were unorganized. They had nothing to fall back on when misfortune overtook them. They were full of class pride, and poverty for them was more than material want; it was a stigma, a brand; it meant the loss not only of status but of self-respect. Before their eyes there unfolded the horrible prospect of steady degradation, with the gutter as the final resting place. *Little Man, What Now?* Hans Fallada's moving novel about humble German folk who fought a losing battle against economic adversity, tells a story that makes the spread of Nazism all too understandable. The misfortunes that befell Fallada's characters were typical of what happened to millions of honest, self-respecting and hard-working Germans who wanted only a modest livelihood to sustain themselves and their families but who found all the cards stacked against them.

In their desperation, the victims of the depression turned not only upon themselves but upon those more fortunate than they. Little shopkeepers tearfully liquidating their businesses cursed the ever flourishing department stores. People who saw the modest savings of a lifetime dwindle and disappear learned to hate their affluent neighbors. Jobless clerks envied their bosses. Hordes of university graduates found the doors of opportunity securely closed against them and thought malevolently about those on the inside. Even before the depression, Germany had had far too many doctors and lawyers. When hard times came along, marginal practitioners went under. For the more embittered of these there was no solace save the hope of dragging others down with them. The peasants were having a rough time of it, too, but they knew from past experience that their pleas for assistance would go unheeded. Staggering under the burden of taxation, working with implements all too often purchased with borrowed money, and faced with the possibility of losing even their modest homesteads as a result of the calamitous toboggan of farm prices, they found little to sustain them in this dark hour and even less to look forward to. Never before, in time of peace, had the mass of Germans suffered so.

The depression staggered the republic. It unleashed forces which the Nazis harnessed for their own purposes. They eventually created a totalitarian dictatorship in Germany. Then they turned the world topsy-turvy. But it all began with the depression. The key to Hitler's rise lies there.

3

The closing days of 1929 brought a marked aggravation of the government's financial difficulties. Foreign credit was being drastically curtailed, short-term loans were not being renewed, and Young plan payments would soon be due. Revenue from taxation, which was lower per capita than in France or Great Britain, was falling below budgetary requirements, while disbursements for such things as public works and social welfare were still at their predepression level. To meet the situation, taxes would have to be increased and expenditures mercilessly slashed. The propertied groups championed anew the idea of cutting insurance payments to the unemployed, but the Social Democrats remained strongly opposed and urged retrenchment elsewhere. Sharp differences of opinion also arose over the question of instituting a capital levy and boosting the income tax. Class considerations were obviously uppermost in the minds of those who spoke for the various parliamentary factions.

A complicating element was the fact that the unemployment insurance fund, upon which there were now ever increasing demands because of growing joblessness, could be maintained only with the help of large loans from the state. But the latter was scarcely in a position to extend such loans. Early in 1930, the employers' associations renewed their agitation against the unemployment insurance act. Once again they demanded a cut in unemployment payments. Their paramount aim, however, was a general reduction in taxes and wages. As before, the trade unions and the Social Democrats vigorously dissented. The struggle came to a head when the Mueller government introduced a bill authorizing the Reich Institute for Labor Mediation and Unemployment Insurance to increase the premiums from three and one-half to four per cent and stipulating that appropriate legislative action would have to precede any reduction in unemployment benefits. The Social Democrats warmly supported the measure; but the People's party, freed from the moderating influence of Stresemann, promptly came out against it. Inter-party negotiations followed, and finally a compromise proposal was framed. It was largely the work of Heinrich Bruening, the chairman of the Centrist deputation in the Reichstag. Under this arrangement, the premiums were not, for the moment, to be increased. The Reich was to come to the rescue of the unemployment insurance fund by lending it 150 million marks. If further loans should prove necessary, they were to be granted with the understanding that the government would either increase the premiums or establish a balance between the income and disbursements of the Institute for Labor Mediation and Unemployment Insurance. Because the second of these alternatives was more likely to be adopted if the depression continued, and because a balance between income and disbursements could not be achieved without reducing unemployment benefits, the trade unions strongly opposed the Bruening proposal and demanded its rejection. The leaders of the Social Democratic party were not of one mind on this question. Mueller and Severing argued that the terms of the Bruening proposal did not make it certain that unemployment payments would be cut. That was something only the future could decide. In the meantime it was necessary, in the interests of the working-class, to keep the present coalition cabinet alive. But the more radical spokesmen of the party, headed by Wissell, felt otherwise. They feared that acceptance of the Bruening proposal would, in the end, doom unemployment insurance altogether. They were, besides, none too happy over the existing coalition with the non-socialist parties and wished to see it terminated. The attitude of the trade unions proved decisive. Rather than risk an open conflict with them, Mueller and Severing yielded. The Social Democratic party, through its representatives in the cabinet, served notice that it would now demand enactment of the government's original bill. At once the Centrists and the People's party objected. Split wide open by this controversy, the Mueller cabinet resigned on March 27, 1930.

4

In choosing Mueller's successor, Hindenburg was swayed by the counsel of General Kurt von Schleicher. This remarkable man occupied a position of power and influence in the elaborate hierarchy of the Reichswehr. He owed his success to two things: an unusual talent for organization and intrigue; and the unfailing good-will of highly-placed patrons. Schleicher came from an old Brandenburg family and, like most boys of his class, was sent to the military academy. There he made a brilliant record and attracted the favorable notice of General Groener. The latter was so impressed with the young man's gifts that he made him his protégé. Upon leaving the cadet corps Schleicher entered President Hindenburg's old regiment, the Third Foot Guards. He had the good fortune of becoming the mess-mate and close friend of Hindenburg's son, Oskar. During the future field marshal's first retirement in Hanover, Schleicher was a frequent guest of the Hindenburgs. He made a tremendous hit with the statuesque head of the household. This was scarcely surprising, for Schleicher was a clever fellow and could be charming whenever it suited his purpose. In 1913, thanks to Groener, the ambitious and calculating Brandenburger was appointed to the general staff. Except for one short interval in 1917, Schleicher sat behind a desk throughout the war. When Groener succeeded Ludendorff as First Quartermaster General of the German army, he hastened to make Schleicher, who was then thirty-six years old, his personal aide-de-camp. When the war was over, Groener had his protégé transferred to the ministry of war. Together with other staff officers who, like himself, continued to work under Groener's direction, Schleicher helped to create the foundations for the new Reichswehr. At the time of the Kapp putsch, he remained loyal to the legitimate government. The appointment of Seeckt as commander-in-chief of the Reichswehr brought no change in Schleicher's status. He retained his post in the ministry of war, continuing all the while to demonstrate abilities of a high order. His talents did not go unrecognized. He became Seeckt's right-hand man and handled with impressive skill the many important assignments that came his way. In 1923 he was promoted to the rank of lieutenant-colonel. He speedily justified this mark of confidence by doing an excellent organizing job in connection with the enforcement of martial law during the hectic winter of 1923-24. The ensuing years found Schleicher making the most of his contacts and indulging freely his penchant for intrigue. His smoothness and his capacity for patient and meticulous work were put to the best possible use. In all this, he pursued a single aim: to make himself the behind-the-scenes boss of the Reichswehr.

What Schleicher wanted was power without responsibility. The advent of Hindenburg to the presidency of the Reich brought him closer to his goal. Through Oskar, who now served as his father's personal adjutant, Schleicher was able to gain admittance to the presidential palace at will. He became intimate with all the members of Hindenburg's entourage, notably Otto Meissner, who had been Ebert's secretary and was serving the old field marshal in the same capacity. The duties of this office were not impressive on paper, but Meissner, a strong personality with a decided flair for intrigue, had made himself a power to be reckoned with. Hindenburg almost always consulted his formidable amanuensis before taking action on issues of any importance. When Schleicher and Meissner decided it would be more profitable to collaborate than to compete for Hindenburg's favor, a deal was made and all the presidential favorites, including, of course, Oskar, were counted in. The result was the formation of the so-called palace camarilla which came to exert tremendous influence and eventually took Hindenburg completely in tow.

It was Schleicher's ambition to control the Reichswehr from his unobtrusive niche in the ministry of war. But his chances were poor so long as Seeckt remained at the head of the army. For Seeckt had a mind of his own and was distinctly not the type to play second-fiddle to anybody. This irked not only Schleicher but Hindenburg as well, and so the old man was glad to dismiss Seeckt in the wake of the uproar caused by the presence of the Crown Prince's eldest son at the army maneuvers in 1926. The far more pliable General Heye succeeded Seeckt, and he in turn was succeeded in 1930 by Schleicher's close friend, General Baron von Hammerstein-Equord. Another stroke of good fortune for Schleicher was the fall of Gessler early in 1928. For the man who now took over the ministry of war was none other than his faithful patron, Groener. In 1929 Schleicher was made a major-general. Simultaneously, Groener created for him a special post in the ministry of war. His official title was "Chief of the ministerial office" and his functions were similar to those discharged by secretaries of state in other ministries. The new post carried with it multifarious duties and enormous power. It put Schleicher in control of the intelligence services and of all relations between the national parliament and the armed forces. As time went on, the scope of the job expanded and the influence of the man who held it grew apace. He established contact with individuals belonging to diverse political camps but was careful not to identify himself with any particular group or party.

Schleicher's ambition was not confined to the Reichswehr. While continuing to shun the political spotlight, he aspired to an important and possibly a decisive role in the larger national arena. He believed that the existing parties had demonstrated their incapacity to serve the country and that therefore new movements which were more constructive in outlook would have to be called into being. With this in mind he did everything he could to encourage the revolt of some of the younger members of the Nationalist party against Hugenberg's leadership. It was in the home of one of the general's close friends that Treviranus and his group decided to force a showdown with Hugenberg. Schleicher welcomed the formation of the People's Conservative Association. He hoped to make it the nucleus of a nation-wide organization embracing the younger elements of all the non-socialist parties. This organization would be headed by men who had fought in the trenches and who, by virtue of this common experience, would be able to provide the leadership so sorely lacking in the older parties. In Schleicher's opinion, the man best qualified to lead the organization was Bruening. It is therefore not surprising that Hindenburg asked him to take the place vacated by Mueller.

5

Bruening was born in Muenster, the son of middle-class parents who enjoyed considerable prestige locally. He was a devout Catholic and throughout his career maintained close contact with the clerical group in his own party. He served as an officer during the war and received the Iron Cross, first class, for coolness under fire. Because he preferred a constitutional monarchy to a republic, he opposed the November revolution; this fact was subsequently stressed by his enemies on the Left. After the war, he entered politics as a member of the

Center and quickly established himself as an expert on economics and finance. In 1921, he took charge of the affairs of the Christian trade unions and worked in this capacity under the over-all direction of Stegerwald. Bruening did not excel as a public speaker. Logic and intelligence he possessed in abundance, but they hardly made up for his oratorical deficiencies. He was cold and taciturn; in his own party he was respected but not loved. He had the look of a cloistered ascetic, of someone too withdrawn to be at home in the hurly-burly of the political arena. Yet this forty-six-year-old bachelor was no amateur when it came to political horse-trading, and he could be hard as nails when occasion demanded. Besides, he had plenty of courage. No statesman ever needed it more.

Bruening had large objectives, but he was permitted to achieve very little. He wished to continue, in foreign affairs, the policy of fulfillment espoused by Rathenau and Stresemann. Yet it fell to him to inaugurate the policy of repudiation. Albeit a conservative, he sincerely believed in parliamentary government. But it was he who, under the pressure of an economic crisis that grew daily more ominous, dealt the first shattering blow to the foundations of German democracy. He felt keenly the suffering of his people and strove with all his might to bring them contentment and well-being. Yet in the end he satisfied no one because the cure he prescribed called for terrible sacrifices.

Bruening received his mandate from Hindenburg on March 28, 1930. Egged on by the palace camarilla, the old man was now prepared to reduce the Reichstag to the state of impotence which had been its fate under the imperial constitution of 1871. He wished, in effect, to assume the role formerly discharged by the German emperor. He told Bruening that, in view of the current parliamentary difficulties, he did not think it wise to construct the new government on the basis of a Reichstag coalition. This was tantamount to saying that the principle of ministerial responsibility would be disregarded and that a presidential dictatorship would be resorted to, if necessary. Bruening, despite his predilection for democratic methods, offered no objection because he believed that a strong government was imperative under existing circumstances. The Centrist organ, *Germania,* hastened to explain that he wished to secure the co-operation of all the political forces in the country. On March 29, Bruening's efforts to organize a cabinet seemed on the verge of complete failure. The chief stumbling-block was the attitude of Schiele, with whom Bruening had been conferring. Schiele insisted on three things as the *sine qua non* of his entry into the government: 1) *Osthilfe,* i.e., financial aid for hard-pressed landowners in the eastern provinces; 2) a high protective tariff for the benefit of agriculture; and 3) downward revision of social insurance payments. Bruening demurred, and a deadlock ensued. At this point, Hindenburg intervened. He favored *Osthilfe* and wanted Schiele to assume the portfolio of food and agriculture. He urged Bruening to make concessions to the agrarian leader's point of view. Further negotiations followed; they resulted in a victory for Schiele. Difficulties also arose in connection with the filling of the three other key ministries: finance, economics and interior. They, too, were finally surmounted.

The composition of the new cabinet was announced on March 30. The following were holdovers from the Mueller government: Hermann Dietrich (Democratic party), vice-chancellor and minister of economics; Curtius, foreign affairs; Wirth, interior; Paul Moldenhauer (People's party), finance; Groener, war; Stegerwald, labor; Georg Schaetzel (Bavarian People's party), posts. The newcomers, besides Schiele, were Theodor von Guérard (Center), transport; Bredt, justice; and Treviranus, occupied territories. The last-named ministry was abolished on October 1, 1930. The Center, flanked by the People's party, held a dominating position. The most conspicuous absentees were the Social Democrats. The parties represented in the Bruening cabinet accounted for 249 Reichstag seats—a clear majority. But whether they would work together remained to be seen. Especially dubious was the attitude of Hugenberg. He could be relied upon to exact a heavy price for his party's support. Besides, he did not relish the presence of Treviranus in the cabinet. This, however, was more than offset by Hindenburg's readiness to stand by Bruening. The field marshal conceived no affection for his austere chancellor. But he agreed with Schleicher that the Centrist chieftain was the man to lead Germany at this difficult hour.

On April 1, 1930, Bruening presented his program to the Reichstag. As he rose to speak, he was greeted by cries of "Hunger chancellor!" from the Communist benches. In cold, measured tones, he read his statement. It ran as follows: In conformity with Hindenburg's request, the new cabinet was not tied to any coalition. Nonetheless, the political forces represented in the Reichstag could not be ignored. The cabinet had been formed for the purpose of discharging as speedily as possible the many vital tasks that confronted the Reich. This would be the last attempt to accomplish these tasks with the aid of the present Reichstag. No change was contemplated in the realm of foreign policy. The recovery of Germany could be attained only through co-operation with all other nations. The three main objectives of the government's diplomacy would be: 1) loyal fulfillment of existing agreements; 2) clarification and development of Germany's relations with those states that were friendly to her; and 3) encouragement of international co-operation, especially in the economic field, in order to alleviate Germany's present material hardships. The ultimate goal was an economically sound and politically free Germany, one that enjoyed equality of rights, that was at liberty to complete the work of reconstruction and play an important role in the community of nations. As for the internal situation, the new government would give special attention to the prevailing economic and social difficulties and to the radical movements that stemmed from them. To deal with these movements, it was not enough to invoke police measures. A constructive economic program would be required. The government was mindful of President Hindenburg's recent appeal for national unity. Bitter disputes over questions of foreign policy had divided the German people. Now that these disputes had been settled, the government would seek to effect a reconciliation between the various parties. It was also determined to carry out all the provisions of the Young plan. The most urgent needs of the moment were sound finances and help for impecunious *Laender* and municipalities. Without a speedy solution of the nation's financial problems, there could be no alleviation of the economic crisis and no reduction of unemployment. The appropriations called for under the cabinet's budgetary program were part of a larger whole. This included continued subsidization of unemployment insurance as well as new taxes and reduced government expenditures. The economies contemplated by the cabinet were not, in the slightest degree, inspired by an anti-social attitude. They were designed to make possible a lowering of the realty taxes which weighed so heavily on the urban and rural middle classes. The German government took to heart the plight of these classes. It intended to do everything it could to assist them. The elimination of duplication and waste in all fields of public administration would provide the means for continuing existing social policies. The government regarded the maintenance of such policies as an absolute necessity. Agriculture, which was likewise in desperate straits, required immediate financial aid. Especially critical were the conditions in the eastern provinces; every effort would be made to alleviate them. The government was firmly resolved to carry out this program. It would employ, if necessary, all the constitutional means at its disposal. The Reichstag would have to place itself above considerations of party. For only an objective attitude toward the government's program could assure the future of the German people.

The stern, almost peremptory tone of Bruening's address nettled the Social Democrats. They wondered what he was up to. They reasoned that if he really wanted a working agreement with the Reichstag, he would not have resorted to threats. But new elections in the midst of the current economic crisis could have only one result: an increase in the strength of the anti-republican parties on the Right and on the Left. And this, in turn, would mean a chaotic parliament. When the Social Democrats withdrew from the government coalition late in March, they experienced a feeling of relief. They were glad to be rid of official responsibility. They expected to do much better for themselves as an opposition group at a time when those who held power were almost certain to come to grief. But the need to protect the republic and the hard-won social gains of the working class seemed to dictate a more positive policy.

When Bruening finished speaking, Loebe, the president of the Reichstag, announced that the Communists had introduced a no-confidence resolution. In the debate which followed, Breitscheid, the Social Democratic spokesman, took a vigorous line. His party, he said, was not in the least frightened by the necessity of opposing the new cabinet. Government against or without the Social Democrats was impossible. Certain people had impatiently awaited the dissolution of the Great Coalition formed under Mueller. A very high authority (this, of course, was an allusion to Hindenburg) had intervened to carry out their wishes. In the process, the constitution had been subjected to an interpretation that was not in accord with its text and spirit. Breitscheid expressed concern over the entry of Schiele into the cabinet and, in the name of his party, demanded more information regarding the government's plans to aid agriculture. He ventured the prediction that once the new masters of the Reich addressed themselves to the tasks at hand, they would either continue the work of their predecessors or disrupt the nation's finances altogether. The possibility of a change in foreign policy likewise disturbed Breitscheid. He called attention to the fact that the Treviranus group was demanding the resignation of Curtius. He also pointed out that the Bruening cabinet contained three individuals who had voted against the Young plan. Adverting once again to domestic politics, he charged that Article 48 of the constitution was being abused. At no time, he insisted, had there been any threat to the safety of the land. But Treviranus—this was a matter of public record—had stated that he was entering the cabinet in order to avail himself of Article 48. Breitscheid warned Bruening that he had in his ministry men who regarded this clause of the constitution as a stepping-stone to dictatorship. He implored the chancellor to dissociate himself from them. In the meanwhile, however, the Social Democratic party was introducing a no-confidence motion. It was aware of all the possible consequences of its action. It had no fear of new elections; it was ready for a fresh recourse to the tribunal of public opinion. What it wanted was orderly progress on the basis of the constitution and unity among the friends of the republic.

Breitscheid's closing remark was in effect a plea for the restoration of the Great Coalition. It fell on deaf ears. Co-operation with the Social Democrats was bound to mean concessions to their point of view in the economic and social realm. This the dominant elements in the Bruening government and the men around Hindenburg would not allow. Besides, Breitscheid's emphasis on his party's readiness for new elections was regarded as sheer bluff. No one knew better than the Social Democrats that an election in the midst of a grave economic crisis would strengthen the extremists on Right and Left and jeopardize the republic. The Center, without further ado, gave its unqualified approval to Bruening's declaration. The People's party welcomed his assurance that the present foreign policy would be continued. It likewise applauded the introduction of a comprehensive financial program and the promise of rigid economies in all spheres. The followers of Bredt stressed the point that confidence in the president had led them to join the cabinet. Their main concern, they said, was to procure protection for the interests of the middle classes. If the government should prove unco-operative, it would forfeit the support of the Economic party. The latter appreciated the need for certain temporary expedients whose purpose was largely psychological. But it assumed that Bruening would not fail in the end to institute sweeping financial reforms. The Democrats deplored the failure of the parties to reach an agreement in regard to unemployment insurance. For this they blamed the Social Democrats. They were not enthusiastic about the new cabinet, which contained individuals who till now had fought the internal and foreign policies of the republic. But they were prepared to submerge their doubts and misgivings because they felt that everything possible should be done to avert a political crisis. They regarded the Bruening government as a purely transitional one, destined to remain in office until a majority coalition had been reestablished. The Communist party denounced the chancellor and his ministers as exploiters of the masses. It warned that it would endeavor to force a dissolution of the Reichstag and to turn the people against the government. The Nazis, too, pronounced the new cabinet totally unacceptable.

Bruening's reply to his socialist and liberal critics was significant. He said that the government would decide, in each individual case, whether the use of Article 48 was legally admissible. Recourse would be had to it only when there was no longer any hope that the Reichstag and the parties would fulfill their mission. The ultimate decision in this matter rested, therefore, with the representatives of the people.

The big and crucial question-mark was the attitude of the Nationalists. Most of them were inclined to support the new cabinet. One of their leaders, Schiele, was a member of the government, and the chancellor had made it clear that he intended to protect the interests of agriculture. For this reason, the Junker *Landbund* was friendly to Bruening. Hugenberg felt otherwise. He insisted that the party should go along with the Nazis in saying no to everything the government might propose. The newspapers which he controlled argued that the interests of the nation must come before those of agriculture. But the landowning group headed by Westarp prevailed. Hugenberg, accepting defeat as gracefully as he could, informed the Reichstag on April 3, 1930, that the Nationalists would vote against the no-confidence resolutions. They would not, however, assume the slightest responsibility for the actions of the Bruening government. They disliked most of the ministers. They feared that the policy of fulfillment would be maintained. They disapproved of continued collaboration between the Social Democrats and the bourgeois parties in Prussia. The cabinet's financial program, which had been inherited from Mueller, did not suit them. In due course, Hugenberg concluded, his party would take appropriate action. The same day, the no-confidence motions were defeated by a vote of 253 to 187. The Nationalists sided with the government. The Nazis, who had remained adamant in their opposition to Bruening, were furious. Hitler hastened to announce the dissolution of the committee that had been formed to combat the Young plan. The Nazi-Nationalist partnership ceased to exist. But it was destined, before long, to be revived.

Chapter 30

THE INAUGURATION OF THE PRESIDENTIAL DICTATORSHIP

I

ON APRIL 6, 1930, Bruening addressed the executive committee of the Center. His remarks afforded a clear indication of his state of mind and of his approach to the political issues of the moment. He claimed that he had done everything in his power to prevent the crisis which precipitated Mueller's fall. His party, he pointed out, had repeatedly declared that its main concern was to save the Great Coalition and to insure the proper functioning of the parliamentary system. Just when success in these negotiations seemed imminent, the Social Democrats had balked. They would have to employ different methods if they did not wish to destroy all possibility of collaboration with the Center. There could be no doubt that the Mueller cabinet had taken too weak a line with the parties. The Reichstag had bogged down; and as it grew less effective, the parties became more disunited. All this automatically strengthened the position of the president. The latter was adhering strictly to the stipulations of the constitution. But it must be remembered that this document endowed him with powers which could be called into use whenever the Reichstag failed to do its duty. These powers would be employed solely for the purpose of rescuing parliament and democracy. Such was the intention of the new government. It was averse to experiments, but it was resolved to wage an energetic battle in behalf of the German people and of the existing political system. No stone would be left unturned to win this battle. The cabinet had the backing of the president, and behind him stood the great majority of the nation.

Bruening proceeded to fulfill one of his promises to Schiele. High protective tariffs for the benefit of agriculture were proposed. Simultaneously, action was taken to pave the way for the imposition of new duties on consumption and for an increase in the turnover tax. This program was adopted by the Reichstag on April 14, 1930. At Hugenberg's behest, a minority of the Nationalist deputies joined the opposition. Especially close was the vote on the new tax measures. The Social Democratic party made a strenuous but futile effort to defeat them, charging that they would weigh most heavily on the great mass of low-income consumers. Equally unsuccessful was its attempt to prevent a reduction in the outlay for unemployment insurance and to boost the income-tax rates for all persons earning more than 8,000 marks annually.

The victory of the cabinet had been won by too small a margin to be of any great comfort to the president and his chancellor. The defection of a comparatively insignificant number of deputies would have sufficed to upset the apple-cart. Moreover, the tie between the parties now supporting the government was extremely tenuous. Bruening was under pressure to satisfy, at one and the same time, Junkers, heavy industry, middle-class people and peasants. The meeting of the leaders of the Nationalist party on April 25, 1930, boded no good for the government. Questions of strategy were reexamined. At the close of the conference, a resolution was adopted thanking Hugenberg for adhering to the program previously announced by the party. The delegates took this opportunity to declare very bluntly that they were opposed to the present cabinet. They deplored, they said, the action of those Nationalist deputies who had voted in favor of the government's tax program. They conceded that this action had been inspired by justifiable concern over the plight of agriculture, but it was nonetheless incompatible with the position taken by Hugenberg, the party's leader. Bruening, despite his concessions to the landowners, was thus denied further Nationalist support. This meant that he would be unable to muster a parliamentary majority for his new financial measures. And such measures were already in preparation because it was clear that the program enacted on April 14 was wholly inadequate for the purpose of eliminating the budgetary deficit.

The government's original proposals included lower taxes on certain of the most blighted branches of the nation's economy. But this concession was withdrawn because of the mounting disparity between public receipts and expenditures. The minister of finance, Molden-hauer, explained the cabinet's action to the Reichstag on May 2, 1930. He called attention to the heavy costs of unemployment insurance and to the fact that the revenue of the state was far below official estimates. The lightening of the tax burden would therefore have to be deferred until the budget had been balanced. In the meantime, appropriations for poor relief and unemployment insurance were likely to be slashed. Stringent economies were imperative. Several ways to achieve them had been suggested. One of these was to fix a maximum beyond which public expenditures might not go. Another was to reduce the number of federal civil servants and the pensions to which they were entitled. A third possible expedient was the establishment of a uniform salary scale for the Reich, the *Laender* and the municipalities.

The Social Democrats bitterly attacked this program. They accused Bruening of pursuing a policy that was directed against the working classes. They demanded to know the government's views in regard to the proposed construction of a second pocket battleship. The costs of building this vessel, they claimed, were equal to the sum which the non-socialist parties had refused to add to the unemployment insurance fund. Had Mueller's program for combating the economic crisis been adopted, a reduction of the tax burden would now be possible. The Centrists sprang to Bruening's defense. They ridiculed the Social Democrats' outcry against higher indirect taxes. They declared themselves in favor of aid to the poor, but insisted that the task of balancing the budget must come first. 435 million marks were being allocated, nonetheless, for unemployment relief. This, they contended, was sufficient to refute the charge that the Bruening government was not greatly concerned about the plight of the jobless. This contention was echoed by the spokesman for the People's party. The cabinet, he said, was in no way motivated by hostility to labor. The Democrats, for their part, conceded the necessity of doing something to assist agriculture; but they indicated that they would refuse to support a policy of subventions to rescue the bankrupt estates of eastern Germany. The Communists concentrated their fire on the Social Democrats. The latter, they asserted, were only pretending to oppose the government; Bruening was merely carrying out the "reactionary" program of his predecessor.

Another parliamentary battle developed over the government's request for plenary financial powers. The Social Democrats took this opportunity to absolve themselves of all blame for the crisis which resulted in Mueller's fall. They averred that their demand for an enlargement of the unemployment insurance fund, which the other parties had wished to postpone until the autumn, had been inspired by a desire to improve the country's financial situation and was in no sense an irresponsible gesture. They insisted that the plenary-powers bill be declared an amendment to the constitution. If this were done, a majority of two-thirds would be required to enact it. In reply, Bruening and his colleagues underlined their determination to deal with current financial questions in a strictly constitutional manner. They pointed out that in 1923, when the country wallowed in a crisis comparable to the one now being experienced, the Reichstag, by an overwhelming majority, adopted a plenary-powers bill. The present government was confronted with the necessity of acting quickly and vigorously. To facilitate matters, a sharper distinction would have to be drawn between the functions of the cabinet, which provided leadership and assumed responsibility, and those of the Reichstag. The latter legislated and exercised over-all control; it could, if it did not like the way things were being done, bring about the fall of the ministry. Once again, the Social Democrats failed. Despite their spirited opposition, the plenary-powers bill was passed.

The estimates for the Reich ministry of economics likewise precipitated a debate of considerable significance. The Social Democrats argued that the collective interests of the nation should not be subordinated to the special interests of agriculture. Germany, they pleaded, must lead the way in lowering tariff barriers. A protectionist tariff policy, such as the government was now advocating, would endanger the well-being of the masses. Turning to another aspect of the current crisis, they insisted that one of the main causes of widespread unemployment in Germany was the over-rapid and exaggerated rationalization of industry. One way to meet the situation was to shorten the working week. They denied that wage reductions would create more employment. The existing wage level was not too high, and any attempt to lower it would have to be repelled. Less pay for the workers meant decreased purchasing power and a smaller home market. The government must curb the power of the cartels, which were obstructing all efforts to establish a fair price level. The Nationalists, as was to be expected, sharply dissented. They declared that high prices were due not to the existence of cartels but to the excessive costs of social insurance. The Economic party, which hitherto had sided with the cabinet, subscribed to the contention that exaggerated rationalization and trustification had helped to bring on the present crisis. However, it contended that the chief culprits were not the industrialists but the Social Democrats. It went on to warn that if expenditures were not drastically curtailed, it would be unable to support the government's budgetary proposals.

2

At this time trade-union leaders and spokesmen for the country's largest employers' organizations met to discuss the current crisis. They explored above all the possibility of reviving the national economy by means of a general reduction of price and wage levels. Both sides exhibited an unusual amount of good-will, and the conversations went further than any previous attempts by capital and labor to achieve a working agreement. The employers sought a revision of existing wage scales. They contended that there was no other way to lessen the costs of production. The workers, for their part, demanded lower prices. The immediate objective, it was agreed, was a decrease in unemployment, which had reached the three-million mark. On June 12, 1930, the Rhenish and Westphalian producers of iron and steel instituted reductions in prices ranging from four to seven marks a ton. Simultaneously, they reminded the Bruening government that such a move would be successful in combating unemployment and restoring prosperity only if the state refrained from increasing those taxes that weighed most heavily on industry. Matching the action of their employers, about 200,000 workers in the Westphalian metal industry took a seven and one-half per cent cut in wages. This gesture evoked high hopes throughout the nation, but the feeling that better days might be ahead proved short-lived. In June, 1930, the United States enacted the Hawley-Smoot tariff which instituted the highest rates in American history, increasing the duty on a number of commodities more than twenty per cent. This constituted a hard blow to the German export trade, which already was in a bad slump. And the prosperity of the country depended in large measure on what happened to its foreign trade.

3

Still another battle between Bruening and his Reichstag adversaries was foreshadowed by the cabinet's action of June 5, 1930. On that

day it adopted a new financial program to replace the already inadequate one agreed upon only a few months earlier. The government
now figured on an average of 1,600,000 recipients of unemployment
benefits and 400,000 recipients of poor relief (this left about a million
jobless unaccounted for), thus making a total of two million persons
as against 1,400,000, the number hitherto reckoned with. At the beginning of May, 1930, the deficit in the unemployment insurance fund
stood at 450 million marks. An additional 150 million marks had to
be found for the poor relief fund. The revenues earmarked for both
these funds fell far below expectations. Another complication was the
necessity of setting aside 100 million marks for the purpose of financing
a public works program. In its effort to balance the budget, the government was prepared to resort to drastic measures. It proposed
emergency levies on bachelors, individuals with fixed salaries and
businessmen who earned fees as directors of corporations. It called for
an increase of one per cent (which meant raising the rate from three
and one-half to four and one-half per cent) in unemployment insurance
premiums. This, together with loans and increased contributions from
the Reich, bade fair to rescue the unemployment insurance fund from
its desperate plight. Economies in the administration of the fund were
proposed as a means of achieving a considerable saving. The sale of
preferred state railway shares and speedier collection of the proceeds
from the cigarette tax were likewise counted on to yield sizable sums.
According to Moldenhauer, the aims of the government's financial
program were threefold: solution of the unemployment problem; the
restoration of agriculture to a sound position, with emphasis on aid to
the hard-hit eastern provinces; a balanced budget. He explained to
the cabinet on June 13 that to combat unemployment the government
was launching a public works program. First of all, however, the
budget had to be balanced. Only by cutting production costs and
prices could the current financial difficulties be overcome and the labor
situation improved. Such action would have to be accompanied by a
drastic reduction of non-essential public expenditures in the Reich,
states and municipalities. Moldenhauer defended the projected levy
on persons with fixed salaries. People in secure economic positions, he
contended, must make a sacrifice in the current crisis, since sacrifices
were also being demanded of wage earners. Other ways of dealing
with the situation, such as an addition to the income tax, would only
increase the burdens impeding production and make it impossible
to reduce price levels and combat unemployment.

There was much public discussion of the government's program. Widespread opposition quickly developed not only to the "mulcting" of persons with fixed salaries but to the proposed levy on bachelors and directors of corporations. Most of the parties represented in the cabinet joined in the outcry and their spokesmen predicted that the Reichstag would refuse to go along with the government. Big-business circles were particularly vehement in their denunciations of the proposal to boost the cost of unemployment insurance. Bruening's adversaries argued that the added revenue which the government expected from its program would fail to materialize. It was also charged in quarters hostile to the chancellor that the current negotiations between the industrialists and the trade unions would be seriously jeopardized by the proposed emergency levy, that such a step would counteract the efforts to keep prices and wages down. Reflecting the obdurate attitude of its right wing, the People's party caused another boiling over of the political pot by declaring in unequivocal language that it would vote against the emergency levy. This gesture rendered the position of Moldenhauer untenable. With his own party standing four-square against the tax program which he had described as the only road to salvation, he would have to do one of two things: either withdraw from the cabinet or read himself out of the party by continuing to battle for what he believed. He chose the first of these alternatives and resigned as minister of finance on June 18, 1930. He was succeeded by Dietrich, who relinquished his post as minister of national economy to one of his subordinates.

The departure of Moldenhauer brought no lessening of the clamor against the program that bore his name. On the contrary, the battle over the government's financial proposals rose to a new pitch of fury. Stegerwald, the minister of labor, was very much in the thick of the struggle. He emphatically denied the charge made by the employers that the high cost of unemployment insurance and labor arbitration was the chief cause of the economic crisis. The Nationalists added to the excitement by insisting that the plight of the unemployment insurance fund was hopeless. The People's party also harped on this theme. It called for elimination of the Reich's unlimited obligation to lend money to the fund and enlarged on the wisdom of postponing the contemplated increase in the unemployment insurance rates. For vastly different reasons the Social Democrats likewise ranged themselves against Bruening's proposals. They charged that the government's very dilatory handling of the deficit in the unemployment insurance fund was due to one-sided concern with the needs of a capitalist economy. The Communists echoed this charge, arguing with wonted sharpness that Stegerwald was making himself the tool of the employers.

4

The swift deterioration of the country's economic situation exacerbated existing tensions and animosities and led to an ominous increase in the number of clashes between rival extremist groups. For most of these disturbances, which became more and more serious, the Nazis were responsible. Taking note of the situation and contending that the state was strong enough to prevent the spread of such disturbances, the Prussian minister of the interior, Albert Grzesinski hastened to intervene. On January 16, 1930, he issued a circular forbidding outdoor meetings and parades.

But the Nazis were in no mood to allow a government decree to cramp their style. They were in high spirits because of their showing in the recent Thuringian elections. Those elections afforded the first clear indication of what was happening to German political life as a result of the depression. They recorded the first phase of the shift in public sentiment since the Reichstag elections of 1928. The impact of the economic crisis on Thuringia dealt a disastrous blow to the old bourgeois parties in that state. This part of Germany contained a large number of small secondary industries and home crafts which found the going extremely rough once the depression had set in. The big industrial undertakings were having their troubles, too, but they were better equipped than the small concerns to adjust themselves to the critical drop in demand. Moreover, employees in big factories, which were virtually non-existent in Thuringia, were well organized and consequently not likely to detach themselves from their traditional Social Democratic or Communist moorings. The small industrial enterprises were confronted with the prospect of total extinction. The men who were active in them, from the employers to the humblest workers, listened greedily to anyone who promised to save them. Equally receptive were the villagers who plied handicrafts at miserable rates of pay and who saw even this pitiful source of livelihood threatened by the depression. The Nazis told these people what they wanted to hear and profited handsomely. The Thuringian diet elections occurred on December 8, 1929. The Social Democrats, who remained far and away the strongest party, lost ground. So did the Communists, the

Nationalists and the middle parties. The Nazis increased their representation from two to six. They still constituted a negligible quantity in the total membership of the diet, but the trend toward right-wing extremism was unmistakable and apparently gaining momentum. On January 23, 1930, one of the Nazi leaders, Wilhelm Frick, became minister of the interior and of education in the new Thuringian cabinet. This regime was supported by a coalition composed of the Nationalists, the People's party, the Economic party, the local Peasant party and the National Socialists.

On March 13, 1930, the Reichstag gave consideration to a bill for the protection of the republic and for the suppression of political disturbances. Severing, the federal minister of the interior, urged the adoption of the measure. The government, he conceded, could count on both the army and the police. But the fact remained that there were still many Germans who might be tempted to tamper with the Weimar constitution. The country therefore needed a law similar to the one which had been enacted after the murder of Rathenau. Severing scored the attitude of the Nationalists. A few years ago, he pointed out, they had advocated the prolongation of the law of 1922 on the ground that the state had to be shielded against the Communists. But at the present time they took a different line. They sought to deny the state the protection which it manifestly required. When the Reich was without the kind of law now under consideration, the right of assembly and the freedom of the press were abused by extremists on the Right and on the Left. It was impossible, Severing argued, to tolerate any longer the antics of demagogues who went about poisoning the mind of the masses. Public order was in constant jeopardy. In Prussia alone 300 policemen had been wounded and fourteen killed during the past year. For this state of affairs the Communists and the Nazis were jointly responsible. The former were girding themselves for a decisive onslaught. The Nazis were attempting to spread their subversive gospel among members of the Reichswehr. To deal effectively with these threats to the existing regime, the government would have to be given the requisite powers.

A heated debate ensued in the Reichstag. The opponents of the measure left the hall in order to prevent a vote. The final reading took place on March 15, but once again action had to be postponed. Three days later, the measure was finally adopted by a vote of 265 to 150. A sharp conflict, arising out of the application of the new law, developed between the German government and Frick. This controversy, which attracted widespread notice, revolved about a number of issues. One of these was the status of the Thuringian sections of the "Eagle and Falcon," a reactionary organization known to be hostile to the republic. Severing wanted the Thuringian authorities to take action against this organization; but Frick refused, and he was supported in his stand by his colleagues in the cabinet. Another bone of contention was the reported appointment of Nazis as police officials in Thuringia.

With the accession of Bruening to the chancellorship and the assumption of the ministry of the interior by Wirth, the controversy between the Reich and Thuringia seemed headed for speedy adjustment. An agreement was reached in April, 1930, after the Thuringian government had explicitly declared that Nazis were not being taken into the Thuringian police. But in a few weeks a new conflict arose. It began when Frick recommended the saying of racist prayers in the Thuringian schools. Wirth protested sharply against this action on May 11. He also used the occasion to censure the appointment, in violation of the assurance so recently given, of Nazis to leading positions in the police administration of Thuringia. Failure to obtain satisfaction from Frick led Wirth on June 6, 1930, to halt the subsidy which the Reich habitually granted Thuringia in order to help it maintain its police establishment. The Social Democrats urged strong action against Frick. One of their spokesmen in the Reichstag, Sollmann, eloquently stated the party's position. Germany, he declared, must free herself from political gangsterism on the Right and on the Left. Every Sunday, blood was shed on the streets of German cities and towns. This could be tolerated no longer. The Nazis admitted that they wished to throttle the republic. Against such foes the authorities must proceed mercilessly. This was all the more imperative because of what was going on at the present time within the bourgeois parties. The pauperization of the intelligentsia, the middle class and the peasants was driving these elements of German society to seek new ideologies. The old non-socialist parties were wobbly because their economic and social principles were on the rocks. Outmoded party programs could not prevent a social upheaval. The struggle between the haves and the have-nots was now raging within the bourgeois parties. And millions of these people were in danger of swallowing a nihilist philosophy of despair. Nazi social radicalism, with its anti-Marxist, anti-socialist and anti-communist bias and its stress on nationalism, was proving effective among impoverished white-collar people.

Wirth's refusal to continue the police subsidy to Thuringia was applauded by all the moderate bourgeois parties. They agreed that the Nazis were unfit to hold public office and bitterly condemned the introduction of politically angled prayers in the Thuringian schools. Only the Nationalists criticized Wirth's action. While the Reichstag hall resounded to denunciations of Nazi gangsterism, the men of the swastika continued to provoke disorders in every part of the land. Once again, on June 12, 1930, the Prussian minister of the interior was forced to intervene. He forbade the Nazis to wear uniforms and emblems. He likewise made it illegal to sport canes or any other symbols of membership in the National Socialist party. The police were instructed to use drastic means if necessary to enforce this measure, which was aimed primarily at the SA formations and was similar to the Prussian decree of 1929 ordering the dissolution of the Communist Front Fighters' Organization. Nevertheless, Nazi-inspired disorders continued.

The extent to which Hitlerism was profiting politically by the current depression was convincingly demonstrated by the outcome of the Saxon elections of June 22, 1930. The Nazis increased their representation in the diet from five to fourteen and thus became the second strongest party in Saxony, being surpassed only by the Social Democrats, who remained far ahead of all rivals with thirty-two seats. Hitler's men polled 20,000 more votes than the Communists, who gained only one additional seat to raise their total to thirteen. The Nazis scored at the expense of the Nationalist and the People's parties, both of which lost heavily. Another serious casualty was the Democratic party. The downward course of its fortunes in the Reich and in the *Laender* was rapidly making it a negligible quantity in the political life of the nation.

5

The impending evacuation of the Rhineland, scheduled to be completed by June 30, 1930, was frequently alluded to by government spokesmen, but the public at large, weighed down by preoccupation with the economic crisis, showed little interest. It was before a Reichstag confronted with vexatious and apparently insoluble domestic problems that Curtius underlined the significance of this long-awaited event. The liberation of German soil, he declared on June 25, was only part of a larger foreign policy, the fundamental objectives of which had been repeatedly stated in the past. The Reich would continue its efforts to achieve complete freedom and equality. It would do everything in its power to secure satisfaction for its vital needs. But in so doing it would have to remain mindful of the fact that it had a very great interest in the safeguarding of peace. The consummation of the last phase of the evacuation evoked appropriate but hardly fervid expressions of contentment. Hindenburg and the German government issued a manifesto signalizing the occasion, and Loebe, the president of the Reichstag, made a suitable speech. But how little this happy event served to lessen domestic tensions and quarrels was shown by the action of the Nationalists, who proposed a no-confidence motion against Curtius. The motion was defeated on July 1, 1930, by a vote of 283 to 127. The Communists introduced a similar resolution directed against Stegerwald. It too, was defeated. But the precariousness of the government's position was thrown into sharp relief by the decision of the Social Democratic deputies to abstain from voting.

The attitude of the nation's largest party testified to the mounting bitterness of the struggle between Bruening and his adversaries. On June 28, 1930, he announced that the government had decided to withdraw its financial proposals and was submitting others which would have to be acted upon with maximum speed. The new scheme retained the tax on unmarried persons. It increased by five per cent the tax on all annual incomes over 8,000 marks. It called for a cut in public expenditures, including the salaries paid to government employees. The Social Democrats promptly voiced their opposition to this program. They maintained that greater reductions in government expenditures could be effected. First of all, appropriations for the Reichswehr could be diminished. They pointed out that although the Reichswehr had been in existence for only slightly more than a decade, it already was paying out pensions that amounted to seventy-two million marks. Officers, mostly colonels and lieutenant-colonels, received the bulk of this sum. Another possible economy, argued the Social Democrats, was the discontinuance of federal subventions to the *Laender*. There were also gaps to be filled in the inheritance tax. Likewise not to be overlooked was the collection of back taxes from the owners of large landed estates. The best way to raise money, they contended, was to augment the income tax. An increase of five per cent was not enough. They favored the idea of forced contributions to the state; but they insisted that the specific measure proposed by the government, i.e., a slash in the salary of civil servants, was not just. Ill advised, too, were the current plans for a general reduction of the wage level. The entire program, they claimed, was designed to spare the propertied classes. The Communists made the same charge. The government, they said, wished to plunder the poor in order to give everything to the rich. If it had its way, the working classes would find themselves shouldering the burdens imposed by the Young plan.

For diametrically different reasons, the Nationalists pronounced the new proposals utterly unacceptable. Reverting with fanatical monomania to their old refrain, they charged that the catastrophic state of the nation's finances was the direct result of the Young plan. But the new reparation settlement was not the only factor. Equally at fault were the disastrous economic and financial policies pursued during the last few years under Social Democratic influence. The idea of a levy on government employees and the proposed increase in the income tax were both reprehensible. According to the Nationalists, financial stability could be achieved by reducing non-essential expenditures, lowering the taxes on real property and incomes and assessing public enterprises. No less uncompromising was the attitude of the Economic party, which introduced a motion calling for the dissolution of the Reichstag.

The country's plight obviously demanded swift and drastic remedial action. But the current deadlock gave every indication of continuing indefinitely. At a most critical moment in its history, the Reich found itself paralyzed by the weaknesses inherent in its social and political structure. The depression intensified class antagonisms and encouraged exaggerated factionalism. It thus helped to render the nation incapable of unified, non-partisan effort. The seriousness of the situation was not lost on Bruening. In the face of apparently insurmountable opposition, he resolved to make one more appeal to the Reichstag. The nation, he declared on July 15, 1930, wanted a decision, not more talk and negotiation. The program to which he and his colleagues were committed had not everywhere been fully understood. Germany was in the midst of a very serious economic crisis. The problems which the government was called upon to solve were far more difficult than those that had confronted the country in 1923. The proposals that were now before the Reichstag could be carried out only if the budgetary deficit were met. This held true for such urgently needed remedial measures as *Osthilfe* and the maintenance of unemployment benefits. If one believed that in the long run the government's program would put an end to unemployment, then there ought to be no further delay in sanctioning it. If the Reichstag failed to do its duty now, it would be impossible in the autumn to effectuate the great reforms now under consideration. Once the government was sure that the budget would be balanced, it would be able to tackle the problem of overhauling completely the country's financial system. The states and municipalities would have to be made responsible for the raising as well as the disbursement of revenue. But all the government's efforts to overcome the crisis would be futile if parliament refused to do its part. This was a big moment for the Reichstag. If it manifested a proper sense of responsibility now, it would be doing more for the preservation of parliamentarism and democracy than had been done in all the preceding years. Democracy and parliamentarism would be better served by the courageous assumption of responsibility for unpopular measures than by any other kind of legislative action. To retain its power, influence and prestige, parliament must at all times be capable of fearless behavior. Should the Reichstag fail on this occasion to display the requisite courage, the government, acting in the interests of democracy, would employ all the constitutional means at its disposal to overcome the budgetary deficit. This was Bruening's way of saying that if he should not succeed in obtaining a parliamentary majority for his financial program, he would invoke Article 48 of the federal constitution.

The Social Democrats replied to this challenge in language of equal vigor. The government, they asserted, was in a blind alley and the only thing it could do now was to beat a retreat; yet this was exactly what the chancellor was refusing to do. They assailed once again the government's entire fiscal program and declared they would vote against it. Bruening, they pointed out, had threatened to use all available constitutional means should his proposals be rejected; but what the constitution actually called for, under the circumstances now prevailing, was the resignation of the cabinet. They warned Bruening not to abuse Article 48 in order to put into effect measures rejected by the Reichstag. They contended that the government had not yet exhausted all constitutional resources. Specifically, it had not yet sought to draw upon the strength of the Reichstag's largest party, the Social Democrats. If the non-socialist parties should refuse to admit representatives of the working class to the cabinet, the government, with only a minority supporting it, would have no choice but to withdraw. If the new cabinet should find it impossible to muster a Reichstag majority, then new elections would have to be ordered and the people given a chance to resolve the impasse. Such was the language of the Social Democrats, but their bid for a working understanding with the government came to nought. Thereupon they reiterated their determination to fight the cabinet's fiscal proposals tooth and nail.

The Nationalists likewise persisted in their attitude of opposition. So did the Communists. They denounced Bruening's speech as "the announcement of a Fascist dictatorship." The Center, the Democrats, the Bavarian Populists and the Economic party declared they would support the new financial program, although the latter two groups warned that they were not altogether satisfied with it. With the Social Democrats, Nationalists and Communists saying nay, the government faced certain defeat in the Reichstag. Hindenburg now intervened. Invoking the powers vested in him by virtue of Article 48, he authorized Bruening to resort to emergency decrees if parliament should refuse to sanction the government's proposals. He also empowered the chancellor to dissolve the Reichstag if a majority of the deputies should vote to abrogate the emergency decrees or adopt a no-confidence resolution against the government. Hindenburg's move was a far-reaching and fateful one. It meant that dictatorial means were to replace the democratic process in resolving the conflict. Those who favored this move, and they were a small minority in the country, defended it as the only way to avert a complete political and economic breakdown. The opposition refused to be cowed. On July 16, the Reichstag rejected an essential part of the government's fiscal program. The vote was 256 to 193. The Social Democrats, the Nationalists, the Communists and the Nazis made up the anti-Bruening majority. On this occasion, the Social Democrats once again defied the government in spirited fashion. They denounced its avowed intention to resort to Article 48 as contrary to the constitution. That article, they contended, was designed to assist the state and not a government that had gotten into difficulties of its own making. They warned that they would promptly demand the abrogation of the emergency decrees. Casting aside the niceties of parliamentary discourse, they accused Bruening of attempting to destroy the democratic foundations of the constitution.

On the evening of July 16, 1930, Hindenburg and Bruening carried out their threat. The government, instead of resigning in the wake of an adverse vote, put its financial program into effect by means of emergency decrees. For the first time since the founding of the republic, the principle of ministerial responsibility had been violated.

Two days later a motion calling for abrogation of the decrees was passed by a vote of 236 to 221. The Social Democrats spearheaded this counteroffensive in the lower house. The issue, they declared, was clear: to preserve democracy and the parliamentary system, to prevent the president of the Reich from ruling against the wishes of the people's representatives. Bruening promptly retaliated by ordering the dissolution of the Reichstag. The government fixed September 14, 1930, as the date of the new elections. Simultaneously, it issued a manifesto to the people. The Reichstag, it charged, had refused to grant the means needed by the government to do its work. The majority parties were disunited and therefore incapable of assuming the responsibilities of government. It was now up to the German people to determine the future of the nation.

The seriousness of the crisis escaped no one, but the question of responsibility for it became the object of considerable contention. It was widely believed both in and outside Germany that the crisis sprang from the determination of Bruening and his colleagues in the cabinet to exclude the Social Democrats from the government. These circles argued that all of Bruening's political difficulties from the moment he assumed the chancellorship were due above all to his unfriendly attitude toward the country's largest party. Government spokesmen, on the other hand, denounced the behavior of the Social Democrats as a disservice to the state and to the democratic cause.

The Social Democratic motion demanding the revocation of the emergency decrees had prevailed in the Reichstag thanks to Alfred Hugenberg. The latter managed to swing enough Nationalist votes against Bruening to account for the 236-to-221 outcome. He insisted on going all-out against the government in spite of the pleas of some of his party colleagues. His decision to make common cause with the Social Democrats, the Communists and the Nazis against the chancellor caused a new split in the Nationalist party. Count Westarp and several other bigwigs resigned their membership and announced their intention of forming a new group. The secessionists were for the most part big landowners who had long been demanding financial aid for German agriculture. They feared that Hugenberg's tactics would make it impossible for them to secure such aid. They complained that Hugenberg and those who obeyed him were wantonly throwing away important advantages for the landowning class. They accused him of betraying the Nationalist cause and of co-operating with the "Jewish" parties—by which they meant the bankers—against the agrarian elements. The Westarp group united with the followers of Treviranus to bolster the latter's Conservative People's party.

On July 26, 1930, Hindenburg issued, as emergency decrees, a number of measures submitted to him by Bruening after the dissolution of the Reichstag. These measures, whose purpose was stated to be the alleviation of the country's financial, economic and social ills, went further than those which the Reichstag had rejected. They included a sizable reduction of certain public expenditures; an increase in the unemployment insurance rate, in the income tax and in the tax on bachelors; and a special levy on all civil servants. Permission was granted the municipalities to impose a head tax and to boost the excise on beer. Generous subsidies for agriculture in the eastern provinces were authorized. The government was empowered to take action against the cartels if they should refuse to lower prices. Notice was served that the state would no longer make up deficits in the unemployment insurance fund. It proposed, from now on, to content itself with furnishing only a fixed sum; and if the deficit persisted, not more than one-half of the amount needed to rectify matters would be provided by the government. The other half would have to be raised either by increasing the premiums still further or by reducing insurance benefits.

Chapter 31

THE NAZIS SCORE THEIR FIRST MAJOR TRIUMPH

I

THE dissolution of the Reichstag on July 18, 1930, opened the way for a new test of the strength and stability of parliamentary democracy in Germany. Heartening to the republican elements was the disruption of the Nationalist party in the wake of the newest division within its ranks. But the current economic depression improved the prospects of the republic's other enemies, the Nazis and the Communists. The followers of Hitler entered the fray with well filled party coffers, thanks to financial aid from a few Rhenish industrialists. The latter feared that their workers, under the impact of the depression, would gravitate more and more toward left-wing extremism and hoped to use the Nazis as a bulwark against Bolshevism.

A rich harvest awaited the demagogue. The human flotsam of the depression was his almost for the asking. The prescription for success was simple: promise bread and jobs. The biggest prize was the lower middle class. The Communist party made little effort to win the support of these unfortunates. Had it competed for their favor, it would have been wasting its time. For their class pride and antipathy to Bolshevism were deeply ingrained. They found the Nazis more congenial. Hitler's men were, after all, people of their own kind. They instinctively trusted them. With these men there was no risk of losing identification with the middle class. With these men one went forward, recaptured dignity, security, prestige. They listened to Hitler, drank in his prophecies. He promised them everything and they believed. To do otherwise was to shut the only avenue of escape from their misery. Support me, he said, and all will be well. I will give you jobs. I will restore you to your old place in German society. I will destroy those who are responsibile for your misfortunes. I will protect you. Hitler knew how to awaken and canalize their latent hostilities. He appealed to their prejudices and rancors with brutal directness. He lashed out at "high capitalism," the ruthless money barons, the Shylocks of big-time finance. He inveighed against the Jews. He pictured the republic as a principal cause of the nation's misery. It was run, he said, by knaves and traitors who despised the German people and sought to enslave them.

Extraordinarily clever and full of psychological insight was the propaganda which the Nazis beamed at the peasantry. There were, of course, the usual tirades against the money-lenders, the speculators, the urban middlemen and the "slavery of interest." Care was also taken to promise material relief. The bottom had dropped out of agricultural prices and by the middle of 1930 the peasants were really in a very bad way. But the Nazis did not commit the mistake made by the Communists: they did not pitch their propaganda exclusively on a material note, on the familiar strain of the inevitable struggle between landed magnates and rural underdogs. Rather, they knew the German peasant well enough to realize that the things that mattered most to him were tradition and independence. They knew there was a strain of mysticism in the peasant character. They were well aware, too, that what the peasant cherished above all else was the feeling that he was his own master. The Bolshevists had discovered to their grief that these men of the soil were strangely indifferent to Marxist slogans. The Nazis, guided by their expert on agricultural affairs, Walther Darré, perceived that the German peasant was still steeped in mythology and paganism, that he still lived by certain primitive notions which had nothing in common with the rationalism of the modern world. From this they arrived at the conclusion that the occupation of the peasant was not really an economic one at all. Its aim was not to acquire gain but to maintain a certain way of life. The farmers were told that National Socialism sought to restore them to the place which was their due, the very highest in German society. For upon them devolved the supremely sacred mission of renewing the physical vitality of the nation. This appeal to the peasant's self-esteem paid handsome political dividends. The same was true of the promise to restore the farmer's independent status and to emancipate him from the control of the city. Security of tenure was dangled before his eyes and he was assured that the distinctive, indeed unique, character of his calling would receive long-overdue recognition. Everything about the peasant and his way of life was exalted. The result of this brilliantly conceived and adroitly administered propaganda was the progressive conversion of the rural masses to Nazism.

The Fuehrer also eyed the ferment that was going on in the ranks of the nation's proletariat. What was happening there was enough to gladden the heart of any demagogue. Jobless workers, not knowing which way to turn, seemed ready for almost anything. Some of them were fed up with their rutted trade-union executives, who long ago had ceased to display imagination and energy. They were fed up, too, with their paltry unemployment insurance allowances and the exasperating red tape they had to go through to get them. These men were in earnest when they said they were through with the old leaders and the old ideas.

Could Hitler capitalize on all this? He quickly discovered that the pickings were slim. Dyed-in-the-wool proletarians with long socialist and trade-union affiliations behind them disdained his transparent claptrap. However, not all the workers saw through Hitler's palaver, and some who did shut their eyes and pretended not to see. These were the ones, an insignificant fraction of German labor, that went over to the enemies of their class lock, stock and barrel.

Hitler appealed to the national pride and xenophobia of the German people. At a moment when acute economic adversity was sapping the country's morale and self-esteem, he glorified the Germanic race and promised power and glory for the Reich. He conjured up visions of an aroused and rearmed Germany casting off the chains of the Treaty of Versailles and recapturing the great position in the world which was her due. This was superb propaganda and beautifully timed. It evoked a tremor of response in all Germans, regardless of class or party. For they were unanimous in their detestation of the settlement of 1919 and in their longing to see Germany great and strong again. They were convinced, one and all, that the Reich had been shabbily treated. They merged their woes with those of the Fatherland. The thought of a Germany triumphant and invincible provided an escape from personal frustration.

2

While the great mass of German workers were successfully withstanding the blandishments of the Nazis, they found themselves subjected to an incessant barrage of Communist propaganda. With

Moscow furnishing the directives, Bolshevist orators and publicists hammered away at one theme: Down with the Social Democrats, the "social Fascists" who had betrayed the German proletariat. They professed not to take the Nazis seriously. The latter were crude fellows, nothing but bull-in-the-china-shop Fascists peddling bromides as old as demagoguery itself. If they turned out to be really dangerous, their turn would come later. First one must get on with the main business, which was to break the Social Democrats' grip on German labor. So eager were the Communists to harass the Social Democrats that they even consented to a tacit comradeship-in-arms with Nazi disturbers of the peace. Some German Bolshevists found these tactics repugnant and others thought them the essence of folly. They were told that Moscow had so ordered. Thereafter they held their peace.

The majority of Germany's industrial workers proved impervious to Communist propaganda. But not so the rebellious minority. These men embraced the hammer and sickle and sallied forth into the streets and meeting-places to give battle for their new faith. The Communist party became stronger than at any time since the first months of the republic. From Moscow came organizers and funds. Expectations soared among party leaders. They were still wedded to legal tactics. They had no plans for a frontal attack on the republic. They did not contemplate a putsch. But they had the Social Democrats on the run and nothing else mattered for the moment.

The Bolshevist ferment within a section of the German proletariat represented no immediate threat to the propertied classes. But the latter were not disposed to take a dispassionate view of the situation. It was enough for them that proletarian radicalism was palpably on the increase. Beginning with the summer of 1930, they lived in constant dread of this peril from below. Everything else paled into utter insignificance. This feeling, fed by alarmist conjecture regarding the temper of the nation's unemployed, speedily developed into something akin to panic. It was shared by everyone who had or thought he had a stake in the existing economic and social order. Small landed proprietors fettered by mortgages and debts were just as fearful as Junker magnates. Marginal middle-class people shared the apprehensions of industrialists and financiers. They all agreed that Communism had to be eliminated root and branch. This red scare proved a great boon to Hitler. It was destined to bring him financial assistance from most of the coal and steel barons of western Germany; it also helped to make National Socialism popular in middle-class circles.

3

All indications pointed to an election campaign far more turbulent than any which had preceded it. An endless series of disorders, highlighted by clashes between Nazis and Communists, kept the nation on edge. Most of the parties came out with their old familiar slogans in the apparent belief that such time-worn shibboleths had lost little of their magic. On July 19, 1930, Hugenberg initiated the verbal fireworks. He issued a strongly-worded proclamation castigating the Young plan and socialism and urging all patriotic Germans to rally to the defense of the Fatherland. The Communists and Nazis also launched their campaigns with inflammatory appeals to the electorate. The Communists leavened their inveterate anti-capitalist and anti-bourgeois propaganda with the oft-repeated promise that, if victorious, they would declare null and void all the obligations arising out of the Treaty of Versailles. In taking this line, they were obviously attempting to steal some of the chauvinist thunder of their brown-shirted adversaries. The spotlight was held by the Nazis. Hitherto most of their sympathizers had come from the younger elements on the extreme Right. But now they were attracting support from dissatisfied groups within all the bourgeois parties, groups that believed that the current economic and social crisis was the result of the parliamentary system and that only some form of dictatorship could save the country.

Early in the campaign middle-class liberals effected a regrouping of their forces in an effort to bolster their position and improve their chances in the forthcoming elections. The Democratic party had been doing so badly in recent years and months that some sort of reorganization was deemed imperative by its leaders. Moreover, a section of the People's party which strongly disapproved of the policies urged by that group's right wing stood ready to collaborate with the Democrats in forming a new party dedicated to liberal ideas in both the political and social spheres. These dissident members of the People's party argued that Stresemann, had he lived long enough, would have worked for such an alignment. Conferences between them and spokesmen for the Democrats led on July 27, 1930, to the founding of the German State party. Most of the organizational work involved was performed by three men: Erich Koch-Weser, the chairman of the Democratic party; Hermann Dietrich, Reich minister of finance and a leading Democrat; and Baron Rochus von Rheinbaben, one of the most respected members of the People's party and Stresemann's biographer.

The new party promptly issued a manifesto. The German people, it declared, would have to create a more effective instrument of their will than the last Reichstag. Many individuals doubted the possibility of achieving a proper expression of the nation's desires by parliamentary means. They demanded a dictatorship and were preparing to set one up. Some wanted a dictatorship of the proletariat; others espoused a plutocratic dictatorship; still others wished to see the country brought under the heel of a Nazi dictatorship. The founders of the new party did not believe that the German people were so far gone as to surrender themselves to lawlessness and violence. But it was unfortunately true that the existing parties had failed to create a sense of national unity. The last Reichstag had, at the decisive moment, shown itself to be merely a collection of special interests and not the expression of the national will. The German people were politically more mature than their parties. Unity that went beyond previous attempts to bring together all moderate elements was imperative. The State party sought to create that unity. It stood by the Weimar constitution. It was inspired by the principle of political equality and social justice for all citizens. It wished to mobilize the political strength of the country on behalf of a democratic evolution of the German republic. The party was for private enterprise, but it was also for the protection of the people against the encroachments of big business, especially the cartels. It wished to safeguard social insurance. The party believed that the various economic groups in the country should be afforded an opportunity to participate on a responsible basis in the economic and political life of the nation. Agriculture had to be helped in the crisis through which it was currently passing. The peasantry had to be strengthened. The eastern provinces had to be succored. Government expenditure had to be reduced. The system of taxation had to be so ordered as to achieve an equitable distribution of burdens. The party wanted a foreign policy that would safeguard the country's vital interests and underline the wisdom of co-operating with other countries in a spirit of peace. Now that the Rhineland had been freed, Germany must convince the world of the untenableness of the "dictates" of Versailles and St. Germain. The strengthening of Germandom abroad and the protection of German minorities were likewise matters of paramount importance. National defense was an inescapable necessity in view of the ceaseless military preparations of Germany's neighbors.

The founders of the State party hoped to win the support of all citizens who were fed up with the wrangling of existing political groups. They were hopeful, too, of rallying the liberal youth of the country to their banner. Extremists on the Right and Left were loud in their ridicule of the new party. They claimed that it was foredoomed because it was seeking to embrace too many incompatible elements. But its leaders paid scant heed to these prophecies of woe. They believed that enough Germans would subscribe to the principles of the State party to make it a force to be reckoned with.

A few days later the Democratic party voted itself out of existence and transferred its political organization to the new group. What actually took place was, in large measure, merely a change of name; for the bulk of the State party consisted of former Democrats who believed that their task of obtaining new recruits would be facilitated by the acquisition of a fresh label.

While middle-class liberalism was attempting to give itself a new lease on life, Kaas and Bruening sought to prepare their party for the forthcoming contest at the polls. A conference of Centrist leaders took place on July 29, 1930. The principal address was delivered by Kaas. Speaking with unusual pungency and sternness, he denied the oft-repeated charge that Bruening had deliberately brought about the fall of the Mueller cabinet. Equally false, he declared, was the assertion that Bruening, from the very beginning of his chancellorship, had decided to treat the Reichstag as a negligible quantity and to rule dictatorially. The Center did not wish to overthrow the existing democracy. On the contrary, it wished to preserve it. It had no desire to destroy parliamentarism; it was merely anxious to see it improved and disciplined. Kaas warned the Social Democrats that he would put an end to the Centrist-socialist coalition in Prussia if they persisted in opposing the federal government. Bruening also addressed the gathering. He contended that invocation of Article 48 was not a dictatorial measure. Rather, it was the one means of educating the Germans politically. The new Reichstag would have to decide whether it wished to effectuate all the financial reforms needed to achieve a balanced budget. One thing was certain: the cabinet, not the parties, must lead.

Another striking development that came during the first weeks of the campaign was the effort to unite all the middle parties. The initiative was taken by Ernst Scholz, the leader of the People's party. At the end of July he called a conference at which, in addition to his own group, the Economic, State and Conservative People's parties were represented. The Centrists did not participate in these negotiations, preferring to campaign as an independent group. It was the feeling of Scholz and of Koch-Weser that the multiplicity of political parties and the consequent division of the moderate forces would play into the hands of the extremists. But although the two men saw eye to eye on the broader aspects of the issue, they could not agree on a practical scheme to implement this community of outlook. On August 7, 1930, efforts to effect a fusion of the State and People's parties came to nought. For this the uncompromising attitude of Scholz was largely to blame. He insisted that the State party should give up its name and become an integral part of his group. By keeping its own political organization intact, he argued, the People's party would be in a better position to reach a working understanding with right-wing groups after the elections. The State party rejected these terms. It feared that acceptance of them would render impossible any kind of collaboration with the Social Democrats. Equally futile were the conversations between Scholz and spokesmen for the Economic and Conservative People's parties. The divergences were too numerous and serious to permit an outright merger. However, the three parties did agree to issue a joint election manifesto in an effort to eliminate unnecessary recrimination during the campaign and to facilitate co-operation between them in the new Reichstag. The manifesto asserted that the carrying out of the financial program espoused by Hindenburg and Bruening was the most urgent task confronting the nation. The signatories pledged themselves to battle for this program not only during the current campaign but after the elections as well.

4

The vicissitudes of the campaign lent special significance to the manner in which the various contestants comported themselves on August 11, 1930, the eleventh anniversary of the Weimar constitution. Bruening utilized the occasion to emphasize once again the need for national unity. The work of strengthening the republic, he said, required the services of every German. In an obvious reference to the Social Democrats, he declared that no one who was sincere would be denied participation in this work. A far more elaborate and eloquent presentation of the government's case was made by Josef Wirth, the minister of the interior. The German people, he stated in the most positive fashion, would find it impossible to acquiesce in any form of government other than democracy. However, the current political crisis indicated that much still remained to be done to improve the functioning of the democratic system in Germany.

The problem of co-ordinating and organizing the political liberties conferred on the citizens by the republican constitution of Weimar has not yet been completely solved, and we must still find an answer to the question of how these far-reaching individual liberties can be devoted to producing firm government leadership. This is the foremost internal problem confronting us in the existing situation of economic depression.

Wirth urged the youth of the country to reject Fascism and Communism. The fact that so many young people were demanding a dictatorship was deplorable but entirely comprehensible. It was not difficult, he said, to understand the admiration evoked by Mussolini and the appeal exercised by Leninist anti-capitalism. But what had to be borne in mind was that dictatorship of the Right or the Left constituted a grave threat to the status of the individual. If the youth of Germany found Bolshevism and Fascism attractive, it was perhaps because of a desire to be rid of the Treaty of Versailles, because of disgust with the Reichstag and because of a failure to reach any clear conclusions. Young voters, Wirth declared, should not remain sullenly aloof even if they disapproved of the composition of the Reichstag; they must be neither intolerant nor cynical.

Constitution Day evoked in the socialist and liberal press the usual affirmations of loyalty to the democratic regime. But newspapers reflecting other political persuasions either maintained stony silence or indulged in unflattering allusions to the Weimar document. According to the reactionary *Hamburger Nachrichten*, the republican constitution was "no excuse for a national holiday." It pronounced the day's festivities "artificial and foreign to the hearts of the people." It charged that the constitution was "a makeshift produced under the pressure of Germany's foes from the outside and that of the Spartacists at home who sought to establish a dictatorship of the proletariat." It did, however, concede that such a dictatorship had been prevented by the Social Democrats. The *Essen Zeitung*, one of the organs of Rhenish-Westphalian heavy industry, declared that Germany could be saved only by a return to strict "constitutionalism." What this sheet wanted was a regime which would put an end to the "socialistic experimentation now being indulged in at the expense of capital, industry and private property." If a republic could do the job, well and good. Indeed, a republic was preferable to a dictatorship. The trouble right now, however, was that Germany was not a constitutional republic but a pseudo-democracy that was failing to meet the country's needs.

The views expressed by the *Essen Zeitung* were symptomatic of the political divergences to be found among the nation's industrialists. On one thing they were all agreed: the need for a "strong" government which would protect the propertied classes, undermine the position of organized labor and ward off the Bolshevist threat. But they differed on how to achieve this end. The majority of them believed that the Weimar system, if forcefully administered and leavened with the proper amount of social conservatism, would prove adequate. Others, notably Fritz Thyssen, the head of the United Steel Works, Emil Kirdorf, the director of the Rhenish-Westphalian Coal Syndicate, Carl Bechstein, the famous piano manufacturer, and Hugo Bruckmann, the owner of a well-known printing establishment in Munich, believed that National Socialism was the answer and supported the movement financially long before Hitler came to power. But even among the magnates of the Ruhr, who were, on the whole, more pro-Nazi than industrial leaders from other sections of the country, there were individuals who made no secret of their antipathy to Hitler. An outstanding example was Krupp, head of the great armament factory in Essen. He remained violently opposed to the Fuehrer until the latter's assumption of the chancellorship in January, 1933. Many of the nation's most powerful industrialists continued to support the Nationalists. But even this proved a windfall for the Nazis. For Hugenberg, to whom the big corporations sent their donations, placed a portion of this money at Hitler's disposal. The conflict of political loyalties that prevailed in business circles was well illustrated by the action of the Federation of German Industry. On August 16, 1930, this organization, which embraced the bulk of the country's industrialists, urged its members to vote for candidates who espoused financial reforms and supported the republic. It also put in a good word for those parties that opposed collectivism, that favored private property and private industry, and that sought to revive business and reduce unemployment.

5

As the campaign approached a climax, it became increasingly evident that the drift of popular sentiment was toward extremism. The State party, which sought to make itself the rallying point for liberals, evoked very little response. The same was true for the other middle parties and for the Nationalists, too. The Nazis, who had no such worries, exploited the country's reluctance to make further reparation payments. Hitler's platform demanded that "all German statesmen responsible for the Dawes and Young plans be cited before the people's tribunal and punished for defrauding the nation." The Nazi chieftain adapted the motifs of his oratory to the outlook and needs of the particular part of the country in which he happened to be campaigning. In the rural areas he proclaimed himself the friend of the exploited farmer and the implacable foe of the parasitical money-lender. In the towns and cities he harped on such familiar themes as anti-Semitism, the Versailles "dictate" and reparation. His subordinates, especially those who belonged to the party's left wing, courted popular favor by denouncing "high capitalism," the "slavery of interest" and the evils of industrial bigness. Common to all these Nazi harangues was the promise of prosperity and jobs. Hitler had at his disposal the best electioneering apparatus of any of the leading parties, thanks to donations from Thyssen, Kirdorf, Hugenberg and men of their ilk.

Communist orators and publicists likewise played up the onerous terms of the Young plan. The heaviest burdens, they wailed, would fall on the proletariat. Their primary purpose, in taking this line, was to embarrass the Social Democrats. The latter solicited popular support by underlining their efforts to safeguard unemployment insurance and to protect the existing wage level. Their main hope, as usual, was the trade unions, but mass unemployment was placing a heavy strain upon the morale of those sections of organized labor that traditionally voted for Social Democratic candidates.

The drift toward extremism contained a threat not only to the moderate parties but to the Nationalists as well. But Hugenberg, blinded by his fanatical hatred of the republic, saw in Hitler only an ally whom he could dominate and whose usefulness was bound to increase with every new Nazi success. Besides, the Nationalist leader hoped that the growth of the Nazi movement would be at the expense of parties other than his own. Inauspicious, too, were the prospects of the Conservative People's party. Treviranus and Westarp certainly did not help their cause by going to the electorate with slogans that were almost a verbatim reproduction of the Nationalist program. They demanded the abrogation of the Young plan. They insisted upon a drastic revision of Germany's frontiers. The victors of 1918, they declared, would have to expunge the war-guilt clause and carry out their promise to disarm. They called for a redefinition of the relations between the Reich and the *Laender* and emphasized the necessity of rushing financial aid to debt-ridden landowners in the eastern provinces. Such was the program of the group that had pronounced Hugenberg's policy bankrupt and issued a call for positive, constructive conservatism. The Conservative People's party, like the Nationalists, was unable to compete with the Nazis. To exploit the rich political opportunities opened up by the depression, two things were needed: mass appeal and an elaborate party apparatus. Both of these the Treviranus-Westarp group lacked. Above all, it shunned extremism, but extremism was precisely what millions of unhappy and bewildered Germans were ready for.

The campaign reached a crescendo of turbulence on the eve of the elections. Berlin was the scene of exceptionally serious disorders. A Nazi parade through one of the working-class sections of the city ran afoul of Communist riflemen perched on housetops. A pitched battle ensued and casualties were heavy. The fighting spread to other parts of the capital. Similar clashes occurred in several provincial cities. The brawls were nearly always between Nazis and Communists, but occasionally the men of the swastika combined with their proletarian rivals against the Social Democrats. The SA was active in breaking up mass meetings organized by the moderate parties. The victims of these outrages did not reply in kind. Violence was alien to the Social Democrats and to the parties supporting Bruening. They endeavored to fight this battle as they had fought all preceding ones, with decorum, with appeals to reason, with facts and figures. Their mentality, their outlook, their techniques were distinctly out of tune with the wild emotionalism that seemed to have gripped a large part of the nation.

6

Some thirty-five million Germans went to the polls on September 14, 1930. In the little booths where they marked their ballots, they did something which sent a tremor of amazement and fear around the world. Using the democratic process as their instrument, they plunged their country into what was to be the first phase of a totalitarian revolution. The Nazis provided the biggest sensation. They polled more than 6,400,000 votes and elected 107 deputies. In 1928, their supporters had come to a paltry 809,000 and only twelve of their candidates had been successful. But now, on the morrow of this latest contest, Hitler's party was the second strongest in the Reichstag, being topped only by the Social Democrats, who lost a goodly number of seats. Almost as spectacular were the gains of the Communist party. Its candidates attracted 4,587,000 votes—an increase of nearly forty per cent over the total polled in 1928. Instead of the fifty-four deputies who had represented them in the old Reichstag, the Bolshevists now had seventy-seven lusty-throated, hard-bitten comrades to do their bidding. This contingent ranked third in size but proved a worthy second to the Nazis in boisterousness and rowdyism.

If September 14, 1930, was a sad day for the Weimar republic, it was a slap in the face for its current chancellor. Bruening's pleas to the electorate had boomeranged in humiliating fashion. His own party believed in him as strongly as ever, but everywhere else the feeling toward him ranged from grudging sufferance to clawing hostility. With the Social Democrats still sullen and collaboration with the Nazis and Communists unthinkable, the Centrist leader could only wring his hands in despair. But between him and disaster there stood, as before, the ponderous hulk of the octogenarian president. So long as Hindenburg upheld him, he could carry on in defiance of the Reichstag. But how long would the old man remain on his side? How long would the Reichswehr and the palace camarilla regard him with an unjaundiced eye? He was none too sure, but for the time being more urgent matters claimed his attention. The depression was getting worse daily and the battle against it had to be pressed to the exclusion of all else. He set his face grimly toward the future, resolved to give scant heed to the yappings of his detractors. Perhaps the country might yet be saved from economic ruin and political chaos. His task it was to try.

Chapter 32

THE SOCIAL DEMOCRATS TOLERATE BRUENING

I

THE spectacular gains registered by the followers of Hitler heightened public interest in the fate of three Reichswehr officers who were accused of treasonable activity on behalf of the National Socialist party. The trial of these men before the Supreme Court at Leipzig opened on September 23, 1930. The prosecution charged that the accused had sought to alter the constitution by force and had fomented insubordination and discontent in the army. It was revealed that they had approached the Nazis in order to concoct plans for the "liberation" of the Fatherland. Their action was inspired by the belief that fulfillment of the Treaty of Versailles ran counter to the will of the nation. Moreover, they deplored the retirement of Seeckt, whose ouster they ascribed to political intrigues. After conferring with Nazi leaders in Munich, the accused had endeavored to disseminate Fascist propaganda in the army and had even organized Nazi cells. It was clear from the testimony that many of the younger Reichswehr officers were strongly pro-Nazi.

The high point of the trial came on September 25, when Hitler himself appeared to give evidence. He emphatically denied that he had ever intended to provoke disaffection in the armed forces and proclaimed himself opposed to such action. In answer to questions about the nature and aims of his party, he declared:

Our political movement, which wishes to acquire the power of the state by legal means, places the martial idea before everything . . . We want the Reichswehr to become again a great German people's army.

The Reichswehr, he went on, should protect the nation, not the state. As for the men who had established the republic, they would be given no quarter.

When our party emerges victorious by legal means, a new Supreme Court will replace this one, and the criminals of November, 1918, will find their reward. Then heads will roll.

The trial lasted twelve days. The court found the accused guilty of treason and sentenced them to eighteen months' detention in a fortress. The three men, so ran the verdict, had decided that the Reichswehr was moving too far to the Left and had conferred with Nazi leaders regarding ways and means of counteracting this trend. They had then sought to convert other officers to their views. Their real purpose, apparently, was to keep the Reichswehr from opposing an eventual putsch by right-wing patriotic associations. They hoped, in this fashion, to facilitate a Nazi attempt to overthrow the government. On the day the verdict was announced, great crowds assembled outside the court building and demonstrated in favor of the prisoners. They shouted "Revenge!" and "Germany, Wake Up!" The Nazi press denounced this "political judgment." In an obvious allusion to Groener and Schleicher, whom it held responsible for the fate of the accused, it lashed out furiously against the "Berlin bureau generals."

Groener, who made no secret of his anti-Nazi sentiments, refused to be cowed. In reply to right-wing criticisms of his action in having the three officers tried by a court instead of settling the matter through the usual disciplinary channels, he stated:

The manner of the army's service to the Fatherland shall not be decided by party programs but only by the President and the leaders appointed by him. They alone are able clearly to perceive the necessities of state. Who undermines their authority wrongs the army and the Fatherland.

Groener gave further indication of his determination to stamp out political activity in the Reichswehr by ordering the dismissal of an artilleryman who had been spreading National Socialist propaganda among members of the armed forces. Groener asserted, in justifying this action, that the Nazis were seeking to modify the existing regime by unconstitutional means.

Groener's insistence on the principle, so rigidly adhered to by Seeckt, that the army should not meddle in politics, did not find favor with his scheming and ambitious subordinate, Schleicher. The latter was now apparently convinced, thanks to the evidence brought out during the trial of the three officers, that the Reichswehr could not be trusted to take a strong line against the Nazis. He promptly opened negotiations with Captain Roehm and urged the admission of Nazis to the government. He assumed that Hitler's followers would become less dangerous once they had been persuaded to accept some responsibility for the course of public affairs.

While Schleicher began to nurture the idea of bringing the Nazis into the cabinet, certain of Hitler's associates hammered away at the all-or-nothing theme. Shortly after the elections, Goebbels renewed the old charges against Bruening's program. He contended that it would result in the destruction of the German people. The Nazi party, he proclaimed, would either take over the government or remain in opposition. The Fuehrer himself skirted the question of sharing power with other parties. The future of National Socialism seemed roseate indeed, and it was upon this happy prospect that he preferred for the moment to dwell. He told a cheering audience on October 4, 1930, that the Nazi movement was open to all who wished to join the fight for a new German soul. The recent elections, he declared, represented a big stride toward the final goal: drastic reformation of the nation by legal means. The German people would now have to choose between liberty and honor on the one hand and Bolshevism on the other.

2

The Social Democrats found themselves in an uncomfortable dilemma. They detested Bruening's financial program, but they also feared the possible consequences of a new political crisis which was bound to ensue if they remained in opposition to the present government. They finally decided to tolerate the Bruening cabinet for the time being. Though continuing to protest against the government's plan to reduce its financial responsibility for unemployment insurance and other hard-won workers' benefits, they gave priority to the necessity of defending the country's republican institutions against extremists on both Right and Left. This decision was precipitated by Bruening's belligerent announcement on September 30, 1930. He declared that in order to put his fiscal program through, he would fight the Reichstag tooth and nail. This he was resolved to do even if, in the process, a dictatorship would have to be created. The threat of a dictatorship, made with Hindenburg's backing, conjured up unpleasant possibilities for the Social Democrats. They could scarcely overlook the strength of the Nazis and the possibility of a deal between them and Bruening, a deal that might prove fatal to the republic. So toleration of Bruening was decided upon in spite of his unacceptable views on the subject of unemployment insurance. The leaders of the party also feared to risk another dissolution and new elections. A third factor in their decision was the desire to keep alive the Social Democratic-Centrist coalition in Prussia. This coalition, which for some time the Nationalists and the Nazis had been trying to disrupt, now loomed as the principal bulwark of the German republic.

3

The Nazis were infuriated by Bruening's threat to put his financial reforms into effect without the consent of parliament. Executing one of those about-faces for which they were subsequently to become famous, they now made themselves the champions of the Reichstag's rights against the chancellor. The *Voelkischer Beobachter* provided the leitmotif of their protests when it declared:

We solemnly warn Herr von Hindenburg not to put himself in opposition to the German people in the interest of the Centrist party and a few bankrupt politicians. If the Bruening government dares to take such a course, it will become an illegal government and arouse the population also to take recourse to illegality.

The Stahlhelm added to the excitement by demanding the overthrow of the "Marxist dictatorship" in Prussia. Bruening's political difficulties were aggravated at this moment by the rising tide of opposition to the Young plan and the widespread demand for its revision. This clamor against reparation, which had been initiated by the Nationalists, the Nazis and the Communists, was now being supported by the middle parties. Many Germans of moderate outlook believed that new taxes or wage cuts could be obviated by the immediate stoppage of reparation payments. All the while the country's economic difficulties were growing worse despite the government's heroic efforts to combat the trend. In the autumn of 1930 the number of unemployed was well beyond the three-million mark. Of these about two million received unemployment insurance benefits. The rest had to get along as best they could.

The debate over how to solve the unemployment problem raged

with unabated fury. On October 8, 1930, the Federation of German Industry adopted a resolution reiterating that organization's demand for far-reaching reductions in wages and in public expenditures. Only by cutting government and production costs to the bone, it contended, could the way be opened for the reabsorption into private industry of large numbers of unemployed. The trade unions did not take kindly to this insistence upon further wage reductions. The bitterness which pervaded certain sections of German labor constituted a serious threat to the preservation of industrial peace at a time when uninterrupted production was a vital necessity. Significant in this connection was the action of Berlin's metal workers. On October 14, 1930, they went on strike after a board of arbitration had recommended a sizable lowering of their starting wage. They stayed away from their jobs for two weeks. Their mood was a grim portent of what could be expected to happen in other branches of the national economy as the living standards of the masses continued to decline.

4

The new Reichstag convened on October 13, 1930. The Nazi deputies, clad in brown uniforms and arrayed in military formation, marched arrogantly into the hall. Without further ado, they created so much disorder that the proceedings had to be repeatedly suspended. They professed only contempt for the decorum with which parliamentary bodies ordinarily conducted their business. The Communists contributed to the excitement by demanding speedy consideration of the no-confidence motions which were being introduced by the opposition parties. While all this was going on in the Reichstag, Nazi-instigated clashes occurred in the center of the capital. Brown-shirted hoodlums broke the windows of Jewish shops and turned the display rooms topsy-turvy. Two days later, the Reichstag reconvened for the purpose of choosing its presiding officer. The Social Democrats backed Loebe for re-election to the post which he had held so long. The People's party nominated Scholz. In an inflammatory speech, the Communist deputy, Ernst Torgler, put forward the name of his party's veteran leader, Wilhelm Pieck. Frick, speaking on behalf of the Nazi delegation, argued that the recent elections had demonstrated that the German people favored the establishment of an anti-Marxist front. In the course of his remarks, he called Loebe a "slacker." This evoked tumultuous protests from the Social Democratic benches.

After quiet had been restored, Frick announced that the Nazis would support Scholz, who, he pointedly stated, had served at the front during the war. Loebe, nonetheless, was elected, although he failed to receive a majority of the votes cast.

On October 16, Bruening appeared before the Reichstag to ask support for his financial program. When he entered the hall, the Communists greeted him with cries of "Down with the Hunger Chancellor!" Unperturbed by the patent hostility of large sections of his audience, Bruening called for effective and prompt action to counteract the steadily worsening economic crisis. The government, he explained, had prepared an elaborate plan. The essential condition for the success of this plan was the continuance in effect of the emergency decrees issued on July 26, 1930. But motions had already been introduced demanding the abrogation of those decrees. The government urged rejection of these motions on the ground that abrogation of the decrees would aggravate conditions throughout the country. The decrees were doing a great deal of good already. They were making possible the preservation of social insurance and the extension of financial assistance to agriculture in the eastern provinces. Their elimination would render the economic crisis insurmountable. New appropriations were needed to meet the increased costs of unemployment insurance. Revenue from taxation continued to fall far below expectations, and the coming year would bring an even greater disparity between income and expenditure. Only extraordinary measures could provide a solution. Conventional fiscal methods would prove unavailing. One of the most serious difficulties was the tightness of the money market. Many Germans, displaying a deplorable lack of patriotism, were shipping capital out of the country. Such lack of confidence was imposing a severe strain upon the financial resources of the Reich and contributing to the spread of unemployment. The government found itself compelled to turn to foreign sources of credit. After long negotiation, it had managed to secure a two-year loan.

The primary objective of his program, Bruening continued, was a balanced budget. This he proposed to achieve by placing unemployment insurance on a self-sufficient basis, instituting stringent economies, reshaping taxation policies so as not to discourage industrial production and redefining the financial relations between the Reich and the various local governments. In its efforts to effect a reduction of wage and price levels, the cabinet did not contemplate a permanent lowering of real wages. In its concern for the welfare of the people, it was behind none of its predecessors. But a broadly conceived social policy could contribute to the general well-being and improve the lot of manual and white-collar workers only if it rested on solid economic foundations. An anemic national economy and an unbalanced budget stood in the way of such a policy. They also hampered the fight against unemployment. But so long as Germans remained without work through no fault of their own, the government would attempt to take care of them. Uniquely critical was the plight of agriculture in the eastern provinces. The five-year *Osthilfe* program laid before the last Reichstag had not been put into effect because final action had been prevented by the dissolution of parliament. It would be carried out as soon as the present Reichstag provided the necessary authorization.

Turning to international affairs, Bruening declared that the country's supreme objective was the attainment of national freedom. This could be achieved, he insisted, only by pursuing the path of peace. The government categorically opposed "a policy of adventures." Since the Young plan went into effect, Germany's economic condition had steadily grown worse. The authors of the new reparation settlement recognized that Germany's ability to pay depended on the state of her commerce and finances. Their attitude on this question was heartily shared by the Reich. But the fact remained that many Germans, especially the younger generation, continued to resent the treatment accorded their country by other powers. The first blow to their hopes for international understanding had been the violation of Wilson's Fourteen Points. Since then their disillusionment had been kept alive by the failure of the Allies to carry out those provisions of the Treaty of Versailles which were favorable to Germany's interests. The enforced disarmament of the Reich had not been followed by the disarmament of other nations. Indeed, many countries were constantly increasing their armaments and thus jeopardizing the peace and security of the world. This was "an intolerable situation." The government, for its part, would do everything it could to build up Germany's defenses within the limits prescribed by the treaty. It would also exert itself to the utmost to keep the Reichswehr, which was the backbone of the national community and of the state, free from the influence of parties and politics. In this hour of need, there was no room for internal disunity. Antagonisms engendered in the course of the recent electoral campaign must be laid aside. The heavy sacrifices which the

German people were being asked to make would "pave the way to freedom and recovery."

Hermann Mueller stated the position of the Social Democrats. As the former chancellor rose to address the Reichstag on October 17, the Nazi and Nationalist deputies ostentatiously left the hall. Mueller made it clear that he and his comrades would not support the no-confidence motions before the house. The actions of the party, he averred, would be governed by existing realities. It would decide for itself when to withhold its support from the present cabinet. The Nazi-Nationalist opposition was seeking, above all, to obtain control of Prussia, which in 1923 frustrated the Hitler-Ludendorff putsch and saved the Reich. The Social Democrats were determined to do everything in their power to protect the republican constitution. They did not like certain features of Bruening's financial program. They were most anxious to see the entire matter handled in strictly parliamentary fashion. They deplored the flight of capital from the country and doubted Hitler's sincerity in clamoring for a revision of the Young plan. The National Socialist movement was attempting to provoke civil war, but it would find the workers firmly united in their resolve to combat reaction. Spokesmen for the middle parties pronounced the government's program acceptable. Some of them voiced misgivings regarding certain specific proposals, but they indicated that this would not keep their groups from voting in the affirmative.

The prolonged debate came to a close on October 18. The efforts of the Nazis, Nationalists and Communists to prevent the referral of the emergency decrees to the appropriate Reichstag committee were defeated by a vote of 339 to 220. A motion to table the no-confidence resolutions sponsored by the opposition parties was carried by a less impressive margin: 318 to 236. Having taken care of all the urgent matters on its docket, the Reichstag proceeded to vote itself a recess until the beginning of December. Thanks to the support of the Social Democrats, the Bruening government had emerged with flying colors from its first encounter with the new parliament.

5

During the ensuing weeks, the cabinet put the finishing touches to its financial program. On December 1, 1930, Hindenburg issued a new batch of emergency decrees. Two days later the budget for 1931-32 was laid before the Reichstag. It was explained and defended by

Dietrich, who stressed the need for further sacrifices. He declared that the government, in casting about for ways and means to meet the expected deficit, had decided not to overburden industry, since increased production was the nation's most pressing need. The heavier tax program envisaged would affect, above all, the sale of non-essential consumers' goods. Drastic economies, especially as regards unemployment insurance, were likewise a basic feature of the new estimates. Approval of the budget as it now stood would contribute mightily to the strengthening of the government's credit abroad and make possible an energetic prosecution of the battle to revive the nation's economy. A sharp increase in unemployment was to be expected during the winter. If the Reichstag did its part, the worst would soon be over. It was too bad that one had to resort to emergency decrees. For this, parliament was responsible. A body which contained large parties whose attitude was completely negative, who refused to shoulder responsibility for anything, risked losing its influence.

It was Dietrich who on one occasion raised this question: was the Reich merely a conglomeration of disparate interests, or was it a truly national community with a being and purpose that transcended the desires and needs of the many groups that composed it? So far but little unity had been displayed in the face of the worst crisis in the nation's history. The debate on the new budget indicated no change for the better. The opposition parties continued their sniping tactics. Gottfried Feder, speaking for the Nazis, charged that the government had no right to remain in office because it had not received a formal vote of confidence from the Reichstag. To clarify the situation, his party had decided to introduce a no-confidence motion. The Communists exhibited their usual truculence. They asserted that a Fascist dictatorship, which enjoyed the support of the Social Democrats, was already in existence. The Nationalists aped the Nazis in developing a sudden love for the constitution. The rights of parliament, they wailed, were being throttled. Rule by Article 48 was flagrantly illegal. Something had to be done about the Young plan. There could be no real improvement in the country's economic situation without a drastic revision of that intolerable settlement. The Economic party executed an about-face. It joined the opposition and gave emphasis to its dissatisfaction with the latest financial proposals by procuring the withdrawal of its leader, Bredt, from the Bruening cabinet. The other middle parties and the Social Democrats voiced objections to certain features of the government's program but indicated they would support it, nonetheless. On December 6 the various no-confidence resolutions were defeated by a vote of 291 to 256. By a slightly larger margin the Reichstag likewise rejected a motion calling for abrogation of the recent emergency decrees. Six days later, after a series of tumultuous episodes precipitated by Nazi vituperation and hatemongering, the Reichstag adjourned for the winter holidays. The men of the swastika had little to show for their obstructionist tactics in parliament. But they did score one very resounding victory on a question which exercised them mightily: they forced the government to halt the showing of the American film version of Erich Remarque's *All Quiet on the Western Front*. Pacifism had been a potent force in Germany during the greater part of the twenties and had achieved trenchant expression in Remarque's book. Now it was being forced to recede before the ever-mounting Nazi tide. Hitler scored another victory on an issue which had been a continuous source of vexation for months. Shortly before Christmas the Reich and Thuringia finally settled their differences—on the latter's terms. The federal police subvention was resumed. The Thuringian government proffered assurances of good behavior, but only the hopelessly naive could take them seriously.

6

The ill feeling created by the outrageous language and behavior of the Nazi deputies in the Reichstag was reflected in the speech which Mgr. Kaas made at a meeting of Centrist leaders in Cassel on January 4, 1931. "If we," he declared, "were not restrained by a sense of responsibility, we would, for pedagogical reasons, make room for the Nazis, in order that the German people might become aware of their bloody ignorance. But the experiment seems risky, for I do not believe that afterwards there will be anything left to save." However, the Nazis were not alone culpable. All the opposition parties were indulging in complaints and laments. They kept deriding those who possessed fortitude enough to assume political responsibility. According to Mgr. Kaas, Bruening had only one aim: to restore the strength of the Reich. A few days later Dietrich dwelt upon the same theme in an address delivered before members of his party in Stuttgart. The government, he said, reposed its faith in the vitality and future of the German people. It had no intention of relinquishing office. On the contrary, it was resolved not to allow itself to be led astray by the insanity which had taken hold of large sections of the nation. It would continue the battle calmly and energetically.

Bruening himself sounded a similar note when he addressed the leaders of the Catholic trade unions in Cologne late in January, 1931. Democracy and parliamentarism, he said, were undergoing a crisis. In the pre-depression days, when there were large financial surpluses, people found it easy to sing the praises of democracy. But when good times ceased, defections from the cause of parliamentarism multiplied. As a consequence, one saw in Germany a great many persons who had once been ardent republicans but who now stood far to the Right in national politics. The present government was waging the fight for democracy firmly, serenely, without useless talk. It believed in the German people who, at crucial moments, knew instinctively what had to be done. They were not as devoid of political wisdom as the leaders of certain parties liked to believe. They would not assent so quietly to heavy economic sacrifices if they were not impelled thereto by a sense of responsibility. The urgent necessity of the moment was to implant this sense of responsibility in the members of the Reichstag. The sport of introducing in parliament hundreds of purely propagandistic motions had to be halted. The duty of a deputy was to tell his constituents the truth and not to make unfulfillable promises. The plight in which the country now found itself was due not only to the costs of reparation but to the fatuous tendency of Germans to believe that, after losing the war, they could live better and spend more than in the pre-1914 years. Buildings had been erected which would have been financially out of the question before the war. Huge sums had been lavished on projects that turned out to be unwise and unproductive. There was but one thing to do now, and that was to return to more thrifty ways. The government, for its part, would not be dissuaded by threats and calumnies from following "the path of solid reconstruction." It was true that the reparation burden could not be borne indefinitely. But first the Reich would have to equip itself economically and financially for the battle to secure further concessions. What was needed in this connection was the courage to make unpopular decisions.

The fortitude with which Bruening was so richly endowed was subjected to a new test when the Reichstag reconvened on February 3, 1931. Seemingly impervious to the government's appeals for national unity, the opposition parties promptly resumed their efforts to hamstring the work of parliament and make life as miserable as possible for the cabinet. The Communists touched off the verbal fireworks by demanding that the ban against the Red Front Fighters' League be lifted. Once again they accused the middle parties of plotting to set up a dictatorship in Germany. The Nazis, not to be outdone by their rivals on the extreme Left, introduced a motion calling for dissolution of the Reichstag. All the opposition groups hastened to submit no-confidence resolutions. From the Nazi benches came an endless stream of boos, catcalls and insulting remarks. The government's spokesmen were mercilessly heckled when they rose to ask swift approval of the new financial measures. The passions, the hatreds and resentments which permeated large sections of the German people were faithfully mirrored in these proceedings. German parliamentarism appeared to be on the verge of an ignominious breakdown.

A sad day was dawning for a good many political reputations in Germany, but not for Bruening's. The integrity and courage of the chancellor shone more brightly than ever at this hour. Though he was the man who had invoked the necessity of rule by emergency decrees, he was able to impress all but the most prejudiced with the sincerity of his faith in the democratic process. It was indubitably his wish to see parliament resume, at the earliest possible moment, the functions assigned to it by the constitution. He had resorted to Article 48 only because he was convinced that the salvation of his crisis-ridden country required action which the Reichstag, paralyzed by party bickerings, had proved itself incapable of taking. His faith in democracy was matched by his abhorrence of demagoguery. Few questions lent themselves so easily to unscrupulous and self-seeking misrepresentation as that of reparation. The Nazis, Communists and Nationalists had made this issue a football of politics and were still pressing for obviously impossible solutions in the hope of winning popular acclaim. To such tactics Bruening obdurately refused to stoop. He told the Reichstag on February 5, 1931, that the government would not be swayed by internal considerations in deciding how and when to secure a revision of the Young plan. It would not, for the sake of popularity, allow itself to be forced into doing something which, in the long run, would hurt rather than help the German people. "We are firmly determined," he said, "to stick to this point of view under all circumstances and to accept the unpopularity that goes with it."

As was to be expected, Bruening's exhortations for speedy and united action had little effect on the opposition parties. The debate in the

Reichstag became more and more agitated and moved inexorably toward an explosive crescendo. The Communists bitterly attacked the government's handling of the unemployment problem and proclaimed that only the establishment of a Soviet regime could insure victory for the rights of the working classes. In a speech punctuated by boisterous applause from the Nazi benches, Goebbels flayed the Bruening cabinet and dared it to issue a call for new elections. From such a contest, he prophesied, the Nazis would emerge with 180 seats. The National Socialist party would under no circumstances deviate from its policy of stubborn opposition. The means it employed were legal but the goal it sought was not. What it would do with the power acquired by legal methods was its own affair. When Goebbels finished, the Nazi deputies gave him a frenzied ovation and then marched out of the hall. The reaction of the Reichstag majority to all this was well expressed by the next speaker, Sollmann, when he remarked: "After the unrestrained emotional outburst which we have just witnessed, we may well wonder where the boundaries of politics end and those of psychiatry begin."

On February 7, 1931, the no-confidence resolutions introduced by the Nazis and the Communists were defeated by a vote of 293 to 221. The Nazi request for immediate dissolution of the Reichstag was likewise turned down. Three days later the parliamentary struggle reached a comic-opera climax. The Nazis pronounced the Reichstag devoid of all authority and declared that they would have nothing more to do with it. Adding that they would return to their benches only when some particularly foul crime was about to be perpetrated against the German people, the brown-shirted deputies departed *en masse*. The Nationalist members of the Reichstag staged a sympathy strike by absenting themselves for one day. The Communists, however, remained glued to their seats. Accusing the Nazis and Nationalists of hypocrisy, they proclaimed their resolve to remain in the hall to the very last in order to keep up the fight against the Young plan and for a Bolshevist Germany.

The support given him by the Social Democrats had once again enabled Bruening to withstand the assaults of the opposition. But friction between the government and the country's largest party was not wanting. The main source of difficulty was Bruening's wage policy. The Social Democrats objected to the lowering of wages, claiming that the economic crisis would only be aggravated thereby. They likewise complained that promised reductions in the price level had failed to materialize. Dissatisfaction among the rank and file of the trade unions was intense. The Social Democrats were therefore compelled to take a firm stand on this issue. The new appropriations for the armed services were another bone of contention. In return for their promise not to oppose these appropriations, the Social Democrats demanded a number of concessions in the economic and social sphere, above all a twenty per cent increase in the tax on property in excess of 50,000 marks. But Bruening flatly refused to grant such concessions; and in the end the Social Democrats abandoned their insistence on a *quid pro quo*. The Reichstag completed its current legislative business on March 26, 1931, and forthwith voted to adjourn until the middle of October. This seemed an unduly long recess—especially at a time when the need for speedy legislative action was constant. By thus abdicating in favor of the executive branch of the government, parliament virtually invited further resort to rule by emergency decrees.

Chapter 33

FINANCIAL DISTRESS, THE HARZBURG FRONT AND HITLER'S DUESSELDORF SPEECH

I

THE winter of 1930-31 witnessed a continuation of the downward trend in the nation's economy. The remedial measures so far instituted had proved of little avail. Those about to be put into effect would take time to make their beneficent influence felt. Something had to be done to accelerate the process of recovery. One area of action suggested itself: Austro-German relations. In Germany, sentiment in favor of Anschluss was as strong as ever. In little rump Austria, where economic and financial difficulties were chronic, the suffering caused by the depression had intensified the long-standing desire for union with the Reich. Here loomed rich possibilities. To exploit them involved risks, but the rewards of success made the gamble worthwhile. For the scheme which Bruening had in mind could be justified on incontrovertible economic grounds. Without a doubt it would facilitate the slow uphill battle which had absorbed all his energies from the moment he took office.

Ever since the onset of the depression, well informed circles everywhere had agreed on one point: that the existence of trade barriers between the various states of Europe contributed to the prevailing economic difficulties and blocked the road to recovery. But political antipathies and economic nationalism made the lowering of these barriers virtually impossible. Many outstanding statesmen saw the need for action. One of these was Aristide Briand. The depression, he urged, could be overcome only if all countries abandoned their lone-wolf tactics and worked together. In September, 1930, he broached the idea of a European federal union before the assembly of the League of Nations. This seemed the best way to guarantee international economic co-operation. The first reaction was not altogether unfavorable, and in internationalists of every land the hope was kindled that an ancient dream might yet come true. But in the end Briand's suggestion, which alone could have saved Europe from anarchy, was interred. The various governments and peoples of that hate-ridden continent distrusted each other too much to subscribe to so farsighted a solution of their difficulties. They preferred, in time-honored fashion, to drift toward catastrophe.

National antipathies were certainly much in evidence in Europe, but between Austria and Germany there existed the closest of ties: those of race, language and culture. And transcending even these was the pressing sense of need, the realization that union would aid them in combating the economic crisis. Politically, too, Austria and Germany had much in common. They were both democracies, both victims of Allied map remaking. In each of them socialism played an important role, and the working masses who furnished the sinews of Austrian and German trade unionism were strongly in favor of Anschluss. True, clericals and legitimists in Austria frowned on the idea of union with the great neighbor to the north, but they were outnumbered and overruled. Though both nations ardently desired Anschluss, their governments knew it was out of the question for the time being. Foreign opposition was insuperable. Austro-German union had been expressly forbidden by the Treaties of Versailles and St. Germain. France, Italy and Czechoslovakia were determined to uphold that ban. Under the stress of financial difficulties which had sent her begging for foreign assistance, Austria had promised her creditors to do nothing which might compromise her independence. Since she was perenially in need of financial transfusions, she knew it would be most ill-advised to go back on her word.

But Bruening and his friends in Vienna had something up their sleeves which they thought, or at any rate hoped, would be less objectionable. They would form an Austro-German customs union. The whole thing would be on an exclusively economic plane. There would be no political or territorial merger. Each country would retain full sovereignty and independence. There would be no infringement of the Treaties of Versailles and St. Germain, no repudiation of Austria's promise to her creditors. But for Germany and Austria, the proposed arrangement would be a godsend. By co-ordinating their tariff policies, the two countries would be in a better position to fight the depression. And though territorial union, their real and ultimate objective, would still be unaccomplished, a long step toward it would have been taken. Thus, on both the economic and diplomatic fronts, a grea victory would be won.

However, all these lovely plans and expectations came to nought. The Austro-German project was sprung on the world in March, 1931. Care was taken to emphasize that there had been no intention to confront Europe with a *fait accompli*. But the reaction abroad was far from encouraging. The governments of France, Italy and Czechoslovakia, contending that the proposed customs union was really a step toward political and territorial Anschluss, promptly protested. The Germans insisted with righteous warmth that the independence of Austria would not be jeopardized, but no one believed them. France mobilized her financial as well as her diplomatic resources to block the plan. She jabbed hard at the shaky economies of Germany and Austria, forcing them even closer to the verge of collapse.

The matter was finally referred to the world court. Then things began to happen in Central Europe. First came the collapse of the *Kreditanstalt*, Austria's greatest banking institution. In practically no time at all, cries of anguish came pouring out of Germany, which had close financial ties with the *Kreditanstalt* and all its subsidiaries. The severe banking crisis that blanketed the Reich in the wake of the Austrian debacle was aggravated by jittery American financiers, who hurried to recall their short-term loans. Germany teetered on the brink of bankruptcy.

Everything that had happened in this incredibly short span appeared to vindicate the German stand for a customs union. But above all it pointed to the need for prompt and drastic action to aid the Germanic states and thus save all Europe and the world from financial catastrophe. On June 16, 1931, the Bank of England came through with a sizable loan to Austria. Four days later President Herbert Hoover, mindful of the danger to American investments in Germany, proposed a one-year suspension of all reparation and war-debt payments. London and Berlin immediately welcomed the American suggestion. The French, who had not been consulted in advance and who would be the ones to suffer most from any cessation of reparation payments, postponed their acceptance for a few weeks. To satisfy them, certain conditions were agreed upon: Germany was to spend the savings effected under the one-year moratorium for economic and not for mili-

tary purposes; and she was to fulfill the terms of the Young plan when
the moratorium was over.

In the meantime the flight of capital from Germany continued at an
appalling rate. Germans as well as foreigners contributed to this process. With callous indifference to the results of their action, they shipped
every penny they could lay their hands on to safe places abroad. The
great Darmstadt and National Bank closed its doors on July 13, 1931.
All the other banks followed suit on orders from the government,
which placed the country's foreign exchange under its exclusive control. At the London economic conference which opened on July 20,
1931, Bruening begged for a long-term loan. But the Bank of England,
which was suffering huge withdrawals of gold, could do nothing. The
United States, for its part, was concentrating on the task of getting
American funds out of Germany. France was in a position to help
her traditional enemy. She had piled up a tremendous gold reserve.
However, she insisted on certain political concessions—above all, a
German pledge to abstain from tampering with the peace treaties until
after the repayment of the loan—as the price of financial assistance.
Nazi leaders, who were watching for a chance to throw a monkey
wrench into the proceedings, promptly wired Bruening that the French
terms were absolutely unacceptable. But the unhappy chancellor knew
this as well as they. He left the British capital empty-handed.

But help was on the way. An international committee of experts
appointed to examine the German situation submitted its report in
August, 1931. It urged the continuation of all short-term loans for a
period of six months. The Reich's creditors, fearful of what a total
German collapse might do to their own economies, adopted the experts' recommendation. This "standstill agreement" was extended in
1932 and annually thereafter during the next few years. Thanks to
belated assistance from abroad, Bruening succeeded in piloting his
country through the terrible financial crisis which had come within an
ace of plunging Central Europe into irreparable chaos. But additional
hardships had to be imposed on the nation. The feeling against Bruening became a phobia. Nevertheless, he clung doggedly to office. He
had a job to do, and he was determined to finish it.

2

The Austro-German customs union had to be abandoned in the face
of unremitting foreign hostility. The opposition of France was the
decisive factor. The Germans were far too mindful of French military

might and too dependent on the good-will of gold-rich Paris to persist. On September 3, 1931, Curtius, the foreign minister of the Reich, announced that the controversial project was being dropped. Two days later the world court, by a vote of 8 to 7, condemned the Austro-German scheme. France, Italy and Czechoslovakia exulted. The champions of Anschluss gave free vent to their disappointment and rage. The Reich, they charged in agonized tones, had been given another slap in the face. Who, they queried, was determining German foreign policy? Certainly not the German people. Curtius, disheartened by the turn of events, resigned early in October. Bruening decided to reshuffle his cabinet. From Hindenburg he received authorization to form a new government which, like its predecessor, would be independent of the political parties. But he found it impossible to persuade certain persons to accept the posts which he had marked out for them. He offered the ministry of war to Schleicher, but the latter was not yet disposed to come out into the open. Leading members of the People's party, when approached by Bruening, categorically refused to join the cabinet. Their unwillingness to co-operate reflected the dissatisfaction of heavy industry with certain phases of the government's financial program. No less unyielding was Gessler, whose collaboration Bruening ardently solicited. The former head of the war ministry was in poor health and had no desire to resume the burdens of public office. The cabinet was finally reconstituted on October 9. Wirth and Guérard were dropped. The only newcomer was Professor Hermann Warmbold, a man of conservative outlook who took over the ministry of economics. To his duties as chancellor, Bruening added those of foreign minister. Groener, who remained at his old post, also agreed to assume the ministry of interior which Wirth had vacated. Treviranus was transferred to the ministry of transport.

The second Bruening cabinet evoked little enthusiasm among the Social Democrats. But they consoled themselves with the thought that certain notorious enemies of labor, who had been mentioned as ministerial possibilities, were not in it. The Nazis and the Nationalists made no secret of their displeasure. They denounced the new government as completely unrepresentative of the popular will and prophesied that it would fare no better than its predecessor. Events speedily verified this prophecy. For the travail which seemed fated to be Bruening's lot was far from over. Indeed, worse, much worse, was yet to come.

Less than seven years later Hitler took Austria. He did what democratic Germany had been forbidden to do. The powers that aborted the customs union project in 1931 did nothing to stop the Nazi invaders in 1938. Had Bruening been permitted to have his way, both he and the German republic would have gained sorely needed prestige. The battle against the depression would have been greatly facilitated, especially if other nations had followed the Austro-German example and put an end to their ruinous tariff policies. One of the Reich's principal grievances against the settlement of 1919 would have lost at least some of its acuity. But in 1931, as in the years that followed, the requisite statesmanship and courage were lacking.

3

Harzburg is an unpretentious town in Brunswick. On October 11, 1931, it played host to a great conclave. Represented were the Nazis, the Nationalists, the pan-Germans, the Stahlhelm and the Junker *Landbund*. On hand, too, were generals, admirals, members of princely families and spokesmen for the heavy industry of Rhenish Westphalia. Nothing comparable in the way of a political gathering had taken place in Germany since the days of the November Revolution. Topping the list of prominent personalities was Adolf Hitler. Other notables present were Alfred Hugenberg, Fritz Thyssen, Franz Seldte and Hjalmar Schacht. The purpose of the meeting was to unite all right-wing elements in a common drive to oust the Bruening cabinet and set up a "truly national government." The reasons which led the Nazis to join the other opposition groups were stated by Frick shortly before the proceedings at Harzburg got under way. Fusion of the country's national elements, he explained, was contemplated in order to facilitate the assumption of power by those who were really entitled to govern. True, some members of the party disliked the idea of making common cause with other factions. But these critics were forgetting that in the beginning Mussolini, too, acquiesced in the establishment of a coalition government. The Nazis were prepared to follow his example, and within the union which would result from this decision they, and they alone, would play the leading role. The Bruening cabinet was nearing the end of its rope. But before administering the final blow, the national opposition would have to rally to its cause all those who were still unable to make up their minds.

The Harzburg meeting was opened by Hugenberg. With evident relish the Nationalist leader warmed up to his theme: Germany must be saved from the Red peril. He described Braun and Severing, the principal Social Democratic members of the Prussian cabinet, as "the German Kerenskys." The Reich, he went on, stood at the parting of the ways. It would have to choose either the Russian or the German road. For years the national opposition had cried out against the refusal of successive governments to halt "the bloody terror of Marxism." It had protested against the spread of "cultural Bolshevism," the disintegration caused by the class struggle, the exclusion of the "national forces" from power. It had time and again stressed the iniquity of policies which were devitalizing Germany and subjecting her to alien rule. In order to save the country from Bolshevism and economic bankruptcy, the national opposition was prepared to take over political control in Prussia and in the Reich. It would reject co-operation from no one who honestly wished to help, but it would do nothing which might prolong the life of the Weimar system. It demanded the immediate resignation of the Bruening and Braun cabinets and the issuance of a call for new elections.

Hitler spoke in a similar vein. He predicted that either Bolshevism or nationalism would triumph in Germany. He dwelt at considerable length on the duties of a statesman. The political structure of Germany, he said, must be completely overhauled. He declared that the national opposition did not want war because its leaders were former soldiers who knew what war really meant. But no people could surrender the right to fight to the last man should the necessity for such exertions arise.

At Harzburg a mighty combination was formed. It had wealth, prestige and influence. And, thanks to Hitler, it had numbers, too. The strength it could muster far surpassed that of its principal rival, organized labor. The inexorable growth of mass unemployment, the lack of militant and far-sighted leadership in the trade unions and the perennial feud between Social Democrats and Communists rendered the working-classes of Germany incapable of defending the existing political order. Between the Harzburg Front and power there stood only the wooden giant in the presidential palace. He controlled the Reichswehr, and whoever controlled the Reichswehr controlled the state. He alone, by virtue of his constitutional prerogatives, could invite the leaders of the national opposition to form a government. And it was who could keep a minority cabinet in office by continuing to invoke the authority vested in him by Article 48.

4

The alliance between Hitler and industrialists like Thyssen, Kirdorf and Voegler was strengthened at Harzburg. It was broadened and cemented on January 27, 1932, when the Fuehrer, at Thyssen's invitation, addressed the Industry Club in Duesseldorf. For two and a half hours he harangued the assembled coal and steel barons of western Germany. He sought to dispel once and for all the misgivings engendered in a good many of these men by the radical outpourings of Nazi left-wingers. He was out to prove that the Nazis were safe from the point of view of big business, that their occasional diatribes against "high capitalism," trusts and the "slavery of interest" were just so much electioneering eye-wash and not to be taken seriously. This was Hitler's first contact with the entire body of Rhenish-Westphalian industrialists, and he was resolved to make the most of it.

He told his listeners that any political system which subjected the talented few to the majority could not properly be called the rule of the people. Such a system was in reality the rule of the weak, the stupid, the mediocre and the fainthearted. A nation, he contended, must permit itself to be ruled by its ablest men. Power must not be entrusted to a "chance majority" which of necessity was alien to the tasks of government. Democracy would lead to the "destruction of a people's true values." Countries which surrendered themselves to the rule of the masses were doomed to lose their greatness and ultimately even their ability to defend themselves against the rest of the world.

Private property, Hitler went on, could be justified morally and ethically on the ground that the economic achievements of individuals were not equal. But one could hardly subscribe to this view, he urged, and at the same time hold that men were equal in the political sphere. The principle of inequality that prevailed in the economic realm had to be extended to politics. Failure to do so would result in the transfer of the egalitarian principle from politics to economics. But the economic analogue of political democracy was Communism. Moreover, bungling in the political sphere could destroy even the best economic system. There were no two ways about it: diametrically opposed to each other stood the nefarious principle of democracy and the constructive "principle of the authority of personality" or, better still, the "principle of achievement."

The Fuehrer dwelt at considerable length on the Red menace. Bolshevism, he warned, was "not merely a mob storming about in some of our streets in Germany but . . . a conception of the world which is in the act of subjecting to itself the entire Asiatic continent." Already triumphant in Russia, it would, if not halted, "shatter the whole world" and transform it "as completely as in times past did Christianity." German businessmen would be foolish to underestimate the danger, for in time Russian industry would be able to compete with that of the Reich.

The crisis in which Germany was currently wallowing stemmed, according to Hitler, not only from external causes but from "our internal . . . aberration of spirit, our internal division, our internal collapse." This was clear from the mentality of the nation's unemployed. These millions of human beings were being driven by enforced idleness to regard Bolshevism as the logical outcome of their misery. Emergency decrees could not avert catastrophe. Increased production was not the road to salvation for the simple reason that consumption would always lag behind man's capacity to turn out more goods. Economic crises could be solved not by economic expedients but by the exercise of political power. "It was the power-state," Hitler argued, "which created for the business world the general conditions for its subsequent prosperity." It was putting the cart before the horse to assume that business methods could enable Germany to regain her "power-position." The truth of the matter was that the reacquisition of power would have to precede economic recovery. And, conversely, economic systems went to pieces only after the state, the repository of power, had broken down.

Hitler maintained that a solution would have to be found for the problem created by the division of the German people into patriots and Bolshevists. One half of the nation believed in private property, in the Fatherland, in the state, in courage and in God. The other half maintained that private property was theft, despised the Fatherland, aspired to smash the state, derided courage and repudiated God. German Bolshevists preferred Russia to their own country. For Marxism "knows no German nation, knows no national state, but knows only the International." These internal conflicts, which were devitalizing the nation, could not be overcome by legislative action. What was needed was "a new mental outlook" that would revivify the people. This new outlook was to be found in the National Socialist movement. Without the Nazis and their mighty organizational apparatus, Germany ere now would have fallen prey to Bolshevism. Patriotic Germans ought no longer to be in doubt regarding their

attitude toward a party which practised what it preached, which
stood for nationalism and strong leadership, which repudiated internationalism and democracy, which acknowledged "only the principles of
responsibility, command and obedience." The National Socialist
movement was inexorably resolved to extirpate Marxism in Germany.
For twelve years it had been engaged in this struggle. It was prepared
to continue it on an even larger scale.[1]

Today we stand at the turning-point of Germany's destiny. . . . Either
we shall succeed in working out a body-politic hard as iron from this con-
glomerate of parties, associations, unions and conceptions of the world, from
this pride of rank and madness of class, or else, lacking this internal consolidation, Germany will fall into final ruin. . . . Today no one can escape the
obligation to complete the regeneration of the German body-politic. Every
one must show his personal sympathy, must take his place in the common
effort. If I speak to you today it is not to ask for your votes or to induce
you on my account to do this or that for the party. No, I am here to ex-
pound a point of view, and I am convinced that the victory of this point of
view would mean the only possible starting-point for a German recovery.

The all-important thing, Hitler reiterated, was to lead the nation back
to faith and ideals. For once that had been done, Germans would pay
less attention to their material privation. Proof of this was to be found
in the self-sacrificing attitude of the young men who composed the
SA and the SS. If the faith which inspired them were shared by the
rest of the nation, the salvation of Germany would be assured.

Hitler's speech, judged in terms of what it was designed to do, was
an astute performance. And it was remarkably effective. It won him
the financial support of Germany's most powerful industrialists. Till
now, only a handful of the nation's plutocrats had been in his corner.
After the Duesseldorf speech, practically all Rhenish-Westphalian captains of industry were rooting for him. They were convinced that
Hitler was their man. True, he had his peculiarities; many of his
closest associates were disreputable characters; his brown-shirted minions were given to gangsterism. But the fact remained that he could
be trusted to defend the propertied classes against the surge of radicalism from below. More than that, he was committed to a dynamic
offensive against political democracy; and if he were successful, the
men at the top of the economic hierarchy would have at their disposal
an authoritarian regime which would not rest until Marxism and Bol-

---

[1] Quoted in *The Speeches of Adolf Hitler April 1922-August 1939*, by Norman H.
Baynes (Oxford University Press).

shevism had been destroyed root and branch. The dangers stemming from the presence of millions of unemployed would be removed. Freedom of enterprise would be assured. So would unhindered exploitation of labor and accumulation of profits. Judged in terms of results, the Duesseldorf speech was one of Hitler's greatest triumphs. It gave his movement, already anchored in the lower middle class, access to the wealth and influence of the nation's top strata. There were still hurdles to surmount on the road that led to power, but the distance that separated the Nazis from their goal had been perceptibly shortened. Little wonder then that January 27, 1932, has been called by Nazi spokesmen "a memorable day in the history of the NSDAP."

Chapter 34

HINDENBURG'S RE-ELECTION AND THE
ADVANCE OF THE NAZI TIDE

I

THE formation of the Harzburg Front posed a mighty threat to the position of Bruening. But another and even more immediate danger was beginning to take shape. Schleicher, who at one time had hoped to build a new and powerful movement around the Centrist leader, was now of a different mind. The poor showing of the Conservative People's party in the elections of 1930 and Bruening's refusal to give cabinet posts to Nazis apparently convinced the general that he would have to find some other way to accomplish his designs. In the opinion of Schleicher, the Reichswehr "could not wage a war on two fronts." It could not, at one and the same time, smash Bolshevism and curb the Nazis. The latter would have to be invited to co-operate with all the other "national" forces in the land. They would have to be offered a certain number of places in the cabinet of the Reich. Schleicher himself had divided feelings about the Hitlerites. He still wished to deflate them by maneuvering them into an assumption of at least some of the responsibility for unpopular governmental policies. But he also persuaded himself that, under proper tutelage and control, they might become a positive, constructive force.

Toward the close of 1931, Schleicher began to undermine Bruening's position. Simultaneously, he sought to strengthen his own forces. He cultivated the good-will of the press and tightened his hold on certain of the federal ministries. He also established closer relations with right-wing intellectuals, notably those who wrote for magazines like *Die Tat* and *Der Widerstand*. The influence he wielded in the presidential palace was, of course, his most formidable weapon. He made ready to use it at the earliest possible moment. Bruening's political troubles were enhanced by further aggravation of the nation's economic ills. Early in December, 1931, the number of unemployed passed the five-million mark and gave every indication of going far beyond that figure. On December 8 Hindenburg signed an emergency decree "for securing the national economy and finances and preserving the public peace." It instituted further reductions in prices, wages, salaries and interest rates and increased the turnover tax. This marked what the government described as the final step in the policy of deflation. Section II of the decree forbade the wearing of political uniforms and insignia. It also tightened existing regulations in regard to the possession of arms. In an address to the nation, Bruening explained and defended the provisions of this measure. He urged upon foreign governments the need for united action in dealing with the world economic crisis. Partial solutions, he warned, would do more harm than good. The next few weeks would prove decisive. The tendency of each country to barricade itself behind tariff walls was intensifying the economic difficulties of all. What was needed was an international understanding, but until it was reached, each government would have to follow the course marked out for it by economic realities within its own frontiers. To his own compatriots he addressed the following warning:

The inclination toward a purely emotional consideration of policies must not prevail over calm reflection. . . . Should Germany attempt to pursue unattainable objectives, she would destroy herself. . . . The government must not and will not shrink from combating with iron energy the threatening disintegration of the nation's strength. It will tolerate no power other than the constitutional one. The president and government of the Reich alone exercise power. It will be invoked with ruthless severity, even to the extent of proclaiming martial law, if necessary, against all who attack the constitutional authorities. The leader of the National Socialist party stressed the legality of his political methods and aims. But in the sharpest possible contrast with his words stand the violent assertions of other equally responsible leaders of the party who incite to senseless civil war at home and foolish moves abroad. When a man declares that once he has achieved power by legal means, he will break through the barriers, he is not really adhering to legality. . . . As a responsible statesman I protest most vigorously against such a view.

Hitler was stung by Bruening's rebuke. Should the German people, he retorted, authorize the National Socialists to introduce a new constitution, Bruening would not be able to stop them. When a constitution outlived its usefulness, it was modified. But while they were struggling for power, he and his followers would remain within the bounds of legality. Hitler's attitude irked some of the secondary leaders of the party. They preferred a march on Berlin. But the Fuehrer had not forgotten the beer-hall fiasco of 1923 and did not relish the idea of another putsch. He was convinced that the methods he was now employing would, in the end, pay the highest political dividends. So he urged the fire-eaters in his entourage to be patient. The day of peaceful accession to power, he told them, would not be long in coming.

2

The question of the next presidential election loomed on the nation's horizon. High government officials were visibly disturbed. They dreaded the thought of an election at this time. Political extremism was so rampant that almost anything might happen. Besides, an election was an expense which the Reich could ill afford. The country must be spared this ordeal. It must not be thrown into a turmoil at a moment when it so urgently needed unity and calm. In the opinion of Bruening and his associates, there was only one thing to do: prolong Hindenburg's term of office for a year or two until the nation had had a chance to surmount its economic difficulties and regain some measure of composure. The idea was sound but not easy to execute. Extension of Hindenburg's term beyond the legal seven years had to be sanctioned by the Reichstag. Moreover, because such legislation was in the nature of an amendment to the constitution, it would require a two-thirds majority. To get that many votes, the government would need the support of the Nazi deputies, something it had been unable to secure for any of its measures.

Bruening decided to talk to Hitler, to put the matter up to him in such a way as to make refusal difficult. He saw the Fuehrer on January 7, 1932. The interview proved inconclusive. Hitler reserved his reply in order to give himself a chance to discuss the matter with Hugenberg. The latter strongly opposed prolongation of Hindenburg's term. He argued that it would constitute a demonstration of confidence in Bruening and strengthen his position. Hitler conferred with his lieutenants, who showered him with divergent counsels. One group, contending that Hindenburg would be unbeatable in any contest for popular favor, urged that the future of the party would be better served by agreeing to a political truce. This was violently contradicted by other Nazi leaders, who argued that the party would do itself incalculable harm if it eschewed a chance to go before the people. The man who took the lead in pressing this view was Roehm, and eventually his exhortations prevailed. In a note which he addressed to Bruening, Hitler stated that he was unable to comply with the government's request. He contended that the proposed extension of Hindenburg's term of office would be a violation of the constitution. Moreover, the present Reichstag was no longer a true expression of the popular will. Hitler took exception to the argument, advanced by Bruening when the two men conferred in Berlin, that considerations of foreign policy (above all, the need to insure the success of the current negotiations in regard to reparation) made it inadvisable to hold a presidential election at this time. He charged that the anxiety of the Bruening government to postpone the election stemmed from "motives of political self-preservation." In Hitler's view, the very circumstances adduced by the government in support of its negative position rendered the election "an urgent necessity." With brutal frankness he described as beneficial to German foreign policy any development that might precipitate the downfall of the existing political system. Simultaneously, he warned that if Bruening did not resign, the Nazis would enter the contest for the presidency. And, momentarily forgetting his much publicized resolve to gain power by legal means, he declared in an address at Munich: "If the present regime does not make way for us, we will remove it."

Hitler's attitude forced the country to subject itself to the excitement and expense of a presidential election. The field marshal, showing his eighty-four years and weary of office, had to be persuaded by his advisers to stand for re-election. Bruening offered to resign in an effort to induce the Nazis and the Nationalists to support Hindenburg. But, in return for such support, the Nazis demanded control of the government. Hindenburg, who had conceived a violent dislike for Hitler, flatly refused. Bruening girded himself for the battle with extraordinary enthusiasm. His main concern was to keep Hitler permanently out of power. He looked beyond Hindenburg's expected victory at the polls. The field marshal's death had to be reckoned with as a none too distant possibility. Before it occurred, something would have to be done to wreck Hitler's chances forever. Following this train of thought, Bruening urged the establishment of a constitutional monarchy patterned on British lines. The throne, he suggested, should go to one of the sons of the former Crown Prince. But nothing was done to effectuate this plan.

Nazi spokesmen affected, from the very outset, complete confidence regarding the outcome of the presidental contest. They claimed no less than twenty million voters. Privately, however, they conceded that their chances were none too good. Influential members of the party urged Hitler to run for the presidency. The Fuehrer was personally opposed to the idea, since defeat was likely to diminish his prestige. It seemed smarter politics to put up a secondary leader—someone like Frick, for example. On February 15, 1932, while the Nazis were pondering questions of strategy, Hindenburg formally announced that he would be a candidate for re-election. He said:

> The fact that the request that I should do so has reached me not from a party but from wide sections of the community causes me to look upon my declaration of consent in the light of a duty.

The Nationalists and the Nazis promptly berated him for his decision to run under the auspices of the pro-republican elements. The Communists likewise voiced their disapproval. But all the other parties came out squarely for the field marshal. The Social Democrats declared that the central issue was the battle against Fascism. Accordingly, they were prepared to support Hindenburg with all the resources at their command.

On February 22, 1932, Goebbels announced at a Nazi meeting in Berlin that Hitler would be the party's candidate. Since German citizenship was a prerequisite, the government of Brunswick, which was now controlled by the National Socialists, appointed Hitler to an official post on February 25. This automatically made him a subject of the Reich. The Stahlhelm's second-in-command, Colonel Theodor Duesterberg, was the choice of the Nationalists. These old-line conservatives preferred Hitler to Hindenburg, but decided to run their own candidate in the hope of increasing the strength of their party. Thaelmann was once again the Communist standard-bearer. A fifth candidate in the person of Gustav Winter entered the race. Winter represented a small group that demanded the revalorization of pre-inflation bank notes.

The contest between Hindenburg and Hitler caused tremendous excitement. The Nazis fought with their usual resourcefulness and pugnacity. Bruening bore the brunt of the campaign for Hindenburg.

He rose to the occasion with leonine energy. Centrists, socialists and liberals worked wholeheartedly with him. The trade unions proved a tower of strength. All upholders of democracy were unanimous in regarding the aged president, whom they had tried so hard to defeat in 1925, as the white hope of the republic. Government spokesmen counted on the magic of his name. Hard times and mass unemployment were on the side of the Nazis. They were also on the side of the Communists. Only the Nationalists could expect no profit from the unprecedented crisis through which Germany was passing.

Bruening made a number of speeches in Hindenburg's behalf. One of his major addresses was delivered at Duesseldorf on March 8, 1932. On this occasion, he declared that if Germany were not in such difficult straits, he would have turned the government over to the parties of the Right. But in view of the unfulfillable promises made by the spokesmen of those parties, the bulk of the nation would very likely refuse to support them. The masses, he feared, might then go over to the Communists. Two days later, Hindenburg addressed the nation. He stressed the point that he had decided to run only after careful reflection and in the belief that it was his patriotic duty to do so. A negative decision, he said, would have paved the way for the election of either Hitler or Thaelmann. Such a calamity had to be prevented.

The voting took place on March 13, 1932. The results were as follows:

Hindenburg	18,661,736
Hitler	11,338,571
Thaelmann	4,982,079
Duesterberg	2,557,876
Winter	111,470

Hindenburg failed by four tenths of one per cent to secure an absolute majority. Hitler's total was impressive. But even if he were to get all of Duesterberg's votes in the run-off contest, he would still be far behind Hindenburg. The result in Greater Berlin was especially interesting. Here Hindenburg ran far ahead of all his rivals, but Thaelmann received nearly 30,000 more votes than Hitler. Nevertheless, the Nazis were justified in regarding the outcome as an important landmark in the growth of their movement. They had obtained almost five million additional adherents since the Reichstag elections of 1930. This was a gain of close to eighty per cent. But many neutral observers believed that they had reached their peak. The Nazis paid no heed to such talk. Affecting a confidence they could scarcely have felt, they predicted a clear-cut victory for Hitler in the second election. The Communist party, surprisingly enough, appeared to have made but little progress since September, 1930. Despite eighteen months of acute economic depression, the Bolshevist cause had won considerably less than half a million new converts.

The German people returned to the polls on April 10, 1932. The Nationalists withdrew their candidate and gave their blessing to Hitler. Thaelmann remained in the contest. Although Hindenburg's supporters knew the president was sure to win, they endeavored to pile up as big a vote as possible. They were thinking of the moral effect which a crushing victory would have upon the Nazis. The latter, for their part, worked zealously to better their showing. This they did in order to be in a position to claim that their movement was still moving forward. They were also anxious to bolster their own spirits for the impending elections in Prussia and in other states of the Reich. The outcome, as expected, was a victory for Hindenburg. He boosted his total to 19,360,000. But this represented an increase of only 700,000. The Nazis, on the other hand, professed themselves eminently satisfied. The Fuehrer had emerged with 13,400,000 supporters: a gain of two million in less than a month. And since part of the Nationalist vote went to the field marshal and something like a million Communist votes disappeared altogether, the Nazi gain took on added significance. The elections results seemed to give the lie to Hitler's contention that Germany had to be rescued from the Red peril. Nevertheless, fear of Bolshevism continued to permeate the upper strata of German society.

Enough Germans had voted for Hindenburg to give him a majority of roughly 2,000,000 over the combined Hitler-Thaelmann following. His elevation to the presidency for a second term caused the democratic elements in the country to breathe a sigh of relief. These people were living in a dream world. So anxious were they to believe in Hindenburg that they shut their eyes to certain unpleasant truths. The chief of these was that the old man had become the spearhead of the conservative counterrevolution. He was now completely under the thumb of the Junkers and the militarists. He shared their conception of government and society. Like them he clung to the old Prussian ideals of authority, hierarchy and discipline. But the friends of democracy continued to view him in a vastly different light. They deluded themselves into believing that with him standing guard, the republic would have a fighting chance to hold its enemies at bay. They looked to him for leadership in the troubled days ahead. They were ready to support him with all the resources at their command. Their only fear was that he might die before the battle for democracy reached its crucial phase. His life and that of the republic seemed to hang by the same slender thread. The march of events was soon to shatter this colossal self-deception.

3

On the morrow of Hindenburg's re-election, the government gave a short-lived demonstration of vigor. For some time, the ministers of the interior of most of the German states had been urging Groener to dissolve the SA and SS. They insisted that there was no other way to halt the wave of unbridled gangsterism which everywhere was undermining respect for law and order. Schleicher advised Groener to comply with this request. The matter was laid before Bruening, who decided to take the action demanded. His decision received the unanimous approval of the cabinet. On April 13, 1932, Hindenburg signed an emergency decree "for the safeguarding of the authority of the state." This measure, which was countersigned by Bruening and Groener, ordered the immediate dissolution of all Nazi military organizations. The official explanation stressed the fact that the SA and the SS constituted a private army and as such were inimical to public order and safety.

The mere existence of such a fighting organization, which forms a "state within a state," is . . . a source of constant disturbance for peaceful citizens. . . . It is exclusively the business of the state to maintain organized forces. The toleration of such a partisan organization . . . inevitably leads to clashes and to conditions comparable with civil war. . . . Any private organization of this kind is essentially illegal. Moreover, there is always the danger that such an organization, owing to its nature, may some day drag the party into illegal activities.

Hitler irately declared that the Nazi reply to this decree would be "not a parade but a kick." The day of retribution, he warned, would be April 24, when the Prussian elections were scheduled to take place. The Nazis exploited to the full the "persecution" of their movement. They presented themselves to the nation as martyrs being crucified by Bruening and used this lachrymose line to bolster their campaign in Prussia. Would the same fate, people wondered, overtake the Reichsbanner? The Nazis and the Nationalists were demanding the dissolution of this organization; but the latter, in an effort to forestall such action, promptly disbanded its semi-military formations. Nevertheless, pressure was exerted on Hindenburg, and the president, in a letter which was made public, asked Groener to look into the matter and make appropriate recommendations. Bruening and Groener agreed that the Reichsbanner, which was very different from the SA and the SS, which respected law and order and supported the existing regime, should not be dissolved, especially after it had voluntarily disbanded its semi-military formations. But they decided to place all organizations which continued to maintain military formations of any kind under the control of the Reich ministry of the interior.

The somewhat unfriendly tone of the president's letter to Groener and the fact that it was made public testified to the existence of a rift between Hindenburg and Groener which was manifestly due to Schleicher's intrigues. For Schleicher was now working not only against Bruening but against Groener, too. As a matter of fact, after the issuance of the decree dissolving the SA and the SS, Schleicher and his henchman, General von Hammerstein-Equord, informed Groener in rather peremptory fashion that the Reichswehr no longer trusted him. Schleicher, who had recommended the action against Hitler's private army, thus abruptly reversed himself. Behind closed doors he pronounced the step unwise and accused Bruening of having committed a serious blunder. He told Hindenburg that Groener and Bruening had played directly into Hitler's hands. The field marshal allowed himself to be convinced that they had made a fool of him, that they had deliberately forced him into an untenable position by getting him to sign the anti-Nazi decree.

4

In the meantime, the campaign in Prussia had gone into high gear. The Nazis made all sorts of vague promises and carefully shunned definite commitments. They led each of their prospective converts to believe that he would get what he wanted if Hitler's candidates won. Monarchists dreamed of a return of the Hohenzollerns through the presidency. Landowners were cajoled into thinking that they would be able to get rid of their mortgages. Industrialists had visions of a disrupted labor movement and higher profits. Civil servants hoped for increased pay. Small shopkeepers were encouraged to assume that they would no longer have to worry about the department stores.

Former Communists were enticed by the possibility of some form of "national" Bolshevism.

The elections took place on April 24, 1932. The Nazis scored a tremendous success in Prussia, Bavaria, Wuerttemberg, Anhalt and Hamburg—together, about four-fifths of the Reich. Most important, of course, was the result in Prussia, where approximately 420 Diet seats were divided as follows:

Nazis	162
Nationalists	31
Social Democrats	93
Center	67
Communists	57
People's party	7
State party	2

The Nazis and the Center had between them a clear majority. Hitler, as the leader of the strongest party, promptly claimed the right to govern in Prussia. The Center announced that it was prepared to co-operate with any group which was willing "to serve the welfare of the whole nation on the basis of the constitution." It insisted that it would continue to oppose any arrangement which might lead to the establishment of a party dictatorship. But since this was the admitted aim of the Nazis, a parliamentary impasse ensued. As a consequence, the Braun cabinet, resting on the Centrist-Social Democratic coalition, remained in office for the time-being.

Chapter 35

PAPEN SUCCEEDS BRUENING

I

WITH the Nazis growing constantly stronger and with Schleicher intriguing against him, Bruening's prospects seemed bleak indeed. The domestic situation offered not a single ray of hope. The number of unemployed was in the neighborhood of six million. The budgetary deficit attained gigantic proportions. Foreign affairs presented a less discouraging picture. A spectacular triumph, such as he had vainly sought in the field of Austro-German relations, still seemed within the realm of possibility. Two vital international issues were on the tapis: the reparation problem and the German demand for parity in armaments. A victory for Bruening in both or either of these questions would do much to restore his prestige.

Germany's economic plight made it unlikely that she would be able to resume reparation payments upon the expiration of the Hoover moratorium. This view was not confined to Germans. It was shared by Allied fiscal experts. There was therefore good reason to suppose that reparation payments would be canceled altogether. This was Bruening's avowed goal. Its attainment would ease the Reich's financial situation; and the nation would know whom to thank. The readiness of foreign circles to concede the fairness of Germany's demand placed Bruening within sight of his objective. But his hopes were blasted by the Allied decision to postpone the reparation conference until June, 1932. Not Bruening but his anti-republican successor was to be the recipient of Allied favors. Deprived of the triumph he so desperately needed, Bruening attempted to make the most of his own spirited stand for total cancellation. With an eye to domestic opinion he asserted in unequivocal terms that Germany would be unable to meet her reparation obligations when the moratorium expired. But his countrymen were not impressed. They had heard similar statements before. They wanted action, not words.

Early in February, 1932, the first general disarmament conference met in Geneva. Germany demanded recognition of her right to equality in armaments. The French objected and a deadlock ensued. Weeks and even months went by as the futile wrangling continued. Bruening, however, did not give up. Eventually, his labors bore fruit. But just as he seemed on the verge of securing important concessions, he was balked here, too, by the long arm of Schleicher. The latter told the French ambassador in Berlin that Bruening was about to fall and that therefore there was no point in negotiating with him. Tardieu, the French premier, was none too keen to accommodate Bruening. Besides, he was in the midst of a preelection campaign and wished to give it his undivided attention. So he welcomed Schleicher's admonition. He proceeded to make a great deal more of an attack of laryngitis than he might have done had no encouragement come from Berlin. He refused to go to Geneva, where Bruening and the representatives of the other powers had been conferring. Without France nothing could be accomplished. So the chancellor returned to Germany empty-handed. His last trump was gone.

2

The climactic crisis in Bruening's career as chancellor was ushered in on May 12, 1932, when the no-confidence motion offered by the opposition parties was defeated in the Reichstag by a vote of 287 to 257. The Centrist-Social Democratic coalition was still functioning effectively. On the same day, however, it was announced that Groener was going to resign as minister of war. But he would continue as minister of the interior. Groener's departure from the post which controlled the Reichswehr was a victory for Schleicher. It was also a victory for the Nazis, who had been violently assailing the general for his action against the SA and the SS. They jubilantly hailed his resignation as the "beginning of the end of the November system."

Bruening's enemies readied themselves for the kill. Schleicher warned Hindenburg that the chancellor's policies were socialistic. He contended that Bruening was unable to handle the Nazis. The job, he said, required someone far stronger. Important Ruhr industrialists helped to tighten the noose around Bruening's neck by complaining of his attempts to keep prices down. They also railed against the social policies sponsored by Stegerwald, Bruening's labor minister and a stanch trade-unionist. Bruening himself quickened the tempo of the conspiracy by suggesting that some of the insolvent estates in East Prussia be partitioned to provide relief for the jobless. At once the field marshal's Junker neighbors denounced the plan as "agrarian Bolshevism." Through Oskar Hindenburg, they brought great pressure to bear on the president. The latter, who loved his own estate at Neudeck, needed little persuading to embrace the view that Bruening's scheme was utterly subversive.

The end came with dramatic suddenness. On May 29, 1932, Hindenburg asked Bruening to resign. The Centrist leader complied the following day. He was the first chancellor of the republic to resign because he did not have the president's confidence, just as he had been the first chancellor to hold office on the strength of that confidence. All preceding chancellors had resigned when the majority in the Reichstag refused to support them or when it was clear that a majority would be unobtainable. Now, however, presidential absolutism was a basic feature of German political life. For two years Bruening had struggled to bring order out of chaos. He succumbed to an overwhelming combination of circumstances and forces, but only after he had given an unforgettable demonstration of tenacity and resourcefulness. His efforts at home were stymied by the worst economic crisis in the nation's history. He was hounded by foes who kept yapping at his heels and exulted in his every misfortune. From the heads of other nations he obtained scant satisfaction. And even when he had managed, after much time and effort, to achieve the virtual cancellation of reparation, the fruits of this success were denied him. When the curtain was finally rung down on his ill-starred career, few there were to sing his praises.

The dismissal of Bruening sealed the fate of German democracy. True, he had not hesitated to govern in undemocratic fashion and to defy the representatives of the people. He had been sustained in office by the forces of reaction and had permitted himself to be used by them for their own purposes. But he believed in the democratic principle and hoped to see it resurrected when the need for emergency measures had vanished. From time to time he had managed to obtain a parliamentary majority. Indeed, his was the last government to receive the backing, however intermittently and reluctantly vouchsafed, of a freely elected Reichstag majority. Thereafter popular rule, already undermined by resort to presidential fiat, became a mockery. More elections were held, but the voice of the people was no longer the voice of God. The republic was betrayed by its chief executive who less than two months earlier had been re-elected to protect it. It was ground under foot by the Junker-militarist-industrialist clique before Hitler took over.

3

Colonel Franz von Papen was fifty-three years old in 1932. He had wit, charm and savoir faire. He was a great favorite at the aristocratic *Herrenklub* in Berlin where his talents as a conversationalist stood him in excellent stead. He was very rich. His family belonged to the Catholic nobility of Westphalia. By marriage he acquired considerable industrial interests in the Saar. Like most members of his class he went into the army as a matter of course. During the war he served as German military attaché in Washington. He filled this post with more zeal than wisdom. He engaged in illegal activities and even lent himself to conspiracies against the United States. His repeated violations of American neutrality finally caught up with him. He was recalled at the request of President Wilson. The charge was sabotage.

Papen continued to dabble in politics after the advent of the republic. He belonged to the ultra-conservative wing of the Center and was part owner of *Germania,* its principal organ. He was a member of the Prussian Diet from 1921 until April, 1932. He frowned on the pro-republican attitude of most of his party comrades. He condemned their practise of collaborating with socialists and liberals. For years he tried to get them to abandon this practise and to align themselves with the reactionary parties. Like his fellow-aristocrats, he affected great alarm over "cultural Bolshevism," a catchall covering everything the old ruling classes disliked. His holdings in the Saar led him to look kindly on the idea of a Franco-German rapprochement. He wanted to make diplomacy the handmaiden of property rights. But this bending of the knee to economic realities failed to separate him from the irreconcilables who talked only about avenging the defeat of 1918.

Papen was extremely popular in his own set. But even his best friends hardly thought him cut out for a brilliant political career. Statesmanship was not his long suit. He rose above the run-of-the-mine members of his class only because Schleicher decided that he should. The gray eminence of the war ministry was constantly on the lookout for new puppets. The Westphalian aristocrat caught his eye. He seemed to have the making of an ideal tool. Schleicher was still reluctant to step too far into the limelight. He did not want the chancellorship for himself. He preferred to give it to a pliable henchman because power without responsibility continued to be his objective. As his plot against Bruening thickened, he began to point to Papen as the man of the hour, God's gift to Germany. He sang his praises before the people who counted: Hindenburg, Hugenberg, Hitler, leaders of the Junker *Landbund*, army chieftains. The president took an instant liking to Schleicher's new protégé. The way was smoothed for Papen's assumption of the chancellorship. But one big hurdle still remained to be cleared: the obstructionist attitude of the Nazis. Hitler seemed intent on going his own way, shunning all commitments which might jeopardize his freedom of action. He wanted supreme power for himself and realized that his chances of obtaining it would be endangered if he consented to entangling alliances. His cue was to stick to his purely negative line, denouncing, attacking everything and everyone. But without Nazi support or sufferance, Papen would find himself walking a political tightrope. The Centrists and the Social Democrats were sure to make trouble, while the Hugenberg Nationalists, his only trustworthy allies, were of dubious value because they were slipping fast.

Schleicher made good use of his contacts with the Nazis. He told them of his plan to oust Bruening and install a cabinet made up exclusively of Hindenburg's friends. He promised that the ban on the SA would be lifted. The Reichstag would be dissolved. The Nazis would be left free to carry on exactly as they pleased in the pre-election campaign. Hitler saw a chance to turn the tables on Schleicher, to be the user instead of the used. He accepted the general's offer. He agreed to "tolerate" Bruening's successor. But he had no intention of keeping his word. He expected the new elections to swell his parliamentary representation mightily. He would then hold the whip-hand. But Schleicher was not altogether deceived. He had no intention of standing idly by while the Hitlerites moved toward new triumphs. On the eve of Bruening's dismissal, he assured Hindenburg that the new government would either control the Nazis or destroy them.

4

Papen became chancellor on May 31, 1932. He packed his cabinet with titled reactionaries from the *Herrenklub*. The list of appointments read so much like a page out of the German nobility's "Who's Who?" that the public dubbed Papen and his colleagues the "Almanach de Gotha" cabinet. Militarists and industrialists were likewise well represented. It was in theory a non-party cabinet, but actually most of its members had been active Nationalists under Hugenberg. The dominant member of the government was Schleicher, who finally came out into the open and assumed the ministry of war. Professor Warmbold, who was connected with the German Dye Trust, retained his post as minister of economics. Hugo Schaeffer, the new labor minister, was a director of the Krupp firm. The ministry of the interior went to the East Prussian Junker, Baron Wilhelm von Gayl, who had been a leader of the Free Corps in 1919. Baron Magnus von Braun was the new minister of food and agriculture. Clearly, the ruling classes of the pre-1918 period were back in the political saddle. The government contained not a single representative of labor; this was something unique in the annals of the German republic.

The reaction to the new cabinet was intensely unfavorable. The Center did not dissemble its hostility. It publicly disavowed Papen, who thereupon resigned from the board of the *Germania*. The Social Democrats charged that the new masters of the Reich were planning to abolish unemployment insurance and the collective wage agreement. Germany, according to the Communists, was now under the heel of an out-and-out dictatorship. Even some of the Nationalist papers were unfriendly. One of them went so far as to attack Papen because of his association with French capitalists; another flatly asserted that the Nationalist party had had nothing to do with the formation of this cabinet of barons. The Nazis, for their part, dismissed the new government as a purely transitional one.

It was clearly Schleicher's purpose to create a broad national front of all non-Marxist elements, including the Nazis. Thus on June 2, 1932, Papen expounded to the country Hindenburg's belief that the burdens being imposed on the German people could be borne only if "all the spiritual forces to be found in Germany" were united. On the following day Schleicher himself issued the following proclamation to the Reichswehr:

I shall devote my strength to making the Reichswehr capable of defending Germany's frontiers and insuring the national security. I shall further see to it that those spiritual and physical forces in our people which form the indispensable foundation of the country's defense are strengthened.

5

On June 4, 1932, on the advice of the cabinet, Hindenburg dissolved the Reichstag, thus fulfilling the promise made to the Nazis. The reason given for this action was that the Reichstag no longer reflected the national will. Simultaneously, Papen issued a proclamation to the country. The government, he stated, was seeking to effect an amalgamation of all the patriotic elements in the country. Germany had been brought to financial ruin by the Treaty of Versailles, by the economic crisis and by "the mismanagement of parliamentary democracy." Successive governments had endeavored to help both capital and labor by means of more and more state socialism. They had attempted to convert the state into "a kind of welfare institute" and thus had undermined the nation's moral strength. This "moral disintegration of the people, aggravated by class warfare and cultural Bolshevism," would have to be checked.

The entire tone of Papen's proclamation was Nazi. He was obviously trying to placate Hitler by talking his language. He was also attempting to steal the Nazis' thunder. His slurring allusions to the "charity state" infuriated the Social Democrats. They declared war to the hilt against this "little clique of feudal monarchists, come to power by backstairs methods with Hitlerist help, which now announces the class-war from above."

The Nazis, in the meanwhile, chafed at the government's delay in lifting the ban on the SA and SS. On June 14, 1932, the *Angriff* warned that National Socialist toleration of the government would end suddenly unless the matter was attended to instantly. Further threats proved unnecessary. On the following day, Hindenburg fulfilled the second part of the bargain with the Nazis by removing the prohibition against Hitler's military formations. The entire cabinet shared Schleicher's belief that the Nazis could not be suppressed but that they could be controlled and exploited. The general persisted in regarding National Socialism as a movement that might be made to serve the best interests of the Fatherland.

The Nazis had gotten what they wanted. They refused, nonetheless, to change their tactics. On June 23, 1932, the *Angriff* violently assailed the government's plan to reduce unemployment payments and impose new taxes. This was good electioneering strategy, but it was hardly compatible with the promise given by the Nazis before Papen's accession. Goebbels made his party's stand crystal-clear. The Nazis, he said, did not create the Papen cabinet; they were therefore not disposed to tolerate it. They had not fought for power all these years merely to help others take over the government.

Hitler and his aids boasted that they had a chance to win more than one half of the electorate in the forthcoming contest. But Schleicher and Papen did not think so. This was basic to their calculations. They conceded that National Socialism was very strong, but they clung to the belief that it would be unable to capture a majority of the voters. If they were right, Hitler would have to come to them if he wished to share power. They could then lay down their conditions. Thus the Nazis, once they joined the cabinet, would remain under the control of Schleicher and his conservative friends. The latter believed that Hitler would accept such an arrangement if his party failed to win a majority in the elections. They assumed that the office-hungry Nazis would decide that half a loaf was better than none.

6

The political situation was complicated at this moment by indications that the chancellor was preparing to intervene in the Prussian muddle. Shortly after taking office, Papen asked the Prussian Diet to elect a premier without delay. Braun was still carrying on pending the formation of a new government. But action on this issue continued to be blocked by the inability of the Nazis and the Centrists to reach a mutually satisfactory accord. Papen knew full well that the prevailing impasse in Prussia made compliance with his demand impossible, since no party or group of parties in the Diet was capable of mustering a stable majority. Papen's purpose was to precipitate a crisis and then make it a pretext for appointing a commissioner who would govern Prussia in the name of the Reich. He would thus bring the powerful Prussian police under the control of the federal government and deprive the Social Democratic party of its last political stronghold. When informed of Papen's démarche in Prussia, the other German states at once became uneasy and voiced the fear that the remnants of their independence were going to be taken away from them. They were not reassured by the persistence of the impasse in the Prussian Diet, which, at the insistence of the Nazis, once again postponed the election of a new premier in spite of Papen's demand for quick action. The pretext for intervention remained, and that it would be utilized before long could scarcely be doubted.

7

An important international conference opened in Lausanne on June 16, 1932. One of its aims was to achieve a final settlement of the vexatious reparation problem. The Germans and the French engaged in one of their habitual diplomatic wrangles. The Papen government, pointing to the Reich's economic and financial difficulties, demanded the complete cancellation of reparation payments. France demurred. She wanted to see the Young plan formally continued but admitted that the payments would have to be drastically reduced. The controversy waxed hot and heavy, and for a time it looked as if the conferees would have to go home with their business still unfinished. In the end common sense prevailed. A compromise solution was adopted on July 9. The creditor states agreed to discard the Young plan in return for a promise by Germany to pay three billion gold marks into a general fund for European reconstruction. The Lausanne settlement rang down the curtain on the reparation imbroglio. It was the last in the series of Allied recessions from the claims originally made upon Germany.

Papen emphasized the magnitude of this victory in an effort to improve his government's chances in the forthcoming elections. The fate of Germany, he declared somewhat grandiloquently in a public address, had hung in the balance. However, everything had gone well at Lausanne. Reparation and the Young plan had been discarded. There remained, to be sure, the obligation to pay a maximum of three billion gold marks. But this money would benefit Germany as well as other countries. Besides, it was to be payable by means of special German bonds which were to be issued only after economic equilibrium had been restored in the Reich. Papen also took this opportunity to claim equality of rights for Germany. He said that the question of war guilt had been discussed by spokesmen for the various governments, and although no general willingness to accept Germany's thesis had been shown, the issue had been definitely placed before the world.

Most Germans realized that the virtual cancellation of reparation so soon after the adoption of the Young plan constituted a significant triumph. But the Nazis refused to concede anything of the sort. They bitterly assailed the Lausanne agreement. They vowed that they would never recognize this "new tribute pact," which was described as "catastrophic" by the *Angriff*. To have taken any other line would have weakened their bid for support from all disgruntled elements in the Reich.

Chapter 36

PAPEN'S COUP IN PRUSSIA AND THE
ELECTIONS OF JULY, 1932

I

THE weeks which preceded the Reichstag elections were hectic. Political murder and assault on an unprecedented scale were reported from every part of the country. As usual, the disturbances were highlighted by clashes between Nazis and Communists, and once again it was the men of the swastika who were the chief trouble-makers. But this did not prevent them from claiming that they were the innocent victims of Bolshevist gangsterism. They charged that the Communists, with Russian members of the Cheka at their head, were launching a reign of terror. The Nazis clamored for a free hand in order to protect themselves against these "unprovoked" attacks. They contended that the police had lost control of the situation and insisted that the Storm Troops be given permission "to clear the streets." They also demanded the suppression of the Communist party. Hitler's hoodlums did not confine their brutalities to Reds. They clashed with members of the Reichsbanner and attacked the editorial offices of the *Vorwaerts*. The republicans and their adversaries staged numerous parades. In one demonstration uniformed Nazis and Stahlhelm men marched with a Reichswehr battalion past a group of reviewers which included the divisional commander and Lieutenant-General Fedor von Bock, who represented Schleicher. As the disorders continued to mount, the Social Democrats turned to Hindenburg for help. They sent him a strongly-worded protest against the policy of the Papen government, which, "largely through the raising of the ban on the Brown Army and its uniforms . . . , has produced conditions tantamount to civil war in Germany."

This virtual civil war reached its climax in the bloody Altona riots of July 17, 1932. In Altona, an industrial community adjacent to Hamburg, the Nazis organized a procession through some of the poorer working-class sections. They knew in advance that the Communists would be infuriated by such a provocative gesture in the very heart of the town's reddest area. As the uniformed Nazis came into view, they were fired upon from roofs, windows and balconies. The Nazis and their police escort returned the fire. Several people were killed and many were wounded. Upon receiving word of what had happened, the government reimposed the ban on open-air demonstrations and processions. It took the position that the Communists were responsible for the latest disorders, and in authoritative quarters there was talk of standing the culprits against a wall.

The Altona riots gave Papen a pretext for carrying out his plan to oust the Social Democrats from the Prussian government and to bring the country's largest state under the direct control of the Reich. After receiving from Hindenburg the necessary authorization, Papen summoned the members of the Prussian cabinet, who appeared at the chancellery on the morning on July 20, 1932. The government of the Reich, he informed them, felt that law and order were not being preserved in Prussia. Consequently, acting on the basis of emergency powers delegated by President Hindenburg, it had removed from office Braun, the Prussian premier, and Severing, his minister of the interior. It had appointed the chancellor of the Reich to serve as federal commissioner for Prussia. Severing was incensed. He vigorously denied the charge that the Prussian government was unable to perform its duty and that public order was not being maintained. He declared that he would not yield unless compelled to do so by force. He then left Papen's office and returned to the Prussian ministry of the interior, where he steadfastly declined to surrender his post. The federal government thereupon proclaimed a state of emergency in Berlin and in the province of Brandenburg and conferred supreme executive power, which meant virtually dictatorial authority, upon General Gerd von Rundstedt, local divisional commander of the Reichswehr. Simultaneously, it published a decree making Papen Reich commissioner for Prussia and authorizing him to remove the Prussian ministers from their offices. The decree was accompanied by an explanatory statement which ascribed the recent disorders to Communist agitation and charged that in Prussia "resolute leadership against the Communist movement" had been lacking. "There is a well-founded suspicion," it went on, "that high Prussian departments . . . no longer possess the independence necessary for the fulfillment of their tasks."

General Rundstedt issued an order demanding unquestioning obedience from everyone and warning that failure to heed his commands would be severely punished. The general went to the office of Grzesinski, Berlin's Social Democratic chief of police, and informed him and his aids that they had been dismissed. When they objected to leaving, they were removed by an officer and ten men to the nearby police barracks. There they were detained until the evening, when they were released. Their posts were promptly given to reactionary members of the officers' corps. On the evening of the same day, July 20, a representative of the Reich commissioner, the new chief of police and a police captain went to Severing and asked him to surrender his office, which he again refused to do. His visitors told him that force would be used. Thereupon he yielded. Simultaneously, other members of the Prussian cabinet were ousted. Men of conservative outlook were appointed to replace them. Provincial governors and police chiefs throughout Prussia, most of whom belonged to the Social Democratic party, were likewise supplanted by Rightists.

In the course of this crowded and momentous day, the Prussian government, headed by Braun, publicly assailed the appointment of a Reich commissioner as unconstitutional and affirmed its resolve to appeal to the supreme court of the Reich. It announced that, pending action by this tribunal, it would seek a temporary injunction to prevent Papen from going ahead with his plans. But Papen and Schleicher were already in control of the Reich's largest state and of the best police force in all the world. A gigantic stride toward the authoritarian regime envisaged by the cabinet of barons had been taken. The Social Democrats had lost their last stronghold. What would the party's answer be? And what would the trade unions do? Would they do what they had done in 1920 at the time of the Kapp putsch? Would they stage a general strike and thus force their adversaries to beat a retreat? Or would they take Papen's coup lying down, content themselves with ineffectual verbal protests and hope for miraculous delivery from an apparently impending doom? The leaders of the trade unions decided in favor of the latter course. They lacked militancy and dynamic purpose and therefore disapproved of the general strike as an instrument of class war. They were anxious to hold on to their comfortable jobs as trade-union executives and feared that those jobs would be jeopardized if the actions of the government were resisted. Moreover, the trade unions had been weakened by the depression and were not as well equipped as formerly to sustain a general strike. Finally, the Communists were urging a general strike, and anything the Communists favored was ipso facto suspect among moderate trade-unionists, who detested Bolshevism and its methods. The men who spoke for the bulk of organized labor insisted that, for the time being, attention would have to be concentrated on trying to win the coming elections. The Papen government, they said, must not be given a pretext for cancelling those elections. The adoption of this strategy added fuel to the flame of discord within the ranks of the German proletariat. The Social Democrats warned their followers against heeding the exhortations of irresponsible agitators (this was an obvious reference to the Communists) and urged them to maintain discipline and shun provocation. Berlin remained fairly quiet on the morrow of the "rape" of Prussia. What there was in the way of excitement resulted from the activities of the Communists. They distributed leaflets calling for a general strike. They held a number of meetings; at one of these, a revolution was demanded. The police arrested the distributors of the handbills, broke up the meetings and suppressed the *Rote Fahne* for five days.

2

Papen's coup provoked deep pessimism in democratic circles. The feeling was widespread that what had happened was the "real Kapp putsch," that the revolution of November, 1918, had been undone at one fell swoop. This feeling was strengthened by the refusal of the supreme court to grant the Prussian government's plea for a temporary injunction. Papen's victory was complete. He had dealt a staggering blow to the cause of federalism in Germany. He had given Social Democracy and organized labor their worst defeat since the founding of the republic. But that was not all. The government, it was widely believed, had improved its chances in the forthcoming elections. Once again it had stolen some of the Nazis' thunder. In still another bid for popular support, Schleicher addressed the nation on July 26, 1932. He attacked France's attitude on the question of armaments and warned that Germany would provide for her own security if equality were denied her. He extolled the military virtues, but hastened to add that he was not in favor of martial law or military dictatorship. He said he would never permit the Reichswehr to deviate from its impartial attitude and from the idea that it must serve only the nation as a whole. The army would do nothing more than obey the orders of Hindenburg, its supreme commander. A government supported by bayonets would end in failure. The Reichswehr, which represented no party, class or interest, would not protect "outworn economic forms or untenable ownership conditions." Schleicher was thus intimating his acceptance of the economic and social ideas championed by Nazi left-wingers. This was an astute move on his part, an attempt to exploit the growing anti-capitalist feeling in the country which had contributed so heavily to Hitler's successes at the polls.

Papen took a similar line in a last-minute appeal to the nation. His government, he said, stood above the political parties and was completely independent of them. He reaffirmed Schleicher's demand for equality in armaments and echoed his remark about "outworn economic forms." He said that people, in forming their judgments, must get away from the "unfruitful controversy over the terms capitalism and socialism." The guiding principle from now on should be: "general utility comes before individual utility." The protection of property rights must be understood in this sense. The government was friendly to private enterprise, but the latter would have to demonstrate its ability to exist without financial help from the state. All businesses hitherto subsidized by the state would be returned to private control. The government also contemplated certain political reforms. Papen alluded, in this connection, to the inadequacy of the "emergency structure of Weimar" and declared that the constitution would have to be basically revised.

3

Hitler conducted a whirlwind campaign. On July 15, 1932, he began an airplane tour of Germany. During the ensuing fortnight he addressed fifty mass meetings—more than three daily. Nazi electioneering tactics followed the now familiar pattern. But there was far greater co-ordination of effort as the nation-wide network of party cells swung into high gear. Hitler's propagandists operated with the smooth efficiency of a well-oiled machine. They carried the battle to every man, woman and child. They organized mammoth meetings that were masterpieces of stagecraft. Perfect timing and skillfully contrived light and sound effects contributed to the success of their work. The millions of dispossessed and unemployed were receptive. They found Gregor Strasser especially persuasive. The Nazis' foremost left-winger talked to them and to the country generally about the shortcomings of the prevailing economic system. The antipathy of the masses to capitalism, he was wont to explain, did not mean that they were hostile to property rights derived from labor and thrift. It likewise did not mean that they sympathized with "the stupid and destructive tendencies of the International." This feeling was simply the nation's protest against an economic system that did not function properly. The fact of the matter was that the country produced enough to feed everyone. If the present system of distribution was defective, then some other system would have to be introduced. Strasser vigorously championed the idea of settling the needy on the land and of instituting compulsory labor service for all German citizens twenty-one years of age. On one important issue, he saw eye to eye with those industrialists who were pressing for inflation. Like them, he advocated abandonment of the gold standard. However, he assailed the big trusts as inimical to the vital needs of the people. The Nazis, he stated emphatically, recognized and accepted the German labor movement. They regarded socialism as a way of protecting individuals and groups against exploitation. In one of his most provocative and widely publicized speeches, Strasser declared:

The nationalization of the railways, the municipalization of the tramways, the electric light and gas works, Baron vom Stein's liberation of the peasants, the Prussian officers' principle of achievement, the incorruptible German professional official . . . all that is the expression of German socialism as we conceive and demand it.

The Nazi conception of socialism was obviously a hodgepodge calculated to entice the maximum number of voters. It had very little in common with the ideas espoused by the Social Democrats and the Communists. Strasser, like many of his associates, talked endlessly about the synthesis of nationalism and socialism, which, he claimed, had been effected by the NSDAP. He spoke feelingly about the dignity and rights of labor. Nazism, he often said, offered not reaction but recovery, not chaos but a new order anchored in the finest traditions of German life. The Nazis were revolutionaries only in the sense that they wished to do away with the "decaying, immoral ideas" of the French Revolution. They wished, too, to see the workers shielded from capitalist exploitation and the people as a whole liberated from the incubus of ruinous speculation. They were not bent on persecuting the Jews; all that they had in mind was the elimination of Jewish capitalists from the leadership of the nation.

Strasser's exertions were paralleled by those of his comrades. Goebbels performed brilliantly as propagandist and agitator. He stood out as one of the movement's ablest orators. Goering contributed showmanship and his great talents as an organizer. He was no amateur when it came to rabble-rousing. He was far from being a silvertongued orator, but his war record, blunt soldierly manner and penchant for horseplay always assured him an appreciative audience. Roehm made himself invaluable as Hitler's chief of staff. His handling of the Storm Troops was not always beyond criticism, and his sexual irregularities continued to be a source of embarrassment to certain of his associates. The Fuehrer, however, seemed to love him dearly and extolled the manner in which he discharged his duties as generalissimo of the SA.

4

The outcome of the elections of July 31, 1932, was spectacular in the extreme. The biggest sensation was the showing of the Communists. They gained heavily, principally at the expense of the faltering Social Democrats. The latter were paying through the nose for their failure to resist the "rape" of Prussia. Many of their supporters, shocked by their do-nothing attitude, transferred their allegiance to the Communists. The elections revealed that bourgeois liberalism was virtually extinct in Germany. Of this the pitiful showing made by the State party was proof. But friends of the republic could take solace in the success of the Centrists, who acquired additional seats in the Reichstag. They could also derive comfort from the sorry plight of the Nationalists. Hugenberg's followers saw their representation reduced to thirty-seven. They and the People's party, which dwindled almost to the vanishing point, boasted a combined strength of forty-four out of a total of 608 Reichstag seats. The Papen-Schleicher cabinet could count only on these two factions. As expected, the Nazis scored large gains, but they failed to secure a majority. However, their 230 seats made them far and away the single biggest group in the Reichstag. The size of their popular support indicated clearly that the advance of the movement had been slowed. For their total barely surpassed the vote amassed by Hitler in the second presidential contest. Judged in terms of vote-getting, National Socialism had stood virtually still during the last three and a half months. This seemed to vindicate the attitude of those observers who had been saying that the Nazis were already at their zenith.

Chapter 37

PAPEN VERSUS HITLER

I

ON THE morrow of the elections, the *Voelkischer Beobachter* warned that it was no longer possible to form a German government without the National Socialists. Simultaneously, Papen issued a statement which indicated his readiness to invite the Nazis to participate actively in the reconstruction of the country. He and his colleagues in the cabinet professed to regard the results of the elections as fresh proof of the need for a presidial government composed of individuals who enjoyed Hindenburg's confidence and eschewed close party affiliations. But they were prepared to concede that the admission of a few Nazis to the cabinet would be politically expedient, to say the least. They assumed that the National Socialist tide had reached its highest point. The Fuehrer's hope of winning a majority of the electorate seemed foredoomed. Papen and Schleicher therefore felt strong enough to insist that the Nazis would have to enter the cabinet on conditions laid down by the government or not at all.

The overwhelming majority of Germans had no use whatever for the cabinet of barons. The elections proved that. But Papen had no intention of resigning. Under the existing presidential dictatorship, the principle of ministerial responsibility to the people's representatives no longer prevailed. Besides, Hindenburg had grown extremely fond of Papen and was most anxious to keep him in office. Schleicher, for his part, had not yet decided to dispense with Papen's services. Aided and abetted by this powerful twain, Papen put forward the claim that his government, which had just been repudiated at the polls, was not

affected one way or the other by the distribution of strength in the
new Reichstag.

2

Hitler's next move was awaited with intense interest. Many of his
followers were champing at the bit. Where, they queried, were the
spoils of victory, the miracles and power their leader had promised?
They could not understand what he was waiting for. How many more
elections would he have to win before he brought himself to seize
control of the state? And what of the future? The fact could not be
blinked that the movement had progressed but little since Hindenburg's re-election. Having absorbed the middle-class vote, it had
reached the point where further growth would be slow and painful.
The resistance of trade-unionists, Catholics and old-line Nationalists
was likely to prove insurmountable. From now on the party would have
to work hard for every additional vote. The days of mass conversions
to the Nazi gospel were apparently over. Besides, the conditions of the
struggle would soon change for the worse. Unless the Papen-Schleicher
government bungled things badly, economic conditions in Germany
were bound to improve slowly but steadily. This would rob the movement of its most potent talking point and dry up the principal sources
of its strength. Then there was the disconcerting fact that the cabinet
had already stolen much of the Fuehrer's thunder. Papen had obtained
the virtual cancellation of reparation payments. And now he and his
colleagues were clamorously demanding equality in armaments and
the deletion of the war-guilt clause. The future of National Socialism
therefore looked bleak indeed. But there was a way out, if only Hitler
would take it. That way was to use force. The exponents of a putsch
complained that the Fuehrer was too much of a pacifist, too much
concerned about the legality of his actions. They contended that never
again would he have at his disposal so large and devoted a following.
Sentiment for direct action was especially strong among the Storm
Troopers. Reflecting the attitude of their commanders, who recalled
with pleasure their experiences as members of the Free Corps, they
were all for severing the Gordian knot with a display of brute strength.
But Hitler had a better memory and a better grasp of existing realities
than these champions of a march on Berlin. He kept thinking of what
had happened on the morning of November 9, 1923, and how everything had gone wrong between himself and Kahr. He was sure that
an insurrection now would turn out to be as much of a fiasco as the

beer hall putsch in Munich. He told his more impatient followers that what they were suggesting would mean suicide for the party and urged them to keep calm.

3

At the beginning of August, 1932, negotiations were initiated for a reorganization of the cabinet. But they ran afoul of the Nazis' demand for the chancellorship and the principal ministries, a demand which Hindenburg, as everyone knew, would not accede to. Over the week-end of August 5-8, Schleicher had an informal talk with Hitler. The latter came away with the impression that the Reichswehr chieftain was prepared to back his claim to the chancellorship. On the 9th, the general conferred with Papen. The following day Hindenburg arrived from his estate in East Prussia and promptly closeted himself with the chancellor, who reported to him on the state of the negotiations. Simultaneously, the Nazis issued an official statement in which they reiterated their demand for the chancellorship. They made it clear that they would not accept "an insufficient share" of power and argued that Hitler should be placed at the head of a "cabinet of personalities." They professed agreement with Hindenburg's desire to maintain the non-party character of the government, claiming that Nazism was not a party but a national movement. This claim Papen rejected. He declared that Hindenburg stood firmly by the principle that the cabinet must be a presidial one, i.e., one that was completely independent of political parties. The German foreign office also had something to say on the subject of Hitler and the Nazis. Reports coming in from abroad showed that foreign opinion took a very unfavorable view of recent developments in Germany. It was even rumored in some places that certain governments might take drastic action if Hitler hoisted himself into the saddle. Baron Konstantin von Neurath, the foreign minister, talked very bluntly to Papen. He warned him that the foreign office would be unable to assume responsibility for the consequences if the chancellorship were turned over to Hitler.

On the morning of August 13, 1932, Hitler saw Papen and Schleicher. The chancellor minced no words. The presidential system, he declared, must be maintained. It would be unable to command respect if it were headed by a party leader. Such, at any rate, was Hindenburg's attitude. The old field marshal was a stubborn man and there was little one could do with him. Under the circumstances, Hitler would have to be content with something less than the chancellorship. Would he care to become vice-chancellor? The Fuehrer replied that he would not. He wanted full power. Nothing else would satisfy him. In that case, Papen coldly observed, there was only one thing for Hitler to do: he must try to persuade Hindenburg. Hitler flew into a rage. That, he cried, was Papen's job, not his. He knew that Hindenburg was not one of his admirers. But Papen had no intention of serving as Hitler's advocate and told him so in a manner which made further discussion useless.

Still seething, the Fuehrer hurried to the home of Goebbels, where the little cripple and Goering awaited him. It was anything but a cheerful gathering. The conversation was mainly concerned with the art of baiting traps, a subject on which the party's leaders needed little coaching. This time, however, the victims were Nazis. Hitler, accompanied by Roehm and Frick, finally set out for the president's palace. The interview lasted only fifteen minutes and was a chilly affair. Hindenburg asked Hitler whether he, together with other representatives of his party, would enter a cabinet headed by Papen. Hitler said no, reiterating his demand for the chancellorship. What he had in mind, he said, was a position similar to that occupied by Mussolini in Italy after the march on Rome. Hindenburg curtly refused, declaring that his conscience would not permit him to vest the power of the state in a party which intended to use it in one-sided fashion. He proceeded to lecture his visitor in the manner of a teacher addressing wayward children. He expressed regret at Hitler's refusal to fulfill his pre-election promise to support a national government enjoying the trust of the country's chief executive. He admonished the Fuehrer to conduct himself in a chivalrous manner and to remember his responsibility to the Fatherland.

The Nazis' disappointment was intense. Goebbels, who registered the Fuehrer's every emotion with barometric fidelity, foresaw a long period of sweat and tears. "It will mean a hard struggle," he averred, "but we shall triumph in the end. . . . The idea of the Fuehrer as vice-chancellor of a bourgeois cabinet is too ludicrous to be treated seriously. Rather go on struggling for ten years more than accept this offer. . . . The first round is lost. The fight . . . goes on!" Without doubt, Papen had scored a resounding victory. But he was not yet through with the Austrian corporal. He published an official communiqué recounting the Hindenburg-Hitler interview. The nation read that the field marshal had accused the Fuehrer of breaking his word, that he had found it necessary to urge him to behave like a gentleman and to place the

national welfare before personal ambitions. It was a terrible humiliation for Hitler, one that he could not readily live down. He railed
against Papen and Hindenburg. He was less irate with Schleicher,
apparently crediting him with a real desire to effect a working agreement between the Nazis and the government. The general let it be
known that there was nothing final about the rebuff of August 13.
Something, he pointed out, could still be salvaged from the wreckage
of Nazi aspirations. Hitler would have to give up the idea of becoming chancellor. But he or one of his representatives could have an important cabinet post. He had only to say the word.

4

While Hitler was disconsolately pondering his next move, he and his
associates suddenly found themselves in the midst of a new and dramatic crisis. In an effort to terminate the wave of terrorism that was
taking an increasing toll of life, the government, on August 9, 1932,
had issued an emergency decree prescribing summary justice for all
guilty parties. Shortly thereafter, a band of Nazis invaded the home
of a Communist worker in the Upper Silesian village of Potempa
and brutally murdered him. The trial of the nine men charged with
the killing began at Beuthen on August 19. When the prisoners filed
into court they were greeted with ostentatious cordiality by a high-
ranking member of the Nazi party. On August 22, five of the accused
were condemned to death. Two were sentenced to two years' imprisonment; the others were acquitted. The judge who pronounced
the death sentence called attention to the extraordinary barbarity
of the crime. The victim's larynx had been destroyed by kicks
and the carotid artery severed. The court imposed the maximum
penalty on the five self-confessed murderers in spite of Goebbels'
warning that a storm would be unleashed if any of the accused received the death sentence. And indeed, when the verdict became
known, the SA veritably exploded with rage.

All eyes were now turned to the Fuhrer. Would he allow his warriors to die without saying something in their defense? Would he
permit the verdict to go unchallenged? The enormous publicity given
the court's action and the excitement within the party made it imperative for him to do something. He could either take the five assassins
to his bosom and glorify murder or make a public confession of his
inability to protect his followers and thus risk forfeiting their alle-

giance. When he did break his silence, he was careful to underscore the wickedness of the government. The authorities, he charged, were permitting the murder of patriots while the Bolshevists committed every species of atrocity without being brought to book. The sentence imposed by the court at Beuthen was merely part of the vendetta waged by the "reactionary" elements against the liberating forces of National Socialism. Repudiated at the polls, the government was now resorting to legal assassination to accomplish its purpose. Disregarding his oft-repeated promise to adhere to the principle of legality, Hitler sent the following telegram to the five murderers:

My comrades:—In the face of this most monstrous and bloody sentence I feel myself bound to you in infinite loyalty. From this moment, your liberation is a question of our honor. To fight against a government which could allow this is our duty.

Simultaneously, the Fuehrer addressed a manifesto to the Nazi party. He denounced Papen in language of unexampled ferocity. The chancellor, he said, had "inscribed his name upon the history of Germany with the blood of patriotic fighters." Roehm, who visited the convicted assassins, assured them that the Nazis would not allow the execution to take place. This proved no idle boast. The sentence was eventually commuted to lifelong imprisonment. Hitler's attitude horrified all decent, law-abiding Germans. Hindenburg, who strongly resented the vitriolic attack on Papen, was furious. But Hitler was too angry to be careful. Before a number of audiences, he referred with evident relish to the possibility that the president would soon be dead. Such language caused his stock to slump not a little.

Papen struck back at Hitler in a speech which he delivered in Muenster on August 28, 1932. Alluding to the storm of protest against the Beuthen verdict, he said:

I recognize no law that is but the weapon of one class or party. That is a Marxist view which I repudiate, even when it is uttered by National Socialists. It is a blow in the face for every German and Christian conception of right.

Papen proclaimed that he himself stood unfalteringly for the "lawful state," for the "authoritative leadership of the state." In taking this stand, he went on, he was pursuing the aim espoused by millions of National Socialists. Moreover, the government had endeavored to secure the co-operation of the Hitlerian movement, "whose historical services to Germany none could deny." Turning to economic issues, the chancellor underlined the cabinet's conviction that the German currency must not be endangered and that risky experiments must be avoided. Unemployment constituted the central problem. In an effort to solve it, the government planned to stimulate private industry. This would have to be done by advancing large sums to factory owners and by reducing the tax burden resting on productive enterprises. Financial assistance would be extended to all industrial undertakings that took on more workers. With an eye to creating additional jobs, the government would authorize employers to reduce wages. Papen hastened to add that he and his colleagues intended to maintain both the collective wage agreement and the existing system of compulsory arbitration. But he made it clear that hereafter capital and labor would be expected to iron out their difficulties with less and less state interference. The work of national reconstruction could be accomplished only by a government that was authoritative and independent. Interruptions of this work by political parties would not be countenanced. However, the government did not intend to deviate from the constitution or to alter the form of the state. The Weimar document provided, in the office of the president, "the positive pole in the confusion of parties."

The *Voelkischer Beobachter* replied to Papen the very next day. Should the cabinet, it warned, deny power to the National Socialists and dissolve the Reichstag, Germany would be transformed into a military dictatorship. Such a regime was likely to encounter active resistance throughout the country. Would the Reichswehr, Hitler's organ queried, be sent out against the people in order to do the will of a few men holding office in defiance of the national will?

Papen's pronouncement was timed to coincide with certain significant developments within the Nazi movement. The failure of Hitler to take the bull by the horns and gamble on a *coup d'état* was dutifully accepted by the bulk of his followers. But the left-wingers of the party were less tractable. As the likelihood of revolution faded, many of them decided they had had enough of procrastination and "bourgeois" preoccupation with legality. At first individually, and then in sizable groups, these malcontents went over to the Communists. Those who remained in the fold continued to air their dissatisfaction and to rebuke the policy-makers for their timorousness. The Nazi leaders were naturally disturbed. They had visions of further defections. A comprehensive discussion of party strategy ensued. Gregor Strasser had decided views and pressed them with fervor and skill. He regarded the drift to Communism and the impatience of his own left-wingers as a mortal threat to the National Socialist movement. When Hitler's cleaving to legality ruled out the possibility of direct action and produced an apparent impasse, Strasser came out in favor of an agreement with Papen. It was obvious to him that National Socialism had reached its peak. A policy of compromise, he held, was now unavoidable, and the Papen of the Muenster speech was the kind of statesman with whom some sort of a deal should be possible. The chancellor would make an acceptable partner. By collaborating with him for as long as might be necessary, the Nazi movement would be able to save itself.

The situation, as Strasser saw it, simmered down to this: For some time to come, the Fuehrer would have to forget about winning elections and concentrate on obtaining a strong position within the government. If he persisted in his policy of opposition, he was lost. For, with the first phase of economic recovery on the way, the presidential regime had an excellent chance of surviving indefinitely. There was nothing to stop it from ordering one election after another; and in the process National Socialism would go under. But if Hitler secured a foothold in the cabinet and transferred his operations to the inner councils of the state, the superior intelligence and strategy of the Nazis would ultimately prevail. In meeting Papen halfway, the party would not be humbling itself. It had only to accept, on conditions that it considered satisfactory, an offer already made. An attitude of mere toleration toward the government would suffice to consummate the deal. This was Strasser's line, and it was supported by such Nazi bigwigs as Alfred Rosenberg, Gottfried Feder and Wilhelm Frick. But Strasser's principal rivals, Goering and Goebbels, said no. Hitler sided with the burly ex-aviator and the club-footed journalist. Strasser was overruled. Making "Remember Potempa!" its slogan, the party resolved to persist in its policy of total opposition to the government. Goering went to Berlin to perfect the details of a scheme to oust Papen.

5

The new Reichstag was soon to convene. No one doubted that it would make things uncomfortable for the government. But Papen was ready. He obtained full powers from Hindenburg, intending to use them to dissolve the Reichstag if the expected impasse should materialize. The Nazis knew what the chancellor was up to and didn't relish it. Their fear of another dissolution was in sharp contrast with their previous attitude. The awful thing that Strasser had warned against was now imminent: a new election, with every indication pointing to a loss of strength and prestige for National Socialism. Strasser became frantic. He begged Hitler to muzzle Goering. He besought Schleicher, with whom he was on friendly terms, to hurry Papen into making an offer that would prove acceptable to Hitler. Strasser's gnawing uneasiness communicated itself to the general. Schleicher did not like the way Papen was exploiting Hindenburg's dismissal of Hitler. He thought his protégé too complacent about the current crisis. He began to put pressure on him. This marked the beginning of a rift between the two men. Papen was not at all worried. Sure of Hindenburg's support, he felt himself master of the situation. The president had given him a blank check for his dealings with the Reichstag. The Reichswehr, whose allegiance to the old field marshal took precedence over all other loyalties, was ready to move at a signal from him.

The Reichstag met on August 30, 1932. After electing Goering as its speaker, it adjourned until September 12. The Nazis, insisting that the present parliament was capable of carrying on, hoped during this interval to convince Hindenburg that dissolution was not necessary. Papen utilized his short breathing space to make an important move. On September 5, 1932, he issued an emergency decree. It had a dual purpose: to create new jobs and to curb the power of organized labor. The first of these objectives was to be attained by promising bonuses to employers who put additional men on their pay rolls and by pouring large sums into public works. The second was achieved by authorizing the government to modify existing social insurance laws, to revise collective wage contracts and to overhaul the compulsory wage-arbitration system. The decree was received with mixed feelings. Industrialists applauded it, while the workers, fearing the loss of important privileges, did not conceal their consternation.

A few days before the Reichstag reconvened at Goering's call, Hindenburg signed a decree of dissolution and empowered Papen to use it as he saw fit. The chancellor made no secret of the fact that he intended to keep demanding new elections until the opposition had been worn down. But Goering pretended not to care. As soon as the deputies were in their seats, he called for action on a no-confidence motion offered by the Communists. Papen at once sprang to his feet and asked to be heard. Goering ignored him. The chancellor indignantly reiterated his demand, whereupon the portly Nazi sharply informed him that all other business was out of order when a vote was being taken. Papen said no more. He strode to the speaker's table and placed a document upon it. This document was the decree of dissolution. Then he and all his cabinet colleagues departed. The vote on the motion of no-confidence was overwhelmingly against the government: 512 to 42. The Nationalists and the People's party made up the insignificant minority. Goering joyfully announced the result and then, amid much applause, pronounced the decree of dissolution null and void. The government, he explained, had fallen as a result of the vote. Papen took up the challenge with alacrity. He flatly rejected Goering's contention. The vote, he said, was invalid because it took place after the Reichstag had been dissolved. The government had not the slightest intention of deviating from the line of action to which it was committed.

6

In issuing a call for new elections, Papen launched the policy of attrition which he hoped would bring the Nazis to their senses and force Hitler to support the presidential dictatorship. He was confident that the Fuehrer would come a cropper in the forthcoming test at the polls. To make sure that nothing would go wrong with his calculations, Papen had a word with his industrialist friends. The subsidies which had made possible Hitler's lavish campaigns were discontinued. Nazi funds began to dwindle. Money became the party's most urgent need; and where it was to come from nobody knew. This was only one, although easily the most serious of Hitler's problems. Another grew out of the rift between himself and Strasser. But if the Fuehrer's prospects were bad, Papen's were even worse. The cabinet of barons was still very unpopular. It had not the remotest chance of winning a parliamentary majority. But it did expect to increase its meager following. It counted heavily on the possibility that economic recovery would soon be under way. Papen's strong stand on the issue of equal arms for Germany also encouraged wishful thinking in government circles. A satisfactory settlement of this question had not yet been achieved, but the chancellor's aggressive tactics were widely applauded.

The campaign produced an abundance of oratorical fireworks. The Nazi watchword was "Down with the reactionaries!" The need for

Herculean exertions was repeatedly underlined by the party directorate. "Our adversaries," Goebbels noted shortly after the beginning of the campaign, "count on our losing morale and getting fagged out. But we know this and will not oblige them. That is what keeps us going. We would be lost, and all our work would have been in vain, if we gave in now." As usual, the Fuehrer outshouted everyone else. But the self-assurance of palmier days was missing. He talked in the manner of one expecting bad tidings and trying in advance to put the blame on others. He denounced the Hugenberg Nationalists who had deprived him of desperately needed subsidies. He resorted to his old trick of playing up the antagonism between the rich and the poor. He pictured the plutocrats, now the special objects of his ire, as vultures preying on a helpless nation. His followers did not respond very heartily to these verbal broadsides. The party's advent to power had seemed imminent only a short time ago. Now the distance which separated it from the long coveted goal appeared to be increasing daily. Disillusionment and despair spread among the Nazi rank and file. The fight for control of the state was continued at the Fuehrer's command, but the men who waged it were no longer sure of victory. The Communists exploited this disaffection in an effort to win new converts. They also attempted to curry favor with the chauvinist elements in the Nazi party by sounding a strongly patriotic note. They had much to say about the shackles of Versailles and repeatedly called attention to Polish atrocities against the Germans. Papen's campaign utterances emphasized the non-party character of his government. But the fact remained that the only way to express approval of his policies was to support the candidates of the Nationalist party. And since this political faction was by now thoroughly discredited, its appeals to the electorate produced no major shifts in public sentiment.

7

On November 3, 1932, the transport workers of Berlin, faced with a sizable cut in wages, went on strike. This action was instigated by the Communists and disavowed by the Social Democrats. To the surprise of many people, the Nazis announced that they were supporting the strike. The Communists had been scoring heavily among the laboring classes by attacking the wage reductions instituted under Papen. In the hope of beating the Communists at this game and, incidentally, of converting the strike into a great political demonstration against the government, the Nazis decided to take a hand in the affair. According to Goebbels, the reasoning of the party was as follows:

If we hold ourselves aloof from this strike, . . . our position among the working classes, so far firm, will be shaken. Here is another great opportunity to show the public, on the eve of the elections, that the line we have taken . . . is dictated by a true sympathy with the people. For this reason, the National Socialist party purposely eschews the old bourgeois methods.

Nazi headquarters explained that the party would not permit the living standard of German workers to fall below that of Chinese coolies. There were outbreaks of violence which forced the government to call out the city's entire police force. Hitler's followers were treated gently by the authorities. The Communists, as usual, fared otherwise. Fifty-two members of the party were arrested and publication of the *Rote Fahne* was suspended for a week. One of the most curious aspects of the situation was the spectacle of Nazis and Communists standing side by side with collection-boxes in their hands and soliciting pennies "for the strike." Nazi sympathy with the action of the Berlin transport workers alienated many of Hitler's middle-class supporters. Conservative and liberal newspapers made the most of their opportunity. They charged that the Nazis were out-and-out Bolshevists and that the strike had been fomented by them. Goebbels tried very hard to defend the party's point of view. But the damage had already been done.

8

The strike was still in progress when the country went to the polls on November 6, 1932. The results demonstrated that the vast majority of the nation still disliked the presidential dictatorship. But they also disclosed that Papin's tactics were not altogether ineffectual. The number of his supporters in the Reichstag rose to seventy-four. This was unimpressive in absolute terms but the percentual increase was considerable. The government's adherents accounted for almost eleven and one-half per cent of the total vote, which likewise represented an appreciable gain. So Papen felt justified in claiming a personal victory. But far more significant was his success in taking the wind out of Hitler's sails. The Nazi movement, which since 1930 had registered an uninterrupted series of gains, was abruptly thrown into reverse. It lost thirty-four Reichstag seats and its percentage of the electorate dropped from the July high of 37.4 to 33.1. Something like two

million voters deserted the men of the swastika. The process of
wearing the Nazis down and forcing them into submission by means
of repeated elections had gotten off to an auspicious beginning. Indeed, it was questionable whether the party would be able to survive
another dose of this medicine. Goebbels was not overstating the case
when he wrote: "We are now on the eve of desperate effort. . . . The
chief thing is to maintain the party."

The Nazi discomfiture stood out all the more sharply because of
what happened to Hitler's rivals on the extreme Left. No feature of
the election results was more indicative of the volatile state of German
politics than the victory scored by the Communist party. It increased
its Reichstag representation to 100 and captured 16.9 per cent of the
total vote. It battened on defections from the NSDAP. It continued
to siphon recruits from the trouble-ridden Social Democrats. The latter lost twelve seats and saw their share of the electorate drop to 20.4
per cent. The Center got off with only a slight setback but the State
party suffered a knockout blow. It emerged with exactly one seat.

The enemies of Nazism rejoiced. Papen had done what no other
man had been able to do since the onset of the depression: turn back
the National Socialist tide. Political observers in and out of Germany
freely predicted a speedy and ignominious demise for Hitlerism. But
there was something else to worry about: the forward surge of German
Bolshevism. As the Nazi tide receded, would the Communist one continue to advance? In the minds of a great many Germans, this question took precedence over all others.

Chapter 38

SCHLEICHER SUCCEEDS PAPEN

I

THE country eagerly awaited the next act of the fast-moving political drama. What would Hitler do now? And what did Papen have up his sleeve? Would there be a junction of all the conservative forces in the face of the Bolshevist threat? Or would the Nazis and the cabinet of barons continue to snarl and claw at each other? Hitler lost little time in speaking his mind. Immediately after the elections, he addressed a manifesto to his followers. He claimed that the attack on the National Socialist movement had been successfully repelled. Once again, he pointed out, the Papen government had suffered overwhelming defeat, with no less than ninety per cent of the nation ranged against it. With recurring emphasis on the reactionary character of the men in office, Hitler charged that the masses were being driven straight to Bolshevism. He saddled the Papen-Hugenberg clique with responsibility for the election of one hundred Communists to the Reichstag. The Nazi party, he declared, would ruthlessly oppose the enemies of Germany's rebirth. There would be no compromise, no negotiations with them. The Fuehrer's truculent language was patently designed to bolster the spirits of his followers, but it was not strong enough for the Storm Troopers. They were again talking about dispensing with legality if their craving for power should remain thwarted.

Actually the National Socialist party was in desperate straits and its leaders were at their wits' end. Each day brought new evidence of restlessness and dissension within the movement. The shortage of cash remained the most pressing problem. Goebbels made the following entry in his diary on November 11, 1932: "Received a report on the

511

financial situation of the Berlin organization. It is hopeless. Nothing but debts and obligations, together with the complete impossibility of obtaining any reasonable sum of money after this defeat." It was difficult to see how the movement could regain lost ground without expensive propaganda campaigns. Besides, the NSDAP's padded pay rolls had to be protected. Drastic cuts would wreck the entire party machinery. But monetary worries were only part of the story. From every sector of the political battlefront came fresh tidings of woe. Several local elections took place at this time and in all of them the Nazis suffered losses. Indeed, so rapid was the swing of the pendulum that most observers predicted that Hitler's Reichstag representation would fall below 150 in the event of another election. For the Nazi leaders this was a disheartening prospect. Certain individuals within the movement showed no inclination to keep their worries to themselves. Especially vocal were the Nazi members of parliament. These men were for the most part impecunious party wheel-horses who for years had hungered for the security and dignity of political office. Now many of them, after a brief sojourn in the Reichstag, were threatened with the loss of their seats. Their fears and lamentations helped to keep the party in a constant state of jitters.

2

Papen was full of confidence. With Nazi power waning, with Hindenburg and the Junker-industrialist clique wishing him Godspeed, he seemed to hold the whip-hand. But trouble was brewing for the personable chancellor. Schleicher began to find his protégé much too powerful. Papen, having entrenched himself solidly in the president's affections, insisted on being his own master. This was not the role which Schleicher had marked out for him. But there was more to the general's ill-humor than just a thwarted desire for power or pique at being displaced as Hindenburg's prime favorite. He still hoped to establish a great national front. Hitler's co-operation was essential. Without it, Schleicher feared, the presidential dictatorship would continue to be detested by most Germans as a strictly upper-class affair and would have to rely for its perpetuation on the bayonets of the Reichswehr. Papen's tactics, he charged, were all wrong. Further elections would settle nothing and in the end might even create a state of civil war. Schleicher persuaded his cabinet colleagues to join him in demanding Papen's resignation. They, too, were uneasy over the ultimate consequences of the chancellor's policy. They wanted Hindenburg to consult the party leaders and find out whether there was any escape from the current deadlock. Perhaps it would yet be possible to form a coalition government which could command the support of the great majority of the nation.

So far Schleicher's arguments had made little impression on Hindenburg. The old war lord thoroughly approved of Papen's tactics. But Schleicher persisted, impelled by the conviction that disaster would overtake the presidential regime if his counsels went unheeded. He buttressed his contentions with alarmist information supplied by his confidant, Gregor Strasser. The latter elaborated upon the strength of the radical-revolutionary current in the National Socialist movement. He underlined the ceaseless drift of Nazi malcontents to Communism. But he scored most heavily when he warned that Hitler was having a difficult time trying to restrain his own followers. No one could tell how much longer the Fuehrer would be able to have his way.

Spurred by these admonitions, Schleicher and his friends in the cabinet moved toward a showdown. They charged that only personal differences between Papen and Hitler stood in the way of their plans for a national front. They contended that the growing strength of the Bolshevists and the rebellious attitude of many hitherto submissive trade-unionists made the formation of such a front more imperative than ever. The time had come to choose between partnership with the Nazis and a regime sustained solely by the armed forces of the state. Papen professed a willingness to explore all possibilities. He agreed that an effort should be made to form a government of national concentration and promised that personal considerations would not be permitted to stand in the way. He intimated that he was prepared to resign if thereby the parties could be induced to join the cabinet. Papen's sincerity may well be questioned. He was quite convinced of his own indispensability, and what he contemplated now was nothing more than a confirmation of the fact that no real rapprochement between the government and the opposition was possible. He believed that Schleicher's scheme would founder and consequently saw little risk in giving it a try.

3

Papen secured authorization from Hindenburg to consult the party leaders. The ensuing conversations proved as futile as everyone had expected them to be. Only the Nationalists and the People's party, who had all along backed the government, gave an affirmative answer. The other groups turned a deaf ear to Papen's plea for support. They disliked the government's program, but personal antipathy to the chancellor also played a major role in the failure of these negotiations. The Centrists were still angry over the ouster of Bruening and strongly resented Papen's apparent willingness to see the Prussian Junkers regain their former predominance. Hitler remembered with bitterness the events of August 13 and Papen's part in them. He was in no mood to run the risk of further traps and humiliations.

The distrust with which large sections of the nation regarded Papen was not diminished by the intemperate remarks of certain newspapers friendly to the government. These organs expressed the feeling of Nationalist circles when they urged the cabinet not to be restrained by respect for the Weimar constitution. They argued that the government had the law on its side and, more important, the Reichswehr, too. This caused a widespread uneasiness which Papen sought to allay by disclaiming any intention of altering the constitution by illegal means. He claimed that his sole aim was to curb that "exaggerated parliamentarianism" which had "wrought such havoc."

Having established anew the universally known fact that most of the parties would have nothing to do with his government, Papen on November 17, 1932, made the *pro forma* gesture of resigning. An official communiqué stated that the chancellor wished to give the president an opportunity to try his hand at welding the leaders of the various parties into a cabinet of national concentration. The Papen government was to remain in office on a temporary basis while Hindenburg was so engaged. In the course of what was officially termed his farewell audience with Hindenburg, Papen observed that the aim of the presidential system had been to effect a union of all the national forces. Such a coalition would have made possible the formation of a government enjoying the support of the country. This aim had not been achieved. Because he, Papen, stood in the way of its attainment, he felt he should withdraw. He advised Hindenburg to put personal feelings aside and ask Hitler to form a cabinet which could muster a majority in the Reichstag. Knowing that Hitler would be unable to secure a parliamentary majority, Papen experienced no hesitation whatsoever in making this suggestion. The Nazi leader's foredoomed effort to climb into the saddle would clarify the situation. Then this nonsensical jockeying for position would cease. Of this Papen felt reasonably sure. He took it for granted that he would be restored to power.

And the conditions under which he would stage his triumphant resumption of office were likely to be far more favorable than those which had prevailed when he first assumed the chancellorship. He could, therefore, afford to step aside for the moment and allow the tangled political skeins to be unraveled.

4

Hindenburg's decision to take up the task vainly attempted by Papen awakened new hope in the Nazi party. But although Strasser and those who shared his views were intimating that the party might be prepared to take less than it had asked on August 13, the *Voelkischer Beobachter* sang the old refrain. It bluntly demanded the chancellorship for the Fuehrer. The latter reaffirmed this demand when he conferred with Hindenburg on November 19 and again on November 21. The field marshal asked Hitler to ascertain whether a cabinet headed by him would be able to command a majority in the Reichstag. A number of conditions were attached to this request. These included the retention of Schleicher at the war ministry and of Baron von Neurath at the foreign office. Hitler replied that the formation of a majority cabinet was impossible and made several counter-proposals. He agreed to retain Schleicher and Neurath but insisted that Hindenburg appoint him chancellor and grant him full powers. Schleicher tried to persuade Hitler to lower his demands. The Fuehrer, however, refused to budge, whereupon Hindenburg informed him that the grant of full powers was out of the question. The old man explained that his conscience would not permit him to vest so much authority in the leader of a party which stressed its "exclusiveness" and which manifested so much hostility to himself and to the legislative program rendered necessary by the current crisis. Also to be borne in mind, Hindenburg continued, was the certainty that a presidial cabinet headed by Hitler would result in the establishment of a party dictatorship. The Fuehrer angrily charged that from the beginning the negotiations had been foredoomed by Hindenburg's resolve to retain the Papen cabinet, no matter what the cost.

The field marshal's conversations with other party leaders were equally fruitless. By November 25, the decision once again rested with Hindenburg. Would he reinstate Papen? This unquestionably he wanted to do. He hated the idea of parting from his beloved "Fraenzchen." But Schleicher's intervention proved decisive. He stressed the point that a new Papen cabinet would mean either another dissolution of the Reichstag or an attempt to govern unconstitutionally. Public opinion, he argued, was strongly opposed to Papen's continuation in office and to the idea of new elections. To disregard this sentiment was to invite the danger of civil war and rule by the bayonet. Some other chancellor, with a presidial cabinet that was more acceptable to the nation, might succeed in concluding a truce with the parties and in persuading the Reichstag to adjourn. Schleicher once again carried the cabinet with him. Several of the ministers declared that they would not serve under Papen. Hindenburg was compelled to yield.

The great political drama now entered its penultimate phase. Without further ado Hindenburg sent for Schleicher and curtly informed him that he would have to take the chancellorship. The events of the last few days had destroyed the old friendship between the two men. Suspicion and a slow, cold anger gripped the president. He saw his erstwhile favorite in a new and unflattering light. Schleicher had turned against Papen. For this Hindenburg never forgave him. The "king-maker" in the ministry of war had at last overreached himself. He had followed a tortuous path in his efforts to achieve power without responsibility. At this juncture he wished to make another straw man, Hjalmar Schacht, head of the new government. But Hindenburg's command could not be ignored. Schleicher had no choice but to accept the chancellorship and all the responsibility that went with it.

Chapter 39

THE ADVENT OF HITLER

I

SCHLEICHER was appointed chancellor on December 3, 1932. Warmbold, Braun and Neurath retained their posts. Gayl and Schaeffer were dropped. These two men, together with Papen, were chiefly responsible for the unpopularity of the previous cabinet. The public blamed them for the recent decrees regarding labor conditions and social insurance. Seemingly insurmountable difficulties plagued Schleicher from the very beginning. He had no organized following of his own. Not a single party or faction in the land was for him. In this respect he was much worse off than Papen, who had always been able to count on the Nationalists and the People's party. Hindenburg and the palace camarilla viewed the new chancellor with a jaundiced eye. They maintained close contact with Papen, who was eager to unseat his former sponsor. The new Reichstag was likely to prove rebellious.

Even before he assumed his new office, Schleicher opened negotiations that were designed to achieve some kind of working agreement with the major political and economic groups in the country. He talked with Social Democratic and Centrist leaders. He contacted trade-union spokesmen and representatives of employers' associations. He sought, through Strasser, to bring the Nazis into his camp. Schleicher's aim was to secure the co-operation of many different sections of the population, to establish a broad social foundation for his cabinet. He had hopes of labor support following his conversations with trade-union leaders. The latter stressed the workers' desire to see the government undertake the financing of public employment schemes. The Bavarian People's party announced its willingness to give the new government a fair chance. Schleicher counted heavily on

Strasser, to whom he offered the vice-chancellorship. Strasser continued to favor a policy of collaboration and once again urged his views upon Hitler and other leaders of the party. Acceptance of Schleicher's offer, he pointed out, might be the way to salvage something before it was too late. Nazi strength was declining rapidly. The Fuehrer and his aids were terribly upset by the catastrophe which had just overtaken the party in the Thuringian elections. Equally depressing was the outcome of recent contests in Bremen and Hamburg. These reverses prompted Goebbels to write in his diary: "The situation in the Reich is disastrous." The party's financial difficulties were more acute than ever. All this could be adduced in support of Strasser's thesis. Nevertheless, both Goering and Goebbels opposed co-operation with Schleicher, and Hitler, after some hesitation, sided with them. There remained the possibility of a major split in the party if Strasser could wield sufficient influence. This possibility figured significantly in Schleicher's calculations once it became clear that Hitler would refuse to tolerate the new government. If the left-wingers went over to Schleicher, the latter's position would be greatly strengthened and that of the Nazis seriously, perhaps even fatally, undermined.

2

The Reichstag met on December 6, 1932. Goering, who was re-elected its presiding officer, promptly launched into a diatribe against the Papen government. He charged that it had destroyed respect for the "authoritative leadership of the state." The right to govern, he proclaimed, emanated from the people; bayonets could not be substituted for the national will. Schleicher's elevation to the chancellorship pushed the Reichswehr into the country's political controversies, and this the Nazis deplored. "The army," Goering asserted, "belongs to the whole nation." The former aviator's remarks boded ill for Schleicher's efforts to reach a working agreement with the Reichstag. But the Nazis, and this was the general's trump, were anxious to avoid another dissolution and consequently shunned a head-on collision with the cabinet. Thus it was that the Reichstag rejected two motions. One of these, offered by the Social Democrats, called upon the government to make its declaration of policy forthwith. The other, sponsored by the Communists, asked that a no-confidence resolution be placed on the agenda for the following day. On December 9, after a series of free-for-all clashes between Nazis and Communists, the Reichstag adjourned, leaving it to Goering and the standing committee on procedure to determine the date of its next meeting. Before adjourning, the Reichstag passed a Nazi-sponsored bill making the president of the supreme court acting president of the Reich in the event of the death or incapacitation of the chief executive. This was directed against Schleicher, since under existing law it was the chancellor who assumed the functions of the president in such a situation. The Reichstag like-wise enacted a Centrist bill revoking that provision of the decree of September 5, 1932, which authorized wage reductions in plants that took on new workers. Schleicher ostentatiously accepted this measure in an effort to demonstrate his friendliness to labor, whose favor he was still courting. The Reichstag completed its work by adopting an am-nesty bill supported by the Nazis, the Communists and the Social Democrats, all of whom wished to see the jails emptied of their party comrades.

The great sensation of the day was the absence of Strasser from the Reichstag. An official Nazi statement explained that Hitler had given him "three weeks' recuperative leave." But the real explanation was that Strasser, frustrated in his effort to induce the party to co-operate with Schleicher and irked by Goering's and Goebbel's intrigues against him, simply decided that he had had enough. On December 8, 1932, the Fuehrer, with whom he had already had several lengthy discus-sions, suggested another heart-to-heart talk. Instead of complying with this invitation, Strasser sent his chief a letter in which he warned that National Socialism was treading a course that led straight to chaos and ruin. Declaring that he could no longer stomach such tactics, he for-mally resigned all his party offices. Having thus unburdened himself, Strasser left for the south. The leaders of the party made no secret of their pessimism. On the night of December 8, 1932, Goebbels wrote: "It is difficult to be cheerful. We are all rather downcast, especially in view of the danger of the whole party's falling to pieces, and of all our work being in vain. We are confronted with the great test." The Fuehrer himself was heard to say: "If the party breaks up, I'll end matters with my pistol in three minutes." His anxiety proved ground-less, Strasser's action failed to split the party. After the Reichstag ad-journed, all the Nazi deputies gathered in Goering's home and reaf-firmed their loyalty to the Fuehrer.

3

Strasser's discomfiture dealt a heavy blow to Schleicher's hopes. But this was in part offset by the fact that the Reichstag had adjourned without adopting a no-confidence resolution. The chancellor now had a breathing space during which he would be able to launch his program. At this juncture he scored a spectacular diplomatic success for which he himself had paved the way when he held the post of minister of war in the Papen cabinet. On August 8, 1932, he had declared that Germany would not return to Geneva when the disarmament conference resumed its deliberations unless she were guaranteed equality of rights. The other governments took the warning to heart. An acceptable formula was eventually worked out and enunciated in the five-power declaration of December 11, 1932. Germany's claim to equality in armaments was recognized in principle. The objective so passionately pursued for years had at last been achieved.

Schleicher made his bid for popular favor in a radio speech on December 15, 1932. He asked the nation to forget that he was a soldier and to think of him as "the impartial trustee of the interests of all in an emergency." No government could for long carry on, he said, unless it had the backing of the masses of the population. His paramount aim was to provide work. He had recommended to the president the appointment of a Reich commissioner whose task it would be to draw up the necessary plans and see that they were carried out. This job-making program would have to be financed without resort to inflation. New taxes and further wage cuts were not contemplated for the current fiscal year. The system of agricultural import quotas instituted by Papen for the sole benefit of the big landowners was to be discontinued. Millions of marks were to be spent on internal colonization in the eastern provinces. 1,300,000 acres of land were to be set aside for this purpose. In order to make things easier during the coming winter, the government planned to reduce the price of meat and coal and, possibly, of milk and bread as well. At one point in his speech, Schleicher remarked that he supported neither capitalism nor socialism. The only thing that mattered was to do the right thing at the right time without worrying about economic dogmas. He did, however, declare himself in favor of trade unionism and insisted that economic burdens should be borne equally by all classes. Conscription, he contended, was a good thing, but he explicitly disclaimed any intention of setting up a military dictatorship. He was interested not in changing the constitution but in reorganizing the nation.

Only in moderate bourgeois circles was the reaction to Schleicher's address favorable. The Social Democrats and the trade unions showed no inclination to meet him halfway. The Nazis remained blatantly hostile. They attacked him bitterly in the Prussian Diet, where he was accused of bringing about the fall of Seeckt, Gessler, Groener, Bruening and Papen. Schleicher, nevertheless, clung to the belief that a policy of concessions might yet win him the sufferance of his foes. He restored recent wage and relief cuts. He granted greater freedom of the press and of assembly. He lightened the penalties for breaches of public order. He made it possible for several thousand political prisoners released under the terms of the amnesty law to get to their homes in time for the Christmas holidays. In a transparent effort to placate the Nazis, he requested the police to warn non-German Communists residing in the Reich that they faced expulsion. He managed to remain optimistic in the face of apparently insurmountable difficulties. Although he was astute about most things, he failed to appraise correctly the resourcefulness and tenacity of his antagonists. His most grievous mistake was to underestimate Papen. Schleicher took his former protégé altogether too lightly. He was blind to the intensity of Papen's desire for revenge, to the richness of his talent for intrigue.

4

In the elections of November 6, 1932, one sixth of the voters had registered a preference for Communist candidates. This was a sizable proportion, and it seemed likely to grow. The Communists expected to profit by the disaffection that was rife among both Nazis and Social Democrats. A great many of Hitler's followers, rather than see their hopes for a new world blasted, would not hesitate to cast their lot with the Bolshevists. As a matter of fact, the Fuehrer threatened to urge his adherents to embrace the hammer and sickle if the chancellorship were denied him. An ominous ferment was also at work within the Social Democratic party. The flabby and visionless leadership of this once mighty contingent was causing a steady stream of desertions to the champions of proletarian revolution. The industrialists of western Germany had complied with Papen's suggestion that they withhold further financial support from the Nazis until Hitler agreed to abandon his "all or nothing" position. That had seemed wise at the time. But with Hitler's party in the throes of a crisis that might throw it bodily into Stalin's arms, they began to question the strategy of taming the Fuehrer by depriving him of funds.

Such was their state of mind when Schleicher moved to the center of the political stage. They took an immediate dislike to the new chancellor. His attitude toward labor diverged sharply from theirs. They agreed with Papen that the bane of German life, the cause of all the nation's economic ills, was the rise of the "charity" state. By this they meant a number of things: governmental interference with freedom of enterprise, heavy income taxes, the pampering of labor and the unemployed, the expansion of social services, the multiplication of workers' benefits. They held that the play of economic forces must not be obstructed. Schleicher's efforts to curry favor with the laboring elements made him extremely unpopular in big-business circles, where he was dubbed the "social general." Heavy industry objected strongly to his wage and anti-inflationary policies. It disliked his interest in broad problems of social reorganization. It raged because he appointed a minister of labor who was more sympathetic to the workers than the man who had held the post in the preceding cabinet. The fact that he was an aristocrat and a militarist could not obscure his "subversive" proclivities. Indeed, his influence in high army circles made him doubly dangerous. What if he should succeed in arranging an alliance between the Reichswehr and the trade unions? Not that anything of the sort was likely; but fear of it was in the air. "Schleicher must go!" became the slogan of those who spoke for heavy industry.

The hostility of the Junker aristocracy constituted a more immediate and potent threat to Schleicher's position. On January 11, 1933, the *Landbund* published a vitriolic denunciation of the chancellor's agrarian policy. It was incensed by the refusal of the government to institute a higher tariff on imported foodstuffs and to extend the quota system. Its wishes in these matters were being stoutly opposed by the export industries, which feared foreign reprisals if the Junkers had their way. Thus the long-standing conflict between two of the nation's most powerful classes flared anew. The *Landbund* hurled some very serious charges at Schleicher. It accused him of allowing German agriculture to deteriorate to a point "hardly conceivable under a purely Marxist government." It flayed what it called "the plundering of agriculture in favor of the money-bag interests of the export industry, with its international leanings." What really lay back of this explosion of rage was the loathing with which the big landowners regarded Schleicher's land settlement scheme. This was a revival of Bruening's plan, which the Junkers had so violently opposed. Once again they rallied swiftly to the defense of their class interests. Once again they played upon Hindenburg's fears by fulminating against "agrarian Bolshevism." As usual, the president's son seconded their efforts. The immediate objective of the *Landbund* was the removal of Schleicher from the chancellorship. There seemed little reason to doubt the success of its efforts.

5

The closing weeks of 1932 were filled with sadness and despair for the men of the swastika. Nazi fortunes were at their lowest point since the onset of the depression. The party's debt was estimated to be in the neighborhood of twelve million marks. All sorts of economies had to be practised; and in the streets of towns and cities throughout the land one encountered thousands of SA men holding out collection-boxes and abjectly soliciting alms. There were many who could not stand the gaff. Some of these offered to sell party secrets to anti-Nazi groups and newspapers; other simply deserted and cast their lot with more affluent organizations. The party's master-minds pondered the narrowing possibilities of escape from a doom that seemed all but inevitable. Hitler remained averse to the idea of a putsch. The lesson which Kahr and Lossow had taught him in 1923 on the blood-stained pavements of Munich was still fresh in his mind. The recession of popular favor which recent elections had signalized was likely to continue. The future seemed to hold only the prospect of more elections and more humiliating setbacks. The complete disintegration of the National Socialist movement appeared a matter of months and no more. "Everywhere," Goebbels lamented, "the rats flee from the sinking ship." The following entries in his diary speak for themselves: [1]

December 10. The feeling in the party is still divided. All are waiting for something to happen.

December 15. It is very difficult to hold the Storm Troopers and the party officials on a straight course. It is high time we attained to power although for the moment there is not the slightest chance of it.

December 20. We must summon all our forces once more to hold the organization together. . . .

December 21. Troubles and worries call for attention in the party. This sort of thing always follows an internal crisis; but one has to keep cool. Our money difficulties continue, but we are fighting them stoutly.

December 22. We must cut down the salaries of our district leaders, as otherwise we cannot make shift with our finances. . . . It would be an injustice on the part of Fate were this movement not permitted to attain to power.

December 23. I am at home alone, pondering over my life. The past was sad, and the future looks dark and gloomy; all chances and hopes have quite disappeared.

[1] Quoted in *My Part in Germany's Fight*, by Joseph Goebbels, translated by Kurt Fiedler (Hurst and Blackett, Ltd.).

It was at this moment that Papen came to the rescue. He played the leading role in what turned out to be the most momentous conspiracy of modern times. He it was who canalized the hostility to Schleicher and facilitated the restoration of the Harzburg Front. Papen was delighted to serve in this capacity. His hatred of Schleicher, compounded of jealousy and a desire for revenge, was implacable. He was ambitious. He planned to make the removal of Schleicher the entering wedge for his own return to power. His prospects were bright. He enjoyed the confidence of his fellow plutocrats. He was still Hindenburg's prime favorite and on excellent terms with the palace camarilla. He was sure that he could work with Hitler.

Goebbels recorded the beginning of the conspiracy. On December 29, 1932, he made the following entry in his diary: "The Fuehrer may have a discussion with Papen in a few days' time. That would offer us a new opportunity." Ribbentrop, who was a close friend of Papen, speeded the rapprochement between the former chancellor and Hitler. Papen found the bankrupt and dilemma-ridden Nazis very receptive. He invited Hitler to a meeting at the home of the Cologne banker, Baron Kurt von Schroeder. The historic conference took place on January 4, 1933. Papen discussed the necessity of forming a government of national concentration. The Harzburg Front was formally reconstituted. A group of Rhenish-Westphalian industrialists headed by Thyssen undertook to pay a large part of the Nazi debt. Papen did not promise Hitler the chancellorship. On the contrary, Papen wished to find out whether Hitler would agree to support a cabinet headed by someone other than himself. The Fuehrer indicated that he would not demand the chancellorship if a suitable person became minister of war.

When Schleicher learned of the meeting, he reproached Papen bitterly. The chancellor was in the midst of negotiations with Strasser, who had just returned from Italy. The Nazi left-winger agreed to join the Schleicher cabinet and sent Hitler word to this effect. The latter was alarmed; he feared that Strasser's entry into the government might do irreparable harm to the National Socialist movement. Another ominous portent, from Hitler's point of view, was the apparent readiness of Hugenberg to ally himself with Schleicher. But on January 15, 1933, the Nazis scored a success in the Lippe elections. Hitler's spirits rose. At once he served notice on Papen that his party would demand greater concessions in return for its promise to enter a cabinet of national concentration. This was tantamount to saying that he would have to be given the chancellorship. But Hindenburg was strongly opposed to anything of the sort. His aversion to Hitler had in no way diminished. He wanted Papen to succeed Schleicher. Hugenberg, too, preferred Papen and let it be known that he would refuse to sanction Hitler's elevation to the chancellorship.

In the meantime, Schleicher had suffered a major reverse. The Centrists, on whose support he had been counting, informed him that they would not join any cabinet which included Hugenberg. Thereafter, the general's position deteriorated rapidly. On January 21, 1933, Goebbels wrote: "The work in anticipation of the downfall of the Schleicher cabinet is well in hand. Even the form in which the Fuehrer is to take over power is seriously discussed." Three days later he enlarged with evident relish upon the progress of the conspiracy:

Several discussions with the men, who in future will be of importance, have cleared the ground. Generally speaking there is conformity among them, but as yet we need to do a bit of weeding out before we definitely reach our goal. One thing is certain; feeling in general is everywhere against the present cabinet. . . . Schleicher's position is much endangered now. . . . His downfall will come overnight. . . .

On January 25, Goebbels noted jubilantly:

It looks pretty bad for Schleicher. His downfall is expected on Saturday (January 28). He is defending himself desperately, but to no purpose any more. Even the Nationalists are now against him. He is absolutely isolated. All his grand plans have gone awry.

Schleicher, however, was not yet prepared to concede defeat. He still hoped to put his economic and social program into effect. Time was what he needed. But the Reichstag was due to reconvene on January 31, 1933. If the Nazis were threatened with another dissolution, they might acquiesce in a second adjournment. Schleicher asked Hindenburg for the power to dissolve parliament. The chancellor pointed out that his government would be unable to defend itself vis-à-vis the Reichstag if it did not secure this power in advance. He also remarked that without an order of dissolution, he would be unsuccessful in his efforts to prevent a discussion of the *Osthilfe* scandals recently unearthed by the Reichstag's budget committee. To Schleicher's dismay, Hindenburg refused to grant the authority in question. The president's sternly negative attitude attested the efficacy of Papen's machinations. Realizing that the game was up, Schleicher resigned. This was on January 28, 1933.

6

Hindenburg hoped that Hitler would now assent to a Papen cabinet. But Schleicher, in taking leave of the president, urged the appointment of Hitler as head of the new government. Meissner took the same line. The Centrists indicated their willingness to tolerate a Hitler cabinet provided it conformed rigidly to parliamentary principles. Hugenberg, however, continued to say no. Hitler, for his part, declared that he would accept nothing less than the chancellorship. The attitude of Papen proved decisive. He allowed Hitler to have his way, but only on certain conditions. The Fuehrer was to govern in strictly parliamentary fashion. The presidential authority was to remain supreme. Only three cabinet posts were to go to Nazis. Papen was to be vice-chancellor and was always to be present at conferences between Hitler and Hindenburg. Neurath was to remain at the foreign office, but the ministry of war was reserved for General Werner von Blomberg, a Nazi sympathizer. The ministries of economics and agriculture were assigned to Hugenberg, who now withdrew his objections to a Hitler cabinet. Franz Seldte, the Stahlhelm leader, was to take charge of the labor ministry. The Fuehrer would thus be surrounded by old-line conservatives who, it was generally anticipated, would restrain him and prevent one-sided use of his power. He would be—so reasoned his Nationalist allies—chancellor in name only. The new vice-chancellor, as the prime instrument and interpreter of the president's will, would be the real head of the government. Such was the arrangement which Papen and Meissner urged Hindenburg to accept. The old man finally yielded.

At noon, on January 30, 1933, Hitler and Papen were received by Hindenburg. Papen informed the field marshal that Hitler had succeeded in forming a government of national concentration. The oath of office was administered then and there. The Fuehrer put his hand in Hindenburg's and promised to uphold the constitution and rule by legal means. During the night a great torchlight procession filed past the Reich chancellery. Hindenburg and Hitler looked on and acknowledged the cheers of the demonstrators. Hindenburg seemed to be enjoying the spectacle in his grim, impassive way. Hitler was beside himself with joy. These two men, their new relationship cemented by shouts of approval from the exhilarated masses below, symbolized the unity which at long last prevailed among the reactionary foes of the republic.

SOME BIBLIOGRAPHICAL SUGGESTIONS

NEWSPAPERS

Allgemeine Zeitung
Berliner Lokal Anzeiger
Berliner Tageblatt
Frankfurter Zeitung
Germania
Hamburger Nachrichten
Koelnische Volkszeitung
Koelnische Zeitung
Rote Fahne
Voelkischer Beobachter
Vorwaerts

PERIODICALS AND YEARBOOKS

Archiv fuer die Geschichte des Sozialismus und der Arbeiterbewegung
Der deutsche Gedanke
Deutsche Revue
Deutsche Rundschau
Deutscher Revolutions-Almanach
Deutsches biographisches Jahrbuch
Deutschland: Jahrbuch fuer das deutsche Volk
Deutschlands Erneuerung
Die Gesellschaft
Die Grenzboten
Die Hilfe
Hochland
Illustrierte Zeitung
Jahrbuch der deutschen Sozialdemokratie
Die Neue Rundschau
Die Neue Zeit
Nord und Sued

Politisches Jahrbuch
Preussische Jahrbuecher
Schulthess' europaeischer Geschichtskalender
Sozialistische Monatshefte
Stimmen der Zeit
Sueddeutsche Monatshefte
Die Tat
Die Zukunft

PARLIAMENTARY DEBATES

Verhandlungen des Reichstags 1914-1918
Die deutsche Nationalversammlung 1919-1920
Verhandlungen des Reichstags 1920-1932

OTHER PRIMARY SOURCES

Allen, Henry T. *My Rhineland Journal.* Boston, 1923.
Allgemeiner Kongress der Arbeiter- und Soldatenraete Deutschlands. Vom 16. bis 21. Dezember 1918 im Abgeordnetenhause zu Berlin. Berlin, 1919.
Barth, Emil. *Aus der Werkstatt der deutschen Revolution.* Berlin, 1920.
Bernstorff, Count Johann. *Memoirs.* New York, 1936.
Bouton, S. M. *And the Kaiser Abdicates!* New Haven, 1920.
Braun, Otto. *Von Weimar zu Hitler.* New York (Europa Verlag), 1940.
Brockdorff-Rantzau, Graf Ulrich von. *Dokumente.* Berlin, 1922.
Buero des Reichswahlleiters. *Hauptergebnisse der Wahlen zum Reichstag am 31. Juli 1932.* Berlin, 1932.
D'Abernon, Viscount Edgar Vincent. *The Diary of an Ambassador.* New York, 1929-31. 3 vols.
Dawes, Charles G. *A Journal of Reparations.* London, 1939.
Dawes, Rufus C. *The Dawes Plan in the Making.* Indianapolis, 1925.
Deutsche Waffenstillstands-Kommission des Auswaertigen Amts. *Der Waffenstillstand 1918-1919.* Berlin, 1928. 3 vols.
Dietrich, Otto. *Mit Hitler in die Macht. Persoenliche Erlebnisse mit meinem Fuehrer.* Munich, 1934.
Duisberg, Carl. *Abhandlungen, Vortraege und Reden aus den Jahren 1922-1933.* Berlin, 1933.
Ebert, Friedrich. *Kaempfe und Ziele.* Dresden, 1927.
——. *Schriften, Aufzeichnungen, Reden.* Dresden, 1926. 2 vols.
Eisner, Kurt. *Gesammelte Schriften.* Berlin, 1919. 2 vols.
——. *Schuld und Suehne.* Berlin, 1919.
——. *Unterdruecktes aus dem Weltkrieg.* Munich, 1919.
Endres, Fritz, ed. *Hindenburg: Briefe, Reden Berichte.* Ebenhausen, 1934.

Erkelenz, Anton. *Demokratie und Parteiorganisation*. Berlin, n.d.
——. *Junge Demokratie*. Berlin, 1925.
Erzberger, Matthias. *Erlebnisse im Weltkrieg*. Stuttgart, 1920.
——. *The League of Nations. The Way to the World's Peace*. New York, 1919.
——. *Der Voelkerbund als Friedensfrage*. Berlin, 1919.
Feder, Gottfried. *Der deutsche Staat auf nationaler und sozialer Grundlage*. Munich, 1933.
——. *Hitler's Official Programme and Its Fundamental Ideas*. London, 1934.
——. *Kampf gegen die Hochfinanz*. Munich, 1933.
Fischer-Baling, Eugen. *Volksgericht, die deutsche Revolution von 1918 als Erlebnis und Gedanke*. Berlin, 1932.
Foch, Ferdinand. *Memoirs*. New York, 1931.
Forsthoff, Ernst, ed. *Deutsche Geschichte seit 1918 in Dokumenten*. Stuttgart, 1938. Vol. I.
Goebbels, Joseph. *Der Angriff. Aufsaetze aus der Kampfzeit*. Munich, 1936.
——. *My Part in Germany's Fight*. London, 1935.
Goering, Hermann. *Aufbau einer Nation*. Berlin, 1934.
Graefe, Albrecht von. *Damals in Weimar 1919*. Berlin, 1929.
Great Britain. War Office. *Reports by British Officers on the Economic Conditions Prevailing in Germany. December 1918—March 1919*. London, 1919.
——. *Further Reports by British Officers on the Economic Conditions Prevailing in Germany. April, 1919*. London, 1919.
Grzesinski, Albert C. *Inside Germany*. New York, 1939.
Haase, Ernst, ed. *Hugo Haase. Sein Leben und Wirken*. Berlin, 1929.
Harnisch, Johannes W. *Skizzen und Stimmungen aus dem Weimar der Nationalversammlung*. Berlin, 1919.
Haussmann, Conrad. *Aus Conrad Haussmanns Politischer Arbeit*. Hrsg. von seinen Freunden. Frankfort on the Main, 1923.
——. *Schlaglichter. Reichstagsbriefe und Aufzeichnungen*. Frankfort on the Main, 1924.
Helfferich, Karl T. *Der Weltkrieg*. Berlin, 1919. 3 vols.
——. *Fort mit Erzberger!* Berlin, 1919.
——. *Gegen Erzberger. Rede vor der Strafkammer in Moabit, 20. Januar 1920*. Berlin, 1920.
——. *Die Politik der Erfuellung*. Munich, 1922.
——. *Reichstagsreden 1922-1924*. Berlin, 1925.
Hindenburg, Paul von. *Aus meinem Leben*. Leipzig, 1920.
Hitler, Adolf. *Mein Kampf*. Boston, 1939.
——. *The Speeches of Adolf Hitler April 1922—August 1939*. Edited by Norman H. Baynes. London, 1942. 2 vols.

Hitler-Prozess. Verhandlungsbericht der Muenchener Neuesten Nach-richten. Munich, 1924. 2 vols.

Hoffmann, Major General Max. *War Diaries and other Papers.* London, 1929. 2 vols.

Hugenberg, Alfred. *Streiflichter aus Vergangenheit und Gegenwart.* Berlin, 1927.

International Labor Office, Geneva. *The Programme and Organization of the Christian Trade Unions of Germany* (Congress at Essen, 20-24 November, 1920). Geneva, 1921.

———. *Works Councils in Germany.* Geneva, 1921.

Keim, Lieut. Gen. August. *Erlebtes und Erstrebtes.* Hanover, 1925.

Klotz, Helmut, ed. *The Berlin Diaries.* London, 1934.

Kraus, Herbert and Roediger, Gustav, eds. *Urkunden zum Friedensvertrag zu Versailles vom 28. Juni 1919.* Berlin, 1920-21. 2 vols.

Landesausschuss der S.P.D. in Bayern, ed. *Hitler und Kahr. Aus dem Untersuchungsausschuss des bayrischen Landtags.* Munich, 1928.

Liebknecht, Karl. *Briefe aus dem Felde, aus der Untersuchungshaft und aus dem Zuchthaus.* Berlin, 1922.

———. *Politische Aufzeichnungen aus seinem Nachlass. Geschrieben in den Jahren 1917-1918.* Berlin, 1921.

———. *Speeches of Karl Liebknecht, with a Biographical Sketch.* New York, 1927.

———. *Reden und Aufsaetze.* Hamburg, 1921.

Ludecke, Kurt G. W. *I Knew Hitler.* New York, 1937.

Ludendorff, Erich. *Ludendorff's Own Story, August 1914—November 1918.* New York, 1919. 2 vols.

———. *Kriegfuehrung und Politik.* Berlin, 1922.

———. *Urkunden der Obersten Heeresleitung ueber ihre Taetigkeit, 1916-1918.* Berlin, 1922.

Ludendorff, Margarethe. *Als ich Ludendorffs Frau war.* Munich, 1929.

Luther, Hans. *Wirtschaftsfragen der Gegenwart.* Jena, 1932.

Lutz, R. H., ed. *Fall of the German Empire, 1914-1918.* Stanford, 1932.

Max, Prince of Baden. *Memoirs.* London, 1928. 2 vols.

Mueller, Hermann. *Die Novemberrevolution. Erinnerungen.* Berlin, 1928.

Mueller, Karl Alexander von. *Vom alten zum neuen Deutschland. Aufsaetze und Reden 1914-1938.* Stuttgart, 1938.

Mueller, Richard. *Der Buergerkrieg in Deutschland. Geburtswehen der Republik.* Berlin, 1925.

———. *Vom Kaiserreich zur Republik.* Berlin, 1924-25. 2 vols.

Niemann, Alfred. *Kaiser und Revolution. Die entscheidenden Ereignisse im Grossen Hauptquartier.* Berlin, 1922.

Noske, Gustav. *Von Kiel bis Kapp. Zur Geschichte der deutschen Revolution.* Berlin, 1920.

Payer, Friedrich. *Von Bethmann-Hollweg bis Ebert. Erinnerungen und Bilder*. Frankfort on the Main, 1923.

Preuss, Hugo. *Deutschlands republikanische Reichsverfassung*. Berlin, 1923.

————. *Reich und Laender. Bruchstuecke eines Kommentars zur Verfassung des deutschen Reiches*. Berlin, 1928.

————. *Um die Reichsverfassung von Weimar*. Berlin, 1924.

Radek, Karl. *In den Reihen der deutschen Revolution 1909-1919*. Munich, 1921.

Rathenau, Walther. *Briefe*. Dresden, 1927. Vol. II.

————. *Gesammelte Reden*. Berlin, 1924.

————. *Politische Briefe*. Dresden, 1929.

Rauschning, H. *Hitler Speaks*. London, 1940.

Reinhard, Oberst a. D. *1918-19. Die Wehen der Republik*. Berlin, 1933.

Reparation Commission. *Report of the First Committee of Experts*. Paris, 1924.

————. *The Experts' Plan for Reparation Payments*. Paris, 1926.

Reynolds, B. T. *Prelude to Hitler*. London, 1933.

Roehm, Ernst. *Die Geschichte eines Hochverraeters*. Munich, 1930.

Rosenberg, Alfred. *Der Mythus des 20. Jahrhunderts*. Munich, 1930.

Salomon, Felix. *Die deutschen Parteiprogramme*. Leipzig, 1924. Vols. II and III.

Schacht, Hjalmar. *The Stabilization of the Mark*. London, 1927.

————. *The End of Reparations*. New York, 1931.

Scheidemann, Philipp. *Der Zusammenbruch*. Berlin, 1921.

————. *The Making of New Germany. The Memoirs of Philipp Scheidemann*. New York, 1929. 2 vols.

Seeckt, Hans von. *Aus meinem Leben, 1918-1936*. Leipzig, 1940.

————. *Deutschland zwischen West und Ost*. Hamburg, 1933.

————. *Gedanken eines Soldaten*. Berlin, 1929.

————. *Landesverteidigung*. Berlin, 1930.

————. *Die Reichswehr*. Leipzig, 1933.

Stadtler, Eduard. *Als Antibolschevist 1918-19*. Duesseldorf, 1935.

Statistisches Reichsamt. *Die deutsche Zahlungsbilanz der Jahre 1924-1933*. Berlin, 1934.

————. *Industrielle Produktion*. Berlin, 1928.

Statistik des deutschen Reichs: Die Wahl des Reichspraesidenten am 13. Maerz und 10. April 1932. Berlin, 1932.

Stein, Adolf. *Zwischen Staatsmaennern, Reichstagsabgeordneten und Vorbestraften*. Berlin, n.d.

Stein, Ludwig. *Aus dem Leben eines Optimisten*. Berlin, 1930.

Strasser, Otto. *Hitler and I*. Boston, 1940.

Stresemann, Gustav. *Macht und Freiheit. Vortraege, Reden und Aufsaetze*. Halle, 1918.

——. *Reden und Schriften. Politik—Geschichte—Literatur 1897-1926.* Dresden, 1926. 2 vols.

——. *Von der Revolution bis zum Frieden von Versailles. Reden und Aufsaetze.* Berlin, 1919.

Sutton, Eric, ed. *Gustav Stresemann. His Diaries, Letters and Papers.* New York, 1935-40. 3 vols.

The Treaties of Peace, 1919-1923. New York, 1924. 2 vols.

Thyssen, Fritz. *I Paid Hitler.* New York, 1941.

Treuberg, Hetta Graefin. *Zwischen Politik und Diplomatie. Memoiren.* Strassburg, 1921.

Troeltsch, Ernst. *Spektator-Briefe. Aufsaetze ueber die deutsche Revolution und die Weltpolitik 1918-1922.* Tuebingen, 1924.

Die Ursachen des deutschen Zusammenbruchs im Jahre 1918. Berlin, 1925-1929. 12 vols.

Vorgeschichte des Waffenstillstands. Amtliche Urkunden. Hrsg. im Auftrag des Reichsministeriums von der Reichskanzlei. Berlin, 1919.

Weber, Max. *Gesammelte politische Schriften.* Berlin, 1921.

Wermuth, Adolf. *Ein Beamtenleben. Erinnerungen.* Berlin, 1922.

Westarp, Graf. *Die Regierung des Prinzen Max von Baden und die konservative Partei.* Berlin, n.d.

——. *Konservative Politik im letzten Jahrzehnt des Kaiserreiches.* Berlin, 1935. Vol. II.

Wilhelm, Crown Prince of the German Empire and of Prussia. *Memoirs.* New York, 1922.

Wilhelm II, German Emperor. *Memoirs.* New York, 1922.

Wirsing, Giselher. *Zwischeneuropa und die deutsche Zukunft.* Jena, 1932.

Wirth, Joseph. *Reden waehrend der Kanzlerschaft.* Berlin, 1925.

Wolff, Theodor. *Through Two Decades.* London, 1936.

Wrisberg, Ernst von. *Der Weg zur Revolution 1914-1918.* Leipzig, 1921.

SECONDARY WORKS

Abel, Theodore Fred. *Why Hitler Came Into Power: An Answer Based on the Original Life Stories of Six Hundred of His Followers.* New York, 1938.

Aereboe, Friedrich. *Der Einfluss des Krieges auf die landwirtschaftliche Produktion in Deutschland.* Stuttgart, 1927.

Alexander, T. and Kandel, I. L. *Reorganization of Education in Prussia.* New York, 1927.

Alexander, T. and Parker, B. *The New Education in the German Republic.* New York, 1929.

Ali Akbar, Saiyid. *The German School System.* Calcutta, 1932.

Alter, Junius. *Nationalisten. Deutschlands nationales Fuehrertum der Nachkriegszeit.* Leipzig, 1930.

American Academy of Political and Social Science. *Social and Industrial Conditions in the Germany of Today*. Philadelphia, 1920.

Angas, Lawrence L. B. *Germany and Her Debts. A Critical Examination of the Reparation Problem*. London, 1923.

Angell, James W. *The Recovery of Germany*. New Haven, 1929.

Anschuetz, Gerhard. *Die Verfassung des deutschen Reichs vom 11. August 1919*. Berlin, 1930.

Apolant, Hans A. *Die Wirtschaftsfriedliche Arbeitnehmerbewegung Deutschlands*. Berlin, 1928.

Arndt, Adolf. *Die Verfassung des deutschen Reichs*. Berlin, 1927.

Bachem, Karl. *Vorgeschichte, Geschichte und Politik der deutschen Zentrumspartei*. Cologne, 1932. Vol. IX.

Bachmann, Hans. *Die deutsche Volkswirtschaft vor und nach dem Weltkriege*. Zurich, 1921.

Bade, Wilfrid. *Joseph Goebbels*. Luebeck, 1933.

Baeumer, Gertrud. *Deutsche Schulpolitik*. Karlsruhe, 1928.

Bauer, Heinrich. *Stresemann, ein deutscher Staatsmann*. Berlin, 1930.

Baumont, Maurice. *The Fall of the Kaiser*. London, 1931.

Baumont, Maurice and Berthelot, Marcel. *L'Allemagne. Lendemains de guerre et de révolution*. Paris, 1922.

Bayles, William D. *Caesars in Goose Step*. New York, 1940.

Becker, Carl H. *Secondary Education and Teacher Training in Germany*. New York, 1931.

Beckerath, Erwin von and others. *The Present Economic State of Germany*. Worcester (Mass.), 1932.

Beckerath, Herbert von. *Modern Industrial Organization*. New York, 1933.

———. *Reparationsagent und deutsche Wirtschaftspolitik*. Bonn, 1928.

Benaerts, Pierre. *Les Origines de la Grande Industrie allemande*. Paris, 1933.

Benoist-Méchin, Baron Jacques. *History of the German Army since the Armistice*. Zurich, 1939.

Berckholtz, Walter. *Der Staatscharakter der deutschen Laender nach der Reichsverfassung vom 11. August 1919*. Oberviechtach, 1928.

Berg, Emil. *Des deutschen Volkes Schicksalsweg: Diktatur oder Untergang*. Leipzig, 1928.

Berger, Marcel and Allard, Paul. *Les Dessous du traité de Versailles*. Paris, 1933.

Bergmann, Karl. *The History of Reparations*. London, 1927.

Bergmann, Konrad A. *Das ethische Bildungziel der hoeheren Schule*. Karlsruhe, 1925.

Bergstraesser, Ludwig. *Geschichte der politischen Parteien in Deutschland*. Mannheim, 1926.

Bernhard, Georg. *Le Suicide de la république allemande*. Paris, 1933.

Bernstein, Eduard. *Die deutsche Revolution*. Berlin, 1921.

Bezirksausschuss des allgemeinen deutschen Gewerkschaftsbundes Berlin-Brandenburg-Grenzmark. *Die wirtschaftlichen Unternehmungen der Arbeiterbewegung*. Berlin, 1928.

Bhatt, G. U. *The System of Education in Germany since the War*. Bombay, 1935.

Billung, R. *N.S.D.A.P. Die Geschichte einer Bewegung*. Munich, 1931.

Birdsall, Paul. *Versailles Twenty Years After*. New York, 1941.

Blachly, Frederick F., and Oatman, Miriam E. *The Government and Administration of Germany*. Baltimore, 1928.

Blood-Ryan, H. W. *Franz von Papen. His Life and Times*. London, 1939.

————. *Goering, the Iron Man of Germany*. London, 1938.

Blos, Wilhelm. *Von der Monarchie zum Volksstaat*. Stuttgart, 1922-1923. 2 vols.

Bopp, K. R. *Hjalmar Schacht: Central Banker*. Columbia (Mo.), 1939.

Boehme, Theodor. *Die christlich-nationale Gewerkschaft*. Stuttgart, 1930.

Boetcher, Hans. *Zur revolutionaeren Gewerkschaftsbewegung in Amerika, Deutschland und England*. Jena, 1922.

Bonin, Walter von. *Die volkswirtschaftliche Bedeutung und die praktische Auswirkung des deutschen Betriebsraetegesetzes*. Greifswald, 1927.

Bonn, Moritz Julius. *Der neue Plan als Grundlage der deutschen Wirtschaftspolitik*. Munich, 1930.

Bonnell, Allen T. *German Control over International Economic Relations 1930-1940*. Urbana, 1940.

Borght, Richard van der, ed. *Die Bodenreform*. Berlin, 1919.

Bourceret, Albert. *Les Associations professionnelles ouvrières en Allemagne*. Paris, 1933.

Bozi, Alfred and Sartorius, Otto, eds. *Die deutsche Wirtschaft*. Berlin, 1926.

Brady, R. A. *The Rationalization Movement in German Industry*. Berkeley, 1933.

Bredt, Victor. *Der deutsche Reichstag im Weltkrieg*. Berlin, 1926.

Braun, Kurt. *Die Konzentration der Berufsvereine der deutschen Arbeitgeber und Arbeitnehmer und ihre rechtliche Bedeutung*. Berlin, 1922.

Brigl-Matthiasz, K. *Das Betriebsraeteproblem*. Berlin, 1926.

Brinckmeyer, Hermann. *Die Rathenaus*. Munich, 1922.

————. *Hugo Stinnes*. New York, 1921.

Brooks, Sidney. *America and Germany 1918-1925*. New York, 1925.

Bruck, Werner F. *Social and Economic History of Germany from William II to Hitler 1888-1938*. Cardiff, 1938.

Brunet, René. *The New German Constitution*. New York, 1922.

Buecher, Hermann. *Finanz-und Wirtschaftsentwicklung Deutschlands in den Jahren 1921 bis 1925*. Berlin, 1925.

Buehler, Ottmar. *Die Reichsverfassung vom 11. August 1919.* Leipzig, 1922.

Butler, Rohan D. *The Roots of National Socialism.* New York, 1942.

Calker, Fritz van. *Wesen und Sinn der Politischen Parteien.* Tuebingen, 1928.

Cambon, Victor. *L'Allemagne nouvelle.* Paris, 1923.

Carroll, Mollie Ray. *Unemployment Insurance in Germany.* Washington, 1929.

Cassau, Jeanette. *Die Arbeitergewerkschaften. Eine Einfuehrung.* Halberstadt, 1927.

Cassau, Theodor. *Die Gewerkschaftsbewegung.* Halberstadt, 1925.

Chamberlin, Waldo. *Industrial Relations in Germany, 1914-1939. Annotated Bibliography of Materials in the Hoover War Library.* Palo Alto, 1942.

Clark, Robert T. *The Fall of the German Republic.* London, 1935.

Clarke, Charles H. *Germany Yesterday and To-Morrow.* London, 1923.

Coar, John Firman. *The Old and the New Germany.* New York, 1924.

Coupaye, Joseph M. L. *La Ruhr et l'Allemagne.* Paris, 1922.

Czech-Jochberg, Erich. *Hitler Reichskanzler.* Oldenburg, 1933.

Daniels, Harold G. *The Rise of the German Republic.* London, 1927.

Danton, George H. *Germany Ten Years After.* Boston, 1928.

Darcy, Paul. *L'Allemagne toujours armée.* Paris, 1933.

Darmstaedter, Friedrich. *Rechtsstaat oder Machtstaat? Eine Frage nach der Geltung der Weimarer Verfassung.* Berlin, 1932.

David, Eduard. *Sozialismus und Landwirtschaft.* Leipzig, 1922.

Dawson, Sir Philip. *Germany's Industrial Revival.* London, 1926.

Dawson, William H. *Germany under the Treaty.* London, 1933.

Delahanty, Thomas W. *The German Dyestuffs Industry.* Washington, 1924.

Delbrueck, Joachim von. *Clemens von Delbrueck.* Berlin, 1922.

Demeter, Karl. *Das deutsche Heer und seine Offiziere.* Berlin, 1935.

Deutsche paedagogische Auslandstelle, Berlin. *The German Educational System.* Leipzig, 1932.

Dix, Arthur. *Wirtschaftskrieg und Kriegswirtschaft. Zur Geschichte des deutschen Zusammenbruchs.* Berlin, 1920.

———. *Die deutschen Reichstagswahlen 1871-1930 und die Wandlungen der Volksgliederung.* Tuebingen, 1930.

Dombrowski, Eric. *German Leaders of Yesterday and To-Day.* New York, 1920.

Douglass, Paul F. *The Economic Dilemma of Politics. A Study of the Consequences of the Strangulation of Germany.* New York, 1932.

Dutch, Oswald. *The Errant Diplomat. The Life of Franz von Papen.* London, 1940.

Emerson, Rupert. *State and Sovereignty in Modern Germany.* New Haven, 1928.

Enderes, Bruno von. *Die Wirtschaftliche Bedeutung der Anschlussfrage.* Leipzig, 1929.

Erdberg-Krczenciewski, Robert A. W. von. *Fuenfzig Jahre freies Volksbildungswesen.* Berlin, 1924.

Esslen, Joseph B. *Die Politik des auswaertigen Handels.* Stuttgart, 1925.

Eulenburg, Franz, ed. *Neue Grundlagen der Handelspolitik.* Munich, 1925.

———. *Probleme der deutschen Handelspolitik.* Jena, 1925.

Fechenbach, Felix. *Der Revolutionaer Kurt Eisner.* Berlin, 1929.

Federn-Kohlhaas. *Walther Rathenau. Sein Leben und Wirken.* Dresden, 1928.

Feine, Hans Erich. *Das Werden des deutschen Staates. Eine verfassungsgeschichtliche Darstellung.* Stuttgart, 1936.

Fletcher, Arthur W. *Education in Germany.* Cambridge (Eng.), 1934.

Flink, Salomon. *The German Reichsbank and Economic Germany. A Study of the Policies of the Reichsbank in their Relation to the Economic Development of Germany, with Special Reference to the Period after 1923.* New York, 1930.

Fraenkel, E. *Betriebsraete und Arbeitsgerichtsgesetz.* Berlin, 1927.

Fraina, Louis C. *The Social Revolution in Germany.* Boston, n.d.

Francke, Kuno. *German After-War Problems.* Cambridge, 1927.

Freytagh-Loringhoven, Axel Freiherr von. *Die Weimarer Verfassung in Lehre und Wirklichkeit.* Munich, 1924.

Fribourg, André. *La Victoire des vaincus.* Paris, 1938.

Fricke, Rolf. *Die Ursachen der Arbeitslosigkeit in Deutschland.* Berlin, 1931.

Fried, Hans Ernest. *The Guilt of the German Army.* New York, 1942.

Fritsch, Konrad. *Die Funktionen des Reichspraesidenten, (nach der neuen Reichsverfassung vom 11. August 1919 verglichen mit den Funktionen des ehemaligen deutschen Kaisers.)* Stettin, 1921.

Fuerstenberg, Hans. *Germany Four Years After Stabilization.* New York, 1927.

Galéra, Karl Siegmar, Baron von. *Geschichte unserer Zeit.* Leipzig, 1930. 4 vols.

Ganzer, Karl Richard. *Vom Ringen Hitlers um das Reich, 1924-1933.* Berlin, 1935.

Garrett, Garet. *The Rescue of Germany.* New York, 1931.

Gedye, G. E. R. *The Revolver Republic.* London, 1930.

Gerlach, J. *Der Betriebsvertretungsgedanke in seiner Eutwicklung und praktischen Verwicklung.* Giessen, 1930.

German Government. *Germany's Economy, Currency and Finance. A Study Addressed by Order of the German Government to the Commit-*

tee of Experts, as Appointed by the Reparation Commission. Berlin, 1924.

Gesellschaft fuer soziale Reform (Berlin). *Der wirtschaftliche Wert der Sozialpolitik.* Jena, 1931.

Giese, Friedrich. *Deutsches Staatsrecht.* Berlin, 1930.

———. *Die Verfassung des deutschen Reiches.* Berlin, 1931.

Giese, Friedrich, Neuwiem, Erhard, and Cahn, Ernst. *Deutsches Verwaltungsrecht.* Berlin, 1930.

Giustiniani, Gaston. *Le commerce et l'industrie devant la dépréciation et la stabilisation monétaire. L'expérience allemande.* Paris, 1927.

Glum, Friedrich. *Der deutsche und der franzoesische Reichswirtschaftsrat.* Berlin, 1929.

Goetz-Girey, R. *Les Syndicats ouvriers allemands après la guerre.* Paris, 1936.

Goldsmith, Margaret L. and Voigt, Frederick. *Hindenburg. The Man and the Legend.* London, 1930.

Graham, Frank D. *Exchange, Prices and Production in Hyper-Inflation. Germany, 1920-1923.* Princeton, 1930.

Graham, Malbone W. *New Governments of Central Europe.* New York, 1924.

Great Britain, Ministry of Labour. *The Unemployment Problem in Germany.* London, 1931.

Grimme, Adolf, ed. *Wesen und Wege der Schulreform.* Berlin, 1930.

Gritzbach, Erich. *Hermann Goering: The Man and His Work.* London, 1939.

Gueydan de Roussel, Guillaume. *L'Évolution du pouvoir exécutif en Allemagne (1919-1934).* Paris, 1935.

Guillebaud, C. W. *The Works Council. A German Experiment in Industrial Democracy.* Cambridge (Eng.), 1928.

Haberland, Guenther. *Elf Jahre staatlicher Regelung der Ein- und Ausfuhr: Eine systematische Darstellung der deutschen Aussenhandelsregelung in den Jahren 1914-1925.* Leipzig, 1927.

Hanke, Georg. *Weltkrieg-Niedergang und Aufbruch der deutschen Nation. Ein Fuehrer durch die neueste Geschichte von 1914-1933.* Berlin, 1933.

Harms, Bernhard. *Die Zukunft der deutschen Handelspolitik etc.* Jena, 1925.

Hart, F. T. *Alfred Rosenberg. Der Mann und sein Werk.* Munich, 1935.

Hass, Hermann. *Sitte und Kultur im Nachkriegsdeutschland.* Hamburg, 1932.

Hasselbach, Ulrich von. *Die Entstehung der N.S.D.A.P. 1919-1923.* Breslau, 1931.

Hatschek, Julius. *Deutsches und preussisches Staatsrecht.* Berlin, 1922-23. 2 vols.

Heiden, Konrad. *Der Fuehrer.* New York, 1944.

————. *A History of National Socialism.* London, 1934.

————. *Hitler.* New York, 1936.

Helmreich, Theodore C. *The Unemployment Program of the German Government, 1930-1934.* Urbana, 1936.

Heneman, Harlow James. *The Growth of the Executive Power in Germany: A Study of the German Presidency.* Minneapolis, 1934.

Herford, Charles H. *The Post-War Mind of Germany and Other European Studies.* Oxford, 1927.

Hermant, Max. *Les Paradoxes économiques de l'Allemagne moderne, 1918-1931.* Paris, 1931.

Herring, Charles E.; Parmelee, Maurice; and Scovell, Robert J. *German Reparations, Budget, and Foreign Trade.* Washington, 1922.

Herz, Ludwig. *Die Abdankung (Schriften zum deutschen Zusammenbruch, 1918).* Leipzig, 1924.

Hesnard, O. *Les Partis politiques en Allemagne.* Paris, 1923.

Heuss, Theodor. *Friedrich Naumann. Der Mann, das Werk, die Zeit.* Stuttgart, 1937.

————. *Hitlers Weg.* Stuttgart, 1932.

Hindenburg, Major Gert von. *Hindenburg 1847-1934. Soldier and Statesman.* London, 1935.

Hinrichs, Bernhard. *Die Grenzen der Verfassungsautonomie der deutschen Laender.* Berlin, 1930.

Hoetzsch, O. *Germany's Domestic and Foreign Policies.* London, 1929.

Hohmann, Walther. *1914-1934. Zwanzig Jahre deutscher Geschichte.* Frankfort on the Main, 1937.

Holt, John B. *German Agricultural Policy 1918-1934. The Development of a National Philosophy toward Agriculture in Postwar Germany.* Chapel Hill, 1936.

Hoevel, Paul. *Grundfragen deutscher Wirtschaftspolitik.* Berlin, 1935.

Hoover, Calvin B. *Germany Enters the Third Reich.* New York, 1933.

Horkenbach, Cuno, ed. *Das deutsche Reich von 1918 bis heute.* Berlin, 1930.

Huber, Ernst R. *Heer und Staat.* Hamburg, 1938.

Hué, Otto. *Die Sozialisierung der deutschen Kohlenwirtschaft.* Berlin, 1921.

Jaeckh, Ernst. *The New Germany.* London, 1927.

Jonuschat, Hans. *Die Steuerpolitik der Parteien im Reichstag.* Berlin, 1927.

Kampffmeyer, Paul. *Friedrich Ebert, ein Lebensbild.* (Pp. 11-128 of Friedrich Ebert, *Schriften, Aufzeichnungen, Reden,* Vol. I). Dresden, 1926.

Kaster, Johannes. *Die Stellung der deutschen Katholiken zur Gewerkschaftsfrage.* Gladbach, 1921.

Kellermann, Fritz. *The Effect of the World War on European Education, with Special Attention to Germany.* Cambridge, 1928.

Kessler, Count Harry. *Germany and Europe*. New Haven, 1923.

———. *Walter Rathenau*. New York, 1930.

King, Joseph. *The German Revolution. Its Meaning and Menace*. London, 1933.

Kleinow, Polizeioberst a. D. *Der Polizeifuehrer in den Nachkriegsjahren*. Luebeck, n. d.

Kloeber, Wilhelm von. *Vom Weltkrieg zur nationalen Revolution. Deutsche Geschichte 1914-1933*. Munich, 1935.

Knickerbocker, Hubert R. *The German Crisis*. New York, 1932.

Koch-Weser, Erich. *Germany in the Post-War World*. Philadelphia, 1930.

Koenigswald, Harald von. *Revolution 1918*. Breslau, 1933.

Koeves, Tibor. *Satan in Top Hat. The Biography of Franz von Papen*. New York, 1941.

Kosok, Paul. *Modern Germany: A Study of Conflicting Loyalties*. Chicago, 1933.

Kraus, Herbert. *Germany in Transition*. Chicago, 1924.

———. *The Crisis of German Democracy. A Study of the Spirit of the Constitution of Weimar*. Princeton, 1932.

Kroellreutter, Otto. *Die politischen Parteien im modernen Staate*. Breslau, 1926.

Krueger, Hanna. *Die unbequeme Frau. Kaethe Schirrmacher in Kampf fuer die Freiheit der Frau und die Freiheit der Nation, 1865-1930*. Berlin, 1936.

Krueger, Wilhelm. *Staat, Gesellschaft und Wirtschaft in der Weimarer Verfassung*. Giessen, 1931.

Krumbach, Josef H., ed. *Franz Ritter von Epp: Ein Leben fuer Deutschland*. Munich, 1939.

Krumbholz, Paul. *Geschichte des weimarischen Schulwesens*. Berlin, 1934.

Kuczynski, R. R. *American Loans to Germany*. New York, 1927.

———. *Deutschland und Frankreich. Ihre Wirtschaft und ihre Politik, 1923-24*. Berlin, 1924.

———. *Postwar Labor Conditions in Germany*. Washington, 1925.

Lederer, Emil, ed. *Das Kartellproblem*. Munich, 1930-32. Vol. III.

———. *Technischer Fortschritt und Arbeitslosigkeit*. Tuebingen, 1931.

Lehmann-Russbueldt, Otto. *Aggression. The Origin of Germany's War Machine*. London, 1942.

Leipart, Theodor. *Karl Legien, ein Gedenkbuch*. Berlin, 1929.

Lengyel, Emil. *Hitler*. New York, 1932.

Leverkuehn, Paul. *Posten auf ewiger Wache. Aus dem abenteuerreichen Leben des Max von Scheubner-Richter*. Essen, 1938.

Lewinsohn, Richard. *Die Umschichtung der europaeischen Vermoegen*. Berlin, 1925.

Linnfeld, Helmut. *Beitraege zur Vorgeschichte der Novemberrevolution von 1918*. Hamburg, 1933.

Lipinski, Richard. *Die Sozialdemokratie von ihren Anfaengen bis zur Gegenwart.* Berlin, 1927. 2 vols.

Loewenstein, Prince Hubertus. *The Tragedy of a Nation. Germany 1918-1934.* New York, 1934.

Lorenz, Robert. *The Essential Features of Germany's Agricultural Policy from 1870 to 1937.* New York, 1941.

Lorwin, L. L. *Labor and Internationalism.* New York, 1929.

Luckau, Alma. *The German Delegation at the Paris Peace Conference.* New York, 1941.

Luehr, Elmer. *The New German Republic.* New York, 1929.

Luther, Hans. *Von Deutschlands eigener Kraft.* Berlin, 1928.

Lutz, R. H. *The German Revolution, 1918-1919.* Palo Alto, 1922.

Maercker, Georg. *Vom Kaiserheer zur Reichswehr.* Leipzig, 1921.

Marck, Siegfried. *Reformismus und Radikalismus in der deutschen Sozialdemokratie.* Berlin, 1927.

——. *Sozialdemokratie.* Berlin, 1931.

Marcks, Erich, and Eisenhart Rothe, Ernst von. *Paul von Hindenburg als Mensch, Staatsmann, Feldheer.* Berlin, 1933.

Mattern, Johannes. *Principles of the Constitutional Jurisprudence of the German National Republic.* Baltimore, 1928.

McConagha, William Albert. *Development of the Labor Movement in Great Britain, France and Germany.* Chapel Hill, 1942.

McPherson, W. H. *Collaboration between Management and Employees in German Factories.* University of Chicago Ph.D. Thesis. Chicago, 1935.

——. *Works Councils under the German Republic.* Chicago, 1939.

Meakin, Walter. *The New Industrial Revolution.* London, 1928.

Meinecke, Friedrich. *Nach der Revolution.* Munich, 1919.

Meissner, Otto. *Das Staatsrecht des Reichs und seiner Laender.* Berlin, 1923.

Mendelssohn-Bartholdy, Albrecht. *The War and German Society.* New Haven, 1937.

Meyer, Diedrich. *Die deutsche Reichsverfassung von 1919.* Bielefeld, 1922.

Meyer, Max H. *Die Weltanschauung des Zentrums in ihren Grundlinien.* Leipzig, 1919.

Michael, Louis Guy. *Agricultural Survey of Europe: Germany.* Washington, 1926.

Michels, R. K. *Cartels, Combines, and Trusts in Post-War Germany.* New York, 1928.

Mommsen, Wilhelm and Franz, Guenther. *Die deutschen Parteiprogramme.* Leipzig, 1931.

Monath, Armin. *Obrigkeitsstaat und Volksstaat.* Marburg-Lahn, 1934.

Morgan, J. H. *The Present State of Germany.* Boston, n.d.

Moulton, Harold G. and McGuire, Constantine E. *Germany's Capacity to Pay. A Study of the Reparation Problem.* New York, 1923.

Moulton, Harold G. *The Reparation Plan.* New York, 1924.

Mowrer, Edgar Ansel. *Germany Puts the Clock Back.* New York, 1933.

Muehlen, N. *Schacht: Hitler's Magician.* New York, 1939.

Naphtali, Fritz. *Wirtschaftsdemokratie.* Berlin, 1928.

National Industrial Conference Board. *Rationalization of German Industry.* New York, 1931.

——. *Unemployment Insurance and Relief in Germany.* New York, 1932.

——. *The Situation in Germany at the Beginning of 1933.* New York, 1933.

Neumann, Franz. *European Trade Unionism and Politics.* New York, 1936.

Neumann, Sigmund. *Die deutschen Parteien: Wesen und Wandel nach dem Kriege.* Berlin, 1932.

Niemann, Alfred. *Die Entthronung Kaiser Wilhelms II.* Leipzig, 1924.

——. *Hindenburg. Vom Kadett zum Feldmarschall.* Leipzig, 1926.

——. *Der Weg Kaiser Wilhelms II. Vom Thron in die Fremde.* Stuttgart, 1932.

Nipperdey, Prof. Hans Carl, ed. *Die Grundrechte und Grundpflichten der Reichsverfassung. Kommentar zum zweiten Teil der Reichsverfassung.* Berlin, 1929-30. 3 vols.

Northrop, Mildred B. *Control Policies of the Reichsbank, 1924-1933.* New York, 1938.

Nowak, Karl Friedrich. *Versailles.* New York, 1929.

Oertzen, Friedrich Wilhelm von. *Die deutschen Freikorps 1918-1923.* Munich, 1936.

Olden, Rudolf. *Hindenburg.* Paris, 1935.

——. *Hitler.* New York, 1936.

——. *Stresemann.* Berlin, 1929.

Oliveira, A. Ramos. *A People's History of Germany.* London, 1942.

Oppenheimer, Heinrich. *The Constitution of the German Republic.* London, 1923.

Ott, Karl. *Die hoehere Schule.* Karlsruhe, 1924.

Pantlen, Hermann. *Der Wiedereintritt Deutschlands in die Weltschiffahrt.* Berlin, 1927.

Pernot, Maurice. *L'Allemagne aujourd'hui.* Paris, 1927.

Philips, August, Jr. *Economic Aspects of Reparations and Inter-Allied Debts.* Leyden, 1930.

Picht, Werner and Rosenstock, Eugen. *Im Kampf um die Erwachsenenbildung 1912-1926.* Leipzig, 1926.

Pinner, Felix. *Deutsche Wirtschaftsfuehrer.* Charlottenburg, 1925.

Pistorius, Theodor von. *Staats- und Verwaltungskunde.* Stuttgart, 1926.

Plaut, Theodor. *Deutsche Handelspolitik.* Leipzig, 1924.

Pogge, Ernst. *Das Verhaeltnis zwischen Reich und Laender.* Harburg-Wilhelmsburg, 1934.

Poll, Bernhard. *Deutsches Schicksal 1914-1918. Vorgeschichte und Geschichte des Weltkrieges.* Berlin, 1937.

Poole, Kenyon E. *German Financial Policies, 1932-39.* Cambridge, 1939.

Posse, Ernst H. *Die politischen Kampfbuende Deutschlands.* Berlin, 1931.

Prailauné, H. N. de. *L'Unitarisme et le fédéralisme dans la constitution allemande du 11 août 1919.* Paris, 1922.

Price, M. Philips. *Germany in Transition.* London, 1923.

Quaatz, Reinhold G. and Spahn, Martin. *Deutschland unter Militaer-Finanz- und Wirtschafts-Kontrolle.* Berlin, 1925.

Quigley, Hugh and Clark, R. T. *Republican Germany.* New York, 1928.

Raphael, Gaston. *Le Roi de la Ruhr. Hugo Stinnes.* Paris, 1924.

Rauschning, Hermann. *Men of Chaos.* New York, 1942.

———. *The Revolution of Nihilism.* New York, 1939.

Raushenbush, H. S. *The March of Fascism.* New Haven, 1939.

Reber, James Q. *Stresemann's Foreign Policy.* University of Chicago M. A. Thesis. Chicago, 1935.

———. *War and Diplomacy in the German Reich, 1870-1938.* University of Chicago Ph.D. Thesis. Chicago, 1939.

Reichsarbeitsministerium. *Deutsche Sozialpolitik 1918-1928.* Berlin, 1929.

Reinhold, Peter P. *The Economic, Financial and Political State of Germany since the War.* New Haven, 1928.

Renner, Karl. *Wege der Verwirklichung.* Berlin, 1929.

Reventlow, Ernst zu. *Minister Stresemann, als Staatsmann und Anwalt des Weltgewissens.* Munich, 1926.

Révész, Imre. *Walther Rathenau und sein oekonomisches Werk.* Zurich, 1926.

Rewoldt, Karl Heinrich. *Das Staatsnotrecht im deutschen Staatsrecht.* Breslau, 1933.

Rheinbaben, Rochus Freiherr von. *Stresemann. Der Mensch und der Staatsmann.* Dresden, 1928.

Riegel, Julius. *Zur Frage der deutschen Oberschule.* Nuremberg, 1921.

Rivaud, Albert. *Les Crises allemandes (1919-1931).* Paris, 1932.

———. *Le Relèvement de l'Allemagne 1918-1938.* Paris, 1939.

Roemer, Wilhelm. *Die Entwicklung des Raetegedankens in Deutschland.* Berlin, 1921.

Roepke, Wilhelm. *German Commercial Policy.* London, 1934.

Rohr, Hans Olof von. *Der Einfluss der deutschen Laender auf die Gestaltung der Reichsverfassung von 1919.* Goettingen, 1931.

Roll, Erich. *Spotlight on Germany. A Survey of her Economic and Political Aims.* London, 1933.

Roques, Paul. *Le Contrôle militaire interallié en Allemagne. septembre 1919—janvier 1927*. Paris, 1927.

Rosenberg, Arthur. *The Birth of the German Republic*. London, 1931.

———. *History of the German Republic*. London, 1936.

Rosinski, Herbert. *The German Army*. London, 1940.

Rudin, Harry R. *Armistice, 1918*. New Haven, 1944.

Runkel, F. *Die deutsche Revolution*. Leipzig, 1919.

Saitzew, Manuel, ed. *Die Arbeitslosigkeit der Gegenwart*. Munich, 1932-33. 3 vols.

Sass, Johannes. *Die 27 deutschen Parteien und ihre Ziele*. Hamburg, 1931.

Schacht, Hjalmar. *Grundsaetze deutscher Wirtschaftspolitik*. Oldenburg, 1932.

Schauff, Johannes. *Die deutschen Katholiken und die Zentrumspartei. Eine politisch-statistische Untersuchung der Reichstagswahlen seit 1871*. Cologne, 1928.

Scheler, Max; Heimann, Eduard and Baumgarten, Arthur. *Walther Rathenau*. Cologne, 1922.

Schiff, Victor. *The Germans at Versailles*. London, 1930.

Schmidt, Carl T. *German Business Cycles, 1924-1933*. New York, 1934.

Schmidt-Pauli, Edgar von. *Die Maenner um Hitler*. Berlin, 1932.

———. *General v. Seeckt*. Berlin, 1937.

———. *Geschichte der Freikorps 1918-1924*. Stuttgart, 1936.

Schmitt, Carl. *Hugo Preuss. Sein Staatsbegriff und seine Stellung in der deutschen Staatslehre*. Tuebingen, 1930.

Schmoller, Gustav. *Walther Rathenau und Hugo Preuss*. Munich, 1922.

Schuerer, Heinz. *Die politische Arbeiterbewegung Deutschlands in der Nachkriegszeit 1918-1923*. Leipzig, 1933.

Schulte, Karl Anton, ed. *Nationale Arbeit. Das Zentrum und sein Wirken in der deutschen Republik*. Berlin, 1930.

Schultze, Ernst. *Tributzahlung und Ausfuhrkraft*. Leipzig, 1929.

Schultze-Pfaelzer, Gerhard. *Hindenburg*. New York, 1932.

———. *Von Spa nach Weimar*. Leipzig, 1929.

Schuman, F. L. *Germany since 1918*. New York, 1937.

Schumann, Harry. *Karl Liebknecht*. Dresden, 1923.

Schwarz, Arnold R. *Die deutsche Ausfuhrkontrolle nach dem Kriege*. Griefswald, 1923.

Schwarz, Paul. *This Man Ribbentrop*. New York, 1943.

Schweyer, Franz. *Politische Geheimverbaende*. Freiburg i. B., 1925.

Seidel, Richard. *The Trade Union Movement of Germany*. Amsterdam, 1928.

Seillière, Ernest. *Les Pangermanistes d'après-guerre*. Paris, 1924.

Sellschopp, Hermann. *Die Grenzen der Diktatur auf Grund der Weimarer Reichsverfassung*. Rostock, 1932.

Sering, Max. *Das Friedensdiktat von Versailles und Deutschlands wirtschaftliche Lage.* Berlin, 1920.

———. *Germany Under the Dawes Plan.* London, 1929.

———. *Die Vererbung des laendlichen Grundbesitzes in der Nachkriegszeit.* Munich, 1930. Vol. I.

Shotwell, James T. *What Germany Forgot.* New York, 1940.

Shuster, George N. *The Germans. An Inquiry and an Estimate.* New York, 1932.

Siebert, Rolf. *Das Abkommen vom 15. November 1918 und die Zentral-Arbeitsgemeinschaft der industriellen und gewerblichen Arbeitgeber und Arbeitnehmer Deutschlands.* Berlin, 1932.

Simons, Walter. *Hugo Preuss.* Berlin, 1930.

Spethmann, Hans. *Die Grosswirtschaft an der Ruhr.* Breslau, 1925.

Stampfer, Friedrich. *Die vierzehn Jahre der ersten deutschen Republik.* Karlsbad, 1936.

Stegemann, Hermann. *Der Kampf um den Rhein.* Stuttgart, 1924.

———. *The Mirage of Versailles.* New York, 1928.

Steinmetz, Paul. *Die deutsche Volkshochschulbewegung.* Karlsruhe, 1929.

Stern, Boris. *Works Council Movement in Germany. U.S. Bureau of Labor. Statistics, Bulletin No. 383.* Washington, 1925.

Stern-Rubarth, Edgar. *Graf Brockdorff-Rantzau. Wanderer zwischen zwei Welten. Ein Lebensbild.* Berlin, 1929.

———. *Stresemann, der Europaeer.* Berlin, 1929.

———. *Three Men Tried. . . . Austen Chamberlain, Stresemann, Briand, and Their Fight for a New Europe.* London, 1939.

Stolper, Gustav. *German Economy, 1870-1940, Issues and Trends.* New York, 1940.

Stroebel, H. *Socialisation in Theory and Practice.* London, 1922.

———. *The German Revolution and After.* New York, 1923.

Stuemke, Bruno. *Die Entstehung der deutschen Republik.* Frankfort on the Main, 1923.

Sturmthal, Adolf F. *The Tragedy of European Labor 1918-1939.* New York, 1943.

Swift, Fletcher H. *Germany. The Financing of Institutions of Public Instruction in Germany 1927-1937.* Berkeley, 1939.

Thomée, Major Gerhard. *Der Wiederaufstieg des deutschen Heeres, 1918-1938.* Berlin, 1939.

Tiedemann, H. *Sowjetrussland und die Revolutionisierung Deutschlands 1917-1919.* Berlin, 1936.

Tschuppik, Karl. *Ludendorff. Die Tragoedie des Fachmanns.* Vienna, 1931.

Ullmann, Hermann. *Durchbruch zur Nation. Geschichte des deutschen Volkes 1919-1933.* Jena, 1933.

Umbreit, Paul. *Der Krieg und die Arbeitsverhaeltnisse.* Berlin, 1928.

Vagts, Alfred. *A History of Militarism*. New York, 1937.

Vallentin, Antonina. *Stresemann*. New York, 1931.

Venter, Robert. *Die oeffentlich-rechtliche Betaetigung von Berufs- und Interessenverbaenden und ihre staatspolitische Bedeutung*. Marburg, 1932.

Verein fuer Sozialpolitik, Berlin. *Verhandlungen des Vereins fuer Sozialpolitik in Dresden 1932. Deutschland und die Weltkrise*. Munich, 1932.

Vermeil, Edmond. *La Constitution de Weimar et le principe de la démocratie allemande*. Strasbourg, 1923.

——. *L'Allemagne contemporaine (1919-1924)*. Paris, 1925.

——. *Doctrinaires de la révolution allemande 1918-1938*. Paris, 1938.

Viereck, Peter. *Metapolitics. From the Romantics to Hitler*. New York, 1941.

Villard, Oswald Garrison. *The German Phoenix: The Story of the Republic*. New York, 1933.

Volkmann, E. O. *Am Tor der neuen Zeit*. Oldenburg, 1933.

——. *Der Marxismus und das deutsche Heer im Weltkriege*. Berlin, 1925.

——. *Revolution ueber Deutschland*. Oldenburg, 1930.

Wagenfuehr, Rolf. *Die Bedeutung des Aussenmarktes fuer die deutsche Industriewirtschaft; die Exportquote der deutschen Industrie von 1870 bis 1936*. Berlin, 1936.

Wagner, Ludwig. *Hitler: Man of Strife*. New York, 1942.

Wahrmund, Konrad. *Dr. Karl Helfferich als Gelehrter, Wirtschaftspolitiker und Staatsmann*. Leipzig, 1938.

Waldeyer-Hartz, Hugo von. *Admiral von Hipper*. London, 1933.

Watkins, Frederick M. *The Failure of Constitutional Emergency Powers under the German Republic*. Cambridge, 1939.

Weber, Marianne. *Max Weber. Ein Lebensbild*. Tuebingen, 1926.

Welter, Erich. *Die Ursachen des Kapitalmangels in Deutschland*. Tuebingen, 1931.

Wenck, Martin. *Friedrich Naumann. Ein Lebensbild*. Berlin, 1920.

Wentzcke, Paul. *Ruhrkampf. Einbruch und Abwehr im Rheinisch-westfaelischen Industriegebiet*. Berlin, 1930.

Wertheim, A. *Der Einfluss der Arbeiterschaft auf die Betriebsleitung in Deutschland*. Erlangen, 1926.

Weterstetten, Rudolph and Watson, A. M. K. *The Biography of President von Hindenburg*. New York, 1930.

Wheeler-Bennett, John W. *The Forgotten Peace*. New York, 1939.

——. *The Wreck of Reparations, Being the Political Background of the Lausanne Agreement, 1932*. London, 1933.

——. *Wooden Titan*. New York, 1936.

Wiggs, Kenneth I. *Unemployment in Germany since the War*. London, 1933.

Winnig, August. *Das Reich als Republik 1918-1928*. Stuttgart, 1929.

Wittmayer, Leo. *Die Weimarer Reichsverfassung.* Tuebingen, 1922.

Wolgast, Ernst. *Zum deutschen Parlamentarismus. "Der Kampf um Artikel 54 der deutschen Reichsverfassung."* Berlin, 1929.

Woytinsky, Wladimir S. *Zehn Jahre neues Deutschland.* Berlin, 1929.

Wunderlich, Frieda. *Der Kampf um die Sozialversicherung.* Berlin, 1930.

――――. *Labor under German Democracy, Arbitration 1918-1933.* New York, 1940.

――――. *Versicherung, Fuersorge und Krisenrisiko.* Leipzig, 1932.

Young, George. *The New Germany.* New York, 1920.

Ziegler, Wilhelm. *Die deutsche Nationalversammlung, 1919-1920, und ihr Verfassungswerk.* Berlin, 1932.

――――. *Versailles. Die Geschichte eines missglueckten Friedens.* Hamburg, 1933.

――――. *Volk ohne Fuehrung. Das Ende des Zweiten Reiches.* Hamburg, 1938.

Ziervogel, Max. *Die Gestaltung der Organisationsform der freien Gewerkschaften.* Giessen, 1924.

Zwing, Karl. *Geschichte der deutschen freien Gewerkschaften.* Jena, 1922.

――――. *Soziologie der Gewerkschaftsbewegung.* Jena, 1925.

INDEX